# DIGITAL IMAGE PROCESSING

**Ikvinderpal Singh**
Lecturer,
PG Deptt of Computer Sc. & Applications,
Khalsa. College,
Amritsar.

**Baljinder Singh**
Lecturer,
PG Deptt of Computer Sc. & Applications,
Khalsa. College,
Amritsar.

**KHANNA BOOK PUBLISHING CO. (P) LTD.**

*::: Publisher of Engineering and Computer Books :::*

**Head Office** : 4C/4344, Ansari Road, Darya Ganj, New Delhi-110002
**Phone** : 011-23244447/48 Fax : 011-23244447
**Regd. Office** : 1694-95, Nai Sarak, Delhi-110006
**Phone** : 011-23283211 Fax : 011-23256658
**E-Mail** : contact@khannabooks.com
**Website** : www.khannabooks.com, www.khannapublishers.com

ISBN: 978-93-80016-21-4
Reprint 2015



Published by:
**Khanna Book Publishing Co. (P) Ltd.**
4C/4344, Ansari Road, Darya Ganj, New Delhi-110 002
Phone: 011-23244448 Telefax: 011-23244447
E-mail: contact@khannabooks.com
Website: www.khannabooks.com

*Printed in India by:*
*S.P.S.* Printers & Binders, Delhi

# DEDICATION

No project could ever get in progress much less accomplished, without help from a lot of fantastic people. We would like to express gratitude to our reverential parents. We are grateful to Almighty God who has given us strength to take and complete this project.

To my mother Smt. Sharanjeet Kaur and father S. Jasjit Singh, biggest embrace and warm thanks to my grandmother Narinderjeet Kaur, and to my dear students who have encouraged me to complete this project.

***IKVINDERPAL SINGH***

To my mother Smt. Amarjit Kaur and father S. Gurbaksh Singh, biggest embrace and warm thanks to my sisters and to my dear students who have encouraged me to complete this project.

***BALJINDER SINGH***

# Preface

This book is intended for beginners, intermediate level, and all those who want to learn or expand their knowledge in Image Processing. A complementary objective was to prepare a book that is self-contained and easily readable by individuals with a basic background in digital image processing, mathematical analysis, and image signal representation like the Fourier transform, the frequency domain, and image data formats.

This book presents a wide variety of standard Image Processing Techniques like image enhancement, image restoration, image compression etc. Indeed, we are strongly believed that Image Processing is field of both intellectual interest and practical value to all such students and young professionals. Hardware architecture and designing for image processing provides an understanding of the mechanism of the standard image processor chips. We also explain various techniques of color image processing like color image signal representation, color system transformations etc.

The main focus of the current treatment is on examples of areas that use digital image processing. The applications of digital signal processing (DSP) in information and communication technology is pervasive and include Picture Data Archival, Computer Vision, and Medical Imaging etc.

Every effort has been made to present material in a clear and consistent manner so that it can be read and applied with ease.

**Best of luck!**

# Acknowledgements

We express our deep gratitude to Dr. Karanjit Singh Kahlon, Professor and Head, Department of Computer Science & Engineering, G.N.D.U., Dr. Hardeep Singh, Professor, Department of Computer Science & Engineering, G.N.D.U., Dr. Gurvinder Singh, Reader, DCSE, GNDU, Amritsar, Prof. Amardeep Gupta, Head, Computer Sc, DAV College, Amritsar, Prof. Nishey Behal, Head, DAV College for Boys, Jalandhar city , Mr. Avtar Singh Sandhu, Mr. Jagbir Singh, Mr. Kawarpal Singh Mr. Avtar Singh Riar, Mr. Sukhwant Singh and our colleagues for their valuable co-operation and guidance. We are grateful to the entire team of M/s Khanna Book Publishing Co. (P) Ltd. for their encouragement and motivation during this project.

# Special Thanks

Our special thanks go to Dr. Daljit Singh, Principal, Khalsa College, Amritsar for their valuable guidance and timely support during the compilation of this book.

# DIGITAL IMAGE PROCESSING

## CONTENTS

# DIGITAL IMAGE PROCESSING

# CHAPTER 1

# BACKGROUND

## 1.1 INTRODUCTION

The term digital image processing generally refers to processing of a two dimensional picture by a digital computer. In a broader context, it implies digital processing of any two – dimensional data. A digital image is an array of real or complex numbers represented by a finite number of bits. Figure 1.1 shows a computer laboratory used for digital image processing. An image given in the form of a transparency, slide, photograph or chart is first digitized and stored as a matrix of binary digits in computer memory.

This digitized image can then be processed and/or displayed on a high-resolution television monitor. For display, the image is stored in a rapid-access buffer memory which refreshes the monitor at 30 frames to produce a visible continuous display mini-or micro computer are used to communicate and control all the digitization, storage , processing and display operations via a computer network (such as the Ethernet). Program inputs to the computer are made through a terminal, and the outputs are available on a terminal, television monitor, or a printer/plotter Figure 1.2 shows the steps in typical image processing sequence.

Digital image processing has a broad spectrum of applications, such as remote sensing via satellites and other spacecrafts , image transmission and storage for business applications, medical processing, radar, sonar and acoustic image processing , robotics and automated inspection of industrial parts.

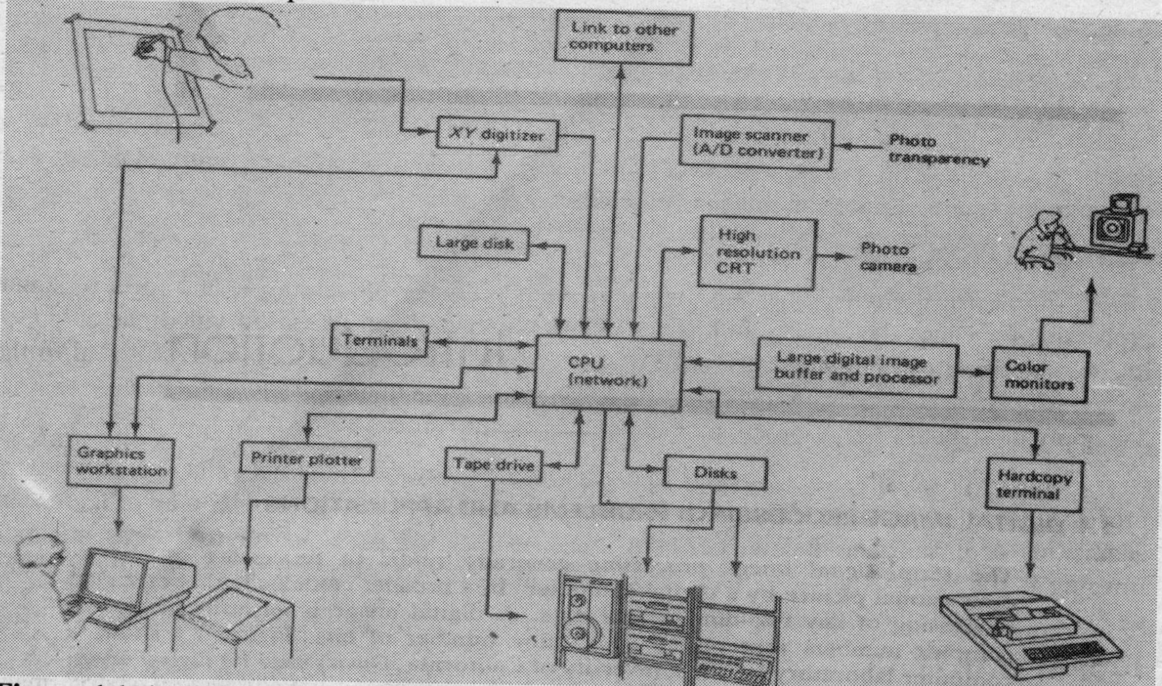


**Figure 1.1 A digital image processing system (Signal and image processing Laboratory, University of California)**

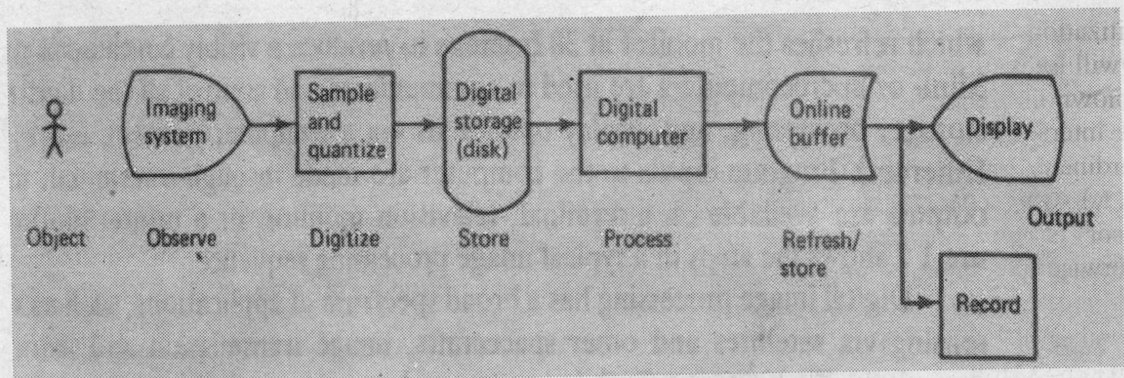


**Figure 1.2 A typical digital image processing sequence**

Image acquired by satellites are useful in tracking of earth resources; geographical mapping; prediction of agricultural crops, urban growth and weather, flood and fire control; and many other environmental applications. Space image applications include recognition and analysis of objects contained in images obtained from deep space-probe missions. Image transmission and storage applications occur in broadcast television , teleconferencing, transmission of facsimile images (printed documents and graphics) for office automation, communication over computer network, closed-circuit television based security monitoring systems, and in military communications. In medical applications one is concerned with processing of chest x-rays, cineangiograms, projection images of transaxial tomography, and other medical images that occur in radiology, nuclear magnetic resonance (NMR), and ultrasonic scanning. These images may be used for patient screening and monitoring or for detection of tumors or other disease in patients.

Radar and sonar images are used for diction and recognition of various types of targets or in guidance and maneuvering of aircraft of missile system. There are many other applications ranging from robot vision for industrial automation to image synthesis for cartoon making or fashion design. In other words, whenever a human or a machine or any other entity receives data of two or more dimensional, an image is processed.

## 1.2 IMAGE PROCESSING

In electrical engineering and computer science, image processing is any form of signal processing for which the input is an image, such as photographs or frames of video; the output of image processing can be either an image or a set of characteristics or parameters related to the image. Most image-processing techniques involve treating the image as a two-dimensional signal and applying standard signal-processing techniques to it.

Image processing usually refers to digital image processing, but optical and analog image processing are also possible. This article is about general techniques that apply to all of them. The acquisition of images (producing the input image in the first place) is referred to as imaging. Imaging is the representation or reproduction of an object's outward form; especially a visual representation (i.e., the formation of an image).

### 1.2.1 DIGITAL IMAGE DEFINITIONS

A digital image a[m, n] described in a 2D discrete space is derived from an analog image a(x, y) in a 2D continuous space through a sampling process that is frequently referred to as digitization. The mathematics of that sampling process will be described in Section 2. For now we will look at some basic definitions associated with the digital image. The effect of digitization is shown in Figure 1.3 The 2D continuous image a(x, y) is divided into N rows and M columns. The intersection of a row and a column is termed a pixel. The value assigned to the integer coordinates [m, n] with {m=0,1,2,...,M-1} and {n=0,1,2,...,N-1} is a[m, n]. In fact, in most cases a(x, y)--which we might consider to be the physical signal that impinges on the face of a 2D sensor--is actually a function of many variables including depth (z), color (λ), and time (t). Unless otherwise stated, we will consider the case of 2D, monochromatic, static images in this chapter.

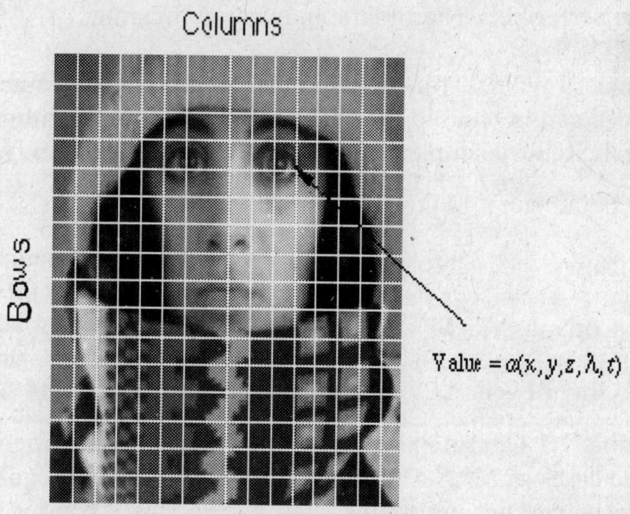


**Figure 1.3 Digitization of a continuous image. The pixel at coordinates [m=10, n=3] has the integer brightness value 110**

The image shown in Figure 1.3 has been divided into N = 16 rows and M = 16 columns. The value assigned to every pixel is the average brightness in the pixel rounded to the nearest integer value. The process of representing the amplitude of the 2D signal at a given coordinate as an integer value with L different gray levels is usually referred to as amplitude quantization or simply quantization.

### 1.2.2 IMAGING METHODOLOGIES AND TECHNOLOGIES

- Chemical imaging, the simultaneous measurement of spectra and pictures
- Creation of a disk image, a file which contains the exact content of a non-volatile computer data storage medium. See also disk cloning
- Digital imaging, creating digital images, generally by scanning, or through digital photography
- Document imaging, replicating documents commonly used in business
- Geophysical imaging
- Medical imaging, creating images of the human body or parts of it, to diagnose or examine disease
    - Magnetic resonance imaging
- Molecular imaging
- Optical imaging

- Personal imaging, real-time sharing of personal experience through images
- Radar imaging, or imaging radar, for obtaining an image of an object, not just its location and speed
- Reprography, reproduction of graphics through electrical and mechanical means
  - Cinematography
  - Photography, the process of creating still images
  - Xerography, the method of photocopying
- Speckle imaging, a method of shift-and-add for astronomical imaging
- Stereo imaging, an aspect of sound recording and reproduction concerning spatial locations of the performers Thermograph, infrared imaging

### 1.2.3 COMMON VALUES

There are standard values for the various parameters encountered in digital image processing. These values can be caused by video standards, by algorithmic requirements, or by the desire to keep digital circuitry simple. Table 1.1 gives some commonly encountered values.

| Parameter | Symbol | Typical values |
|---|---|---|
| Rows | N | 256,512,525,625,1024,1035 |
| Columns | M | 256,512,768,1024,1320 |
| Gray Levels | L | 2,64,256,1024,4096,16384 |

**Table 1.1 Common values of digital image parameters**

Quite frequently we see cases of $M=N=2^K$ where $\{K = 8, 9, 10\}$. This can be motivated by digital circuitry or by the use of certain algorithms such as the (fast) Fourier transform (see Section 3.3).The number of distinct gray levels is usually a power of 2, that is, $L=2^B$ where B is the number of bits in the binary representation of the brightness levels. When $B>1$ we speak of a gray-level image; when $B=1$ we speak of a binary image. In a binary image there are just two gray levels which can be referred to, for example, as "black" and "white" or "0" and "1".

### 1.2.4 CHARACTERISTICS OF IMAGE OPERATIONS

- Types of operations
- Types of neighborhoods

There is a variety of ways to classify and characterize image operations. The reason for doing so is to understand what type of results we might expect to achieve with a given type of operation or what might be the computational burden associated with a given operation.

#### 1.2.4.1 TYPES OF OPERATIONS

The types of operations that can be applied to digital images to transform an input image a[m, n] into an output image b[m, n] (or another representation) can be classified into three categories as shown in Table 1.2.

| Operation | Characterization | Generic Complexity/Pixel |
|---|---|---|
| * Point | - the output value at a specific coordinate is dependent only on the input value at that same coordinate. | constant |
| * Local | - the output value at a specific coordinate is dependent on the | $P^2$ |

| | input values in the neighborhood of that same coordinate. | |
|---|---|---|
| * Global | - the output value at a specific coordinate is dependent on all the values in the input image. | $N^2$ |

**Table 1.2. Types of image operations. Image size = N x N; neighborhood size = P x P. Note that the complexity is specified in operations per pixel**

This is shown graphically in Figure 1.4.

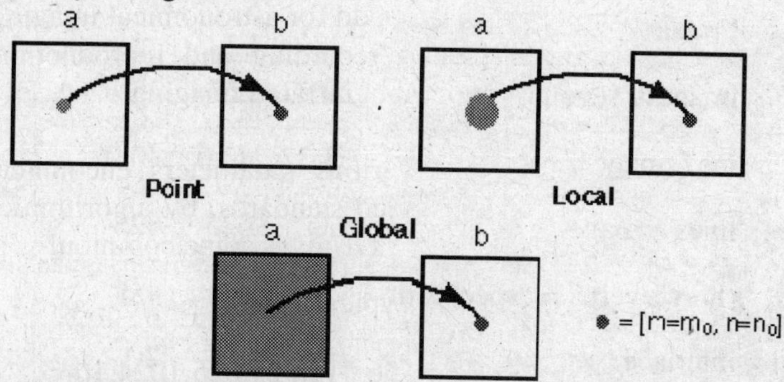


**Figure 1.4. Illustration of various types of image operations**

### 1.2.4.2 TYPES OF NEIGHBORHOODS

Neighborhood operations play a key role in modern digital image processing. It is therefore important to understand how images can be sampled and how that relates to the various neighborhoods that can be used to process an image.

* **Rectangular sampling** - In most cases, images are sampled by laying a rectangular grid over an image as illustrated in Figure 1.5. This results in the type of sampling shown in Figure 1.5 (a)(b).

* **hexagonal sampling** - An alternative sampling scheme is shown in Figure 1.5(c) and is termed hexagonal sampling.

Both sampling schemes have been studied extensively and both represent a possible periodic tiling of the continuous image space. We will restrict our attention, however, to only rectangular sampling as it remains, due to hardware and software considerations, the method of choice.

Local operations produce an output pixel value $b[m=m_o, n=n_o]$ based upon the pixel values in the neighborhood of $a[m=m_o, n=n_o]$. Some of the most common neighborhoods are the 4-connected neighborhood and the 8-connected neighborhood in the case of rectangular sampling and the 6-connected neighborhood in the case of hexagonal sampling illustrated in Figure 1.5.

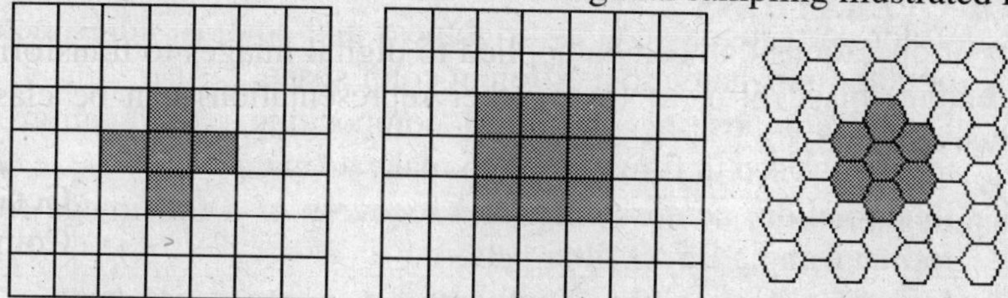

**Figure 1.5a** **Figure 1.5b** **Figure 1.5c**

**Figure1.5. Rectangular sampling Rectangular sampling hexagonal sampling 4-connected 8-connected 6-connected**

### 1.2.5 VIDEO PARAMETERS

It is appropriate--given that many static images are derived from video cameras and frame grabbers-- to mention the standards that are associated with the three standard video schemes that are currently in worldwide use - NTSC, PAL, and SECAM. This information is summarized in Table 3.

| Standard | NTSC | PAL | SECAM |
|---|---|---|---|
| Property | | | |
| images / second | 29.97 | 25 | 25 |
| ms / image | 33.37 | 40.0 | 40.0 |
| lines / image | 525 | 625 | 625 |
| (horiz./vert.) = aspect ratio | 4:3 | 4:3 | 4:3 |
| interlace | 2:1 | 2:1 | 2:1 |
| us / line | 63.56 | 64.00 | 64.00 |

**Table 1.3. Standard video parameters**

In an interlaced image the odd numbered lines (1,3,5,...) are scanned in half of the allotted time (e.g. 20 ms in PAL) and the even numbered lines (2,4,6,...) are scanned in the remaining half. The image display must be coordinated with this scanning format.

The reason for interlacing the scan lines of a video image is to reduce the perception of flicker in a displayed image. If one is planning to use images that have been scanned from an interlaced video source, it is important to know if the two half-images have been appropriately "shuffled" by the digitization hardware or if that should be implemented in software. Further, the analysis of moving objects requires special care with interlaced video to avoid "zigzag" edges.

The number of rows (N) from a video source generally corresponds one-to-one with lines in the video image. The number of columns, however, depends on the nature of the electronics that is used to digitize the image. Different frame grabbers for the same video camera might produce M = 384, 512, or 768 columns (pixels) per line.

### 1.2.6 IMAGE PROCESSING OPERATIONS

1. Euclidean geometry transformations such as enlargement, reduction, and rotation
2. Color corrections such as brightness and contrast adjustments, quantization, or color translation to a different color space
3. Digital compositing or optical compositing (combination of two or more images). Used in filmmaking to make a "matte"
4. Interpolation, demosaicing, and recovery of a full image from a raw image format using a Bayer filter pattern
5. Image registration, the alignment of two or more images
6. Image differencing and morphing
7. Image recognition, for example, extract the text from the image by using optical character recognition

8. Image segmentation
9. High dynamic range imaging by combining multiple images
10. Geometric hashing for 2-D object recognition with affine invariance

## 1.2.7 WHAT IS DIGITAL IMAGE PROCESSING

An image may be defined as a two-dimensional function, f (x, y), where x and y are spatial (plane) coordinates, and the amplitude of f at any pair of coordinates (x, y) is called the intensity or gray level of the image at that point. When x, y, and the amplitude values of f are all finite, discrete quantities, we call the image a digital image. The field of digital image processing refers to processing digital images by means of a digital computer. Note that a digital image is composed of a finite number of elements, each of which has a particular location and value. These elements are referred to as picture elements, image elements, pels, and pixels. Pixel is the term most widely used to denote the elements of a digital image.

Vision is the most advanced of our senses, so it is not surprising that images play the single most important role in human perception. However, unlike humans, who are limited to the visual band of the electromagnetic (EM) spectrum, imaging machines cover almost the entire EM spectrum, ranging from gamma to radio waves. They can operate on images generated by sources that humans are not accustomed to associating with images. These include ultrasound, electron microscopy, and computer-generated images. Thus, digital image processing encompasses a wide and varied field of applications.

There is no general agreement among authors regarding where image processing stops and other related areas, such as image analysis and computer vision, start. Sometimes a distinction is made by defining image processing as a discipline in which both the input and output of a process are images. We believe this to be a limiting and somewhat artificial boundary. For example, under this definition, even the trivial task of computing the average intensity of an image (which yields a single number) would not be considered an image processing operation. On the other hand, there are fields such as computer vision whose ultimate goal is to use computers to emulate human vision, including learning and being able to make inferences and take actions based on visual inputs. This area itself is a branch of artificial intelligence (AI) whose objective is to emulate human intelligence. The field of AI is in its earliest stages of infancy in terms of development, with progress having been much slower than originally anticipated. The area of image analysis (also called image understanding) is in between image processing and computer vision. There are no clear-cut boundaries in the continuum from image processing at one end to computer vision at the other. However, one useful paradigm is to consider three types of computerized processes in this continuum: low-, mid-, and high-level processes.

Low-level processes involve primitive operations such as image preprocessing to reduce noise, contrast enhancement, and image sharpening. A low-level process is characterized by the fact that both its inputs and outputs are images. Mid-level processing on images involves tasks such as segmentation (partitioning an image into regions or objects), description of those objects to reduce them to a form suitable for computer processing, and classification (recognition) of individual objects. A mid-level process is characterized by the fact that its inputs generally are images, but its outputs are attributes extracted from those images (e.g., edges, contours, and the identity of individual objects). Finally, higher-level processing involves "making sense" of an ensemble of recognized objects, as in image analysis, and, at the far end of the continuum, performing the cognitive functions normally associated with vision.

Based on the preceding comments, we see that a logical place of overlap between image processing and image analysis is the area of recognition of individual regions or objects in an image. Thus, what we call in this book digital image processing encompasses processes whose inputs and outputs are images and, in addition, encompasses processes that extract attributes from images, up to and including the recognition of individual objects. As a simple illustration to clarify these concepts, consider the area of automated analysis of text. The processes of acquiring an image of the area containing the text, preprocessing that image, extracting (segmenting) the individual characters, describing the characters in a form suitable for computer processing, and recognizing those individual characters are in the scope of what we call digital image processing in this book. Making sense of the content of the page may be viewed as being in the domain of image analysis and even computer vision, depending on the level of complexity implied by the statement "making sense." As will become evident shortly, digital image processing, as we have defined it, is used successfully in a broad range of areas of exceptional social and economic value. The concepts developed in the following chapters are the foundation for the methods used in those application areas.

## 1.2.8 ORIGINS OF DIGITAL IMAGE PROCESSING

One of the first applications of digital images was in the newspaper industry, when pictures were first sent by submarine cable between London and New York. Introduction of the Bartlane cable picture transmission system in the early 1920s reduced the time required to transport a picture across the Atlantic from more than a week to less than three hours. Specialized printing equipment coded pictures for cable transmission and then reconstructed them at the receiving end. Figure 1.6 was transmitted in this way and reproduced on a telegraph printer fitted with typefaces simulating a halftone pattern.

Some of the initial problems in improving the visual quality of these early digital pictures were related to the selection of printing procedures and the distribution of intensity levels. The printing method used to obtain Fig. 1.6 was abandoned toward the end of 1921 in favor of a technique based on photographic reproduction made from tapes perforated at the telegraph receiving terminal. Figure 1.7 shows an image obtained using this method. The improvements over Fig. 1.6 are evident, both in tonal quality and in resolution.

**Figure 1.6 A digital picture produced in 1921 from a coded tape by a telegraph printer with special type faces**

**Figure 1.7 A digital picture made in 1922 from a tape punched after the signals had crossed the Atlantic twice. Some errors are visible**

The early Bartlane systems were capable of coding images in five distinct levels of gray. This capability was increased to 15 levels in 1929. Figure 1.8 is typical of the type of images that could be obtained using the 15-tone equipment. During this period, introduction of a system for developing a film plate via light beams that were modulated by the coded picture tape improved the reproduction process considerably.

Although the examples just cited involve digital images, they are not considered digital image processing results in the context of our definition because computers were not involved in their creation. Thus, the history of digital image processing is intimately tied to the development of the digital computer. In fact, digital images require so much storage and computational power that progress in the field of digital image processing has been dependent on the development of digital computers and of supporting technologies that include data storage, display, and transmission.

The idea of a computer goes back to the invention of the abacus in Asia Minor, more than 5000 years ago. More recently, there were developments in the past two centuries that are the foundation of what we call a computer today. However, the basis for what we call a modern digital computer dates back to only the 1940s with the introduction by John von Neumann of two key concepts: (1) a memory to hold a stored program and data, and (2) conditional branching. These two ideas are the foundation of a central processing unit (CPU), which is at the heart of computers today. Starting with von Neumann, there were

**Figure 1.8 Unretouched cable picture of Generals Pershing and Foch, transmitted in 1929 from London to New York by 15-tone equipment**

a series of key advances that led to computers powerful enough to be used for digital image processing. Briefly, these advances may be summarized as follows: (1) the invention of the transistor by Bell Laboratories in 1948; (2) the development in the 1950s and 1960s of the high-level programming languages COBOL (Common Business-Oriented Language) and FORTRAN (Formula Translator); (3) the invention of the integrated circuit (IC) at Texas Instruments in 1958; (4) the development of operating systems in the early 1960s; (5) the development of the microprocessor (a single chip consisting of the central processing unit, memory, and input and output controls) by Intel in the early 1970s; (6) introduction by IBM of the personal computer in 1981; and (7) progressive miniaturization of components, starting with large scale integration (LI) in the late 1970s, then very large scale integration (VLSI) in the 1980s, to the present use of ultra large scale integration (ULSI). Concurrent with these advances were developments in the areas of mass storage and display systems, both of which are fundamental requirements for digital image processing.

The first computers powerful enough to carry out meaningful image processing tasks appeared in the early 1960s. The birth of what we call digital image processing today can be traced to the availability of those machines and the onset of the space program during that period. It took the combination of those two developments to bring into focus the potential of digital image processing concepts. Work on using computer techniques for improving images from a space probe began at the Jet Propulsion Laboratory (Pasadena, California) in 1964 when pictures of the moon transmitted by Ranger 7 were processed by a computer to correct various types of image distortion inherent in the on-board television camera. Figure 1.9 shows the first image of the moon taken by Ranger 7 on July 31, 1964 at 9:09 A.M. Eastern Daylight Time (EDT), about 17 minutes before impacting the lunar surface (the markers, called reseau marks, are used for geometric corrections. This also is the first image of the moon taken by a U.S. spacecraft. The imaging lessons learned with Ranger 7 served as the basis for improved methods used to enhance and restore images from the Surveyor missions to the moon, the Mariner series of flyby missions to Mars, the Apollo manned flights to the moon, and others.

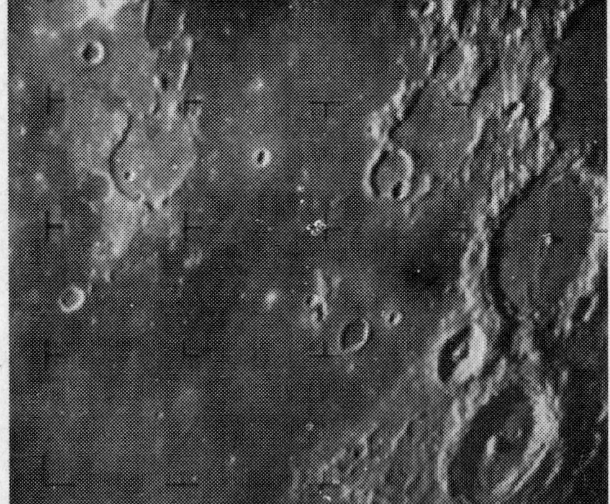

**Figure 1.9 The first picture of the moon by a U.S. spacecraft. Ranger 7 took this image on July 31, 1964 at 9:09 A.M. EDT, about 17 minutes before impacting the lunar surface.**

In parallel with space applications, digital image processing techniques began in the late 1960s and early 1970s to be used in medical imaging, remote Earth resources observations, and astronomy. The invention in the early 1970s of computerized axial tomography (CAT), also called computerized tomography (CT) for short, is one of the most important events in the application of image processing in medical diagnosis. Computerized axial tomography is a process in which a ring of detectors encircles an object (or patient) and an X-ray source, concentric with the detector ring, rotates about the object.

The X-rays pass through the object and are collected at the opposite end by the corresponding detectors in the ring. As the source rotates, this procedure is repeated. Tomography consists of algorithms that use the sensed data to construct an image that represents a "slice" through the object. Motion of the object in a direction perpendicular to the ring of detectors produces a set of such slices, which constitute a three-dimensional (3-D) rendition of the inside of the object. Tomography was invented independently by Sir Godfrey N. Hounsfield and Professor Allan M. Cormack, who shared the 1979 Nobel Prize in Medicine for their invention. It is interesting to note that X-rays were discovered in 1895 by Wilhelm Conrad Roentgen, for which he received the 1901 Nobel Prize for Physics. These two inventions, nearly 100 years apart, led to some of the most active application areas of image processing today.

From the 1960s until the present, the field of image processing has grown vigorously. In addition to applications in medicine and the space program, digital image processing techniques now are used in a broad range of applications. Computer procedures are used to enhance the contrast or code the intensity levels into color for easier interpretation of X-rays and other images used in industry, medicine, and the biological sciences. Geographers use the same or similar techniques to study pollution patterns from aerial and satellite imagery. Image enhancement and restoration procedures are used to process degraded images of unrecoverable objects or experimental results too expensive to duplicate.

In archeology, image processing methods have successfully restored blurred pictures that were the only available records of rare artifacts lost or damaged after being photographed. In physics and related fields, computer techniques routinely enhance images of experiments in areas such as high-energy plasmas and electron microscopy. Similarly successful applications of image processing concepts can be found in astronomy, biology, nuclear medicine, law enforcement, defense, and industrial applications.

These examples illustrate processing results intended for human interpretation. The second major area of application of digital image processing techniques mentioned at the beginning of this chapter is in solving problems dealing with machine perception. In this case, interest focuses on procedures for extracting from an image information in a form suitable for computer processing. Often, this information bears little resemblance to visual features that humans use in interpreting the content of an image. Examples of the type of information used in machine perception are statistical moments, Fourier transform coefficients, and multidimensional distance measures.

Typical problems in machine perception that routinely utilize image processing techniques are automatic character recognition, industrial machine vision for product assembly and inspection, military recognizance, automatic processing of fingerprints, screening of X-rays and blood samples, and machine processing of aerial and satellite imagery for weather prediction and environmental assessment.

### 1.2.9 COMPONENTS OF AN IMAGE PROCESSING SYSTEM

As recently as the mid-1980s, numerous models of image processing systems being sold throughout the world were rather substantial peripheral devices that attached to equally substantial host computers. Late in the 1980s and early in the 1990s, the market shifted to image processing hardware in the form of single boards designed to be compatible with industry standard buses and to fit into engineering workstation cabinets and personal computers. In addition to lowering costs, this market shift also served as a catalyst for a significant number of new companies whose specialty is the development of software written specifically for image processing.

Although large-scale image processing systems still are being sold for massive imaging applications, such as processing of satellite images, the trend continues toward miniaturizing and blending of general-purpose small computers with specialized image processing hardware. Figure 1.10 shows the basic components comprising a typical general-purpose system used for digital image processing. The function of each component is discussed in the following paragraphs, starting with image sensing.

With reference to sensing, two elements are required to acquire digital images. The first is a physical device that is sensitive to the energy radiated by the object we wish to image. The second, called a digitizer, is a device for converting the output of the physical sensing device into digital form. For instance, in a digital video camera, the sensors produce an electrical output proportional to light intensity. The digitizer converts these outputs to digital data.

Specialized image processing hardware usually consists of the digitizer just mentioned, plus hardware that performs other primitive operations, such as an arithmetic logic unit (ALU), which performs arithmetic and logical operations in parallel on entire images. One example of how an ALU is used is in averaging images as quickly as they are digitized, for the purpose of noise reduction. This type of hardware sometimes is called a front-end subsystem, and its most distinguishing characteristic is speed. In other words, this unit performs functions that require fast data throughputs (e.g., digitizing and averaging video images at 30 frames/s) that the typical main computer cannot handle.

The computer in an image processing system is a general-purpose computer and can range from a PC to a supercomputer. In dedicated applications, sometimes specially designed computers are used to achieve a required level of performance, but our interest here is on general-purpose image processing systems. In these systems, almost any well-equipped PC-type machine is suitable for off- line image processing tasks.

Software for image processing consists of specialized modules that perform specific tasks. A well-designed package also includes the capability for the user to write code that, as a minimum, utilizes the specialized modules. More sophisticated software packages allow the integration of those modules and general-purpose software commands from at least one computer language.

Mass storage capability is a must in image processing applications. An image of size 1024 * 1024 pixels, in which the intensity of each pixel is an 8-bit quantity, requires one megabyte of storage space if the image is not compressed. When dealing with thousands, or even millions, of images, providing adequate storage in an image processing system can be a challenge. Digital storage for image processing applications falls into three principal categories: (1) short- term storage for use during processing, (2) on-line storage for relatively fast recall, and (3) archival storage, characterized by infrequent access. Storage is measured in bytes (eight bits), Kbytes (one thousand bytes), Mbytes (one million bytes), Gbytes (meaning giga, or one billion, bytes), and Tbytes (meaning tera, or one trillion, bytes).

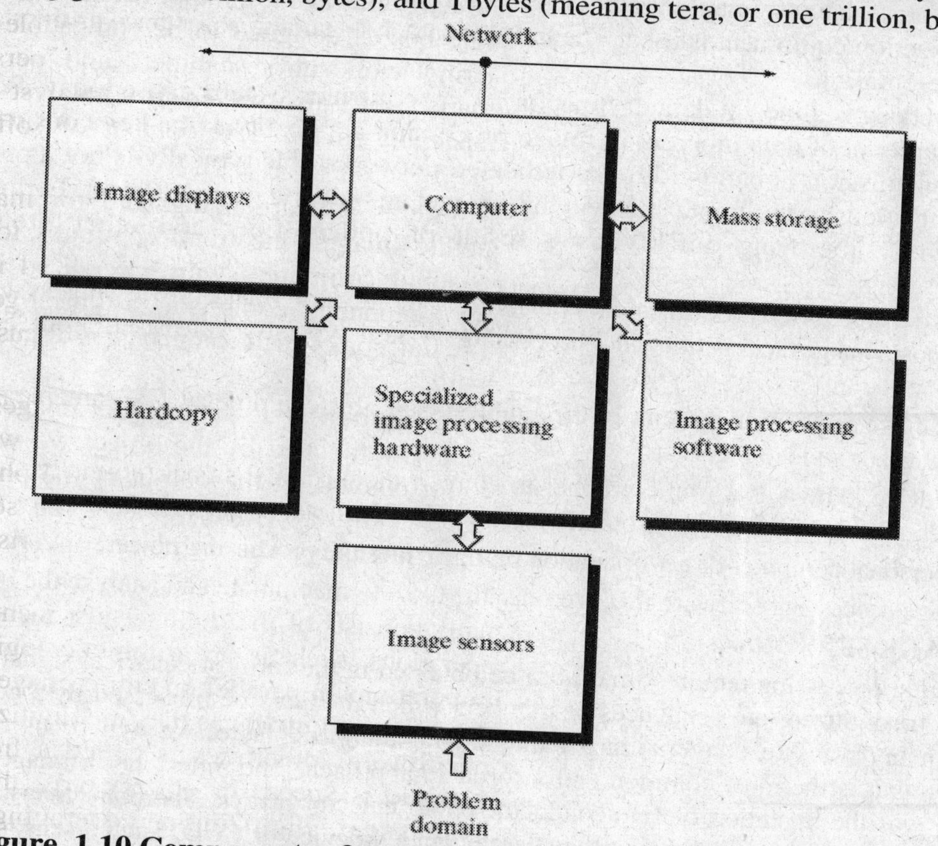


**Figure 1.10 Components of a general purpose image processing system**

One method of providing short-term storage is computer memory. Another is by specialized boards, called frame buffers, that store one or more images and can be accessed rapidly, usually at video rates (e.g., at 30 complete images per second). The latter method allows virtually instantaneous image zoom, as well as scroll (vertical shifts) and pan (horizontal shifts). Frame buffers usually are housed in the specialized image processing hardware unit shown in Fig. 1.10. Online storage generally takes the form of magnetic disks or optical-media storage. The key factor characterizing on-line storage is frequent access to the stored data. Finally, archival storage is characterized by massive storage requirements but infrequent need for access. Magnetic tapes and optical disks housed in "jukeboxes" are the usual media for archival applications.

Image displays in use today are mainly color (preferably flat screen) TV monitors. Monitors are driven by the outputs of image and graphics display cards that are an integral part of the computer system. Seldom are there requirements for image display applications that cannot be met by display cards available commercially as part of the computer system. In some cases, it is necessary to have stereo displays, and these are implemented in the form of headgear containing two small displays embedded in goggles worn by the user.

Hardcopy devices for recording images include laser printers, film cameras, heat-sensitive devices, inkjet units, and digital units, such as optical and CD-ROM disks. Film provides the highest possible resolution, but paper is the obvious medium of choice for written material. For presentations, images are displayed on film transparencies or in a digital medium if image projection equipment is used. The latter approach is gaining acceptance as the standard for image presentations.

Networking is almost a default function in any computer system in use today. Because of the large amount of data inherent in image processing applications, the key consideration in image transmission is bandwidth. In dedicated networks, this typically is not a problem, but communications with remote sites via the Internet are not always as efficient. Fortunately, this situation is improving quickly as a result of optical fiber and other broadband technologies.

This section briefly outlines the capabilities of modern image processing systems. A general purpose image acquisition and processing system typically consists of four essential components:

1. An image acquisition system. In the simplest case, this could be a CCD camera, a flatbed scanner, or a video recorder.
2. A device known as a frame grabber to convert the electrical signal (normally an analog video signal) of the image acquisition system into a digital image that can be stored.
3. A personal computer or a workstation that provides the processing power.
4. Image processing software that provides the tools to manipulate and analyze the images.

### 1.2.9.1 IMAGE SENSORS

Digital processing requires images to be obtained in the form of electrical signals. These signals can be digitized into sequences of numbers which then can be processed by a computer. There are many ways to convert images into digital numbers. Here, we will focus on video technology, as it is the most common and affordable approach. The milestone in image sensing technology was the invention of semiconductor photo detector arrays. There are many types of such sensors, the most common being the charge coupled device or CCD. Such a sensor consists of a large number of photosensitive elements. During the accumulation phase, each element collects electrical charges, which are generated by absorbed photons. Thus the collected charge is proportional

**Figure 1.11 Modern semiconductor cameras : (a) Complete CMOS camera on a chip with digital and analog output (b) High-end digital 12-bit CCD camera, pixel fly**

to the illumination. In the read-out phase, these charges are sequentially transported across the chip from sensor to sensor and finally converted to an electric voltage. For quite some time, CMOS image sensors have been available. But only recently have these devices attracted significant attention because the image quality, especially the uniformity of the sensitivities of the individual sensor elements, now approaches the quality of CCD image sensors.

CMOS imagers still do not reach up to the standards of CCD imagers in some features, especially at low illumination levels (higher dark current). They have, however, a number of significant advantages over CCD imagers. They consume significantly less power, subareas can be accessed quickly, and they can be added to circuits for image preprocessing and signal conversion. Indeed, it is possible to put a whole camera on a single chip (Figure 1.11). Last but not least, CMOS sensors can be manufactured more cheaply and thus open new application areas. Generally, semiconductor imaging sensors are versatile and powerful devices:

• **Precise and stable geometry**. The individual sensor elements are precisely located on a regular grid. Geometric distortion is virtually absent. Moreover, the sensor is thermally stable in size due to the low linear thermal expansion coefficient of silicon (2 ·10–6/K). These features allow precise size and position measurements.

• **Small and rugged**. The sensors are small and insensitive to external influences such as magnetic fields and vibrations.

• **High sensitivity**. The quantum efficiency, i. e., the fraction of elementary charges generated per photon, can be close to one (R2 and R1). Even standard imaging sensors, which are operated at room temperature, have a low noise level of only 10-100 electrons. Thus they show an excellent sensitivity. Cooled imaging sensors can be used with exposure times of hours without showing a significant thermal signal.

However, commercial CCDs at room temperature cannot be used at low light levels because of the thermally generated electrons. But if CCD devices are cooled down to low temperatures, they can be exposed for hours. Such devices are commonly used in astronomy and are about one hundred times more sensitive than photographic material.

• **Wide variety**. Imaging sensors are available in a wide variety of resolutions and frame rates (R2 and R1). The largest built CCD sensor as of 2001 originates from Philips. In a modular design with 1k × 1k sensor blocks, they built a 7k × 9k sensor with 12 × 12 μm pixels . Among the fastest high-resolution imagers available is the 1280 × 1024 active-pixel CMOS sensor from Photo bit with a peak frame rate of 500Hz (660 MB/s data rate).

• **Imaging beyond the visible**. Semiconductor imagers are not limited to the visible range of the electromagnetic spectrum. Standard silicon imagers can be made sensitive far beyond the visible wavelength range (400–700 nm) from 200nm in the ultraviolet to 1100nm in the near infrared. In the infrared range beyond 1100 nm, other semiconductors such an GaAs, InSb, HgCdTe are used (_R3) since silicon becomes transparent. Towards shorter wavelengths, specially designed silicon imagers can be made sensitive well into the x-ray wavelength region.

### 1.2.9.2 IMAGE ACQUISITION AND DISPLAY

A frame grabber converts the electrical signal from the camera into a digital image that can be processed by a computer. Image display and processing nowadays no longer require any special hardware. With the advent of graphical user interfaces, image display has become an integral part of a personal computer or workstation. Besides the display of grayscale images with up to 256 shades (8 bit), also true-color images with up to 16.7 million colors (3 channels with 8 bits each), can be displayed on inexpensive PC graphic display systems with a resolution of up to 1600 × 1200 pixels.

Consequently, a modern frame grabber no longer requires its own image display unit. It only needs circuits to digitize the electrical signal from the imaging sensor and to store the image in the memory of the computer. The direct transfer of image data from a frame grabber to the memory (RAM) of a microcomputer has become possible since 1995 with the introduction of fast peripheral bus systems such as the PCI bus. This 32-bit wide and 33Mhz fast bus has a peak transfer rate of 132 MB/s. Depending on the PCI bus controller on the frame grabber and the chipset on the motherboard of the computer, sustained transfer rates between 15 and 80 MB/s have been reported. This is sufficient to transfer image sequences in real time to the main memory, even for color images and fast frame rate images. The second generation 64-bit, 66MHz PCI bus quadruples the data transfer rates to a peak transfer rate of 512 MB/s. Digital cameras that transfer image data directly to the PC via standardized digital interfaces such as Firewire (IEEE 1394), Camera link, or even fast Ethernet will further simplify the image input to computers. The transfer rates to standard hard disks, however, are considerably lower. Sustained transfer rates are typically lower than 10 MB/s. This is inadequate for uncompressed real-time image sequence storage to disk. Real-time transfer of image data with sustained data rates between 10 and 30 MB/s is, however, possible with RAID arrays.

### 1.2.9.3 COMPUTER HARDWARE FOR FAST IMAGE PROCESSING

The tremendous progress of computer technology in the past 20 years has brought digital image processing to the desk of every scientist and engineer. For a general-purpose computer to be useful for image processing, four key demands must be met: high-resolution image display, sufficient memory transfer bandwidth, sufficient storage space, and sufficient computing power. In all four areas, a critical level of performance has been reached that makes it possible to process images on standard hardware. In the near future, it can be expected that general-purpose computers can handle volumetric images and/or image sequences without difficulties. In the following, we will briefly outline these key areas. General-purpose computers now include sufficient random access memory (RAM) to store multiple images. A 32-bit computer can address up to 4GB of memory. This is sufficient to handle complex image processing tasks even with large images. Nowadays, also 64-bit computer systems are available.

They provide enough RAM even for demanding applications with image sequences and volumetric images. While in the early days of personal computers hard disks had a capacity of just 5–10 MB, nowadays disk systems with more than ten thousand times more storage capacity (40–200 GB) are standard. Thus, a large number of images can be stored on a disk, which is an important requirement for scientific image processing. For permanent data storage and PC exchange, the DVD is playing an important role as a cheap and versatile storage medium. One DVD can hold almost 5GB of image data that can be read independent of the operating system on MS Windows, Macintosh, and UNIX platforms. Cheap DVD writers allow anyone to produce DVDs.

Within the short history of microprocessors and personal computers, computing power has increased tremendously. From 1978 to 2001 the clock rate has increased from 4.7MHz to 1.6GHz by a factor of 300. The speed of elementary operations such as floating-point addition and multiplication has increased even more because on modern CPUs these operations have now a throughput of only a few clocks instead of about 100 on early processors. Thus, in less than 25 years, the speed of floating point computations on a single microprocessor increased more than a factor of 10 000. Image processing could benefit from this development only partly. On modern 32-bit processors it became increasingly inefficient to transfer and process 8-bit and 16-bit image data. This changed only in 1997 with the integration of multimedia techniques into PCs and workstations.

The basic idea of fast image data processing is very simple. It makes use of the 64-bit data paths in modern processors for quick transfer and processing of multiple image data in parallel. This approach to parallel computing is a form of the single instruction multiple data (SIMD) concept. In 64-bit machines, eight 8-bit, four 16-bit or two 32-bit data can be processed together. Sun was the first to integrate the SIMD concept into general-purpose computer architecture with the visual instruction set (VIS) on the Ultra- Sparc architecture.

In January 1997 Intel introduced the Multimedia Instruction Set Extension (MMX) for the next generation of Pentium processors (P55C). The SIMD concept was quickly adopted by other processor manufacturers. Motorola, for instance, developed the AltiVec instruction set. It has also become an integral part of new 64-bit architectures such as in IA-64 architecture from Intel and the x86-64 architecture from AMD. Thus, it is evident that SIMD-processing of image data has become a standard part of future microprocessor architectures. More and more image processing tasks can be processed in real time on standard microprocessors without the need for any expensive and awkward special hardware.

However, significant progress for compilers is still required before SIMD techniques can be used by the general programmer. Today, the user either depends on libraries that are optimized by the hardware manufacturers for specific hardware platforms or he is forced to dive into the details of hardware architectures for optimized programming.

### 1.2.9.4 SOFTWARE AND ALGORITHMS

The rapid progress of computer hardware may distract us from the importance of software and the mathematical foundation of the basic concepts for image processing. In the early days, image processing may have been characterized more as an "art" than as a science. It was like tapping in the dark, empirically searching for a solution. Once an algorithm worked for a certain task, you could be sure that it would not work with other images and you would not even know why.

Fortunately, this is gradually changing. Image processing is about to mature to a well developed science. The deeper understanding has also led to a more realistic assessment of today's capabilities of image processing and analysis, which in many respects is a still world away from the capability of human vision.

It is a widespread misconception that a better mathematical foundation for image processing is of interest only to the theoreticians and has no real consequences for the applications. The contrary is true. The advantages are tremendous.

In the first place, mathematical analysis allows a distinction between image processing problems that can and those that cannot be solved. This is already very helpful. Image processing algorithms become predictable and accurate, and in some cases optimal results are known. New mathematical methods often result in novel approaches that can solve previously intractable problems or that are much faster or more accurate than previous approaches. Often the speed up that can be gained by a fast algorithm is considerable. In some cases it can reach up to several orders of magnitude. Thus fast algorithms make many image processing techniques applicable and reduce the hardware costs considerably.

## 1.3 DIGITAL TRANSMISSION SYSTEMS

In this section digital transmission will be briefly explained. Besides the analog wireless broadcasting systems based on amplitude and frequency modulation, DAB2 (Digital Audio Broadcasting) has been introduced in several countries. On the other hand, the internet has pushed audio/video distribution, internet radio and video via cable networks.

### 1.3.1 TERRESTRIAL DIGITAL BROADCASTING (DAB)

With the introduction of terrestrial digital broadcasting, the quality standards of a compact disc will be achieved for mobile and stationary reception of radio signals. Therefore, the data rate of a two-channel AES/EBU signal from a transmitting studio is reduced with the help of a source coder. Following the source coder (SC), additional information (AI) like the type of program (music/speech) and traffic information is added.

A multicarrier technique is applied for digital transmission to stationary and mobile receivers. At the transmitter, several broadcasting programs are combined in a multiplexer (MUX) to form a multiplex signal. The channel coding and modulation is carried out by a multi-carrier transmission technique. The DAB receiver (Figure 1.16) consists of the demodulator (DMOD), the demultiplexer (DMUX) and the source decoder (SD). The SD provides a linearly quantized PCM signal (Pulse Code Modulation). The PCM signal is fed over a Digital-to-Analog Converter (DA Converter) to an amplifier connected to loudspeakers.

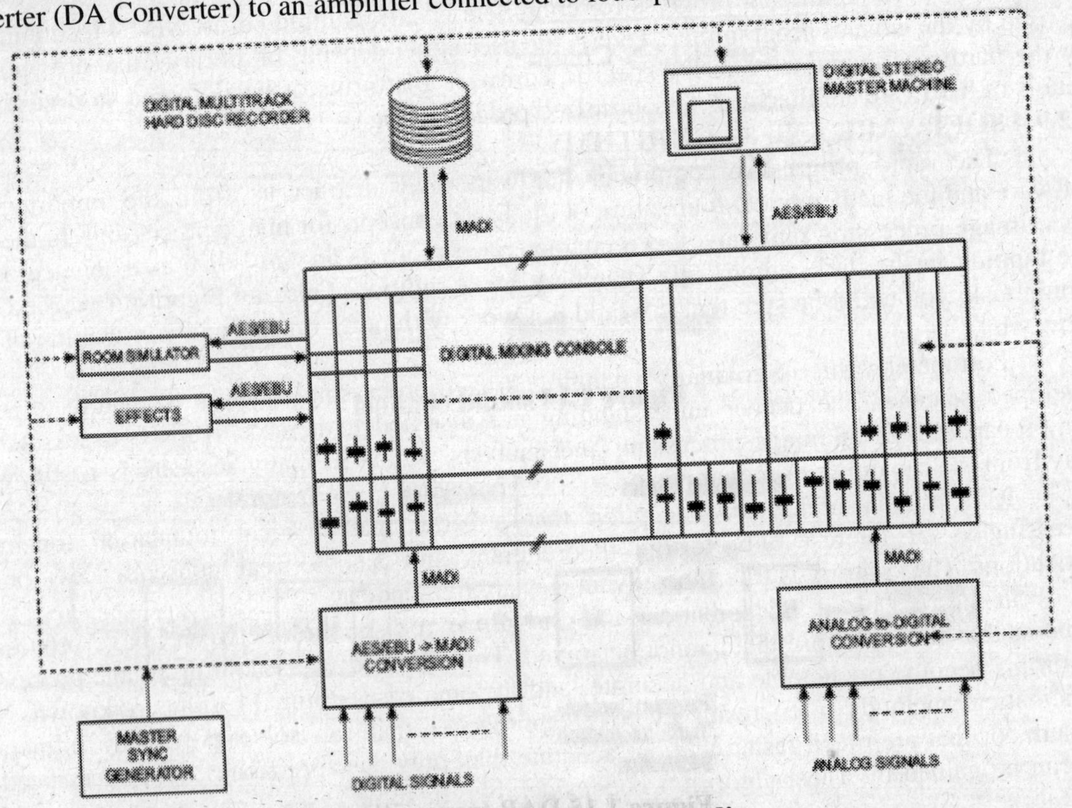


**Figure 1.12 Digital sound studio**

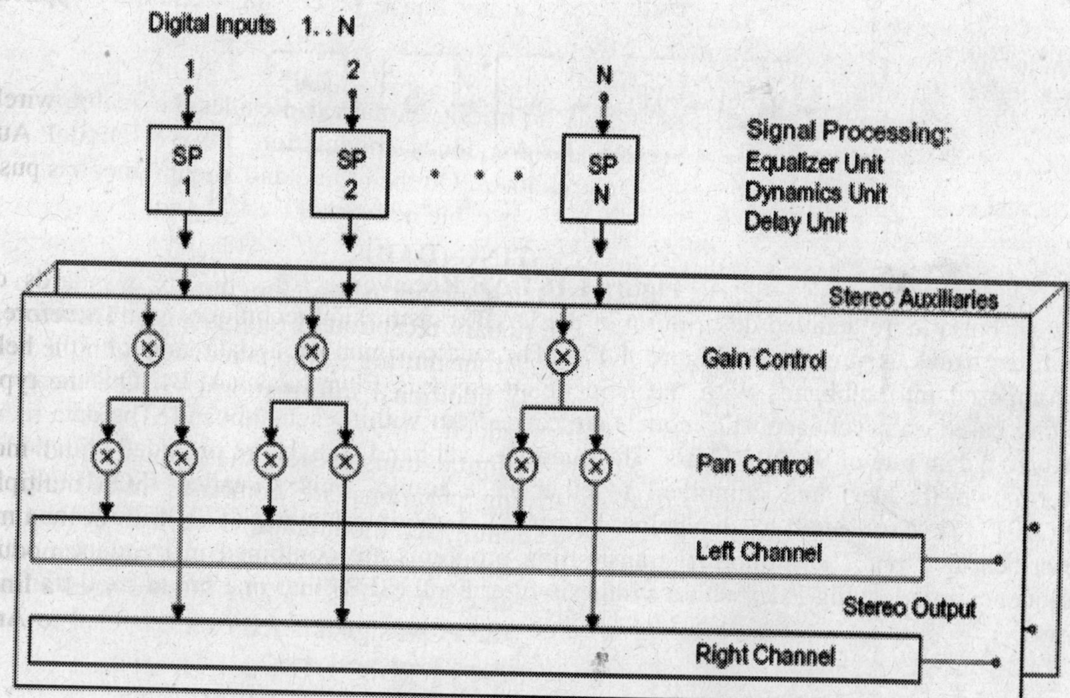


**Figure 1.13 N-Channel Sound mixing console**

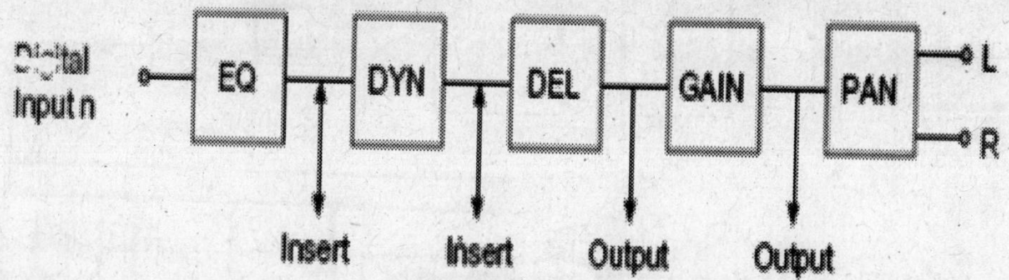


**Figure 1.14 sound channel**

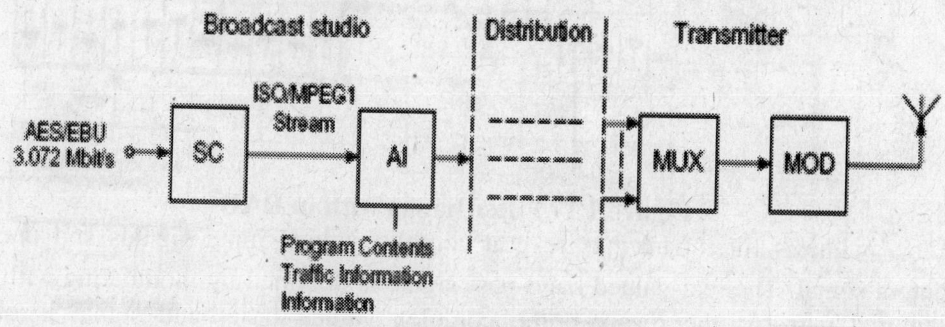


**Figure 1.15 DAB transmitter**

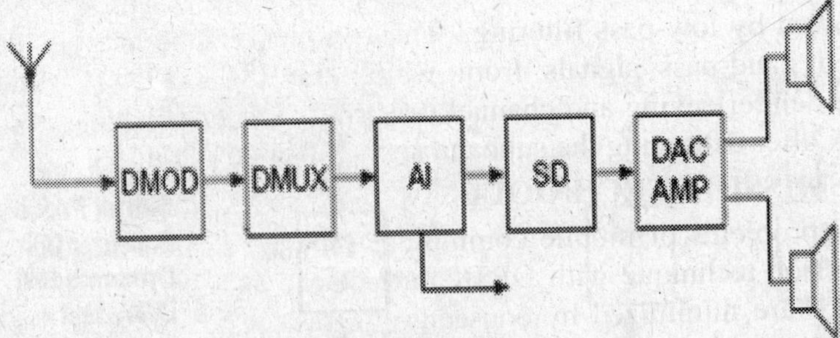


**Figure 1.16 DAB Receiver**

For a more detailed description of the DAB transmission technique, an illustration based on filter banks is presented (Figure 1.17). The audio signal at a data rate of 768 kbit/s is decomposed into subbands with the help of an analysis filter bank (AFB). Quantization and coding based on psychoacoustic models are carried out within each subband. The data reduction leads to a data rate of 96–192 kbit/s. The quantized subband signals are provided with additional information (header) and combined together in a frame. This so-called ISOMPEG1 frame [ISO92] is first subjected to channel coding (CC). Time-interleaving (TIL) follows and will be described later on. The individual transmitting programs are combined in frequency multiplex (frequency-interleaving FIL) with a synthesis filter bank (SFB) into one broad-band transmitting signal.

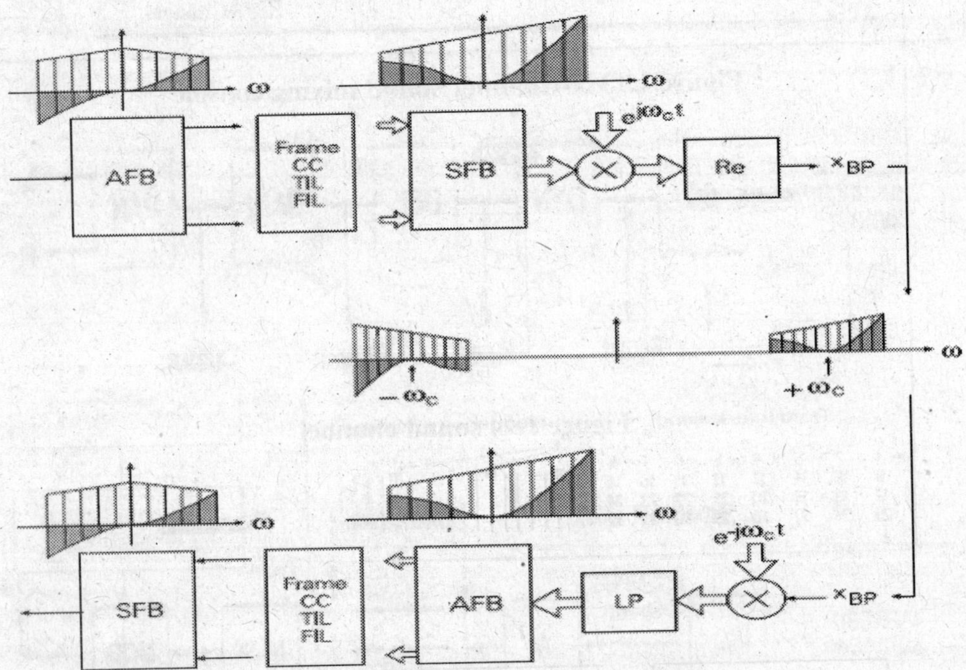


**Figure 1.17 Filter banks with in DAB**

The synthesis filter bank has several complex-valued input signals and one complex-valued output signal. The real-valued band-pass signal is obtained by modulating with $e^{j\omega_c t}$ and taking the real part. At the receiver, the complex valued base-band signal is obtained by demodulation followed by low-pass filtering. The complex-valued analysis filter bank provides the complex-valued band-pass signals from which the ISO-MPEG1 frame is formed after frequency and time deinterleaving and channel decoding. The PCM signal is combined using the synthesis filter bank after extracting the subband signals from the frame.

### 1.3.2 DAB TRANSMISSION TECHNIQUE

The special problems of mobile communications are dealt with using a combination of the OFDM transmission technique with DPSK modulation and time and frequency interleaving. Possible disturbances are minimized by consecutive channel coding. The schematic diagram in Figure 1.18 shows the relevant subsystems. For example, the transmission of a program P1 which is delivered as an ISO-MPEG1 stream is shown in Figure 1.18. The channel coding doubles the data rate. The typical characteristics of a mobile communication channel like time and frequency selectivity are handled by using time and frequency interleaving with the help of a multicarrier technique.

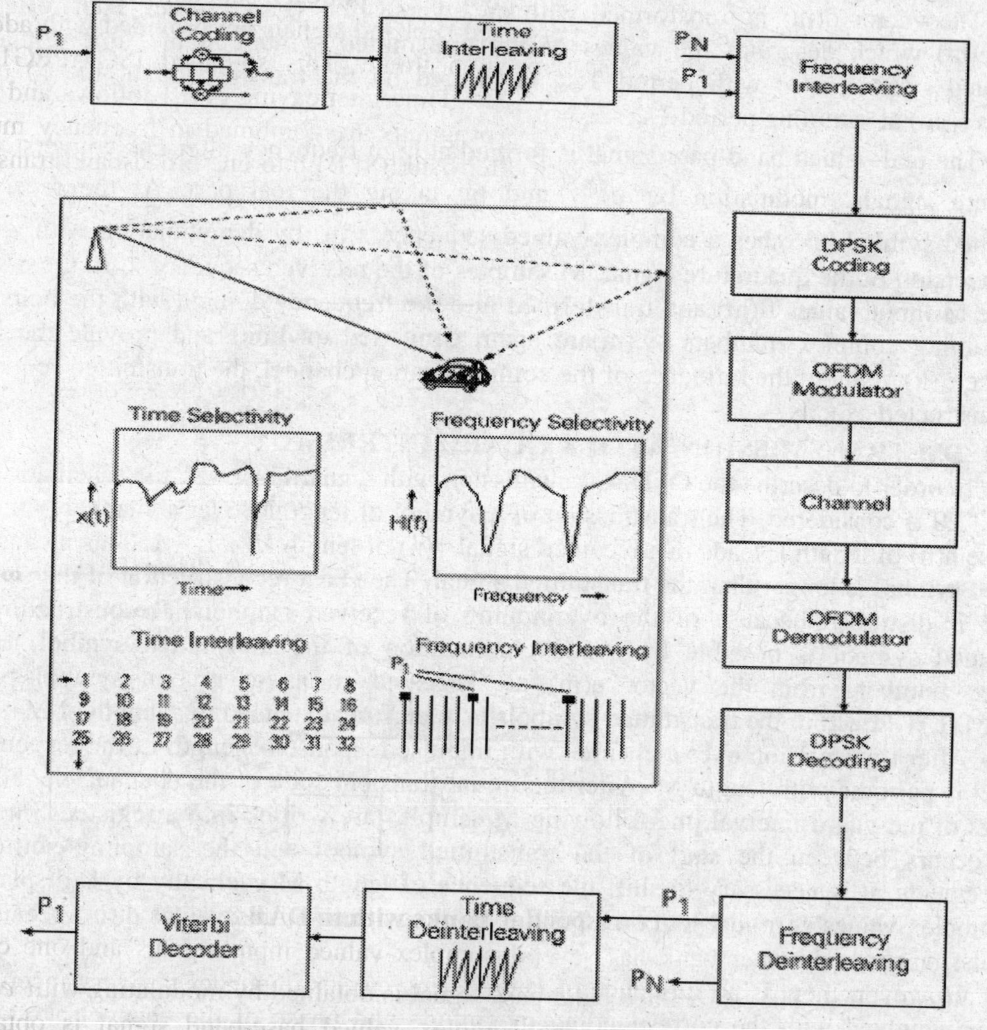


**Figure 1.18 Transmission Technique**

The burst disturbances of consecutive bits are reduced to single bit errors by spreading the bits over a longer period of time. The narrow-band disturbances affect only individual carriers by spreading the transmitter program P1 in the frequency domain, i.e. distribution of transmitter programs of carrier frequencies at a certain displacement. The remaining disturbances of the mobile channel are suppressed with the help of channel coding, i.e. by adding redundancy, and decoding with a Viterbi decoder. The implementation of an OFDM transmission is discussed in the following.

### 1.3.3 OFDM TRANSMISSION

The OFDM transmission technique is shown in Figure 1.19. The technique stands out owing to its simple implementation in the digital domain. The data sequence $C_t(k)$ which is to be transmitted, is written block wise into a register of length 2M. The complex numbers from d1(m) to dM(m) are formed from two consecutive bits (dibits). Here the first bit corresponds to the real part and the second to the imaginary part. The signal space shows the four states for the so-called QPSK. The vector d(m) is transformed with an inverse FFT (Fast Fourier Transform) into a vector e(m) which describes the values of the transmitted symbol in the time domain. The transmitted symbol $x_t(n)$ with period $T_{sym}$ is formed by the transmission of the M complex numbers $e_i(m)$ at sampling period Ts.

The real-valued band-pass signal is formed at high frequency after DA conversion of the quadrature signals, modulation by $e^{j\omega_e t}$ and by taking the real part. At the receiver, the transmitted symbol becomes a complex-valued sequence $x_r(n)$ by demodulation with $e^{-j\omega_e t}$ and AD conversion of the quadrature signal. M samples of the received sequence $x_r(n)$ are distributed over the M input values fi(m) and transformed into the frequency domain with the help of FFT. The resulting complex numbers $g_i(m)$are again converted to dibits and provide the received sequence $c_r(k)$ Without the influence of the communication channel, the transmitted sequence can be reconstructed exactly.

### 1.3.4 OFDM TRANSMISSION WITH A GUARD INTERVAL

In order to describe the OFDM transmission with a guard interval, the schematic diagram in Fig. 1.20 is considered. The transmission of a symbol of lengthM over a channel with impulse response h(n) of length L leads to a received signal y(n) of length M + L – 1. This means that the received symbol is longer than the transmitted signal. The exact reconstruction of the transmitted symbol is disturbed because of the overlapping of received symbols. Reconstruction of the transmitted symbol is possible by cyclic continuation of the transmitted symbol. Here, the complex numbers from the vector e(m) are repeated so as to give a symbol period of $T_{sym}=(M+L)T_s$. Each of the transmitted symbols is, therefore, extended to a length of M + L.

After transmission over a channel with impulse response of length L, the response of the channel is periodic with length M. After the initial transient state of the channel, i.e. after the L samples of the guard interval, the following M samples are written into a register. Since a time delay occurs between the start of the transmitted symbol and the sampling shifted by L displacements, it is necessary to shift the sequence of length M cyclically by L displacements. The complex values $g_i(m)$ do not correspond to the exact transmitted values di(m) because of the transmission channel h(n).

However, there is no influence of neighboring carrier frequencies. Every received value $g_i(m)$ is weighted with the corresponding magnitude and phase of the channel at the specific carrier frequency. The influence of the communication channel can be eliminated by differential coding of consecutive dibits. The decoding process can be done according to $z_i(m) = g_i(m) g_i^*(m-1)$ The dibit corresponds to the sign of the real and imaginary parts.

The DAB transmission technique presented stands out owing to its simple implementation with the help of FFT algorithms. The extension of the transmitted symbol by a length L of the channel impulse response and the synchronization to collect the M samples out of the received symbol have still to be carried out. The length of the guard interval must be matched to the maximum echo delay of the multipath channel. Owing to differential coding of the transmitted sequence, an equalizer at the receiver is not necessary.

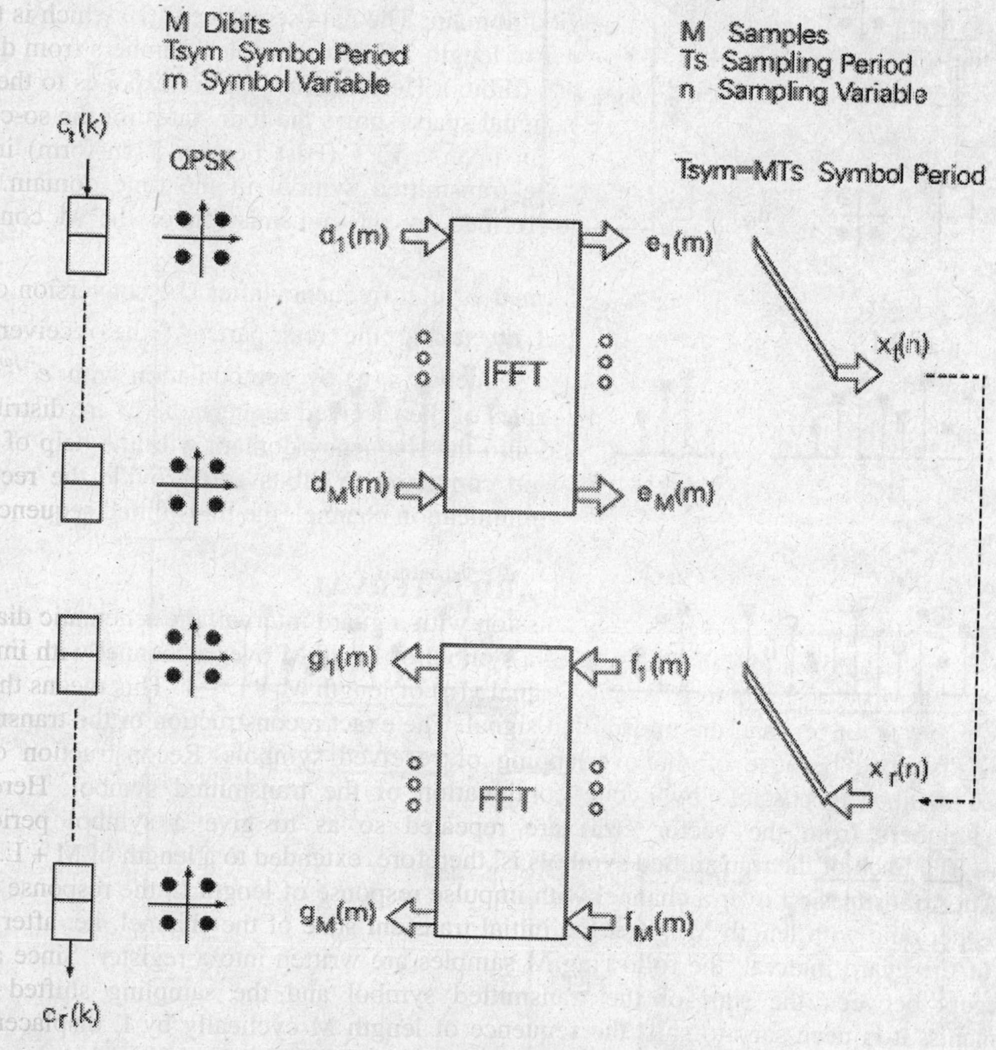


Figure 1.19 OFDM Transmissions

## 1.3.5 DIGITAL RADIO MONDIALE (DRM)

In the interest of national and international broadcasting stations a more widespread program delivery across regional or worldwide regions is of specific importance. This is accomplished by analog radio transmission in the frequency range below 30 MHz. The limited audio quality of the amplitude modulation technique (channel bandwidth 9– 10 kHz) with an audio bandwidth of 4.5 kHz leads to a low acceptance rate for such kind of audio broadcasting. The introduction of the digital transmission technique Digital Radio Mondiale will replace the existing analog transmission systems. The digital transmission is based on OFDM and the audio coding MPEG4-AAC in combination with SBR (Spectral Band Replication).

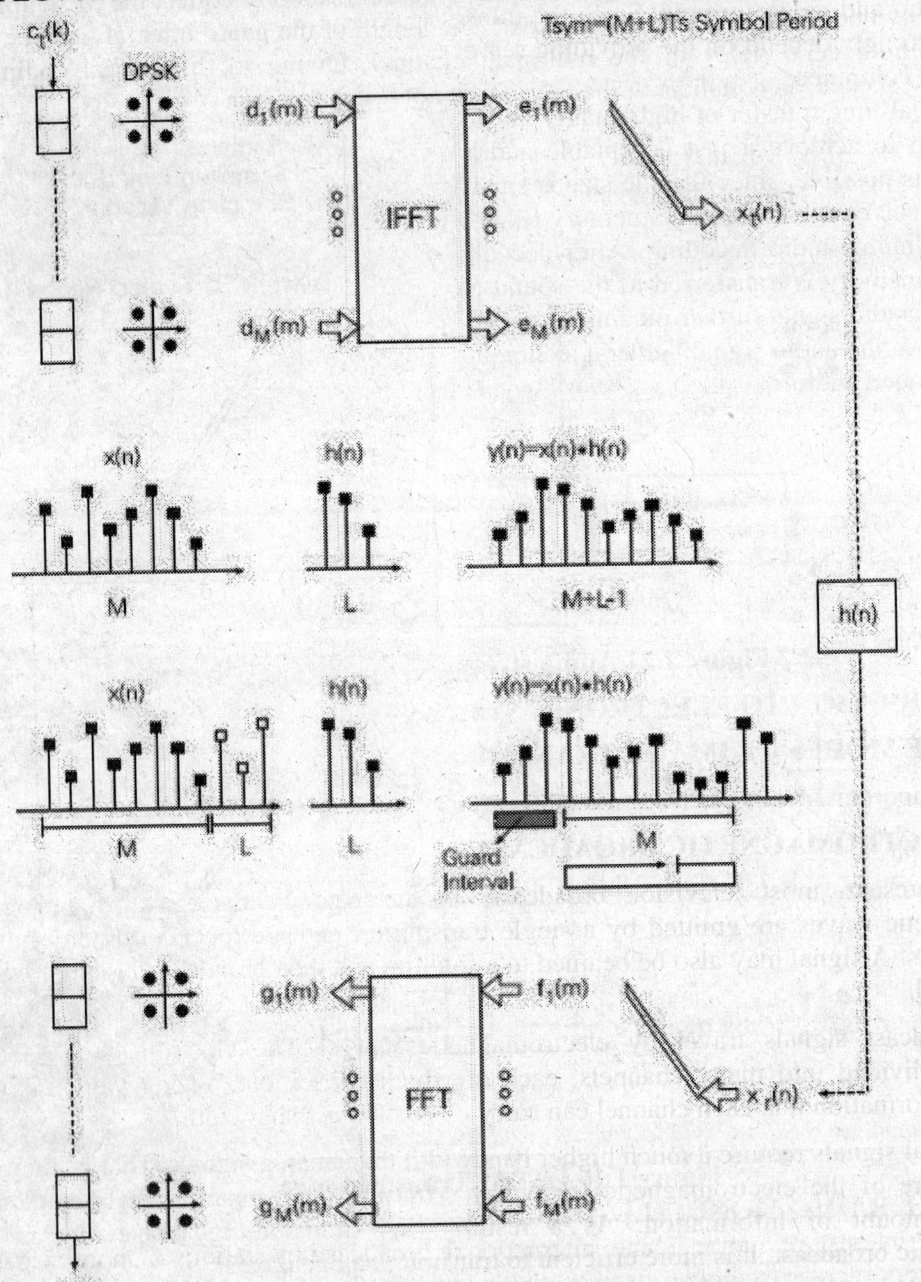


**Figure 1.20 OFDM Transmission with a guard interval**

### 1.3.6 INTERNET AUDIO

The growth of the internet offers new distribution possibilities for information, but especially for audio and video signals. The distribution of audio signals is mainly driven by the MP3 format (MPEG-1 Audio Layer III or in proprietary formats of different companies. The compressed transmission is used because the data rate of home users is still low compared to lossless audio and video formats. Since the transmission is based on file transfer of packets, the data rates strongly depend on the providing server, the actual internet traffic and the access point of the home computer.

A real-time transfer of high quality music is still not possible. If the audio compression is high enough to achieve a just acceptable audio quality, a real-time transfer with a streaming technology is possible, since the file size is small and a transmission needs less time (Fig. 1.21). For this a receiver needs a double memory filled with incoming packets of a coded audio file and a parallel running audio decoding. After decoding of a memory with a sufficiently long audio portion the memory is transferred to the sound card of the computer. During sound playback of the decoded audio signal further incoming packets are received and decoded. Packet loss can lead to interrupts in the audio signal. Several techniques for error concealment and protocols allow the transfer of coded audio.

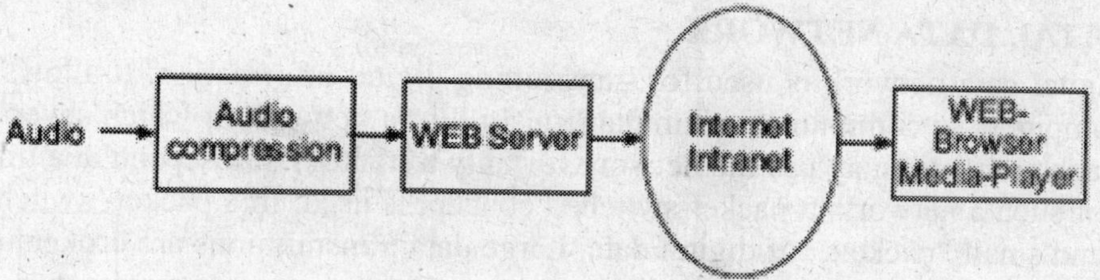


**Figure 1.21 Audio streaming via the internet**

## 1.4 INTRODUCTION TO ELECTRONIC SYSTEMS FOR IMAGE TRANSMISSION

### 1.4.1 THREE MODES OF IMAGE TRANSMISSION

Here three important means of electronic image transmission are discussed.

#### 1.4.1.1. ELECTROMAGNETIC BROADCAST

At present, most television broadcasts in the United States are of analog video. Electromagnetic waves are emitted by a single transmitter, and are received by any number of local receivers. A signal may also be beamed to a satellite and then broadcast directly to receivers on the ground.

Broadcast signals travel by electromagnetic waves. The electromagnetic frequency spectrum is divided into many channels, each of which carries one analog video signal. The amount of information that each channel can carry – is called its bandwidth.

Digital signals require a much higher bandwidth than analog signals. That is, they require a greater share of the electromagnetic frequency spectrum than analog signals containing an equivalent amount of information. As a result, when transmitting images by means of electromagnetic broadcast, it is more efficient to transmit analog signals.

Another method for transmission of analog video signals is point-to- point microwave link. Microwaves are electromagnetic waves with shorter wavelengths than those used for conventional television broadcast. A special receiving station is needed to pick up a microwave broadcast. Since microwaves do not propagate well, transmitter and receiver must be placed in a direct line of sight.

Microwave transmission works well for communication between two locations, over relatively short distances. Standard electromagnetic broadcasts are generally intended for public use, and are therefore not well suited to the uses of interactive image access. Microwave broadcast systems, however, are generally closed, and intended for communication between two specific points. A microwave link connects MIT to Harvard University.

#### 1.4.1.2. CABLE TELEVISION

In the same way as electromagnetic waves can be used to transmit more than one video signal, a cable link may also carry multiple signals. Just as the airwaves can carry several video signals at once, the frequency spectrum of a cable is also divided into a number of channels. Cable television systems use a cable to connect remote receiving sites. An advantage of a cable system is that it does not use public airwaves, and is therefore well-suited to the purpose of transmitting images in a local context. Many such systems exist commercially in the United States. At MIT, a cable television system spans the entire campus, allowing campus- wide access to several video channels.

#### 1.4.1.3. DIGITAL DATA NETWORK

A digital data network is used for transmitting digital information. It allows many users and many computers to communicate simultaneously. For a network in which several computers are linked, each computer may use the network for only a fraction of a second at a time. To allow smooth use of such a network, a packet-switched concept is used. In a packet- switched network, computers send small "packets" of digital data. Large data transmissions are broken up into many packets. Packets on a data network typically have a maximum size of approximately .5 Kilobytes equal to 500 characters of data. Although the transmission of individual packets occurs extremely quickly, the rate at which packets may be sent varies with the number of computers competing for the use of the network. A network is said to be "slow" if enough computers are using it at once to cause noticeable difficulty in sending packets of data.

To transmit an image over a digital network, the image must first be converted to a digital format. There are many formats and algorithms for the digital storage of images, but each format results in a simple digital data file. The size of digital image files typically varies between 50K (Kilobytes) and 500K. Thus, transmitting a single digital image requires sending between 100 and 1000 separate packets on the network.

#### 1.4.1.4. FIBER-OPTIC CABLE

A fiber-optic cable system uses laser light to carry signals through extremely fine glass threads. An advantage to a fiber-optic link is that it has an extremely high bandwidth. That is, it can be used to transmit information at a higher rate than an equivalent electromagnetic or metallic medium. Its high bandwidth makes it ideal for both analog and digital data transmission. It is especially well suited for use as part of a packet-switched data network.

At MIT, the data network which ties together the computers on campus uses a fiber-optic cable as its "spine . This cable runs the entire length of the campus, and allows high-speed digital communication between computers through the use of a packet-switched system.

## 1.4.2 DISPLAY IMAGES

### 1.4.2.1. VISUAL DISPLAY UNIT

A visual display unit, often called simply a monitor or display, is a piece of electrical equipment which displays images generated from the video output of devices such as computers, without producing a permanent record. Most newer monitors typically consist of a [TFT-LCD](thin film transistor liquid crystal display) with older monitors based around a cathode ray tube (CRT). Almost all of the mainstream new monitors being sold on market now are LCD. The monitor comprises the display device, simple circuitry to generatc and format a picture from video sent by the signals source, and usually an enclosure. Within the signal source, either as an integral section or a modular component, there is a display adapter to generate video in a format compatible with the monitor.

**Figure 1.22 19" LG flat-panel LCD monitor.**

### 1.4.2.2. IMAGING TECHNOLOGIES

As with television, many different hardware technologies exist for displaying computer-generated output:

- Liquid crystal display (LCD). TFT LCDs are currently the most popular display device for computers.
    - Passive LCDs are noted for poor contrast and slow response. They were used in laptops until the mid 1990s.
    - Thin film transistor LCDs generate much better images. Nearly all modern LCD monitors are TFTs.
- Cathode ray tube (CRT)
    - Raster scan computer monitors produce images using pixels. These were the most popular display device for older computers.
    - Passive LCDs are noted for poor contrast and slow response. They were used in laptops until the mid 1990s.
    - Thin film transistor LCDs generate much better images. Nearly all modern LCD monitors are TFTs.
- Cathode ray tube (CRT)
    - Raster scan computer monitors produce images using pixels. These were the most popular display device for older computers.
    - Vector displays, as used on the Vectrex, scientific and radar applications, and several early arcade machines such as Asteroids use CRT displays because of

requirement for a deflection system, although a raster-based display may be used, too.

  - o Television sets were used by most early personal and home computers, connecting composite video to the television set using a modulator. Resolution and image quality were strongly limited by the display capabilities of television.

- Plasma display
- Video projectors use CRT, LCD, DLP, LCoS, and other technology to emit light to a projection screen. Front projectors use screens as reflectors to send light back, while rear projectors use screens as diffusers to refract light forward. Rear projectors are often integrated into the same case as their screen.
- Surface-conduction electron-emitter display (SED)
- Organic light-emitting diode (OLED) display
- Penetron military aircraft displays

### 1.4.2.3. CATHODE RAY TUBE

The CRT or cathode ray tube, is the picture tube of a monitor. The back of the tube has a negatively charged cathode. The electron gun shoots electrons down the tube and onto a charged screen. The screen is coated with a pattern of phosphor dots that glow when struck by the electron stream. Each cluster of three dots, one of each color, is one pixel.The image on the monitor's screen is usually made up from at least tens of thousands of such tiny dots glowing on command from the computer. The closer together the pixels are, the sharper the image on screen can be. The distance between pixels on a computer monitor screen is called its dot pitch and is measured in millimeters. Most monitors have a dot pitch of 0.28 mm or less.

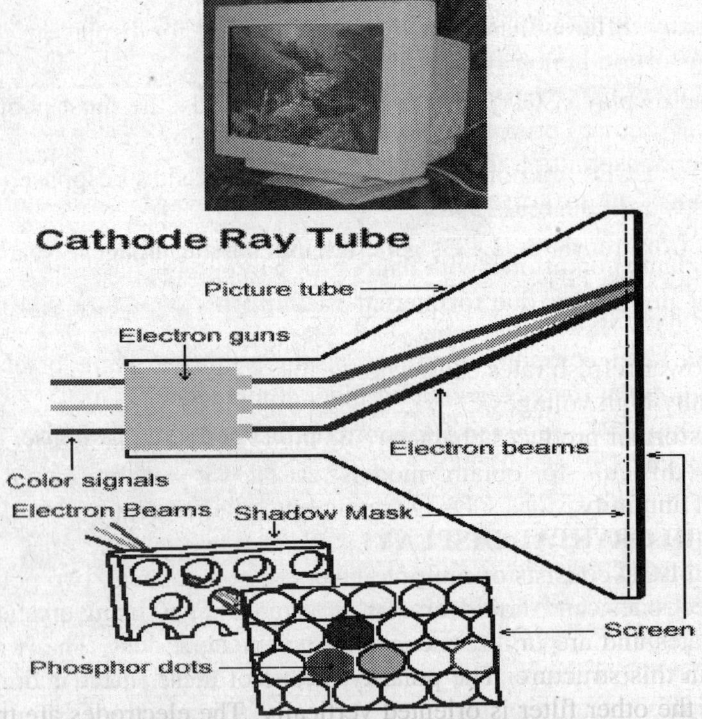


**Figure 1.23 Cathode Ray Tube**

There are two electromagnets around the collar of the tube which deflect the electron beam. The beam scans across the top of the monitor from left to right, is then blanked and moved back to the left-hand side slightly below the previous trace (on the next scan line), scans across the second line and so on until the bottom right of the screen is reached. The beam is again blanked, and moved back to the top left to start again.

This process draws a complete picture, typically 50 to 100 times a second. The number of times in one second that the electron gun redraws the entire image is called the refresh rate and is measured in hertz (cycles per second). It is common in television or very early computer equipment, to use a technique called interlacing, in which all the odd-numbered lines of an image are traced, and then all the even-numbered lines; the circuitry of such an interlaced display need be capable of only half the speed of a non-interlaced display. An interlaced display, particularly at a relatively low refresh rate, can appear to some observers to flicker, and may cause eyestrain.

**ADVANTAGES**

- Very high contrast ratio. 20,000:1 or greater, much higher than many modern LCDs and plasma displays.
- High speed response.
- Excellent Additive color, wide gamut and low black level limited only by external environment.
- Can display natively in almost any resolution and refresh rate.
- Near zero color, saturation, contrast or brightness distortion. Excellent viewing angle.
- No inputs lag.
- A reliable, proven display technology.

**DISADVANTAGES**

- Large size and weight (a 40" unit weighs over 200lbs).
- Geometric distortion in non-flat CRTs.
- Older CRTs are prone to burn-in.
- Warm up time required prior to peak luminance and proper color rendering.
- Greater power consumption than similarly sized displays, such as LCD.
- Screened devices are prone to moiré effect at highest resolution (does not apply to triple-tube projection)
- Intolerant of damp conditions, with dangerous wet failure characteristics.
- Small risk of implosion (due to internal vacuum) if the picture tube is broken in aging sets.
- Use under Lower refresh rates causes noticeable flicker.
- Internal lethally high voltages.
- Flyback transformer produces characteristic high-pitched noise when close to set.
- Increasingly difficult to obtain models at HDTV resolutions, due to consumers' perception of antiquity.

### 1.4.2.4. LCD (LIQUID CRYSTAL DISPLAY)

A pixel on an LCD consists of multiple layers of components: two polarizing filters, two glass plates with electrodes, and liquid crystal molecules. The liquid crystals are sandwiched between the glass plates and are in direct contact with the electrodes. The two polarizing filters are the outer layers in this structure. The polarity of one of these filters is oriented horizontally, while the polarity of the other filter is oriented vertically. The electrodes are treated with a layer of polymer to control the alignment of liquid crystal molecules in a particular direction. These rod-like molecules are arranged to match the horizontal orientation on one side and the vertical orientation on the other, giving the molecules a twisted, helical structure. Twisted nematic liquid crystals are naturally twisted, and are commonly used for LCD's because they react predictably to temperature variation and electric current.

**Figure 1.24 Liquid Crystal Display**

When the liquid crystals are in its natural state, light passing through the first filter will be rotated (in terms of polarity) by the twisted molecule structure, which allows the light to pass through the second filter. When voltage is applied across the electrodes, the liquid crystal structure is untwisted to an extent determined by the amount of voltage. An extremely large voltage will cause the molecules to untwist completely, such that the polarity of any light passing through will not be rotated and will instead be perpendicular to the filter polarity. This filter will block the passage of light because of the difference in polarity orientation, and the resulting pixel will be black. The amount of light allowed to pass through at each pixel can be controlled by varying the corresponding voltage accordingly. In a color LCD each pixel consists of a red, green, and blue subpixel, which requires appropriate color filters in addition to the components mentioned previously. Each subpixel can be controlled individually to display a large range of possible colors for a particular pixel.

The electrodes on one side of the LCD are arranged in columns, while the electrodes on the other side are arranged in rows, forming a large matrix that controls every pixel. Each pixel is designated a unique row-column combination, and the pixel can be accessed by the control circuits using this combination. These circuits send charge down the appropriate row and column, effectively applying a voltage across the electrodes at a given pixel. Simple LCD's such as those on digital watches can operate on what is called a passive-matrix structure, in which each pixel is addressed one at a time.

This results in extremely slow response times and poor voltage control. A voltage applied to one pixel can cause the liquid crystals at surrounding pixels to untwist undesirably, resulting in fuzziness and poor contrast in this area of the image. LCD's with high resolutions, such as large-screen LCD televisions, require an active-matrix structure. This structure is a matrix of thin-film transistors, each corresponding to one pixel on the display. The switching ability of the transistors allows each pixel to be accessed individually and precisely, without affecting nearby pixels. Each transistor also acts as a capacitor while leaking very little current, so it can effectively store the charge while the display is being refreshed.

**THE FOLLOWING ARE TYPES OF LC DISPLAY TECHNOLOGIES:**

- **Twisted Nematic (TN)**: This type of display is the most common and makes use of twisted nematic-phase crystals, which have a natural helical structure and can be untwisted by an applied voltage to allow light to pass through. These displays have low production costs and fast response times but also limited viewing angles, and many have a limited color gamut that cannot take full advantage of advanced graphics cards. These limitations are due to variation in the angles of the liquid crystal molecules at different depths, restricting the angles at which light can leave the pixel.

- **In-Plane Switching (IPS)**: Unlike the electrode arrangement in traditional TN displays, the two electrodes corresponding to a pixel are both on the same glass plate and are parallel to each other. The liquid crystal molecules do not form a helical structure and instead are also parallel to each other. In its natural or "off" state, the molecule structure is arranged parallel to the glass plates and electrodes. Because the twisted molecule structure is not used in an IPS display, the angle at which light leaves a pixel is not as restricted, and therefore viewing angles and color reproduction are much improved compared to those of TN displays. However, IPS displays have slower response times. IPS displays also initially suffered from poor contrast ratios but has been significantly improved with the development of Advanced Super IPS (AS - IPS).
- **Multi-Domain Vertical Alignment (MVA)**: In this type of display the liquid crystals are naturally arranged perpendicular to the glass plates but can be rotated to control light passing through. There are also pyramid-like protrusions in the glass substrates to control the rotation of the liquid crystals such that the light is channeled at an angle with the glass plate. This technology results in wide viewing angles while boasting good contrast ratios and faster response times than those of TN and IPS displays. The major drawback is a reduction in brightness.
- **Patterned Vertical Alignment (PVA)**: This type of display is a variation of MVA and performs very similarly, but with much higher contrast ratios

**ADVANTAGES**

- Slim profile
- Lighter and less bulky than rear-projection televisions
- Is not susceptible to burn-in: Burn-in refers to the television displaying a permanent ghost-like image due to constant, prolonged display of the image. Light-emitting phosphors lose their luminosity over time and when frequently used, the low-luminosity areas become permanently visible.
- LCDs reflect very little light, allowing them to maintain contrast levels in well-lit rooms and no be affected by glare.
- Slightly lower power usage than equivalent sized Plasma displays.
- Can be wall-mounted

**DISADVANTAGES**

- Poor black level: Some light passes through even when liquid crystals completely untwist, so the best black color that can be achieved is varying shades of dark gray, resulting in worse contrast ratios and detail in the image
- Narrower viewing angles than competing technologies. It is nearly impossible to use an LCD without some image warping occuring.
- LCDs rely heavily on thin-film transistors, which are easily damaged, resulting in a defective pixel. The number of defective pixels at which the LCD is determined to be unusable varies (see ISO 13406-2). LCDs currently have a rejection rate of about 50% but this is improving. A larger screen size requires more transistors, which increases the chances of yielding a defective LCD. Technology advancements are slowly easing this problem.

- Typically have slower response times than Plasmas, which can cause ghosting and blurring during the display of fast-moving images.

### 1.4.2.5. PLASMA DISPLAY

A plasma display is made up of many thousands of gas-filled cells that are sandwiched in between two glass plates, two sets of electrodes, dielectric material, and protective layers. The address electrodes are arranged vertically between the rear glass plate and a protective layer. This structure sits behind the cells in the rear of the display, with the protective layer in direct contact with the cells. On the front side of the display there are horizontal display electrodes that sit in between a magnesium-oxide (MgO) protective layer and an insulating dielectric layer.

The MgO layer is in direct contact with the cells and the dielectric layer is in direct contact with the front glass plate. The horizontal and vertical electrodes form a grid from which each individual cell can be accessed. Each individual cell is walled off from surrounding cells so that activity in one cell does not affect another. The cell structure is similar to a honeycomb structure except with rectangular cells.

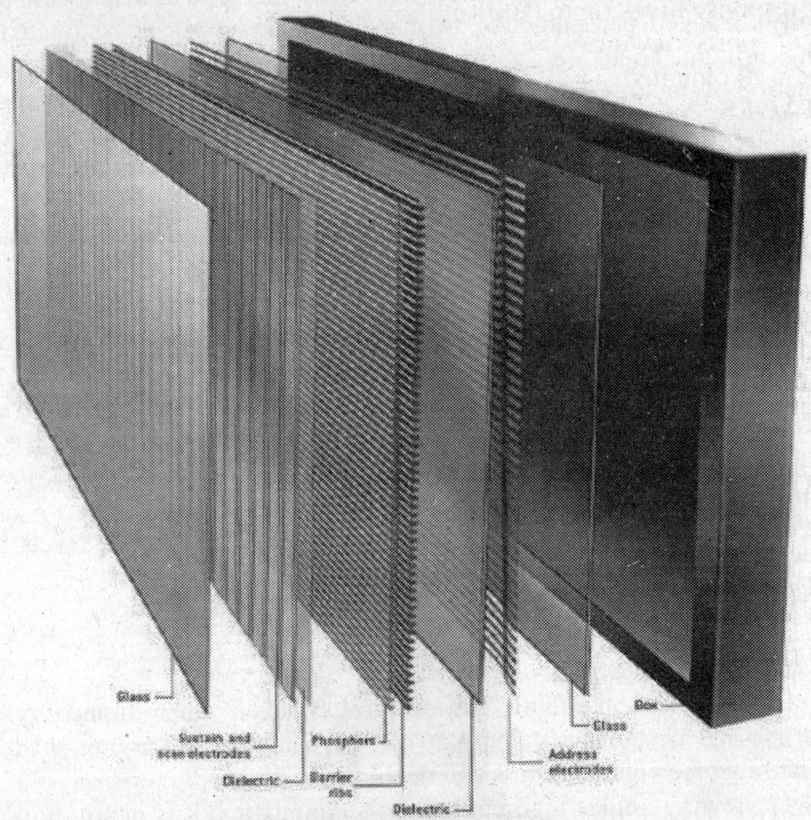


**Figure 1.25 Plasma Display**

To illuminate a particular cell, the electrodes that intersect at the cell are charged by control circuitry and electric current flows through the cell, stimulating the gas (typically xenon and neon) atoms inside the cell. These ionized gas atoms, or plasmas, then release ultraviolet photons that interact with a phosphor material on the inside wall of the cell. The phosphor atoms are stimulated and electrons jump to higher energy levels. When these electrons return to is natural state energy is released in the form of visible light. Every pixel on the display is made up of three subpixel cells. One subpixel cell is coated with red phosphor, another is coated with green phosphor, and the third cell is coated with blue phosphor. Light emitted from the subpixel cells is blended together to create an overall color for the pixel. The control circuitry can manipulate the intensity of light emitted from each cell, and therefore can produce a large spectrum of colors. Light from each cell can be controlled and changed rapidly to produce a high-quality moving picture.

**ADVANTAGES**

- Slim profile
- Lighter and less bulky than rear-projection televisions
- Achieves better color reproduction than LCDs (68 billion ($2^{36}$) versus 16.7 million ($2^{24}$))
- Produces deep, true blacks allowing for superior contrast ratios (upto 1:1,000,000)
- Far wider viewing angles than those of LCD (upto 178°), images do not suffer from degradation at high angles unlike LCD's
- Faster response times (upto 0.001 milliseconds) make Plasmas ideal for fast motion video (films or sports viewing)
- Can be wall mounted

**DISADVANTAGES**

- Susceptible to Screen burn-in and image retention (however newer models have built-in technologies to prevent this such as pixel shifting)
- Phosphors lose luminosity over time, resulting in gradual decline of absolute image brightness (newer models are less susceptible to this, having lifespans exceeding 60,000 hours, far longer than older CRT technology)
- Generally do not come in smaller sizes than 32 inches
- Susceptible to reflection glare in bright rooms
- Heavier than LCD due to the requirement of a glass screen to hold the gases
- Damage to the glass screen can be permanent and far more difficult to repair than an LCD.

### 1.4.2.6. DIGITAL MONITORS

Early digital monitors are sometimes known as TTLs because the voltages on the red, green, and blue inputs are compatible with TTL logic chips. Later digital monitors support LVDS, or TMDS protocols.

**Figure 1.26 TTL Monitors**

IBM PC with green monochrome display.

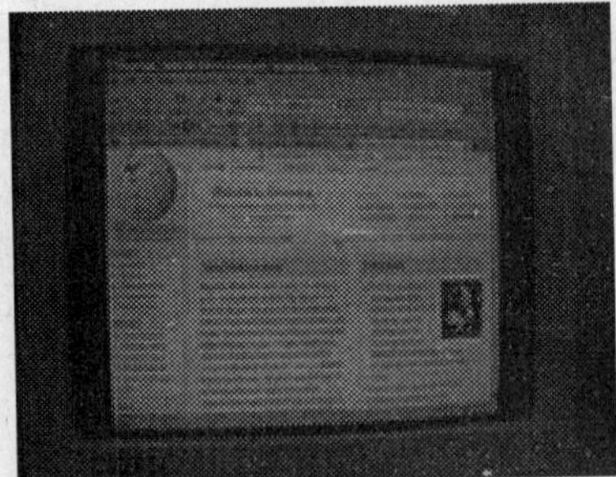

**Figure 1.27 Monochrome Monitor**

An amber monochrome computer monitor, manufactured in 2007, which uses a 15-pin SVGA connector just like a standard color monitor. Monitors used with the MDA, Hercules, CGA, and EGA graphics adapters used in early IBM PC's (Personal Computer) and clones were controlled via TTL logic. Such monitors can usually be identified by a male DB-9 connector used on the video cable. The disadvantage of TTL monitors was the limited number of colors available due to the low number of digital bits used for video signaling.

Modern monochrome monitors use the same 15-pin SVGA connector as standard color monitors. They are capable of displaying 32-bit grayscale at 1024x768 resolutions, making them able to interface with modern computers.TTL Monochrome monitors only made use of five out of the nine pins. One pin was used as a ground, and two pins were used for horizontal/vertical synchronization. The electron gun was controlled by two separate digital signals, a video bit, and an intensity bit to control the brightness of the drawn pixels. Only four shades were possible; black, dim, medium or bright.CGA monitors used four digital signals to control the three electron guns used in color CRTs, in a signaling method known as RGBI, or Red Green and Blue, plus Intensity. Each of the three RGB colors can be switched on or off independently. The intensity bit increases the brightness of all guns that are switched on, or if no colors are switched on the intensity bit will switch on all guns at a very low brightness to produce a dark grey. A CGA monitor is only capable of rendering 16 colors.

The CGA monitor was not exclusively used by PC based hardware. The Commodore 128 could also utilize CGA monitors. Many CGA monitors were capable of displaying composite video via a separate jack.EGA monitors used six digital signals to control the three electron guns in a signaling method known as RrGgBb. Unlike CGA, each gun is allocated its own intensity bit. This allowed each of the three primary colors to have four different states (off, soft, medium, and bright) resulting in 64 colors.

### 1.4.2.7. SINGLE COLOR SCREENS

Display colors other than white were very popular on monochrome monitors in the 1980s. These colors were more comfortable on the eye. This was particularly an issue at the time due to the lower refresh rates in use at the time causing flicker, plus the use of less comfortable color schemes than used with most of today's software. Green screens were the most popular color, with amber displays also availabl:. 'Paper white' was also in use, which was a warm white.

### 1.4.2.8. MODERN TECHNOLOGY

### (i) ANALOG MONITORS

Most modern computer displays can show an infinite number of different colors in the RGB color space by changing red, green, and blue analog video signals in continuously variable intensities. These have been almost exclusively progressive scan since the middle 1980s. While many early plasma and liquid crystal displays have exclusively analog connections, all signals in such monitors pass through a completely digital section prior to display.

**Figure 1.28 Analog Monitor**

While many similar connectors (13W3, BNC, etc...) were used on other platforms, the IBM PC and compatible systems long ago standardized on the VGA connector. All of these connectors deliver nearly flawless high resolution video which vastly outclasses that of a TV.

**(ii) DIGITAL AND ANALOG COMBINATION**

The first popular external digital monitor connectors, such as DVI-I and the various breakout connectors based on it, included both analog signals compatible with VGA and digital signals compatible with new flat-screen displays in the same connector. This made the connector nearly painless for users of both technologies.

**(iii) DIGITAL MONITORS**

Newer connectors are being made which have digital only video signals. Many of these, such as HDMI and DisplayPort, also feature integrated audio and data connections. One less popular

**Figure 1.29 Digital Monitor**

feature most of these connectors share are DRM encrypted signals, although the HDCP technology responsible for implementing the protection was necessarily rudimentary to meet cost constraints, and was primarily a barrier aimed towards dissuading average consumers from creating exact duplicates without a noticeable loss in image quality.

### 1.4.2.9. TOUCH SCREEN

These monitors use touching of the screen as an input method. Items can be selected or moved with a finger, and finger gestures may be used to convey commands. This does however mean the screen needs frequent cleaning due to image degradatión from fingerprints.

**Figure 1.30 Touch Screen**

### 1.4.2.10. TABLET SCREENS

A combination of a monitor with a graphics tablet. Such devices are typically unresponsive to touch, but may offer sensitivity to one or more special tools' pressure, tilt, controls, opposite ends, and multiple tools.

**Figure 1.31 Tablet Screens**

### 1.4.2.11. VIDEO PROJECTOR

A video projector takes a video signal and projects the corresponding image on a projection screen using a lens system. All video projectors use a very bright light to project the image, and most modern ones can correct any curves, blurriness, and other inconsistencies through manual settings. Video projectors are widely used for conference room presentations, classroom training, home theatre and live events applications. Projectors are widely used in many schools and other educational settings, connected to an interactive white board to interactively teach pupils.

**Figure 1.32 Video Projector**

Projected image from a video projector in a home cinema.

### 1.4.2.12. LARGE-SCREEN TELEVISION TECHNOLOGY

Large-screen television technology developed rapidly in the late 1990s and 2000s. Various thin screen technologies are being developed, but only the liquid crystal display (LCD), plasma display (PDP) and Digital Light Processing (DLP) were released on the public market. These technologies have almost completely displaced cathode ray tubes (CRT) in television sales, due to the necessary bulkiness of the cathode ray tubes. However, just released technologies like Organic light-emitting diode (OLED) and not-yet released technologies like Surface-conduction Electron-emitter Display (SED) or Field Emission Display (FED) are making their way to replace the first flat screen technologies in picture quality. The diagonal screen size of a CRT television is limited to about 40 inches because of the size requirements of the cathode ray tube, which fires a beam of electrons onto the screen, creating a viewable image. A larger screen size requires a longer tube, making a CRT television with a large screen (50 to 80 inches) unrealistic because of size. The aforementioned technologies can produce large-screen televisions that are much thinner.

### 1.4.2.13. PROJECTION TELEVISION

A projection television uses a projector to create a small image from a video signal and magnify this image onto a viewable screen. The projector uses a bright beam of light and a lens system to project the image to a much larger size. A Front-projection television uses a projector that is separate from the screen which could be a suitably-prepared wall, and the projector is placed in front of the screen. The setup of a Rear-projection television is in some ways similar to that of a traditional television, the projector is contained inside the television box and projects the image from behind the screen.

**Figure 1.33 56 inch DLP rear projection Television**

### 1.4.2.14. FLAT PANEL DISPLAY

**Figure 1.34 Flat Panel Display**

Flat panel displays encompass a growing number of technologies enabling video displays that are lighter and much thinner than traditional television and video displays that use cathode ray tubes, and are usually less than 4 inches (100 mm) thick. They can be divided into two general categories: Volatile or Static.

Flat panel displays balance their smaller footprint and trendy modern look with high production costs and in many cases inferior images compared with traditional CRTs. In many applications, specifically modern portable devices such as laptops, cellular phones, and digital cameras, whatever disadvantages exist are overcome by the portability requirements.

### 1.4.2.15. LASER VIDEO DISPLAY

A laser video display, or laser TV, is a rear-projection television that replaces the conventional high-intensity discharge lamps with three colored lasers. The image on the screen is produced like a conventional rear projection system, by scanning the light source across the screen using optoelectronics.

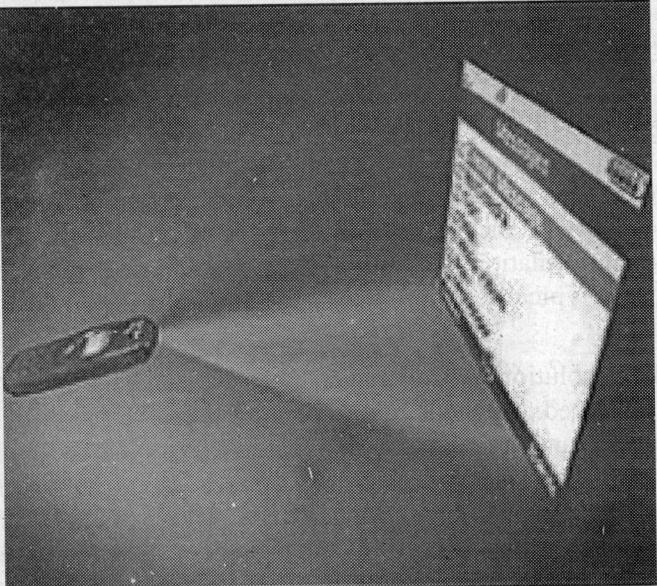

**Figure 1.35 Laser Video Display**

## 1.5 INTRODUCTION TO ELECTRONIC SYSTEMS FOR IMAGE STORAGE

### 1.5.1 ELECTRONIC IMAGE STORAGE

Electronic storage of images can be divided into analog and digital formats.

#### 1.5.1.1. ANALOG STORAGE FORMATS

In analog storage, the shape of the waveform used to reproduce an image is stored. Retrieving an image stored in analog format involves reconstructing the waveform from its representation on the storage medium. There exist different analog formats for the storage of video images. In the United States, nearly all analog storage devices and media store NTSC format video signals.

Two familiar types of analog image devices are videotape and videodisc. These are primarily designed to store a particular type of analog signal, such as NTSC or PAL formats. Some storage methods can provide only linear access to the images which they store. For example, a magnetic videotape must be searched in a linear fashion in order to locate a desired segment. Linear access devices such as videotape are commonly used for the purposes of storing large amounts of analog data. However, for automated storage and/or retrieval, linear access storage methods are generally not adequate. Random access devices are better suited.

Because random access devices allow direct access to any single frame of a sequence of video frames, they are useful for large-scale storage and interactive retrieval. Laser videodisc players are the most common type of random access storage devices. A laser videodisc is randomly accessible because any particular frame of the video signal stored on the disc may be individually retrieved by specifying its unique frame number.

#### 1.5.1.2. DIGITAL STORAGE FORMATS

Digital storage differs greatly from analog storage. To store an image digitally, it is first necessary to convert it to a series of numbers which contain information about all of the parts of the image. These numbers are in turn represented as a stream of ones and zeros, and thus form a digital data stream. Since computers and many related devices are designed to work with digital data, digital image formats work well for storing and manipulating images.

Digital storage devices are designed store any kind of digital information. Images stored in digital formats can usually be manipulated in the same ways as can any other digitally-stored information. Because the information in a digital image must be broken down into many pieces of information, digital images typically require very large amounts of storage space in comparison to other types of digital data.

The greater the resolution of an image, the greater the number of discrete pieces of information that must be stored. Magnetic disks are common storage media for digital data. They are made of metal or plastic, and are coated with a material capable of being magnetized by a disk drive. They exist in many forms, and have varying storage capacities. A floppy diskette used with a small computer may have a capacity of 1 Megabyte of data, while a disk pack used on a large computer system may have a capacity of 1000 Megabytes or more. Read-only optical disks are also an effective means of storing large amounts of data. Read-only disks must be produced in quantity by a manufacturer of optical media, and are therefore best used as means of distributing large databases of information.

Write-once optical disks are used increasingly for storing digital data. Such disks may hold 170 Megabytes to as much as 2000 Megabytes of data apiece. Their extremely large capacity suits them to the storage of large amounts of data.

An important feature of most digital storage media is that they provide random access to the data which they store. That is, information can be retrieved on demand without regard to its physical location on the storage medium. Hence, most large capacity digital storage devices work well for the interactive storage and retrieval of images encoded in digital formats.

### 1.5.1.3. ELECTRONIC IMAGE STORAGE

Electronic storage, often called storage or memory, refers to computer components, electronic devices, and recording media that retain digital data used for computing for some interval of time. Computer data storage provides one of the core functions of the modern computer, that of information retention. It is one of the fundamental components of all modern computers, and coupled with a central processing unit (CPU, a processor), implements the basic computer model used since the 1940s.

**Figure 1.36 1-GB of SDRAM mounted in a personal computer. example of primary storage.**

In contemporary usage, memory usually refers to a form of semiconductor storage known as random access memory (RAM) and sometimes other forms of fast but temporary storage. Similarly, storage today more commonly refers to mass storage - optical discs, forms of magnetic storage like hard disks, and other types slower than RAM, but of a more permanent nature.

Historically, memory and storage were respectively called primary storage and secondary storage. The contemporary distinctions are helpful, because they are also fundamental to the architecture of computers in general. The distinctions also reflect an important and significant technical difference between memory and mass storage devices, which has been blurred by the historical usage of the term storage. Nevertheless, this article uses the traditional nomenclature.

### 1.5.1.4. PURPOSE OF STORAGE

Many different forms of storage, based on various natural phenomena, have been invented. So far, no practical universal storage medium exists, and all forms of storage have some drawbacks. Therefore a computer system usually contains several kinds of storage, each with an individual purpose.

A digital computer represents data using the binary numeral system. Text, numbers, pictures, audio, and nearly any other form of information can be converted into a string of bits, or binary digits, each of which has a value of 1 or 0. The most common unit of storage is the byte, equal to 8 bits. A piece of information can be handled by any computer whose storage space is large enough to accommodate the binary representation of the piece of information, or simply data. For example, using eight million bits, or about one megabyte, a typical computer could store a short novel.

Traditionally the most important part of every computer is the central processing unit (CPU, or simply a processor), because it actually operates on data, performs any calculations, and controls all the other components.

Without a significant amount of memory, a computer would merely be able to perform fixed operations and immediately output the result. It would have to be reconfigured to change its behavior. This is acceptable for devices such as desk calculators or simple digital signal processors. Von Neumann machines differ in that they have a memory in which they store their operating instructions and data. Such computers are more versatile in that they do not need to have their hardware reconfigured for each new program, but can simply be reprogrammed with new in-memory instructions; they also tend to be simpler to design, in that a relatively simple processor may keep state between successive computations to build up complex procedural results. Most modern computers are von Neumann machines.

In practice, almost all computers use a variety of memory types, organized in a storage hierarchy around the CPU, as a tradeoff between performance and cost. Generally, the lower a storage is in the hierarchy, the lesser its bandwidth and the greater its access latency is from the CPU. This traditional division of storage to primary, secondary, tertiary and off-line storage is also guided by cost per bit.

### 1.5.1.5. PRIMARY STORAGE

Primary storage, presently known as memory, is the only one directly accessible to the CPU. The CPU continuously reads instructions stored there and executes them as required. Any data actively operated on is also stored there in uniform manner.

Historically, early computers used delay lines, Williams's tubes, or rotating magnetic drums as primary storage. By 1954, those unreliable methods were mostly replaced by magnetic core memory, which was still rather cumbersome. Undoubtedly, a revolution was started with the invention of a transistor, that soon enabled then-unbelievable miniaturization of electronic memory via solid-state silicon chip technology.

This led to a modern random access memory (RAM). It is small-sized, light, but quite expensive at the same time. (The particular types of RAM used for primary storage are also volatile, i.e. they lose the information when not powered).

**Figure 1.37 Hard disk Drive**

40 GB hard disk drive (HDD); when connected to a computer it serves as secondary storage.

**Figure 1.38 Tape Cartridge**

160 GB SDLT tape cartridge, an example of off-line storage. When used within a robotic tape library, it is classified as tertiary storage instead.

As shown in the diagram, traditionally there are two more sub-layers of the primary storage, besides main large-capacity RAM:

- Processor registers are located inside the processor. Each register typically holds a word of data (often 32 or 64 bits). CPU instructions instruct the arithmetic and logic unit to perform various calculations or other operations on this data (or with the help of it). Registers are technically among the fastest of all forms of computer data storage.
- Processor cache is an intermediate stage between ultra-fast registers and much slower main memory. It's introduced solely to increase performance of the computer. Most actively used information in the main memory is just duplicated in the cache memory, which is faster, but of much lesser capacity. On the other hand it is much slower, but much larger than processor registers. Multi-level hierarchical cache setup is also commonly used—primary cache being smallest, fastest and located inside the processor; secondary cache being somewhat larger and slower.

Main memory is directly or indirectly connected to the CPU via a memory bus. It is actually comprised of two buses (not on the diagram): an address bus and a data bus. The CPU firstly sends a number through an address bus, a number called memory address that indicates the desired location of data. Then it reads or writes the data itself using the data bus. Additionally, a memory management unit (MMU) is a small device between CPU and RAM recalculating the actual memory address, for example to provide an abstraction of virtual memory or other tasks. As the RAM types used for primary storage are volatile (cleared at start up), a computer containing only such storage would not have a source to read instructions from, in order to start the computer.

Hence, non-volatile primary storage containing a small startup program (BIOS) is used to bootstrap the computer, that is, to read a larger program from non-volatile secondary storage to RAM and start to execute it. A non-volatile technology used for this purpose is called ROM, for read-only memory (the terminology may be somewhat confusing as most ROM types are also capable of random access).

Many types of "ROM" are not literally read only, as updates are possible; however it is slow and memory must be erased in large portions before it can be re-written. Some embedded systems run programs directly from ROM (or similar), because such programs are rarely changed. Standard computers do not store non-rudimentary programs in ROM; rather use large capacities of secondary storage, which is non-volatile as well, and not as costly.

## (i) RANDOM-ACCESS MEMORY

Random-access memory (usually known by its acronym, RAM) is a form of computer data storage. Today, it takes the form of integrated circuits that allow stored data to be accessed in any order (i.e., at random). The word random thus refers to the fact that any piece of data can be returned in a constant time, regardless of its physical location and whether or not it is related to the previous piece of data.

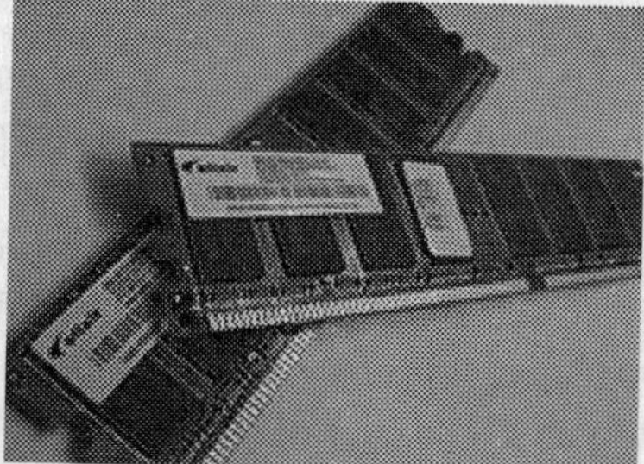

**Figure 1.39 Random Access Memory**

By contrast, storage devices such as tapes, magnetic discs and optical discs rely on the physical movement of the recording medium or a reading head. In these devices, the movement takes longer than data transfer, and the retrieval time varies based on the physical location of the next item.

The word RAM is often associated with volatile types of memory (such as DRAM memory modules), where the information is lost after the power is switched off. Many other types of memory are RAM, too, including most types of ROM and flash memory called NOR-Flash.

## (ii) READ-ONLY MEMORY

Read-only memory (usually known by its acronym, ROM) is a class of storage media used in computers and other electronic devices. Because data stored in ROM cannot be modified (at least not very quickly or easily), it is mainly used to distribute firmware (software that is very closely tied to specific hardware, and unlikely to require frequent updates).

In its strictest sense, ROM refers only to mask ROM (the oldest type of solid state ROM), which is fabricated with the desired data permanently stored in it, and thus can never be modified. However, more modern types such as EPROM and flash EEPROM can be erased and re-programmed multiple times; they are still described as "read-only memory"(ROM) because the reprogramming process is generally infrequent, comparatively slow, and often does not permit random access writes to individual memory locations. Despite the simplicity of mask ROM, economies of scale and field-programmability often make reprogrammable technologies more flexible and inexpensive, so mask ROM is rarely used in new products as of 2007.

## 1.5.1.6. SECONDARY STORAGE

**Figure 1.40 Hard Disk Drive with protective cover removed.**

Secondary storage in popular usage, differs from primary storage in that it is not directly accessible by the CPU. The computer usually uses its input/output channels to access secondary storage and transfers the desired data using intermediate area in primary storage. Secondary storage does not lose the data when the device is powered down—it is non-volatile. Per unit, it is typically also an order of magnitude less expensive than primary storage. Consequently, modern computer systems typically have an order of magnitude more secondary storage than primary storage and data is kept for a longer time there.

In modern computers, hard disks are usually used as secondary storage. The time taken to access a given byte of information stored on a hard disk is typically a few thousandths of a second, or milliseconds. By contrast, the time taken to access a given byte of information stored in random access memory is measured in billionths of a second, or nanoseconds. This illustrates the very significant access-time difference which distinguishes solid-state memory from rotating magnetic storage devices: hard disks are typically about a million times slower than memory. Rotating optical storage devices, such as CD and DVD drives, have even longer access times.

Some other examples of secondary storage technologies are: flash memory (e.g. USB sticks or keys), floppy disks, magnetic tape, paper tape, punch cards, standalone RAM disks, and Zip drives.

The secondary storage is often formatted according to a filesystem format, which provides the abstraction necessary to organize data into files and directories, providing also additional information (called metadata) describing the owner of a certain file, the access time, the access permissions, and other information.

Most computer operating systems use the concept of virtual memory, allowing utilization of more primary storage capacity than is physically available in the system. As the primary memory fills up, the system moves the least-used chunks (pages) to secondary storage devices (to a swap file or page file), retrieving them later when they are needed. As more of these retrievals from slower secondary storage are necessary, the more the overall system performance is degraded.

### 1.5.1.7. TERTIARY STORAGE

**Figure 1.41 Tertiary Storage**

**Large tape library.** Tape cartridges placed on shelves in the front, robotic arm moving in the back. Visible height of the library is about 180 cm.

Tertiary storage or tertiary memory provides a third level of storage. Typically it involves a robotic mechanism which will mount (insert) and dismount removable mass storage media into a storage device according to the system's demands; this data is often copied to secondary storage before use. It is primarily used for archival of rarely accessed information since it is much slower than secondary storage (e.g. 5-60 seconds vs. 1-10 milliseconds). This is primarily useful for extraordinarily large data stores, accessed without human operators. Typical examples include tape libraries and optical jukeboxes.

When a computer needs to read information from the tertiary storage, it will first consult a catalog database to determine which tape or disc contains the information. Next, the computer will instruct a robotic arm to fetch the medium and place it in a drive. When the computer has finished reading the information, the robotic arm will return the medium to its place in the library.

### 1.5.1.8. OFF-LINE STORAGE

Off-line storage, also known as disconnected storage, is a computer data storage on a medium or a device that is not under the control of a processing unit. The medium is recorded, usually in a secondary or tertiary storage device, and then physically removed or disconnected. It must be inserted or connected by a human operator before a computer can access it again. Unlike tertiary storage, it cannot be accessed without human interaction.

Off-line storage is used to transfer information, since the detached medium can be easily physically transported. Additionally, in case a disaster, for example a fire, destroys the original data, a medium in a remote location will be probably unaffected, enabling disaster recovery. Off-line storage increases general information security, since it is physically inaccessible from a computer, and data confidentiality or integrity cannot be affected by computer-based attack techniques. Also, if the information stored for archival purposes is accessed seldom or never, off-line storage is less expensive than tertiary storage.

In modern personal computers, most secondary and tertiary storage media are also used for off-line storage. Optical discs and flash memory devices are most popular, and to much lesser extent removable hard disk drives. In enterprise uses, magnetic tape is predominant. Older examples are floppy disks, Zip disks, or punched cards.

**Figure 1.42 1GB DDR RAM memory module**

### 1.5.2. CHARACTERISTICS OF STORAGE

Storage technologies at all levels of the storage hierarchy can be differentiated by evaluating certain core characteristics as well as measuring characteristics specific to a particular implementation. These core characteristics are volatility, mutability, accessibility, and addressibility. For any particular implementation of any storage technology, the characteristics worth measuring are capacity and performance.

#### 1.5.2.1. VOLATILITY

**Non-volatile memory**

Will retain the stored information even if it is not constantly supplied with electric power. It is suitable for long-term storage of information. Nowadays used for most of secondary, tertiary, and off-line storage. In 1950s and 1960s, it was also used for primary storage, in the form of magnetic core memory.

**Volatile memory**

Requires constant power to maintain the stored information. The fastest memory technologies of today are volatile ones (not a universal rule). Since primary storage is required to be very fast, it predominantly uses volatile memory.

#### 1.5.2.2. DIFFERENTIATION

**Dynamic memory**

A form of volatile memory which also requires the stored information to be periodically re-read and re-written, or refreshed, otherwise it would vanish.

**Static memory**

A form of volatile memory similar to DRAM with the exception that it never needs to be refreshed.

#### 1.5.2.3. MUTABILITY

**Read/write storage or mutable storage**

Allows information to be overwritten at any time. A computer without some amount of read/write storage for primary storage purposes would be useless for many tasks. Modern computers typically use read/write storage also for secondary storage.

**Read only storage**

Retains the information stored at the time of manufacture, and write once storage (Write Once Read Many) allows the information to be written only once at some point after manufacture. These are called immutable storage. Immutable storage is used for tertiary and off-line storage. Examples include CD-ROM and CD-R.

**Slow write, fast read storage**

Read/write storage which allows information to be overwritten multiple times, but with the write operation being much slower than the read operation. Examples include CD-RW and flash memory.

#### 1.5.2.4. ACCESSIBILITY

**Random access**

Any location in storage can be accessed at any moment in approximately the same amount of time. Such characteristic is well suited for primary and secondary storage.

**Sequential access**

The accessing of pieces of information will be in a serial order, one after the other; therefore the time to access a particular piece of information depends upon which piece of information was last accessed. Such characteristic is typical of off-line storage.

### 1.5.2.5. ADDRESSABILITY

**Location-addressable**

Each individually accessible unit of information in storage is selected with its numerical memory address. In modern computers, location-addressable storage usually limits to primary storage, accessed internally by computer programs, since location-addressability is very efficient, but burdensome for humans.

**File addressable**

Information is divided into files of variable length, and a particular file is selected with human-readable directory and file names. The underlying device is still location-addressable, but the operating system of a computer provides the file system abstraction to make the operation more understandable. In modern computers, secondary, tertiary and off-line storage use file systems.

**Content-addressable**

Each individually accessible unit of information is selected with a hash value, or a short identifier with a number pertaining to the memory address the information is stored on. Content-addressable storage can be implemented using software (computer program) or hardware (computer device), with hardware being faster but more expensive option.

### 1.5.2.6. CAPACITY

**Raw capacity**

The total amount of stored information that a storage device or medium can hold. It is expressed as a quantity of bits or bytes (e.g. 10.4 megabytes).

**Density**

The compactness of stored information. It is the storage capacity of a medium divided with a unit of length, area or volume (e.g. 1.2 megabytes per square inch).

### 1.5.2.7. PERFORMANCE

**Latency**

The time it takes to access a particular location in storage. The relevant unit of measurement is typically nanosecond for primary storage, millisecond for secondary storage, and second for tertiary storage. It may make sense to separate read latency and write latency, and in case of sequential access storage, minimum, maximum and average latency.

**Throughput**

The rate at which information can be read from or written to the storage. In computer data storage, throughput is usually expressed in terms of megabytes per second or MB/s, though bit rate may also be used. As with latency, read rate and write rate may need to be differentiated. Also accessing media sequentially, as opposed to randomly, typically yields maximum throughput.

### 1.5.2.8. ENVIRONMENTAL IMPACT

The impact of a storage device on the environment.

**Energy**

- Energy star certified power adapters for storage devices reduce power consumption 30 percent on average
- Storage devices that reduce fan usage, automatically shut-down during inactivity, and low power hard drives can reduce energy consumption 90 percent.
- 2.5 inch hard disk drives often consume less power than larger ones.Low capacity solid-state drives consume less power than DRAM, because they have no moving parts.[8][9][10] Also, memory may use more power than hard disks.

**Recycling**

- Some devices are made of recyclable materials like aluminum, bamboo, or plastics
- Easily disassembled devices are easier to recycle if only certain parts are recyclable
- Packaging may be recyclable and some companies print instructions on the box or use recyclable paper for the instructions instead of waxed paper

**Manufacturing**

- The amount of raw materials (metals, aluminum, plastics, lead) used to manufacture the device
- Excess waste materials and if they are recycled
- Chemicals used in manufacturing
- Shipping distance for the device itself and parts
- Amount of packaging materials and if they are recyclable

### 1.5.2.9. FUNDAMENTAL STORAGE TECHNOLOGIES

As of 2008, the most commonly used data storage technologies are semiconductor, magnetic, and optical, while paper still sees some limited usage. Some other fundamental storage technologies have also been used in the past or are proposed for development.

#### 1. SEMICONDUCTOR

Semiconductor memory uses semiconductor-based integrated circuits to store information. A semiconductor memory chip may contain millions of tiny transistors or capacitors. Both volatile and non-volatile forms of semiconductor memory exist. In modern computers, primary storage almost exclusively consists of dynamic volatile semiconductor memory or dynamic random access memory. Since the turn of the century, a type of non-volatile semiconductor memory known as flash memory has steadily gained share as off-line storage for home computers. Non-volatile semiconductor memory is also used for secondary storage in various advanced electronic devices and specialized computers.

#### 2. MAGNETIC

Magnetic storage uses different patterns of magnetization on a magnetically coated surface to store information. Magnetic storage is non-volatile. The information is accessed using one or more read/write heads which may contain one or more recording transducers. A read/write head only covers a part of the surface so that the head or medium or both must be moved relative to another in order to access data. In modern computers, magnetic storage will take these forms:

- Magnetic disk
    - Floppy disk, used for off-line storage

   - Hard disk, used for secondary storage
- Magnetic tape data storage, used for tertiary and off-line storage

In early computers, magnetic storage was also used for primary storage in a form of magnetic drum, or core memory, core rope memory, thin film memory, twistor memory or bubble memory. Also unlike today, magnetic tape was often used for secondary storage.

**3. OPTICAL**

Optical storage, the typical Optical disc, stores information in deformities on the surface of a circular disc and reads this information by illuminating the surface with a laser diode and observing the reflection. Optical disc storage is non-volatile. The deformities may be permanent (read only media), formed once (write once media) or reversible (recordable or read/write media). The following forms are currently in common use:

- CD, CD-ROM, DVD, BD-ROM: Read only storage, used for mass distribution of digital information (music, video, computer programs)
- CD-R, DVD-R, DVD+R BD-R: Write once storage, used for tertiary and off-line storage
- CD-RW, DVD-RW, DVD+RW, DVD-RAM, BD-RE: Slow write, fast read storage, used for tertiary and off-line storage
- Ultra Density Optical or UDO is similar in capacity to BD-R or BD-RE and is slow write, fast read storage used for tertiary and off-line storage.

Magneto-optical disc storage is optical disc storage where the magnetic state on a ferromagnetic surface stores information. The information is read optically and written by combining magnetic and optical methods. Magneto-optical disc storage is non-volatile, sequential access, slow write, fast read storage used for tertiary and off-line storage.

3D optical data storage has also been proposed.

## 1.5.2.10. ROBOTIC STORAGE

Large quantities of individual magnetic tapes, and optical or magneto-optical discs may be stored in robotic tertiary storage devices. In tape storage field they are known as tape libraries, and in optical storage field optical jukeboxes, or optical disk libraries per analogy. Smallest forms of either technology containing just one drive device are referred to as autoloaders or autochangers.

Robotic-access storage devices may have a number of slots, each holding individual media, and usually one or more picking robots that traverse the slots and load media to built-in drives. The arrangement of the slots and picking devices affects performance. Important characteristics of such storage are possible expansion options: adding slots, modules, drives, robots. Tape libraries may have from 10 to more than 100,000 slots, and provide terabytes or petabytes of near-line information. Optical jukeboxes are somewhat smaller solutions, up to 1,000 slots.

Robotic storage is used for backups, and for high-capacity archives in imaging, medical, and video industries. Hierarchical storage management is a most known archiving strategy of automatically migrating long-unused files from fast hard disk storage to libraries or jukeboxes. If the files are needed, they are retrieved back to disk.

## 1.5.2.11 FLASH MEMORY

A USB flash drive. The chip on the left is the flash memory. The microcontroller is on the right. Flash memory is a non-volatile computer memory that can be electrically erased and reprogrammed. It is a technology that is primarily used in memory cards and USB flash drives for general storage and transfer of data between computers and other digital products. It is a specific type of EEPROM (Electrically Erasable Programmable Read-Only Memory) that is erased and programmed in large blocks; in early flash the entire chip had to be erased at once. Flash memory costs far less than byte-programmable EEPROM and therefore has become the dominant technology wherever a significant amount of non-volatile, solid state storage is needed. Example applications include PDAs (personal digital assistants), laptop computers, digital audio players, digital cameras and mobile phones. It has also gained popularity in the game console market, where it is often used instead of EEPROMs or battery-powered SRAM for game save data.

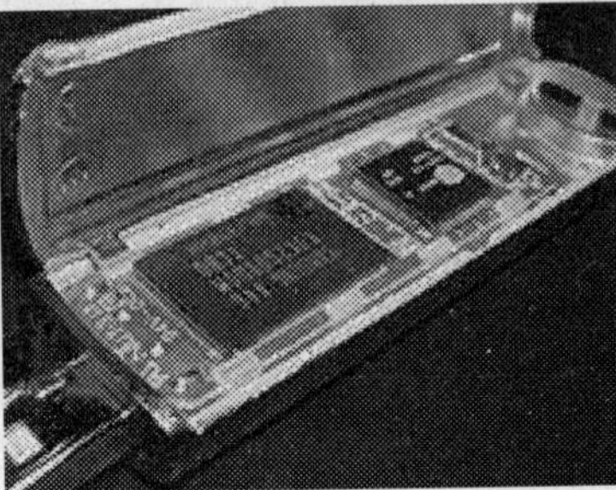

**Figure 1.43 Flash Memory**

Flash memory is non-volatile, which means that no power is needed to maintain the information stored in the chip. In addition, flash memory offers fast read access times (although not as fast as volatile DRAM memory used for main memory in PCs) and better kinetic shock resistance than hard disks. These characteristics explain the popularity of flash memory in portable devices. Another feature of flash memory is that when packaged in a "memory card," it is enormously durable, being able to withstand intense pressure, extremes of temperature, and even immersion in water.

Although technically a type of EEPROM, the term "EEPROM" is generally used to refer specifically to non-flash EEPROM which is erasable in small blocks, typically bytes. Because erase cycles are slow, the large block sizes used in flash memory erasing give it a significant speed advantage over old-style EEPROM when writing large amounts of data.

### 1.5.2.12 MAGNETIC TAPE DATA STORAGE

Magnetic tape has been used for data storage for over 50 years. In this time, many advances in tape formulation, packaging, and data density have been made. Modern magnetic tape is most commonly packaged in cartridges and cassettes. The device that performs actual writing or reading of data is a tape drive. Autoloaders and tape libraries are frequently used to automate cartridge handling.

When storing large amounts of data, tape can be substantially less expensive than disk or other data storage options. Tape storage has always been used with large computer systems. Modern usage is primarily as a high capacity medium for backups and archives. As of 2008, the highest capacity tape cartridges (Sun StorageTek T10000B, IBM TS1130) can store 1 TB of data without using compression.

### 1.5.2.13 COMPACT DISC

A Compact Disc (also known as a CD) is an optical disc used to store digital data, originally developed for storing digital audio. The CD, available on the market since October 1982, remains the standard physical medium for sale of commercial audio recordings to the present day.

Standard CDs have a diameter of 120 mm and can hold up to 80 minutes of audio (700 MB of data). The Mini CD has various diameters ranging from 60 to 80 mm; they are sometimes used for CD singles or device drivers, storing up to 24 minutes of audio.

The technology was later adapted and expanded to include data storage CD-ROM, write-once audio and data storage CD-R, rewritable media CD-RW, Video Compact Discs (VCD), Super Video Compact Discs (SVCD), PhotoCD, PictureCD, CD-i, and Enhanced CD.

CD-ROMs and CD-Rs remain widely used technologies in the computer industry. The CD and its extensions are successful: in 2004, worldwide sales of CD audio, CD-ROM, and CD-R reached about 30 billion discs. By 2007, 200 billion CDs had been sold worldwide.

### 1.5.2.14 DVD

DVD, also known as "Digital Versatile Disc" or "Digital Video Disc", is an optical disc storage media format. Its main uses are video and data storage. DVDs are of the same dimensions as compact discs (CDs) but store more than six times as much data.

Variations of the term DVD often describe the way data is stored on the discs: DVD-ROM (Read Only Memory), has data that can only be read and not written, DVD-R and DVD+R can record data only once and then function as a DVD-ROM. DVD-RW, DVD+RW and DVD-RAM can both record and erase data multiple times. The wavelength used by standard DVD lasers is 650 nm, and thus the light has a red color.

DVD-Video and DVD-Audio discs respectively refer to properly formatted and structured video and audio content. Other types of DVDs, including those with video content, may be referred to as DVD-Data discs.

As next generation High Definition more advanced optical formats such as Blu-ray Disc also use a disc identical in some aspects, the original DVD is occasionally given the retronym SD DVD (for standard definition).However, the trademarked HD DVD discs have been discontinued since Blu-ray absorbed their market share.

### 1.5.2.15 DIGITAL CAMERA

A digital camera (or digicam for short) is a camera that takes video or still photographs, or both, digitally by recording images via an electronic image sensor.

**Figure 1.44 Digital Camera**

Many compact digital still cameras can record sound and moving video as well as still photographs. In the Western market, digital cameras outsell their 35 mm film counterparts.

Digital cameras can do things film cameras cannot: displaying images on a screen immediately after they are recorded, storing thousands of images on a single small memory device, recording video with sound, and deleting images to free storage space. Digital cameras are incorporated into many devices ranging from PDAs and mobile phones (called camera phones) to vehicles. The Hubble Space Telescope and other astronomical devices are essentially specialised digital cameras.

### 1.5.2.16. IMAGE DATA STORAGE

**Figure 1.45 Compact Flash (CF) card, one of many media types used to store digital photographs**

Most digital cameras utilize some form of removable storage to store image data. While the vast majority of the media types are some form of memory card using flash memory (CompactFlash, SD, etc.) there are storage methods that use other technologies such as Microdrives (very small hard disk drives), CD single (185 MB), and 3.5" floppy disks.

**REMOVABLE STORAGE TECHNOLOGIES INCLUDE:**

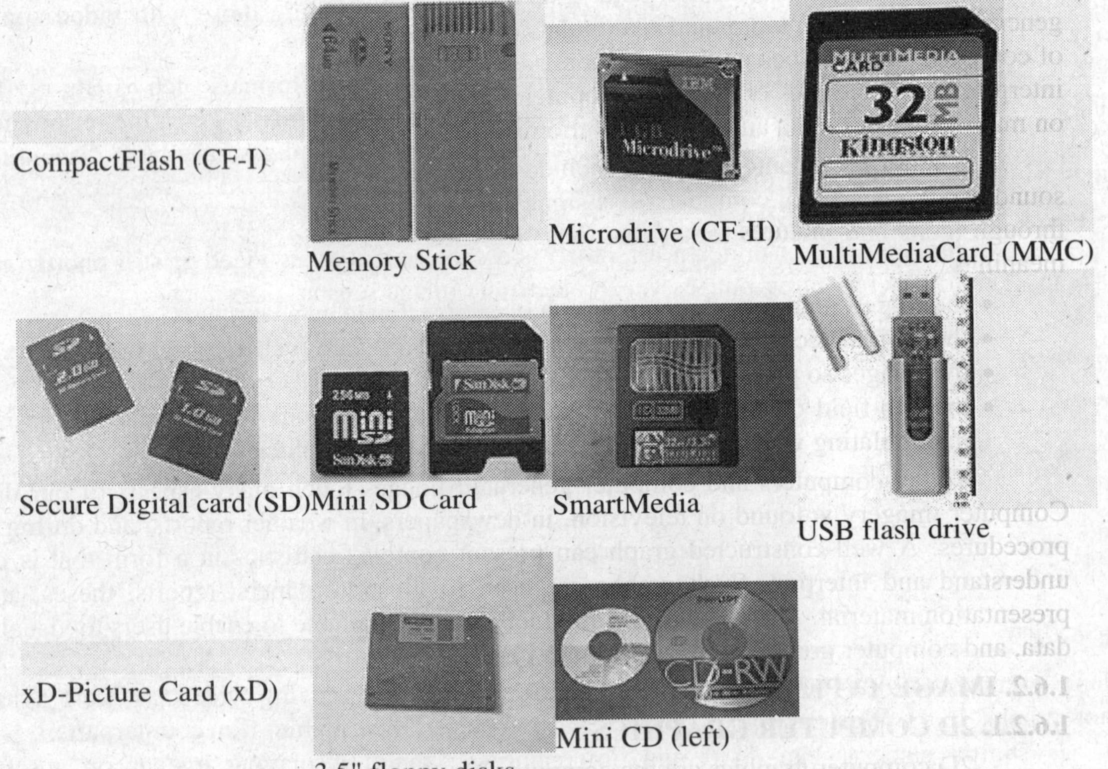


**Figure 1.46 Removable Storage Technologies**

**OTHER FORMATS INCLUDE:**

- Onboard flash memory — Cheap cameras and cameras secondary to the device's main use (such as a camera phone)
- PC Card hard drives — early professional cameras (discontinued)
- Thermal printer — known only in one model of camera that printed images immediately rather than storing

Most manufacturers of digital cameras do not provide drivers and software to allow their cameras to work with Linux or other free software. Still, many cameras use the standard USB storage protocol, and are thus easily usable. Other cameras are supported by the gPhoto project.

### 1.5.2.17. MEMORY CARD

A memory card or flash memory card is a solid-state electronic flash memory data storage device capable of storing digital contents. These are mainly used with digital cameras, handheld and Mobile computers, mobile phones, music players, video game consoles, and other electronics. They offer high re-record-ability, power-free storage, small form factor, and rugged environmental specifications. There are also non-solid-state memory cards that do not use flash memory, and there are different types of flash memory.

## 1.6 COMPUTER PROCESSING AND RECOGNITION OF PICTORIAL DATA

### 1.6.1. COMPUTER GRAPHICS

A 2D projection of a 3D projection of a 4D Pentachoron performing a double rotation about two orthogonal planes.Computer graphics are graphics created using computers and, more generally, the representation and manipulation of pictorial data by a computer. The development of computer graphics has made computers easier to interact with and better for understanding and interpreting many types of data. Developments in computer graphics have had a profound impact on many types of media and have revolutionized the animation and video game industry.

The term computer graphics includes almost everything on computers that is not text or sound. Today nearly all computers use some graphics and users expect to control their computer through icons and pictures rather than just by typing. The term Computer Graphics has several meanings:

- the representation and manipulation of pictorial data by a computer
- the various technologies used to create and manipulate such pictorial data
- the images so produced, and
- the sub-field of computer science which studies methods for digitally synthesizing and manipulating visual content, see study of computer graphics

Today computers and computer-generated images touch many aspects of our daily life. Computer imagery is found on television, in newspapers, in weather reports, and during surgical procedures. A well-constructed graph can present complex statistics in a form that is easier to understand and interpret. Such graphs are used to illustrate papers, reports, theses, and other presentation material. A range of tools and facilities are available to enable users to visualize their data, and computer graphics are used in many disciplines.

### 1.6.2. IMAGE TYPES

### 1.6.2.1. 2D COMPUTER GRAPHICS

2D computer graphics are the computer-based generation of digital images—mostly from two-dimensional models, such as 2D geometric models, text, and digital images, and by techniques specific to them. The word may stand for the branch of computer science that comprises such techniques, or for the models themselves.

**Figure 1.47 Raster graphic sprites (left) and masks (right)**

2D computer graphics are mainly used in applications that were originally developed upon traditional printing and drawing technologies, such as typography, cartography, technical drawing, advertising, etc.. In those applications, the two-dimensional image is not just a representation of a real-world object, but an independent artifact with added semantic value; two-dimensional models are therefore preferred, because they give more direct control of the image than 3D computer graphics, whose approach is more akin to photography than to typography.

### 1.6.2.2. PIXEL ART

Pixel art is a form of digital art, created through the use of raster graphics software, where images are edited on the pixel level. Graphics in most old (or relatively limited) computer and video games, graphing calculator games, and many mobile phone games are mostly pixel art.

### 1.6.2.3. VECTOR GRAPHICS

Vector graphics formats are complementary to raster graphics, which is the representation of images as an array of pixels, as it is typically used for the representation of photographic images. There are instances when working with vector tools and formats is best practice and instances when working with raster tools and formats is best practice. There are times when both formats come together. An understanding of the advantages and limitations of each technology and the relationship between them is most likely to result in efficient and effective use of tools.

### 1.6.2.4. 3D COMPUTER GRAPHICS

3D computer graphics in contrast to 2D computer graphics are graphics that use a three-dimensional representation of geometric data that is stored in the computer for the purposes of performing calculations and rendering 2D images. Such images may be for later display or for real-time viewing. Despite these differences, 3D computer graphics rely on many of the same algorithms as 2D computer vector graphics in the wire frame model and 2D computer raster graphics in the final rendered display.

In computer graphics software, the distinction between 2D and 3D is occasionally blurred; 2D applications may use 3D techniques to achieve effects such as lighting, and primarily 3D may use 2D rendering techniques. 3D computer graphics are often referred to as 3D models. Apart from the rendered graphic, the model is contained within the graphical data file. However, there are differences. A 3D model is the mathematical representation of any three-dimensional object (either inanimate or living).

A model is not technically a graphic until it is visually displayed. Due to 3D printing, 3D models are not confined to virtual space. A model can be displayed visually as a two-dimensional image through a process called 3D rendering, or used in non-graphical computer simulations and calculations.

### 1.6.3. COMPUTER ANIMATION

Computer animation is the art of creating moving images via the use of computers. It is a subfield of computer graphics and animation. Increasingly it is created by means of 3D computer graphics, though 2D computer graphics are still widely used for stylistic, low bandwidth, and faster real-time rendering needs. Sometimes the target of the animation is the computer itself, but sometimes the target is another medium, such as film. It is also referred to as CGI (Computer-generated imagery or computer-generated imaging), especially when used in films. To create the illusion of movement, an image is displayed on the computer screen then quickly replaced by a new image that is similar to the previous image, but shifted slightly. This technique is identical to the illusion of movement in television and motion pictures.

### 1.6.4. CONCEPTS AND PRINCIPLES

#### 1.6.4.1. IMAGE

In common usage, an image or picture is an artifact, usually two-dimensional, that has a similar appearance to some subject—usually a physical object or a person. Images may be two-dimensional, such as a photograph, screen display, and as well as a three-dimensional, such as a statue. They may be captured by optical devices—such as cameras, mirrors, lenses, telescopes, microscopes, etc. and natural objects and phenomena, such as the human eye or water surfaces. A digital image is a representation of a two-dimensional image using ones and zeros (binary). Depending on whether or not the image resolution is fixed, it may be of vector or raster type. Without qualifications, the term "digital image" usually refers to raster images.

#### 1.6.4.2. PIXEL

In digital imaging, a pixel is the smallest piece of information in an image. Pixels are normally arranged in a regular 2-dimensional grid, and are often represented using dots or squares. Each pixel is a sample of an original image, where more samples typically provide a more accurate representation of the original. The intensity of each pixel is variable; in color systems, each pixel has typically three or four components such as red, green, and blue, or cyan, magenta, yellow, and black.

#### 1.6.4.3. GRAPHICS

Graphics are visual presentations on some surface, such as a wall, canvas, computer screen, paper, or stone to brand, inform, illustrate, or entertain. Examples are photographs, drawings, line art, graphs, diagrams, typography, numbers, symbols, geometric designs, maps, engineering drawings, or other images. Graphics often combine text, illustration, and color. Graphic design may consist of the deliberate selection, creation, or arrangement of typography alone, as in a brochure, flier, poster, web site, or book without any other element. Clarity or effective communication may be the objective, association with other cultural elements may be sought, or merely, the creation of a distinctive style.

#### 1.6.4.4. RENDERING

Rendering is the process of generating an image from a model, by means of computer programs. The model is a description of three dimensional objects in a strictly defined language or data structure. It would contain geometry, viewpoint, texture, lighting, and shading information. The image is a digital image or raster graphics image. The term may be by analogy with an "artist's rendering" of a scene. 'Rendering' is also used to describe the process of calculating effects in a video editing file to produce final video output.

**1. 3D PROJECTION**

3D projection is a method of mapping three dimensional points to a two dimensional plane. As most current methods for displaying graphical data are based on planar two dimensional media, the use of this type of projection is widespread, especially in computer graphics, engineering and drafting.

**2. RAY TRACING**

Ray tracing is a technique for generating an image by tracing the path of light through pixels in an image plane. The technique is capable of producing a very high degree of photorealism; usually higher than that of typical scanline rendering methods, but at a greater computational cost.

**3. SHADING**

**Figure 1.48 Shading Example of shading.**

Shading refers to depicting depth in 3D models or illustrations by varying levels of darkness. It is a process used in drawing for depicting levels of darkness on paper by applying media more densely or with a darker shade for darker areas, and less densely or with a lighter shade for lighter areas. There are various techniques of shading including cross hatching where perpendicular lines of varying closeness are drawn in a grid pattern to shade an area. The closer the lines are together, the darker the area appears. Likewise, the farther apart the lines are, the lighter the area appears. The term has been recently generalized to mean that shaders are applied.Dr. Anigbogu

**1.6.4.5. TEXTURE MAPPING**

Texture mapping is a method for adding detail, surface texture, or colour to a computer-generated graphic or 3D model. Its application to 3D graphics was pioneered by Dr Edwin Catmull in 1974. A texture map is applied (mapped) to the surface of a shape, or polygon. This process is akin to applying patterned paper to a plain white box. Multitexturing is the use of more than one texture at a time on a polygon.

**1.6.5. VOLUME RENDERING**

Volume rendering is a technique used to display a 2D projection of a 3D discretely sampled data set. A typical 3D data set is a group of 2D slice images acquired by a CT or MRI scanner. Usually these are acquired in a regular pattern (e.g., one slice every millimeter) and usually have a regular number of image pixels in a regular pattern. This is an example of a regular volumetric grid, with each volume element, or voxel represented by a single value that is obtained by sampling the immediate area surrounding the voxel.

### 1.6.6. 3D MODELING

3D modeling is the process of developing a mathematical, wireframe representation of any three-dimensional object via specialized software. The product is called a "3D model". It can be displayed as a two-dimensional image through a process called 3D rendering or used in a computer simulation of physical phenomena. The model can also be physically created using 3D Printing devices. Models may be created automatically or manually. The manual modeling process of preparing geometric data for 3D computer graphics is similar to plastic arts such as sculpting.

## 1.7 OVERVIEW OF PRACTICAL APPLICATIONS

Today, there is almost no area of technical endeavor that is not impacted in some way by digital image processing. We can cover only a few of these applications in the context and space of the current discussion. However, limited as it is, the material presented in this section will leave no doubt in the reader's mind regarding the breadth and importance of digital image processing. We show in this section numerous areas of application, each of which routinely utilizes the digital image processing techniques developed.

The areas of application of digital image processing are so varied that some form of organization is desirable in attempting to capture the breadth of this field. One of the simplest ways to develop a basic understanding of the extent of image processing applications is to categorize images according to their source (e.g., visual, X-ray, and so on).The principal energy source for images in use today is the electromagnetic energy spectrum. Other important sources of energy include acoustic, ultrasonic, and electronic (in the form of electron beams used in electron microscopy). Synthetic images, used for modeling and visualization, are generated by computer. In this section we discuss briefly how images are generated in these various categories and the areas in which they are applied. Methods for converting images into digital form are discussed in the next chapter.

Images based on radiation from the EM spectrum are the most familiar, especially images in the X-ray and visual bands of the spectrum. Electromagnetic waves can be conceptualized as propagating sinusoidal waves of varying wavelengths, or they can be thought of as a stream of mass less particles, each traveling in a wavelike pattern and moving at the speed of light. Each mass less particle contains a certain amount (or bundle) of energy. Each bundle of energy is called a photon. If spectral bands are grouped according to energy per photon, we obtain the spectrum shown in Fig. 1.49, ranging from gamma rays (highest energy) at one end to radio waves (lowest energy) at the other. The bands are shown shaded to convey the fact that bands of the EM spectrum are not distinct but rather transition smoothly from one to the other.

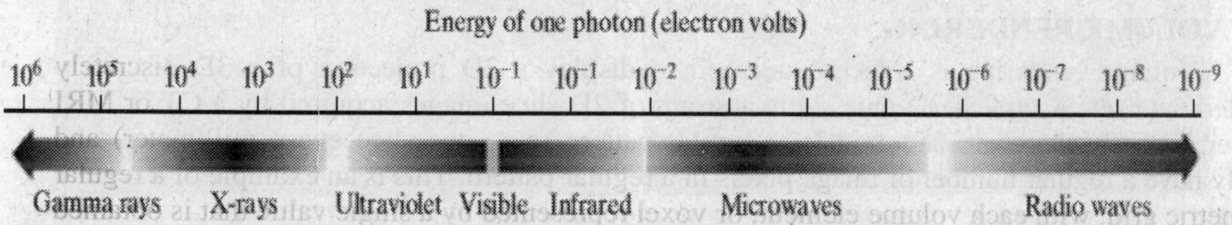


**Figure 1.49 The electromagnetic spectrum arranged according to energy per photon**

### 1.7.1 GAMMA-RAY IMAGING

Major uses of imaging based on gamma rays include nuclear medicine and astronomical observations. In nuclear medicine, the approach is to inject a patient with a radioactive isotope that emits gamma rays as it decays. Images are produced from the emissions collected by gamma ray detectors. Figure 1.50(a) shows an image of a complete bone scan obtained by using gamma-ray imaging. Images of this sort are used to locate sites of bone pathology, such as infections or tumors. Figure 1.50(b) shows another major modality of nuclear imaging called positron emission tomography (PET). The principle is the same

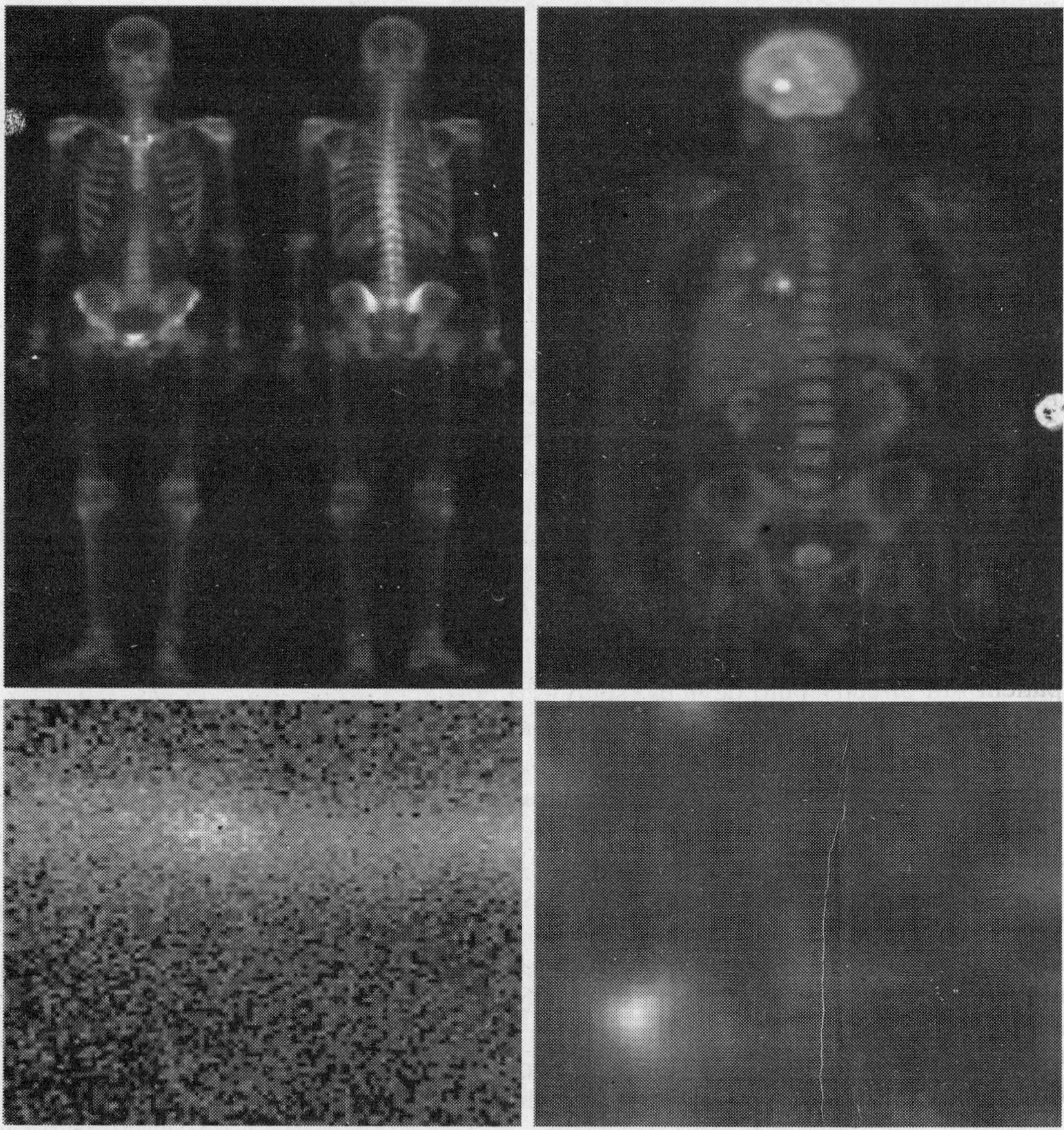

**Figure 1.50 Examples of gamma-ray imaging. (a) Bone scan. (b) PET image. (c) Cygnus Loop. (d) Gamma radiation (bright spot) from a reactor valve**

as with X-ray tomography. However, instead of using an external source of X-ray energy, the patient is given a radioactive isotope that emits positrons as it decays. When a positron meets an electron, both are annihilated and two gamma rays are given off. These are detected and a tomographic image is created using the basic principles of tomography. The image shown in Fig. 1.50(b) is one sample of a sequence that constitutes a 3-D rendition of the patient. This image shows a tumor in the brain and one in the lung, easily visible as small white masses.

A star in the constellation of Cygnus exploded about 15,000 years ago, generating a superheated stationary gas cloud (known as the Cygnus Loop) that glows in a spectacular array of colors. Figure 1.50(c) shows the Cygnus Loop imaged in the gamma-ray band. Unlike the two examples shown in Figs. 1.50(a) and (b), this image was obtained using the natural radiation of the object being imaged . Finally, Fig. 1.50(d) shows an image of gamma radiation from a valve in a nuclear reactor. An area of strong radiation is seen in the lower, left side of the image.

## 1.7.2 X-RAY IMAGING

X-rays are among the oldest sources of EM radiation used for imaging. The best known use of X-rays is medical diagnostics, but they also are used extensively in industry and other areas, like astronomy. X-rays for medical and industrial imaging are generated using an X-ray tube, which is a vacuum tube with a cathode and anode. The cathode is heated, causing free electrons to be released. These electrons flow at high speed to the positively charged anode. When the electrons strike a nucleus, energy is released in the form of X-ray radiation. The energy (penetrating power) of the X-rays is controlled by a voltage applied across the anode, and the number of X-rays is controlled by a current applied to the filament in the cathode. Figure 1.51(a) shows a familiar chest X-ray generated simply by placing the patient between an X-ray source and a film sensitive to X-ray energy. The intensity of the X-rays is modified by absorption as they pass through the patient, and the resulting energy falling on the film develops it, much in the same way that light develops photographic film. In digital radiography, digital images are obtained by one of two methods: (1) by digitizing X-ray films; or (2) by having the X-rays that pass through the patient fall directly onto devices (such as a phosphor screen) that convert X-rays to light. The light signal in turn is captured by a light-sensitive digitizing system.

Angiography is another major application in an area called contrast-enhancement radiography. This procedure is used to obtain images (called angiograms) of blood vessels. A catheter (a small, flexible, hollow tube) is inserted, for example, into an artery or vein in the groin.

The catheter is threaded into the blood vessel and guided to the area to be studied. When the catheter reaches the site under investigation, an X-ray contrast medium is injected through the catheter. This enhances contrast of the blood vessels and enables the radiologist to see any irregularities or blockages. Figure 1.51(b) shows an example of an aortic angiogram. The catheter can be seen being inserted into the large blood vessel on the lower left of the picture. Note the high contrast of the large vessel as the contrast medium flows up in the direction of the kidneys, which are also visible in the image.

Perhaps the best known of all uses of X-rays in medical imaging is computerized axial tomography. Due to their resolution and 3-D capabilities, CAT scans revolutionized medicine from the moment they first became available in the early 1970s

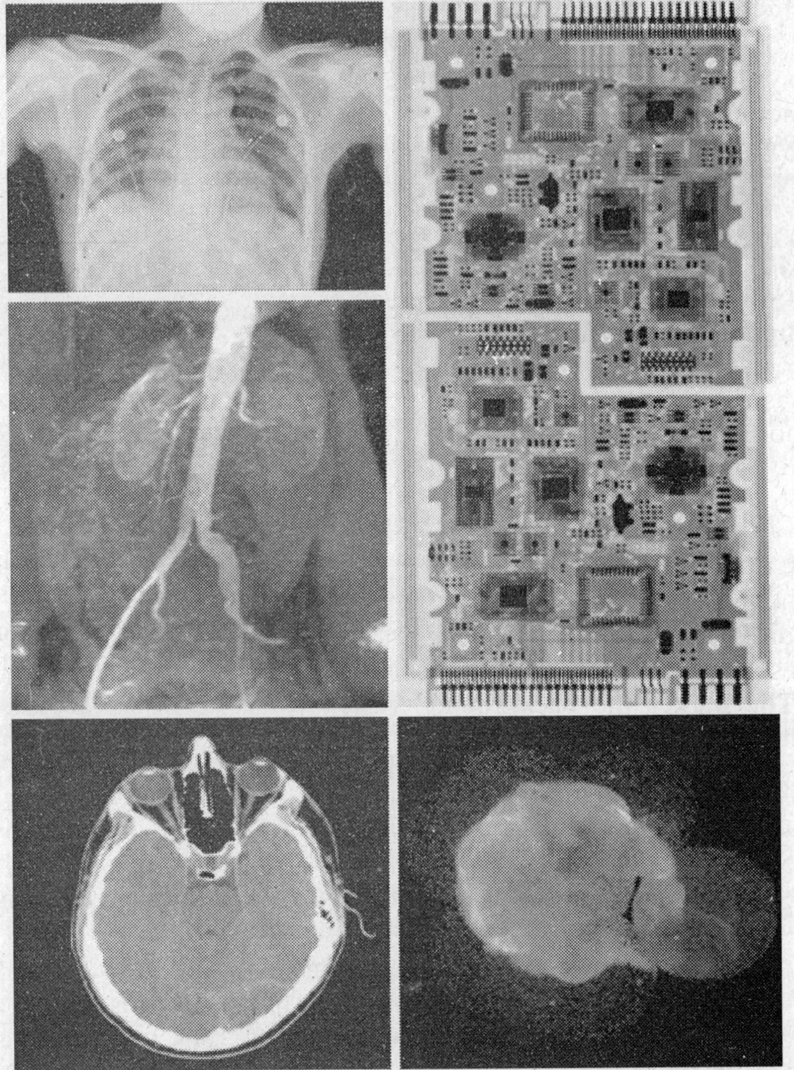

**Figure 1.51 Examples of X-ray imaging. (a) Chest X-ray. (b) Aortic angiogram. (c) Head CT. (d) Circuit boards. (e) Cygnus Loop. (Images courtesy of (a) and (c) Dr. David R. Pickens, Dept. of Radiology & Radiological Sciences, Vanderbilt University Medical Center, (b) Dr. Thomas R. Gest, Division of Anatomical Sciences, University of Michigan Medical School, (d) Mr. Joseph E. Pascente, Lixi, Inc., and (e) NASA**

each CAT image is a "slice" taken perpendicularly through the patient. Numerous slices are generated as the patient is moved in a longitudinal direction. The ensemble of such images constitutes a 3-D rendition of the inside of the patient, with the longitudinal resolution being proportional to the number of slice images taken. Figure 1.51(c) shows a typical head CAT slice image.

Techniques similar to the ones just discussed, but generally involving higher- energy X-rays, are applicable in industrial processes. Figure 1.51(d) shows an X-ray image of an electronic circuit board. Such images, representative of literally hundreds of industrial applications of X-rays, are used to examine circuit boards for flaws in manufacturing, such as missing components or broken traces. Industrial CAT scans are useful when the parts can be penetrated by X-rays, such as in plastic assemblies, and even large bodies, like solid-propellant rocket motors. Figure 1.51(e) shows an example of X-ray imaging in astronomy. This image is the Cygnus Loop of Fig. 1.51(c), but imaged this time in the X-ray band.

### 1.7.3 IMAGING IN THE ULTRAVIOLET BAND

Applications of ultraviolet "light" are varied. They include lithography, industrial inspection, microscopy, lasers, biological imaging, and astronomical observations. We illustrate imaging in this band with examples from microscopy and astronomy.

Ultraviolet light is used in fluorescence microscopy, one of the fastest growing areas of microscopy. Fluorescence is a phenomenon discovered in the middle of the nineteenth century, when it was first observed that the mineral fluorspar fluoresces when ultraviolet light is directed upon it. The ultraviolet light itself is not visible, but when a photon of ultraviolet radiation collides with an electron in an atom of a fluorescent material, it elevates the electron to a higher energy level. Subsequently, the excited electron relaxes to a lower level and emits light in the form of a lower-energy photon in the visible (red) light region. The basic task of the fluorescence microscope is to use an excitation light to irradiate a prepared specimen and then to separate the much weaker radiating fluorescent light from the brighter excitation light. Thus, only the emission light reaches the eye or other detector. The resulting fluorescing areas shine against a dark background with sufficient contrast to permit detection. The darker the background of the nonfluorescing material, the more efficient the instrument.

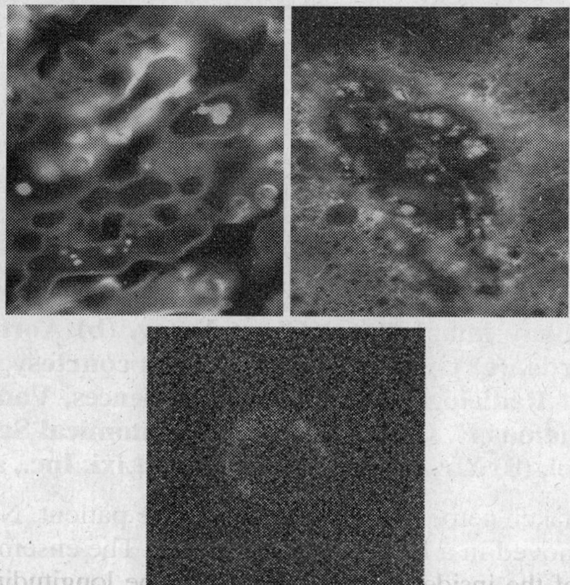

**Figure 1.52 Examples of ultraviolet imaging. (a)Normal corn. (b)Smut corn. (c)Cygnus Loop.**

Fluorescence microscopy is an excellent method for studying materials that can be made to fluoresce, either in their natural form (primary fluorescence) or when treated with chemicals capable of fluorescing (secondary fluorescence). Figures 1.52(a) and (b) show results typical of the capability of fluorescence microscopy. Figure 1.52(a) shows a fluorescence microscope image of normal corn, and Fig. 1.52(b) shows corn infected by "smut," a disease of cereals, corn, grasses, onions, and sorghum that can be caused by any of more than 700 species of parasitic fungi. Corn smut is particularly harmful because corn is one of the principal food sources in the world. As another illustration, Fig. 1.52(c) shows the Cygnus Loop imaged in the high-energy region of the ultraviolet band.

### 1.7.4 IMAGING IN THE VISIBLE AND INFRARED BANDS

Considering that the visual band of the electromagnetic spectrum is the most familiar in all our activities, it is not surprising that imaging in this band outweighs by far all the others in terms of scope of application. The infrared band often is used in conjunction with visual imaging, so we have grouped the visible and infrared bands in this section for the purpose of illustration. We consider in the following discussion applications in light microscopy, astronomy, remote sensing, industry, and law enforcement. Figure 1.53 shows several examples of images obtained with a light microscope. The examples range from pharmaceuticals and microinspection to materials characterization. Even in just microscopy, the application areas are too numerous to detail here. It is not difficult to conceptualize the types of processes one might apply to these images, ranging from enhancement to measurements.

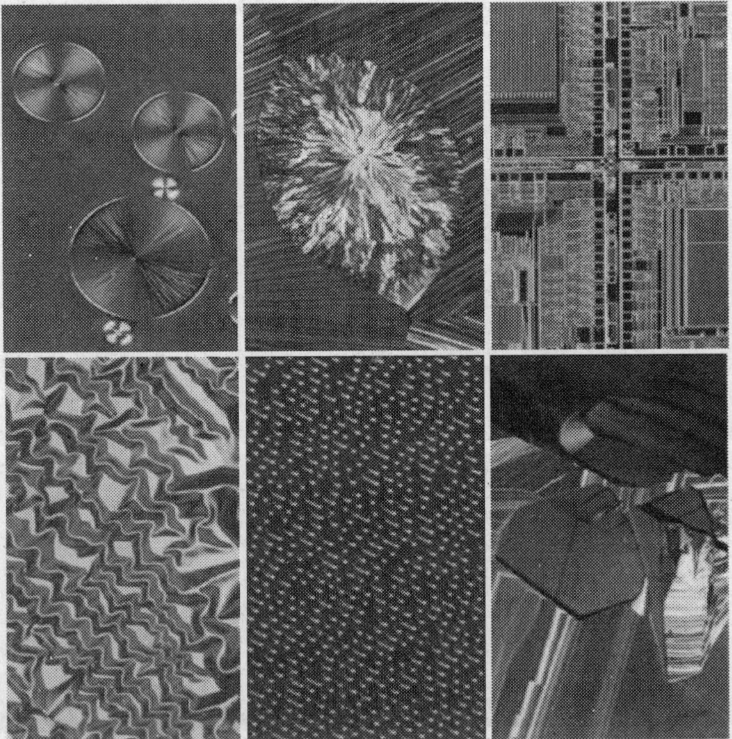

**Figure 1.53 Examples of light microscopy images. (a) Taxol (anticancer agent), magnified**

| Band No. | Name | Wavelength (μm) | Characteristics and Uses |
|---|---|---|---|
| 1 | Visible blue | 0.45–0.52 | Maximum water penetration |
| 2 | Visible green | 0.52–0.60 | Good for measuring plant vigor |
| 3 | Visible red | 0.63–0.69 | Vegetation discrimination |
| 4 | Near infrared | 0.76–0.90 | Biomass and shoreline mapping |
| 5 | Middle infrared | 1.55–1.75 | Moisture content of soil and vegetation |
| 6 | Thermal infrared | 10.4–12.5 | Soil moisture; thermal mapping |
| 7 | Middle infrared | 2.08–2.35 | Mineral mapping |

**Table 1.4 Thematic bands in NASA's LANDSAT satellite**

Another major area of visual processing is remote sensing, which usually includes several bands in the visual and infrared regions of the spectrum. Table 1.4 shows the so-called thematic bands in NASA's LANDSAT satellite. The primary function of LANDSAT is to obtain and transmit images of the Earth from space, for purposes of monitoring environmental conditions on the planet. The bands are expressed in terms of wavelength, with 1 pm being equal to $10^{-6}$ m. Note the characteristics and uses of each band.

In order to develop a basic appreciation for the power of this type of multi- spectral imaging, consider Fig. 1.54, which shows one image for each of the spectral

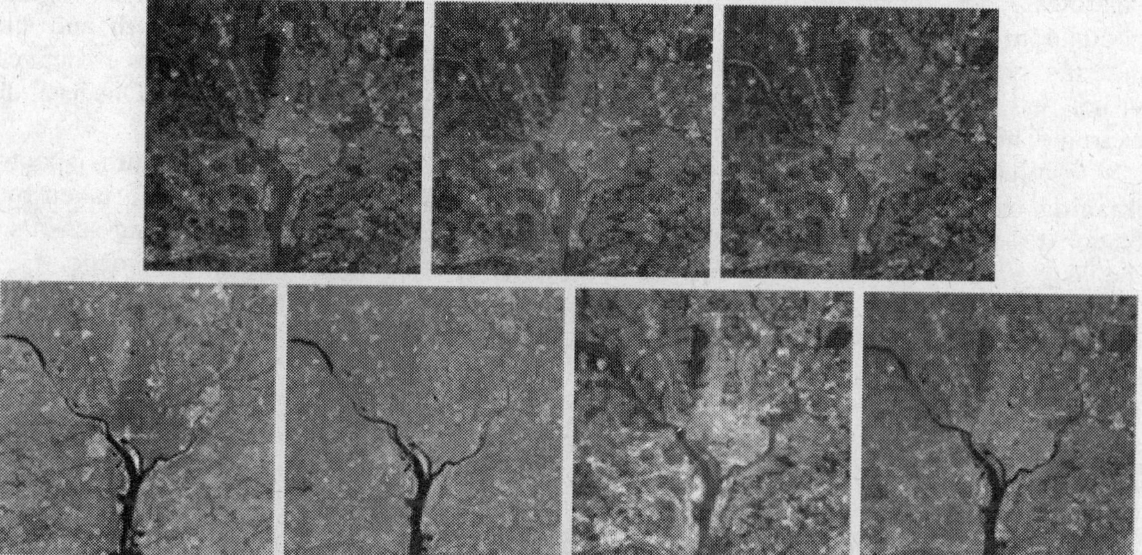

**Figure 1.54 LAND SAT satellite images of the Washington, D.C. area.**

**Figure 1.55 Multispectral image of Hurricane Andrew taken by NOAA GEOS (Geostationary Environmental Operational Satellite) sensors**

bands in Table 1.4. The area imaged is Washington D.C., which includes features such as buildings, roads, vegetation, and a major river (the Potomac) going though the city. Images of population centers are used routinely (over time) to assess population growth and shift patterns, pollution, and other factors harmful to the environment. The differences between visual and infrared image features are quite noticeable in these images. Observe, for example, how well defined the river is from its surroundings in Bands 4 and 5.

Weather observation and prediction also are major applications of multi- spectral imaging from satellites. For example, Fig. 1.53 is an image of a hurricane taken by a National Oceanographic and Atmospheric Administration (NOAA) satellite using sensors in the visible and infrared bands. The eye of the hurricane is clearly visible in this image.

Figures 1.56 and 1.57 show an application of infrared imaging. These images are part of the Nighttime Lights of the World data set, which provides a global inventory of human settlements. The images were generated by the infrared imaging system mounted on a NOAA DMSP (Defense Meteorological Satellite Program) satellite. The infrared imaging system operates in the band 10.0 to 13.4 pm, and has the unique capability to observe faint sources of visible- near infrared emissions present on the Earth's surface, including cities, towns, villages, gas flares, and fires. Even without formal training in image processing, it is not difficult to imagine writing a computer program that would use these images to estimate the percent of total electrical energy used by various regions of the world.

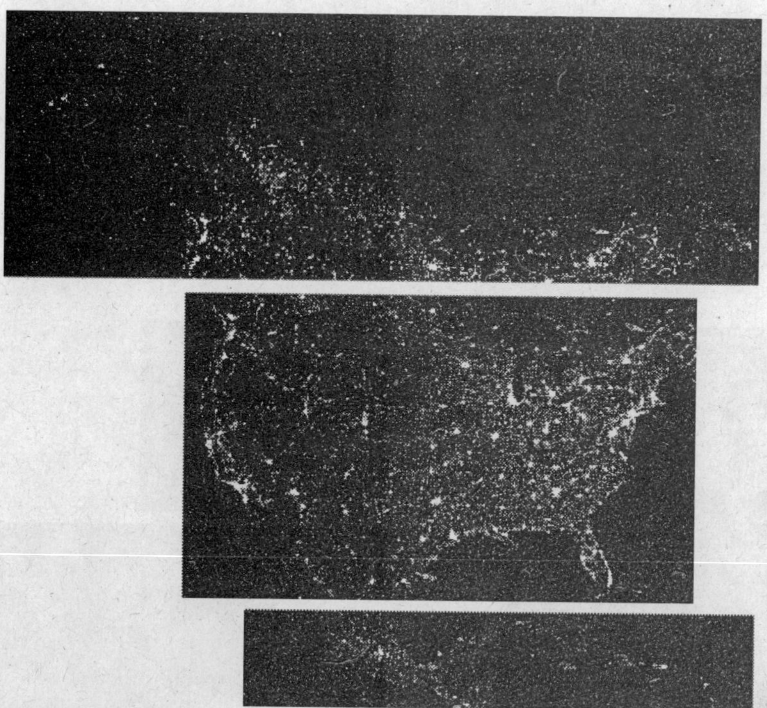

**Figure 1.56 Infrared satellite images of the Americas. The small gray map is provided for reference**

A major area of imaging in the visual spectrum is in automated visual inspection of manufactured goods. Figure 1.58 shows some examples. Figure 1.58(a) is a controller board for a CD-ROM drive. A typical image processing task with products like this is to inspect them for missing parts (the black square on the top, right quadrant of the image is an example of a missing component). Figure 1.58(b) is an imaged pill container. The objective here is to have a machine look for missing pills. Figure 1.58(c) shows an application in which image processing is used to look for bottles that are not filled up to an acceptable level. Figure 1.58(d) shows

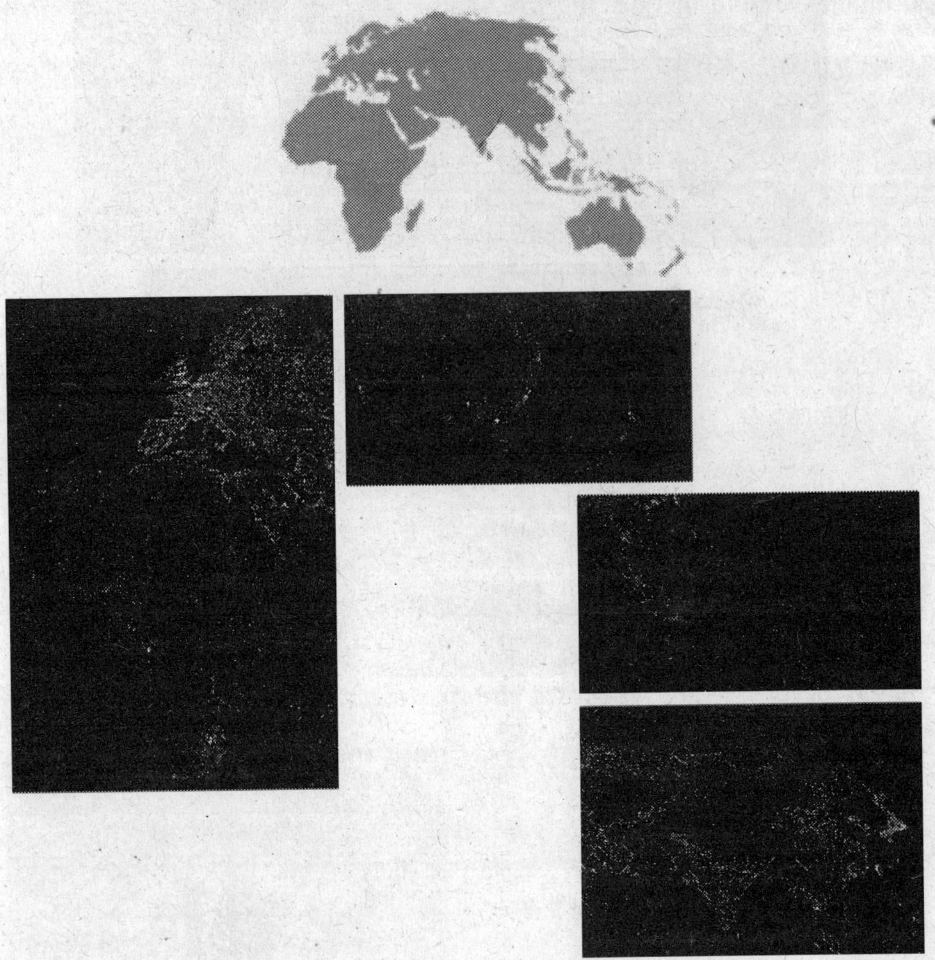

**Figure 1.57 Infrared satellite images of the remaining populated part of the world. The small gray map is provided for reference.**

a clear-plastic part with an unacceptable number of air pockets in it. Detecting anomalies like these is a major theme of industrial inspection that includes other products such as wood and cloth. Figure 1.58(e) shows a batch of cereal during inspection for color and the presence of anomalies such as burned flakes. Finally, Fig. 1.58(f) shows an image of an intraocular implant (replacement lens for the human eye). A "structured light" illumination technique was used to highlight for easier detection flat lens deformations toward the center of the lens. The markings at 1 o'clock and 5 o'clock are tweezers damage. Most of the other small speckle detail is debris. The objective in this type of inspection is to find damaged or incorrectly manufactured implants automatically, prior to packaging.

As a final illustration of image processing in the visual spectrum, consider Fig. 1.59. Figure 1.59(a) shows a thumb print. Images of fingerprints are routinely processed by computer, either to enhance them or to find features that aid in the automated search of a database for potential matches. Figure 1.59(b) shows an image of paper currency. Applications of digital image processing in this area include automated counting and, in law enforcement, the reading of the serial number for the purpose of tracking and identifying bills.

The two vehicle images shown in Figs. 1.59 (c) and (d) are examples of automated license plate reading

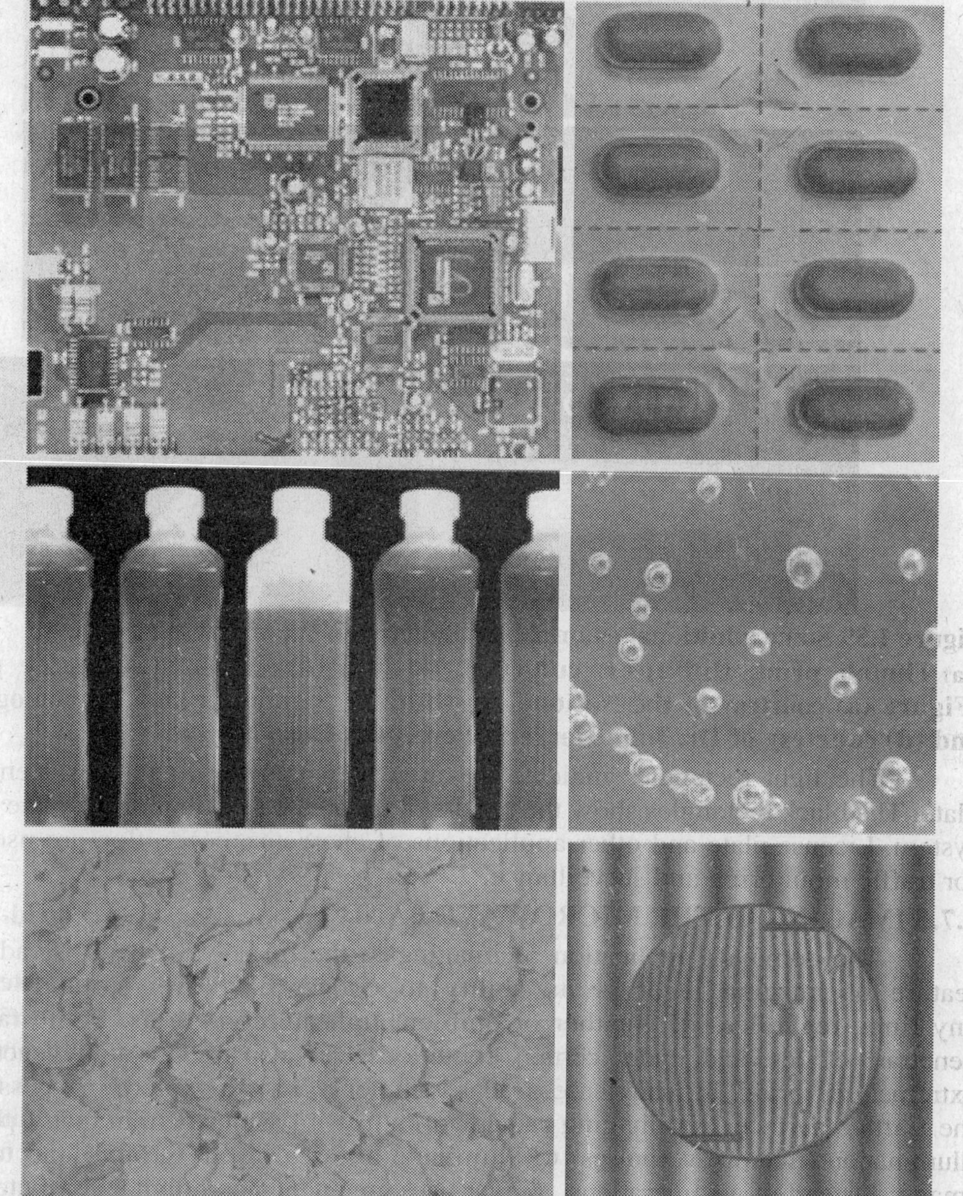

**Figure 1.58 Some examples of manufactured goods often checked using digital image processing. (a) A circuit board controller.**
**(b) Packaged pills.**
**(c) Bottles.**
**(d) Bubbles in clear-plastic product.**
**(e) Cereal.**
**(f) Image of intraocular implant.**

**Figure 1.59 Some additional examples of imaging in the visual spectrum.**
**(a) Thumb print. (b)Paper currency. (c) and (d). Automated license plate read (Figure (a) courtesy of the National Institute of Standards and Technology. Figures and (d) courtesy of Dr. Juan Herrera, Perceptics Corporation.)**

The light rectangles indicate the area in which the imaging system detected plate. The black rectangles show the results of automated reading of the plate content by system. License plate and other applications of character recognition are used extensiv for traffic monitoring and surveillance.

### 1.7.5 IMAGING IN THE MICROWAVE BAND

The dominant application of imaging in the microwave band is radar. The un feature of imaging radar is its ability to collect data over virtually any regio any time, regardless of weather or ambient lighting conditions. Some radar waves penetrate clouds, and under certain conditions can also see through vegetation, ice, extremely dry sand. In many cases, radar is the only way to explore inaccessible regior the Earth's surface. An imaging radar works like a flash camera in that it provides its illumination (microwave pulses) to illuminate an area on the ground and take a snap image. Instead of a camera lens, a radar uses an antenna and digital computer processir record its images. In a radar image, one can see only the microwave energy that was flected back toward the radar antenna.

Figure 1.60 shows a space borne radar image covering a rugged mountainous of southeast Tibet, about 90 km east of the city of Lhasa. In the lower right corner is a valley of the Lhasa River, which is populated by Tibetan farmers and yak herders includes the village of Menba. Mountains in this area reach about 5800 m (19,000 ft) al sea level, while the valley floors lie about 4300 m (14,000 ft) above sea level. Note the cl and detail of the image, unencumbered by clouds or other atmospheric conditions that normally interfere with images in the visual band.

**Figure 1.60 Spaceborne radar image of mountains in southeast Tibet**

## 1.7.6 IMAGING IN THE RADIO BAND

As in the case of imaging at the other end of the spectrum (gamma rays), the major applications of imaging in the radio band are in medicine and astronomy. In medicine radio waves are used in magnetic resonance imaging (MRI). This technique places a patient in a powerful magnet and passes radio waves through his or her body in short pulses. Each pulse causes a responding pulse of radio waves to be emitted by the patient's tissues. The location from which these signals originate and their strength are determined by a computer which produces a two-dimensional picture of a section of the patient. MRI can produce pictures in any plane. Figure 1.61 shows MRI images of a human knee and spine.

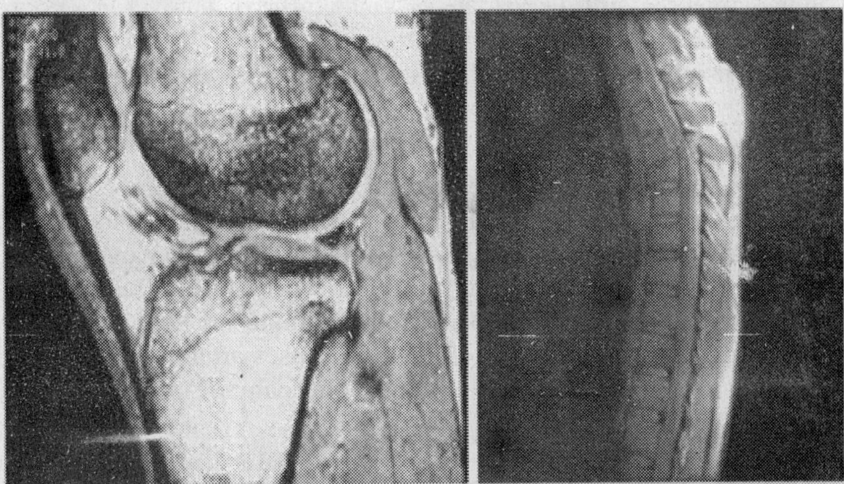

**Figure 1.61 MRI images of a human (a) knee, and (b) spine. (Image (a) courtesy of Dr. Thomas R. Gest, Division of Anatomical Sciences, University of Michigan Medical School, and (b) Dr. David R. Pickens, Department of Radiology and Radiological Sciences, Vanderbilt University Medical Center.)**

The last image to the right in Fig. 1.62 shows an image of the Crab Pulsar in the radio band. Also shown for an interesting comparison are images of the same region but taken in most of the bands discussed earlier. Note that each image gives a totally different "view" of the Pulsar.

### 1.7.7 EXAMPLES IN WHICH OTHER IMAGING MODALITIES ARE USED

Although imaging in the electromagnetic spectrum is dominant by far, there are a number of other imaging modalities that also are important. Specifically, we discuss in this section acoustic imaging, electron microscopy, and synthetic (computer-generated) imaging.

Imaging using "sound" finds application in geological exploration, industry, and medicine. Geological applications use sound in the low end of the sound spectrum (hundreds of Hertz) while imaging in other areas use ultrasound (millions of Hertz). The most important commercial applications of image processing in geology are in mineral and oil exploration. For image acquisition over land, one of the main approaches is to use a large truck and a large flat steel plate. The plate is pressed on the ground by the truck, and the truck is vibrated through a frequency spectrum up to 100 Hz. The strength and speed of the returning sound waves are determined by the composition of the earth below the surface. These are analyzed by computer, and images are generated from the resulting analysis.

For marine acquisition, the energy source consists usually of two air guns towed behind a ship. Returning sound waves are detected by hydrophones placed in cables that are either towed behind the ship, laid on the bottom of the ocean, or hung from buoys (vertical cables). The two air guns are alternately pressurized to ~2000 psi and then set off. The constant motion of the ship provides a transversal direction of motion that, together with the returning sound waves, is used to generate a 3-D map of the composition of the Earth below the bottom of the ocean.

Figure 1.63 shows a cross-sectional image of a well-known 3-D model against which the performance of seismic imaging algorithms is tested. The arrow points to a hydrocarbon (oil and/or gas) trap. This target is brighter than the surrounding layers because of the change in density in the target region is larger.

Seismic interpreters look for these "bright spots" to find oil and gas. The layers above also are bright, but their brightness does not vary as strongly across the layers. Many seismic reconstruction algorithms have difficulty imaging this target because of the faults above it.

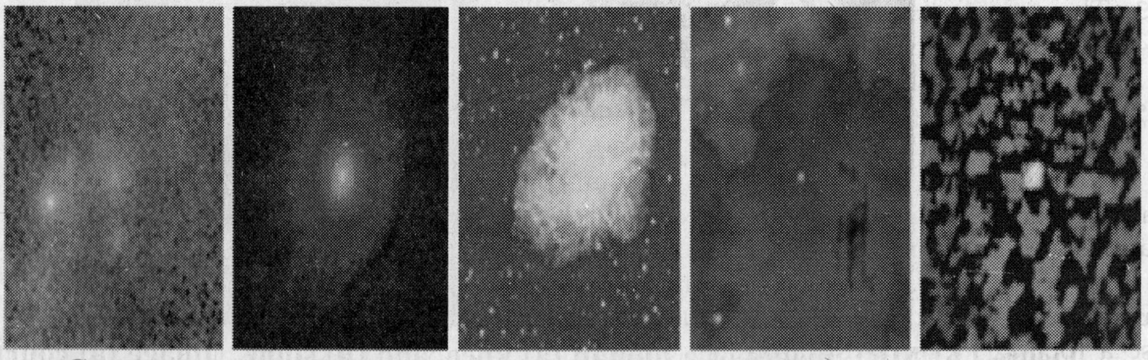


**Figure 1.62 Images of the Crab Pulsar (in the center of images) covering the electromagnetic spectrum**

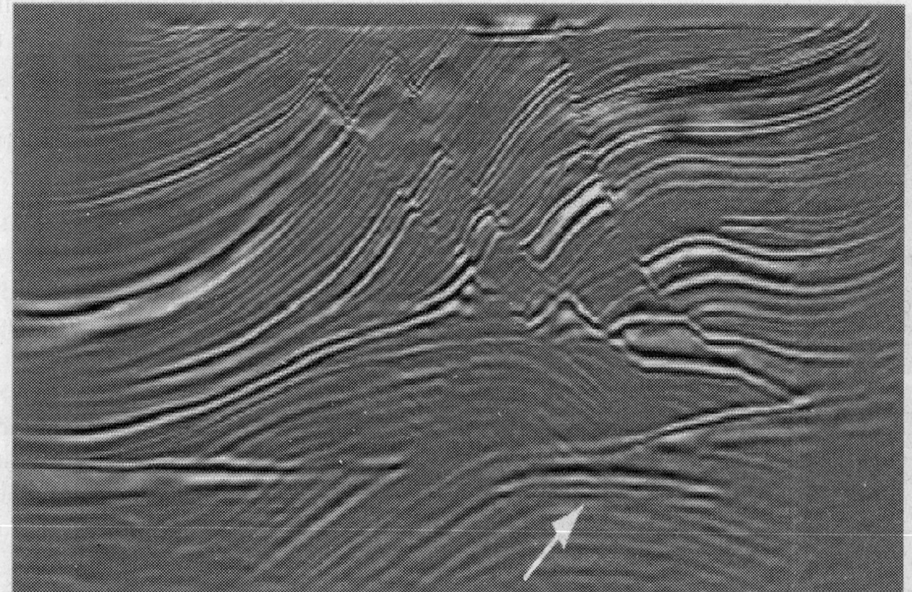

**Figure 1.63 Cross-sectional image of a seismic model. The arrow points to a hydrocarbon (oil and/or gas) trap**

Although ultrasound imaging is used routinely in manufacturing, the best known applications of this technique are in medicine, especially in obstetrics, where unborn babies are imaged to determine the health of their development. A byproduct of this examination is determining the sex of the baby. Ultrasound images are generated using the following basic procedure:

1. The ultrasound system (a computer, ultrasound probe consisting of a source and receiver, and a display) transmits high-frequency (1 to 5 MHz) sound pulses into the body.
2. The sound waves travel into the body and hit a boundary between tissues (e.g., between fluid and soft tissue, soft tissue and bone). Some of the sound waves are reflected back to the probe, while some travel on further until they reach another boundary and get reflected.
3. The reflected waves are picked up by the probe and relayed to the computer.
4. The machine calculates the distance from the probe to the tissue or organ boundaries using the speed of sound in tissue (1540 m/s) and the time of the each echo's return.
5. The system displays the distances and intensities of the echoes on the screen, forming a two-dimensional image.

In a typical ultrasound image, millions of pulses and echoes are sent and received each second. The probe can be moved along the surface of the body and angled to obtain various views. Figure 1.64 shows several examples.

We continue the discussion on imaging modalities with some examples of electron microscopy. Electron microscopes function as their optical counterparts, except that they use a focused beam of electrons instead of light to image a specimen. The operation of electron microscopes involves the following basic steps: A stream of electrons is produced by an electron source and accelerated toward the specimen using a positive electrical potential. This stream is confined.

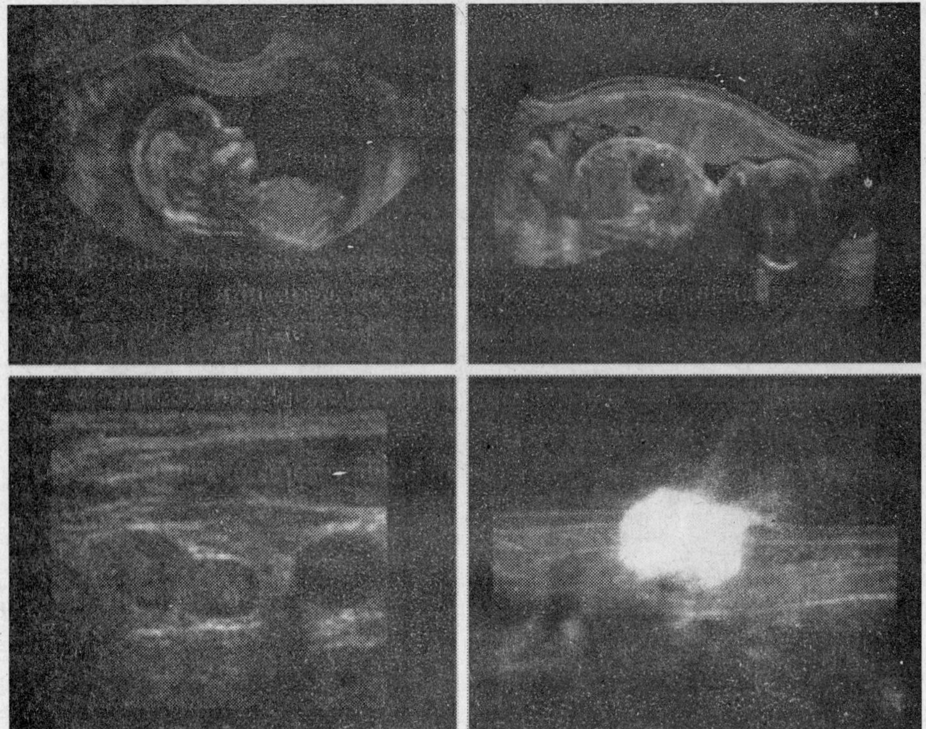

**Figure 1.64 Examples of ultrasound imaging. (a) Baby. (b) Another view of baby. (c)Thyroids.**

and focused using metal apertures and magnetic lenses into a thin, focused, monochromatic beam. This beam is focused onto the sample using a magnetic lens. Interactions occur inside the irradiated sample, affecting the electron beam. These interactions and effects are detected and transformed into an image; much in the same way that light is reflected from, or absorbed by, objects in a scene. These basic steps are carried out in all electron microscopes, regardless of type.

A transmission electron microscope (TEM) works much like a slide projector. A projector shines (transmits) a beam of light through the slide; as the light passes through the slide, it is affected by the contents of the slide. This transmitted beam is then projected onto the viewing screen, forming an enlarged image of the slide. TEMs work the same way, except that they shine a beam of electrons through a specimen (analogous to the slide).The fraction of the beam transmitted through the specimen is projected onto a phosphor screen. The interaction of the electrons with the phosphor produces light and, therefore, a viewable image. A scanning electron microscope (SEM), on the other hand, actually scans the electron beam and records the interaction of beam and sample at each location. This produces one dot on a phosphor screen. A complete image is formed by a raster scan of the bean through the sample, much like a TV camera. The electrons interact with a phosphor screen and produce light. SEMs are suitable for "bulky" samples, while TEMs require very thin samples.

Electron microscopes are capable of very high magnification. While light microscopy is limited to magnifications on the order 1000*, electron microscopes

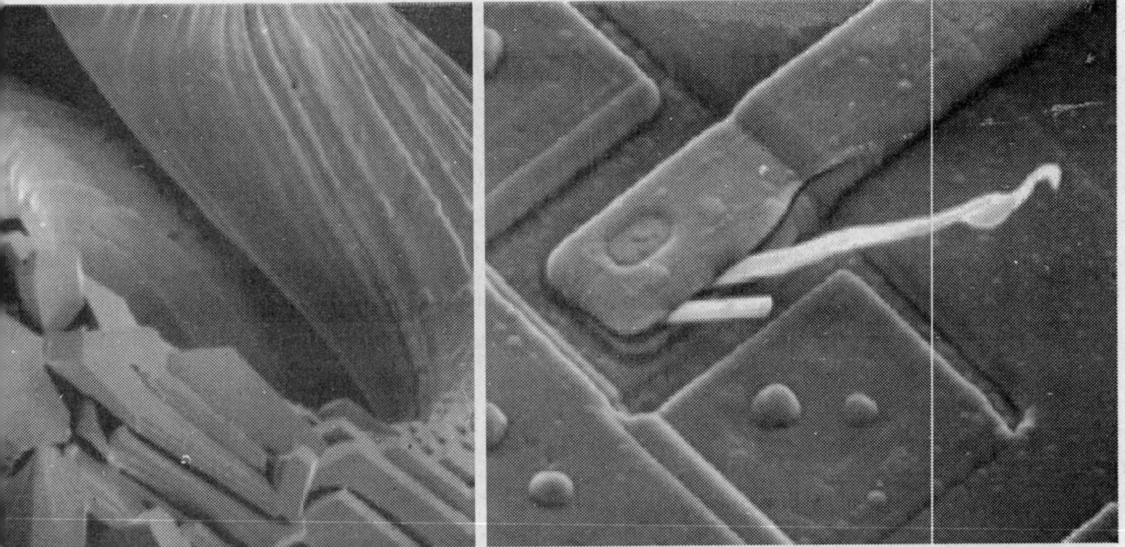

**ıre 1.65 (a) 250 x SEM image of a tungsten filament following thermal failure. (b) 2500 x ⁄I image of damaged integrated circuit. The white fibers are oxides resulting from ·mal destruction**

achieve magnification of 10,000* or more. Figure 1.65 shows two SEM images of cimen failures due to thermal overload.

We conclude the discussion of imaging modalities by looking briefly at images that not obtained from physical objects. Instead, they are generated by computer. Fractals striking examples of computer-generated images. Basically, a fractal is nothing more than terative reproduction of a basic pattern according to some mathematical rules. For ance, tiling is one of the simplest ways to generate a fractal image. A square can be divided into four square subregions, each of which can be further subdivided into four ller square regions, and so on. Depending on the complexity of the rules for filling each square, some beautiful tile images can be generated using this method. Of course, the metry can be arbitrary. For instance, the fractal image could be grown radically out of a ter point. Figure 1.66(a) shows a fractal grown in this way. The reader will recognize image as the theme image used in the beginning page of each chapter in this book, cted because of its artistic simplicity and abstract analogy to a human eye. Figure 5(b) shows another fractal (a "moonscape") that provides an interesting analogy to the ges of space used as illustrations in some of the preceding sections.

Fractal images tend toward artistic, mathematical formulations of "growth" of image elements according to some rules. They are useful sometimes as random textures. nore structured approach to image generation by computer lies in 3-D modeling. This is area that provides an important intersection between image processing and computer phics and is the basis for many 3-D visualization systems (e.g., flight simulators). Figures 5(c) and (d) show examples of computer-generated images. Since the original object is ated in 3-D, images can be generated in any perspective from plane projections of the volume. Images of this type can be used for medical training and for a host of other lications, such as criminal forensics and special effects.

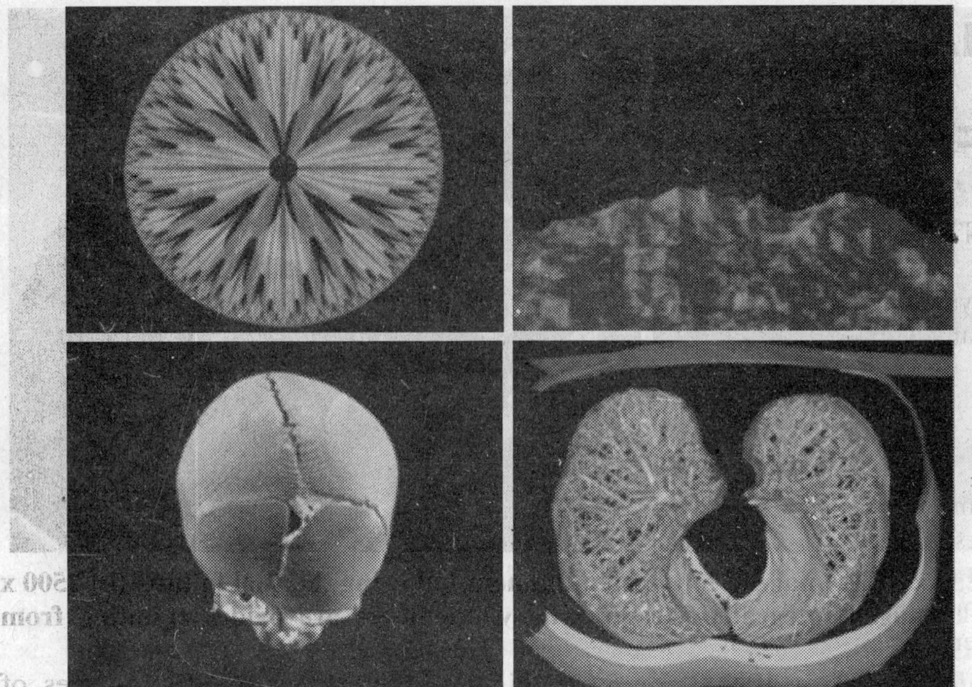

**Figure 1.66 (a) and (b) Fractal images (c) Images generated from 3-D computer models of the object shown**

# QUESTION BANK

Q1. What is Digital image processing? Explain with the help of example.

Q2. Explain the various Imaging Methodologies and Technologies?

Q3. What are the various characteristics of Image processing operations?

Q4. Write short note on Video Parameters.

Q5. Discuss the origins of various digital image processing.

Q6. Briefly explain the components of an image processing system.

Q7. What are the various Digital Transmission Systems?

Q8. Briefly explain the Electronic Systems for Image Transmission & Storage.

Q9. What are the Characteristics of Image storage?

Q10. Explain the Computer Processing and Recognition of Pictorial Data.

Q11. Briefly explain the various Practical Applications of Digital image processing.

# CHAPTER 2

# FUNDAMENTALS OF IMAGE PROCESSING

## 2.1 INTRODUCTION

Modern digital technology has made it possible to manipulate multi-dimensional signals with systems that range from simple digital circuits to advanced parallel computers. The goal of this manipulation can be divided into three categories:

1. Image Processing image in -> image out
2. Image Analysis image in -> measurements out
3. Image Understanding image in -> high-level description out

We will focus on the fundamental concepts of image processing. Space does not permit us to make more than a few introductory remarks about image analysis. Image understanding requires an approach that differs fundamentally from the theme of this book. Further, we will restrict ourselves to two-dimensional (2D) image processing although most of the concepts and techniques that are to be described can be extended easily to three or more dimensions. We begin with certain basic definitions. An image defined in the "real world" is considered to be a function of two real variables, for example, a(x, y) with a as the amplitude (e.g. brightness) of the image at the real coordinate position (x, y). An image may be considered to contain sub-images sometimes referred to as regions-of-interest, ROIs, or simply regions. This concept reflects the fact that images frequently contain collections of objects each of which can be the basis for a region. In a sophisticated image processing system it should be possible to apply specific image processing operations to selected regions. Thus one part of an image (region) might be processed to suppress motion blur while another part might be processed to improve color rendition. The amplitudes of a given image will almost always be either real numbers or integer numbers. The latter is usually a result of a quantization process that converts a continuous range (say, between 0 and 100%) to a discrete number of levels. In certain image-forming processes, however, the signal may involve photon counting which implies that the amplitude would be inherently quantized. In other image forming procedures, such as magnetic resonance imaging, the direct physical measurement yields a complex number in the form of a real magnitude and a real phase. For the remainder of this book we will consider amplitudes as reals or integers unless otherwise indicated.

## 2.2 MATHEMATICAL AND PERCEPTUAL PRELIMINARIES

### 2.2.1 MATHEMATICAL SYSTEMS

Several mathematical systems have been developed. These offer what is virtually a word processing system for mathematicians. Many are screen based, using a Windows system. The advantage of these systems is that you can transpose mathematics pretty well directly from textbooks, and see how it works. Code functionality is not obscured by the use of data structures, although this can make the code appear cumbersome. A major advantage is that the system provides low-level functionality and data visualization schemes, allowing the user to concentrate on techniques alone. Accordingly, these systems afford an excellent route to understand, and appreciate, mathematical systems before the development of application code, and to check that the final code works correctly.

## 2.2 MATHEMATICAL TOOLS

Mathcad, Mathematica, Maple and Matlab are among the most popular of current tools. here have been surveys that compare their efficacy, but it is difficult to ensure precise omparison owing to the impressive speed of development of techniques. Most systems have eir protagonists and detractors, as in any commercial system. Many books use these packages r particular subjects, and there are often handbooks as addenda to the packages. We shall use oth Matlab and Mathcad throughout this text as they two very popular mathematical systems. he website links for the main mathematical packages are given in Table 2.1.

| General | | |
|---|---|---|
| Guide to available mathematical software | NIST | http://gams.nist.gov/ |
| **Vendors** | | |
| Mathcad | MathSoft | http://www.mathcad.com/ |
| Mathematica | Wolfram Research | http://www.wolfram.com/ |
| Matlab | Mathworks | http://www.mathworks.com/ |
| Maple | Maplesoft | http://www.maplesoft.com/ |

**Table 2.1 Mathematical Package websites**

## 2.3 HELLO MATHCAD, HELLO IMAGES!

Mathcad uses worksheets to implement mathematical analysis. The flow of calculation is ery similar to using a piece of paper: calculation starts at the top of a document, and flows left to ght and downwards. Data is available to later calculation (and to calculation to the right), but is ot available to prior calculation, much as is this case when calculation is written manually on aper.

Mathcad uses the Maple mathematical library to extend its functionality. To ensure that uations can migrate easily from a textbook to application, Mathcad uses a WYSIWYG (what ou see is what you get) notation [its equation editor is not dissimilar to the Microsoft Equation Vord) editor]. Mathcad offers a compromise between many performance factors, and is ailable at low cost. There used to be a free worksheet viewer called Mathcad Explorer which erated in read-only mode, which an advantage is lost. An image processing handbook is ailable with Mathcad, but it does not include many of the more sophisticated feature extraction chniques. Images are actually spatial data, data which is indexed by two spatial coordinates. ne camera senses the brightness at a point with coordinates x, y. Usually, x and y refer to the orizontal and vertical axes, respectively. Throughout this text we shall work in orthographic ojection, ignoring perspective, where real-world coordinates map directly to x and y ordinates in an image.

The homogeneous coordinate system is a popular and proven method for handling three mensional coordinate systems (x, y and z, where z is depth). The brightness sensed by the mera is transformed to a signal which is then fed to the A/D converter and stored as a value vithin the computer, referenced to the coordinates x, y in the image. Accordingly, a computer nage is a matrix of points. For a greyscale image, the value of each point is proportional to the rightness of the corresponding point in the scene viewed, and imaged, by the camera. These oints are the picture elements, or pixels.

Consider, for example, the matrix of pixel values in Figure 2.1(a). This can be viewed as surface (or function) in Figure 2.1(b), or as an image in Figure 2.1(c). In Figure 2.1(c) the rightness of each point is proportional to the value of its pixel. This gives the synthesized image f a bright square on a dark background. The square is bright where the pixels have a value round 40 brightness levels; the background is dark, and these pixels have a value near 0 rightness levels. This image is first given a label, pic, and then pic is allocated,:=, to the matrix efined by using the matrix dialogue box in Mathcad, specifying a matrix with eight rows and ight columns. The pixel values are then entered one by one until the matrix is complete alternatively, the matrix can be specified by using a subroutine, but that comes later). Note that either the background nor the square has a constant brightness. This is because noise has been dded to the image. If we want to evaluate the performance of a computer vision technique on an nage, but without the noise, we can simply remove it (one of the advantages of using synthetic nages). The matrix becomes an image when it is viewed as a picture, in Figure 2.1(c). This is one either by presenting it as a surface plot, rotated by zero degrees and viewed from above, or y using Mathcad's picture facility. As a surface plot, Mathcad allows the user to select a reyscale image, and the patch plot option allows an image to be presented as point values.

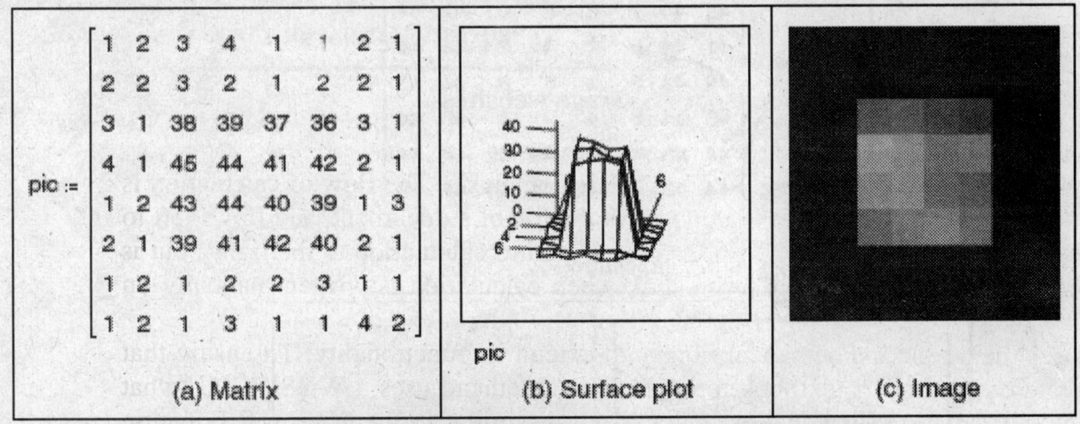


**Figure 2.1 Synthesized Image of a Square**

Mathcad stores matrices in row–column format. The coordinate system used throughout his text has x as the horizontal axis and y as the vertical axis (as conventional). Accordingly, x is he column count and y is the row count, so a point (in Mathcad) at coordinates x, y is actually ccessed as picy_x. The origin is at coordinates x = 0 and y = 0, so pic0_0 is the magnitude of the oint at the origin and pic2_2 is the point at the third row and third column and pic3_2 is the oint at the third column and fourth row, as shown in Code 2.1 (the points can be seen

ic2,2=38 pic3,2=45

ows(pic)=8 cols(pic)=8

**CODE 2.1 ACCESSING AN IMAGE IN MATHCAD**

In Figure 2.1(a). Since the origin is at (0,0) the bottom right-hand point, at the last olumn and row, has coordinates (7,7). The number of rows and the number of columns in a matrix, the dimensions of an image, can be obtained by using the Mathcad rows and cols functions, respectively, and again in Code 2.1. This synthetic image can be processed using the Mathcad programming language, which can be invoked by selecting the appropriate dialogue box. This allows for conventional for, while and if statements, and the earlier assignment operator which is := in non-code sections, is replaced by [back-arrow] in sections of code. A subroutine that inverts the brightness level at each point, by subtracting it from the maximum brightness level in the original image, is illustrated in Code 2.2. This uses for loops to index the rows and the columns, and then calculates a new pixel value by subtracting the value at that point from the maximum obtained by Mathcad's max function. When the whole image has been processed, the new picture is returned to be assigned to the label newpic. The resulting matrix is shown in Figure 2.2(a). When this is viewed as a surface (Figure 2.2(b)), the inverted brightness levels mean that the square appears dark and its surroundings appear white, as in Figure 2.2(c).

```
new_pic:=  for x∈0..cols(pic)-1
             for y∈0..rows(pic)-1
               newpicture_y,x←max(pic)-pic_y,x
           newpicture
```

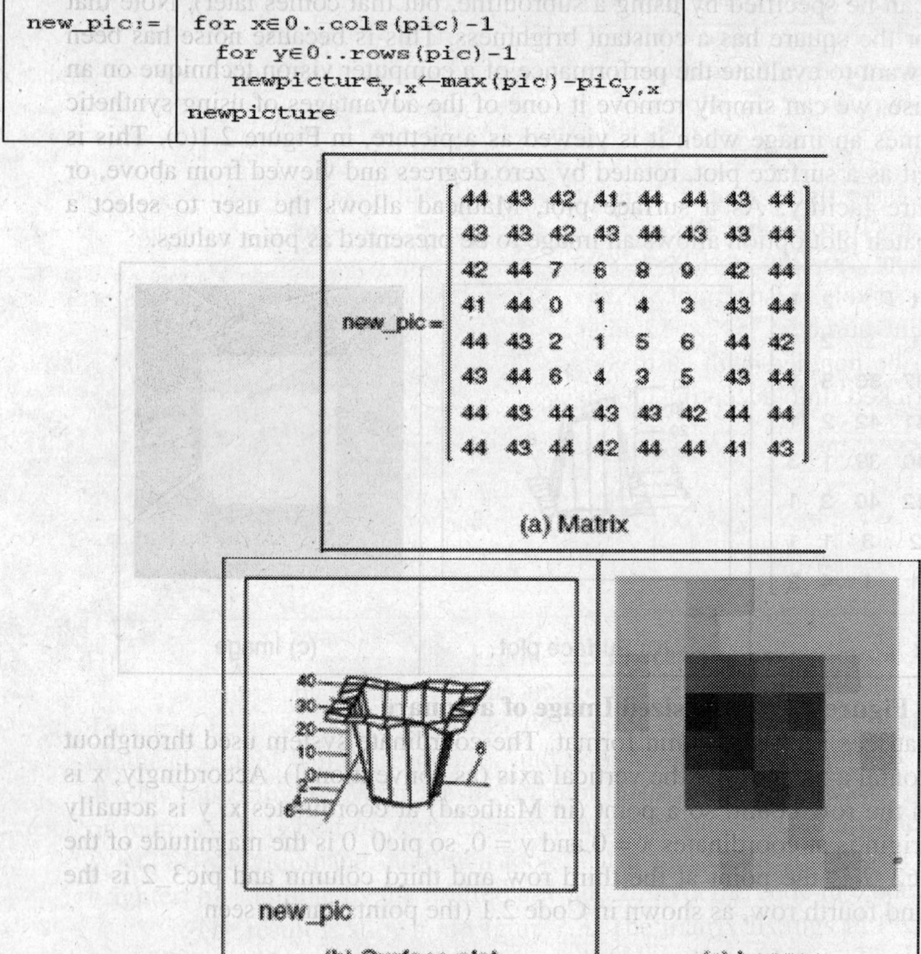


(a) Matrix

(b) Surface plot

(c) Image

**Figure 2.2 Image of a square after division**

## CODE 2.2 PROCESSING IMAGE POINTS IN MATHCAD

Routines can be formulated as functions, so they can be invoked to process a chosen picture, rather than restricted to a specific image. Mathcad functions are conventional; we simply add two arguments (one is the image to be processed, the other is the brightness to be added) and use the arguments as local variables, to give the add function illustrated in Code 2.3. To add a value, we simply call the function and supply an image and the chosen brightness level as the arguments.

```
add_value(inpic,value):= | for x∈0..cols(inpic)-1
                         |   for y∈0..rows(inpic)-1
                         |     newpicture_{y,x} ← inpic_{y,x}+value
                         | newpicture
```

## CODE 2.3 FUNCTION TO ADD A VALUE TO AN IMAGE IN MATHCAD

Mathematically, for an image which is a matrix of N ×N points, the brightness of the pixels in a new picture (matrix), N, are the result of adding b brightness values to the pixels in the old picture, O, given by:

$$N_{x,y} = O_{x,y} + b \qquad \forall_{x,y} \in 1, N \tag{2.1}$$

Real images have many points. Unfortunately, the Mathcad matrix dialogue box only allows matrices that are 10 rows and 10 columns at most, i.e. a 10×10 matrix. Real images can be 512×512, but are often 256×256 or 128×128; this implies a storage requirement for 262×144, 65×536 and 16×384 pixels, respectively. Since Mathcad stores all points as high-precision, complex floating point numbers, 512×512 images require too much storage, but 256×256 and 128×128 images can be handled with ease. Since this cannot be achieved by the dialogue box, Mathcad has to be 'tricked' into accepting an image of this size. Figure 2.3 shows an image

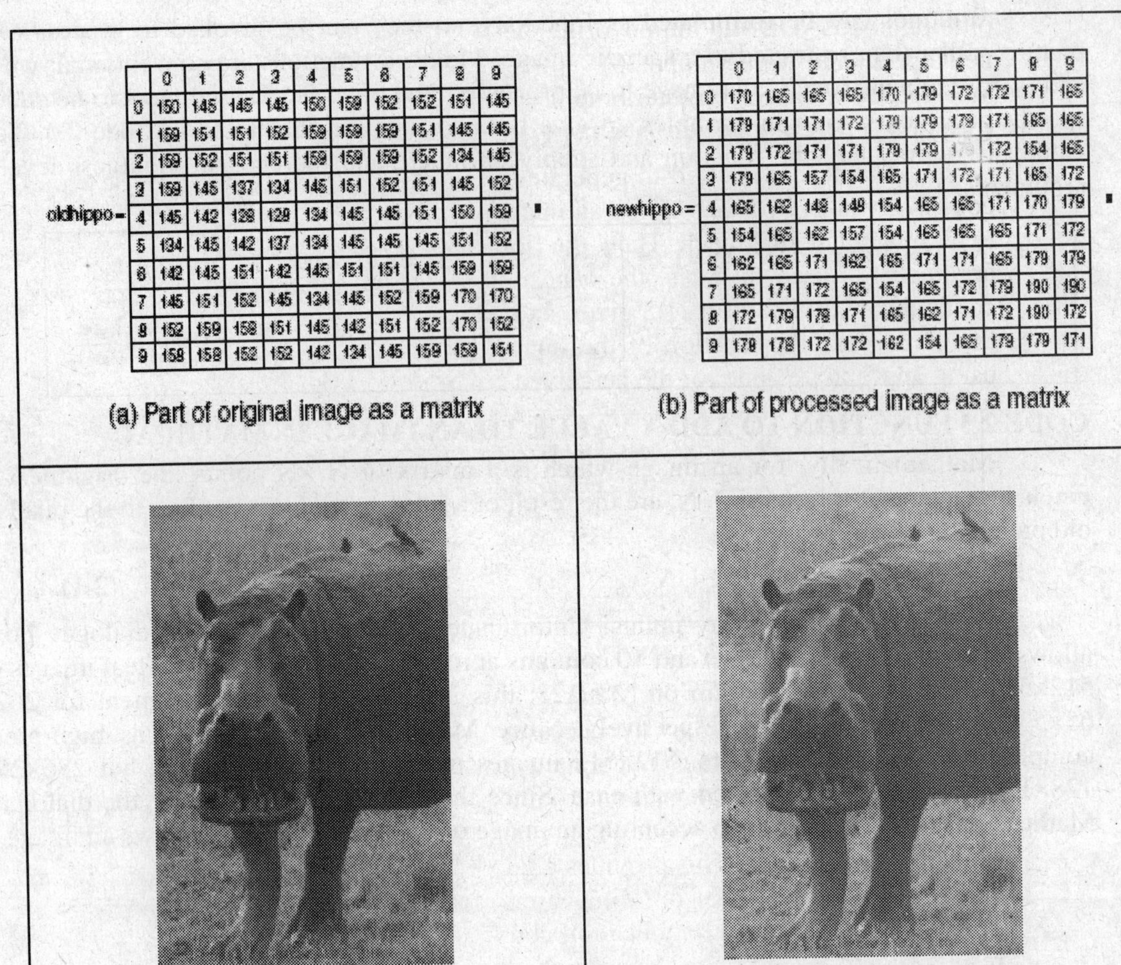

oldhippo =

| | 0 | 1 | 2 | 3 | 4 | 5 | 6 | 7 | 8 | 9 |
|---|---|---|---|---|---|---|---|---|---|---|
| 0 | 150 | 145 | 145 | 145 | 150 | 159 | 152 | 152 | 151 | 145 |
| 1 | 159 | 151 | 151 | 152 | 159 | 159 | 159 | 151 | 145 | 145 |
| 2 | 159 | 152 | 151 | 151 | 159 | 159 | 159 | 152 | 134 | 145 |
| 3 | 159 | 145 | 137 | 134 | 145 | 151 | 152 | 151 | 145 | 152 |
| 4 | 145 | 142 | 129 | 129 | 134 | 145 | 145 | 151 | 150 | 159 |
| 5 | 134 | 145 | 142 | 137 | 134 | 145 | 145 | 145 | 151 | 152 |
| 6 | 142 | 145 | 151 | 142 | 145 | 151 | 151 | 145 | 159 | 159 |
| 7 | 145 | 151 | 152 | 145 | 134 | 145 | 152 | 159 | 170 | 170 |
| 8 | 152 | 159 | 158 | 151 | 145 | 142 | 151 | 152 | 170 | 152 |
| 9 | 158 | 158 | 152 | 152 | 142 | 134 | 145 | 159 | 159 | 151 |

(a) Part of original image as a matrix

newhippo =

| | 0 | 1 | 2 | 3 | 4 | 5 | 6 | 7 | 8 | 9 |
|---|---|---|---|---|---|---|---|---|---|---|
| 0 | 170 | 165 | 165 | 165 | 170 | 179 | 172 | 172 | 171 | 165 |
| 1 | 179 | 171 | 171 | 172 | 179 | 179 | 179 | 171 | 165 | 165 |
| 2 | 179 | 172 | 171 | 171 | 179 | 179 | [illegible] | 172 | 154 | 165 |
| 3 | 179 | 165 | 157 | 154 | 165 | 171 | 172 | 171 | 165 | 172 |
| 4 | 165 | 162 | 149 | 149 | 154 | 165 | 165 | 171 | 170 | 179 |
| 5 | 154 | 165 | 162 | 157 | 154 | 165 | 165 | 165 | 171 | 172 |
| 6 | 162 | 165 | 171 | 162 | 165 | 171 | 171 | 165 | 179 | 179 |
| 7 | 165 | 171 | 172 | 165 | 154 | 165 | 172 | 179 | 190 | 190 |
| 8 | 172 | 179 | 178 | 171 | 165 | 162 | 171 | 172 | 190 | 172 |
| 9 | 178 | 178 | 172 | 172 | 162 | 154 | 165 | 179 | 179 | 171 |

(b) Part of processed image as a matrix

(c) Bitmap of original image

(d) Bitmap of processed image

**Figure 2.3 Processing an image**

captured by a camera. This image has been stored in Windows bitmap (.BMP) form This can be read into a Mathcad worksheet using the READBMP command (in capitals Mathcad cannot handle readbmp), and is assigned to a variable. It is inadvisable to attempt display this using the Mathcad surface plot facility, as it can be slow for images and requires a of memory. It is best to view an image using Mathcad's picture facility or to store it using WRITEBMP command, and then look at it using a bitmap viewer. So, we can make an ima brighter, by addition, by the routine in Code 2.3, via the code in Code 2.4.

The result is shown in Figure 2.3. The matrix listings in Figure 2.3(a) and (b) show t 20 has been added to each point (these only show the top left-hand section of the image where bright points relate to the grass; the darker points on, say, the ear cannot be seen). The effect v be to make each point appear brighter, as seen by comparison of the (darker) original ima (Figure 2.3c) with the (brighter) result of addition (Figure 2.3d). For the moment, we are j seeing how Mathcad can be used, in a simple way, to process pictures.

oldhippo:=READBMP("hippo_orig")
newhippo:=add_value(hippo,20)
WRITEBMP("hippo_brighter.bmp"):=newhippo

**CODE 2.4 PROCESSING AN IMAGE**

Mathcad was used to generate the image used to demonstrate the Mach band effect; th code is given in Code 2.5. First, an image is defined by copying the hippo image (from Code 2. to an image labelled mach. Then, the floor function (which returns the nearest integer less than i argument) is used to create the bands, scaled by an amount appropriate to introduce sufficie contrast (the division by 21.5 gives six bands in the image of Figure 2.3a). The cross-section ar the perceived cross-section of the image were both generated by Mathcad's X–Y plot facilit using appropriate code for the perceived cross-section.

```
mach:=   for x∈0..cols(mach)-1
           for y∈0..rows(mach)-1
             mach_{y,x} ← brightness·floor( x / bar_width )
         mach
```

**CODE 2.5 CREATING THE IMAGE OF FIGURE 2.3(A)**

The translation of the Mathcad code into application can be rather prolix when compare with the Mathcad version by the necessity to include low-level functions. Since these can obscu the basic image processing functionality, Mathcad is used throughout this book to show how th techniques work. The translation to application code is perhaps easier via Matlab, as it offe direct compilation of the code. You can then use the algorithms as a basis for developing yo own application code. This provides a good way to verify that your code actually works: you ca compare the results of your final application code with those of the original mathematic description. If your final application code and the Mathcad implementation are both correct, th results should be the same. Your application code will be much faster than in Mathcad, and wi benefit from the graphical user interface (GUI) that you have developed.

### 2.2.4. HELLO MATLAB

Matlab is rather different from Mathcad. It is not a WYSIWYG system, but instead it more screen based. It was originally developed for matrix functions, hence the 'Mat' in the nam Like Mathcad, it offers a set of mathematical tools and visualization capabilities in a mann arranged to be very similar to conventional computer programs. In some users' views, WYSIWYG system like Mathcad is easier to start with, but there are a number of advantages Matlab, not least the potential speed advantage in computation and the facility for debuggin together with a considerable amount of established support. Again, there is an image processin toolkit supporting Matlab, but it is rather limited compared with the range of techniques expose in this text. Its popularity is reflected in a book dedicated to use of Matlab for image processir (Gonzalez et al., 2003), by perhaps one of the subject's most popular authors.

Essentially, Matlab is the set of instructions that process the data stored in a workspac which can be extended by user-written commands. The workspace stores the different lists of da and these data can be stored in a MAT file; the user-written commands are functions that a stored in M-files (files with extension .M). The procedure operates by instructions at the command line to process the workspace data using either one of Matlab's commands or your own commands. The results can be visualized as graphs, surfaces or images, as in Mathcad. Matlab provides powerful matrix manipulations to develop and test complex implementations.

Thus, matrix expressions are transformed into loop sequences. This helps students without experience in matrix algebra to understand and implement the techniques without dependency on matrix manipulation software libraries. Implementations in this book only serve to gain understanding of the techniques' performance and correctness, and favour clarity rather than speed.

The system runs on Unix/Linux or Windows and on Macintosh systems. A student version is available at low cost. There is no viewer available for Matlab; you have to have access to a system for which it is installed. As the system is not based around worksheets, we shall use a script which is the simplest type of M-file, as illustrated in Code 2.6. To start the Matlab system, type MATLAB at the command line. At the Matlab prompt (>>) type chapter1 to load and run the script (given that the file chapter1.m is saved in the directory you are working in). Here, we can see that there are no text boxes and so comments are preceded by %. The first command is one that allocates data to our variable pic. There is a more sophisticated way to input this in the Matlab system, but that is not available here. The points are addressed in row–column format and the origin is at coordinates y = 1 and x = 1. So we access these points pic3_3 as the third column of the third row and pic 4_3 as the point in the third column of the fourth row. Having set the display facility to black and white, we can view the array pic as a surface.

### 2.2.5 TOOLS

Certain tools are central to the processing of digital images. These include mathematical tools such as convolution, Fourier analysis, and statistical descriptions, and manipulative tools such as chain codes and run codes. We will present these tools without any specific motivation. The motivation will follow in later sections.

- Convolution
- Properties of Convolution
- Fourier Transforms
- Properties of Fourier Transforms
- Statistics
- Contour Representation

#### 2.2.5.1 CONVOLUTION

There are several possible notations to indicate the convolution of two (multi-dimensional) signals to produce an output signal. The most common are:

$$c = a \otimes b = a * b$$

We shall use the first form, $c = a \otimes b$, with the following formal definitions.

In 2D continuous space:

$$c(x,y) = a(x,y) \otimes b(x,y) = \int_{-\infty}^{+\infty}\int_{-\infty}^{+\infty} a(\chi,\varsigma)\, b(x-\chi, y-\varsigma)\, d\chi\, d\varsigma$$

In 2D discrete space:

$$c[m,n] = a[m,n] \otimes b[m,n] = \sum_{j=-\infty}^{+\infty}\sum_{k=-\infty}^{+\infty} a[j,k]\, b[m-j, n-k]$$

### 2.2.5.2 PROPERTIES OF CONVOLUTION

There are a number of important mathematical properties associated with convolution.

* Convolution is commutative.

$c = a \otimes b = b \otimes a$

* Convolution is associative.

$c = a \otimes (b \otimes c) = (a \otimes b) \otimes c = a \otimes b \otimes c$

* Convolution is distributive.

$c = a \otimes (b + d) = (a \otimes b) + (a \otimes d)$

where a, b, c, and d are all images, either continuous or discrete.

### 2.2.5.3 FOURIER TRANSFORMS

The Fourier transform produces another representation of a signal, specifically a representation as a weighted sum of complex exponentials. Because of Euler's formula:

$e^{fq} = \cos(q) + j\sin(q)$

where $j^2 = -1$, we can say that the Fourier transform produces a representation of a (2D) signal as a weighted sum of sines and cosines.

The defining formulas for the forward Fourier and the inverse Fourier transforms are as follows. Given an image a and its Fourier transform A, then the forward transform goes from the spatial domain (either continuous or discrete) to the frequency domain which is always continuous.

Forward - A=F{a}

The inverse Fourier transform goes from the frequency domain back to the spatial domain.

Inverse – $a=F^{-1}\{A\}$

The Fourier transform is a unique and invertible operation so that:

$a=F^{-1}\{F_{\{A\}}\}$ and $A=F\{F^{-1}{}_{\{A\}}\}$

The specific formulas for transforming back and forth between the spatial domain and the frequency domain are given below.

In 2D continuous space:

Forward - $$A(u,v) = \int_{-\infty}^{+\infty}\int_{-\infty}^{+\infty} a(x,y)e^{-f(ux,uy)}dxdy$$

Inverse - $$a(x,y) = \frac{1}{4\Pi^2}\int_{-\infty}^{+\infty}\int_{-\infty}^{+\infty} A(u,v)e^{+f(ux,uy)}dudv$$

In 2D discrete space:

Forward - $$A(\Omega,\Psi) = \sum_{m=-\infty}^{+\infty}\sum_{n=-\infty}^{+\infty} a[m,n]e^{-f(\Omega_m+\Psi_n)}$$

Inverse – $$a[m,n] = \frac{1}{4\Pi^2}\int_{-\Pi}^{+\Pi}\int_{-\Pi}^{+\Pi} A(\Omega,\Psi)e^{+f(\Omega\Pi+\Psi\Pi)}d\Omega d\Psi$$

### 2.2.5.4 PROPERTIES OF FOURIER TRANSFORMS

- Importance of phase and magnitude
- Circularly symmetric signals

- Examples of 2D signals and transforms

There are a variety of properties associated with the Fourier transform and the inverse Fourier transform. The following are some of the most relevant for digital image processing.

1. The Fourier transform is, in general, a complex function of the real frequency variables. As such the transform can be written in terms of its magnitude and phase.

$$A(u,v) = |A(u,v)|e^{j\varphi(u,v)} \qquad A(\Omega,\Psi) = |A(\Omega,\Psi)|e^{j\varphi(\Omega,\Psi)}$$

2. A 2D signal can also be complex and thus written in terms of its magnitude and phase.

$$a(x,y) = |a(x,y)|e^{j\vartheta(x,y)} \qquad a[m,n] = |a[m,n]|e^{j\vartheta[m,n]}$$

3. If a 2D signal is real, then the Fourier transform has certain symmetries.

$$A(u,v) = A^*(-u,-v) \qquad A(\Omega,\Psi) = A^*(-\Omega,-\Psi)$$

The symbol (*) indicates complex conjugation. For real signals eq. leads directly to:

$$|A(u,v)| = |A(-u,-v)| \qquad \phi(u,v) = -\phi(-u,-v)$$

$$|A(\Omega,\Psi)| = |A(-\Omega,-\Psi)| \qquad \phi(\Omega,\Psi) = -\phi(-\Omega,-\Psi)$$

* If a 2D signal is real and even, then the Fourier transform is real and even.

$$A(u,v) = A(-u,-v) \qquad A(\Omega,\Psi) = A(-\Omega,-\Psi)$$

* The Fourier and the inverse Fourier transforms are linear operations.

$$\mathcal{F}\{w_1 a + w_2 b\} = \mathcal{F}\{w_1 a\} + \mathcal{F}\{w_2 b\} = w_1 A + w_2 B$$

$$\mathcal{F}^{-1}\{w_1 A + w_2 B\} = \mathcal{F}^{-1}\{w_1 A\} + \mathcal{F}^{-1}\{w_2 B\} = w_1 a + w_2 b$$

where a and b are 2D signals (images) and $w_1$ and $w_2$ are arbitrary, complex constants.

4. The Fourier transform in discrete space, $A(\Omega,\Psi)$, is periodic in both $\Omega$ and $\Psi$. Both periods are $2\pi$.

$$A(\Omega + 2\pi j, \Psi + 2\pi k) = A(\Omega,\Psi) \qquad j,k \text{ integers}$$

5. The energy, E, in a signal can be measured either in the spatial domain or the frequency domain. For a signal with finite energy:

Parseval's theorem (2D continuous space):

$$E = \int_{-\infty}^{+\infty}\int_{-\infty}^{+\infty} |a(x,y)|^2 \, dx dy = \frac{1}{4\pi^2}\int_{-\infty}^{+\infty}\int_{-\infty}^{+\infty} |A(u,v)|^2 \, du dv$$

Parseval's theorem (2D discrete space):

$$E = \sum_{m=-\infty}^{+\infty}\sum_{n=-\infty}^{+\infty} |a[m,n]|^2 = \frac{1}{4\pi^2}\int_{-\pi}^{+\pi}\int_{-\pi}^{+\pi} |A(\Omega,\Psi)|^2 \, d\Omega d\Psi$$

This "signal energy" is not to be confused with the physical energy in the phenomenon that produced the signal. If, for example, the value a[m, n] represents a photon count, then the physical energy is proportional to the amplitude, a, and not the square of the amplitude. This is generally the case in video imaging.

6. Given three, multi-dimensional signals a, b, and c and their Fourier transforms A, B, and C:

$$c = a \otimes b \quad \overset{F}{\leftrightarrow} \quad C = A \bullet B$$

And

$$c = a \bullet b \quad \overset{F}{\leftrightarrow} \quad C = \frac{1}{4\pi^2} A \otimes B$$

In words, convolution in the spatial domain is equivalent to multiplication in the Fourier (frequency) domain and vice-versa. This is a central result which provides not only a methodology for the implementation of a convolution but also insight into how two signals interact with each other--under convolution--to produce a third signal. We shall make extensive use of this result later.

7. If a two-dimensional signal a(x, y) is scaled in its spatial coordinates then:

$$\text{If} \quad a(x, y) \rightarrow a(M_x \bullet x, M_y \bullet y)$$

$$\text{Then} \quad A(u, v) \rightarrow A\left(\frac{u}{M_x}, \frac{v}{M_y}\right) \Big/ \left|M_x \bullet M_y\right|$$

8. If a two-dimensional signal a(x, y) has Fourier spectrum A(u, v) then:

$$A(u = 0, v = 0) = \int_{-\infty}^{+\infty}\int_{-\infty}^{+\infty} a(x, y)\,dx\,dy$$

$$a(x = 0, y = 0) = \frac{1}{4\pi^2}\int_{-\infty}^{+\infty}\int_{-\infty}^{+\infty} A(u, v)\,dx\,dy$$

9. If a two-dimensional signal a(x, y) has Fourier spectrum A(u, v) then:

$$\frac{\partial a(x, y)}{\partial x} \overset{F}{\leftrightarrow} juA(u, v) \qquad \frac{\partial a(x, y)}{\partial y} \overset{F}{\leftrightarrow} jvA(u, v)$$

$$\frac{\partial^2 a(x, y)}{\partial x^2} \overset{F}{\leftrightarrow} -u^2 A(u, v) \qquad \frac{\partial^2 a(x, y)}{\partial y^2} \overset{F}{\leftrightarrow} -v^2 A(u, v)$$

### 2.2.6 IMPORTANCE OF PHASE AND MAGNITUDE

Equation indicates that the Fourier transform of an image can be complex. This is illustrated below in Figures 2.4a-c. Figure 2.4a shows the original image a[m, n], Figure 2.4b the magnitude in a scaled form as $\log(|A(\Omega,\Psi)|)$, and Figure 2.4c the phase $\varphi(\Omega,\Psi)$.

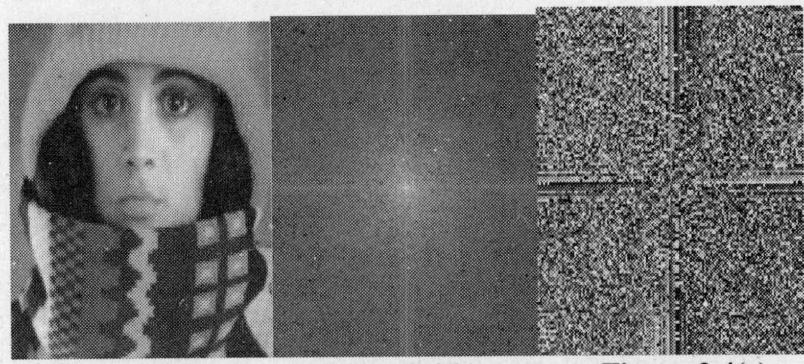

Figure 2.4(a) Figure 2.4(b) Figure 2.4(c)

Original log(|A(Ω,Ψ)|) φ(Ω,Ψ)

Both the magnitude and the phase functions are necessary for the complete reconstruction of an image from its Fourier transform. Figure 2.5a shows what happens when Figure 2.4a is restored solely on the basis of the magnitude information and Figure 2.5b shows what happens when Figure 2.4a is restored solely on the basis of the phase information.

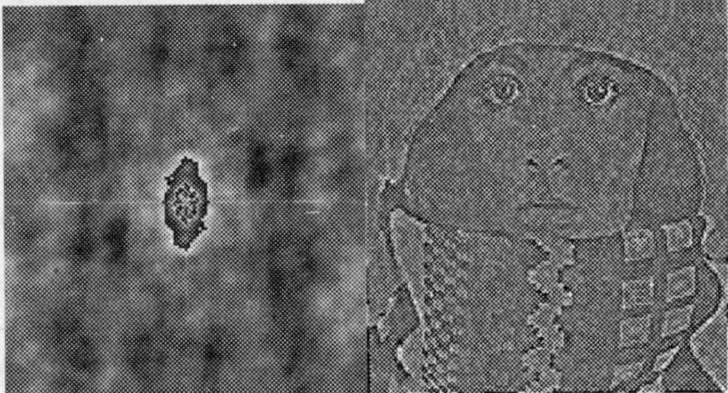

Figure 2.5(a) Figure 2.5(b)

$\varphi(\Omega,\Psi) = 0$ $|A(\Omega,\Psi)|$ = constant

Neither the magnitude information nor the phase information is sufficient to restore the image. The magnitude-only image (Figure 2.5(a)) is unrecognizable and has severe dynamic range problems. The phase-only image (Figure 2.5(b)) is barely recognizable, that is, severely degraded in quality.

### 2.2.7 CIRCULARLY SYMMETRIC SIGNALS

An arbitrary 2D signal a(x, y) can always be written in a polar coordinate system as $a(r,\theta)$. When the 2D signal exhibits a circular symmetry this means that:

$$a(x, y) = a(r,\theta) = a(r)$$

where $r^2 = x^2 + y^2$ and $\tan\theta = y/x$. As a number of physical systems such as lenses exhibit circular symmetry, it is useful to be able to compute an appropriate Fourier representation. The Fourier transform A(u, v) can be written in polar coordinates $A(\omega_r,\xi)$ and then, for a circularly symmetric signal, rewritten as a ankel transform:

$$A(u,v) = \mathcal{F}\{a(x,y)\} = 2\pi\int_0^\infty a(r)J_o(\omega_r r)r\,dr = A(\omega_r)$$

where $\omega_r^2 = u^2 + v^2$ *and* $\tan\xi = v/u$ and $J_o(*)$ is a Bessel function of the first kind of order zero. The inverse ankel transform is given by:

$$a(r) = \frac{1}{2\pi}\int_0^\infty A(\omega_r)J_o(\omega_r r)\omega_r d\omega_r$$

The Fourier transform of a circularly symmetric 2D signal is a function of only the radial frequency, $\omega_r$. The dependence on the angular frequency, $\xi$, has vanished. Further, if a(x,y) = a(r) is real, then it is automatically even due to the circular symmetry. According to equation , $A(\omega_r)$ will then be real and even.

## EXAMPLES OF 2D SIGNALS AND TRANSFORMS

Table 2.2 shows some basic and useful signals and their 2D Fourier transforms. In using the table entries in the remainder of this chapter we will refer to a spatial domain term as the point spread function (PSF) or the 2D impulse response and its Fourier transforms as the optical transfer function (OTF) or simply transfer function. Two standard signals used in this table are u(*), the unit step function, and $J_1$(*), the Bessel function of the first kind. Circularly symmetric signals are treated as functions of r.

## 2.2.8 STATISTICS

- Probability distribution function of the brightnesses
- Probability density function of the brightnesses
- Average
- Standard deviation
- Coefficient-of-variation
- Percentiles
- Mode
- Signal to Noise ratio

In image processing it is quite common to use simple statistical descriptions of images and sub-images. The notion of a statistic is intimately connected to the concept of a probability distribution, generally the distribution of signal amplitudes.

For a given region--which could conceivably be an entire image--we can define the probability distribution function of the brightnesses in that region and the probability density function of the brightness in that region. We will assume in the discussion that follows that we are dealing with a digitized image a[m, n].

### 2.2.8.1 PROBABILITY DISTRIBUTION FUNCTION OF THE BRIGHTNESSES

The probability distribution function, P(a), is the probability that a brightness chosen from the region is less than or equal to a given brightness value a. As a increases from $-\infty$ to $+\infty$, P(a) increases from 0 to 1. P(a) is monotonic, non-decreasing in a and thus dP/da >= 0.

### 2.2.8.2 PROBABILITY DENSITY FUNCTION OF THE BRIGHTNESSES

The probability that a brightness in a region falls between a and $a+\Delta a$, given the probability distribution function P(a), can be expressed as $p(a)\Delta a$ where p(a) is the probability density function:

$$p(a)\Delta a = \left(\frac{dP(a)}{da}\right)\Delta a$$

| | | | |
|---|---|---|---|
| T.2.2.(a) Rectangle | $R_{a,b}(x,y) = \frac{1}{4ab}u(a^2-x^2)u(b^2-y^2)$ | $\overset{F}{\leftrightarrow}$ | $\left(\frac{\sin(2\pi a f_x)}{\pi a f_x}\right)\left(\frac{\sin(2\pi b f_y)}{\pi b f_y}\right)$ |
| T.2.2.(b) Pyramid | $R_{a,b}(x,y) \otimes R_{a,b}(x,y)$ | $\overset{F}{\leftrightarrow}$ | $\left(\frac{\sin(2\pi a f_x)}{\pi a f_x}\frac{\sin(2\pi b f_y)}{\pi b f_y}\right)^2$ |
| T.2.2(c) Pill Box | $P_a(r) = \frac{u(a^2-r^2)}{\pi a^2}$ | $\overset{F}{\leftrightarrow}$ | $2\frac{J_1(2\pi a f)}{\pi a f}$ |
| T.2.2(d) Cone | $P_a(r) \otimes P_a(r)$ | $\overset{F}{\leftrightarrow}$ | $4\left(\frac{J_1(2\pi a f)}{\pi a f}\right)^2$ |
| T.2.2(e) Airy PSF | $PSF(r) = \frac{1}{\pi}\left(\frac{J_1(\omega_c r/2)}{r}\right)^2$ | $\overset{F}{\leftrightarrow}$ | $\frac{2}{\pi}\left(\cos^{-1}\left(\frac{f}{f_c}\right) - \left(\frac{f}{f_c}\right)\sqrt{1-\left(\frac{f}{f_c}\right)^2}\right)u(f_c^2-f^2)$ |
| T.2.2(f)Gaussian | $g_{2D}(r,\sigma) = \frac{1}{2\pi\sigma^2}\exp\left(-\frac{r^2}{2\sigma^2}\right)$ | $\overset{F}{\leftrightarrow}$ | $G_{2D}(f,\sigma) = \exp(-2\pi^2 f^2\sigma^2)$ |
| T.2.2(g)Peak | $\frac{1}{r}$ | $\overset{F}{\leftrightarrow}$ | $\frac{1}{f}$ |
| T.2.2(h) Exponential Decay | $e^{-ar}$ | $\overset{F}{\leftrightarrow}$ | $2\pi a \Big/ \left(\omega^2 + a^2\right)^{3/2}$ |

**Table 2.2: 2D Images and their Fourier Transforms**

Because of the monotonic, non-decreasing character of P(a) we have that:

$$P(a) \geq 0 and \int_{-\infty} p(a)da = 1$$

For an image with quantized (integer) brightness amplitudes, the interpretation of Δa is the width of a brightness interval. We assume constant width intervals. The brightness probability density function is frequently estimated by counting the number of times that each brightness occurs in the region to generate a histogram, h[a]. The histogram can then be normalized so that the total area under the histogram. Said another way, the p[a] for a region is the normalized count of the number of pixels, Λ, in a region that have quantized brightness a:

$$p[a]=\frac{1}{\Lambda}h[a] \quad \text{with} \quad \Lambda=\sum_a h[a]$$

The brightness probability distribution function for the image shown in Figure 2.4a is shown in Figure 2.6a. The (unnormalized) brightness histogram of Figure 2.4a which is proportional to the estimated brightness probability density function is shown in Figure 2.6b. The height in this histogram corresponds to the number of pixels with a given brightness.

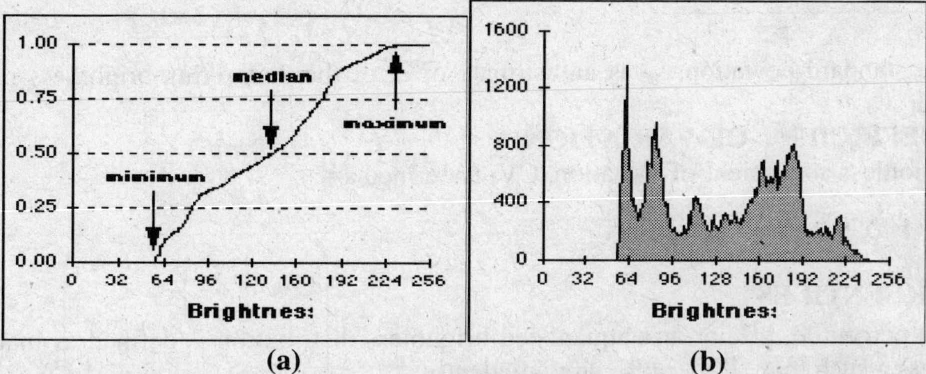


(a) (b)

**Figure 2.6: (a) Brightness distribution function of Figure a with minimum, median, and maximum indicated. See text for explanation. (b) Brightness histogram of Figure 2.6a**

Both the distribution function and the histogram as measured from a region are a statistical description of that region. It must be emphasized that both P[a] and p[a] should be viewed as estimates of true distributions when they are computed from a specific region. That is, we view an image and a specific region as one realization of the various random processes involved in the formation of that image and that region. In the same context, the statistics defined below must be viewed as estimates of the underlying parameters.

### 2.2.8.3. AVERAGE

The average brightness of a region is defined as the sample mean of the pixel brightnesses within that region. The average, $m_a$, of the brightnesses over the Λ pixels within a region ($\Re$) is given by:

$$m_a=\frac{1}{\Lambda}\sum_{(m,n)\in\Re}a[m,n]$$

Alternatively, we can use a formulation based upon the (unnormalized) brightness histogram, h(a) = Λ*p(a), with discrete brightness values a. This gives:

$$m_a=\frac{1}{\Lambda}\sum_a a\cdot h[a]$$

The average brightness, $m_a$, is an estimate of the mean brightness, $u_a$, of the underlying brightness probability distribution.

### 2.2.8.4. STANDARD DEVIATION

The unbiased estimate of the standard deviation, $s_a$, of the brightnesses within a region ($\Re$) with Λ pixels is called the sample standard deviation and is given by:

$$s_a = \sqrt{\frac{1}{\Lambda - 1} \sum_{m,n \in \Re} \left(a[m,n] - m_a\right)^2}$$

$$= \sqrt{\frac{\sum_{m,n \in \Re} a^2[m,n] - \Lambda m_a^2}{\Lambda - 1}}$$

Using the histogram formulation gives:

$$S_a = \sqrt{\frac{\left(\sum_a a^2 * h[a]\right) - \Lambda * m_a^2}{\Lambda - 1}}$$

The standard deviation, $s_a$, is an estimate of $\sigma_a$ of the underlying brightness probability distribution.

### 2.2.8.5. COEFFICIENT-OF-VARIATION

The dimensionless coefficient-of-variation, CV, is defined as:

$$CV = \frac{s_a}{m_a} \times 100\%$$

### 2.2.8.6. PERCENTILES

The percentile, p%, of an unquantized brightness distribution is defined as that value of the brightness a such that: P(a) = p% or equivalently

$$\int_{-\infty}^{a} p(\alpha)d\alpha = p\%$$

Three special cases are frequently used in digital image processing.

1. 0% the minimum value in the region
2. 50% the median value in the region
3. 100% the maximum value in the region

All three of these values can be determined from Figure 2.6a.

### 2.2.8.7. MODE

The mode of the distribution is the most frequent brightness value. There is no guarantee that a mode exists or that it is unique.

### 2.2.8.8. SIGNAL TO NOISE RATIO

The signal-to-noise ratio, SNR, can have several definitions. The noise is characterized by its standard deviation, $s_n$. The characterization of the signal can differ. If the signal is known to lie between two boundaries, $a_{min} \le a \le a_{max}$, then the SNR is defined as:

Bounded signal - $SNR = 20\log_{10}\left(\frac{a_{\max} - a_{\min}}{S_n}\right)dB$

If the signal is not bounded but has a statistical distribution then two other definitions are known:

Stochastic signal - S & N inter-dependent $SNR = 20\log_{10}\left(\frac{m_a}{S_n}\right)dB$

S & N independent $SNR = 20\log_{10}\left(\frac{S_a}{S_n}\right) dB$

where $m_a$ and $s_a$ are defined above.

The various statistics are given in Table 2.3 for the image and the region shown in Figure 2.7.

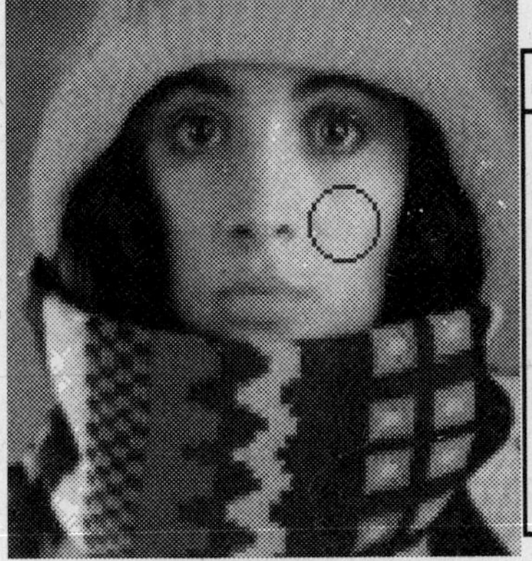

Figure 2.7

| Statistic | Image | ROI |
|---|---|---|
| Average | 137.7 | 219.3 |
| Standard Deviation | 49.5 | 4.0 |
| Minimum | 56 | 202 |
| Median | 141 | 220 |
| Maximum | 241 | 226 |
| Mode | 62 | 220 |
| SNR (db) | NA | 33.3 |

**Table 2.3 Region is the interior of the circle. Statistics from**

A SNR calculation for the entire image based on eq. is not directly available. The variations in the image brightnesses that lead to the large value of s (=49.5) are not, in general, due to noise but to the variation in local information. With the help of the region there is a way to estimate the SNR. We can use the $s\Re$ (=4.0) and the dynamic range, $a_{max}$ - $a_{min}$, for the image (=241-56) to calculate a global SNR (=33.3 dB). The underlying assumptions are that 1) the signal is approximately constant in that region and the variation in the region is therefore due to noise, and, 2) that the noise is the same over the entire image with a standard deviation given by $s_n = s\Re$.

### 2.2.9 CONTOUR REPRESENTATIONS

- Chain code
- Chain code properties
- Crack code
- Run codes

When dealing with a region or object, several compact representations are available that can facilitate manipulation of and measurements on the object. In each case we assume that we begin with an image representation of the object as shown in Figure 2.8a,b. Several techniques exist to represent the region or object by describing its contour.

#### 2.2.9.1. CHAIN CODE

This representation is based upon the work of Freeman. We follow the contour in a clockwise manner and keep track of the directions as we go from one contour pixel to the next. For the standard implementation of the chain code we consider a contour pixel to be an object pixel that has a background (non-object) pixel as one or more of its 4-connected neighbors. The codes associated with eight possible directions are the chain codes and, with x as the current contour pixel position, the codes are generally defined as:

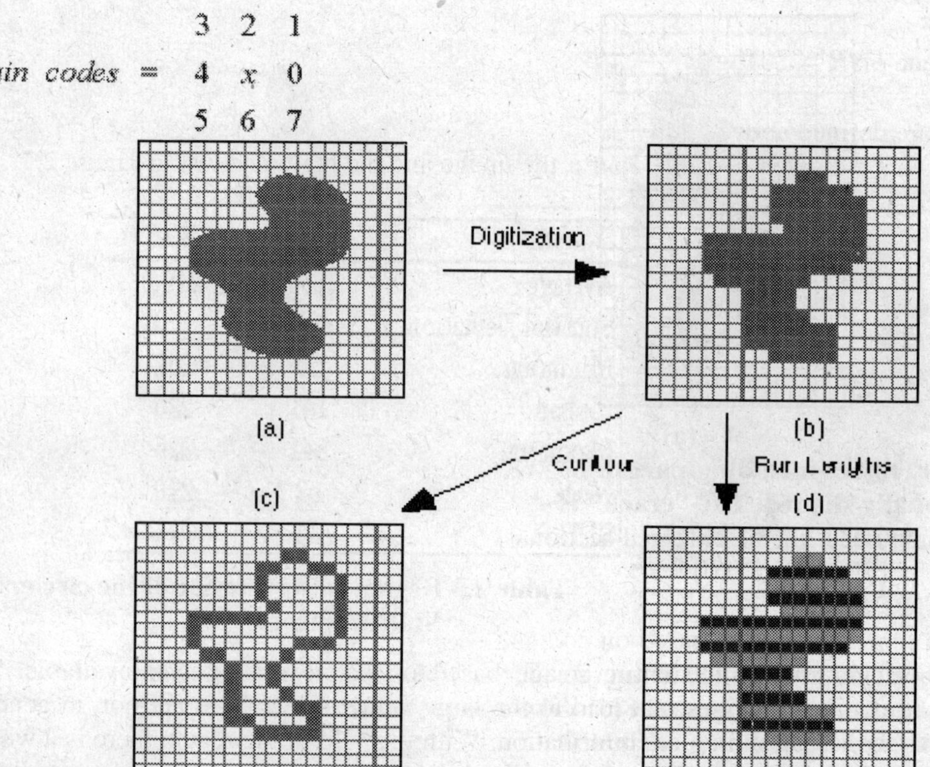


**Figure 2.8: Region (shaded) as it is transformed from (a) continuous to (b) discrete form and then considered as a (c) contour or (d) run lengths illustrated in alternating colors**

### 2.2.9.2. CHAIN CODE PROPERTIES

* Even codes {0,2,4,6} correspond to horizontal and vertical directions; odd codes {1,3,5,7} correspond to the diagonal directions.

* Each code can be considered as the angular direction, in multiples of 45 deg., that we must move to go from one contour pixel to the next.

* The absolute coordinates [m, n] of the first contour pixel (e.g. top, leftmost) together with the chain code of the contour represent a complete description of the discrete region contour.

* When there is a change between two consecutive chain codes, then the contour has changed direction. This point is defined as a corner.

### 2.2.9.3. CRACK CODE

An alternative to the chain code for contour encoding is to use neither the contour pixels associated with the object nor the contour pixels associated with background but rather the line, the "crack", in between. This is illustrated with an enlargement of a portion of Figure 2.8 in Figure 2.9. The "crack" code can be viewed as a chain code with four possible directions instead of eight.

$$
\textit{Crack codes} = \begin{matrix} & 1 & \\ 2 & x & 0 \\ & 3 & \end{matrix}
$$

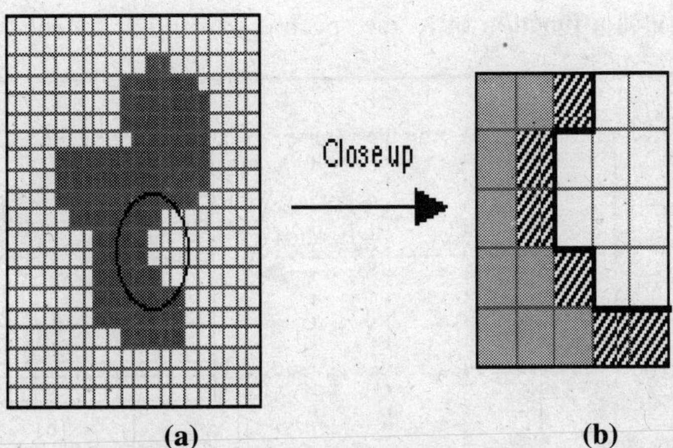


**Figure 2.9: (a) Object including part to be studied. (b) Contour pixels as used in the chain code are diagonally shaded. The "crack" is shown with the thick black line**

The chain code for the enlarged section of Figure 9b, from top to bottom, is {5,6,7,7,0}. The crack code is {3,2,3,3,0,3,0,0}.

**2.2.9.4. RUN CODES**

A third representation is based on coding the consecutive pixels along a row--a run--that belong to an object by giving the starting position of the run and the ending position of the run. Such runs are illustrated in Figure 2.8(d). There are a number of alternatives for the precise definition of the positions. Which alternative should be used depends upon the application and thus will not be discussed here.

## 2.2.10 PERCEPTION

Many image processing applications are intended to produce images that are to be viewed by human observers (as opposed to, say, automated industrial inspection.) It is therefore important to understand the characteristics and limitations of the human visual system--to understand the "receiver" of the 2D signals. At the outset it is important to realize that 1) the human visual system is not well understood, 2) no objective measure exists for judging the quality of an image that corresponds to human assessment of image quality, and, 3) the "typical" human observer does not exist. Nevertheless, research in perceptual psychology has provided some important insights into the visual system. See, for example, Stock ham .

- Brightness Sensitivity
- Spatial Frequency Sensitivity
- Color Sensitivity
- Optical Illusions

### 2.2.10.1 BRIGHTNESS SENSITIVITY

- Wavelength sensitivity
- Stimulus sensitivity

There are several ways to describe the sensitivity of the human visual system. To begin, let us assume that a homogeneous region in an image has an intensity as a function of wavelength (color) given by $I(\lambda)$. Further let us assume that $I(\lambda) = I_o$, a constant.

**1. WAVELENGTH SENSITIVITY**

The perceived intensity as a function of λ, the spectral sensitivity, for the "typical observer" is shown in Figure 2.10 .

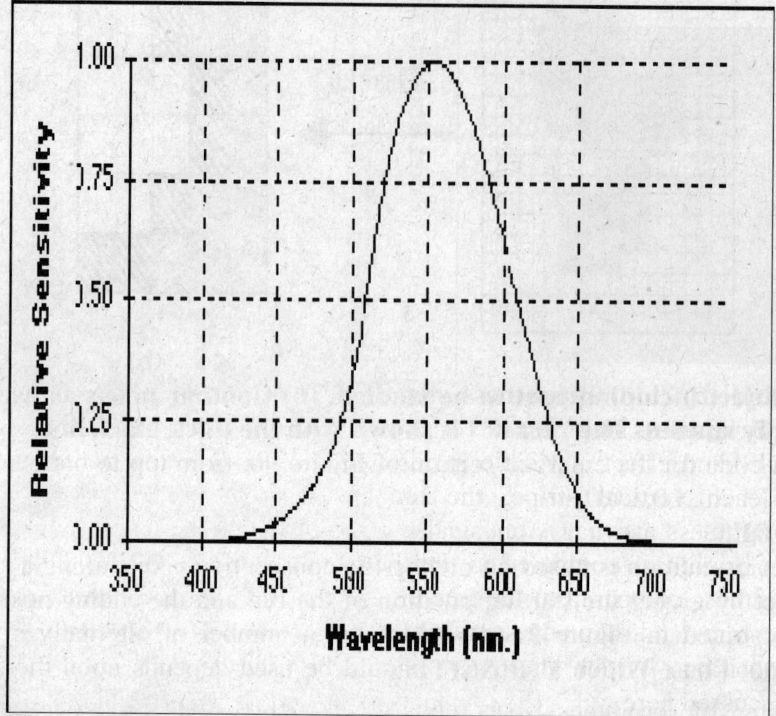


**Figure 2.10: Spectral Sensitivity of the "typical" human observer**

## 2. STIMULUS SENSITIVITY

If the constant intensity (brightness) $I_o$ is allowed to vary then, to a good approximation, the visual response, R, is proportional to the logarithm of the intensity. This is known as the Weber-Fechner law:

$$R = \log(I_o)$$

The implications of this are easy to illustrate. Equal perceived steps in brightness, $\Delta R = k$, require that the physical brightness (the stimulus) increases exponentially. This is illustrated in Figure 2.11(a)(b).

A horizontal line through the top portion of Figure 2.11(a) shows a linear increase in objective brightness (Figure 2.11(b)) but a logarithmic increase in subjective brightness. A horizontal line through the bottom portion of Figure 2.11(a) shows an exponential increase in objective brightness (Figure 2.11(b)) but a linear increase in subjective brightness.

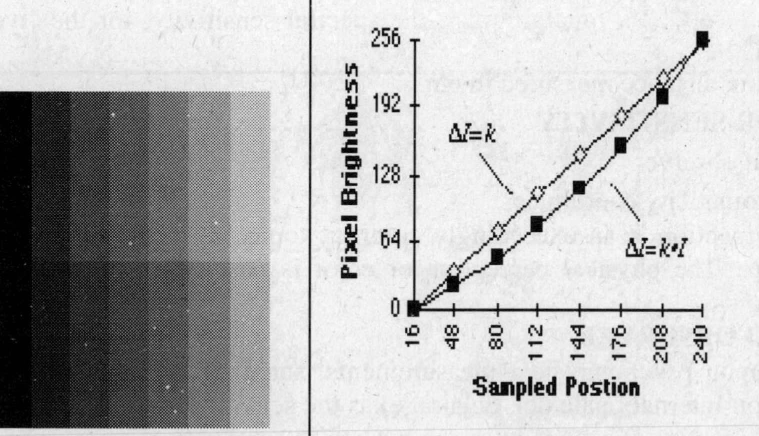


**Figure 2.11(a) and (b) (top) Brightness step ΔI = k Actual brightnesses plus interpolated values (bottom) Brightness step ΔI = k*I**

The Mach band effect is visible in Figure 2.11(a). Although the physical brightness is constant across each vertical stripe, the human observer perceives an "undershoot" and "overshoot" in brightness at what is physically a step edge. Thus, just before the step, we see a slight decrease in brightness compared to the true physical value. After the step we see a slight overshoot in brightness compared to the true physical value. The total effect is one of increased, local, perceived contrast at a step edge in brightness.

### 2.2.10.2 SPATIAL FREQUENCY SENSITIVITY

If the constant intensity (brightness) $I_o$ is replaced by a sinusoidal grating with increasing spatial frequency (Figure 2.12(a)), it is possible to determine the spatial frequency sensitivity. The result is shown in Figure 2.12(b).

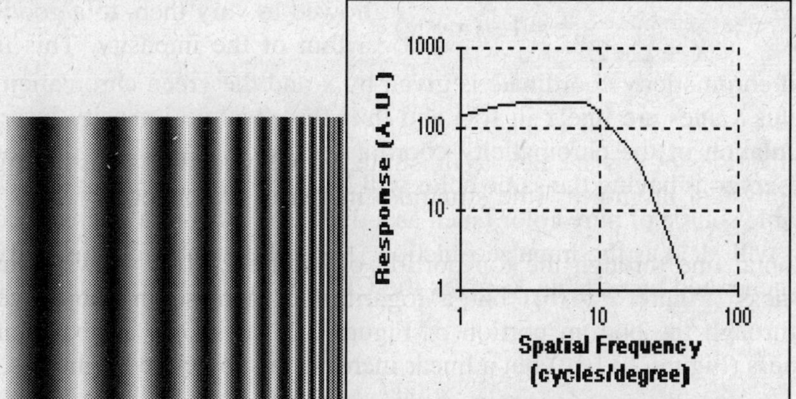


**Figure 2.12(a) and (b) Sinusoidal test grating spatial frequency sensitivity**

To translate these data into common terms, consider an "ideal" computer monitor at a viewing distance of 50 cm. The spatial frequency that will give maximum response is at 10 cycles per degree. (See Figure 12b.) The one degree at 50 cm translates to 50 tan(1deg.) = 0.87 cm on the computer screen. Thus the spatial frequency of maximum response $f_{max}$ = 10 cycles/0.87 cm = 11.46 cycles/cm at this viewing distance. Translating this into a general formula gives:

$$f_{max} = \frac{10}{d \bullet \tan(1^\circ)} = \frac{572.9}{d} \ cycles / cm$$

where d = viewing distance measured in cm.

### 2.2.10.3 COLOR SENSITIVITY

- Standard observer
- CIE chromaticity coordinates

human color perception is an exceedingly complex topic. As such we can only present a brief introduction here. The physical perception of color is based upon three color pigments in the retina.

#### 1. STANDARD OBSERVER

Based upon psychophysical measurements, standard curves have been adopted by the CIE (Commission Internationale del' Eclairage) as the sensitivity curves for the "typical" observer for the three "pigments" $\bar{x}(\lambda), \bar{y}(\lambda), and\ \bar{z}(\lambda)$. These are shown in Figure 2.13. These are not the actual pigment absorption characteristics found in the "standard" human retina but rather sensitivity curves derived from actual data. $\bar{x}(\lambda)$ Figure 2.13: Standard observer color sensitivity curves.

For an arbitrary homogeneous region in an image that has an intensity as a function of wavelength (color) given by $I(\lambda)$, the three responses are called the tristimulus values:

$$X = \int_0^\infty I(\lambda)\bar{x}(\lambda)d\lambda \quad Y = \int_0^\infty I(\lambda)\bar{y}(\lambda)d\lambda \quad Z = \int_0^\infty I(\lambda)\bar{z}(\lambda)d\lambda$$

#### 2. CIE CHROMATICITY COORDINATES

The chromaticity coordinates which describe the perceived color information are defined as:

$$x = \frac{X}{X+Y+Z}, y = \frac{Y}{X+Y+Z}, z = 1-(x+y)$$

The red chromaticity coordinate is given by x and the green chromaticity coordinates by y. The tristimulus values are linear in $I(\lambda)$ and thus the absolute intensity information has been lost in the calculation of the chromaticity coordinates {x, y}. All color distributions, $I(\lambda)$, that appear to an observer as having the same color will have the same chromaticity coordinates.

If we use a tunable source of pure color (such as a dye laser), then the intensity can be modeled as $I(\lambda) = d(\lambda - \lambda_o)$ with d(*) as the impulse function. The collection of chromaticity coordinates {x, y} that will be generated by varying $\lambda_o$ gives the CIE chromaticity triangle as shown in Figure 2.13.

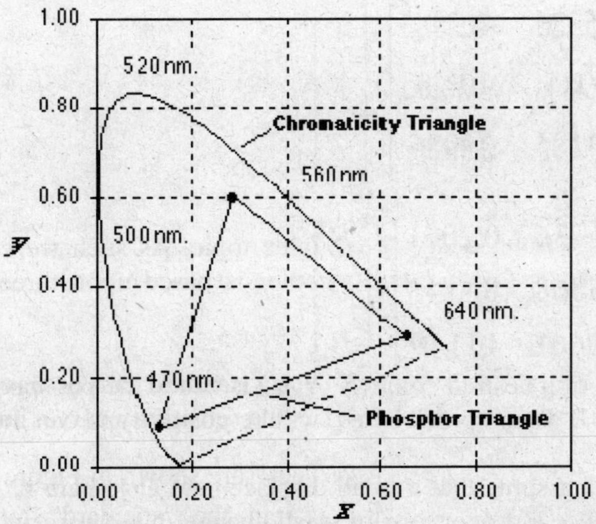


**Figure 2.13: Chromaticity diagram containing the CIE chromaticity triangle associated with pure spectral colors and the triangle associated with CRT phosphors**

Pure spectral colors are along the boundary of the chromaticity triangle. All other colors are inside the triangle. The chromaticity coordinates for some standard sources are given in Table 2.4.

| Source | x | y |
|---|---|---|
| Fluorescent lamp 4800 deg.K | 0.35 | 0.37 |
| Sun 6000 deg.K | 0.32 | 0.33 |
| Red Phosphor (europium yttrium vanadate) | 0.68 | 0.32 |
| Green Phosphor (zinc cadmium sulfide) | 0.28 | 0.60 |
| Blue Phosphor (zinc sulfide) | 0.15 | 0.07 |

**Table 2.4: Chromaticity coordinates for standard sources**

The description of color on the basis of chromaticity coordinates not only permits an analysis of color but provides a synthesis technique as well. Using a mixture of two color sources, it is possible to generate any of the colors along the line connecting their respective chromaticity coordinates. Since we cannot have a negative number of photons, this means the mixing coefficients must be positive. Using three color sources such as the red, green, and blue phosphors on CRT monitors leads to the set of colors defined by the interior of the "phosphor triangle" shown in Figure 2.13.

The formulas for converting from the tristimulus values (X, Y, Z) to the well-known CRT colors (R, G, B) and back are given by:

$$\begin{bmatrix} R \\ G \\ B \end{bmatrix} = \begin{bmatrix} 1.9107 & -0.5326 & -0.2883 \\ -0.9843 & 1.9984 & -0.0283 \\ 0.0583 & -0.1185 & 0.8986 \end{bmatrix} \bullet \begin{bmatrix} X \\ Y \\ Z \end{bmatrix}$$

And

$$\begin{bmatrix} X \\ Y \\ Z \end{bmatrix} = \begin{bmatrix} 0.6067 & 0.1736 & 0.2001 \\ 0.2988 & 0.5868 & 0.1143 \\ 0.0000 & 0.0661 & 1.1149 \end{bmatrix} \bullet \begin{bmatrix} R \\ G \\ B \end{bmatrix}$$

As long as the position of a desired color (X, Y, Z) is inside the phosphor triangle in Figure 2.13, the values of R, G, and B as computed by eq. will be positive and can therefore be used to drive a CRT monitor.

It is incorrect to assume that a small displacement anywhere in the chromaticity diagram (Figure 2.13) will produce a proportionally small change in the perceived color. An empirically-derived chromaticity space where this property is approximated is the (u', v') space:

$$u' = \frac{4x}{-2x+12y+3} \qquad v' = \frac{9y}{-2x+12y+3}$$

and

$$x = \frac{9u'}{6u'-16v'+12} \qquad y = \frac{4v'}{6u'-16v'+12}$$

Small changes almost anywhere in the (u', v') chromaticity space produce equally small changes in the perceived colors.

### 2.2.10.4 OPTICAL ILLUSIONS

The description of the human visual system presented above is couched in standard engineering terms. This could lead one to conclude that there is sufficient knowledge of the human visual system to permit modeling the visual system with standard system analysis techniques. Two simple examples of optical illusions, shown in Figure 2.14, illustrate that this system approach would be a gross oversimplification. Such models should only be used with extreme care.

**Figure 2.14: Optical Illusions**

The left illusion induces the illusion of gray values in the eye that the brain "knows" does not exist. Further, there is a sense of dynamic change in the image due, in part, to the saccadic movements of the eye. The right illusion, Kanizsa's triangle, shows enhanced contrast and false contours neither of which can be explained by the system-oriented aspects of visual perception described above.

### 2.2.11 IMAGE SAMPLING

Converting from a continuous image a(x, y) to its digital representation b[m, n] requires the process of sampling. In the ideal sampling system a(x, y) is multiplied by an ideal 2D impulse train:

$$b_{ideal}[m,n] = a(x,y) \bullet \sum_{m=-\infty}^{+\infty} \sum_{n=-\infty}^{+\infty} \delta(x - mX_o, y - nY_o)$$

$$= \sum_{m=-\infty}^{+\infty} \sum_{n=-\infty}^{+\infty} a(mX_o, nY_o)\delta(x - mX_o, y - nY_o)$$

where $X_o$ and $Y_o$ are the sampling distances or intervals, d(*,*) is the ideal impulse function, and we have used eq. . (At some point, of course, the impulse function d(x, y) is converted to the discrete impulse function d[m, n].) Square sampling implies that $X_o = Y_o$. Sampling with an impulse function corresponds to sampling with an infinitesimally small point. To take the effects of a finite sampling aperture p(x, y) into account, we can modify the sampling model as follows:

$$b[m,n] = \left(a(x,y) \otimes p(x,y)\right) \bullet \sum_{m=-\infty}^{+\infty} \sum_{n=-\infty}^{+\infty} \delta(x - mX_o, y - nY_o)$$

The combined effect of the aperture and sampling are best understood by examining the Fourier domain representation.

$$B(\Omega, \Psi) = \frac{1}{4\pi^2} \sum_{m=-\infty}^{+\infty} \sum_{n=-\infty}^{+\infty} A(\Omega - m\Omega_s, \Psi - n\Psi_s) \bullet P(\Omega - m\Omega_s, \Psi - n\Psi_s)$$

where $\Omega_s = 2\pi/X_o$ is the sampling frequency in the x direction and $\Psi_s = 2\pi/Y_o$ is the sampling frequency in the y direction. The aperture p(x,y) is frequently square, circular, or Gaussian with the associated $P(\Omega,\Psi)$. The periodic nature of the spectrum, described in eq. is clear from eq. .

- Sampling Density for Image Processing
- Sampling Density for Image Analysis

### 2.2.11.1 SAMPLING DENSITY FOR IMAGE PROCESSING

- Sampling aperture

To prevent the possible aliasing (overlapping) of spectral terms that is inherent in eq. two conditions must hold:

* Bandlimited A(u,v) -

$$|A(u,v)| \equiv 0 \quad \text{for} \quad |u| > u_c \quad \text{and} \quad |v| > v_c$$

* Nyquist sampling frequency -

$$\Omega_s > 2 \bullet u_c \quad \text{and} \quad \Psi_s > 2 \bullet v_c$$

where $u_c$ and $v_c$ are the cutoff frequencies in the x and y direction, respectively. Images that are acquired through lenses that are circularly-symmetric, aberration-free, and diffraction-limited will, in general, be bandlimited. The lens acts as a lowpass filter with a cutoff frequency in the frequency domain (eq. ) given by:

$$u_c = v_c = \frac{2NA}{\lambda}$$

where NA is the numerical aperture of the lens and $\lambda$is the shortest wavelength of light used with the lens . If the lens does not meet one or more of these assumptions then it will still be bandlimited but at lower cutoff frequencies than those given in eq. . When working with the F-number (F) of the optics instead of the NA and in air (with index of refraction = 1.0), eq. becomes:

$$u_c = v_c = \frac{2}{\lambda}\left(\frac{1}{\sqrt{4F^2+1}}\right)$$

### 1. SAMPLING APERTURE

The aperture p(x, y) described above will have only a marginal effect on the final signal if the two conditions eqs. and are satisfied. Given, for example, the distance between samples $X_o$ equals $Y_o$ and a sampling aperture that is not wider than $X_o$, the effect on the overall spectrun--due to the A(u, v)P(u, v) behavior implied by eq.--is illustrated in Figure 2.15 for square and Gaussian apertures.

The spectra are evaluated along one axis of the 2D Fourier transform. The Gaussian aperture in Figure 2.15 has a width such that the sampling interval $X_o$ contains $+/-3\sigma$ (99.7%) of the Gaussian. The rectangular apertures have a width such that one occupies 95% of the sampling interval and the other occupies 50% of the sampling interval. The 95% width translates to a fill factor of 90% and the 50% width to a fill factor of 25%.

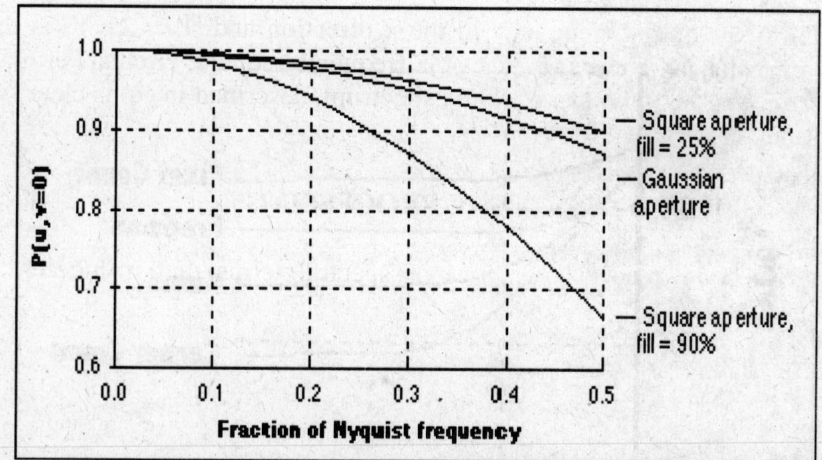


**Figure 2.15: Aperture spectra P(u, v=0) for frequencies up to half the Nyquist frequency. For explanation of "fill" see text.**

## 2.2.11.2. SAMPLING DENSITY FOR IMAGE ANALYSIS

- Sampling for area measurements
- Sampling for length measurements
- Conclusions on sampling

The "rules" for choosing the sampling density when the goal is image analysis--as opposed to image processing--are different. The fundamental difference is that the digitization of objects in an image into a collection of pixels introduces a form of spatial quantization noise that is not band limited. This leads to the following results for the choice of sampling density when one is interested in the measurement of area and (perimeter) length.

### (i) SAMPLING FOR AREA MEASUREMENTS

Assuming square sampling, $X_o = Y_o$ and the unbiased algorithm for estimating area which involves simple pixel counting, the CV of the area measurement is related to the sampling density by :

2D: $\lim_{S\to\infty} CV(S) = k_2 S^{-3/2}$ 3D: $\lim_{S\to\infty} CV(S) = k_3 S^{-2}$

and in D dimensions:

$$\lim_{S\to\infty} CV(S) = k_D S^{-(D+1)/2}$$

where S is the number of samples per object diameter. In 2D the measurement is area, in 3D volume, and in D-dimensions hyper volume.

### (ii) SAMPLING FOR LENGTH MEASUREMENTS

Again assuming square sampling and algorithms for estimating length based upon the Freeman chain-code representation, the CV of the length measurement is related to the sampling density per unit length as shown in Figure 2.16.

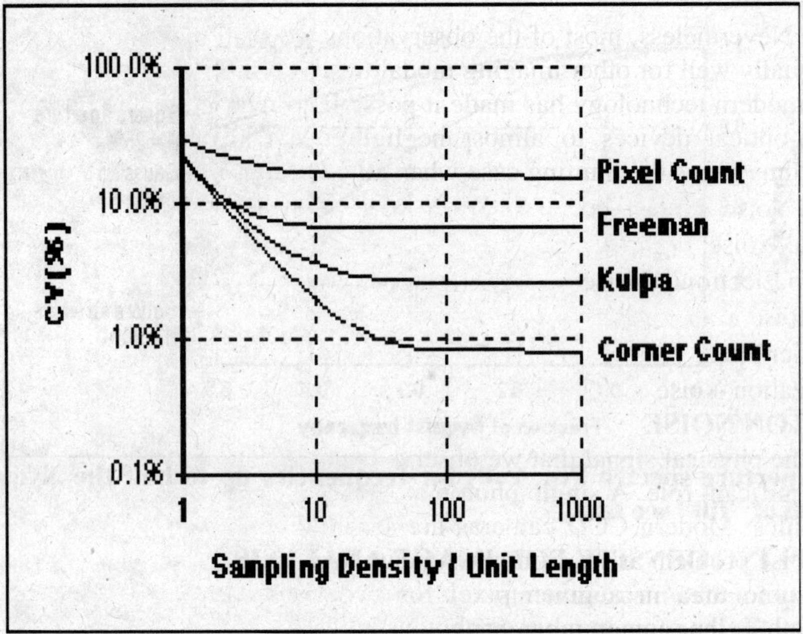


**Figure 2.16: CV of length measurement for various algorithms.**

The curves in Figure 2.16 were developed in the context of straight lines but similar results have been found for curves and closed contours. The specific formulas for length estimation use a chain code representation of a line and are based upon a linear combination of three numbers:

$$L = \alpha \bullet N_e + \beta \bullet N_o + \gamma \bullet N_c$$

where $N_e$ is the number of even chain codes, $N_o$ the number of odd chain codes, and $N_c$ the number of corners. The specific formulas are given in Table 2.5.

| Coefficients | a | β | γ | |
|---|---|---|---|---|
| Formula | | | | Reference |
| Pixel count | 1 | 1 | 0 | [18] |
| Freeman | 1 | $\sqrt{2}$ | 0 | [11] |
| Kulpa | 0.9481 | $0.9481 * \sqrt{2}$ | 0 | [20] |
| Corner count | 0.980 | 1.406 | -0.091 | [21] |

**Table 2.5: Length estimation formulas based on chain code counts ($N_e$, $N_o$, $N_c$)**

## 2.2.12 NOISE

Images acquired through modern sensors may be contaminated by a variety of noise sources. By noise we refer to stochastic variations as opposed to deterministic distortions such as shading or lack of focus. We will assume for this section that we are dealing with images formed from light using modern electro-optics. In particular we will assume the use of modern, charge-coupled device (CCD) cameras where photons produce electrons that are commonly referred to as photoelectrons. Nevertheless, most of the observations we shall make about noise and its various sources hold equally well for other imaging modalities.

While modern technology has made it possible to reduce the noise levels associated with various electro-optical devices to almost negligible levels, one noise source can never be eliminated and thus forms the limiting case when all other noise sources are "eliminated".

- Photon Noise
- Thermal Noise
- On-chip Electronic Noise
- KTC Noise
- Amplifier Noise
- Quantization Noise

### 2.2.12.1. PHOTON NOISE

When the physical signal that we observe is based upon light, then the quantum nature of light plays a significant role. A single photon at λ= 500 nm carries an energy of E = hν = hc/λ = 3.97 x $10^{-19}$ Joules. Modern CCD cameras are sensitive enough to be able to count individual photons. The noise problem arises from the fundamentally statistical nature of photon production. We cannot assume that, in a given pixel for two consecutive but independent observation intervals of length T, the same number of photons will be counted. Photon production is governed by the laws of quantum physics which restrict us to talking about an average number of photons within a given observation window. The probability distribution for p photons in an observation window of length T seconds is known to be Poisson:

$$P(p|\rho,T)=\frac{(\rho T)^{p}e^{-\rho T}}{p!}$$

where ρis the rate or intensity parameter measured in photons per second. It is critical to understand that even if there were no other noise sources in the imaging chain, the statistical fluctuations associated with photon counting over a finite time interval T would still lead to a finite signal-to-noise ratio (SNR). If we use the appropriate formula for the SNR (eq. ), then due to the fact that the average value and the standard deviation are given by:

Poisson process - $average = pT \quad \sigma = \sqrt{pT}$

we have for the SNR:

Photon noise - $SNR = 10\log_{10}(\rho T) \quad dB$

The three traditional assumptions about the relationship between signal and noise do not hold for photon noise:

- photon noise is not independent of the signal;
- photon noise is not Gaussian, and;
- photon noise is not additive.

For very bright signals, where ρT exceeds $10^5$, the noise fluctuations due to photon statistics can be ignored if the sensor has a sufficiently high saturation level.

### 2.2.12.2. THERMAL NOISE

An additional, stochastic source of electrons in a CCD well is thermal energy. Electrons can be freed from the CCD material itself through thermal vibration and then, trapped in the CCD well, be indistinguishable from "true" photoelectrons. By cooling the CCD chip it is possible to reduce significantly the number of "thermal electrons" that give rise to thermal noise or dark current. As the integration time T increases, the number of thermal electrons increases. The probability distribution of thermal electrons is also a Poisson process where the rate parameter is an increasing function of temperature. There are alternative techniques (to cooling) for suppressing dark current and these usually involve estimating the average dark current for the given integration time and then subtracting this value from the CCD pixel values before the A/D converter. While this does reduce the dark current average, it does not reduce the dark current standard deviation and it also reduces the possible dynamic range of the signal.

### 2.2.12.3. ON-CHIP ELECTRONIC NOISE

This noise originates in the process of reading the signal from the sensor, in this case through the field effect transistor (FET) of a CCD chip. The general form of the power spectral density of readout noise is:

Readout noise -
$$S_{nn}(\omega) \propto \begin{cases} \omega^{-\beta} & \omega < \omega_{\min} \quad \beta > 0 \\ k & \omega_{\min} < \omega < \omega_{\max} \\ \omega^{\alpha} & \omega > \omega_{\max} \quad \alpha > 0 \end{cases}$$

where a and $\beta$are constants and $\omega$is the (radial) frequency at which the signal is transferred from the CCD chip to the "outside world." At very low readout rates ($\omega < \omega_{min}$) the noise has a 1/f character. Readout noise can be reduced to manageable levels by appropriate readout rates and proper electronics. At very low signal levels, however, readout noise can still become a significant component in the overall SNR .

### 2.2.12.4. KTC NOISE

Noise associated with the gate capacitor of an FET is termed KTC noise and can be non-negligible. The output RMS value of this noise voltage is given by:

KTC noise (voltage) - $\sigma_{KTC} = \sqrt{\dfrac{KT}{C}}$

where C is the FET gate switch capacitance, k is Boltzmann's constant, and T is the absolute temperature of the CCD chip measured in K. Using the relationships $Q = C.V = N_{e-} * e^{-}$, the output RMS value of the KTC noise expressed in terms of the number of photoelectrons ($N_i$) is given by:

KTC noise (electrons) - $\sigma_{Ne} = \sqrt{\dfrac{KTC}{e^{-}}}$

where $e^{-}$ is the electron charge. For C = 0.5 pF and T = 233 K this gives $N_i$ =252 electrons. This value is a "one time" noise per pixel that occurs during signal readout and is thus independent of the integration time. Proper electronic design that makes use, for example, of correlated double sampling and dual-slope integration can almost completely eliminate KTC noise .

### 2.2.12.5. AMPLIFIER NOISE

The standard model for this type of noise is additive, Gaussian, and independent of the signal. In modern well-designed electronics, amplifier noise is generally negligible. The most common exception to this is in color cameras where more amplification is used in the blue color channel than in the green channel or red channel leading to more noise in the blue channel.

### 2.2.12.6. QUANTIZATION NOISE

Quantization noise is inherent in the amplitude quantization process and occurs in the analog-to-digital converter, ADC. The noise is additive and independent of the signal when the number of levels L >= 16. This is equivalent to B >= 4 bits. For a signal that has been converted to electrical form and thus has a minimum and maximum electrical value, eq. is the appropriate formula for determining the SNR. If the ADC is adjusted so that 0 corresponds to the minimum electrical value and $2^B$-1 corresponds to the maximum electrical value then:

Quantization noise - SNR = ^B+11 dB

For B >= 8 bits, this means a SNR >= 59 dB. Quantization noise can usually be ignored as the total SNR of a complete system is typically dominated by the smallest SNR. In CCD cameras this is photon noise.

### 2.2.13 DISPLAYS

The displays used for image processing--particularly the display systems used with computers--have a number of characteristics that help determine the quality of the final image.

- Refresh Rate
- Interlacing
- Resolution

### 2.2.13.1. REFRESH RATE

The refresh rate is defined as the number of complete images that are written to the screen per second. For standard video the refresh rate is fixed at the values , either 29.97 or 25 images/s. For computer displays the refresh rate can vary with common values being 67 images/s and 75 images/s. At values above 60 images/s visual flicker is negligible at virtually all illumination levels.

### 2.2.13.2. INTERLACING

To prevent the appearance of visual flicker at refresh rates below 60 images/s, the display can be interlaced. Standard interlace for video systems is 2:1. Since interlacing is not necessary at refresh rates above 60 images/s, an interlace of 1:1 is used with such systems. In other words, lines are drawn in an ordinary sequential fashion: 1,2,3,4,...,N.

### 2.2.13.3. RESOLUTION

The pixels stored in computer memory, although they are derived from regions of finite area in the original scene, may be thought of as mathematical points having no physical extent. When displayed, the space between the points must be filled in. This generally happens as a result of the finite spot size of a cathode-ray tube (CRT). The brightness profile of a CRT spot is approximately Gaussian and the number of spots that can be resolved on the display depends on the quality of the system. It is relatively straightforward to obtain display systems with a resolution of 72 spots per inch (28.3 spots per cm.) This number corresponds to standard printing conventions. If printing is not a consideration then higher resolutions, in excess of 30 spots per cm, are attainable.

## 2.3 THE HUMAN VISION SYSTEM

Human vision is a sophisticated system that senses and acts on visual stimuli. It has evolved for millions of years, primarily for defence or survival. Intuitively, computer and human vision appear to have the same function. The purpose of both systems is to interpret spatial data, data that is indexed by more than one dimension. Even though computer and human vision are functionally similar, you cannot expect a computer vision system to replicate exactly the function of the human eye. This is partly because we do not understand fully how the vision system of the eye and brain works, as we shall see in this section.

Accordingly, we cannot design a system to replicate its function exactly. In fact, some of the properties of the human eye are useful when developing computer vision techniques, whereas others are actually undesirable in a computer vision system. But we shall see computer vision techniques which can, to some extent, replicate, and in some cases even improve upon, the human vision system.

You might ponder this, so put one of the fingers from each of your hands in front of your face and try to estimate the distance between them. This is difficult, and I am sure you would agree that your measurement would not be very accurate. Now put your fingers very close together. You can still tell that they are apart even when the distance between them is tiny. So human vision can distinguish relative distance well, but is poor for absolute distance.

Computer vision is the other way around: it is good for estimating absolute difference, but with relatively poor resolution for relative difference. The number of pixels in the image imposes the accuracy of the computer vision system, but that does not come until the next chapter. Let us start at the beginning, by seeing how the human vision system works.

In human vision, the sensing element is the eye from which images are transmitted via the optic nerve to the brain, for further processing. The optic nerve has insufficient bandwidth to carry all the information sensed by the eye. Accordingly, there must be some preprocessing before the image is transmitted down the optic nerve.

The human vision system can be modelled in three parts:

- the eye: this is a physical model since much of its function can be determined by pathology
- a processing system: this is an experimental model since the function can be modelled, but not determined precisely
- analysis by the brain: this is a psychological model since we cannot access or model such processing directly, but only determine behaviour by experiment and inference.

### 2.3.1 THE EYE

The function of the eye is to form an image; a cross-section of the eye is illustrated in Figure 2.17. Vision requires an ability to focus selectively on objects of interest. This is achieved by the ciliary muscles that hold the lens. In old age, it is these muscles which become slack and the eye loses its ability to focus at short distance. The iris, or pupil, is like an aperture on a camera and controls the amount of light entering the eye. It is a delicate system and needs protection, which is provided by the cornea (sclera). This is outside the choroid, which has blood vessels that supply nutrition and is opaque to cut down the amount of light. The retina is on the inside of the eye, which is where light falls to form an image.

By this system, muscles rotate the eye, and shape the lens, to form an image on the fovea (focal point), where the majority of sensors are situated. The blind spot is where the optic nerve starts; there are no sensors there.

Focusing involves shaping the lens, rather than positioning it as in a camera. The lens is shaped to refract close images greatly, and distant objects little, essentially by 'stretching' it. The distance of the focal centre of the lens varies from approximately 14mm to around 17 mm, depending on the lens shape. This implies that a world scene is translated into an area of about 2mm2. Good vision has high acuity (sharpness), which implies that there must be very many sensors in the area where the image is formed.

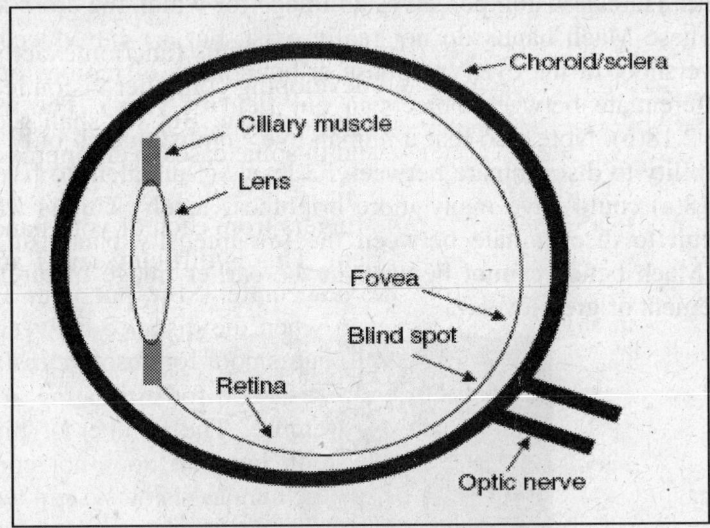


**Figure 2.17 Human eye**

There are nearly 100 million sensors dispersed around the retina. Light falls on these sensors to stimulate photochemical transmissions, which results in nerve impulses that are collected to form the signal transmitted by the eye. There are two types of sensor: first, the rods, which are used for black and white (scotopic) vision; and secondly, the cones, which are used for colour (photopic) vision. There are approximately 10 million cones and nearly all are found within 5 of the fovea. The remaining 100 million rods are distributed around the retina, with the majority between 20 and 5 of the fovea. Acuity is expressed in terms of spatial resolution (sharpness) and brightness/colour resolution and is greatest within 1 of the fovea. There is only one type of rod, but there are three types of cone. These are:

- S (short wavelength): these sense light towards the blue end of the visual spectrum
- M (medium wavelength): these sense light around green
- L (long wavelength): these sense light towards the red region of the spectrum.

The total response of the cones arises from summing the response of these three types of cone, which gives a response covering the whole of the visual spectrum. The rods are sensitive to light within the entire visual spectrum, giving the monochrome capability of scotopic vision. Accordingly, when the light level is low, images are formed away from the fovea, to use the superior sensitivity of the rods, but without the colour vision of the cones. Note that there are very few of the bluish cones, and there are many more of the others. But we can still see a lot of blue (especially given ubiquitous denim!). So, somehow, the human vision system compensates for the lack of blue sensors, to enable us to perceive it. The world would be a funny place with red water! The vision response is logarithmic and depends on brightness adaptation from dark conditions where the image is formed on the rods, to brighter conditions where images are formed on the cones.

One inherent property of the eye, known as Mach bands, affects the way we perceive images. These are illustrated in Figure 2.18 and are the bands that appear to be where two stripes of constant shade join. By assigning values to the image brightness levels, the cross-section of plotted brightness is shown in Figure 2.18(a). This shows that the picture is formed from stripes of constant brightness. Human vision perceives an image for which the cross-section is as plotted in Figure 2.18(c). These Mach bands do not really exist, but are introduced by your eye. The bands arise from overshoot in the eyes' response at boundaries of regions of different intensity (this aids us to differentiate between objects in our field of view). The real cross-section is illustrated in Figure 2.18(b). Note also that a human eye can distinguish only relatively few grey levels. It has a capability to discriminate between 32 levels (equivalent to five bits), whereas the image of Figure 2.18(a) could have many more brightness levels. This is why your perception finds it more difficult to discriminate between the low-intensity bands on the left of Figure 2.18(a). (Note that Mach bands cannot be seen in the earlier image of circles, Figure 2.18(a), owing to the arrangement of grey levels).

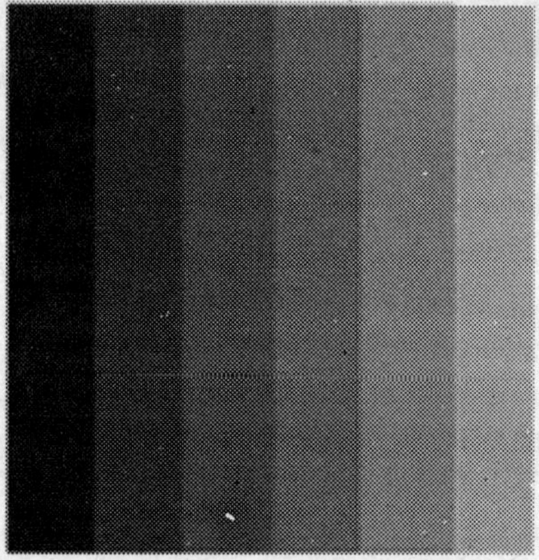

(a) Image showing the Mach band effect

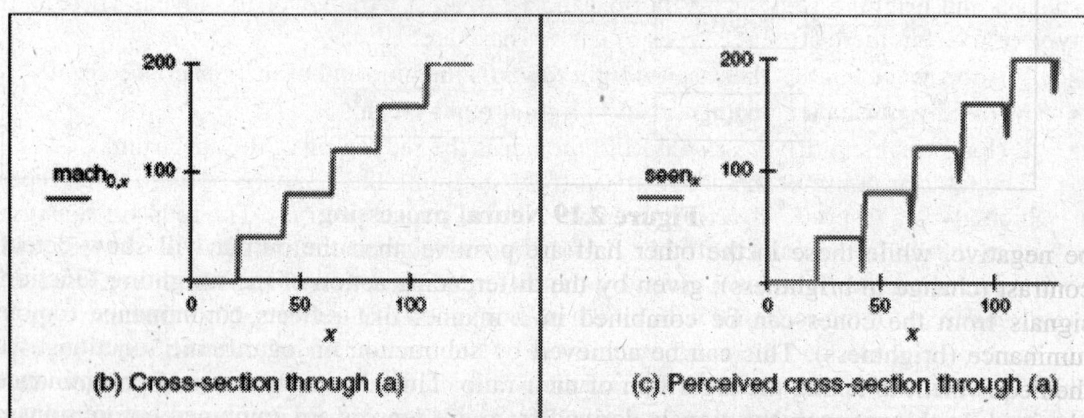


(b) Cross-section through (a)

(c) Perceived cross-section through (a)

**Figure 2.18 Illustrating the Mach band effect**

This is the limit of our studies of the first level of human vision; for those who are interested, Cornsweet (1970) provides many more details concerning visual perception. So we have already identified two properties associated with the eye that it would be difficult to include, and would often be unwanted, in a computer vision system: Mach bands and sensitivity to unsensed phenomena. These properties are integral to human vision. At present, human vision is far more sophisticated than we can hope to achieve with a computer vision system. Infrared guided-missile vision systems can have difficulty in distinguishing between a bird at 100m and a plane at 10 km. Poor birds! (Lucky plane?) Human vision can handle this with ease.

### 2.3.2 THE NEURAL SYSTEM

Neural signals provided by the eye are essentially the transformed response of the wave length dependent receptors, the cones and the rods. One model is to combine these transformed signals by addition, as illustrated in Figure 2.19. The response is transformed by a logarithmic function, mirroring the known response of the eye. This is then multiplied by a weighting factor that controls the contribution of a particular sensor. This can be arranged to allow combination of responses from a particular region. The weighting factors can be chosen to afford particular filtering properties. For example, in lateral inhibition, the weights for the centre sensors are much greater than the weights for those at the extreme. This allows the response of the centre sensors to dominate the combined response given by addition. If the weights in one half are chosen to

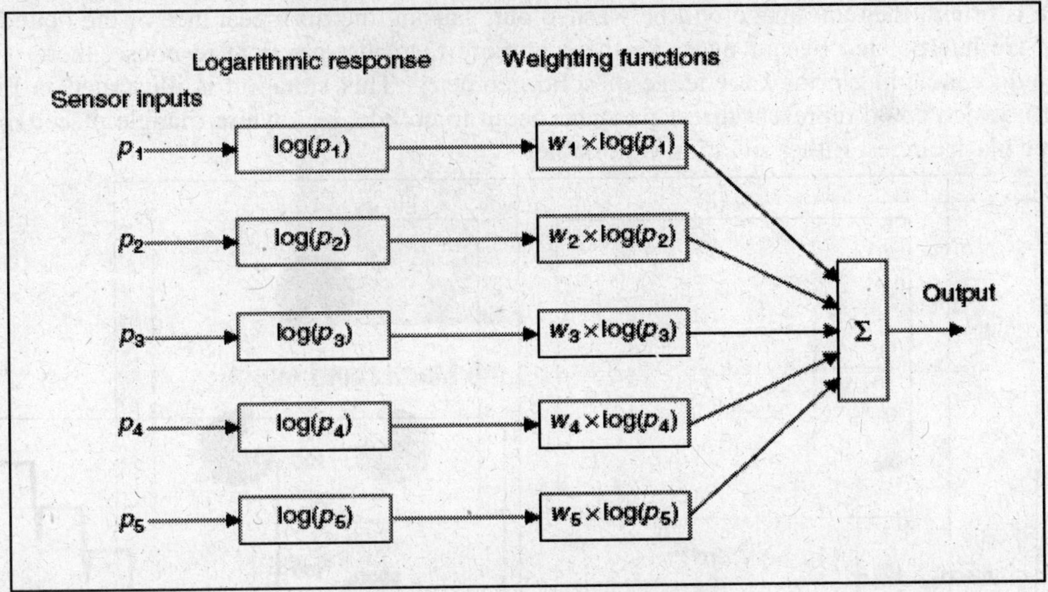


**Figure 2.19 Neural processing**

be negative, while those in the other half are positive, then the output will show detection of contrast (change in brightness), given by the differencing action of the weighting functions. The signals from the cones can be combined in a manner that reflects chrominance (colour) and luminance (brightness). This can be achieved by subtraction of logarithmic functions, which is then equivalent to taking the logarithm of their ratio. This allows measures of chrominance to be obtained. In this manner, the signals derived from the sensors are combined before transmission through the optic nerve. This is an experimental model, since there are many ways possible to combine the different signals together. Visual information is then sent back to arrive at the lateral geniculate nucleus (LGN), which is in the thalamus and is the primary processor of visual information. This is a layered structure containing different types of cells, with differing functions. The axons from the LGN pass information on to the visual cortex. The function of the LGN is largely unknown, although it has been shown to play a part in coding the signals that are transmitted. It is also considered to help the visual system to focus its attention, such as on sources of sound.

### 2.3.3 PROCESSING

The neural signals are then transmitted to two areas of the brain for further processing. These areas are the associative cortex, where links between objects are made, and the occipital cortex, where patterns are processed. It is naturally difficult to determine precisely what happens in this region of the brain. To date, there have been no volunteers for detailed study of their brain's function (although progress with new imaging modalities such as positive emission tomography or electrical impedance tomography will doubtless help). For this reason, there are only psychological models to suggest how this region of the brain operates. It is well known that one function of the human vision system is to use edges, or boundaries, of objects. We can easily read the word in Figure 2.20(a); this is achieved by filling in the missing boundaries in the knowledge that the pattern is likely to represent a printed word. But we can infer more about this image; there is a suggestion of illumination, causing shadows to appear in unlit areas. If the light source is bright, then the image will be washed out, causing the disappearance of the boundaries which are interpolated by our eyes. So there is more than just physical response, there is also knowledge, including prior knowledge of solid geometry. This situation is illustrated in Figure 2.20(b), which could represent three 'pacmen' about to collide, or a white triangle placed on top of three black circles. Either situation is possible.

**Figure 2.20 How human vision uses edges**

It is also possible to deceive human vision, primarily by imposing a scene that it has not been trained to handle. In the famous Zollner illusion (Figure 2.21a), the bars appear to be slanted, whereas in reality they are vertical (check this by placing a pen between the lines): the small cross-bars mislead your eye into perceiving the vertical bars as slanting. In the Ebbinghaus illusion (Figure 2.21b), the inner circle appears to be larger when surrounded by small circles than it is when surrounded by larger circles. There are dynamic illusions too: you can always impress children with the 'see my wobbly pencil' trick. Just hold the pencil loosely between your fingers then, to whoops of childish glee, when the pencil is shaken up and down, the solid pencil will appear to bend. Benham's disk

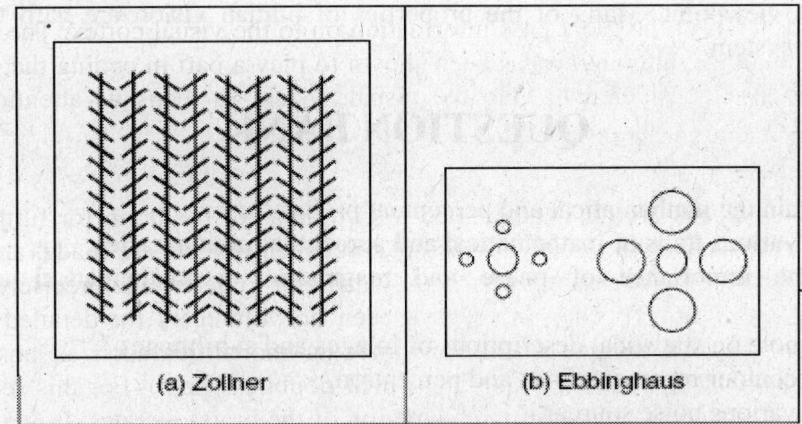


**Figure 2.21 Static illusions**

(Figure 2.22) shows how hard it is to model vision accurately. If you make up a version of this disk into a spinner (push a matchstick through the centre) and spin it anticlockwise, you do not see three dark rings, you will see three coloured ones. The outside one will appear to be red, the middle one a sort of green and the inner one deep blue. (This can depend greatly on lighting, and contrast between the black and white on the disk. If the colours are not clear, try it in a different place, with different lighting.) You can appear to explain this when you notice that the red colours are associated with the long lines and the blue with short lines. But this is from physics, not psychology. Now spin the disk clockwise. The order of the colours reverses: red is associated with the short lines (inside) and blue with the long lines (outside). So the argument from physics is clearly incorrect, since red is now associated with short lines, not long ones, revealing the need for psychological explanation of the eyes' function. This is not colour perception; see Armstrong (1991) for an interesting (and interactive) study of colour theory and perception.

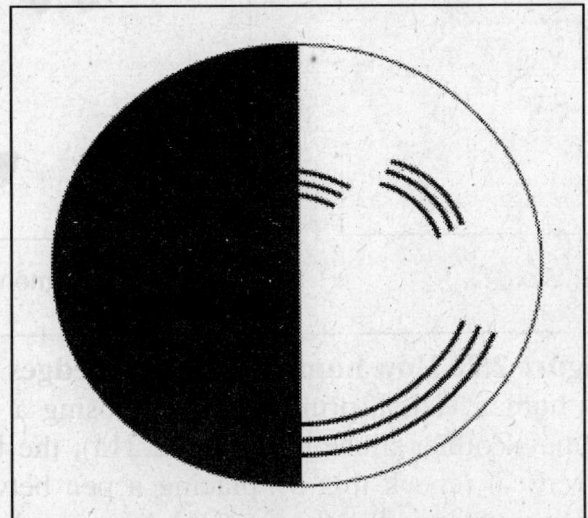

**Figure 2.22 Benham's disk**

There are many texts on human vision. One popular text on human visual perception is by Schwartz (2004) , The Joy of Vision useful, despite its title! Marr's seminal text (Marr, 1982) is a computational investigation into human vision and visual perception, investigating it from a computer vision viewpoint. Many of the properties of human vision are hard to include in a computer vision system.

## QUESTION BANK

Q1. Briefly explain the mathematical and perceptual preliminaries.
Q2. Explain the various tools of mathematical and perceptual preliminaries.
Q3. Discuss the importance of phase and magnitude of mathematical and perceptual preliminaries.
Q4. Write short note on statistical descriptions of images and sub-images.
Q5. Discuss the contour representations and perception.
Q6. Discuss the various noise sources.
Q7. Briefly explain human visual system model.

# CHAPTER 3

# IMAGE SIGNAL REPRESENTATION

## 3.1 INTRODUCTION

In this chapter, we shall look at the basic theory which underlies image formation and processing. We shall start by investigating what makes up a picture and look at the consequences of having a different number of points in the image. We shall also look at images in a different representation, known as the frequency domain. In this, as the name implies, we consider an image as a collection of frequency components. We can operate on images in the frequency domain and we shall also consider different transformation processes. These allow us different insights into images and image processing which will be used in later chapters not only as a means to develop techniques, but also to give faster (computer) processing.

| Main topic | Sub topics | Main points |
|---|---|---|
| Images | Effects of differing *numbers* of points and of number *range* for those points. | Greyscale, colour, resolution, dynamic range, storage. |
| Fourier transform theory | What is meant by the *frequency domain*, how it applies to *discrete* (sampled) images, how it allows us to *interpret* images and the *sampling resolution* (number of points). | Continuous Fourier transform and properties, sampling criterion, discrete Fourier transform and properties, image transformation, transform duals. Inverse Fourier transform. |
| Consequences of transform approach | Basic *properties* of Fourier transforms, *other transforms*, frequency domain *operations*. | Translation (shift), rotation and scaling. Principle of superposition and linearity. Walsh, Hartley, discrete cosine and wavelet transforms. Filtering and other operations. |

## 3.2 IMAGE FORMATION

A computer image is a matrix (a two-dimensional array) of pixels. The value of each pixel is proportional to the brightness of the corresponding point in the scene; its value is usually derived from the output of an analogue-to-digital (A/D) converter. The matrix of pixels, the image, is usually square and an image may be described as $N \times N$ m-bit pixels, where N is the number of points and m controls the number of brightness values. Using m bits gives a range of $2^m$ values, ranging from 0 to $2^m - 1$. If m is 8 this gives brightness levels ranging between 0 and 255, which are usually displayed as black and white, respectively, with shades of grey in between, as they are for the greyscale image of a walking man in Figure 3.1(a). Smaller values of m give fewer available levels, reducing the available contrast in an image.

The ideal value of m is related to the signal-to-noise ratio (bandwidth) of the camera. This is stated as approximately 45 dB for an analogue camera, and since there are 6 dB per bit, 8 bits will cover the available range. Choosing 8 bit pixels has further advantages in that it is very convenient to store pixel values as bytes, and 8 bit A/D converters are cheaper than those with a higher resolution. For these reasons images are nearly always stored as 8 bit bytes, although some applications use a different range. The relative influence of the 8 bits is shown in the image of the walking subject in Figure 3.1. Here, the least significant bit, bit 0 (Figure 3.1b), carries the least information (it changes most rapidly). As the order of the bits increases, they change less rapidly and carry more information. The most information is carried by the most significant bit, bit 7 (Figure 3.1). Clearly, the fact that there is a walker in the original image can be recognized much more reliably from the high-order bits than it can from the other bits (notice too the odd effects in the bits, which would appear to come from lighting at the top of the image).

Colour images follow a similar storage strategy to specify pixels' intensities. However, instead of using just one image plane, colour images are represented by three intensity components. These components generally correspond to red, green and blue (the RGB model), although there are other colour schemes. For example, the CMYK colour model is defined by the components cyan, magenta, yellow and black. In any colour mode, the pixel's colour can be specified in two main ways. First, you can associate an integer value with each pixel, which can be used as an index to a table that stores the intensity of each colour component. The index is used to recover the actual colour from the table when the pixel is going to be displayed, or processed. In this scheme, the table is known as the image's palette and the display is said to be performed by colour mapping. The main reason for using this colour representation is to reduce memory requirements. That is, we only store a single image plane (i.e. the indices) and the palette. This is less than storing the red, green and blue components separately and so makes the hardware cheaper, and it can have other advantages, for example when the image is transmitted.

The main disadvantage is that the quality of the image is reduced since only a reduced collection of colours is actually used. An alternative to represent colour is to use several image planes to store the colour components of each pixel. This scheme is known as true colour and it represents an image more accurately, essentially by considering more colours. The most common format uses 8 bits for each of the three RGB components. These images are known as 24 bit true colour and they can contain 16,777,216 different colours simultaneously. In spite of requiring significantly more memory, the image quality and the continuing reduction in cost of computer memory make this format a good alternative, even for storing the image frames from a video sequence. A good compression algorithm is always helpful in these cases, particularly if images

(a) Original image

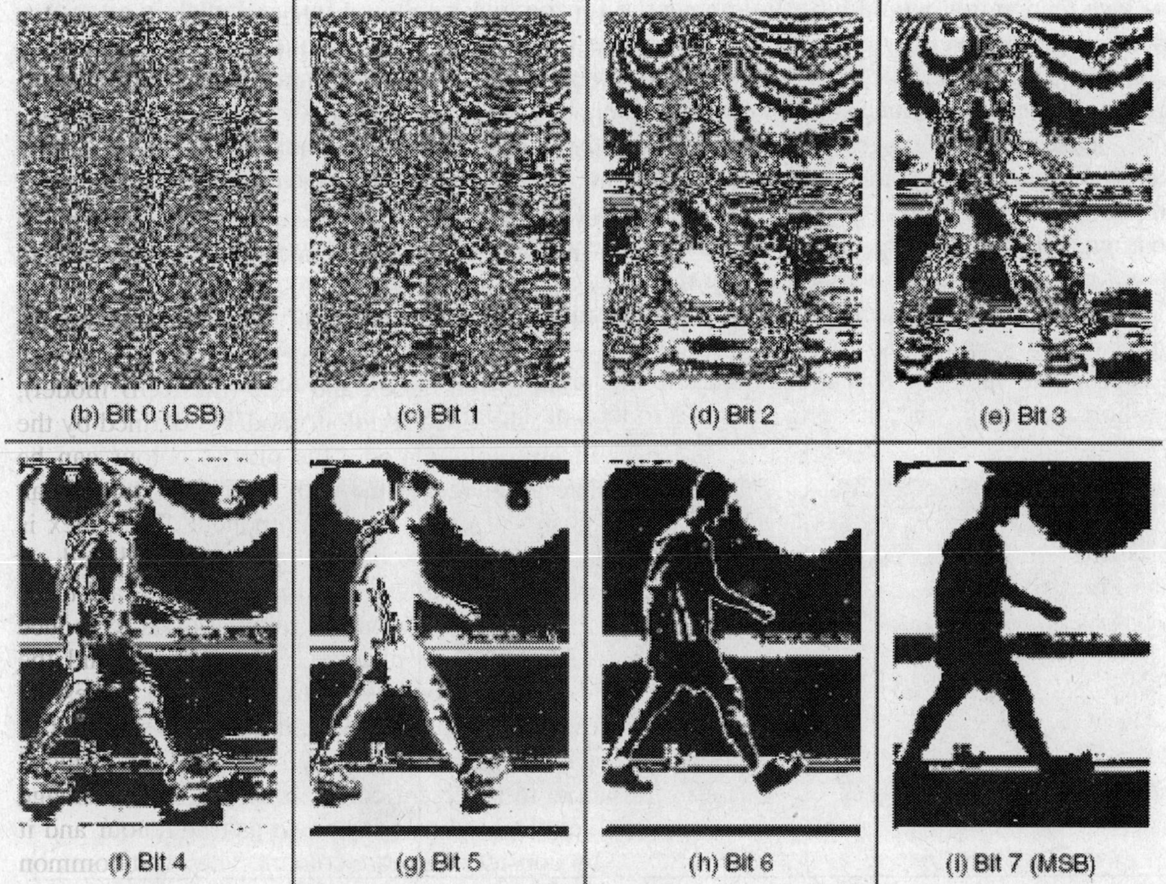


**Figure 3.1 Decomposing an image into its bits**

need to be transmitted on a network. Here we will consider the processing of grey-level images only, since they contain enough information to perform feature extraction and image analysis. Should the image be originally colour, we will consider processing its luminance only, often computed in a standard way. In any case, the amount of memory used is always related to the image size.

Choosing an appropriate value for the image size, N, is far more complicated. We want N to be sufficiently large to resolve the required level of spatial detail in the image. If N is too small, the image will be coarsely quantized: lines will appear to be very 'blocky' and some of the detail will be lost. Larger values of N give more detail, but need more storage space and the images will take longer to process, since there are more pixels. For example, with reference to the image of the walking subject in Figure 3.1(a), Figure 3.2 shows the effect of taking the image at different resolutions. Figure 3.2(a) is a 64×64 image, which shows only the broad structure. It is impossible to see any detail in the subject's face, or anywhere else. Figure 3.2(b) is a 128×128 image, which is starting to show more of the detail, but it would be hard to determine the subject's identity.

The original image, repeated in Figure 3.2(c), is a 256×256 image which shows a much greater level of detail, and the subject can be recognized from the image. (These images come from a research programme aimed to use computer vision techniques to recognize people by their gait; face recognition would have little potential for the low-resolution image, which is often the sort of image that security cameras provide.) If the image were a pure photographic image, some of the much finer detail like the hair would show up in much greater detail. This is because the grains in film are very much smaller than the pixels in a computer image.

Note that the images in Figure 3.2 have been scaled to be the same size. As such, the pixels in Figure 3.2(a) are much larger than in Figure 3.2(c), which emphasizes its blocky structure. The most common choices are for 256×256 images or 512×512. These require 64 and 256 kbytes of storage, respectively. If we take a sequence of, say, 20 images for motion analysis, we will need more than 1 Mbyte to store the 20 256×256 images, and more than 5 Mbytes if the images were 512×512. Even though memory continues to become cheaper , this can still impose high cost. But it is not just cost which motivates an investigation of the appropriate image size, the appropriate value for N. The main question is: are there theoretical guidelines for choosing it? The short answer is 'yes'; the long answer is to look at digital signal processing theory.

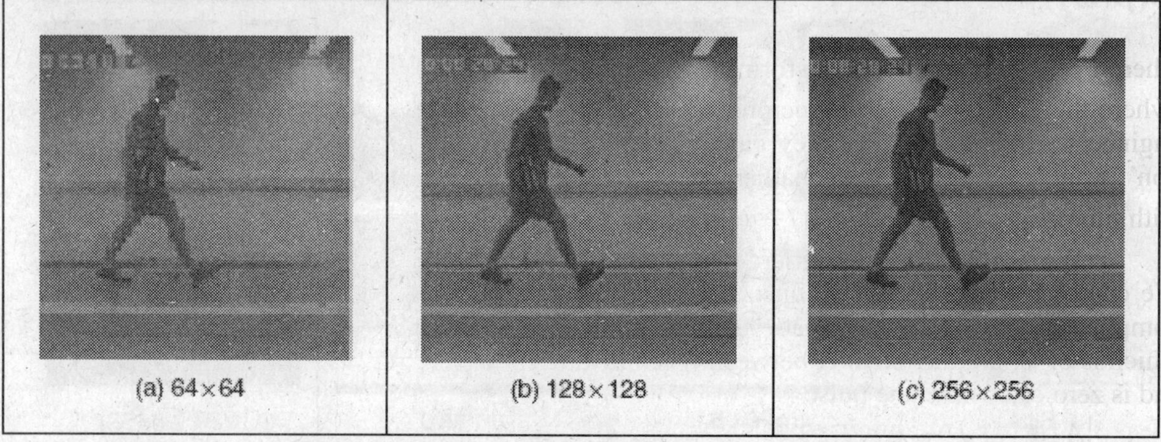
(a) 64×64 (b) 128×128 (c) 256×256

**Figure 3.2 Effects of differing image resolution**

The choice of sampling frequency is dictated by the sampling criterion. Presenting the sampling criterion requires understanding of how we interpret signals in the frequency domain. The way in is to look at the Fourier transform. This is a highly theoretical topic, but do not let that put you off (it leads to image coding, like the JPEG format, so it is very useful indeed).

The Fourier transform has found many uses in image processing and understanding; it might appear to be a complex topic (that's actually a horrible pun!), but it is a very rewarding one to study. The particular concern is the appropriate sampling frequency of (essentially, the value for N), or the rate at which pixel values are taken from, a camera's video signal.

### 3.2.1 THE FOURIER TRANSFORM

The Fourier transform is a way of mapping a signal into its component frequencies. Frequency measures in Hertz (Hz) the rate of repetition with time, measured in seconds (s); time is the reciprocal of frequency and vice versa _Hertz = 1/second's = 1/Hz.

Consider a music centre: the sound comes from a CD player (or a tape, etc.) and is played on the speakers after it has been processed by the amplifier. On the amplifier, you can change the bass or the treble (or the loudness, which is a combination of bass and treble). Bass covers the low-frequency components and treble covers the high-frequency ones. The Fourier transform is a way of mapping the signal from the CD player, which is a signal varying continuously with time, into its frequency components. When we have transformed the signal, we know which frequencies made up the original sound.

So why do we do this? We have not changed the signal, only its representation. We can now visualize it in terms of its frequencies, rather than as a voltage which changes with time. But we can now change the frequencies (because we can see them clearly) and this will change the sound. If, say, there is hiss on the original signal then since hiss is a high-frequency component, it will show up as a high-frequency component in the Fourier transform. So we can see how to remove it by looking at the Fourier transform. If you have ever used a graphic equalizer, you have done this before. The graphic equalizer is a way of changing a signal by interpreting its frequency domain representation; you can selectively control the frequency content by changing the positions of the controls of the graphic equalizer. The equation that defines the Fourier transform, Fp, of a signal p, is given by a complex integral:

$$\Im(p(\omega)) = Fp(\omega) = \int_{-\infty}^{\infty} p(t)e^{-j\omega t}dt \qquad (3.1)$$

where Fp(_) is the Fourier transform; is the angular frequency, $\omega = 2\Pi f$ , measured in radians/s (where the frequency f is the reciprocal of time t_ f = 1/t); j is the complex variable (electronic engineers prefer j to i since they cannot confuse it with the symbol for current – perhaps they don't want to be mistaken for mathematicians!); p(t) is a continuous signal (varying continuously with time); and $e^{-j\omega t} = \cos(\omega t) - j\sin(\omega t)$ gives the frequency components in P(t).

We can derive the Fourier transform by applying Equation 3.1 to the signal of interest. We can see how it works by constraining our analysis to simple signals. (We can then say that complicated signals are just made up by adding up lots of simple signals.) If we take a pulse which is of amplitude (size) A between when it starts at time t =–T/2 and when it ends at t = T/2, and is zero elsewhere, the pulse is:

$$p(t) = \begin{vmatrix} A & if\ -T/2 \le r \le T/2 \\ 0 & Otherwise \end{vmatrix} \qquad (3.2)$$

To obtain the Fourier transform, we substitute for P(t) in Equation 3.1. P(t) = A only for a specified time, so we choose the limits on the integral to be the start and end points of our pulse (it is zero elsewhere) and set P(t) = A, its value in this time interval. The Fourier transform of this pulse is the result of computing:

$$Fp(\omega) = \int_{-T/2}^{T/2} Ae^{-f\omega t}dt \qquad (3.3)$$

When we solve this we obtain an expression for $Fp(\omega)$

$$Fp(\omega) = -\frac{Ae^{-j\omega T/2} - Ae^{j\omega T/2}}{j\omega} \qquad (3.4)$$

By simplification, using the relation $\sin(\theta) = (e^{j\theta} - e^{-j\theta})/2j$ the Fourier transform of the pulse is:

$$Fp(\omega) = \begin{vmatrix} \frac{2A}{\omega}\sin(\frac{\omega T}{2}) & if\omega \ne 0 \\ AT & if\omega = 0 \end{vmatrix} \qquad (3.5)$$

This is a version of the sinc function, sinc(x) = sin(x)/x.. The original pulse, and its transform are illustrated in Figure 3.3. Equation 3.5 (as plotted in Figure 3.3b) suggests that a pulse is made up of a lot of low frequencies (the main body of the pulse) and a few higher frequencies (which give the edges of the pulse). (The range of frequencies is symmetrical around zero frequency; negative frequency is a necessary mathematical abstraction.) The plot of the Fourier transform is called the spectrum of the signal, which can be considered akin to the spectrum of light.

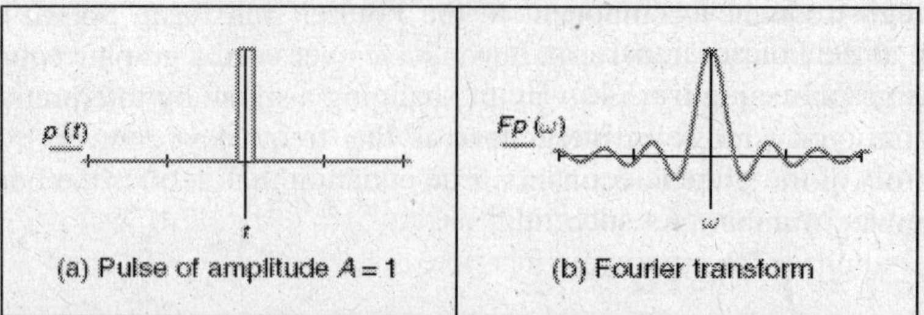


**Figure 3.3 A pulse and its Fourier transform**

So what actually is this Fourier transform? It tells us what frequencies make up a time domain signal. The magnitude of the transform at a particular frequency is the amount of that frequency in the original signal. If we collect together sinusoidal signals in amounts specified by the Fourier transform, we should obtain the originally transformed signal. This process is illustrated in Figure 3.4 for the signal and transform illustrated in Figure 3.3.

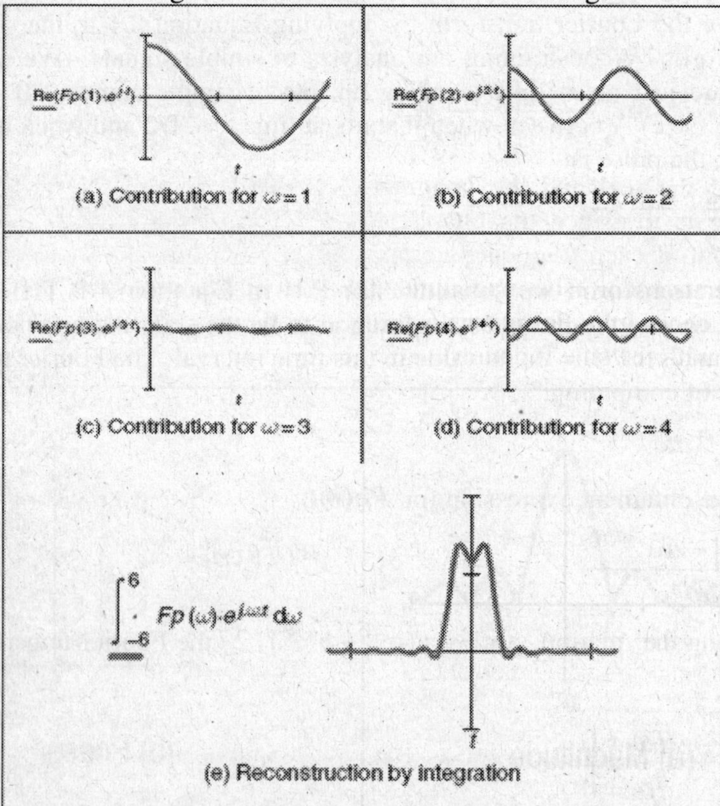


**Figure 3.4 Reconstructing a signal from its transform**

Note that since the Fourier transform is a complex number it has real and imaginary parts, and we only plot the real part here. A low frequency, that for $\omega$=1, in Figure 3.4(a), contributes a large component of the original signal; a higher frequency, that for $\omega$=2 contributes less, as in Figure 3.4(b). This is because the transform coefficient is less for $\omega$=2 than it is for $\omega$=1. There is a very small contribution for $\omega$=3 (Figure 3.4c), although there is more for $\omega$=4 (Figure 3.4d). This is because there are frequencies for which there is no contribution, where the transform is zero. When these signals are integrated together, we achieve a signal that looks similar to the original pulse (Figure 3.4e). Here we have only considered frequencies from $\omega$=-6 to $\omega$=6. If the frequency range in integration were larger, more high frequencies would be included, leading to a more faithful reconstruction of the original pulse. The result of the Fourier transform is a complex number. As such, it is usually represented in terms of its magnitude (or size, or modulus) and phase (or argument). The transform can be represented as:

$$\int_{-\infty}^{\infty} p(t)e^{-j\omega t}dt = \mathrm{Re}[Fp(\omega)] + j\,\mathrm{Im}[Fp(\omega)] \tag{3.6}$$

where Re($\omega$) and lm($\omega$)are the real and imaginary parts of the transform, respectively. The magnitude of the transform is then:

$$\left|\int_{-\infty}^{\infty} p(t)e^{-j\omega t}dt\right| = \sqrt{\mathrm{Re}[Fp(\omega)]^2 + \mathrm{Im}[Fp(\omega)]^2} \tag{3.7}$$

and the phase is:

$$\left\langle \int_{-\infty}^{\infty} p(t)e^{-j\omega t}dt = \tan^{-1}\frac{\mathrm{Im}[Fp(\omega)]}{\mathrm{Re}[Fp(\omega)]} \right. \tag{3.8}$$

where the signs of the real and the imaginary components can be used to determine which quadrant the phase is in (since the phase can vary from 0 to 2$\Pi$ radians). The magnitude describes the amount of each frequency component, while the phase describes timing, when the frequency components occur. The magnitude and phase of the transform of a pulse are shown in Figure 3.5, where the magnitude returns a positive transform, and the phase is either 0 or 2$\Pi$ radians (consistent with the sine function).

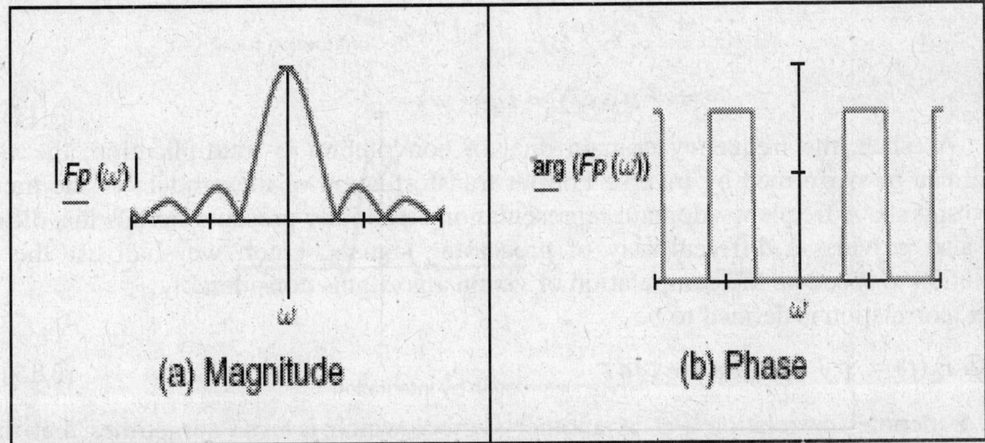


**Figure 3.5 Magnitude and phase of the Fourier transform of a pulse**

To return to the time domain signal, from the frequency domain signal, we require the inverse Fourier transform. This is the process by which we reconstructed the pulse from its transform components. The inverse FT calculates P(t) from Fp($\omega$) according to:

$$p(t) = \Im^{-1}(Fp(\omega)) = \frac{1}{2\pi}\int_{-\infty}^{\infty} Fp(\omega)e^{-j\omega t}d\omega \tag{3.9}$$

Together, Equations 3.1 and 3.9 form a relationship known as a transform pair that allows us to transform into the frequency domain, and back again. By this process, we can perform operations in the frequency domain or in the time domain, since we have a way of changing between them. One important process is known as convolution. The convolution of one signal $P_1(t)$ with another signal $P_2^{(t)}$ where the convolution process denoted by $*$, is given by the integral

$$p_1(t) * p_2(t) = \int_{-\infty}^{\infty} p_1(\tau)p_2(t-\tau)d\tau \tag{3.10}$$

This is the basis of systems theory, where the output of a system is the convolution of a stimulus, say p1, and a system's response, p2, By inverting the time axis of the system response, to give $p_2(t-\tau)$ we obtain a memory function. The convolution process then sums the effect of a stimulus multiplied by the memory function: the current output of the system is the cumulative response to a stimulus. By taking the Fourier transform of Equation 3.10, where the Fourier transformation is denoted by , the Fourier transform of the convolution of two signals is

$$\begin{aligned}\Im[p_1(t) * p_2(t)] &= \int_{-\infty}^{\infty}\left\{\int_{-\infty}^{\infty} p_1(\tau)p_2(t-\tau)d\tau\right\}e^{-j\omega t}dt \\ &= \int_{-\infty}^{\infty}\left\{\int_{-\infty}^{\infty} p_2(t-\tau)e^{-j\omega t}dt\right\}p_1(\tau)d\tau\end{aligned} \tag{3.11}$$

Now, since $\Im[p_2(t-\tau)] = e^{-j\omega t}Fp_2(\omega)$

$$\begin{aligned}\Im[p_1(t) * p_2(t)] &= \int_{-\infty}^{\infty} Fp_2(\omega)p_1(\tau)e^{-j\omega t}d\tau \\ &= Fp_2(\omega)\int_{-\infty}^{\infty} p_1(\tau)e^{-j\omega t}d\tau \\ &= Fp_2(\omega) \times Fp_1(\omega)\end{aligned} \tag{3.12}$$

As such, the frequency domain dual of convolution is multiplication; the convolution integral can be performed by inverse Fourier transformation of the product of the transforms of the two signals. A frequency domain representation essentially presents signals in a different way, but it also provides a different way of processing signals. Later, we shall use the duality of convolution to speed up the computation of vision algorithms considerably.

Further, correlation is defined to be

$$P_1(t) \otimes P_2(t) = \int_{-\infty}^{\infty} P_1(\tau)P_2(t+\tau)d\tau \tag{3.13}$$

where $\otimes$ denotes correlation ($\Theta$ is another symbol which is used sometimes, but there is not much consensus on this symbol). Correlation gives a measure of the match between the two signals $p_2(\omega) and P_1(\omega)$ When $P_2(\omega) = P_1(\omega)$ we are correlating a signal with itself and the process is known as autocorrelation. We shall be using correlation later, to find things in images. Before proceeding further, we also need to define the delta function, which can be considered to be a function occurring at a particular time interval:

$$delta(t-\tau) = \begin{vmatrix} 1 \ if .t = \tau \\ 0 \ otherwise \end{vmatrix} \quad (3.14)$$

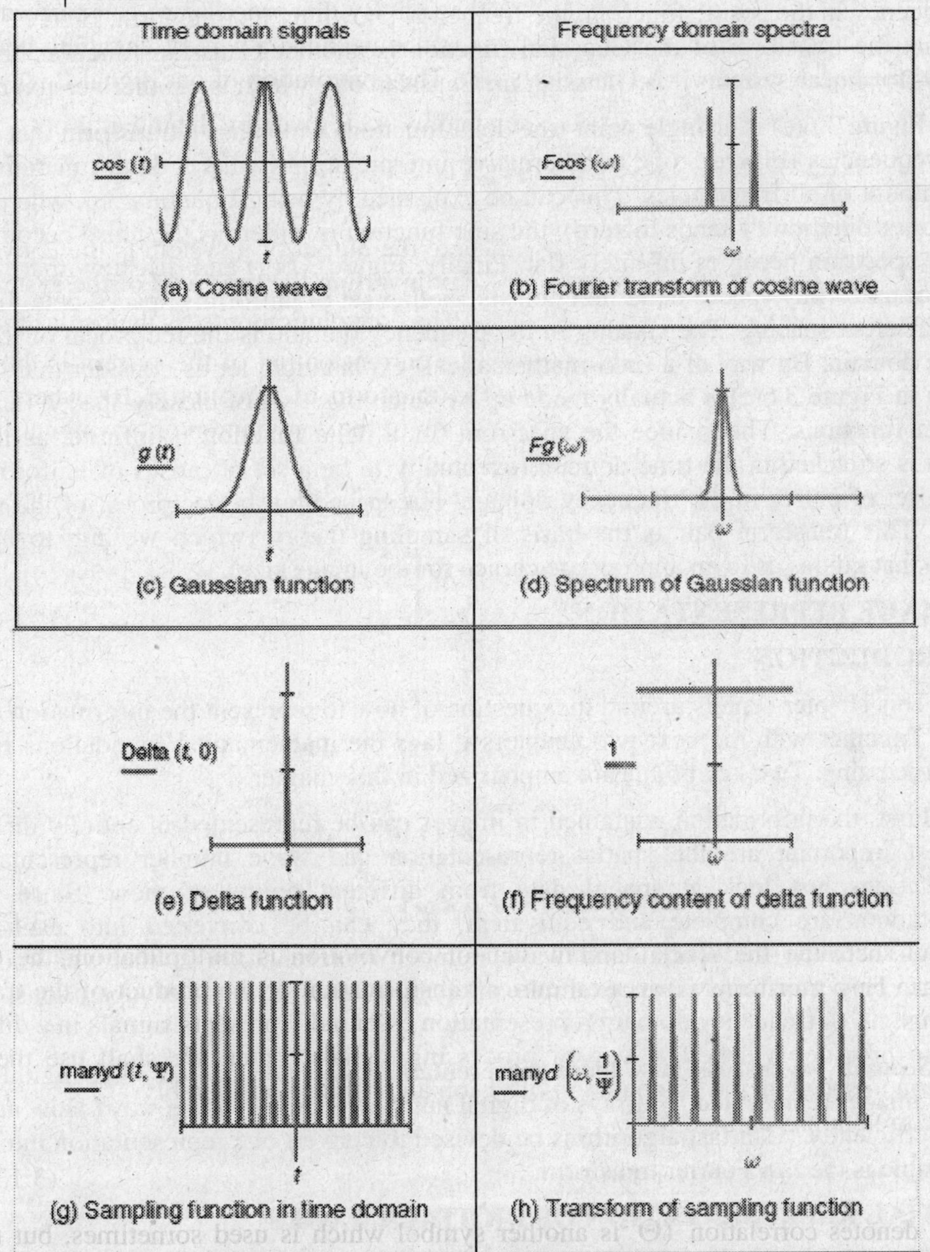


**Figure 3.6 Fourier transform pairs**

The relationship between a signal's time domain representation and its frequency domain version is also known as a transform pair: the transform of a pulse (in the time domain) is a sinc function in the frequency domain. Since the transform is symmetrical, the Fourier transform of a sinc function is a pulse.

There are other Fourier transform pairs, as illustrated in Figure 3.6. First, Figure 3.6(a) and (b) show that the Fourier transform of a cosine function is two points in the frequency domain (at the same value for positive and negative frequency); we expect this since there is only one frequency in the cosine function, the frequency shown by its transform. Figure 3.6(c) and (d) show that the transform of the Gaussian function is another Gaussian function; this illustrates linearity (for linear systems it is Gaussian in, Gaussian out, which is another version of GIGO).

Figure 3.6(e) is a single point (the delta function) which has a transform that is an infinite set of frequencies (Figure 3.6f); an alternative interpretation is that a delta function contains an equal amount of all frequencies. This can be explained by using Equation 3.5, where if the pulse is of shorter duration (T tends to zero), the sinc function is wider; as the pulse becomes infinitely thin, the spectrum becomes infinitely flat. Finally, Figure 3.6(g) and (h) show that the transform of a set of uniformly spaced delta functions is another set of uniformly spaced delta functions, but with a different spacing. The spacing in the frequency domain is the reciprocal of the spacing in the time domain. By way of a (non-mathematical) explanation, let us consider that the Gaussian function in Figure 3.6(c) is actually made up by summing a set of closely spaced (and very thin) Gaussian functions. Then, since the spectrum for a delta function is infinite, as the Gaussian function is stretched in the time domain (eventually to be a set of pulses of uniform height) we obtain a set of pulses in the frequency domain, but spaced by the reciprocal of the time domain spacing. This transform pair is the basis of sampling theory (which we aim to use to find a criterion that guides us to an appropriate choice for the image size).

### 3.2.2 IMAGE REPRESENTATION

### 1. INTRODUCTION

This chapter centers around the question of how to represent the information contained in images. Together with the next two chapters it lays the mathematical foundations for low-level image processing. Two key points are emphasized in this chapter.

First, the information contained in images can be represented in entirely different ways. The most important are the spatial representation and wave number representation. These representations just look at spatial data from different points of view. Since the various representations are complete and equivalent, they can be converted into each other. The conversion between the spatial and wave number representation is the well-known Fourier transform. This transform is an example of a more general class of operations, the unitary transforms.

Second, we discuss how these representations can be handled with digital computers. How are images represented by arrays of digital numbers in an adequate way? How are these data handled efficiently? Can fast algorithms be devised to convert one representation into another? A key example is the fast Fourier transform.

### 2. SPATIAL REPRESENTATION OF DIGITAL IMAGES

#### (i) PIXEL AND VOXEL

Images constitute a spatial distribution of the irradiance at a plane. Mathematically speaking, the spatial irradiance distribution can be described as a continuous function of two spatial variables:

$$E(x1,x2) = E(x). \quad (3.15)$$

Computers cannot handle continuous images but only arrays of digital numbers. Thus it is required to represent images as two-dimensional arrays of points. A point on the 2-D grid is called a pixel or pel. Both words are abbreviations of the word picture element. A pixel represents the irradiance at the corresponding grid position. In the simplest case, the pixels are located on a rectangular grid. The position of the pixel

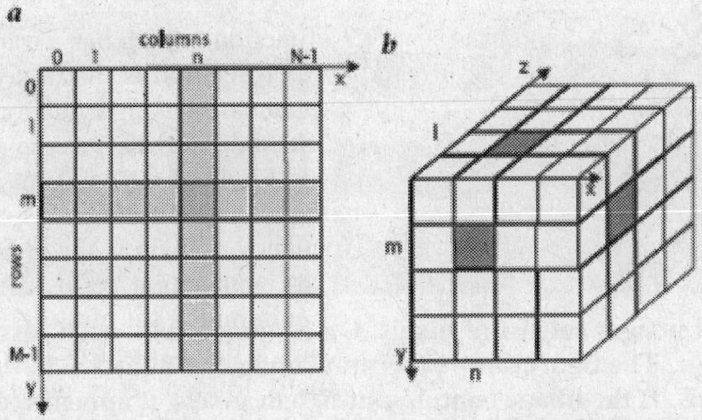


**Figure 3.7 Representation of digital images by array of discrete points on a rectangular grid: (a) 2-D image and (b) 3-D image**

is given in the common notation for matrices. The first index, m, denotes the position of the row, the second, n, the position of the column (Fig. 3.7a). If the digital image contains M × N pixels, i. e., is represented by an M × N matrix, the index n runs from 0 to N – 1, and the index m from 0 to M–1. M gives the number of rows, N the number of columns. In accordance with the matrix notation, the vertical axis (y axis) runs from top to bottom and not vice versa as it is common in graphs. The horizontal axis (x axis) runs as usual from left to right. Each pixel represents not just a point in the image but rather a rectangular region, the elementary cell of the grid. The value associated with the pixel must represent the average irradiance in the corresponding cell in an appropriate way.

Figure 3.8 shows one and the same image represented with a different number of pixels as indicated in the legend. With large pixel sizes (Fig. 3.8(a),(b)), not only is the spatial resolution poor, but the gray value discontinuities at pixel edges appear as disturbing artifacts distracting us from the content of the image. As the pixels become smaller, the effect becomes less pronounced up to the point where we get the impression of a spatially continuous image. This happens when the pixels become smaller than the spatial resolution of our visual system. You can convince yourself of this relation by observing Fig. 3.8 from different distances. How many pixels are sufficient? There is no general answer to this question. For visual observation of a digital image, the pixel size should be smaller than the spatial resolution of the visual system from a nominal observer distance. For a given task the pixel size should be smaller than the finest scales of the objects that we want to study. We generally find, however, that it is the available sensor technology.

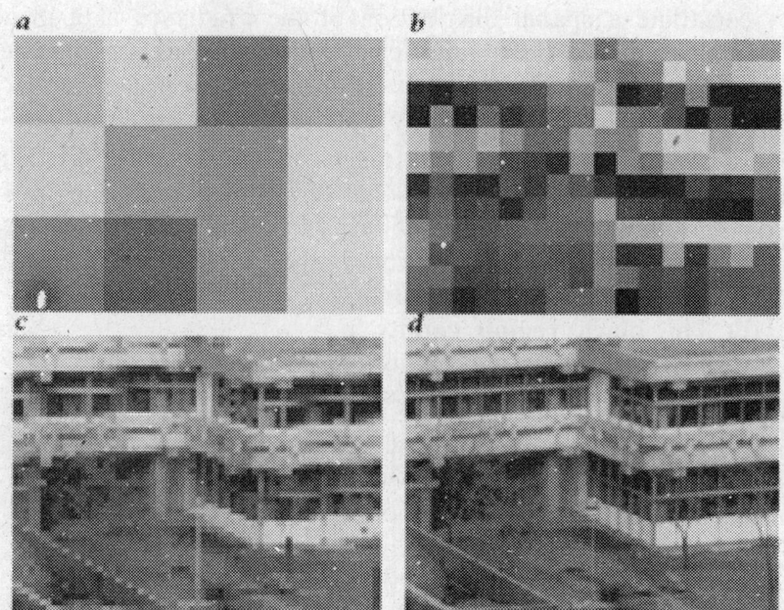


**Figure 3.8 Digital images consist of pixels. On a square grid, each pixel represents a square region of the image. The figure shows the same image with (a) 3 x 4 , (b) 12 x 16 ,(c) 48 x 64 , (d) 192 x 256 pixels. If the image contains sufficient pixels, it appears to be continuous**

that limits the number of pixels rather than the demands from the applications. Even a high-resolution sensor array with 1000 × 1000 elements has a relative spatial resolution of only 10–3. This is a rather poor resolution compared to other measurements such as those of length, electrical voltage or frequency, which can be performed with relative resolutions of far beyond 10–6. However, these techniques provide only a measurement at a single point, while a 1000 × 1000 image contains one million points. Thus we obtain an insight into the spatial variations of a signal. If we take image sequences, also the temporal changes and, thus, the kinematics and dynamics of the studied object become apparent. In this way, images open up a whole new world of information. A rectangular grid is only the simplest geometry for a digital image. Other geometrical arrangements of the pixels and geometric forms of the elementary cells are possible. Finding the possible configurations is the 2-D analogue of the classification of crystal structure in 3-D space, a subject familiar to solid state physicists, mineralogists, and chemists. Crystals show periodic 3-D patterns of the arrangements of their atoms,

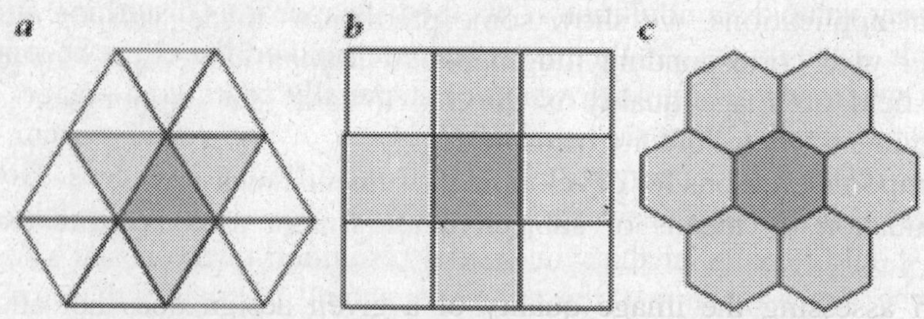


**Figure 3.9 The three possible regular grids in 2-D;**
**(a) triangular grid , (b) square grid and (c) hexagonal grid**

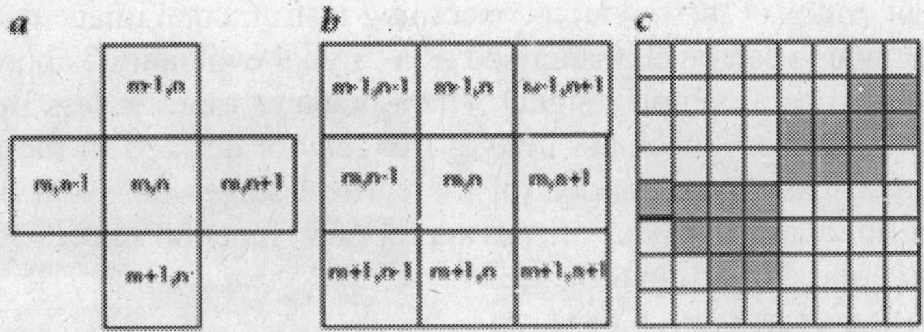


**Figure 3.10 Neighborhoods on a rectangular grid; (a) 4-neighborhood and (b) 8-neighborhood. (c) The black region counts as one object (connected region) in an 8-neighborhood but as two objects in a 4- neighborhood**

ions, or molecules which can be classified by their symmetries and the geometry of the elementary cell. In 2-D, classification of digital grids is much simpler than in 3-D. If we consider only regular polygons, we have only three possibilities: triangles, squares, and hexagons (Fig. 3.9). The 3-D spaces (and even higher-dimensional spaces) are also of interest in image processing. In three-dimensional images a pixel turns into a voxel, an abbreviation of volume element. On a rectangular grid, each voxel represents the mean gray value of a cuboid. The position of a voxel is given by three indices. The first, k, denotes the depth, m the row, and n the column (Fig. 3.10). A Cartesian grid, i.e., hypercubic pixel, is the most general solution for digital data since it is the only geometry that can easily be extended to arbitrary dimensions.

## 3.3 IMAGING SYSTEM SPECIFICATION BUILDING IMAGE QUALITY

Image quality is usually described in terms of the presence of visible distortions of the image such as colour shifts, blur, noise, or blockings. Historically, the most common way to model and predict image quality therefore has been a quantification of the visibility of these distortions, for ex ample using models of early visual processing or using judgments of human subjects obtained in psychophysical experiments. Since this approach seems so obvious, the question of what image quality really is has traditionally been neglected, denying a better interpretation and deeper understanding of what has been measured and modeled during the past. Our aim here is to answer the above question what image quality is, and to present a concept for image quality which is both generic and directly applicable.

The concept is generic in the sense that the approach we use here can equally well be used to describe sound or speech quality. Furthermore, it is directly applicable in the sense that the description we give of image quality, and the algorithms we base upon this description, follow straightforwardly from the answer to the above question. Finally, to show the value of this concept for real applications, we show some predictions made with algorithms based on this concept together with corresponding judgments of human subjects. A major part of research activity in the field of image quality is directed towards the development of reliable, widely applicable, instrumental image quality measures.

There are two important reasons for developing instrumental measures:

(1) quality evaluation by means of subjective assessment tests is quite expensive and time consuming.

(2) a posteriori assessing the image quality of a given design does not allow for an a priori optimization of this design, thus condemning the design of image (re-)production systems to remain an iterative procedure.

At present, much of the research concerning instrumental image quality measures is based upon an approach which can be characterised as a "signal evaluation" approach. In this approach, the image is regarded as a complex signal which deviates more or less from the complex signal that represents the ideal or "original" image. Images are defined in the physical or perceptual domain, in the latter case using models of the earliest stages of visual perception, and quality measures are defined as distances in an appropriate function space, for example, Euclidean distance between actual and original image.

### 3.3.1 WHAT IS IMAGE QUALITY

There can be no good answer to the question "what is image quality?" when the question "what is quality?" has not been answered. Perhaps the most general answer to this last question is "the degree to which something satisfies the requirements imposed on it". Though vague, this answer certainly is intuitively correct. We tend to think of things as "bad", "good", or "excellent" according to the degree to which they exhibit desired characteristics (a book; a house), or according to the degree to which they are adequate for the task we want them to perform (a car; a washing machine).

So, if we wish to answer the question what image quality is, we will need to answer the questions: (1) what are images; (2) what are images used for; and (3) what are the requirements which the use of images imposes on them.

To begin with the answers to the first two questions, there can be no doubt that images are the carriers of visual information about the outside world, and that they are used as input to human visual perception. Visual perception itself is part of the three processes perception, cognition, and action, which together constitute human interaction with the environment (see figure 3.11). Images, therefore, can be regarded as input to the perception stage of interaction. If we use a rather technical view of perception, we may define perception as the stage of human interaction in which attributes

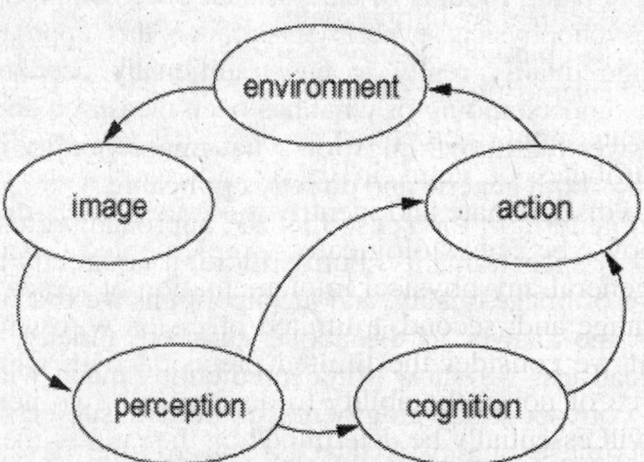


**Figure 3.11: Schematic overview of the interaction process. Images are the carriers of information about the environment, and serve as input to visual perception. The result of visual processing is used as input to cognition (for tasks requiring interpretation of scene content) or as input to action (for example in navigation, where the link between perception and action is mostly direct). Since action will in general result in a changed status of the environment, the nature of the interaction process is cyclic.**

of items in the outside world are measured and internally quantified. The aim of this quantification is essentially two-fold. First, items in the outside world can be discriminated from one another using their internally quantified attributes. The result of this process is an essential step towards the construction of higher-level descriptions of scene geometry and object location, descriptions upon which later processes such as navigation in the scene are based. Second, items in the outside world can be identified by comparing their internally quantified attributes with quantified attributes, stored in memory, of similar items observed in the past. Identification of what is depicted in the image is an essential step in the interpretation of scene content; it determines our semantic awareness of what is in the scene.

So far, what we have found is that images are used as input to the perception stage of human interaction, and that the primary task of perception is to measure and internally quantify attributes of items in the outside world with the aim to discriminate and identify these items. These observations lead us to the answer to the third question: the requirements which the use of images, that is, their use as input to perception, imposes on them, is that, first, the items depicted in the image should be successfully discriminable and, second, the items depicted in the image should be successfully identifiable. We are now able to formulate the following answer to the question what image quality is: (1) The quality of an image is the adequacy of this image as input to visual perception. (2) The adequacy of an image as input to visual perception is given by the discriminability and identifiability of the items depicted in the image.

### 3.3.2 THE INTERNAL QUANTIFICATION OF ATTRIBUTES

If we wish to predict image quality, we will need to specify how discrimination and identification of items is performed, and to do this we need to specify how item attributes are internally quantified. The instrument for the quantification of attribute strength is the metric. Metrics are defined by an origin and a unit, which together constitute the scale, and a scale function, which relates physical attribute strength to the position on the scale, or scale value (Watt 1989, Watt 1991). The scale function is usually assumed to be rigid, that is, constant in time. Essentially all metrics defined by humans are of this type, the reason for this being that we wish to use these metrics to uniquely specify attribute strength in terms of scale value; 1.78 metres should be one and the same length, wherever and whenever it is measured.

As we have pointed out, perception is the stage in human interaction with the environment in which attributes of items in the outside world are measured and internally quantified, with the aim to discriminate and identify these items. The metrics which are used for this task must somehow be physiologically implemented. Any such physiological implementation, and in general any physical implementation of a metric, will inevitably result in, first, a limited scale range and, second, a limited precision with which scale values can be represented. Therefore, if we consider the limited precision with which scale values can be represented to be a source of noise, the ability to discriminate two items using their internally represented scale values will essentially be determined by the ratio of the difference of their scale values to the noise level. This, together with the limited scale range, represents an upper limit to the discriminative power of any physically implemented metric.

Watt (1991) has argued that the discriminative power of a metric can be considerably increased when the scale function of that metric is allowed to be flexible instead of rigid. Flexibility allows for an adaptation of the scale function to what is currently being measured, thus sacrificing a unique specification of measured item attributes for an improved ability to discriminate these items. We found that such metrics exhibit properties which resemble several well-known characteristics of human colour vision, such as adaptation, crispening, and brightness- and colour constancy. However, since flexibility of the scale function no longer allows for a unique specification of measured item attributes, the ability to compare what is observed at the moment with what has been observed in the past is reduced, resulting in a reduced ability to identify. The degree of flexibility of such scale functions can then be used to optimise the overall performance in terms of both discriminability and identifiability.

Since the aim of quantification in perception is to discriminate and identify items, and since discrimination and identification are of such importance to a successful interaction, it is to be expected that the properties of the metrics used for this quantification are optimally, or nearly optimally, chosen. We will therefore adopt the concept of partially flexible metrics here, and start by deriving expressions for metrics which are optimal with respect to either discriminability, identifiability, or a combination of these two. Based on the expressions we derive, we will then formulate expressions for discriminability and identifiability.

To this end, we will regard the outside world as a simple set of items of which the values of a one-dimensional attribute are measured and quantified with the aim to discriminate and identify these items. We will further simplify the situation by assuming that the influence of external noise sources, that is, noise sources acting directly on the attribute strength, may be neglected. In the last part of this paper we will apply the obtained measures for discriminability and identifiability to predict the quality of reproduced black and white images of natural scenes of which the contrast has been manipulated, and compare the predictions with experimentally obtained judgments of human subjects.

### 3.3.3 AN OPTIMAL METRIC FOR OVERALL DISCRIMINABILITY

Assume that, at a certain point in time, the strength of an attribute x is measured for a set of N items. The momentary distribution[1] of the strength of x for the items in the set is given by ii(x, t), where ii(x, t) is scaled to yield unity when integrated over the range X of the attribute strength:

$$\int_X \mu(x, t)dx = 1. \tag{3.16}$$

The measurement results are represented by scale values on an internal scale s. The range of the scale s is given by S, and the scale function s(x, t) which relates attribute strength x to scale value s is monotonic with x, that is, $ds(x, t)/dx > 0$. Furthermore, assume that the precision with which scale values can be represented is limited by the presence of Gaussian noise with mean zero and spread a. Finally, assume that the influence of external noise on the attribute strength x may be neglected.

The questions we now ask are: (1) when the items are to be discriminated using their scale values, what is the overall discriminability of the items in the set (expressed in the overall probability of a topological error) for a given scale function s(x, t); and (2) what scale function s(x, t) will optimise this overall discriminability (that is, minimise the overall probability of a topological error[2])?

#### 3.3.3.1 A MEASURE FOR OVERALL DISCRIMINABILITY

The scale function s(x, t) maps attribute strength x to scale value s. When the attribute strength distribution of the set of N items is given by $\mu(x, t)$, then the corresponding scale value distribution $\eta(s(x, t))$ will be determined by the relation:

$$\eta(s(x, t))ds(x, t) = \mu(x, t)dx, \tag{3.17}$$

so that:

$$\eta\ (s(x, t)) = \mu\ (x, t)\left(\frac{dx(x,t)}{dx}\right)^{-1} \tag{3.18}$$

When the items are ordered by their attribute strengths, we find that the attribute strength differences between subsequent items are in close approximation given by $\Delta x = 1/N\mu\ (x, t)$. The corresponding scale value difference will be given by $\Delta s = 1/\ N\eta\ (s(x, t))$, with $\eta\ (s(x, t))$ given in equation 3.18.

However, due to the presence of noise on the internal scale values, the corresponding scale value s for a certain attribute strength x will be given by a Normal probability density function with mean s(x, t) and spread $\sigma$. For an item with attribute strength x and its successor with attribute strength $x + \Delta x$ we therefore find for the scale value difference a Normal probability density function with mean As = $1/N\eta\ (s(x, t))$ and spread $\sigma\sqrt{2}$. A topological error occurs when As < 0. To find the probability of a topological error, we thus have to integrate the above probability density function from $\Delta s = -\infty$ to $\Delta s = 0$:

$$p_d(x,t)^2 = \int_{\infty}^{0} N(\Delta s; 1/N\eta(s(x,t)), \sigma\sqrt{2})\, d(\Delta s) \tag{3.19}$$

which after substitution of $u = (\Delta s — 1/N\eta\ (s(x, t)))\ \sigma\sqrt{2}$ can be written as:

$$p_d(x, t) = \int_{-\infty}^{-1/N\sigma\sqrt{2}\eta(s(x,t))} N(u; 0, 1)\, du, \tag{3.20}$$

Or

$$p_d(x, t) = \frac{1}{2} - \frac{1}{2}\text{erf}\,\frac{1}{2N\sigma\eta(s(x, t))}. \tag{3.21}$$

The overall probability of a topological error is now given by:

$$P_d(t) = \int_X p_d(x, t)\,\mu(x, t)\, dx. \tag{3.22}$$

Substituting equations 3.21 and 3.18 in this, we obtain:

$$P_d(t) = \int_X \left(\frac{1}{2} - \frac{1}{2}\text{erf}\,\frac{ds(x,t)/dx}{2N\sigma\mu(x,t)}\right)\mu(x, t)\, dx. \tag{3.23}$$

### 3.3.3.2 OPTIMISING OVERALL DISCRIMINABILITY

The question we ask here is: what scale function s(x, t) will minimise the overall probability of a topological error Pd(t) for a given attribute strength distribution $\mu\ (x, t)$? Referring to equation 3.23, we have to solve:

$$\min_{ds(x,t)/dx} \int_X \left( \frac{1}{2} - \frac{1}{2} \text{erf} \frac{ds(x,t)/dx}{2N\sigma\mu(x,t)} \right) \mu(x,t) dx. \tag{3.24}$$

$$\frac{ds(x,t)}{dx} = S\mu(x,t), \tag{3.25}$$

which shows that the optimal scale function s(x, t) depends on the momentary distribution of the attribute strength and therefore should be flexible. For an optimal metric, the ideal, noiseless scale value s for a particular attribute strength x is therefore given by:

$$s = s(x,t) = S \int_{-\infty}^{x} \mu(u,t) du. \tag{3.26}$$

Substituting the above solution in equation 3.23, the overall probability of a topological error for an optimal metric is given by:

$$P_{d,min} = \frac{1}{2} - \frac{1}{2} \text{erf} \frac{S}{2N\sigma}, \tag{3.27}$$

which defines the upper limit of discriminability for given values of S, $\sigma$, and N. In contrast, the lower limit of discriminability is given by the maximum value of Pd(t), which independently of the values of S, $\sigma$ and N is always given by:

$$P_{d,max} = \frac{1}{2}. \tag{3.28}$$

Discriminability may now be specified on a scale from zero (worst) to one (best) by using:

$$D(t) = 1 - \frac{P_d(t) - P_{d,min}}{P_{d,max} - P_{d,min}}. \tag{3.29}$$

## 3.3.4 QUALITY AND INFORMATION PROCESSING

### 3.3.4.1 UNDERSTANDING INFORMATION-PROCESSING SYSTEMS

We adopt the general viewpoint in computational cognition (Newell & Simon 1972, Newell 1990) that (1) the video-cognitive system can be considered to be an information-processing system; and (2) information- processing systems can only be completely understood when they are understood at three distinct levels.

These levels are (1) the semantic level, that is, the level describing the system in terms of computational goals and strategies; (2) the algorithmic level, that is, the level describing the implementation of the computational theory into algorithms and associated representations; and (3) the level of physical implementation, that is, the level describing the physical implementation of these algorithms and representations

As stated above, any information-processing system can only be completely understood when it can be appropriately described at all three levels, which for reasons of simplicity may be designated as the levels of "what & why", "how" and "where". The approach we choose to pursue here is strictly top-down, that is, we first try to gain a fundamental understanding of the "what & why" of the processing of images by the visuo-cognitive system in order to arrive at an understanding of what image quality is, and then proceed with the "how" and "where". Our present purposes are therefore served best with a description of visuo-cognitive information-processing at the semantic level.

### 3.3.4.2 THE QUALITY OF INFORMATION

At a semantic level, the interaction of an observer with his environment can be described by a cycle consisting of three activities:

(1) perception, that is, acquiring information from the environment and constructing an internal representation from it;

(2) cognition, that is, interpreting the obtained internal representation;

(3) action, that is, responding appropriately to this interpretation.

At this point, we may already infer that in order to ensure a proper response to occurrences in the outside world, certain requirements must be imposed upon the information which is acquired from the environment.

When the quality of information is considered to be the degree to which these requirements are satisfied, we arrive at two important conclusions:

(1) the quality of information can only be defined within the context of an observer interacting with his environment

(2) the quality of information refers to the appropriateness of this information as a basis for a proper response to outside world occurrences.

### 3.3.4.3 THE QUALITY OF IMAGES

Realising that images are the medium for visual information, we now focus our attention on the question what requirements should be imposed upon an image. At first thought, the requirements that a "good" image should satisfy would seem to be precision and reliability. The above outlined ideas, however, lead to a somewhat more complicated requirement: for an image to be of "good" quality, the observer's interpretation of this image should be successful, that is, should with high probability be correct. The imposition of this requirement is justified by realising that it is of vital importance that there is no discrepancy between "what really is there" and what the observer assumes is there. The next section will focus on the question how this can be optimally secured.

## 3.3.5 IMAGE QUALITY SEMANTICS

### 3.3.5.1 IMAGE PROCESSING BY THE VISUAL-COGNITIVE SYSTEM

We will subdivide the processing of images by the Visual-cognitive system in three distinct processes:

(1) perception, that is, the construction of a internal representation of the image using primarily low-level knowledge of the visual world;

(2) interpretation, that is, the confrontation ("matching") of this internal representation with memory representations;

(3) task-directed semantic processing of the interpreted scene in order to formulate a response. A diagrammatical depiction of the processing of images by the visual-cognitive system is shown in figure 3.12.

The collection of memory representations of the outside world, which we will from this point onwards refer to as "knowledge of reality", we regard as well-defined but nevertheless fuzzy. As an example of this, consider that although observers "know" what the prototypical characteristics of a certain object are, they usually are unable to define a clear distinction between prototypical and non-prototypical object characteristics. Knowledge of reality therefore may be thought of as accumulated knowledge of (the behaviour of) outside world statistics.

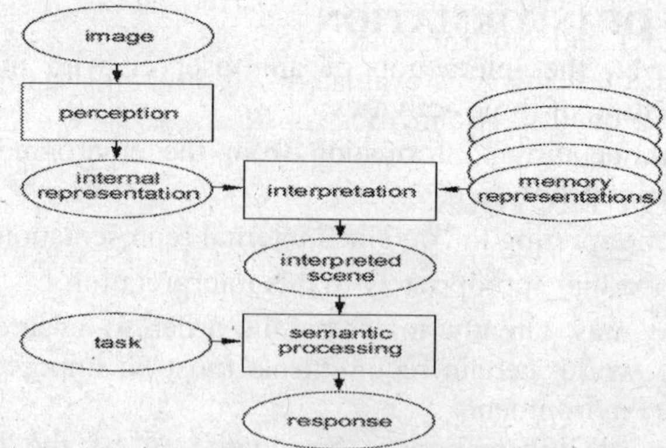


**Figure 3.12: A diagrammatical depiction of visual-cognitive processing of images. In this diagram, ellipses denote representations of information, and rectangles denote processes transforming one representation into another. Note that we consider the "response" to be a formulated sequence of actions, not its manifestation in terms of motoric events**

Instead of referring to a match between the internal representation and a memory representation, we will henceforth more appropriately refer to a match between the internal representation and knowledge of reality.

### 3.3.5.2 NATURALNESS, USEFULNESS AND QUALITY

Given the visual-cognitive processes as outlined above, we now ask how a successful interpretation of an image can be secured best. Returning to figure 3.12, we may readily conclude that for a successful interpretation of an image, the interpretation process should result in a satisfactory match between the internal representation and knowledge of reality.

We therefore quite directly arrive at two principal requirements that an image of "good" quality should satisfy:

1. the internal representation of the image should be sufficiently precise.
2. the degree of correspondence between the internal representation and knowledge of reality as stored in memory should be high.

We are now able to formalise the preceding discussion by defining (1) the usefulness of an image to be the precision[3] of the internal representation of the image; and (2) the naturalness of an image to be the degree of correspondence between the internal representation of the image and knowledge of reality as stored in memory. Using these definitions, we define the quality of an image to be the degree to which the image is both useful and natural.

The sets of requirements that one needs to impose upon an image in order to maximise the usefulness or the naturalness of this image will in general not coincide. For example, detection or discrimination of objects in an image may require "exaggeration" of certain features of this image, resulting in a less natural reproduction of the image. Therefore, given the above definition of image quality, we postulate that the quality of an image will be given by a compromise resulting from simultaneously evaluating to what degree the image satisfies the sets of requirements that lead to maximising the usefulness or the naturalness of the image.

## 3.4 IMAGE QUALITY ASSESSMENT CATEGORIES

There are several techniques and metrics that can be measured objectively and automatically evaluated by a computer program. Therefore, they can be classified as Full

Reference Methods (FR) and No-Reference Methods (NR). In FR image quality assessment methods, the quality of a test image is evaluated by comparing it with a reference image that is assumed to have perfect quality. NR metrics try to assess the quality of an image without any reference to the original one.

### 3.4.1 IMAGE QUALITY FACTORS

**Figure 3.13 Blown highlights are detrimental to image quality. Top: Original image. Bottom: Blown areas highlighted in red**

- Sharpness - determines the amount of detail an image can convey. System sharpness is affected by the lens (design and manufacturing quality, focal length, aperture, and distance from the image center) and sensor (pixel count and anti-aliasing filter). In the field, sharpness is affected by camera shake (a good tripod can be helpful), focus accuracy, and atmospheric disturbances (thermal effects and aerosols). Lost sharpness can be restored by sharpening, but sharpening has limits. Over sharpening, can degrade image quality by causing "halos" to appear near contrast boundaries. Images from many compact digital cameras are oversharpened.
- Noise is a random variation of image density, visible as grain in film and pixel level variations in digital images. It arises from the effects of basic physics— the photon nature of light and the thermal energy of heat— inside image sensors. Typical noise reduction (NR) software reduces the visibility of noise by smoothing the image, excluding areas near contrast boundaries. This technique works well, but it can obscure fine, low contrast detail.
- Dynamic range - Dynamic range (or exposure range) is the range of light levels a camera can capture, usually measured in f-stops, EV (exposure value), or zones (all factors of two in exposure). It is closely related to noise: high noise implies low dynamic range.
- Tonal Response — the relationship between light and pixel level.
- Contrast - also known as gamma, is the slope of the tonal response curve. High contrast usually involves loss of dynamic range— loss of detail, or clipping, in highlights or shadows— when the image is displayed.
- Color accuracy - is an important but ambiguous image quality factor. Many viewers prefer enhanced color saturation; the most accurate color isn't necessarily the most pleasing. Nevertheless it is important to measure a camera's color response: its color shifts, saturation, and the effectiveness if its white balance algorithms.
- Distortion - is an aberration that causes straight lines to curve near the edges of images. It can be troublesome for architectural photography and metrology (photographic applications involving measurement). Distortion is worst in wide angle, telephoto, and

zoom lenses. It often worse for close-up images than for images at a distance. It can be easily corrected in software.

- Light falloff - Also known as vignetting, darkens images near the corners. It can be significant with wide angle lenses.
- Exposure accuracy - You can usually determine it quickly with the help of the histogram, to alter the accuracy you can change the exposure compensation or the way you meter. Exposure accuracy can be an issue with fully automatic cameras and with video cameras where there is little or no opportunity for post-exposure tonal adjustment. Some even have exposure memory: exposure may change after very bright or dark objects appear in a scene.

**Figure 3.14 At full resolution, this image has clearly visible compression artifacts**

- Lateral chromatic aberration - (LCA), also called "color fringing" is a lens aberration that causes colors to focus at different distances from the image center. It is most visible near corners of images. LCA is worst with asymmetrical lenses, including ultrawides, true telephotos and zooms. It is strongly affected by demosaicing.
- Veiling glare - is stray light in lenses and optical systems caused by reflections between lens elements and the inside barrel of the lens. It predicts the severity of lens flare, image fogging (loss of shadow detail and color) as well as "ghost" images that can occur in the presence of bright light sources in or near the field of view.
- Color moiré - is artificial color banding that can appear in images with repetitive patterns of high spatial frequencies, like fabrics or picket fences. It is affected by lens sharpness, the anti-aliasing (lowpass) filter (which softens the image), and demosaicing software. It tends to be worst with the sharpest lenses.
- Artifacts - Software (especially operations performed during RAW conversion) can cause significant visual artifacts, including Data compression and transmission losses (e.g. Low quality JPEG), oversharpening "halos" and loss of fine, low-contrast detail.

### 3.4.2 MEASURES OF IMAGE QUALITY

Comparing restoration results requires a measure of image quality. Two commonly used measures are Mean-Squared Error and Peak Signal-to-Noise Ratio. The mean-squared error (MSE) between two images g(x,y) and $\hat{g}(x, y)$ is:

$$e_{MSE} = \frac{1}{MN}\sum_{n=1}^{M}\sum_{m=1}^{N}[\hat{g}(n,m) - g(n,m)]^2 \qquad (3.30)$$

One problem with mean-squared error is that it depends strongly on the image intensity scaling. A mean-squared error of 100.0 for an 8-bit image (with pixel values in the range 0-255) looks dreadful; but a MSE of 100.0 for a 10-bit image (pixel values in [0,1023]) is barely noticeable.

Peak Signal-to-Noise Ratio (PSNR) avoids this problem by scaling the MSE according to the image range:

$$\mathbf{PSNR} = -10 log_{10} \frac{e_{MSE}}{S^2} \tag{3.31}$$

Where S is the maximum pixel value. PSNR is measured in decibels (dB). The PSNR measure is also not ideal, but is in common use. Its main failing is that the signal strength is estimated as $S^2$, rather than the actual signal strength for the image. PSNR is a good measure for comparing restoration results for the same image, but between-image comparisons of PSNR are meaningless. One image with 20 dB PSNR may look much better than another image with 30 dB PSNR.

MSE and PSNR figures provided in this thesis were calculated after quantization (i.e. after converting floating-point pixel values to integer), but before clipping of the intensity range.

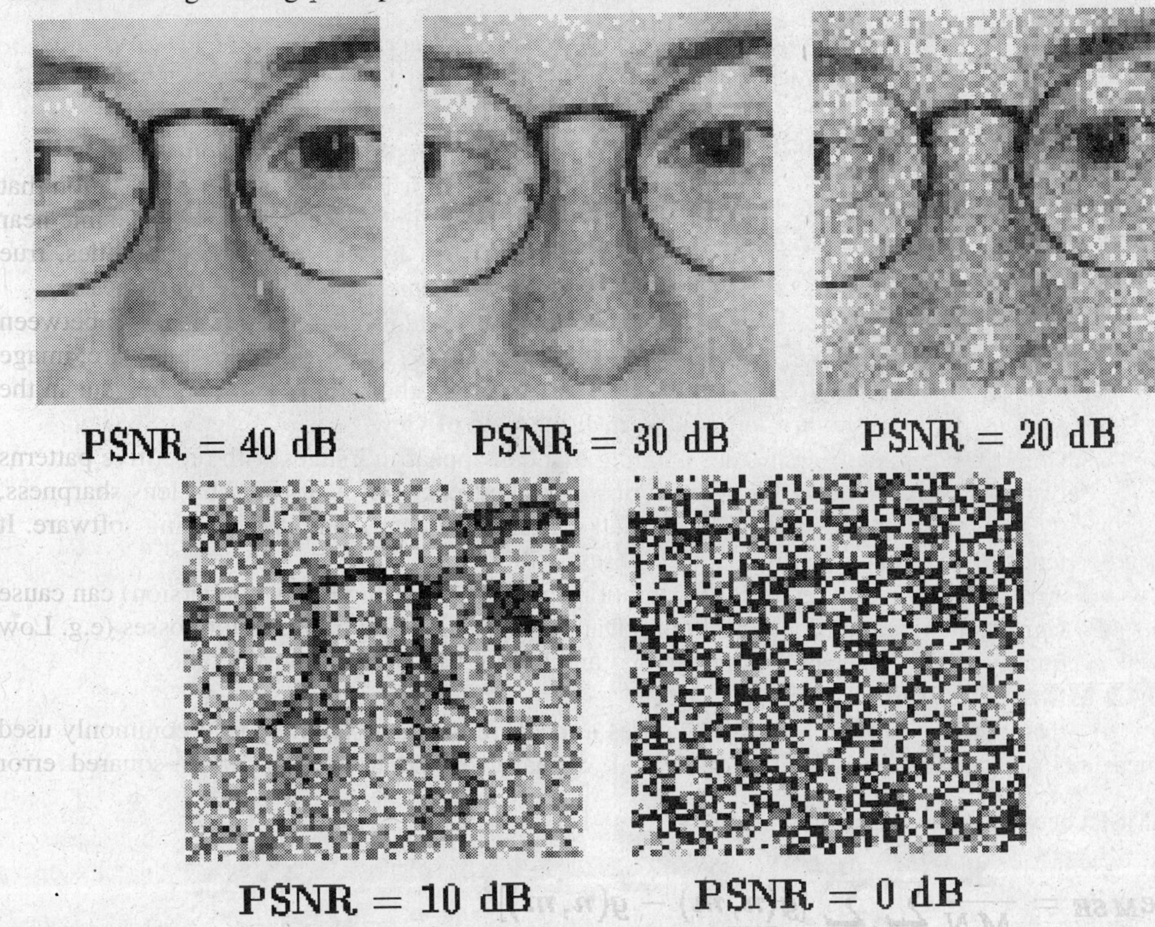


**Figure 3.15: Illustration of the PSNR measure**

### 3.4.2.1 FREQUENCY-DOMAIN SNR BEHAVIOUR

PSNR reduces image quality to a single number. If the number is low, it offers no information about what parts of the signal have been lost. To analyze the restoration more carefully, it is useful to work in the frequency domain. Looking at the signal-to-noise ratio as a function of spatial frequency gives a breakdown of filter performance for features of various scales. One can immediately see whether a filter has trouble with fine or large-scale features.

The Discrete Fourier Transform (DFT) representation of an image g(n,m) is given by:

$$G(u,v) = \sum_{n=0}^{N-1} \sum_{m=0}^{M-1} g(n,m) e^{-2\pi j\left(\frac{un}{N}+\frac{vm}{M}\right)} \tag{3.32}$$

For the purpose of looking at frequency-domain SNR behaviour, it is useful to lump together the coefficients according to normalized spatial frequency, given by:

$$\lambda^{-1} = \sqrt{\frac{N^2 v^2 + M^2 u^2}{M^2 N^2}} \tag{3.33}$$

The range of $\lambda^{-1}$ is $[0, \frac{1}{\sqrt{2}}]$. The inverse of the normalized frequency $(\lambda)$ gives the wavelength of the spatial frequency component. The DC component (or average) of an image corresponds to $\lambda^{-1}$=0. Features on the scale of ten pixels would have $\lambda^{-1} \approx 0.1 (\lambda \approx 10)$, and very fine detailed features (on the scale of 2 pixels) have $\lambda^{-1} \approx 0.5$. The highest possible frequency is $\lambda^{-1} = \frac{1}{\sqrt{2}}$ this corresponds to a checkerboard pattern. Figure 3.16 illustrates some spatial frequency components of various wavelengths and orientations.

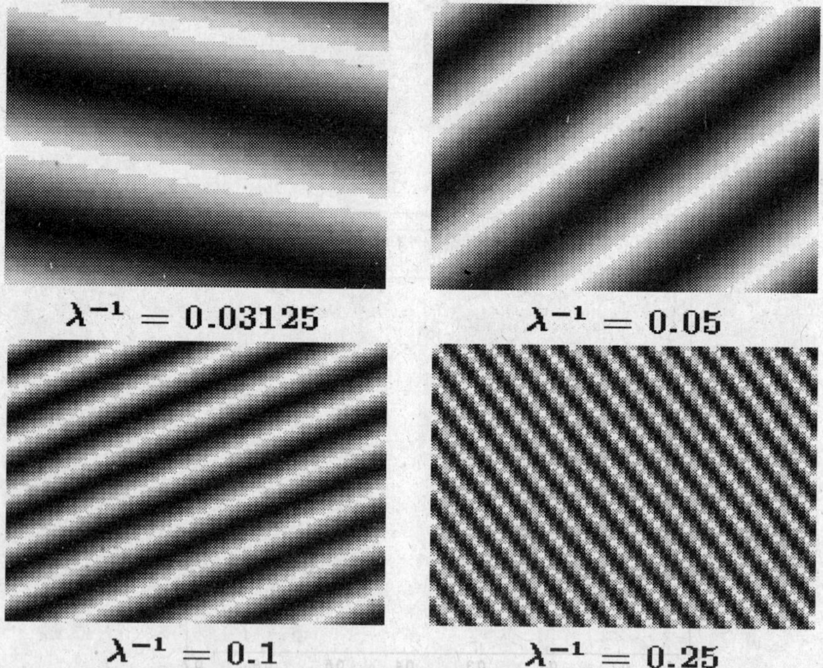


**Figure 3.16: Spatial frequency components of various wavelengths and orientations**

Let s(n,m) be the original image and x(n,m) be a degraded version. To calculate SNR as a function of spatial frequency, the first step is to calculate the difference image:
D(n,m) = s(n,m) – x(n,m)

Then Fourier transforms of s(n,m) and d(n,m) are taken, producing S(u,v) and D(u,v). The frequency domain is then divided into nonoverlapping frequency bands of the form $B_i = [\lambda_i^{-1}, \lambda_{i+1}^{-1}$. Figure 3.17 illustrates this for a sample image.

The average band power $p_i(B_i)$ is calculated by averaging $|S(u,v)|^2$ over all (u,v) in the band. The average power for the difference image, $P_d(B_i)$ is calculated similarly.

ABCDEFGHIJKLMNOPQRSTUVWXYZ
abcdefghijklmnopqrstuvwxyz
1234567890-=!@#$%^&*()_+~[]\{}|:;'",./<>?

**Test image: documents/palatino24pt.vip**

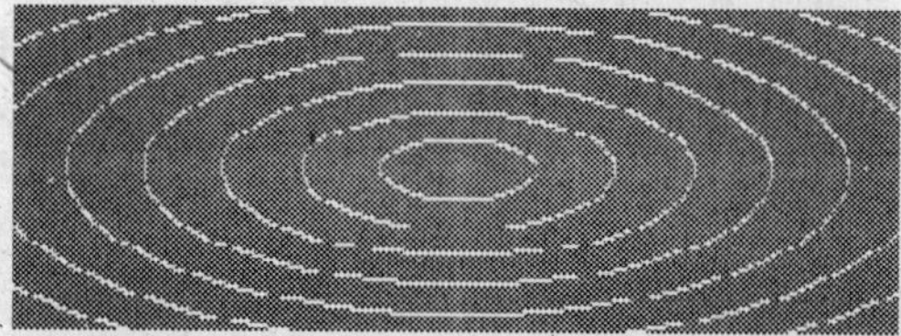

**Fourier spectrum power, with band delimiters superimposed**

**Figure 3.17: Illustration of how the frequency domain is divided into nonoverlapping bands**

The signal-to-noise ratio for each band can then be calculated as:

$$\mathbf{SNR}(B_i) = \frac{P_s(B_i)}{P_d(B_i)} \tag{3.34}$$

**Figure 3.18: Example signal-to-noise ratio plot**

This SNR ratio can be plotted as a function of normalized spatial frequency. Figure 3.18 shows such a plot for the image of Figure 3.17 degraded by additive white Gaussian noise with $\sigma^2 = 400$. This plot illustrates that there is little difference between the Wiener and Lee filter result for low frequencies $\lambda^{-1} \approx 0.1$. However, for higher frequencies $0.3 \leq \lambda^{-1} \leq 0.7$ the Lee filter has much better performance.

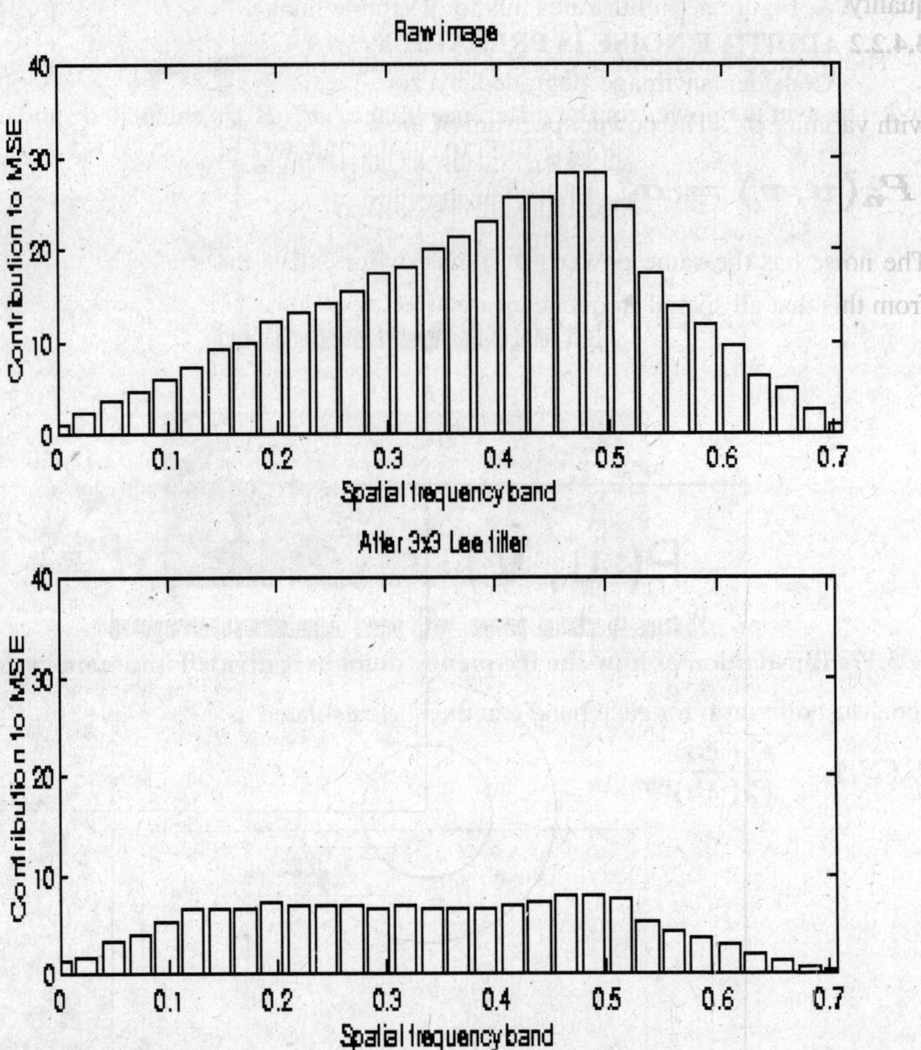


**Figure 3.19: Example plot showing how MSE is distributed over frequency bands. The top figure illustrates that noise power is proportional to band area**

These SNR plots can be somewhat deceptive, since they do not convey how much noise is left in each band. From Figure 3.18, one might conclude that the very high frequency bands $0.5 \leq \lambda^{-1} \leq 0.7$ need improvement the most, since they have the lowest SNR. A better approach is to look at how the total MSE is distributed over frequency bands (Figure 3.19). The top plot shows how each band contributes to the total MSE for the raw image. Since additive white noise has a flat power spectrum, the contribution of each band is proportional to its area in the frequency domain. From the bottom plot, it is clear that comparatively little noise remains in the very high and very low frequency bands. The bands $0.1 \leq \lambda^{-1} \leq 0.5$ need the most improvement. The frequency-domain SNR still does not give a complete picture of the image restoration result. For example, it does not distinguish between visually important and unimportant features. For this reason, it is important to look at the images themselves for a subjective estimate of image quality.

### 3.4.2.2 ADDITIVE NOISE IS PRIMARILY A LOCAL PROCESS

Consider an image degraded by zero-mean, Additive White Gaussian Noise (AWGN) with variance $\sigma_n^2$. The power spectrum of the noise is:

$$P_n(u, v) = \sigma_n^2 \tag{3.35}$$

The noise has the same power ($\sigma_n^2$) everywhere in the frequency domain. One might conclude from this that all spatial frequencies are affected equally by the noise, but this is misleading.

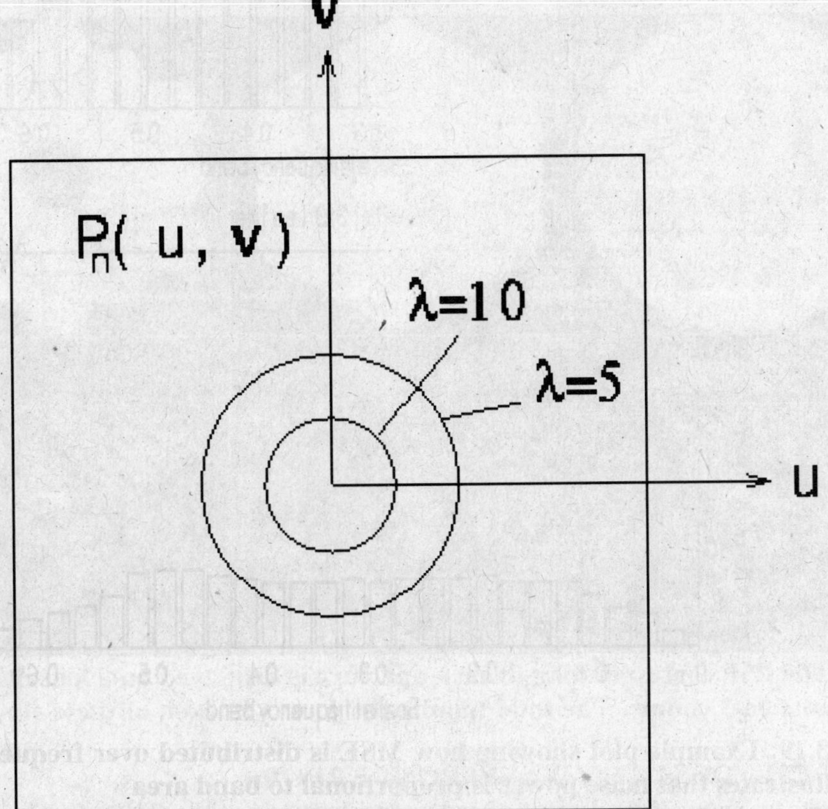


**Figure 3.20:** Frequency-domain view of additive noise

Figure 3.20 illustrates the noise power spectrum. Low frequencies lie (roughly) inside the circle $\lambda = 10$ ($\lambda$) is the wavelength of the frequency component, in pixels). The amount of noise power inside this circle can be approximated by comparing its area to the area of the transform. The circle area is $\pi(1/10)^2 \approx 0.0314$.

The domain of the transform is $[-0.5,+0.5]^2$, which has area 1. So the fraction of noise which lies at wavelengths above 10 pixels is only 0.0314, or about 3%. Similarly, only 12.6% of the noise lies at wavelengths above 5 pixels. The signal strength is typically very strong for wavelengths below 10 pixels, so the effect of the low-frequency noise on the signal-to-noise ratio is minor.

### 3.4.2.3 IMPACT OF THE PUPIL SHAPE ON THE PSF

To lowest order the PSF of an imaging system is determined by two things: the pupil shape and the wave front errors. Often, the shape of the pupil is well known and relatively simple, as in the case of a circular or annular aperture. However, more complex pupils are increasingly common for large systems (the JWST and Keck pupils are prime examples). Errors in the wave front can arise from a variety of sources, including imperfections in the systems optics (which tend to be static or semi-static) or atmospheric variations (as in the case for ground-based observations), and can be extremely difficult to determine. Here, we illustrate how the pupil shape affects the PSF, building from an open circular pupil of diameter ~6.5 m (left), a hexagonal pupil of diameter ~ 6.5 m (center), and a realistic representation of the JWST pupil (right).

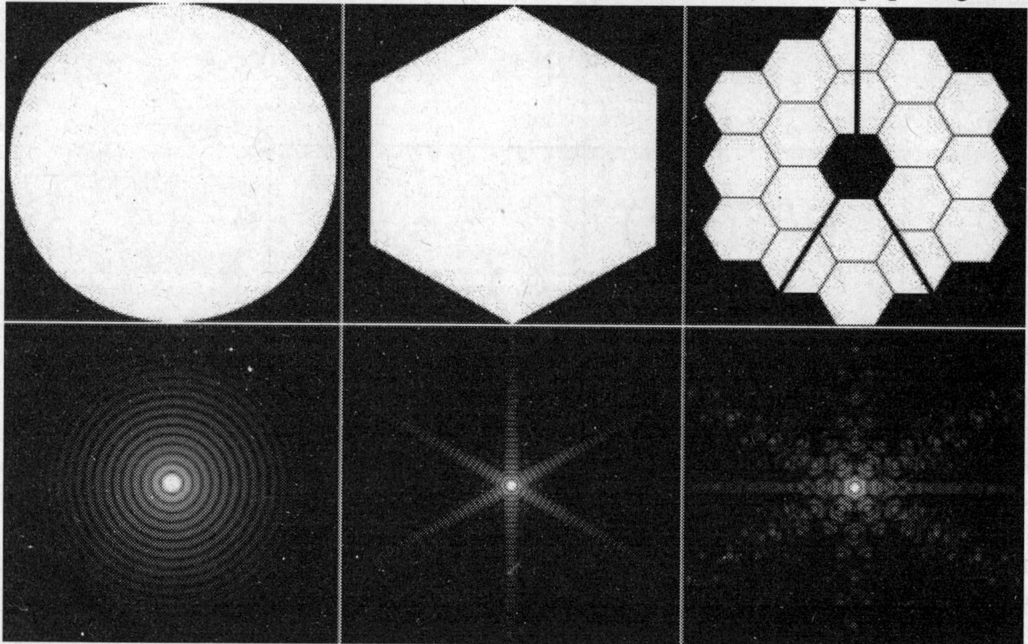

**Figure 3.21 The PSF corresponding to each aperture is displayed on a logarithmic grayscale from 1.0e-7 to 1.0e-3 counts. The total number of counts in each of these simulated PSFs is 1.0**

### 3.4.2.4 PSF DEPENDENCE ON WAVEFRONT ERRORS

In order to quantify the impact of expected variations of the PSF over time, we consider a number of different realizations of the JWST PSF provided to us by the JWST Project. These PSFs differ in the specific distribution of the wavefront error across the pupil; all satisfy, in a statistical sense, Revision T of the wavefront error budget, both in total rms wavefront error and in its distribution as a function of wavenumber (cycles across the pupil). As long as the error budget is satisfied, comparing these PSFs provides an upper limit to the PSF differences that could be encountered in the normal course of observations; the reason is that some wavefront errors, primarily higher frequencies and those arising inside NIRCam, are likely to be highly correlated between different times, and therefore using completely independent realizations can overestimate the temporal variation in the properties of the PSF.

**Figure 3.22 we compare two JWST Rev T OTE error budget Optical Path Difference (OPD) files (top) and their associated PSFs (bottom) for a wavelength of 2.0 microns**

In the above figure, we compare two JWST Rev T OTE error budget Optical Path Difference (OPD) files (top) and their associated PSFs (bottom) for a wavelength of 2.0 microns. OPDs are displayed on a linear grayscale from -400 to 400 nm, while PSFs are displayed on a logarithmic grayscale from 1.0e-6 to 1.0e-3. The OPDs include wavefront error (WFE) contributions from the JWST Optical Telescope Element (OTE), the Integrated Science Instrument Module (ISIM), and the Near-Infrared Camera (NIRCam). The RMS WFE of both OPDs is ~110 nm. While the differences in total RMS WFE are small, the impact of these differences on the resultant PSFs is measurable.

Overall Image Quality

Despite the potential challenges apparent with a relatively complicated PSF like the one we expect for JWST, we do expect that the overall image quality of JWST will still be very good. we show a comparison between simulated JWST + NIRCam images actual HST Advanced Camera for Surveys images of the Hubble Ultra-Deep Field. These images, kindly made available by Massimo Stiavelli, shows that JWST can achieve depth and resolution in the far visible and near-IR that will be better than achievable with HST for the wavelengths they have in common.

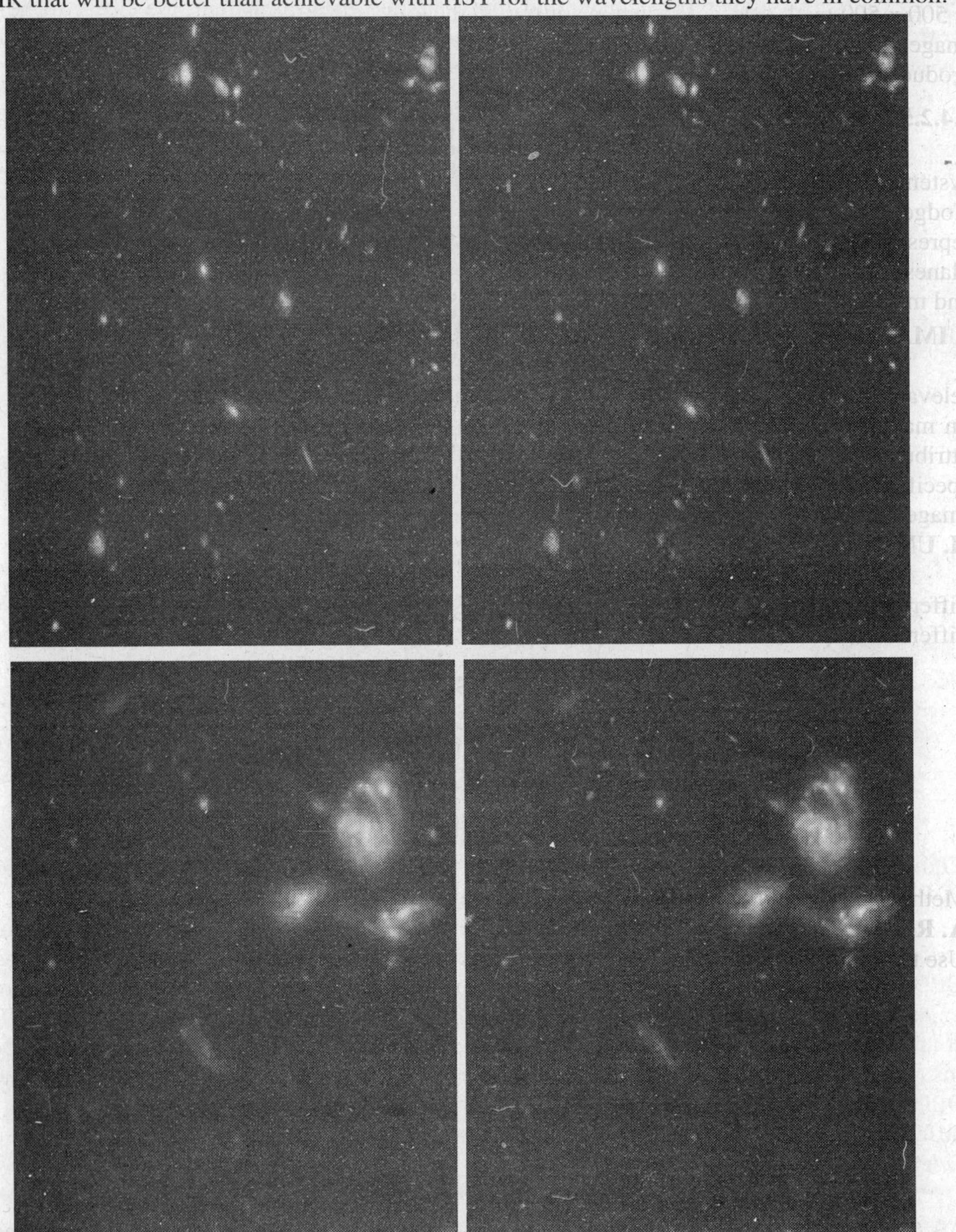

**Figure 3.23 an ACS image of the HUDF field (top left) in V-, I-, and Z-band, compared with a simulated JWST/NIR Cam image in F0707W, F090W, and F115W (top right)**

The figure above shows an ACS image of the HUDF field (top left) in V-, I-, and Z-band, compared with a simulated JWST/NIR Cam image in F0707W, F090W, and F115W (top right). A 500 x 500 pixel detail of the galaxy group in the upper-right of the field is shown beneath each image. Even though JWST is not optimized for optical observations, its large primary mirror produces a PSF that is small enough to compare favorably with HST/ACS imaging.

### 3.4.2.5 POINT SPREAD MODELING USING JWPSF

There are numerous tools available to model the point spread function from an optical system. Many of the simulated PSFs shown here made use of the JWPSF software tool (Cox and Hodge 2006). JWPSF was initially written as a user-friendly means to model the PSF at representative locations in the JWST optical train (including the respective instrument focal planes) at a variety of wavelengths. JWPSF was written in the Python programming language, and makes use of freely available compilers and software for analysis and visualization.

### I. IMAGE QUALITY

Image Quality and Clarity are general terms used to refer to the degree of visibility of relevant information in an image. Although these terms are rather vague, many physicists work on mathematical models of the imaging process which attempt to combine more specific image attributes (ie, resolution, contrast, and noise) into a single image metric which is appropriate for a specified imaging task (such as detection, classification, activity or size quantitation, etc.) The image metric is typically some sort of signal-to-noise ratio.

### II. UNSHARPNESS

Unsharpness and resolution refer to the degree of blurring along the boundaries between different regions of the image (usually defined by different patient organs or, in nuclear medicine, different radiopharmaceutical uptake distributions):

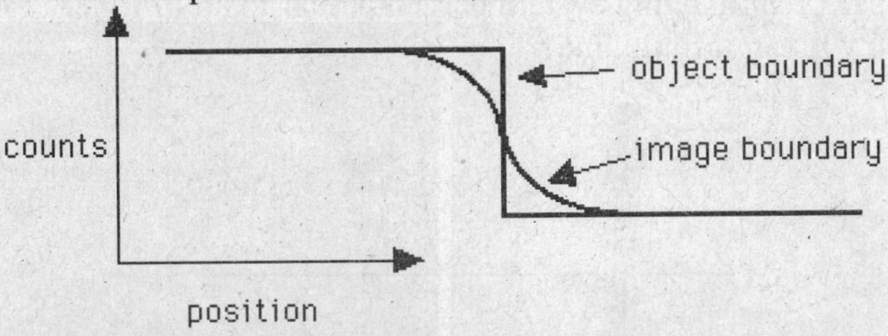


Methods for measuring the resolution of an imaging system

### A. RESOLVING POWER

Use two point sources of the isotope to be imaged:

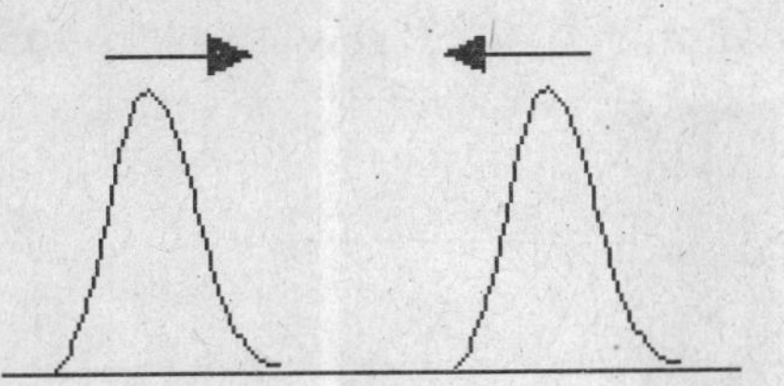

Move the sources toward each other and measure the separation at which the images of the two points cannot be distinguished.

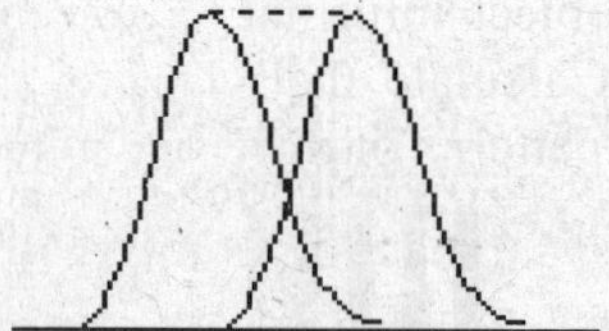

Note that the images will blur together completely at a separation approximately equal to the full-width at half maximum (FWHM) of the image of the point. When the resolution is specified as a single number, that number is usually the FWHM of the point-source image.

**B. POINT-SPREAD FUNCTION (PSF)**

The multidimensional image of a point source (2D for planar imaging, 3D for tomographic SPECT or PET imaging):

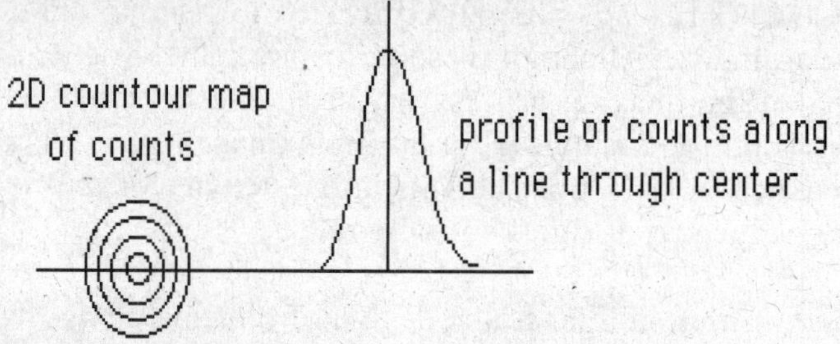


**C. LINE-SPREAD FUNCTION (LSF)**

The 1D response of an imaging system perpendicular to an infinitely long line source (the convolution of the PSF with an infinite line):

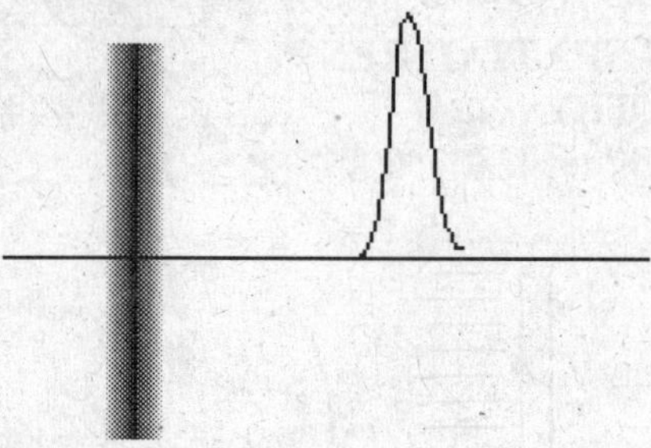

**D. EDGE-RESPONSE FUNCTION (ERF)**

The 1D response of an imaging system perpendicular to a straight boundary between two infinitely long regions (the convolution of the LSF with a step function):

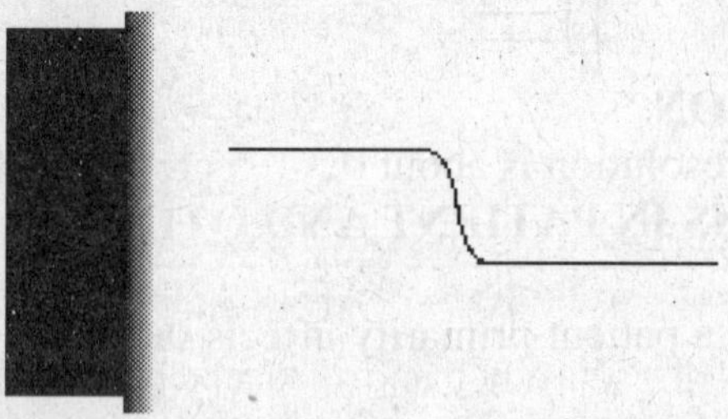

**E. MODULATION TRANSFER FUNCTION (MTF)**

The fidelity with which object information is transferred to the image as a function of spatial frequency in the object. Calculate the MTF as the Fourier transform of the PSF. Or, measure the MTF by imaging bar patterns of different spatial frequencies:

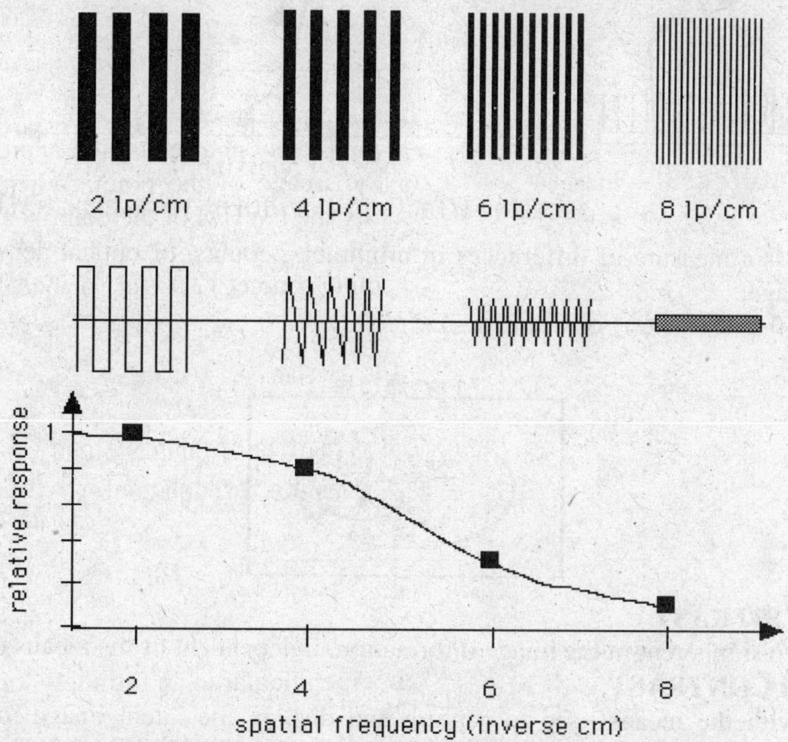


**F. FACTORS DEGRADING SPATIAL RESOLUTION**

**1. COLLIMATOR RESOLUTION**

Collimator resolution is typically 0.8 -> 2.5 cm FWHM in a patient and worsens with distance from collimator:

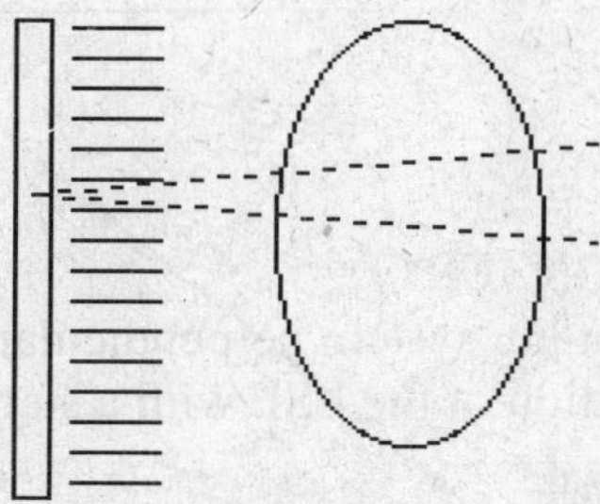

**2. INTRINSIC RESOLUTION**

A gamma camera's intrinsic resolution is about 0.3-0.5 cm FWHM.

**3. SCATTER OF PHOTONS IN PATIENT AND OTHER MATERIALS BEFORE BEING DETECTED**

Scatter of photons in a patient primarily affects the shape of the long "tails" on a realistic system PSF:

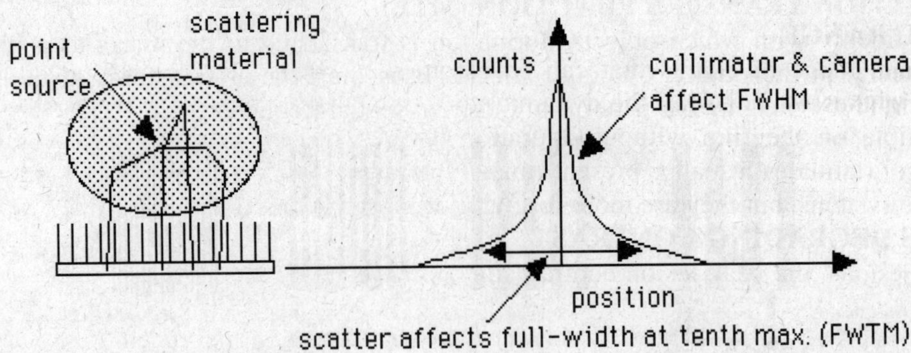


Contrast is a measure of differences in brightness, counts, or optical density in adjacent regions of the image:
C = (D1 - D2) / {0.5*(D1+D2)} or C = (D1 - D2) / D2

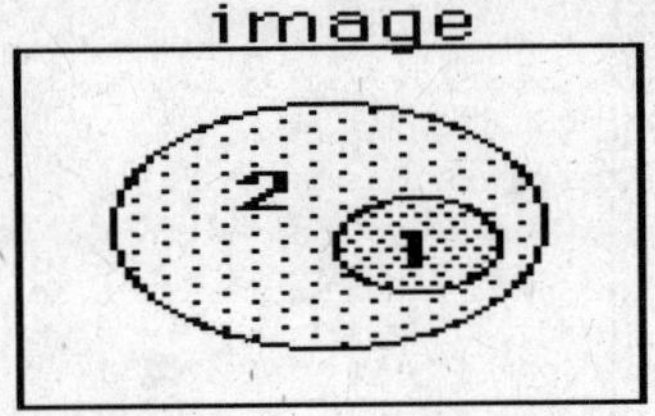


**A.SUBJECT CONTRAST**

The contrast inherent in the image information, independent of the means of display.

**B. DISPLAYED CONTRAST**

Varies with the means used to capture and display the latent image information. For filmed images, the displayed contrast will depend on the H&D curve, which relates optical density to film exposure. For computer displays, the displayed contrast will depend on the type of grayscale or colorscale used to transform the counts in each pixel to luminance on the display monitor. This transformation can also be changed with the "window" and "level" (or contrast and brightness) computer controls.

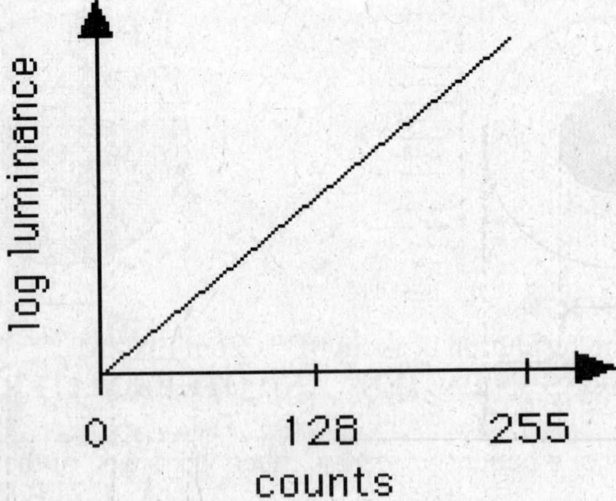

## C. DYNAMIC RANGE

The total range of counts that can be recorded between the minimum and maximum displayable brightnesses. For film, the dynamic range is called latitude , the range of exposures which are visible on the film without saturation (overexposure). Displays (films) with wide dynamic range (latitude) usually present image features with worse contrast than narrow dynamic-range systems, but they are more forgiving of sloppy technique.

## D. FACTORS DEGRADING CONTRAST

(a) For small lesions, the peak lesion contrast may be reduced by the system's spatial resolution (FWHM):

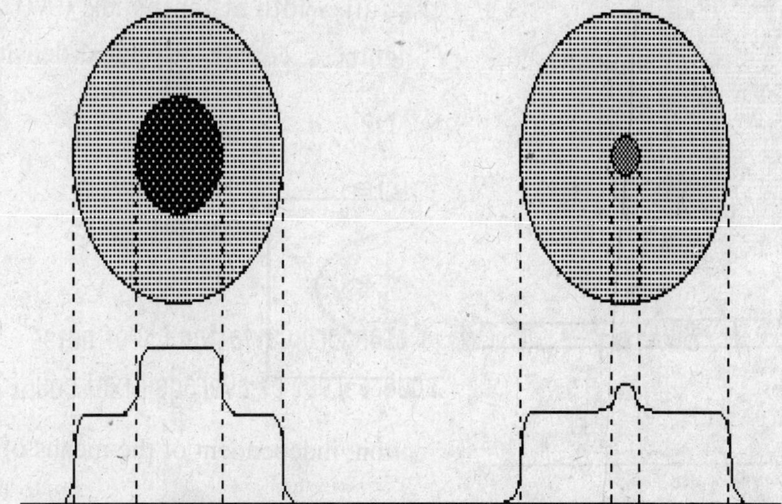

(b) For all lesion sizes, contrast is reduced by scatter in the patient (and other materials). The scatter tails on the PSF give rise to a broad, uniform (almost flat) scatter background which is added to the image of primary (unscattered) photons. This is perhaps the most significant source of contrast reduction in nuclear medicine.

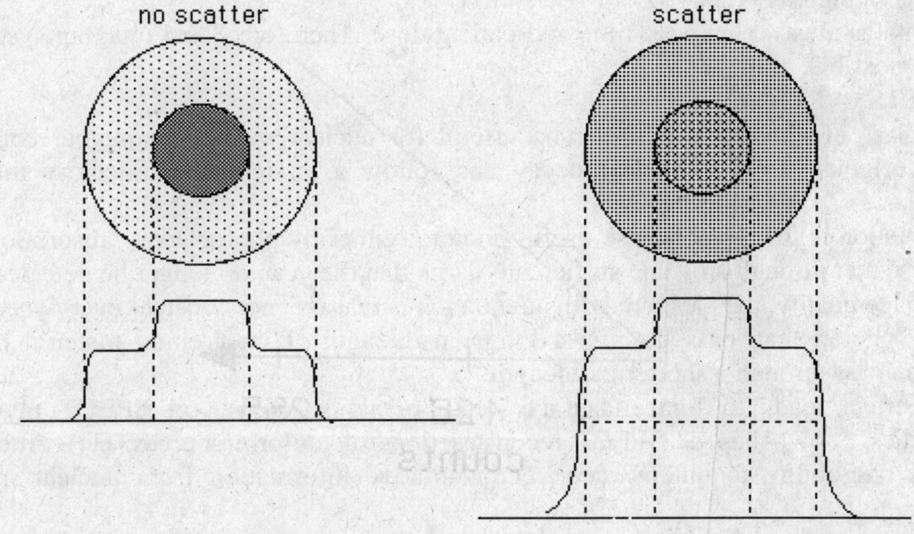

## IV. IMAGE NOISE

Image noise is the degree of variation of pixel values caused by the statistical nature of radioactive decay and detection processes. Even if we acquire an image of a uniform (flat) source on an ideal gamma camera with perfect uniformity and efficiency, the number of counts detected in all pixels of the image will not be the same.

The counting noise in nuclear medicine is Poisson noise, so that the pixel noise variance is equal to the mean number of counts expected in a given region of the image. Standard deviation is the square-root of the variance.

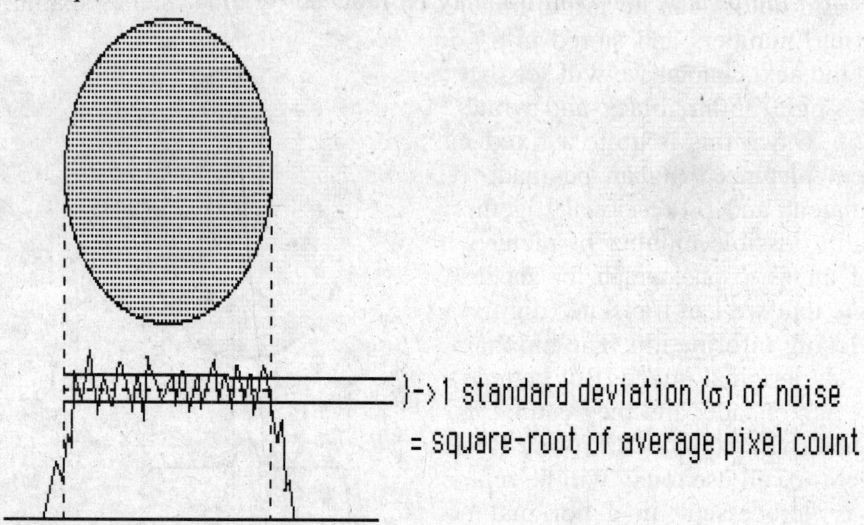


If a lesion is present, the signal-to-noise ratio (SNR) is a measure of how far (in units of standard deviations of noise) the lesion protrudes above (or below) the average background level. A lesion SNR of about 2 would be marginally detectable. A SNR of about 3 would be fairly easily detectable. One would always like to obtain as many counts as possible to reduce the percentage of image noise:

% image noise = ( sigma / N ) x 100% = 100/sqrt(N)

The limitations (as always) are scan time and patient dose. Therefore, ideal imaging systems are as efficient as possible.

## V. ARTIFACTS (ATTENUATION)

The class of photons which is most useful for nuclear medicine imaging consists of photons that originate from a nuclear decay and follow a straight-line trajectory through a collimator hole.

Attenuation is the loss of these useful photons, either by photoelectric absorption in the patient, or by scatter through an angle sufficiently large that they can no longer be detected.
In terms of image quality, the problem with attenuation is that it is not constant everywhere in the image. Fewer photons can pass through a longer pathlength of intervening material (eg, soft tissue) than can pass through a shorter pathlength.

This effect leads to image artifacts (eg, "breast shadows" on SPECT myocardial perfusion studies, "bowl-shaped" SPECT reconstructions of uniform sources, etc). Attenuation also degrades our ability to obtain accurate quantitative information from nuclear medicine images.

## 3.5 ROLE OF COMPUTERS

### 3.5.1 COMPUTER PLAYS VERY IMPORTANT ROLE IN IMAGE PROCESSING.

### 1. DIGITAL PHOTOS

Computers work well with numbers, and they can in principle handle any problem that can be translated into numbers. This is not just true for problems with a mathematical flavor. It is also true for photos. A photograph, after all, is just a large collection of dots on a piece of paper. Each dot can have brightness and perhaps a color. The number of possible dots, brightness values, and colors can be large, but is usually limited. This means that any photo can be translated into numbers and stored in a computer. How many numbers does it take to define a photo? In the next chapter we will see that roughly 20 million numbers can record all the information on a single 35mm black-and-white negative, where each number has a value between 0 and 255. Since this is quite a fixed number, we can even calculate the maximum number of different pictures that can be made on a 35mm negative. It is estimated that all photographers, amateur and professional together, take about 10 billion or $10^{10}$ pictures per year. The maximum possible number of pictures is 25620,000,000. At our current rate, then, we will not run out of things to photograph for another 1048,164,799 years, give or take a few. It is actually remarkable that we can translate (digitize) a photograph, any photograph, into a set of numbers without losing information. The numbers are much like a negative: at any time they can be used to recreate the original image. But better still, these digital negatives are much easier to store. They do not age or fade, and they can be manipulated just as easily in a computer as real negatives can be manipulated in a darkroom. It is not unlikely that within the next ten years the conventional camera we all use today will be replaced by a digital camera that takes photos on a floppy disk that is "processed" in a nor mal personal computer with the type of software presented in this book. The photos can be shown on a television set or printed with a high- resolution film printer that may someday be as standard as the dot matrix printer of a personal computer today. There are signs that this development is under way. Equipment for image recording and replay has over the years become smaller and smaller, so much so that the difference in size between the latest video "camcorders" and a nor mal SLR (single-lens reflex) photo camera has become almost negligible. In the fall of 1986 companies such as RCA, Hitachi, NEC, and Toshiba introduced the first digital video recorders that internally sample and digitize video images. So far, the digital capabilities of these recorders are used mostly for special effects such as high-quality freeze frame, slow motion, and "insert pictures" (a second video image inserted in the corner of the screen). The move , however, is in the direction of a completely digital video system, and with that it will become very easy to hook up a video recorder to a computer and capture video images on a computer disk.

### 2. DIGITAL CAMERAS

Digital SLR cameras have been in development for almost ten years. It first became possible to build these cameras with the availability of large CCD arrays. The CCD or charge-coupled device was invented by Willard S. Boyle and George E. Smith at Bell Labs in the early 1970s (the patent is dated December 31, 1974). It works much like a photocell, translating brightness values into electrical signals. By packing thousands of these CCD elements onto a chip, a solid-state image sensor can be constructed that can almost instantly sample an image and encode it into an electrical or even a digital signal. The first application of the CCD image sensors was in solid-state video and television cameras. The resolution of the image sensor depends trivially on the number of CCD elements in the array. The largest CCD device currently available is a 2048×2048 array made by Tektronix, Inc. It measures 2.5 inches square, which makes it also the largest integrated circuit made to date.

The CCD image sensors have a number of important advantages over other types of photo detectors, and even over conventional photographic film. First, they have a much higher quantum efficiency, that is, they are more sensitive to light. They also have a superior linearity and a large dynamic range, which means that there is a simple fixed relation between the brightness of an image and the response of a CCD element for a wide range of brightness values. Finally, the CCD sensors produce a high-quality and stable signal, with very little noise. They have, in fact, only one real disadvantage. The larger cells are still hard to make and are therefore expensive.

**Figure 3.24 Willard S. Boyle (l.) and George E. Smith Demonstration of the First CCD Camera in Dec. 1974**

The first truly digital cameras for making photographs have yet to be built. Kodak's subsidiary Videk has developed a high-resolution black-and-white CCD camera, named the Megaplus, that comes close to such a general purpose digital camera. The camera is built around a 1340× 1037 dot image sensor and produces digital output. So far, though, the Megaplus camera has no independent image storage capability; it is meant to be used as a scanner with a fixed connection to a personal computer. The first version being marketed by Videk is also quite expensive (over $10,000).

A low-resolution alternative to a fully digital camera is already available today: the still video camera. It has a CCD image sensor, it records photos on floppy disk instead of film, and in fact the only difference from a real digital camera is that it is based on video technology rather than computer technology. Let us look in a little more detail at some of these cameras, though it is good to keep in mind that they cannot compete with the price and resolution of conventional photo cameras and films just yet.

## 3. STILL VIDEO CAMERAS

Several large companies, most notably Canon, Fuji, Kodak, and Sony, have developed, or are in the process of developing, a new generation of SLR photo cameras using CCD image sensors and video technology. In 1980 Sony demonstrated the first "still video image" camera, the Mavica, at the Photokina in Germany. Canon soon followed with a still video camera called the RC-701. An experimental version was tested in practice during the Los Angeles Olympic Games in 1984. In May 1986 Canon announced it as a commercial product, and with that it became the first such camera actually being sold. Sony began marketing the Mavica camera in October 1987. Kodak followed with a prototype still video camera in the first half of 1988.

**Figure 3.25 Canon RC-701 camera**

Shown above is a picture of Canon's RC-701 camera. It looks like a nor mal SLR photo camera, it has all the same controls, but it takes photos on a floppy disk instead of on a film. All main companies are working on a line of products to support the new still video imaging systems. Canon, Sony, and Kodak all have dev eloped still video recorders and players that accept the new photo floppy disks. All three companies also have dev eloped still video image pr inter systems for producing hardcopy output.

The floppy disk for mat for the still video cameras has been standardized among the major companies. The roll-film of the future is a small 2×2 inch floppy disk that can store up to 50 color photos. To ease the transfer of images to and from video recorders, the photos are stored in video for mat, not in digital for m. An immediate consequence of this choice is that the resolution of the still video cameras is rather crude. The CCD image sensor in the cameras is capable of recording approximately 780×490 dots per image. The effective resolution of a video image, how ever, is typically not higher than 480 dots per line and 480 lines per image. To make matters worse, the Canon still video camera records only one of the two "fields" that make up a video frame, e.g., only the odd-numbered lines of the picture. This reduces the effective resolution of the pictures to about 480× 240 dots per image. The Kodak prototype camera and the Sony Mavica camera do not have this restriction, but also the resolution of a full video frame is still a far cry from the roughly 4000× 3000 dots of a conventional film.

The reason for this poor resolution is clearly not in the cameras but in the recording for mat chosen and its origin in video technology. To compete with conventional films the resolution of the new cameras will have to get at least 5 times higher, and the price will have to get at least that much lower. There is, however, reason to believe that this can and will happen. One possibility is that the next generation of digital cameras will use truly digital storage of data on miniature floppy disks that can be read directly by a personal computer. The other possibility is the adoption, at least for digital photography, of the new high-definition television standard (HDTV) that has, quite independently, also been in preparation for several years. The HDTV standard would double the resolution of television and video images. Below we will talk a little more about the type of equipment that is available for digital photography right now.

## 4. SCANNERS AND DIGITIZERS

The simplest method to digitize a photograph is to send it to a graphics lab that has good scanning equipment. For a modest fee, say between $10 and $15, they will digitize a print or a slide and provide you with a floppy disk or a computer tape in the for mat you specify.

Another possibility is to buy a graphics board for the specific personal computer that you own (e.g., one of the TARGA boards for the AT&T personal computers). Most graphics boards have a frame-grabbing capability, that is, they have a video input port that allows you to digitize video frames directly from a video recorder or video camera. The resolution will be lower than what you can get from a good scanner, but the convenience of having your own digitizer on line will be a definite plus.

By far the best method is, of course, to purchase your own photo-scanner or digitizer. For not too much money you can buy small, low-resolution scanners that connect directly to a personal computer. They are advertised in many popular journals, such as Byte magazine. Commercially available high-resolution scanners range in price from a few hundred to a few hundred thousand dollars. As can be expected, the more money you spend, the better scanner you can buy. A good scanner that connects to an IBM PC or an Apple Macintosh, for instance, is the SpectraFax 200, made by the SpectraFax Corporation, in Naples, Florida. The scanner can digitize 8×10 inch color prints at 200 dots per inch, and costs about $4000.

The scanner that was used to digitize photos for this book costs about $30,000. It can scan both opaque and transparent images (i.e., both prints and negatives) at up to 750 dots per inch (8 bits per dot) over an image area of maximally 8×10 inches. It is sold by Imagitex Inc., in Nashua, New Hampshire. Most digitizers of this type hold a single array of photo cells or CCD elements that can be moved mechanically along the length of a picture. Line by line the picture can then be scanned, with a resolution that is determined by the number of cells in the array. The electrical characteristics of the photo cell change under the influence of the light that falls on it. The scanner obtains a reading from each cell in the array that corresponds to the brightness of the image at the precise spot within the image that was focused on the cell. The cheaper scanners have fewer cells in the array and a smaller range of brightness values that can be distinguished. if you want to be able to process images of acceptable quality you need a system that can produce 512×512 dots (pixels) or more, with at least 8 bits per dot for black-and-white images, and at least 24 bits per dot for color images (8 bits each for red, green, and blue).

## 5. VIDEO PRINTERS AND FILM PRINTERS

After you have scanned in the image and processed it in the digital darkroom that lives in your home computer, the image must somehow be put back on film or paper. The cheapest solution is simply to snap a picture from the monitor of your system with a Polaroid camera, but you are not likely to be satisfied for long with the quality of such prints.

A good solution is again to send a floppy disk or a tape with the digital output to a graphics lab and have them produce a high-quality image with good equipment. The graphics lab in this case performs the function of the camera store where you would go with a conventional film to have prints made. The problem for the time being is that there are not many graphics labs that process digital images. But that may change.

An alternative is to use a still video image printer that will allow you to produce a medium-resolution print of any video image. Still video image printers are sold by Sony, Kodak, and Canon. The price is around $4000 for the printer and about $1 per print made.

The best, but also the most expensive, solution is to buy your own high-resolution digital film printer that allows you to write back images onto either Polaroid film or 35mm negatives. A digital film printer reads the encoded image and varies the brightness of a light beam that writes the picture back to film in accordance with the processed information stored in the computer. As with scanners, there are cheap solutions that work slowly, at low resolution or with only a few brightness values that can be written back to film, and there are expensive solutions that can work miracles. The most expensive film pr inters, such as the ones used to make animation movies at the Disney Studios, can cost up to half a million dollars. The one that was used to prepare this book is the QCR D4/2 system made by Matrix Instruments Inc. in Orangeburg, New York. It has a maximum resolution of 4096×4096 dots with a brightness range from 0 to 255. It is relatively slow: it takes about 20 minutes to put a color image back on film at full resolution. Compared to its (up to 50 times) faster brothers it is also relatively cheap. It costs about $20,000.

## 6. COMPUTER-AIDED DESIGN

Computer-aided design (CAD) is the use of computer technology for the design of objects, real or virtual. The design of geometric models for object shapes, in particular, is often called computer-aided geometric design (CAGD).

However CAD often involves more than just shapes. As in the manual drafting of technical and engineering drawings, the output of CAD often must convey also symbolic information such as materials, processes, dimensions, and tolerances, according to application-specific conventions.

CAD may be used to design curves and figures in two-dimensional ("2D") space; or curves, surfaces, or solids in three-dimensional ("3D") objects. CAD is an important industrial art extensively used in many applications, including automotive, shipbuilding, and aerospace industries, industrial and architectural design, prosthetics, and many more. CAD is also widely used to produce computer animation for special effects in movies, advertising, technical manuals. The modern ubiquity and power of computers means that even perfume bottles and shampoo dispensers are designed using techniques unheard of by shipbuilders of 1960s. Because of its enormous economic importance, CAD has been a major driving force for research in computational geometry, computer graphics (both hardware and software), and discrete differential geometry.

**Figure 3.26 An oblique view of a four-cylinder inline crankshaft with pistons**

The term graphic design can refer to a number of artistic and professional disciplines which focus on visual communication and presentation. Various methods are used to create and combine symbols, images and/or words to create a visual representation of ideas and messages. A graphic designer may use typography, visual arts and page layout techniques to produce the final result. Graphic design often refers to both the process (designing) by which the communication is created and the products (designs) which are generated.

Common uses of graphic design include magazines, advertisements, product packaging and web design. For example, a product package might include a logo or other artwork, organized text and pure design elements such as shapes and color which unify the piece. Composition is one of the most important features of graphic design especially when using pre-existing materials or diverse elements.

## 7. VIRTUAL REALITY

**Figure 3.27 U.S. Navy personnel using a VR parachute trainer**

Virtual reality (VR) is a technology which allows a user to interact with a computer-simulated environment, whether that environment is a simulation of the real world or an imaginary world. Most current virtual reality environments are primarily visual experiences, displayed either on a computer screen or through special or stereoscopic displays, but some simulations include additional sensory information, such as sound through speakers or headphones. Some advanced, haptic systems now include tactile information, generally known as force feedback, in medical and gaming applications. Users can interact with a virtual environment or a virtual artifact (VA) either through the use of standard input devices such as a keyboard and mouse, or through multimodal devices such as a wired glove, the Polhemus boom arm, and omnidirectional treadmill. The simulated environment can be similar to the real world, for example, simulations for pilot or combat training, or it can differ significantly from reality, as in VR games. In practice, it is currently very difficult to create a high-fidelity virtual reality experience, due largely to technical limitations on processing power, image resolution and communication bandwidth. However, those limitations are expected to eventually be overcome as processor, imaging and data communication technologies become more powerful and cost-effective over time.

Virtual Reality is often used to describe a wide variety of applications, commonly associated with its immersive, highly visual, 3D environments. The development of CAD software, graphics hardware acceleration, head mounted displays; database gloves and miniaturization have helped popularize the notion. In the book The Metaphysics of Virtual Reality, Michael Heim identifies seven different concepts of Virtual Reality: simulation, interaction, artificiality, immersion, telepresence, full-body immersion, and network communication. The definition still has a certain futuristic romanticism attached. People often identify VR with Head Mounted Displays and Data Suits.

## 8. DIGITAL ART

Digital art most commonly refers to art created on a computer in digital form. In an expanded sense, "digital art" is a term applied to contemporary art that uses the methods of mass production or digital media.[2] The impact of digital technology has transformed traditional activities such as painting, drawing and sculpture, while new forms, such as net art, digital installation art, and virtual reality, have been recognized artistic practices.[3] More generally the term digital artist is used to describe an artist who makes use of digital technologies in the production of art. Digital artists are artists who make digital art using computer graphics software, digital photography technology and computer assisted painting to create art.

## 9. DIGITAL TECHNIQUES

Digital art can be purely computer-generated (such as fractals and algorithmic art) or taken from other sources, such as a scanned photograph or an image drawn using vector graphics software using a mouse or graphics tablet. Though technically the term may be applied to art done using other media or processes and merely scanned in, it is usually reserved for art that has been non-trivially modified by a computing process (such as a computer program, microcontroller or any electronic system capable of interpreting an input to create an output); digitized text data and raw audio and video recordings are not usually considered digital art in themselves, but can be part of the larger project of computer art and information art. Artworks are considered digital painting when created in similar fashion to non-digital paintings but using software on a computer platform and digitally outputting the resulting image as painted on canvas. The availability and popularity of photograph manipulation software has spawned a vast and creative library of highly modified images, many bearing little or no hint of the original image. Using electronic versions of brushes, filters and enlargers, these "neographers" produce images unattainable through conventional photographic tools. In addition, digital artists may manipulate scanned drawings, paintings, collages or lithographs, as well as using any of the above-mentioned techniques in combination. Artists also use many other sources of electronic information and programs to create their work.

3D graphics are created via the process of designing complex imagery from geometric shapes, polygons or NURBS curves to create 3 dimensional shapes, objects and scenes for use in various media such as film, television, print, rapid prototyping and the special visual effects. There are many software programs for doing this. The technology can enable collaboration, lending itself to sharing and augumenting by a creative effort similar to the open source movement, and the creative commons in which users can collaborate in a project to create unique pieces of art.

The mainstream media uses a lot of digital art in advertisements and computers are used extensively in film to produce special effects. Desktop publishing has had a huge impact on the publishing world, although that is more related to graphic design. Computers are also commonly used to make music, especially electronic music, since they present a powerful way to arrange and create sound samples. It is possible that general acceptance of the value of digital art will progress in much the same way as the increased acceptance of electronically produced music over the last three decades.

Digital Photography and digital printing is now an acceptable medium of creation and presentation by major museums and galleries, and the work of digital artists is gaining ground, through robotic installation, net art, immersive virtual reality and software art. But the work of artists who produce digital paintings and digital printmakers is beginning to find acceptance, as the output capabilities advance and quality increases. Internationally, many museums are now beginning to collect digital art such as the San Jose Museum of Art and the Victoria and Albert Museum print department also has a reasonable but small collection of digital art. One reason why the established art community finds it difficult to accept digital art is the erroneous perception of digital prints being endlessly reproducible. Many artists though are erasing the relevant image file after the first print, thus making it a unique artwork.

Some say we are now in a postdigital era, where digital technologies are no longer a novelty in the art world, and "the medium is the message"(Marshall McLuhan). Digital tools have now become an integral part of the process of making art. As silicon-dry digital media converges with wet biological systems, Roy Ascott has pointed to the emergence of a "moistmedia" substrate for 21st century art.

Computer-generated art is art created with a computer, from models created by the artist. The term is usually applied to works created entirely with a computer. Movies make heavy use of computer-generated graphics; they are called computer-generated imagery (CGI) in the film industry. In the 1990s, and early 2000s CGI advanced enough so that for the first time it was possible to create realistic 3D computer animation. The film The Phantom Menace was widely noted for its heavy use of computer graphics.

There are two main paradigms in computer generated imagery. The simplest is 2D computer graphics which reflect how you might draw using a pencil and a piece of paper. In this case, however, the image is on the computer screen and the instrument you draw with might be a tablet stylus or a mouse. What is generated on your screen might appear to be drawn with a pencil, pen or paintbrush. The second kind is 3D computer graphics, where the screen becomes a window into a virtual environment, where you arrange objects to be "photographed" by the computer. Typically a 2D computer graphics use raster graphics as their primary means of source data representations, whereas 3D computer graphics use vector graphics in the creation of immersive virtual reality installations. A possible third paradigm is to generate art in 2D or 3D entirely through the execution of algorithms coded into computer programs and could be considered the native art form of the computer. That is, it cannot be produced without the computer. Fractal art, Datamoshing , algorithmic art and Dynamic Painting are examples.

## 3.6 IMAGE DATA FORMATS

Image file formats are standardized means of organizing and storing images. This entry is about digital image formats used to store photographic and other images; (for disk-image file formats see Disk image). Image files are composed of either pixel or vector (geometric) data that are rasterized to pixels when displayed (with few exceptions) in a vector graphic display. The pixels that compose an image are ordered as a grid (columns and rows); each pixel consists of numbers representing magnitudes of brightness and color.

### 3.6.1 IMAGE FILE SIZES

Image file size—expressed as the number of bytes—increases with the number of pixels composing an image, and the colour depth of the pixels. The greater the number of rows and columns, the greater the image resolution, and the larger the file. Also, each pixel of an image increases in size when its colour depth increases—an 8-bit pixel (1 byte) stores 256 colours, a 24-bit pixel (3 bytes) stores 16 million colors, the latter known as true color.

Image compression uses algorithms to decrease the size of a file. High resolution cameras produce large image files, ranging from hundreds of kilobytes to megabytes, per the camera's resolution and the image-storage format capacity. High resolution digital cameras record 8 megapixel (1MP = 1,000,000 pixels / 1 million) images, or more, in truecolor. For example, an image recorded by an 8 MP camera; since each pixel uses 3 bytes to record truecolor, the uncompressed image would occupy 24,000,000 bytes of memory—a great amount of digital storage for one image, given that cameras must record and store many images to be practical. Faced with large file sizes, both within the camera and a storage disc, image file formats were developed to store such large images. An overview of the major graphic file formats follows below.

### 3.6.2 IMAGE FILE COMPRESSION

**There Are Two Types Of Image File Compression Algorithms: Lossless And Lossy**.

1. **Lossless compression algorithms** reduce file size without losing image quality, though they are not compressed into as small a file as a lossy compression file. When image quality is valued above file size, lossless algorithms are typically chosen.

**Figure 3.28 Lossless Image Compressions**

2. **Lossy compression algorithms** take advantage of the inherent limitations of the human eye and discard invisible information. Most lossy compression algorithms allow for variable quality levels (compression) and as these levels are increased, file size is reduced. At the highest compression levels, image deterioration becomes noticeable as "compression artifacting".

**Figure 3.29 Lossy Image Compression**

### 3.6.2 MAJOR GRAPHIC FILE FORMATS

Including proprietary types, there are hundreds of image file types. The PNG, JPEG, and GIF formats are most often used to display images on the Internet. These graphic formats are listed and briefly described below, separated into the two main families of graphics: raster and vector. In addition to straight image formats, Metafile formats are portable formats which can include contain both raster and vector information. Examples are application-independent formats such as WMF and EMF.

The metafile format is an intermediate format. Most Windows applications open metafiles and then save them in their own native format. Page description language refers to formats used to describe the layout of a printed page containing text, objects and images. Examples are PostScript, PDF and PCL.

#### 3.6.2.1 RASTER FORMATS

These formats store images as bitmaps (also known as pixmaps). For a description of the technology aside from the format, see Raster graphics.

**1. JPEG**

JPEG (Joint Photographic Experts Group) files are (in most cases) a lossy format; the DOS filename extension is JPG (other operating systems may use JPEG). Nearly every digital camera can save images in the JPEG format, which supports 8 bits per color (red, green, blue) for a 24-bit total, producing relatively small files. When not too great, the compression does not noticeably detract from the image's quality, but JPEG files suffer generational degradation when repeatedly edited and saved. Photographic images may be better stored in a lossless non-JPEG format if they will be re-edited, or if small "artifacts" (blemishes caused by the JPEG's compression algorithm) are unacceptable. The JPEG format also is used as the image compression algorithm in many Adobe PDF files.

The Exif (Exchangeable image file) format is an algorithm incorporated in the JPEG software used in most cameras. Its purpose is to record and to standardize the exchange of data between digital cameras and editing and viewing software. The data is recorded for individual images and includes such things as: camera settings, time and date, shutter speed, exposure, image size, compression, name of camera, color information, etc. When images are viewed or edited by image editing software, all of this image information can be displayed.

**2. TIFF**

The TIFF (Tagged Image File Format) is a flexible format that normally saves 8 bits or 16 bits per color (red, green, blue) for 24-bit and 48-bit totals, respectively, using either the TIFF or the TIF filenames. The TIFF's flexibility is both blessing and curse, because no single reader reads every type of TIFF file. TIFFs are lossy and lossless; some offer relatively good lossless compression for bi-level (black & white) images.

Some digital cameras can save in TIFF format, using the LZW compression algorithm for lossless storage. The TIFF image format is not widely supported by web browsers. TIFF remains widely accepted as a photograph file standard in the printing business. The TIFF can handle device-specific colour spaces, such as the CMYK defined by a particular set of printing press inks. OCR (Optical Character Recognition) software packages commonly generate some (often monochromatic) form of TIFF image for scanned text pages.

**3. RAW**

RAW refers to a family of raw image formats that are options available on some digital cameras. These formats usually use a lossless or nearly-lossless compression, and produce file sizes much smaller than the TIFF formats of full-size processed images from the same cameras. The raw formats are not standardized or documented, and differ among camera manufacturers. Many graphic programs and image editors may not accept some or all of them, and some older ones have been effectively orphaned already. Adobe's Digital Negative specification is an attempt at standardizing a raw image format to be used by cameras, or for archival storage of image data converted from proprietary raw image formats.

**4. PNG**

The PNG (Portable Network Graphics) file format was created as the free, open-source successor to the GIF. The PNG file format supports truecolor (16 million colors) while the GIF supports only 256 colors. The PNG file excels when the image has large, uniformly colored areas. The lossless PNG format is best suited for editing pictures, and the lossy formats, like JPG, are best for the final distribution of photographic images, because JPG files are smaller than PNG files. Many older browsers currently do not support the PNG file format, however, with Mozilla Firefox or Internet Explorer 7, all contemporary web browsers now support all common uses of the PNG format, including full 8-bit translucency (Internet Explorer 7 may display odd colors on translucent images ONLY when combined with IE's opacity filter). The Adam7-interlacing allows an early preview, even when only a small percentage of the image data has been transmitted. PNG, an extensible file format for the lossless, portable, well-compressed storage of raster images.

PNG provides a patent-free replacement for GIF and can also replace many common uses of TIFF. Indexed-color, grayscale, and truecolor images are supported, plus an optional alpha channel. PNG is designed to work well in online viewing applications, such as the World Wide Web, so it is fully stream able with a progressive display option. PNG is robust, providing both full file integrity checking and simple detection of common transmission errors. Also, PNG can store gamma and chromaticity data for improved color matching on heterogeneous platforms.

**5. GIF**

GIF (Graphics Interchange Format) is limited to an 8-bit palette, or 256 colors. This makes the GIF format suitable for storing graphics with relatively few colors such as simple diagrams, shapes, logos and cartoon style images. The GIF format supports animation and is still widely used to provide image animation effects. It also uses a lossless compression that is more effective when large areas have a single color, and ineffective for detailed images or dithered images.

**6. BMP**

The BMP file format (Windows bitmap) handles graphics files within the Microsoft Windows OS. Typically, BMP files are uncompressed, hence they are large; the advantage is their simplicity, wide acceptance, and use in Windows programs.

**7. PPM, PGM, PBM, PNM**

Netpbm format is a family including the portable pixmap file format (PPM), the portable graymap file format (PGM) and the portable bitmap file format (PBM). These are either pure

ASCII files or raw binary files with an ASCII header that provide very basic functionality and serve as a lowest-common-denominator for converting pixmap, graymap, or bitmap files between different platforms. Several applications refer to them collectively as the PNM format (portable any map).

### 3.6.2.2 VECTOR FORMATS

Raster image formats above (where the data describes the characteristics of each individual pixel), vector image formats contain a geometric description which can be rendered smoothly at any desired display size.

Vector file formats can contain bitmap data as well. 3D graphic file formats are technically vector formats with pixel data texture mapping on the surface of a vector virtual object, warped to match the angle of the viewing perspective.

At some point, all vector graphics must be rasterized in order to be displayed on digital monitors. However, vector images can be displayed with analog CRT technology such as that used in some electronic test equipment, medical monitors, radar displays, laser shows and early video games. Plotters are printers that use vector data rather than pixel data to draw graphics.

### 1. CGM

CGM (Computer Graphics Metafile) is a file format for 2D vector graphics, raster graphics, and text, and is defined by ISO/IEC 8632. All graphical elements can be specified in a textual source file that can be compiled into a binary file or one of two text representations. CGM provides a means of graphics data interchange for computer representation of 2D graphical information independent from any particular application, system, platform, or device. It has been adopted to some extent in the areas of technical illustration and professional design, but has largely been superseded by formats such as SVG and DXF.

### 2. SVG

SVG (Scalable Vector Graphics) is an open standard created and developed by the World Wide Web Consortium to address the need (and attempts of several corporations) for a versatile, scriptable and all-purpose vector format for the web and otherwise. The SVG format does not have a compression scheme of its own, but due to the textual nature of XML, an SVG graphic can be compressed using a program such as gzip. Because of its scripting potential, SVG is a key component in web applications: interactive web pages that look and act like applications.

### 3. ODG

ODG (Open Document Graphics) is an open standard.

OTHER IMAGE FILE FORMATS OF VECTOR TYPE INCLUDE:

- Encapsulated PostScript
- PDF
- SWF
- Windows Metafile
- XML Paper Specification (XPS)

### 3.6.3 DIGITAL IMAGE DATA FORMATS

In order to properly process remotely sensed data, the analyst must know how the data is organized and stored on digital tapes and how computers and software process the data. Understanding existing digital data formats is essential before the data can be processed. There are many different data formats used for storing digital remotely sensed data. Many commercial data suppliers such as EOSAT and SPOT provide radio metrically corrected data in a customer specified format. There are four major data formats used by government and commercial data suppliers:

1. Band Interleaved by Pixel (BIP) Format
2. Band Interleaved by Line (BIL) Format
3. Band Sequential (BSQ) Format
4. Run-Length Encoding Format

Most digital data are stored on nine-track tape (800, 1600, and 6250 bpi), 4- or 8-mm tape, or on optical disks. The nine-track and 4- or 8-mm tapes must be read serially while it is possible to randomly select areas of interest from within the optical disk. This may result in significant savings of time when unloading remote sensor data. The 4- and 8-mm tape and compact disks are very efficient storage mediums, as opposed to the large number of nine-track tapes required to store most images (Jensen, 1996).

### 3.6.3.1 BAND INTERLEAVED BY PIXEL FORMAT (BIP)

One of the earliest digital formats used for satellite data is band interleaved by pixel (BIP) format. This format treats pixels as the separate storage unit. Brightness values for each pixel are stored one after another. It is practical to use if all bands in an image are to be used. The table below shows the logic of how the data is recorded to the computer tape in sequential values for a four band image in BIP format.

All four bands are written to the tape before values for the next pixel are represented. Any given pixel located on the tape contains values for all four bands written directly in sequence. This format may be awkward to use if only certain bands of the imagery are needed. Often data in BIP format is organized into four separate panels, or tiles, consisting of vertical strips each 840 lines wide in the x direction and 2,342 lines long in the y direction. In order to read all four bands of the image, all four panels must be pieced together to form the entire scene (Campbell, 1987).

**Band Interleaved by Pixel Format (BIP)**

| | | | | | | | | | | |
|---|---|---|---|---|---|---|---|---|---|---|
| Line 1 | Pixel 1 | Band 1 | | Line 1 | Pixel 2 | Band 1 | | Line 1 | Pixel 3 | Band 1 |
| Line 1 | Pixel 1 | Band 2 | | Line 1 | Pixel 2 | Band 2 | | Line 1 | Pixel 3 | Band 2 |
| Line 1 | Pixel 1 | Band 3 | | Line 1 | Pixel 2 | Band 3 | | Line 1 | Pixel 3 | Band 3 |
| Line 1 | Pixel 1 | Band 4 | | Line 1 | Pixel 2 | Band 4 | | Line 1 | Pixel 3 | Band 4 |

### 3.6.3.2 BAND INTERLEAVED BY LINE FORMAT (BIL)

Just as the BIP format treats each pixel of data as the separate unit, the band interleaved by line (BIL) format is stored by lines. The table below, shows the logic of how the data is recorded to the computer tape in sequential values for a four band image in BIL format.

| Band Interleaved by Line Format (BIL) | | | | | | | | | | |
|---|---|---|---|---|---|---|---|---|---|---|
| Line 1 | Band 1 | Line 1 | Band 2 | Line 1 | Band 3 | Line 1 | Band 4 | | | |
| | Line 2 | Band 1 | Line 2 | Band 2 | Line 2 | Band 3 | Line 2 | Band 4 | | |
| | | Line 3 | Band 1 | Line 3 | Band 2 | Line 3 | Band 3 | Line 3 | Band 4 | |
| | | | Line 4 | Band 1 | Line 4 | Band 2 | Line 4 | Band 3 | Line 4 | Band 4 |

Each line is represented in all four bands before the next line is recorded. Like the BIP format, it is a useful to use if all bands of the imagery are to be used in the analysis. If some bands are not of interest, the format is inefficient if the data are on tape, since it is necessary to read serially past unwanted data.

### 3.6.3.3 BAND SEQUENTIAL FORMAT (BSQ)

The band sequential format requires that all data for a single band covering the entire scene be written as one file. Thus, if an analyst wanted to extract the area in the center of a scene in four bands, it would be necessary to read into this location in four separate files to extract the desired information. Many researchers like this format because it is not necessary to read serially past unwanted information if certain bands are of no value, especially when the data are on a number of different tapes. Random-access optical disk technology, however, makes this serial argument obsolete.

### 3.6.3.4 RUN-LENGTH ENCODING (RLE)

Run-length encoding is a band sequential format that keeps track of both the brightness value and the number of times the brightness value occurs along a given scan line. For example, if a body of water were encountered with brightness values of 10 for 60 pixels along a scan line, this could be stored in the computer in integer (213) format as 060010, meaning that the following 60 pixels will each have a brightness value of 10. Storing the two values 60 and 10 would require far less memory on disk or tape than storing 60 number 10s. However, if the data are exceptionally heterogeneous, with very few similar brightness values, this format is no better than the others.

### 3.6.3.5 DATA EXCHANGE STANDARDS

Data exchange is characterized as data import and data export. The data exchange process is not typically reciprocal, but rather, users import data purchased from data exporters (providers). These are usually government agencies or commercial data sources. To be successful, GIS users must know how to cope with the heterogeneous data environment. For data export, each internal data model must be converted to a specific file structure on disk or other media. The process is reversed for data import. The goal of data exchange is to transfer information to enable understanding of the phenomena being represented (Robinson, 1986).

There are three basic design strategies that can be used by data exchange software:

1. Direct Translation (Figure 3.31)
2. Switchyard Conversion (Figure (3.32)

3. Neutral Format (Figure (3.33)

**Band Sequential (BSQ)**
**Computer Compatible Tape Format**

**Single Volume Set** — Volume 1: Header File, EOF, Band 1, EOF, Band 2, EOF, Band 3, EOF, Band 4, EOF, Band 5, EOF, Band 6, EOF, Band 7, EOV — e.g. on CD ROM or 8 mm

**Multiple Volume Set** — Volume 1: Header File, EOF, Band 1, EOF, Band 2, EOF, Band 3, EOF, Band 4, EOV; Volume 2: Header File, EOF, Band 5, EOF, Band 6, EOF, Band 7, EOV — e.g. on 1600 or 6250 bpi tape

**Figure 3.30 Band Sequential Format (BSQ)**

The band sequential format (BSQ) for storing remotely sensed data on nine-track, 8-mm tapes, and CD ROMs. An ASCII header file contains all the information about the image, including date of acquisition, sensor system, sun elevation, sun azimuth, and resampling logic. Each band of imagery is stored as a distinct file composed of i rows and j columns separated by an end of file (EOF) from all other data. Each volume (e.g. tape or CD ROM) ends with an end-of-volume (EOV) marker. Multiple volumes make up a multiple-volume set (Jensen, 1996).

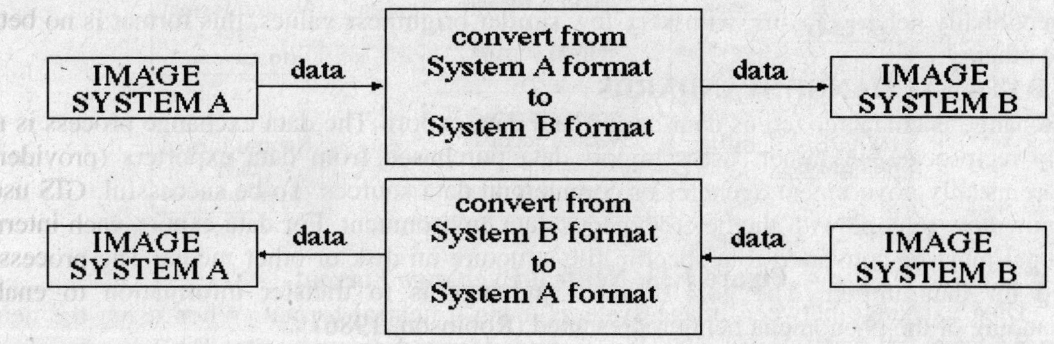


**Figure 3.31: Direct Translation**

Data exchange between image systems using direct translation. This design is an effective method of data exchange because it involves the most efficient path between two systems. It is a good choice when only two systems are involved but requires an understanding of how the two systems work. Routines can be written to fit the data in a desired format. Problems with this design develop when more than two systems are involved. In such a case, alternative routines can be written for each system exchange.

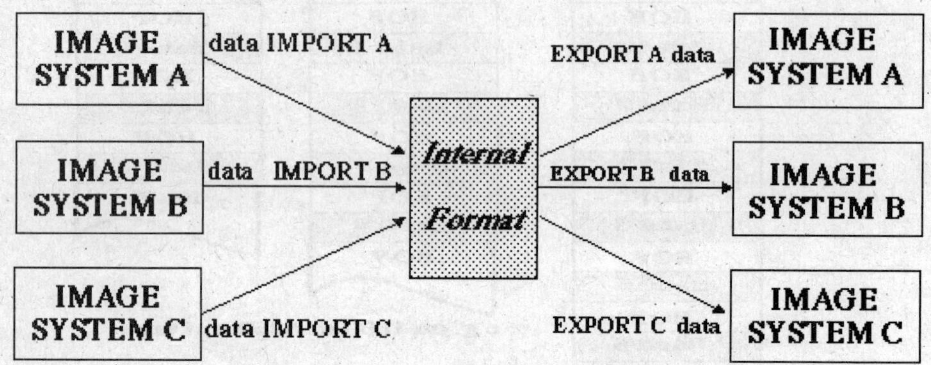


**Figure 3.32 Switchyard Conversion**

Data exchange between image systems using a "data switchyard". This method of data exchange avoids the factorial increase in the number of translation programs associated with direct translation. Data is converted into one internal standard. The software then translates data to the desired export format on output. Only two translation routines are required for all systems. This method works well when a large number of system translations are needed because it reduces the number of routines needed to convert the data. One important thing to consider when using the data switchyard is that attention must be paid to incoming and outgoing characteristics of the data so you don't lose information during the conversion. The central hub of data exchange must be all-inclusive so that you accommodate all the characteristics of the data.

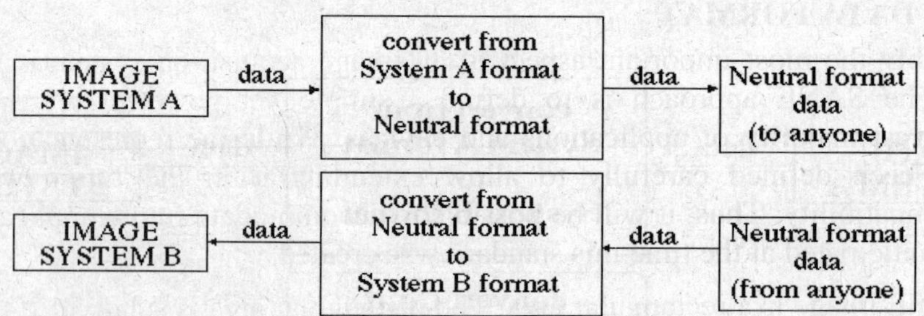


**Figure 3.33: Neutral Exchange Format**

Data exchange between image systems using a neutral format. When using the neutral exchange format, all parties must agree on one standardized common file. The advantage is that only two routines are required (one to read and one to write the exchange format). Problems occur when a routine is unable to effectively encode and decode data to the neutral format and data characteristics are lost. The neutral structure must be all-inclusive and all parties must agree on a common implementation.

| **Band Interleaved by Line Format (BIL)** | | | | | | | | | | |
|---|---|---|---|---|---|---|---|---|---|---|
| Line 1 | Band 1 | Line 1 | Band 2 | Line 1 | Band 3 | Line 1 | Band 4 | | | |
| | Line 2 | Band 1 | Line 2 | Band 2 | Line 2 | Band 3 | Line 2 | Band 4 | | |
| | | Line 3 | Band 1 | Line 3 | Band 2 | Line 3 | Band 3 | Line 3 | Band 4 | |
| | | | Line 4 | Band 1 | Line 4 | Band 2 | Line 4 | Band 3 | Line 4 | Band 4 |

### 3.6.4 IMAGE DATA FORMAT

Arguably the most important aspect of an image acquisition system is how images are represented. The SANE approach is to define a simple yet powerful representation that is sufficient for vast majority of applications and devices. While the representation is simple, the interface has been defined carefully to allow extending it in the future without breaking backwards compatibility. Thus, it will be possible to accommodate future applications or devices that were not anticipated at the time this standard was created.

A SANE image is a rectangular area. The rectangular area is subdivided into a number of rows and columns. At the intersection of each row and column is a quadratic pixel. A pixel consists of one or more sample values. Each sample value represents one channel (e.g., the red channel). Each sample value has a certain bit depth. The bit depth is fixed for the entire image and can be as small as one bit. Valid bit depths are 1, 8, or 16 bits per sample. If a device's natural bit depth is something else, it is up to the driver to scale the sample values appropriately (e.g., a 4 bit sample could be scaled by a factor of four to represent a sample value of depth 8).

## 1. IMAGE TRANSMISSION

The SANE API transmits an image as a sequence of frames. Each frame covers the same rectangular area as the entire image, but may contain only a subset of the channels in the final image. For example, a red/green/blue image could either be transmitted as a single frame that contains the sample values for all three channels or it could be transmitted as a sequence of three frames: the first frame containing the red channel, the second the green channel, and the third the blue channel.

Conceptually, each frame is transmitted a byte at a time. Each byte may contain 8 sample values (for an image bit depth of 1), one full sample value (for an image bit depth of 8), or a partial sample value (for an image bit depth of 16 or bigger). In the latter case, the bytes of each sample value are transmitted in the machine's native byte order. For depth 1, the leftmost pixel is stored in the most significant bit, and the rightmost pixel in the least significant bit.

## 2. BACKEND IMPLEMENTATION

A network-based meta backend will have to ensure that the byte order in image data is adjusted appropriately if necessary. For example, when the meta backend attaches to the server proxy, the proxy may inform the backend of the server's byte order. The backend can then apply the adjustment if necessary. In essence, this implements a ``receiver-makes-right" approach.

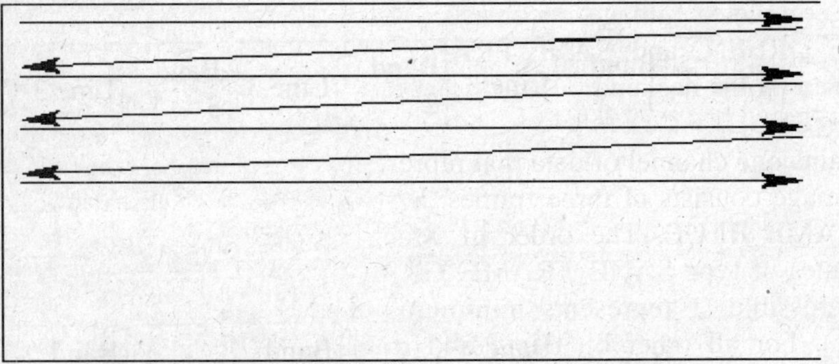

**Figure 3.34: Transfer order of image data bytes**

The order in which the sample values in a frame are transmitted is illustrated in Figure 3.34. As can be seen, the values are transmitted row by row and each row is transmitted from left-most to right-most column. The left-to-right, top-to-bottom transmission order applies when the image is viewed in its normal orientation (as it would be displayed on a screen, for example).

If a frame contains multiple channels, then the channels are transmitted in an interleaved fashion. Figure 3.35 illustrates this for the case where a frame contains a complete red/green/blue image with a bit-depth of 8. For a bit depth of 1, each byte contains 8 sample values of a single channel. In other words, a bit depth 1 frame is transmitted in a byte interleaved fashion.

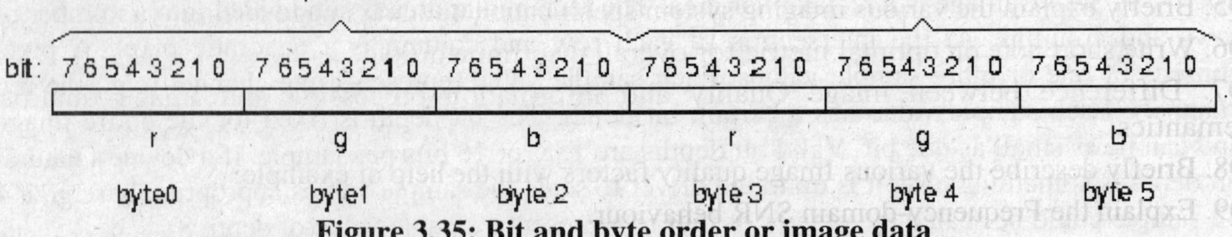


**Figure 3.35: Bit and byte order or image data**

When transmitting an image frame by frame, the front end needs to know what part of the image a frame represents (and how many frames it should expect). For that purpose, the SANE API tags every frame with a type. This version of the SANE standard supports the following frame types:

SANE_FRAME_GRAY:

The frame contains a single channel of data that represents sample values from a spectral band that covers the human visual range. The image consists of this frame only.

SANE_FRAME_RGB:

The frame contains three channels of data that represent sample values from the red, green, and blue spectral bands. The sample values are interleaved in the order red, green, and blue. The image consists of this frame only.

SANE_FRAME_RED:

The frame contains one channel of data that represents sample values from the red spectral band. The complete image consists of three frames: SANE_FRAME_RED, SANE_FRAME_GREEN, and SANE_FRAME_BLUE. The order in which the frames are transmitted chosen by the backend.

SANE_FRAME_GREEN:

The frame contains one channel of data that represents sample values from the green spectral band. The complete image consists of three frames: SANE_FRAME_RED, SANE_FRAME_GREEN, and SANE_FRAME_BLUE. The order in which the frames are transmitted chosen by the backend.

SANE_FRAME_BLUE:

The frame contains one channel of data that represents sample values from the blue spectral band. The complete image consists of three frames: SANE_FRAME_RED, SANE_FRAME_GREEN, and SANE_FRAME_BLUE. The order in which the frames are transmitted chosen by the backend. In frames of type SANE_FRAME_GRAY, when the bit depth is 1 there are only two sample values possible, 1 represents minimum intensity (black) and 0 represents maximum intensity (white). For all other bit depth and frame type combinations, a sample value of 0 represents minimum intensity and larger values represent increasing intensity.

# QUESTION BANK

Q1. Briefly explain image signal representation.

Q2. Discuss the image formation in image processing.

Q3. Briefly explain the Fourier transform in image signal representation.

Q4. Discuss the various image representations in details.

Q5. Briefly explain the various imaging system specification building image quality.

Q6. Write short note on optimal metric for overall discriminability.

Q7. Difference between image Quality and information processing and Image quality semantics.

Q8. Briefly describe the various Image quality factors with the help of example.

Q9. Explain the Frequency-domain SNR behaviour.

Q10. Write short note on Impact of the Pupil Shape on the PSF and PSF Dependence on wavefront errors.

Q11. Explain the Point Spread Modeling using JWPSF.

Q12. Briefly describe the role of computers.

Q13. Discuss the various image data formats.

Q14. Difference between the raster format and vector format.

Q15. Write short note on Band Interleaved by Pixel (BIP) Format ,Band Interleaved by Line(BIL) Format, Band Sequential (BSQ) Format and Run-Length Encoding Format.

# CHAPTER 4

# IMAGE ENHANCEMENT

## 4.1 INTRODUCTION

In image enhancement, the goal is to accentuate certain image features for subsequent analysis or for image display. Examples include contrast and edge enhancement, pseudo coloring, noise filtering, sharpening, and magnifying. Image enhancement is useful in feature extraction, image analysis and visual information display. The enhancement process it self does not increase the inherent information content in the data. It simply emphasizes certain specified image characteristics. Enhancement algorithms are generally interactive and application-dependent.

Image enhancement techniques, such as contrast stretching, map each gray level into another gray level by a predetermined transformation. An example is the histogram equalization method, where the input gray levels are mapped so that the output gray level distribution is uniform. This has been found to be a powerful method of enhancement of low contrast images. Other enhancement techniques perform local neighborhood operations as in convolution, transform operation as in the discrete Fourier transform, and other operations as in pseudo coloring where a gray level image is mapped into color image by assigning different colors to different features.

## 4.2 IMAGE ENHANCEMENT

Image enhancement processes consist of a collection of techniques that seek to improve the visual appearance of an image or to convert the image to a form better suited for analysis by a human or a machine. In an image enhancement system, there is no conscious effort to improve the fidelity of a reproduced image with regard to some ideal form of the image, as is done in image restoration.

Actually, there is some evidence to indicate that often a distorted image, for example, an image with amplitude overshoot and undershoot about its object edges, is more subjectively pleasing than a perfectly reproduced original. For image analysis purposes, the definition of image enhancement stops short of information extraction. As an example, an image enhancement system might emphasize the edge outline of objects in an image by high-frequency filtering. This edge-enhanced image would then serve as an input to a machine that would trace the outline of the edges, and perhaps make measurements of the shape and size of the outline. In this application, the image enhancement processor would emphasize salient features of the original image and simplify the processing task of a data extraction machine. There is no general unifying theory of image enhancement at present because there is no general standard of image quality that can serve as a design criterion for an image enhancement processor. Consideration is given here to a variety of techniques that have proved useful for human observation improvement and image analysis.

### 4.2.1 CONTRAST MANIPULATION

One of the most common defects of photographic or electronic images is poor contrast resulting from a reduced, and perhaps nonlinear, image amplitude range. Image contrast can often be improved by amplitude rescaling of each pixel (1,2). Figure 4.1(a) illustrates a transfer function for contrast enhancement of a typical continuous amplitude low-contrast image. For continuous amplitude images, the transfer function operator can be implemented by photographic techniques, but it is often difficult to realize an arbitrary transfer function accurately. For quantized amplitude images, implementation of the transfer function is a relatively simple task. However, in the design of the transfer function operator, consideration must be given to the effects of amplitude quantization. With reference to Figure 4.1(b), suppose that an original image is quantized to J levels, but it occupies a smaller range.

The output image is also assumed to be restricted to J levels, and the mapping is linear. In the mapping strategy indicated in Figure 4.1 (b), the output level chosen is that level closest to the exact mapping of an input level. It is obvious from the diagram that the output image will have unoccupied levels within its range, and some of the gray scale transitions will be larger than in the original image. The latter effect may result in noticeable gray scale contouring. If the output image is quantized to more levels than the input image, it is possible to approach a linear placement of output levels, and hence, decrease the gray scale contouring effect.

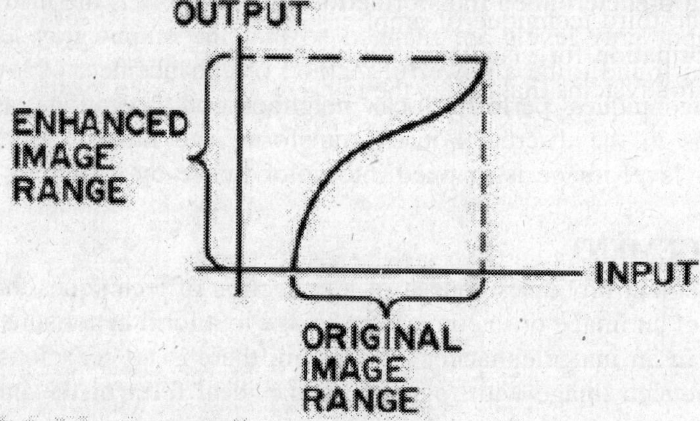


(a) Continuous image contrast enhancement

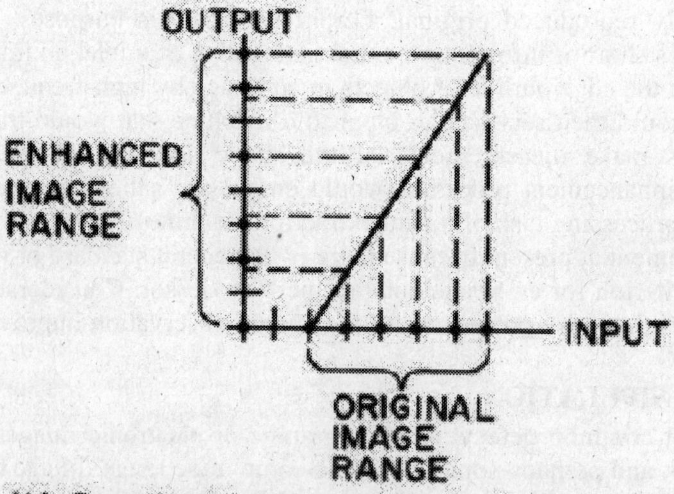


(b) Quantized image contrast enhancement

**Figure 4.1 Continuous and quantized image contrast enhancement**

#### 4.2.1.1. AMPLITUDE SCALING

A digitally processed image may occupy a range different from the range of the original image. In fact, the numerical range of the processed image may encompass negative values, which cannot be mapped directly into a light intensity range. Figure 4.2a illustrates several possibilities of scaling an output image back into the domain of values occupied by the original image. By the first technique, the processed image is linearly mapped over its entire range, while by the second technique, the extreme amplitude values of the processed image are clipped to maximum and minimum limits. The second technique is often subjectively preferable, especially or images in which a relatively small number of pixels exceed the limits. Contrast enhancement algorithms often possess an option to clip a fixed percentage of the amplitude values on each end of the amplitude scale. In medical image enhancement applications, the contrast modification operation shown in Figure 4.2 b, for $a \geq 0$ is called a window-level transformation.

The window value is the width of the linear slope, b-a; the level is located at the midpoint c of the slope line. The third technique of amplitude scaling, shown in Figure 4.2 c, utilizes an absolute value transformation for visualizing an image with negatively valued pixels. This is a useful transformation for systems that utilize the two's complement numbering

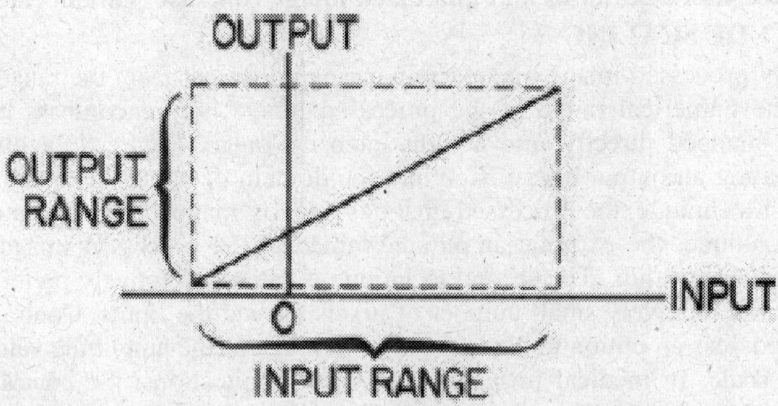


(*a*) Linear image scaling

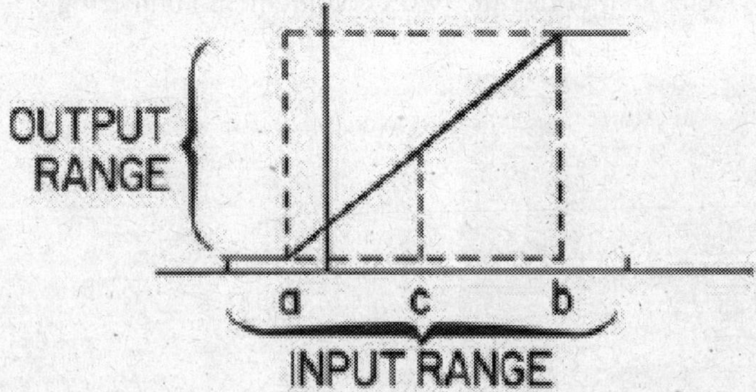


(*b*) Linear image scaling with clipping

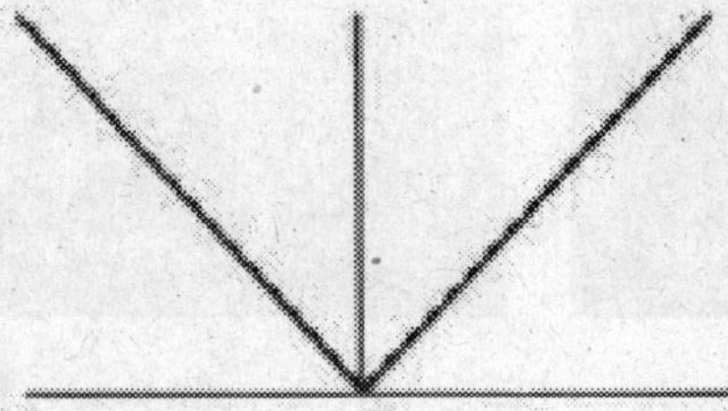

(*c*) Absolute value scaling

**Figure 4.2 Image scaling methods**

(*a*) Linear, full range, – 0.147 to 0.169

(*b*) Clipping, 0.000 to 0.169

(*c*) Absolute value, 0.000 to 0.169

**Figure 4.3 Image scaling of the q component of the yiq representation of the Dolls_gamma color image**

convention for amplitude representation. In such systems, if the amplitude of a pixel overshoots +1.0 (maximum luminance white) by a small amount, it wraps around by the same amount to –1.0, which is also maximum luminance white. Similarly, pixel undershoots remain near black. Figure 4.3 illustrates the amplitude scaling of the Q component of the YIQ transformation .Figure

4.3 (a) presents the result of amplitude scaling with the linear function of Figure 4.2(a) over the amplitude range of the image.

In this example, the most negative pixels are mapped to black (0.0), and the most positive pixels are mapped to white (1.0). Amplitude scaling in which negative value pixels are clipped to zero is shown in Figure 4.3 (b). The black regions of the image correspond to negative pixel values of the Q component. Absolute value scaling is presented in Figure 4.3 (c).

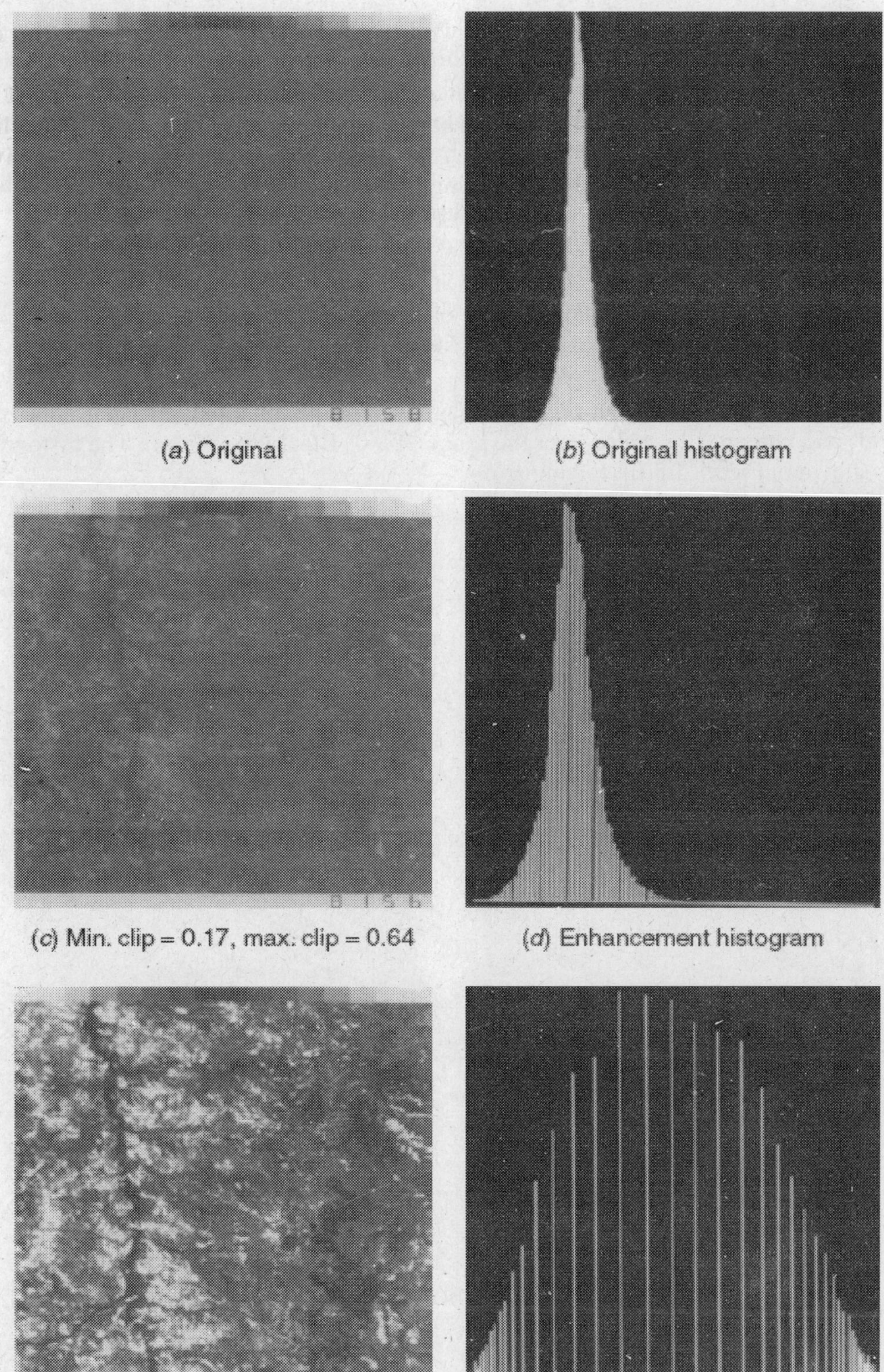

(*a*) Original

(*b*) Original histogram

(*c*) Min. clip = 0.17, max. clip = 0.64

(*d*) Enhancement histogram

(*e*) Min. clip = 0.24, max. clip = 0.35

(*f*) Enhancement histogram

**Figure 4.4 Window-level contrast stretching of an earth satellite image**

Figure 4.4 shows examples of contrast stretching of a poorly digitized original satellite image along with gray scale histograms of the original and enhanced pictures. In Figure 4.4 (c), the clip levels are set at the histogram limits of the original while in Figure 4.4 (e), the clip levels truncate 5% of the original image upper and lower level amplitudes. It is readily apparent from the histogram of Figure 4.4(f) that the contrast- stretched image of Figure 4.4(e) has many unoccupied amplitude levels. Gray scale contouring is at the threshold of visibility.

#### 4.2.1.2. CONTRAST MODIFICATION

Amplitude scaling of images that do not properly utilize the dynamic range of a display; they may lie partly outside the dynamic range or occupy only a portion of the dynamic range. In this section, attention is directed to point transformations that modify the contrast of an image within a display's dynamic range.

Figure 4.5 (a) contains an original image of a jet aircraft that has been digitized to 256 gray levels and numerically scaled over the range of 0.0 (Black) to (White). The histogram of the image is shown in Figure 4.5(b). Examination

(*a*) Original

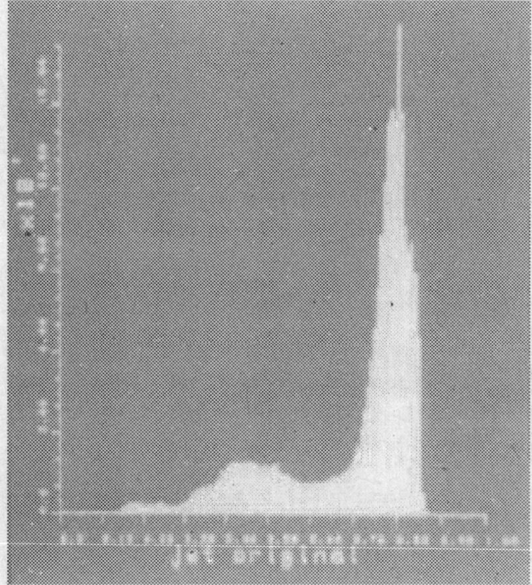


(*b*) Original histogram

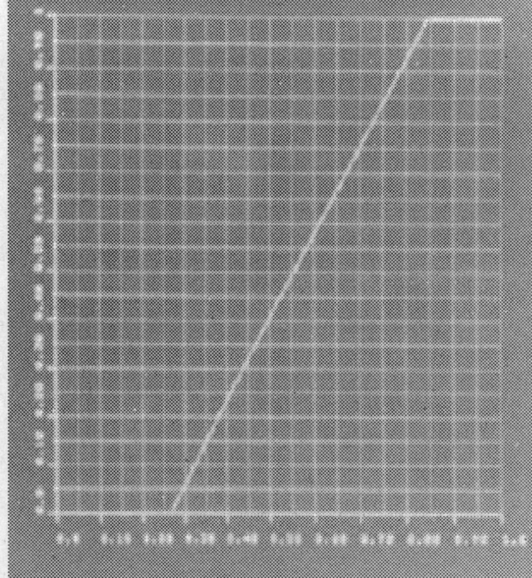

(*c*) Transfer function

(*d*) Contrast stretched

**Figure 4.5 Window-level contrast stretching of the jet_mon image**

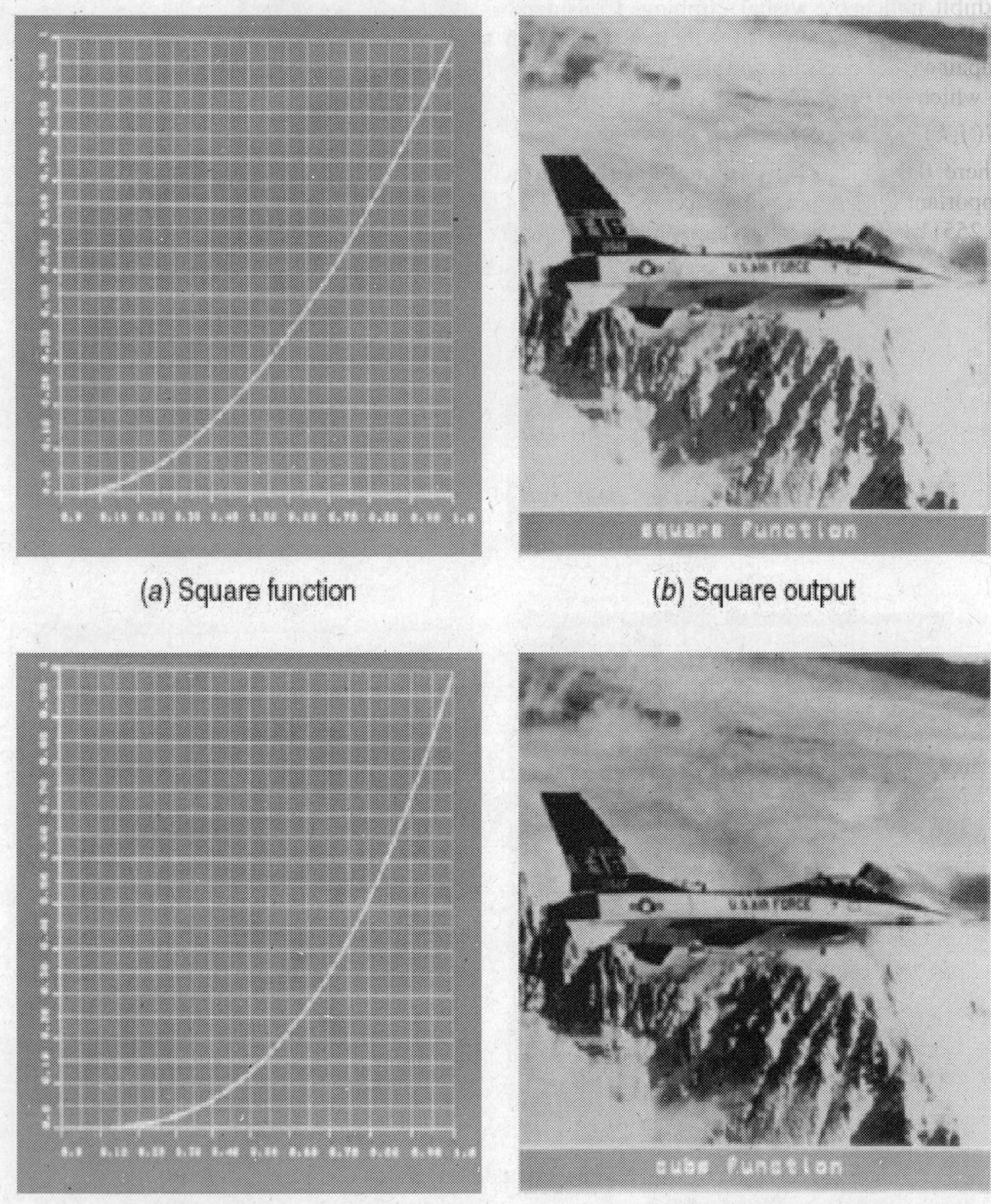


(*a*) Square function (*b*) Square output

(*c*) Cube function (*d*) Cube output

**Figure 4.6 Square and cube contrast modification of the jet_mon image**

of the histogram of the image reveals that the image contains relatively few lower high-amplitude pixels. Consequently, applying the window-level contrast stretching function of Figure 4.5(c) results in the image of Figure 4.5(d), which possesses better visual contrast but does not exhibit noticeable visual clipping. Consideration will now be given to several nonlinear point transformations, some of which will be seen to improve visual contrast, while others clearly impair visual contrast. Figures 4.6 and 4.7 provide examples of power law point transformations in which the processed image is defined by

$$G(j,k) = [F(j,k)]^p \tag{4.1}$$

where $0.0 \leq F(j, k) \leq 1.0$ represents the original image and p is the power law variable. It is important that the amplitude limits of Eq. 4.1 be observed; processing of the integer code (e.g., 0 to 255) by Eq. 4.1 will give erroneous results. The

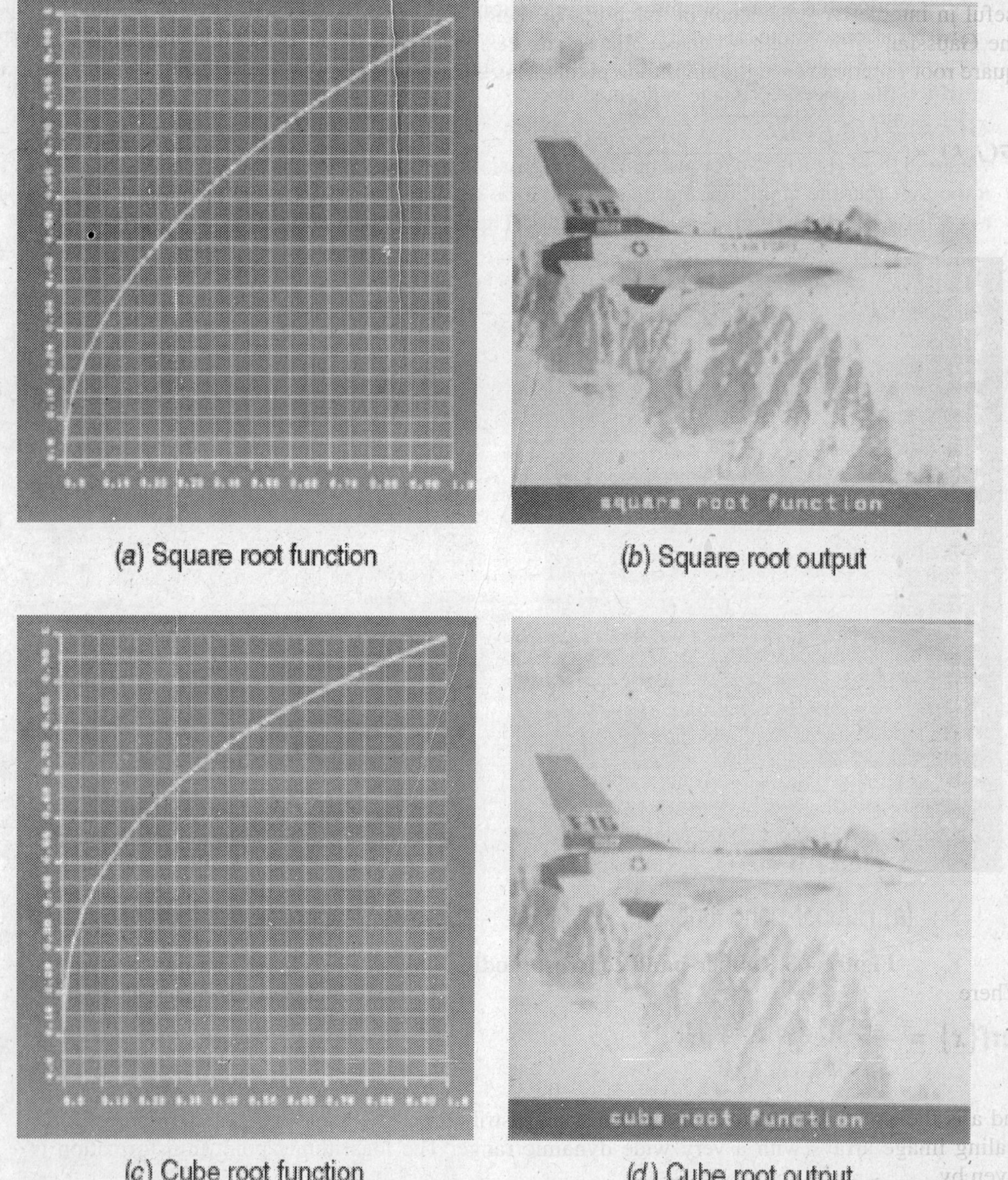


(*a*) Square root function (*b*) Square root output

(*c*) Cube root function (*d*) Cube root output

**Figure 4.7 Square root and cube root contrast modification of the jet_mon image**

square function provides the best visual result. The rubber band transfer function shown in Figure 4.8(a) provides a simple piecewise linear approximation to the power law curves. It is often useful in interactive enhancement machines in which the inflection point is interactively placed. The Gaussian error function behaves like a square function for low-amplitude pixels and like a square root function for high- amplitude pixels. It is defined as

$$G(j,k) = \frac{\operatorname{erf}\left\{\frac{F(j,k)-0.5}{a\sqrt{2}}\right\} + \frac{0.5}{a\sqrt{2}}}{2\operatorname{erf}\left\{\frac{0.5}{a\sqrt{2}}\right\}} \qquad (4.1\text{ (a)})$$

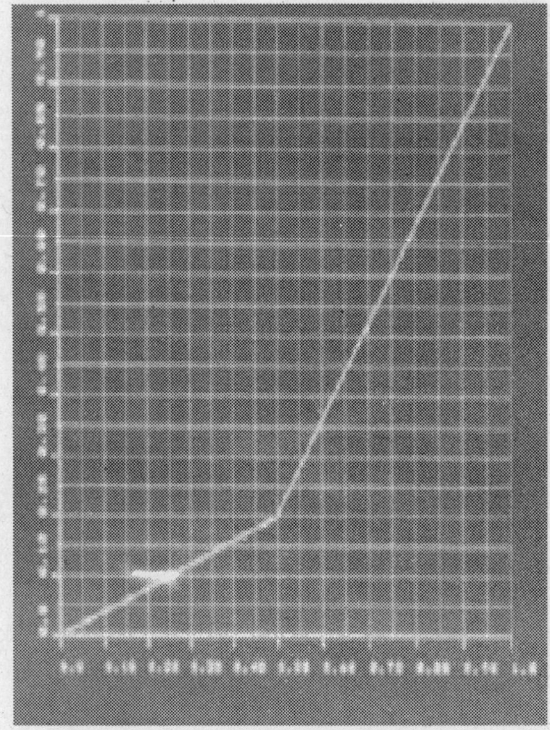

(a) Rubber-band function

(b) Rubber-band output

**Figure 4.8 Rubber-band contrast modification of the jet_mon image**

Where

$$\operatorname{erf}\{x\} = \frac{2}{\sqrt{\pi}} \int_0^x \exp\{-y^2\}\, dy \qquad (4.1\text{ (b)})$$

and a is the standard deviation of the Gaussian distribution. The logarithm function is useful for scaling image arrays with a very wide dynamic range. The logarithmic point transformation is given by

$$G(j,k) = \frac{\log_e\{1.0 + aF(j,k)\}}{\log_e\{2.0\}} \qquad (4.2)$$

under the assumption that $0.0 \le F(j,k) \le 1.0$ where a is a positive scaling factor. There are applications in image processing in which monotonically decreasing and nonmonotonic amplitude scaling is useful. For example, contrast reverse and contrast inverse transfer functions, as illustrated in Figure 4.9, are often helpful in visualizing detail in dark areas of an image. The reverse function is defined as

$$G(j,k) = 1.0 - F(j,k) \tag{4.3}$$

where $0.0 \le f(J,K) \le 1.0.$: The inverse function

$$G(j,k) = 1.0 \quad for 0.0 \le F(j,k) \tag{4.4 (a)}$$

$$G(j,k) = \frac{0.1}{F(j,k)} \qquad for 0.1 \le F(j,k) \le 1.0 \tag{4.4 (b)}$$

is clipped at the 10% input amplitude level to maintain the output amplitude within the range of unity.

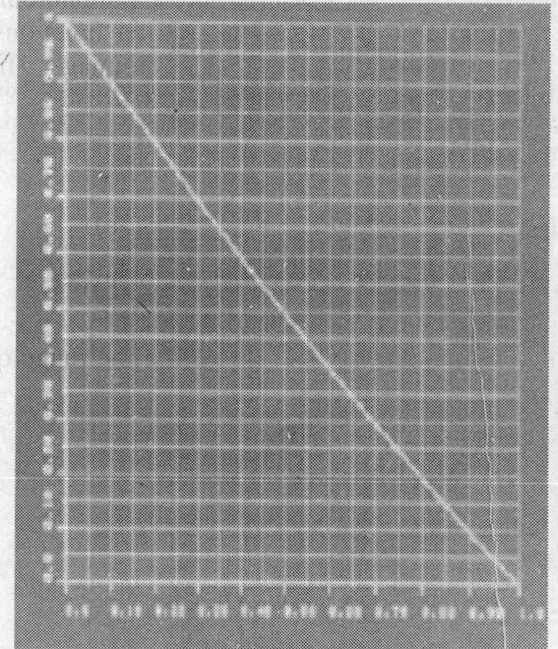

(*a*) Reverse function

(*b*) Reverse function output

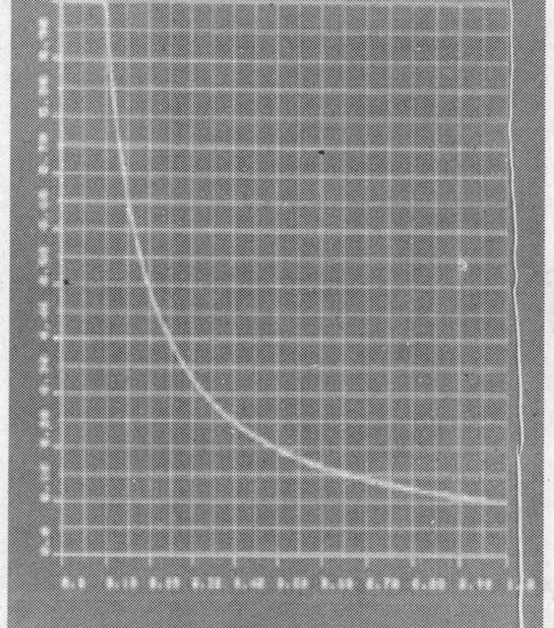

(*c*) Inverse function

(*d*) Inverse function output

**Figure 4.9 Reverse and inverse function contrast modification of the jet_mon image**

Amplitude-level slicing, as illustrated in Figure 4.10, is a useful interactive tool for visually analyzing the spatial distribution of pixels of certain amplitude within an image. With the function of Figure 4.10(a), all pixels within the amplitude passband are rendered maximum white in the output, and pixels outside the passband are rendered black. Pixels outside the amplitude passband are displayed in their original state with the function of Figure 4.10(b).

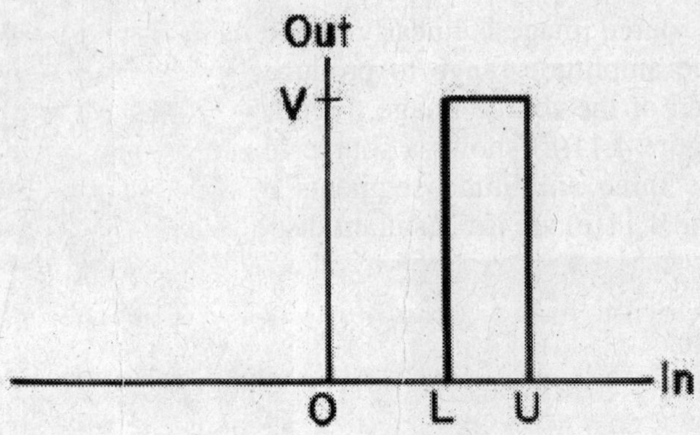

(*a*) Zero background scaling transformation

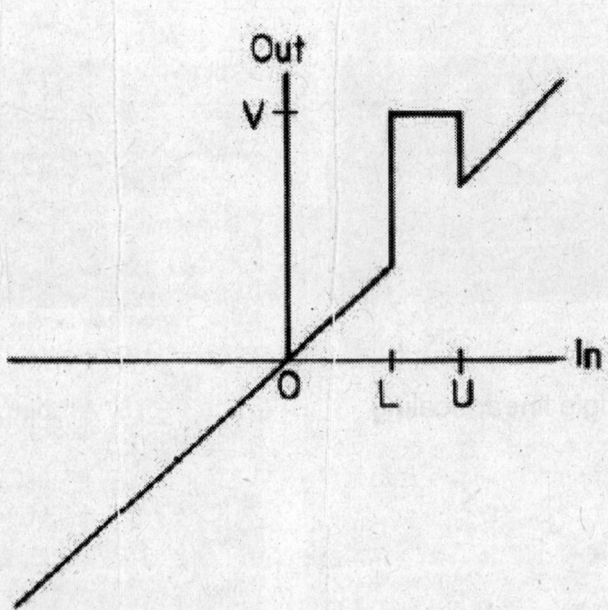

(*b*) Image background scaling transformation

**Figure 4.10 Level slicing contrast modification functions**

**4.2.1.3. WIDE DYNAMIC RANGE IMAGE AMPLITUDE SCALING**

In many imaging applications, a source image sensor may have a much greater dynamic than an associated display device. In such instances, many of the contrast modification procedures presented previously can be used to perform a point transformation of the gray scale of a source image to the gray scale of a destination image to best visualize certain details within the source image. Pardo and Sapiro (3) have proposed a different approach for the visualization of image detail for wide dynamic range source images. In their approach, the source image is amplitude segmented into a small number, N, of amplitude segments.

Then, the source image is linearly scaled using a window-level transform over each non-overlapping source amplitude range to produce N destination images, each of which captures certain image detail of the source image. Figure 4.11 provides an example of this method for N equal to three. Figure 4.11(a) shows a source image linearly scaled over its input range. Figure 4.11(b) shows the three amplitude segments mapped as black, mid-gray and white. Figures 4.11(c), 4.11(d) and 4.11(e) are the resultant displays over the three amplitude ranges.

(a) Single linear scaling

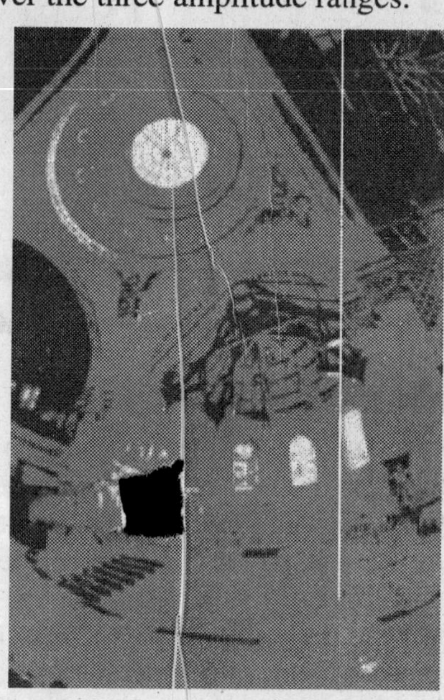

(*b*) Amplitude segments

(c) Low amplitude

(d) Mid-amplitude

(e) High amplitude

**Figure 4.11 Example of multiple destination image scaling of a wide dynamic range source image**

### 4.2.2 HISTOGRAM MODIFICATION

The luminance histogram of a typical natural scene that has been linearly quantized is usually highly skewed toward [illegible] the darkvels; a majority of the pixels possess a luminance less than the average. In such ima[illegible]ges, detaihe darker regions is often not perceptible. One means of enhancing these types of images is a technique called histogram modification, in which the original image is rescaled so that the histogram of the enhanced image follows some desired form. Andrews, Hall and others (4-6) have produced enhanced imagery by a histogram equalization process for which the histogram of the enhanced image is forced to be uniform. Frei has explored the use of histogram modification procedures that produce enhanced images possessing exponential or hyperbolic-shaped histograms.

Ketcham and Hummel have demonstrated improved results by an adaptive histogram modification procedure.

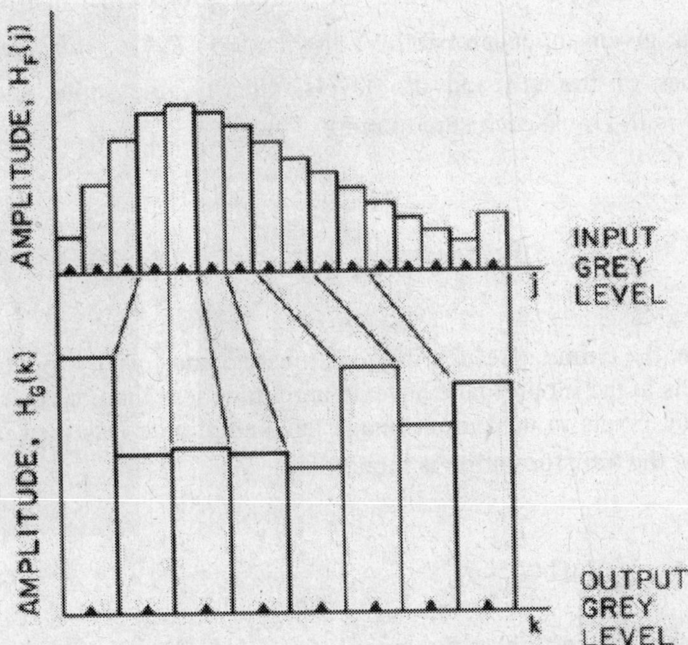


**Figure 4.12 Approximate gray level histogram equalization with unequal number of quantization levels**

### 4.2.2.1. NONADAPTIVE HISTOGRAM MODIFICATION

Figure 4.12 gives an example of histogram equalization. In the figure, $H_F(c)$ for c = 1, 2,..., C, represents the fractional number of pixels in an input image whose amplitude is quantized to the cth reconstruction level. Histogram equalization seeks to produce an output image field G by point rescaling such that the normalized gray-level histogram $H_G(d)=1/D$ for d = 1, 2,..., D. In the example of Figure 4.12, the number of output levels is set at one-half of the number of input levels. The scaling algorithm is developed as follows. The average value of the histogram is computed. Then, starting at the lowest gray level of the original, the pixels in the quantization bins are combined until the sum is closest to the average. All of these pixels are then rescaled to the new first reconstruction level at the midpoint of the enhanced image first quantization bin. The process is repeated for higher-value gray levels. If the number of reconstruction levels of the original image is large, it is possible to rescale the gray levels so that the enhanced image histogram is almost constant. It should be noted that the number of reconstruction levels of the enhanced image must be less than the number of levels of the original image to provide proper gray scale redistribution if all pixels in each quantization level are to be treated similarly. This process results in a somewhat larger quantization error.

It is possible to perform the gray scale histogram equalization process with the same number of gray levels for the original and enhanced images, and still achieve a constant histogram of the enhanced image, by randomly redistributing pixels from input to output quantization bins.

The histogram modification process can be considered to be a monotonic point transformation $g_d = T\{f_c\}$ for which the input amplitude variable $f_1 \leq f_c \leq f_C$ is mapped into an output variable $g_1 \le g_d \le g_D$ such that the output probability distribution follows some desired form for a given input probability distribution $P_R\{g_d = b_d\}$ where ac and $b_d$ are reconstruction values of the cth and dth levels. Clearly, the input and output probability distributions $P_R\{f_c = a_c\}$ must each sum to unity. Thus,

$$\sum_{c=1}^{C} P_R\{f_c = a_c\} = 1 \tag{4.5 (a)}$$

$$\sum_{d=1}^{D} P_R\{g_d = b_d\} = 1 \tag{4.5 (b)}$$

Furthermore, the cumulative distributions must equate for any input index c. That is, the probability that pixels in the input image have an amplitude less than or equal to ac must be equal to the probability that pixels in the output image have amplitude less than or equal to $b_d$, where $b_d = T\{a_c\}$ because the transformation is monotonic.

Hence

$$\sum_{n=1}^{d} P_R\{g_n = b_n\} = \sum_{m=1}^{c} P_R\{f_m = a_m\} \tag{4.6}$$

The summation on the right is the cumulative probability distribution of the input image. For a given image, the cumulative distribution is replaced by the cumulative histogram to yield the relationship

$$\sum_{n=1}^{d} P_R\{g_n = b_n\} = \sum_{m=1}^{c} H_F(m) \tag{4.7}$$

Equation 4.7 now must be inverted to obtain a solution for $g_d$ in terms of $f_c$. In general, this is a difficult or impossible task to perform analytically, but certainly possible by numerical methods. The resulting solution is simply a table that indicates the output image level for each input image level. The histogram transformation can be obtained in approximate form by replacing the discrete probability distributions of Eq. 4.6 by continuous probability densities. The resulting approximation is

$$\int_{g_{min}}^{g} p_g(g)dg = \int_{f_{min}}^{f} pf(f)\,df \tag{4.8}$$

where $p_f(f)$ and $p_g(g)$ are the probability densities of f and g, respectively. The integral on the right is the cumulative distribution function $p_f(f)$ of the input variable f. Hence,

$$\int_{g_{min}}^{g} p_g(g)\,dg = P_f(f) \tag{4.9}$$

In the special case, for which the output density is forced to be the uniform density,

$$p_g(g) = \frac{1}{g_{max} - g_{min}} \tag{4.10}$$

For $g_{min} \le g \le g_{max}$ , the histogram equalization transfer function becomes

$$g = (g_{max} - g_{min})P_f(f) + g_{min} \tag{4.11}$$

Table 4.1 lists several output image histograms and their corresponding transfer functions. Figure 4.13 provides an example of histogram equalization for an x-ray of a projectile. The original image and its histogram are shown in Figure 4.13 (a) and (b), respectively. The transfer function of Figure 4.13(c) is equivalent to the cumulative histogram of the original image. In the histogram equalized result of Figure 4.13,

| Output Probability Density Model | | Transfer Function[a] |
|---|---|---|
| Uniform | $p_g(g) = \frac{1}{g_{max} - g_{min}} \quad g_{min} \le g \le g_{max}$ | $g = (g_{max} - g_{min})P_f(f) + g_{min}$ |
| Exponential | $p_g(g) = \alpha \exp\{-\alpha(g - g_{min})\} \quad g \le g_{min}$ | $g = g_{min} - \frac{1}{\alpha}\ln\{1 - P_f(f)\}$ |
| Rayleigh | $p_g(g) = \frac{g - g_{min}}{\alpha^2}\exp\left\{-\frac{(g - g_{min})^2}{2\alpha^2}\right\} \quad g \ge g_{min}$ | $g = g_{min} + \left[2\alpha^2 \ln\left\{\frac{1}{1 - P_f(f)}\right\}\right]^{1/2}$ |
| Hyperbolic (Cube root) | $p_g(g) = \frac{1}{3}\frac{g^{-2/3}}{g_{max}^{1/3} - g_{min}^{1/3}}$ | $g = \left[g_{max}^{1/3} - g_{min}^{1/3}[P_f(f)] + g_{max}^{1/3}\right]^3$ |
| Hyperbolic (Logarithmic) | $p_g(g) = \frac{1}{g[\ln\{g_{max}\} - \ln\{g_{min}\}]}$ | $g = g_{min}\left(\frac{g_{max}}{g_{min}}\right)^{P_f(f)}$ |

[a]The cumulative probability distribution $P_f(f)$, of the input image is approximated by its cumulative histogram:

$$P_f(f) \approx \sum_{m=0}^{j} H_F(m)$$

**Table 4.1 Histogram Modification Transfer Function**

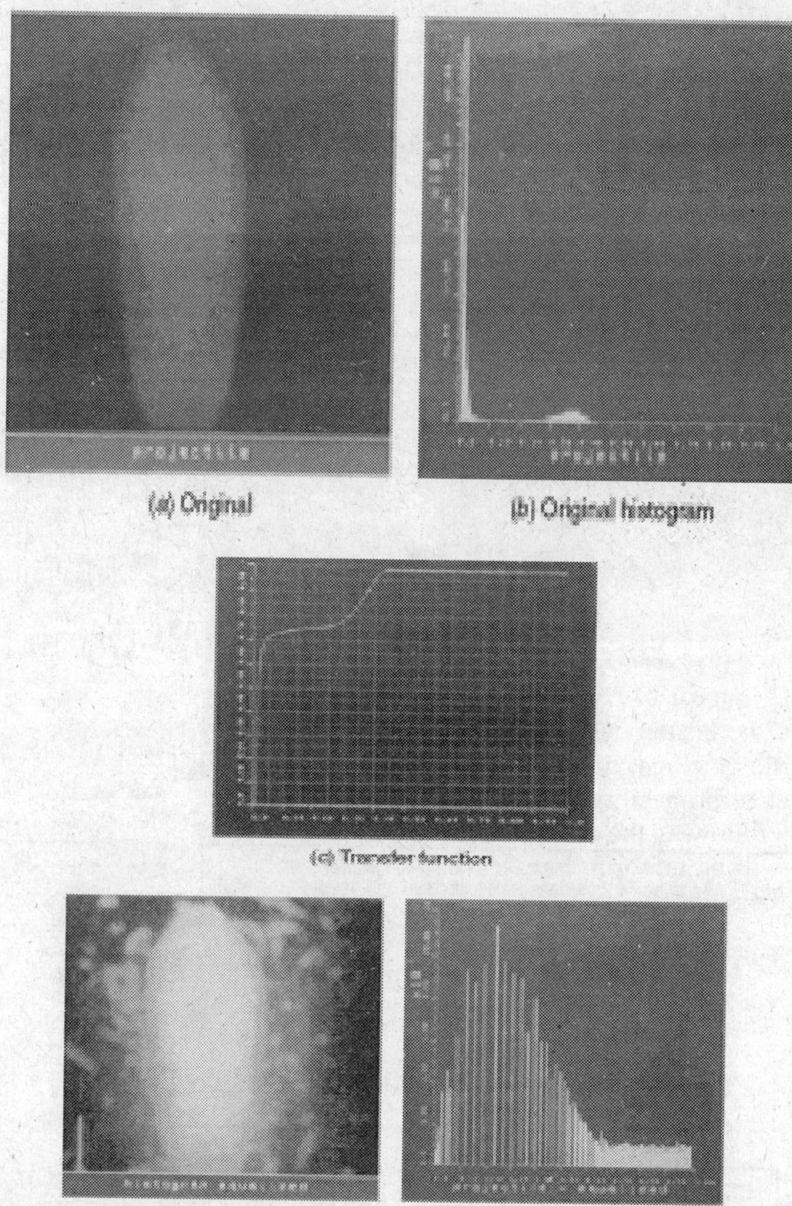
(a) Original (b) Original histogram

(c) Transfer function

(d) Enhanced (e) Enhanced histogram

**Figure 4.13 Histogram equalization of the projectile image**

ablating material from the projectile, not seen in the original, is clearly visible. The histogram of the enhanced image appears peaked, but close examination reveals that many gray level output values are unoccupied. If the high occupancy gray levels were to be averaged with their unoccupied neighbors, the resulting histogram would be much more uniform.

Histogram equalization usually performs best on images with detail hidden in dark regions. Good-quality originals are often degraded by histogram equalization. As an example, Figure 4.14 shows the result of histogram equalization on the jet Image

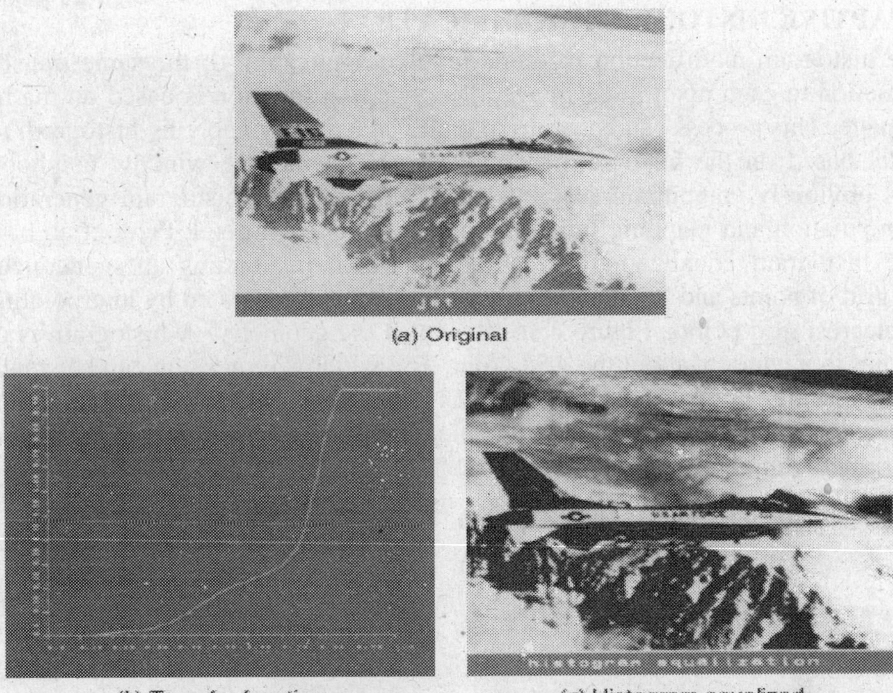


(*a*) Original

(*b*) Transfer function

(*c*) Histogram equalized

**Figure 4.14 Histogram equalization of the jet_mon image**

Frei has suggested the histogram hyperbolization procedure listed in Table 4.1 and described in Figure 4.15 With this method, the input image histograms modified by a transfer function such that the output image probability density is of hyperbolic form. Then the resulting gray scale probability density following the assumed logarithmic or cube root response of the photoreceptors of the eye model will be uniform. In essence, histogram equalization is conceptually performed after the cones of the retina.

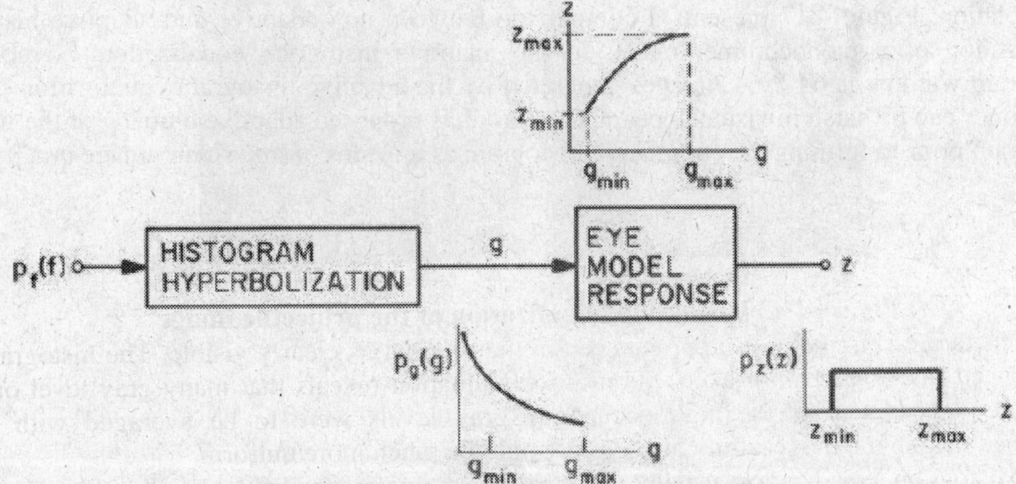


**Figure 4.15 Histogram hyperbolization**

#### 4.2.2.2. ADAPTIVE HISTOGRAM MODIFICATION

The histogram modification methods involve application of the same transformation or mapping function to each pixel in an image. The mapping function is based on the histogram of the entire image. This process can be made spatially adaptive by applying histogram modification to each pixel based on the histogram of pixels within a moving window neighborhood. This technique is obviously computationally intensive, as it requires histogram generation, mapping function computation and mapping function application at each pixel. Pizer et al. have proposed an adaptive histogram equalization technique in which histograms are generated only at a rectangular grid of points and the mappings at each pixel are generated by interpolating mappings of the four nearest grid points. Figure 4.16 illustrates the geometry. A histogram is computed at each grid point in a window about the grid point. The window dimension can be smaller or larger than the grid spacing. Let M00, M10, M01, M11 denote the histogram modification mappings generated at four neighboring grid points. The mapping to be applied at pixel F(j, k) is determined by a bilinear interpolation of the mappings of the four nearest grid points as given by

$$M = (1-a)(1-b)M_{00} + a(1-b)M_{10} + (1-a)bM_{01} + abM_{11} \quad (4.12\ (a))$$

where

$$a = \frac{j-j_0}{j_1-j_0} \quad (4.12\ (b))$$

$$b = \frac{k-k_0}{k_1-k_0} \quad (4.12\ (C))$$

Pixels in the border region of the grid points are handled as special cases of Eq. 4.12. Equation 4.12 is best suited for general-purpose computer calculation. For parallel processors, it is often more efficient to use the histogram generated in the histogram window of Figure 4.16 and apply the resultant mapping function to all pixels in the mapping window of the figure. This process is then repeated at all grid points. At each pixel coordinate (j, k), the four histogram modified pixels obtained from the four overlapped mappings are combined by bilinear interpolation. Figure 4.17 presents a comparison between non adaptive and adaptive histogram equalization of a monochrome image. In the adaptive histogram equalization example, the histogram window is 64 * 64. Images generated by the adaptive histogram equalization process sometimes can be harsh in visual appearance. Stark has proposed adaptive blurring of the window histogram prior to forming the cumulative histogram as a means of improving image quality.

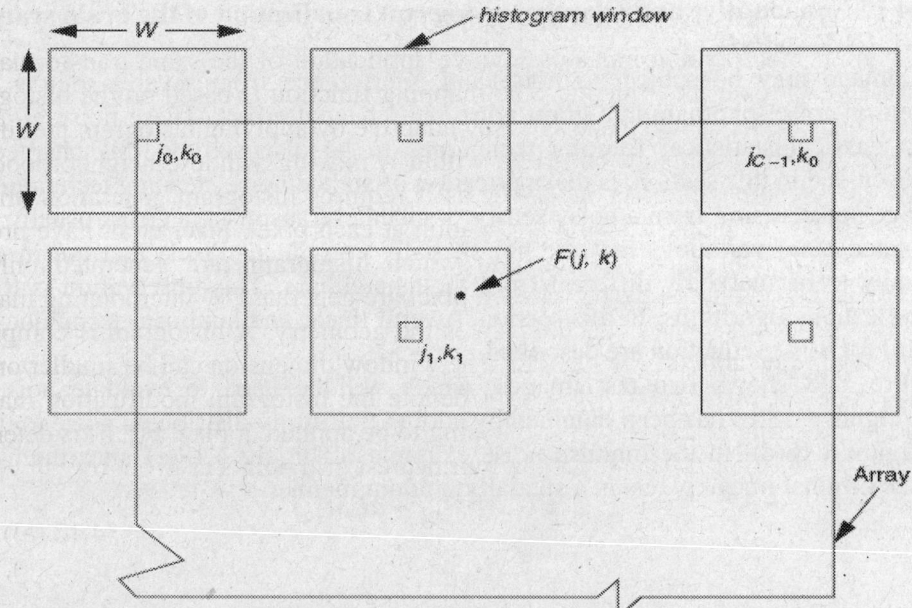


**Figure 4.16 Array geometry for interpolative adaptive histogram modification. Grid point; • pixel to be computed**

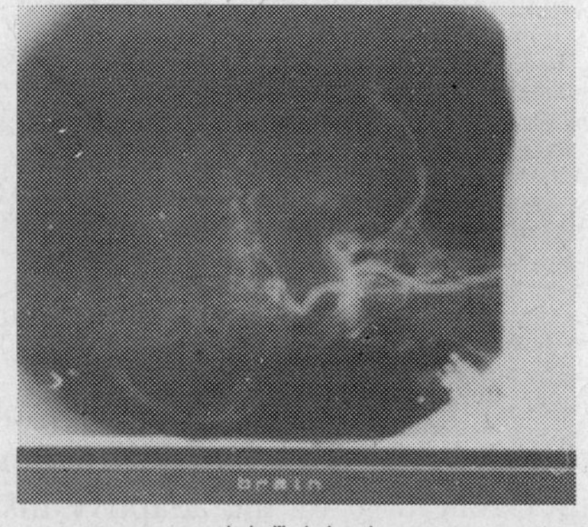


(a) Original

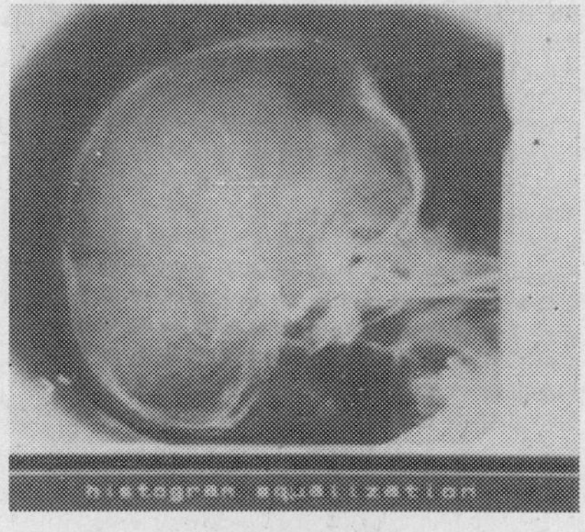


(b) Nonadaptive

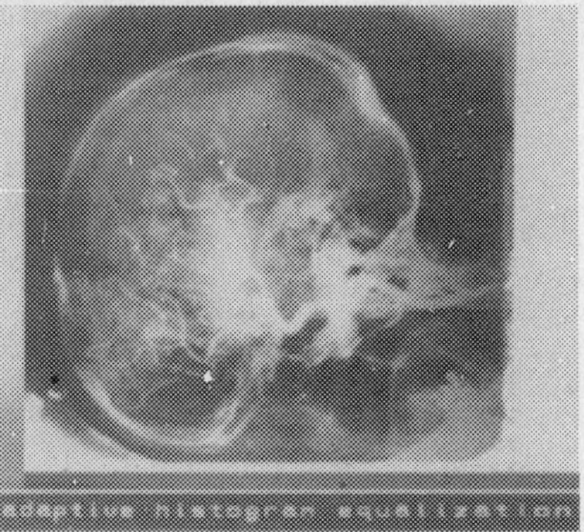


(c) Adaptive

**Figure 4.17 Nonadaptive and adaptive histogram equalization of the brain scan image**

### 4.2.3 NOISE CLEANING

An image may be subject to noise and interference from several sources, including electrical sensor noise, photographic grain noise and channel errors. These noise effects can be reduced by classical statistical filtering techniques to be discussed in this chapter. Another approach, discussed in this section, is the application of ad hoc noise cleaning techniques.

Image noise arising from a noisy sensor or channel transmission errors usually appears as discrete isolated pixel variations that are not spatially correlated. Pixels that are in error often appear visually to be markedly different from their neighbors. This observation is the basis of many noise cleaning algorithms. In this section, several linear and nonlinear techniques that have proved useful for noise reduction are described.

Figure 4.18 shows two test images, which will be used to evaluate noise cleaning techniques. Figure 4.18(b) has been obtained by adding uniformly distributed noise to the original image of Figure 4.18(a). In the impulse noise example of Figure 4.18(c), maximum-amplitude pixels replace original image pixels in a spatially random manner.

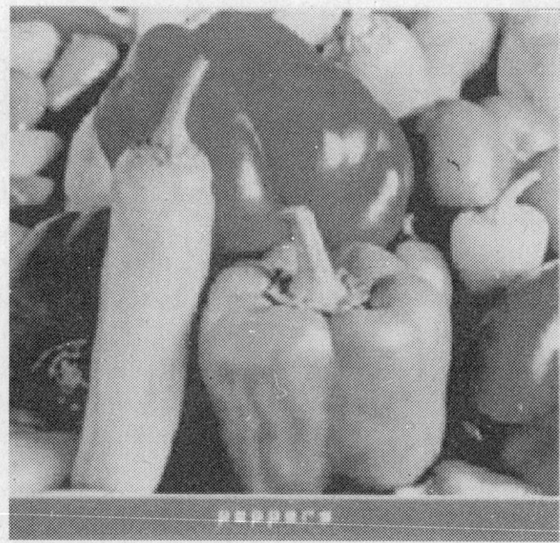


(*a*) Original

(*b*) Original with uniform noise

(*c*) Original with impulse noise

**Figure 4.18 Noisy test images derived from the peppers_mon image**

### 4.2.3.1. LINEAR NOISE CLEANING

Noise added to an image generally has a higher-spatial-frequency spectrum than the normal image components because of its spatial decorrelatedness. Hence, simple low-pass filtering can be effective for noise cleaning. Consideration will now be given to convolution and Fourier domain methods of noise cleaning.

**(i) Spatial Domain Processing**. Following the techniques outlined a spatially filtered output image can be formed by discrete convolution of an input image with a impulse response array according to the relation

$$G(j, k) = \sum \sum F(m,n)H(m + j + c, n + k + c)$$

where C = (L + 1)/2. Whereby the input and output arrays are centered with respect to one another, with the outer boundary of of width pixels set to zero. For noise cleaning, H should be of low-pass form, with all positive elements. Several common pixel impulse response arrays of low-pass form are listed below.

*Mask 1:*

$$\mathbf{H} = \frac{1}{9}\begin{bmatrix} 1 & 1 & 1 \\ 1 & 1 & 1 \\ 1 & 1 & 1 \end{bmatrix} \tag{4.13 (a)}$$

*Mask 2:*

$$\mathbf{H} = \frac{1}{10}\begin{bmatrix} 1 & 1 & 1 \\ 1 & 2 & 1 \\ 1 & 1 & 1 \end{bmatrix} \tag{4.13 (b)}$$

*Mask 3:*

$$\mathbf{H} = \frac{1}{16}\begin{bmatrix} 1 & 2 & 1 \\ 2 & 4 & 2 \\ 1 & 2 & 1 \end{bmatrix} \tag{4.13 (c)}$$

These arrays, called noise cleaning masks, are normalized to unit weighting so that the noise-cleaning process does not introduce an amplitude bias in the processed image. The effect of noise cleaning with the arrays on the uniform noise and impulse noise test images is shown in Figure 4.19 Mask 1 and 3 of Eq. 4.13 are special cases of a parametric low-pass filter whose impulse response is defined as

$$\mathbf{H} = \left(\frac{1}{b+2}\right)^2\begin{bmatrix} 1 & b & 1 \\ b & b^2 & b \\ 1 & b & 1 \end{bmatrix} \tag{4.14}$$

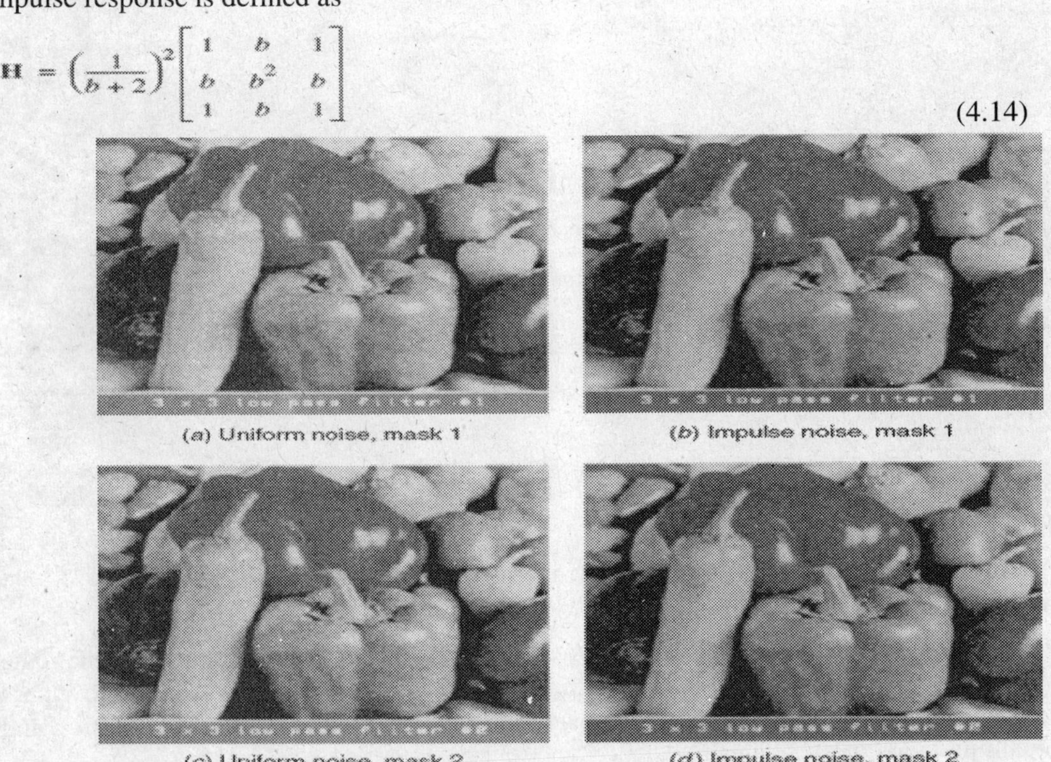

(*a*) Uniform noise, mask 1

(*b*) Impulse noise, mask 1

(*c*) Uniform noise, mask 2

(*d*) Impulse noise, mask 2

(*e*) Uniform noise, mask 3

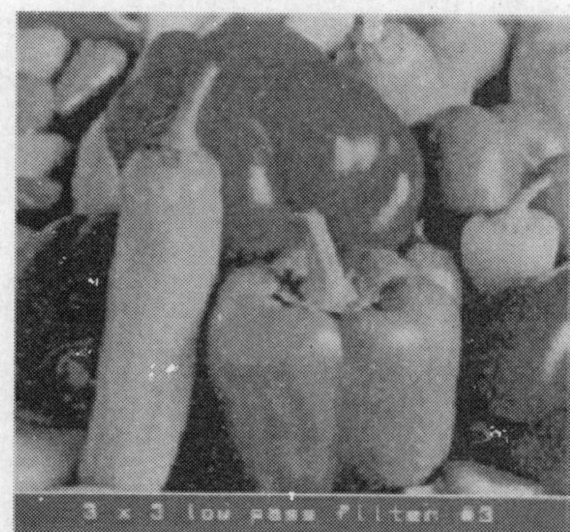


(*f*) Impulse noise, mask 3

**Figure 4.19 Noise cleaning with 3X3 low-pass impulse response arrays on the noisy test images**

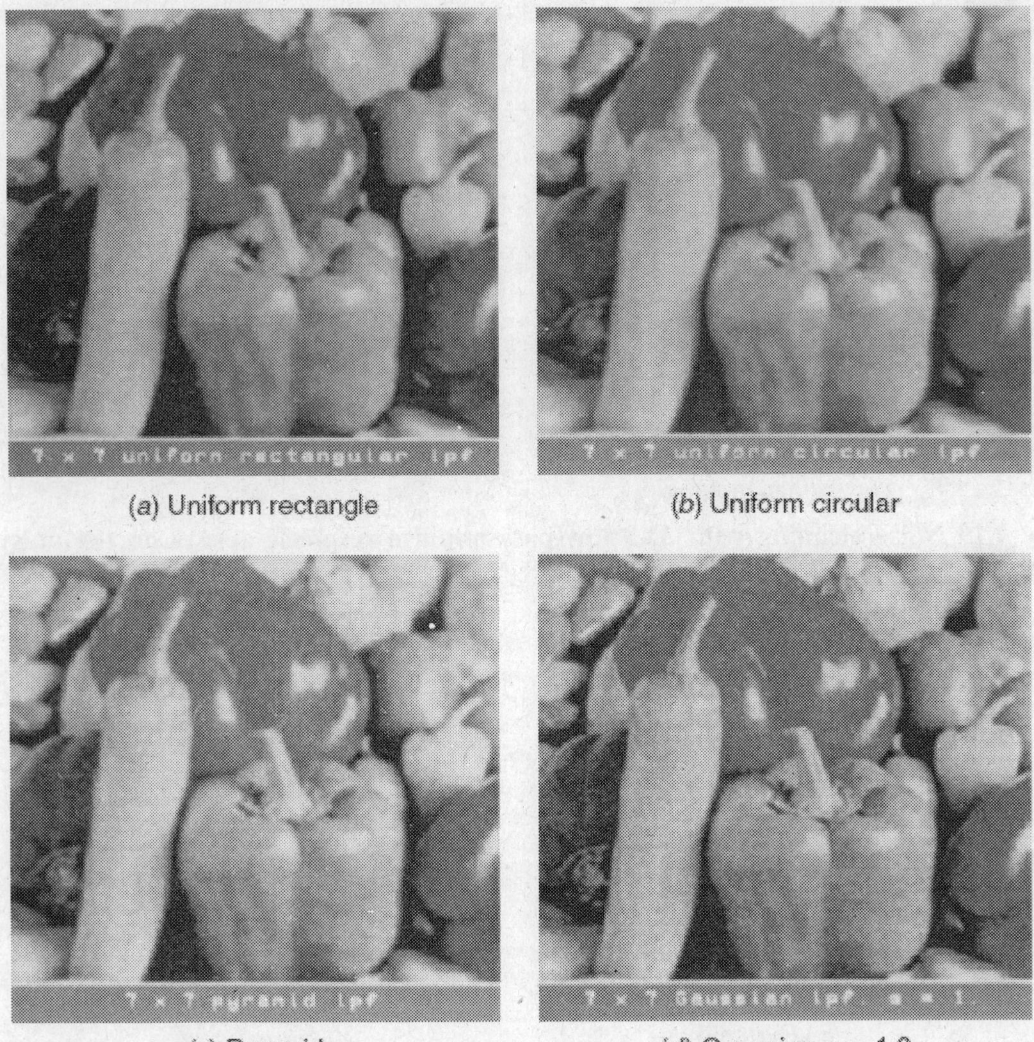


(*a*) Uniform rectangle (*b*) Uniform circular

(*c*) Pyramid (*d*) Gaussian, $s = 1.0$

**Figure 4.20 Noise cleaning with 7X7 impulse response arrays on the noisy test image with uniform noise**

The concept of low-pass filtering noise cleaning can be extended to larger impulse response arrays. Figures 4.20 and 4.21present noise cleaning results for several 7 X 7 impulse response arrays for uniform and impulse noise. As expected, use of a larger impulse response array provides more noise smoothing, but at the expense of the loss of fine image detail.

**(ii) Fourier Domain Processing**. It is possible to perform linear noise cleaning in the Fourier domain using the techniques. Properly executed, there is no difference in results between convolution and Fourier filtering; the choice is a matter of implementation considerations. High-frequency noise effects can be reduced by Fourier domain filtering with a zonal low-pass filter with a transfer function. The sharp cutoff characteristic of the zonal low-pass filter leads to ringing artifacts in a filtered image. This deleterious effect can be eliminated by the use of a smooth cutoff filter,

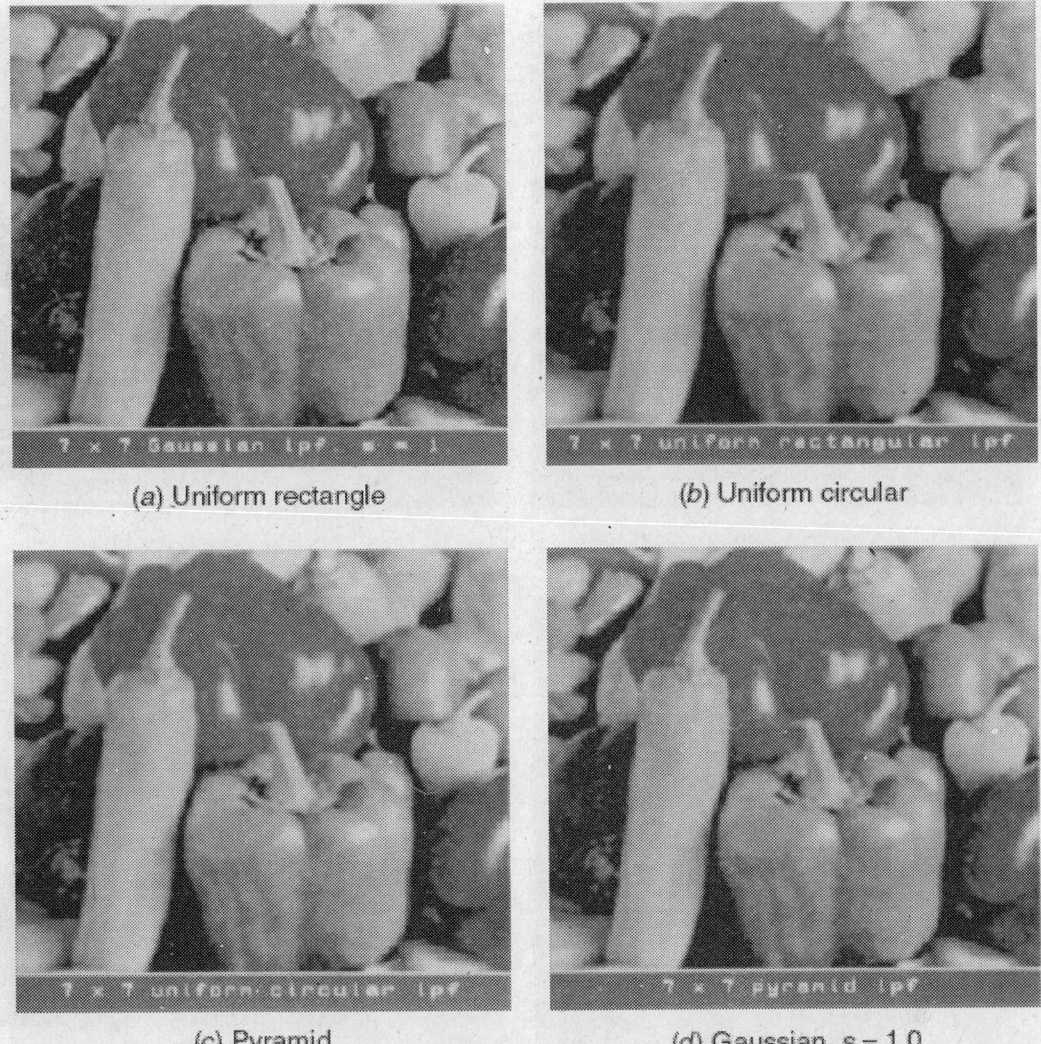


(*a*) Uniform rectangle (*b*) Uniform circular

(*c*) Pyramid (*d*) Gaussian, *s* = 1.0

**Figure 4.21 Noise cleaning with 7X7 impulse response arrays on the noisy test image with impulse noise**

such as the Butterworth low-pass filter whose transfer function. Figure 4.22 shows the results of zonal and Butterworth low-pass filtering of noisy images.

Unlike convolution, Fourier domain processing, often provides quantitative and intuitive insight into the nature of the noise process, which is useful in designing noise cleaning spatial filters. As an example, Figure 4.23(a) a shows an original image subject to periodic interference. Its two-dimensional Fourier transform, shown in Figure 4.23(b), exhibits a strong response at the two points in the Fourier plane corresponding to the frequency response of the interference. When multiplied point by point with the Fourier transform of the original image, the bandstop filter of Figure 4.23 (c) attenuates the interference energy in the Fourier domain. Figure 4.23(d) shows the noise-cleaned result obtained by taking an inverse Fourier transform of the product.

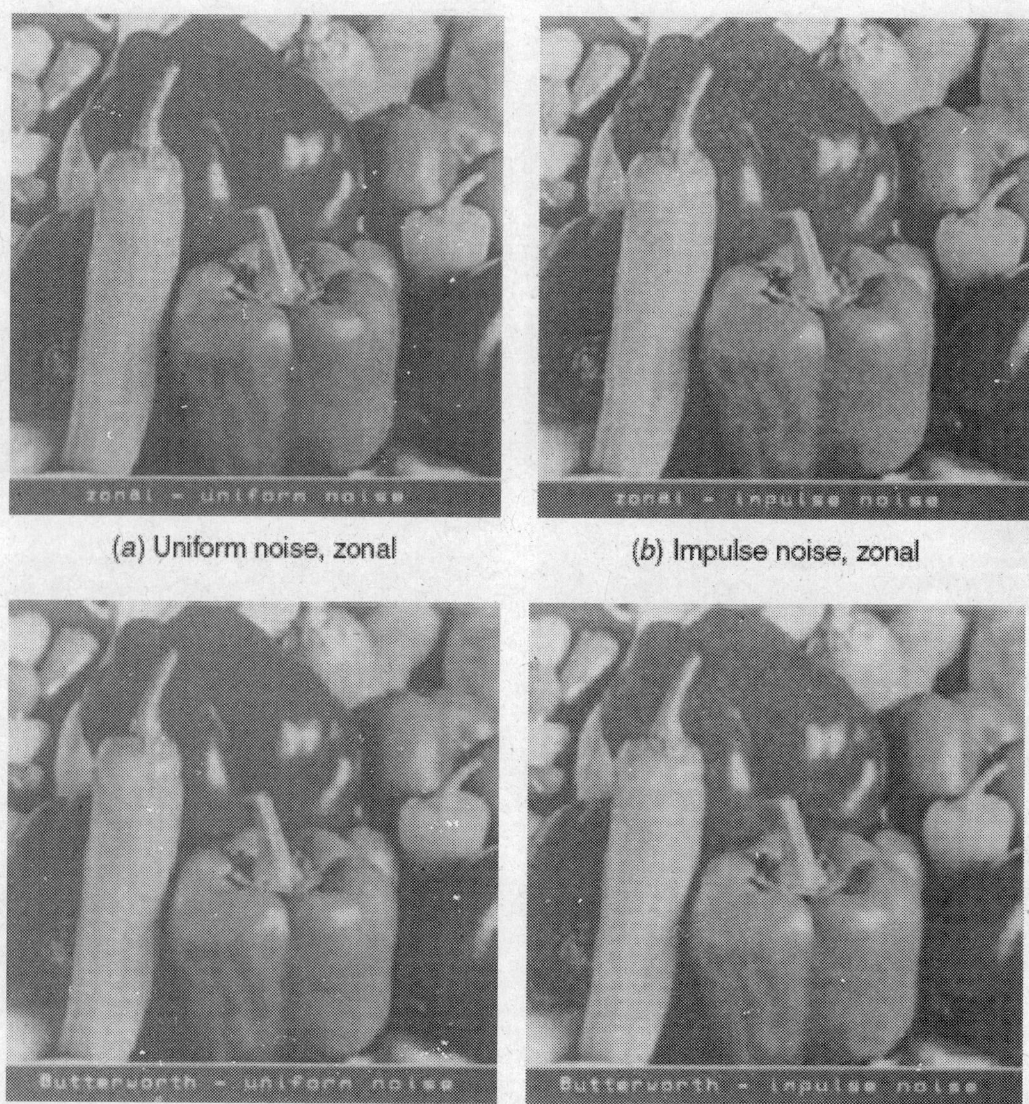


(*a*) Uniform noise, zonal (*b*) Impulse noise, zonal

(*c*) Uniform noise, Butterworth (*d*) Impulse noise, Butterworth

**Figure 4.22 Noise cleaning with zonal and Butterworth low-pass filtering on the noisy test images; cutoff frequency = 64**

**Homomorphic Filtering**. Homomorphic filtering is a useful technique for image enhancement when an image is subject to multiplicative noise or interference. Figure 4.24 describes the process. The input image F(j, k) is assumed to be modeled as the product of a noise-free image S(j, k) and an illumination interference array I(j, k) .

Thus,

$$F(j, k) = I(j, k)S(j, k) \tag{4.15}$$

Ideally, I(j, k) would be a constant for all (j, k). Taking the logarithm of Eq. 4.15 yields the additive linear result

$$\log\{F(j,k)\} = \log\{I(j,k)\} + \log\{S(j,k)\} \tag{4.16}$$

(*a*) Original

(*b*) Original Fourier transform

(*c*) Bandstop filter

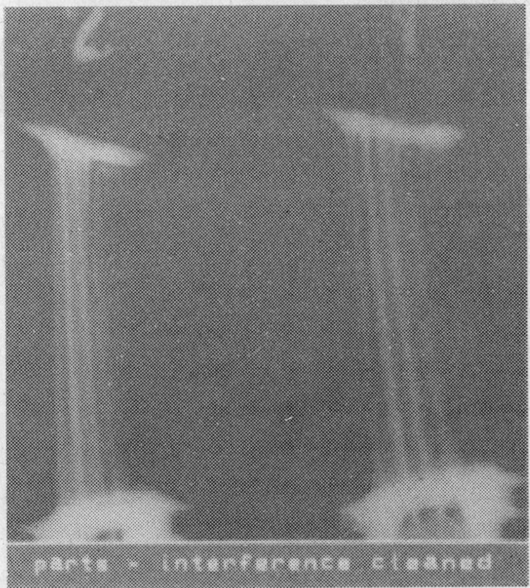


(*d*) Noise cleaned

**Figure 4.23 Noise cleaning with Fourier domain band stop filtering on the parts image with periodic interference**

Conventional linear filtering techniques can now be applied to reduce the log interference component. Exponentiation after filtering completes the enhancement process. Figure 4.25 provides an example of homomorphic filtering. In this example, the illumination field I(j, k) increases from left to right from a value of 0.1 to 1.0.

**Figure 4.24 Homomorphic filtering**

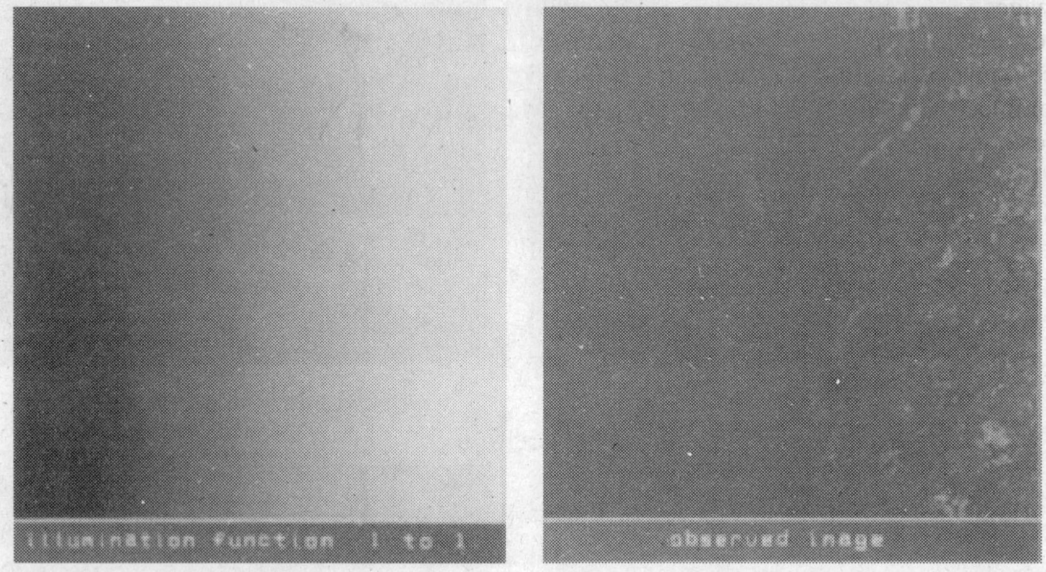


(*a*) Illumination field (*b*) Original

(*c*) Homomorphic filtering

**Figure 4.25. Homomorphic filtering on the washington_ir image with a Butterworth high-pass filter; cutoff frequency = 4**

Therefore, the observed image appears quite dim on its left side. Homomorphic filtering (Figure 4.25(c)) compensates for the nonuniform illumination.

### 4.2.3.2. NONLINEAR NOISE CLEANING

The linear processing techniques described previously perform reasonably well on images with continuous noise, such as additive uniform or Gaussian distributed noise. However, they tend to provide too much smoothing for impulse like noise. Nonlinear techniques often provide a better trade-off between noise smoothing and the retention of fine image detail. Several nonlinear techniques are presented below. Mastin has performed subjective testing of several of these operators.

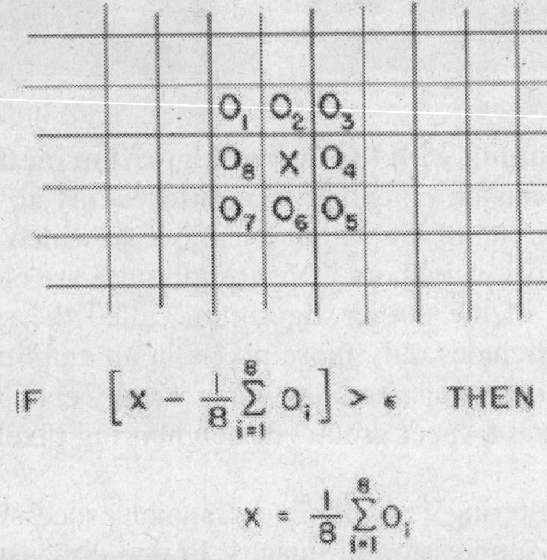


**Figure 4.26 Outlier noise cleaning algorithm**

**Outlier**:- Figure 4.26 describes a simple outlier noise cleaning technique in which each pixel is compared to the average of its eight neighbors. If the magnitude of the difference is greater than some threshold level, the pixel is judged to be noisy, and it is replaced by its neighborhood average. The eight-neighbor average can be computed by convolution of the observed image with the impulse response array

$$H = \frac{1}{8}\begin{bmatrix} 1 & 1 & 1 \\ 1 & 0 & 1 \\ 1 & 1 & 1 \end{bmatrix} \tag{4.17}$$

Figure 4.27 presents the results of outlier noise cleaning for a threshold level of 10%.

(a) Uniform noise

(b) Impulse noise

**Figure 4.27 Noise cleaning with the outlier algorithm on the noisy test images**

The outlier operator can be extended straightforwardly to larger windows. Davis and Rosenfeld have suggested a variant of the outlier technique in which the center pixel in a window is replaced by the average of its k neighbors whose amplitudes are closest to the center pixel. Lee has proposed another variant of the outlier algorithm, called the sigma filter. With the sigma filter, the neighborhood sum includes only those pixels in an amplitude range of $2\sigma$ where $\sigma$ is the standard deviation of the corrupting Gaussian noise. Kenny et al. have proposed the use of the Fisher discriminant to determine a "peer group" of neighboring pixels to be used in the neighbor average.

**(i) Median Filter**. Median filtering is a nonlinear signal processing technique developed by Tukey that is useful for noise suppression in images. In one-dimensional form, the median filter consists of a sliding window encompassing an odd number of pixels. The center pixel in the window is replaced by the median of the pixels in the window. The median of a discrete sequence a1, a2,..., aN for N odd is that member of the sequence for which (N – 1)/2 elements are smaller or equal in value and (N – 1)/2 elements are larger or equal in value. For example, if the values of the pixels within a window are 0.1, 0.2, 0.9, 0.4, 0.5, the center pixel would be replaced by the value 0.4, which is the median value of the sorted sequence 0.1, 0.2, 0.4, 0.5, 0.9. In this example, if the value 0.9 were a noise spike in a monotonically increasing sequence, the median filter would result in a considerable improvement.

On the other hand, the value 0.9 might represent a valid signal pulse for a wide bandwidth sensor, and the resultant image would suffer some loss of resolution. Thus, in some cases the median filter will provide noise suppression, while in other cases it will cause signal suppression. Figure 4.28 illustrates some examples of the operation of a median filter and a mean (smoothing) filter for a discrete step function, ramp function, pulse function and a triangle function with a window of five pixels. It is seen from these examples that the median filter has the usually desirable property of not affecting step functions or ramp functions. Pulse functions, whose periods are less than one-half the window width, are suppressed. But the peak of the triangle is flattened. Operation of the median filter can be analyzed to a limited extent. It can be shown that the median of the product of a constant K and a sequence $f^{(j)}$ is

$$MED\{K[f(j)]\} = K[MED\{f(j)\}] \tag{4.18}$$

However, for two arbitrary sequences $f^{(j)}$ and $g^{(j)}$ , it does not follow that the median of the sum of the sequences is equal to the sum of their medians. That is, in general,

$$MED\{f(j) + g(j)\} \neq MED\{f(j)\} + MED\{g(j)\} \tag{4.19}$$

The sequences 0.1, 0.2, 0.3, 0.4, 0.5 and 0.1, 0.2, 0.3, 0.2, 0.1 are examples for which the additive linearity property does not hold.

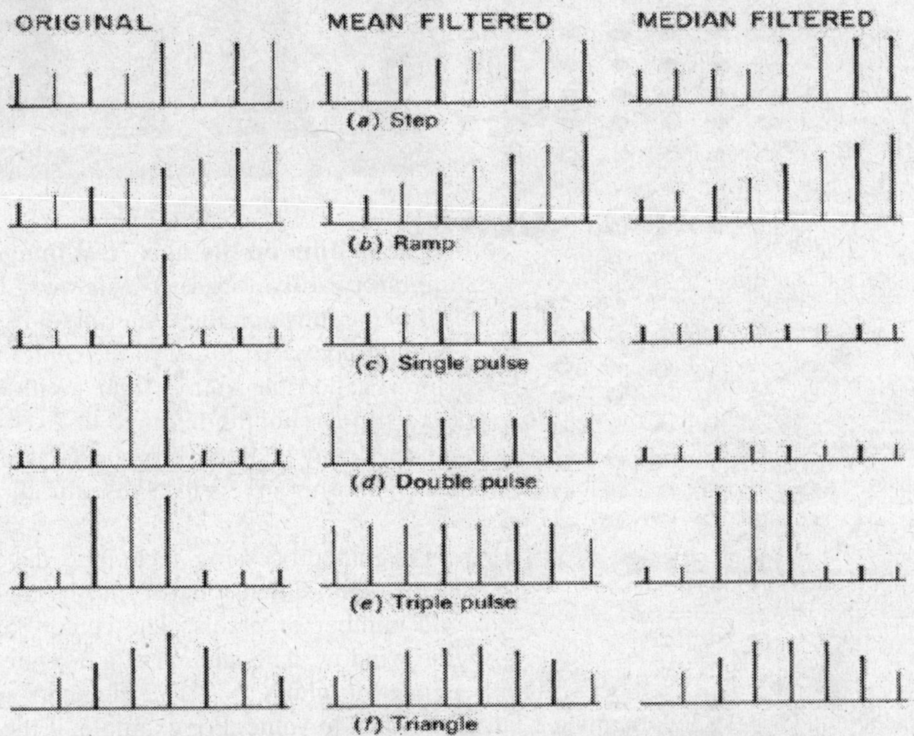


**Figure 4.28 Median filtering on one-dimensional test signals**

There are various strategies for application of the median filter for noise suppression. One method would be to try a median filter with a window of length 3. If there is no significant signal loss, the window length could be increased to 5 for median filtering of the original.

The process would be terminated when the median filter begins to do more harm than good. It is also possible to perform cascaded median filtering on a signal using a fixed-or variable-length window. In general, regions that are unchanged by a single pass of the filter will remain unchanged in subsequent passes.

Regions in which the signal period is lower than one-half the window width will be continually altered by each successive pass. Usually, the process will continue until the resultant period is greater than one-half the window width, but it can be shown that some sequences will never converge.

The concept of the median filter can be extended easily to two dimensions by utilizing a two-dimensional window of some desired shape such as a rectangle or discrete approximation to a circle. It is obvious that a two-dimensional L x L median filter will provide a greater degree of noise suppression than sequential processing with L x 1median filters, but two-dimensional processing also results in greater signal suppression. Figure 4.29 illustrates the effect of two-dimensional median filtering of a spatial peg function with a 3 x 3square filter and a 5 x 5 plus sign–shaped filter. In this example, the square median has deleted the corners of the peg, but the plus median has not affected the corners.

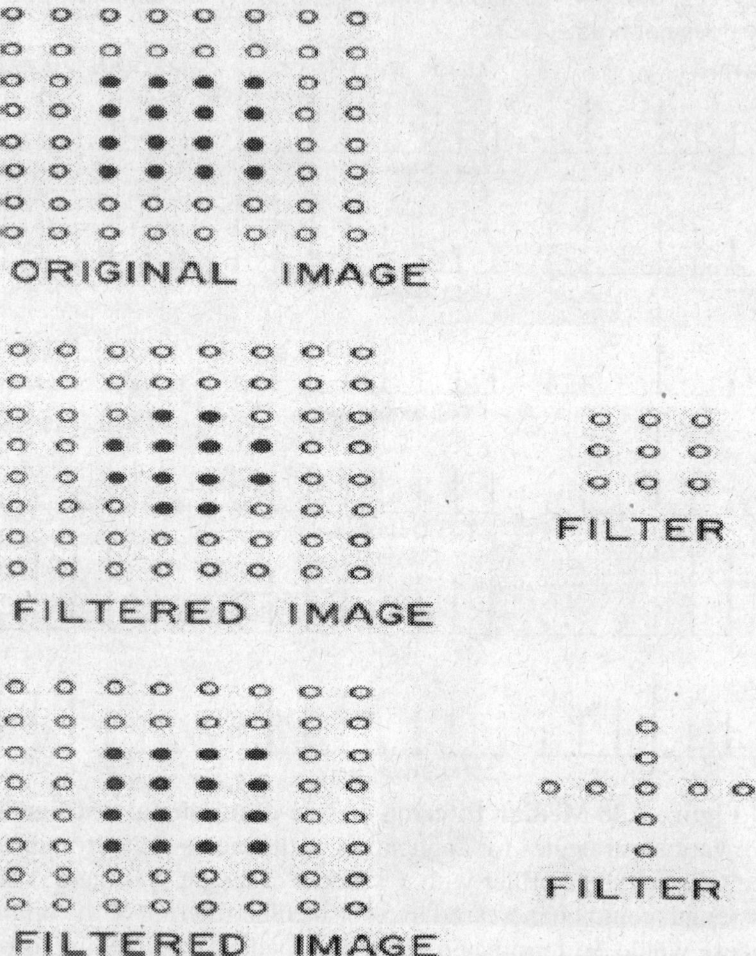


**Figure 4.29 Median filtering on two-dimensional test signals.**

Figures 4.30 and 4.31 show results of plus sign-shaped median filtering on the noisy test images of Figure for impulse and uniform noise, respectively. In the impulse noise example, application of 3 x 3 the median significantly reduces the noise effect, but some residual noise remains. Applying two 3 x 3 median filters in cascade provides further improvement. The 5 x 5 median filter removes almost all of the impulse noise. There is no visible impulse noise in the 7 x 7 median filter result, but the image has become somewhat blurred. In the case of uniform noise, median filtering provides little visual improvement. Huang et al. and Astola and Campbell have developed fast median filtering algorithms. The latter can be generalized to implement any rank ordering.

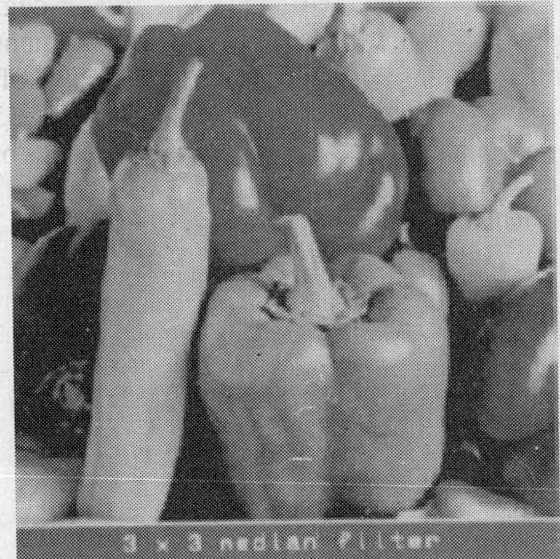


(*a*) 3 × 3 median filter

(*b*) 3 × 3 cascaded median filter

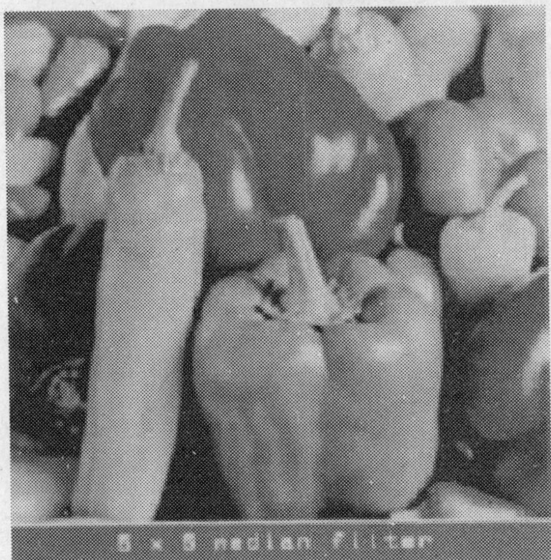


(*c*) 5 × 5 median filter

(*d*) 7 × 7 median filter

**Figure 4.30 Median filtering on the noisy test image with uniform noise**

**(ii) Pseudomedian Filter**. Median filtering is computationally intensive; the number of operations grows exponentially with window size. Pratt et al. have proposed a computationally simpler operator, called the pseudomedian filter, which possesses many of the properties of the median filter.

Let $\{S_L\}$ denote a sequence of elements $S_1, S_2, \ldots, S_L$. The pseudomedian of the sequence is

$$\text{PMED}\{S_L\} = (1/2)\text{MAXIMIN}\{S_L\} + (1/2)\text{MINIMAX}\{S_L\} \tag{4.20}$$

Where for M=(L+1)/2

$$\text{MAXIMIN}\{S_L\} = \text{MAX}\{[\text{MIN}(s_1, \ldots, s_M)], [\text{MIN}(s_2, \ldots, s_{M+1})]$$

$$\ldots, [\text{MIN}(s_{L-M+1}, \ldots, s_L)]\} \tag{4.21 (a)}$$

(*a*) 3 × 3 median filter

(*b*) 5 × 5 median filter

(*c*) 7 × 7 median filter

**Figure 4.31 Median filtering on the noisy test image with uniform noise**

$$\text{MINIMAX}\{S_L\} = \text{MIN}\{[\text{MAX}(s_1, \ldots, s_M)], [\text{MAX}(s_2, \ldots, s_{M+1})]$$

$$\ldots, [\text{MAX}(s_{L-M+1}, \ldots, s_L)]\} \tag{4.21 (b)}$$

Operationally, the sequence of L elements is decomposed into subsequences of M elements, each of which is slid to the right by one element in relation to its predecessor, and the appropriate MAX and MIN operations are computed. As will be demonstrated, the MAXIMIN and MINIMAX operators are, by themselves, useful operators. It should be noted that it is possible to recursively decompose the MAX and MIN functions on long sequences into sliding functions of length 2 and 3 for pipeline computation.

The one-dimensional pseudomedian concept can be extended in a variety of ways. One approach is to compute the MAX and MIN functions over rectangular windows. As with the median filter, this approach tends to over smooth an image. A plus-shape pseudomedian generally provides better subjective results. Consider a plus-shaped window containing the following two-dimensional set elements {SE}

$$\begin{array}{c} y_1 \\ \cdot \\ \cdot \\ \cdot \\ x_1 \;\cdots\; x_M \;\cdots\; x_C \\ \cdot \\ \cdot \\ \cdot \\ y_R \end{array}$$

Let the sequences $\{X_C\}$ and $\{Y_R\}$ denote the elements along the horizontal and vertical axes of the window, respectively. Note that the element $X_M$ is common to both sequences. Then the plus-shaped pseudomedian can be defined as

$$\text{PMED}\{S_E\} = (1/2)\text{MAX}[\text{MAXIMIN}\{X_C\}, \text{MAXIMIN}\{Y_R\}] + (1/2)\,\text{MIN}\,[\text{MINIMAX}\{X_C\}, \text{MINIMAX}\{Y_R\}] \quad (10.3\text{-}11)$$

The MAXIMIN operator in one- or two-dimensional form is useful for removing bright impulse noise but has little or no effect on dark impulse noise. Conversely, the MINIMAX operator does a good job in removing dark, but not bright, impulse noise. A logical conclusion is to cascade the operators. Figure 4.32 shows the results of MAXIMIN, MINIMAX and pseudo median filtering on an image subjected to salt and pepper noise. As observed, the MAXIMIN operator reduces the salt noise, while the MINIMAX operator reduces the pepper noise. The pseudo median provides attenuation for both types of noise. The cascade MINIMAX and MAXIMIN operators, in either order, show excellent results.

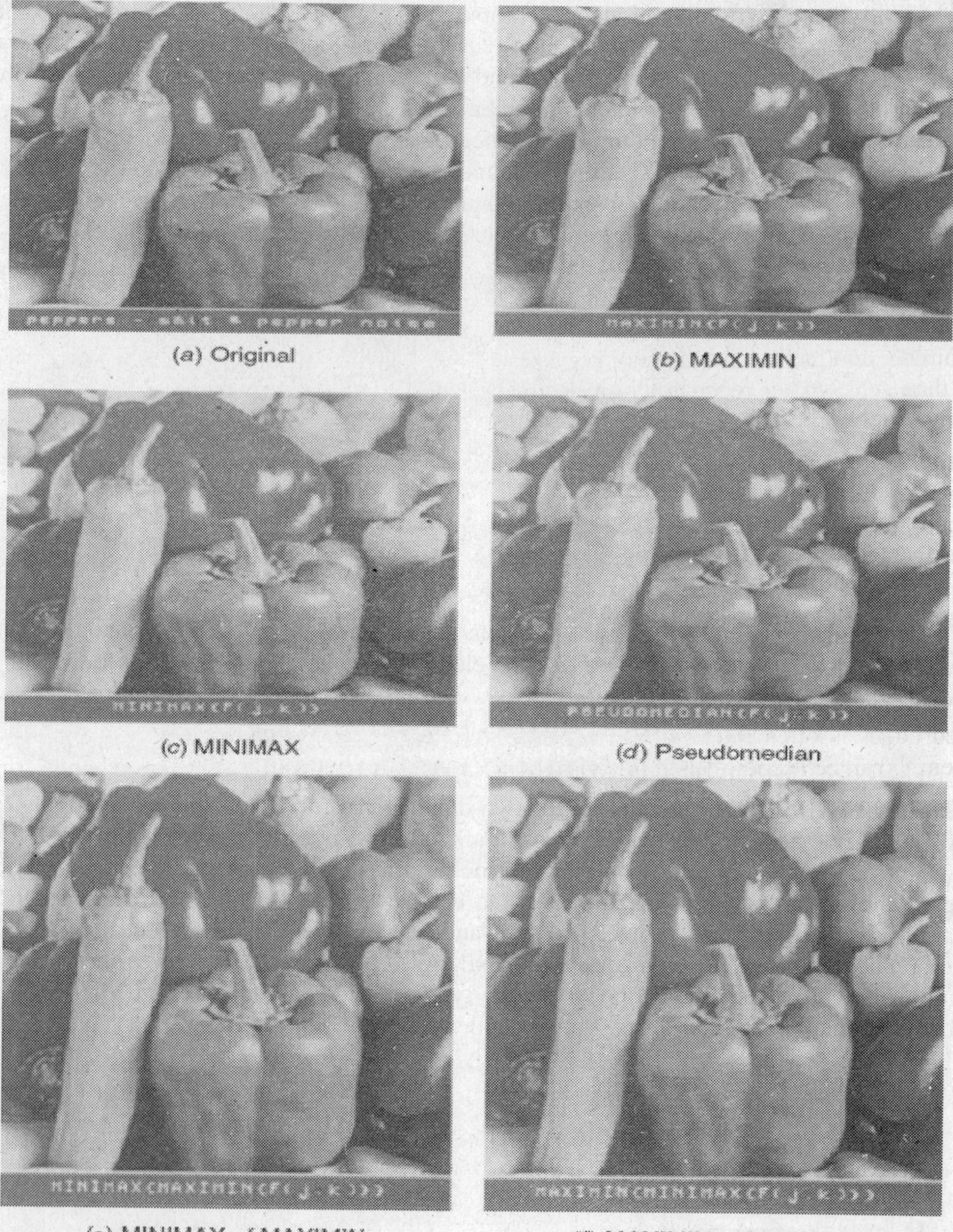


(*a*) Original (*b*) MAXIMIN

(*c*) MINIMAX (*d*) Pseudomedian

(*e*) MINIMAX of MAXIMIN (*f*) MAXIMIN of MINIMAX

**Figure 4.32 5X5 plus-shape MINIMAX, MAXIMIN and pseudomedian filtering on the noisy test images**

**(iii) Wavelet Denoising.** The usefulness of wavelet transforms for image coding derives from the property that most of the energy of a transformed image is concentrated in the trend transform coefficients rather than the fluctuation coefficients. The fluctuation coefficients may be grossly quantized without serious image degradation. This energy compaction property can also be exploited for noise removal.

The basic concept, called wavelet denoising is quite simple. The wavelet transform coefficients are thresholded such that the presumably noisy, low-amplitude coefficients are set to zero. Zhong and Ning have developed a method of classifying wavelet coefficients as being edge-related, regular coefficients or irregular coefficients based upon a measurement of the local statistical self-similarity at different resolution scales. The irregular coefficients are denoised using a minimum mean-squared error estimation method; the edge-related, regular coefficients are processed by a fuzzy weighted mean filter. Balster et al. have proposed a two-threshold wavelet coefficient selection method. The first threshold is used to distinguish coefficients of large magnitude, and the second threshold is used to distinguish coefficients of spatial regularity, which are then selected for reconstruction. Both algorithms have been reported to provide good denoising results

**(iv) Adaptive Processing**. Several methods of adaptive denoising have been developed. Eng and Ma employ a first stage noise detection process to identify pixels that are to undergo no filtering, standard median filtering or fuzzy weighted median filtering in the second stage. Chan et al. have proposed a two-stage scheme in which an adaptive median filter is used to identify pixels that are likely to have been contaminated by noise. In the second stage, the noise candidates are smoothed using a regularization algorithm.

### 4.2.4 EDGE CRISPENING

Psychophysical experiments indicate that a photograph or visual signal with accentuated or crispened edges is often more subjectively pleasing than an exact photometric reproduction. Edge crispening can be accomplished in a variety of ways.

#### 4.2.4.1. LINEAR EDGE CRISPENING

Edge crispening can be performed by discrete convolution, as defined by Eq. 4.14, in which the impulse response array H is of high-pass form. Several common high-pass masks are given below.

*Mask 1:*
$$\mathbf{H} = \begin{bmatrix} 0 & -1 & 0 \\ -1 & 5 & -1 \\ 0 & -1 & 0 \end{bmatrix} \qquad (4.22\text{ (a)})$$

*Mask 2:*
$$\mathbf{H} = \begin{bmatrix} -1 & -1 & -1 \\ -1 & 9 & -1 \\ -1 & -1 & -1 \end{bmatrix} \qquad (4.22\text{ (b)})$$

*Mask 3:*
$$\mathbf{H} = \begin{bmatrix} 1 & -2 & 1 \\ -2 & 5 & -2 \\ 1 & -2 & 1 \end{bmatrix} \qquad (4.22\text{ (c)})$$

These masks possess the property that the sum of their elements is unity, to avoid amplitude bias in the processed image. Figure 4.33 provides examples of edge crispening on a monochrome image with the masks of Eq. 4.22. Mask 2 appears to provide the best visual results.

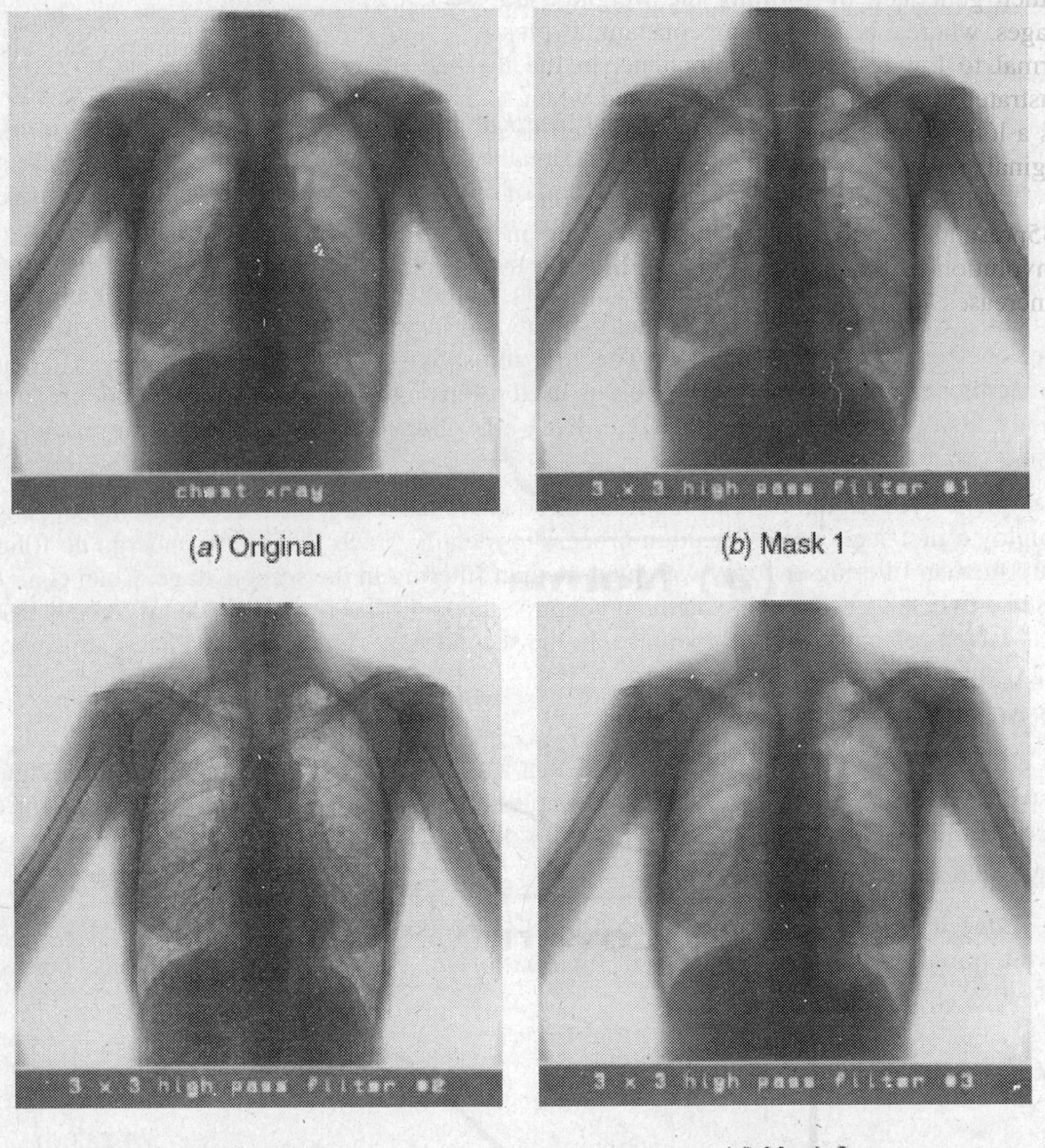


(a) Original (b) Mask 1

(c) Mask 2 (d) Mask 3

**Figure 4.33 Edge crispening with 3 X 3 masks on the chest_xray image**

To obtain edge crispening on electronically scanned images, the scanner signal can be passed through an electrical filter with a high-frequency bandpass characteristic. Another possibility for scanned images is the technique of unsharp masking. In this process, the image is effectively scanned with two overlapping apertures, one at normal resolution and the other at a lower spatial resolution, which upon sampling produces normal and low-resolution images F(j, k) and $F_L$(j, k), respectively. An unsharp masked image

$$G(j,k) = \frac{c}{2c-1} F(j,k) - \frac{1-c}{2c-1} F_L(j,k) \tag{4.23}$$

is then generated by forming the weighted difference between the normal and low resolution images, where c is a weighting constant. Typically, c is in the range 3/5 to 5/6, so that the ratio of normal to low-resolution components in the masked image is from 1.5:1 to 5:1. Figure 4.34 illustrates typical scan signals obtained when scanning over an object edge. The masked signal has a longer-duration edge gradient as well as an overshoot and undershoot, as compared to the original signal.

Subjectively, the apparent sharpness of the original image is improved. Figure 4.35presents examples of unsharp masking in which the low-resolution image is obtained by convolution with a uniform L x L impulse response array. The sharpening effect is stronger as L increases and c decreases.

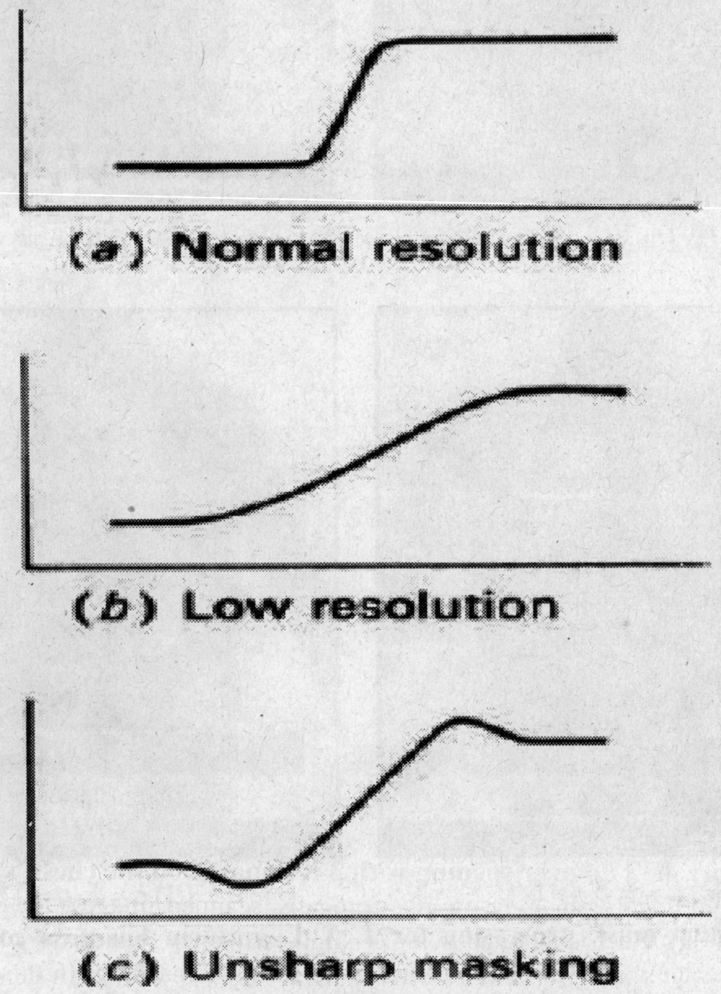


**Figure 4.34 Waveforms in an unsharp masking image enhancement system**

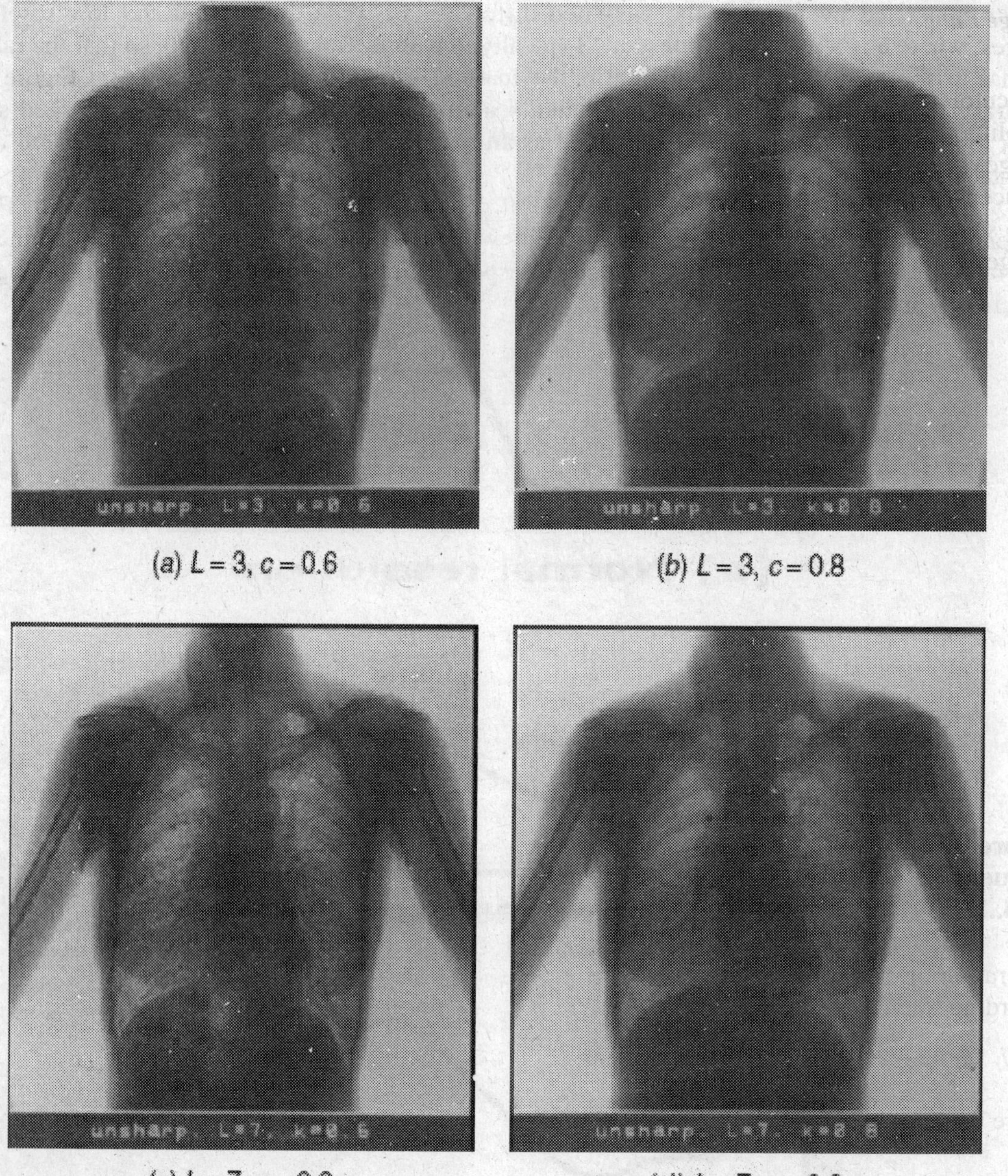


(a) $L = 3, c = 0.6$ (b) $L = 3, c = 0.8$

(c) $L = 7, c = 0.6$ (d) $L = 7, c = 0.8$

**Figure 4.35 Unsharp mask processing for L X L uniform low-pass convolution on the chest_xray image**

Edge crispening using an unsharp masking operator is sensitive to image noise. Polesel et al. have developed an adaptive unsharp masking filter in which contrast enhancement occurs in high detail regions of an image; little or no image sharpening occurs in smooth areas. Linear edge crispening can be performed by Fourier domain filtering.

A zonal high-pass filter with a transfer function suppresses all spatial frequencies below the cutoff frequency except for the dc component, which is necessary to maintain the average amplitude of the filtered image. Figure 4.36 shows the result of zonal high-pass filtering of an image. Zonal high-pass filtering often causes ringing in a filtered image. Such ringing can be reduced significantly by utilization of a high-pass filter with a smooth cutoff response. Figure 4.36 shows the results of zonal and Butterworth high-pass filtering. In both examples, the filtered images are biased to a midgray level for display.

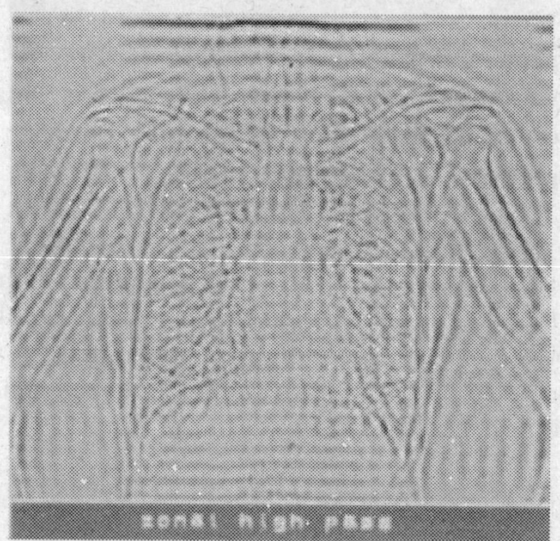


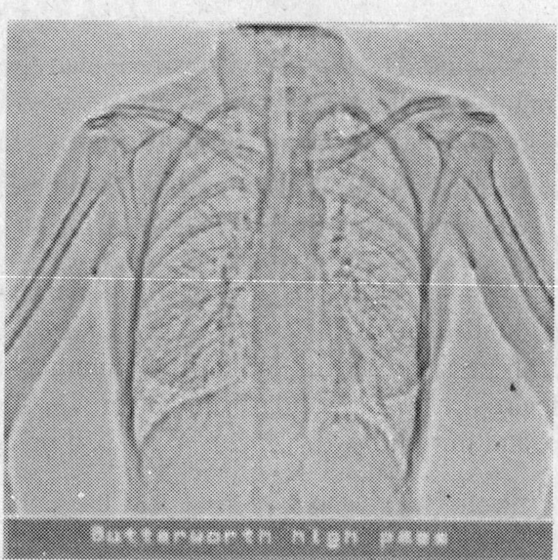


(a) Zonal filtering (b) Butterworth filtering

**Figure 4.36. Zonal and Butterworth high-pass filtering on the chest_xray image; cutoff frequency = 32**

### 4.2.4..2 STATISTICAL DIFFERENCING

Another form of edge crispening, called statistical differencing (38, p. 100), involves the generation of an image by dividing each pixel value by its estimated standard deviation D(j, k) according to the basic relation

$$G(j,k) = \frac{F(j,k)}{D(j,k)} \tag{4.24}$$

where the estimated standard deviation

$$D(j,k) = \frac{1}{W}\left[\sum_{m=j-w}^{j+w} \sum_{n=k-w}^{k+w} [F(m,n) - M(m,n)]^2\right]^{1/2} \tag{4.25}$$

is computed at each pixel over some W x W neighborhood where W = 2w + 1. The function M(j, k) is the estimated mean value of the original image at point (j, k), which is computed as

$$M(j,k) = \frac{1}{W^2} \sum_{m=j-w}^{j+w} \sum_{n=k-w}^{k+w} F(m,n) \tag{4.26}$$

$$M(j,k) = \frac{1}{W^2} \sum_{m=j-w}^{j+w} \sum_{n=k-w}^{k+w} F(m,n) \tag{4.27}$$

The enhanced image G (j, k) is increased in amplitude with respect to the original at pixels that deviate significantly from their neighbors, and is decreased in relative amplitude elsewhere. The process is analogous to automatic gain control for an audio signal.

Wallis has suggested a generalization of the statistical differencing operator in which the enhanced image is forced to a form with desired first- and second-order moments. The Wallis operator is defined by

$$G(j,k) = [F(j,k) - M(j,k)]\frac{A_{max}D_d}{A_{max}D(j,k) + D_d} + [pM_d + (1-p)M(j,k)] \tag{4.28}$$

where $M_d$ and $D_d$ represent desired average mean and standard deviation factors, $A_{max}$ is a maximum gain factor that prevents overly large output values when D (j , k) is small and $0.0 \le p \le 1.0$ is a mean proportionality factor controlling the background flatness of the enhanced image. The Wallis operator can be expressed in a more general form as

$$G(j,k) = [F(j,k) - M(j,k)]A(j,k) + B(j,k) \tag{4.29}$$

Where A (j, k) is a spatially dependent gain factor and B (j , k) is a spatially dependent background factor. These gain and background factors can be derived directly from Eq. 4.28, or they can be specified in some other manner. For the Wallis operator, it is convenient to specify the desired average standard deviation $D_d$ such that the spatial gain ranges between maximum Amax and minimum $A_{min}$ limits. This can be accomplished by setting $D_d$ to the value

$$D_d = \frac{A_{min}A_{max}D_{max}}{A_{max} - A_{min}} \tag{4.30}$$

where $D_{max}$ is the maximum value of D (j, k). The summations of Eqs. 4.26 and 4.27 can be implemented by convolutions with a uniform impulse array. But, overshoot and undershoot effects may occur. Better results are usually obtained with a pyramid or Gaussian-shaped array. Figure 4.37 shows the mean, standard deviation, spatial gain and Wallis statistical differencing result on a monochrome image. Figure 4.38 presents a medical imaging example.

(a) Original

(b) Mean, 0.00 to 0.98

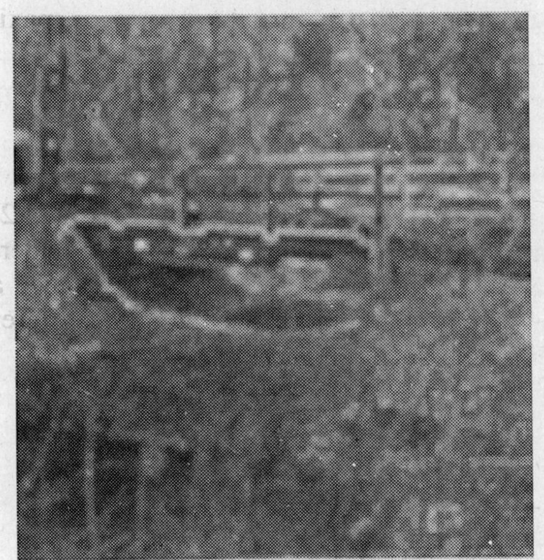
(c) Standard deviation, 0.01 to 0.26

(d) Background, 0.09 to 0.88

(*e*) Spatial gain, 0.75 to 2.35

(*f*) Wallis enhancement, – 0.07 to 1.12

**Figure 4.37 Wallis statistical differencing on the bridge image for $M_d$ = 0.45, $D_d$ = 0.28, p = 0.20, Amax = 2.50, $A_{min}$= 0.75 using a 9X9 pyramid array**

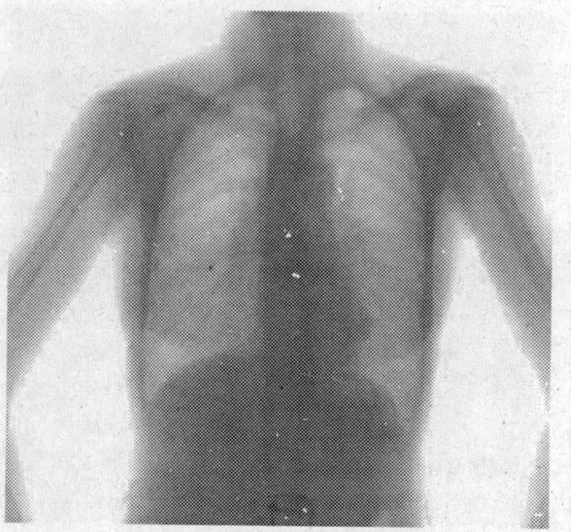

(a) Original

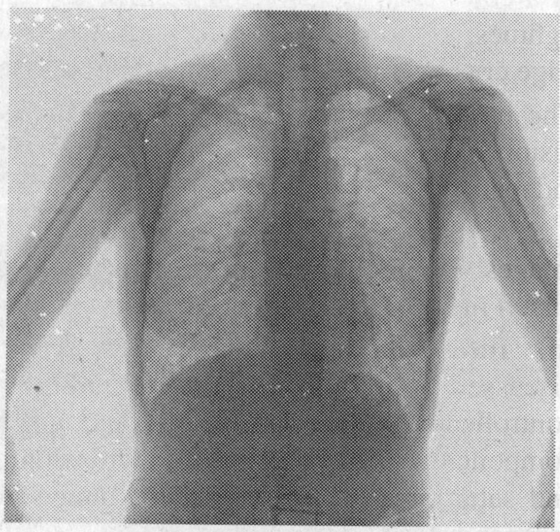

(b) Wallis enhancement

**Figure 4.38 Wallis statistical differencing on the chest_xray image for $M_d$ = 0.64, $D_d$ = 0.22, p = 0.20, $A_{max}$ = 2.50, $A_{min}$ = 0.75 using a 11X11 pyramid array**

## 4.2.5 COLOR IMAGE ENHANCEMENT

The image enhancement techniques discussed previously have all been applied to monochrome images. This section considers the enhancement of natural color images and introduces the pseudocolor and false color image enhancement methods. In the literature, the terms pseudocolor and false color have often been used improperly. Pseudocolor produces a color image from a monochrome image, while false color produces an enhanced color image from an original natural color image or from multispectral image bands.

### 4.2.5.1. NATURAL COLOR IMAGE ENHANCEMENT

The monochrome image enhancement methods described previously can be applied to natural color images by processing each color component individually. This comprises the class of intracomponent processing algorithms. There is also a class of inter-component processing algorithms in which color pixels are combined on a pixel-by-pixel basis. Finally, there is a class of vector processing algorithms.

**(i) Intracomponent Processing**. Typically, color images are processed in the RGB color space. This approach works quite well for noise cleaning algorithms in which the noise is independent between the R, G and B components. Edge crispening can also be performed on an intracomponent basis, but better, and more efficient, results, are often obtained by processing in other color spaces. Contrast manipulation and histogram modification intracomponent algorithms often result in severe shifts of the hue and saturation of color images. Hue preservation can be achieved by using a single point transformation for each of the three RGB components. For example form a sum image S=R + G + B, and then compute a histogram equalization function, which is used for each RGB component. For some image enhancement algorithms, there are computational advantages to processing in a luma-chroma space, such as $YC_bC_r$, or a lightness-chrominance space, such as L*a*b*. As an example, if the objective is to perform edge crispening of a color image, it is usually only necessary to apply the enhancement method to the luma or lightness component. Because of the high-spatial-frequency response limitations of human vision, edge crispening of the chroma or chrominance components may not be perceptible.

The procedure is to transform a RGB tristimulus value original image according to the color vision model to produce a set of three perceptual space images that, ideally, are perceptually independent.

Then, an image enhancement method is applied independently to the perceptual space images. Finally, the enhanced perceptual space images are subjected to steps that invert the color vision model and produce an enhanced color image represented in RGB color space.

**(ii) Intercomponent Processing.** The intracomponent processing algorithms previously discussed provide no means of modifying the hue and saturation of a processed image in a controlled manner. One means of doing so is to transform a source RGB image into a three component image, in which the three components form separate measures of the brightness, hue and saturation (BHS) of a color image. Ideally, the three components should be perceptually independent of one another.

Once the BHS components are determined, they can be modified by amplitude scaling methods. The IHS color coordinate system has been proposed for non-standard color images. There are no standard colorimetric definitions for hue and saturation measures. However, the following ad hoc definition for the L*a*b* color coordinate system of can be utilized:

$$B = L^* \tag{4.31 (a)}$$

$$H = \arctan\{\frac{b^*}{a^*}\} \tag{4.31 (b)}$$

$$S = [a^* + b^*]^{1/2} \tag{4.31 (c)}$$

**(iii) Color Vector Processing**. As shown in Figure, a color vector $v=[R,G,B]^T$ can be formed in three-dimensional color space based upon the R, G and B color components at each pixel (j, k).

Now consider a moving window about the (j, k) pixel, which contains a sequence of color vectors v1, v2,...,vN. For example, for a 3 x 3 window, the neighborhood array is:

$$\begin{bmatrix} v_1 & v_2 & v_3 \\ v_4 & v_5 & v_6 \\ v_7 & v_8 & v_9 \end{bmatrix}$$

For natural, noise-free images with a relatively small window, the vectors vN will be similar in magnitude and direction. For images subject to noise, some of the vectors may differ significantly from one another. Astola, Haavisto and Neuvo have proposed a vector median filter (VMF) as a means of color image denoising. The vector in the window center is replaced by the median of all of the vectors in the window.

### 4.2.5.2. PSEUDOCOLOR

Pseudocolor is a color mapping of a monochrome image array which is intended to enhance the detectability of detail within the image. The pseudocolor mapping of an array F(j , k) is defined as

$$R(j,k) = O_R\{F(j,k)\} \quad (4.32\ (a))$$

$$G(j,k) = O_G\{F(j,k)\} \quad (4.32\ (b))$$

$$B(j,k) = O_B\{F(j,k)\} \quad (4.32\ (c))$$

Where R(j , k) , G (j , k) , B(j , k) are display color components and $O_R\{F(j,k)\}$, $O_G\{F(j,k)\}$, $O_B\{F(j,k)\}$, are linear or nonlinear functional operators. This mapping defines a path in three-dimensional color space parametrically in terms of the array F(j , k) . Figure 4.39 illustrates the RGB color space and two color mappings that originate at black and terminate at white. Mapping A represents the achromatic path through all shades of gray; it is the normal representation of a monochrome image. Mapping B is a spiral path through color space.

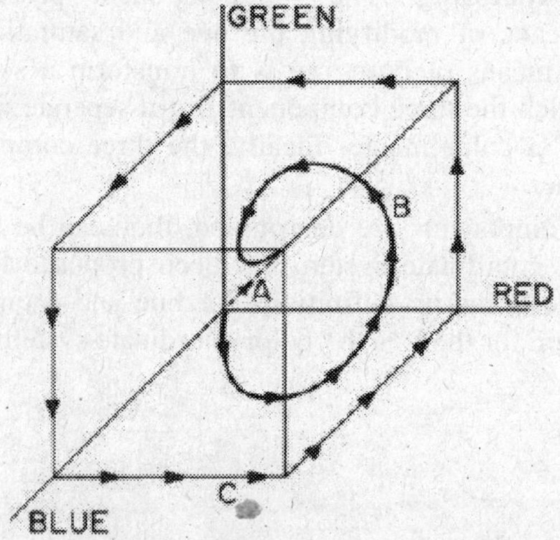


**Figure 4.39 Black-to-white and RGB perimeter pseudocolor mappings**

Another class of pseudocolor mappings includes those mappings that exclude all shades of gray. Mapping C, which follows the edges of the RGB color cube, is such an example. This mapping follows the perimeter of the gamut of reproducible colors as depicted by the uniform chromaticity scale (UCS) chromaticity chart shown in Figure 4.40. The luminance's of the colors red, green, blue, cyan, magenta and yellow that lie along the perimeter of reproducible colors are noted in the figure. It is seen that the luminance of the pseudocolor scale varies between a minimum of 0.114 for blue to a maximum of 0.886 for yellow. A maximum luminance of unity is reached only for white. In some applications, it may be desirable to fix the luminance of all displayed colors so that discrimination along the pseudocolor scale is by hue and saturation attributes of a color only. Loci of constant luminance are plotted in Figure 4.40.

Figure 4.40(a) also includes bounds for displayed colors of constant luminance. For example, if the RGB perimeter path is followed, the maximum luminance of any color must be limited to 0.114, the luminance of blue. At a luminance of 0.2, the RGB perimeter path can be followed except for the region around saturated blue. At higher luminance levels, the gamut of constant luminance colors becomes severely limited. Figure 4.40(b) is a plot of the 0.5 luminance locus. Inscribed within this locus is the locus of those colors of largest constant saturation. A pseudocolor scale along this path would have the property that all points differ only in hue.

With a given pseudocolor path in color space, it is necessary to choose the scaling between the data plane variable and the incremental path distance. On the UCS chromaticity chart, incremental distances are subjectively almost equally noticeable.

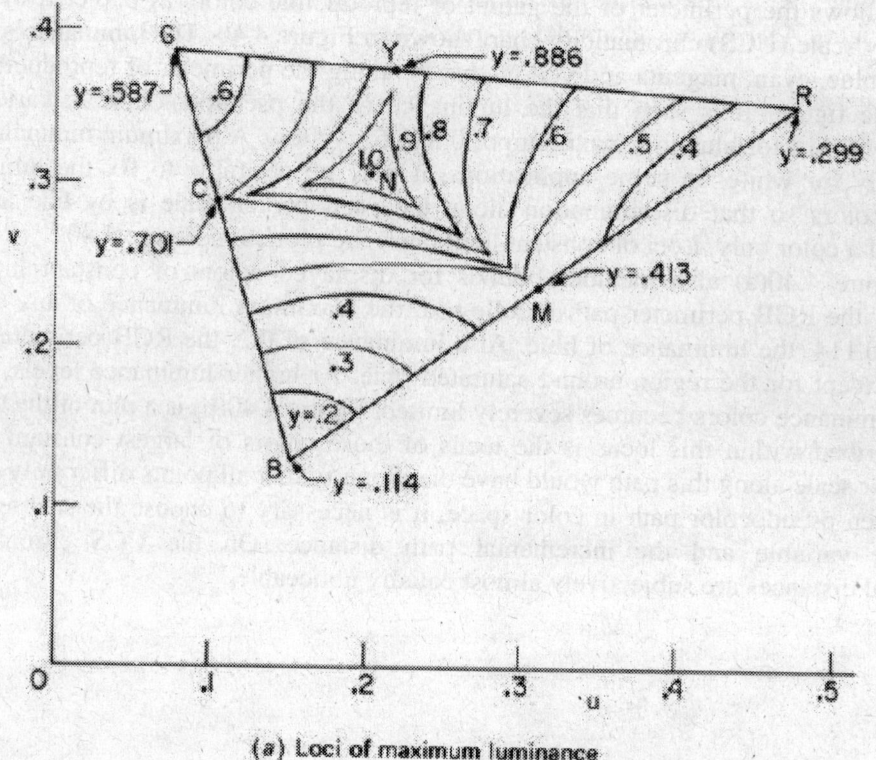


(*a*) Loci of maximum luminance

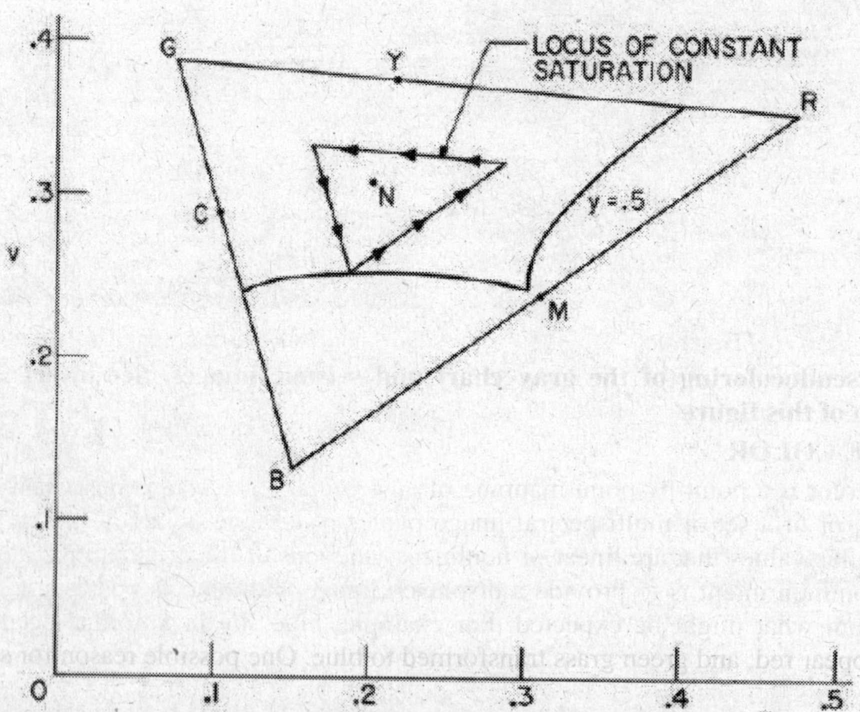


(*b*) Locus of luminance $Y = 0.5$

**Figure 4.40 Luminance loci for NTSC colors**

Therefore, it is reasonable to subdivide geometrically the path length into equal increments. Figure 4.41 shows examples of pseudocoloring of a gray scale chart image and a seismic image.

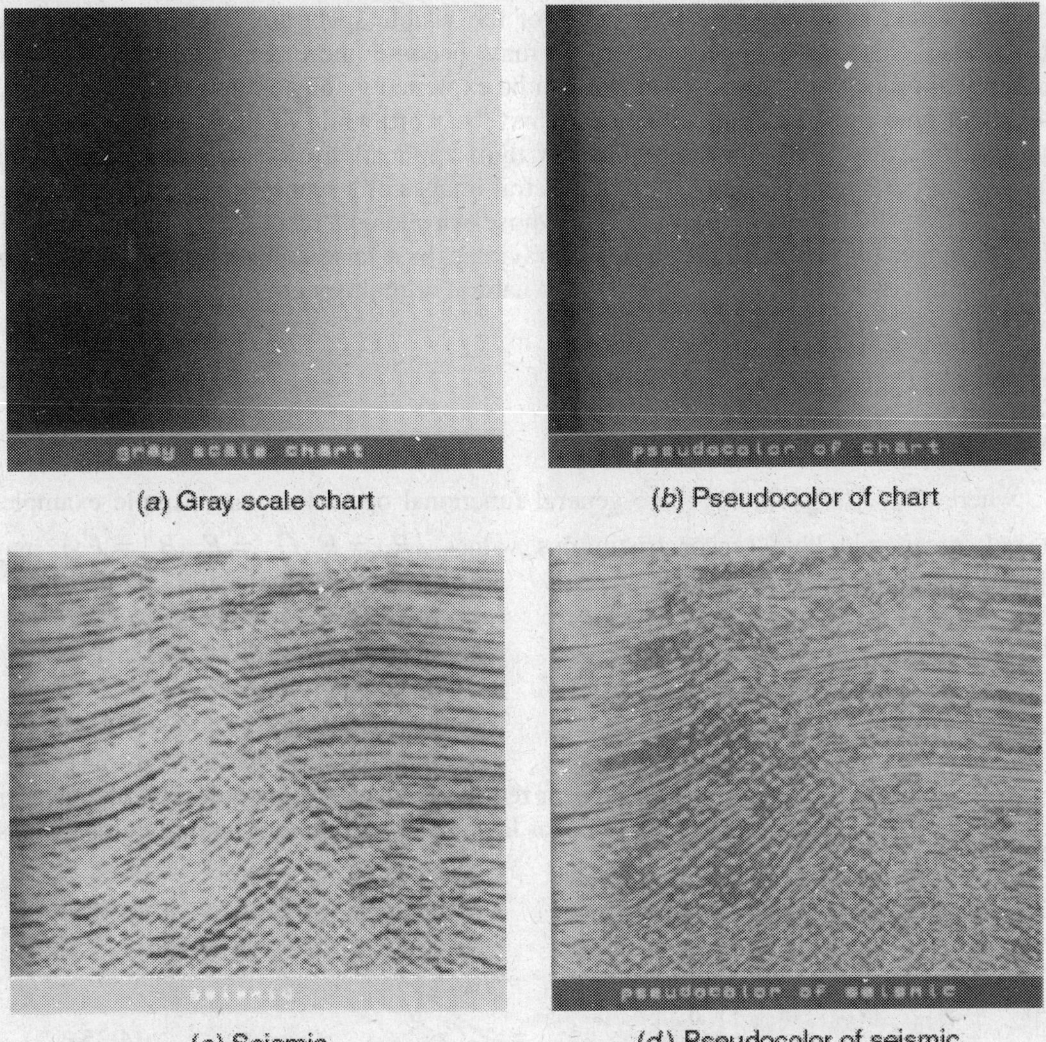


(*a*) Gray scale chart (*b*) Pseudocolor of chart

(*c*) Seismic (*d*) Pseudocolor of seismic

**Figure 4.41 Pseudocoloring of the gray_chart and seismic images. See insert for a color representation of this figure**

### 4.2.5.3. FALSE COLOR

False color is a point-by-point mapping of an original color image, described by its three primary colors, or of a set of multispectral image planes of a scene, to a color space defined by display tristimulus values that are linear or nonlinear functions of the original image pixel values (48 , 49). A common intent is to provide a displayed image with objects possessing different or false colors from what might be expected. For example, blue sky in a normal scene might be converted to appear red, and green grass transformed to blue. One possible reason for such a color mapping is to place normal objects in a strange color world so that a human observer will pay more attention to the objects than if they were colored normally.

Another reason for false color mappings is the attempt to color a normal scene to match the color sensitivity of a human viewer. For example, it is known that the luminance response of cones in the retina peaks in the green region of the visible spectrum. Thus, if a normally red object is false colored to appear green, it may become more easily detectable. Another psychophysical property of color vision that can be exploited is the contrast sensitivity of the eye to changes in blue light. In some situation it may be worthwhile to map the normal colors of objects with fine detail into shades of blue. A third application of false color is to produce a natural color representation of a set of multispectral images of a scene. Some of the multispectral images may even be obtained from sensors whose wavelength response is outside the visible wavelength range, for example, infrared or ultraviolet. In a false color mapping, the red, green and blue display color components are related to natural or multispectral images $F_i$ by

$$R_D = O_R\{F_1, F_2, \ldots\} \quad (4.33 \text{ (a)})$$

$$G_D = O_G\{F_1, F_2, \ldots\} \quad (4.33 \text{ (b)})$$

$$B_D = O_B\{F_1, F_2, \ldots\} \quad (4.33 \text{ (c)})$$

where $O_R\{.\}, O_R\{.\}, O_B\{.\}$ are general functional operators. As a simple example, the set of red, green and blue sensor tristimulus values $(R_S = F_1, G_S = F_2, B_S = F_3)$ may be interchanged according to the relation

$$\begin{bmatrix} R_D \\ G_D \\ B_D \end{bmatrix} = \begin{bmatrix} 0 & 1 & 0 \\ 0 & 0 & 1 \\ 1 & 0 & 0 \end{bmatrix} \begin{bmatrix} R_S \\ G_S \\ B_S \end{bmatrix} \quad (4.34)$$

Green objects in the original will appear red in the display, blue objects will appear green and red objects will appear blue. A general linear false color mapping of natural color images can be defined as

$$\begin{bmatrix} R_D \\ G_D \\ B_D \end{bmatrix} = \begin{bmatrix} m_{11} & m_{12} & m_{13} \\ m_{21} & m_{22} & m_{21} \\ m_{23} & m_{32} & m_{33} \end{bmatrix} \begin{bmatrix} R_S \\ G_S \\ B_S \end{bmatrix} \quad (4.35)$$

This color mapping should be recognized as a linear coordinate conversion of colors reproduced by the primaries of the original image to a new set of primaries. Figure 4.42 provides examples of false color mappings of a pair of images.

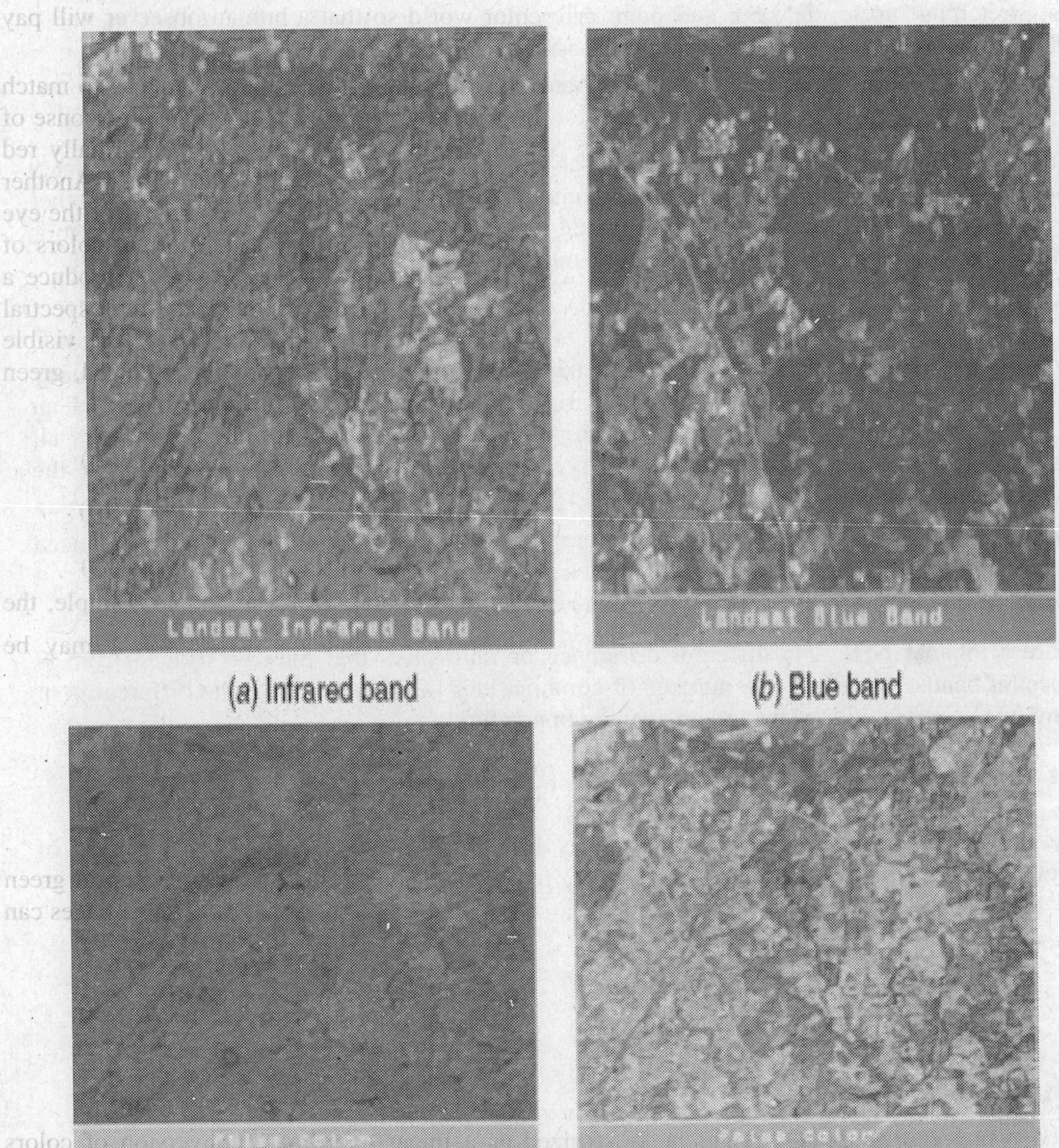


(*a*) Infrared band (*b*) Blue band

(*c*) $R$ = infrared, $G$ = 0, $B$ = blue (*d*) $R$ = infrared, $G$ = 1/2 [infrared + blue], $B$ = blue

**Figure 4.42 False coloring of multispectral images. See insert for a color representation of this figure**

## 4.2.6 MULTISPECTRAL IMAGE ENHANCEMENT

Enhancement procedures are often performed on multispectral image bands of a scene in order to accentuate salient features to assist in subsequent human interpretation or machine analysis. These procedures include individual image band enhancement techniques, such as contrast stretching, noise cleaning and edge crispening, as described earlier. Other methods, considered in this section, involve the joint processing of multispectral image bands.

Multispectral image bands can be subtracted in pairs according to the relation

$$D_{m,n}(j,k) = F_m(j,k) - F_n(j,k) \tag{4.36}$$

in order to accentuate reflectivity variations between the multispectral bands. An associated advantage is the removal of any unknown but common bias components that may exist. Another simple but highly effective means of multispectral image enhancement is the formation of ratios of the image bands. The ratio image between the mth and nth multispectral bands is defined as

$$R_{m,n}(j,k) = \frac{F_m(j,k)}{F_n(j,k)} \tag{4.37}$$

It is assumed that the image bands are adjusted to have nonzero pixel values. In many multispectral imaging systems, the image band $F_n(j, k)$ can be modeled by the product of an object reflectivity function $R_n(j, k)$ and an illumination function $I(j, k)$ that is identical for all multispectral bands. Rationing of such imagery provides an automatic compensation of the illumination factor. The ratio $F_m(j,k)/[F_n(j,k) \pm \Delta(j,k]$, for which $\Delta(j,k)$represents a quantization level uncertainty, can vary considerably if is small. This variation can be reduced significantly by forming the logarithm of the ratios defined by

$$L_{m,n}(j,k) = \log\{R_{m,n}(j,k)\} = \log\{F_m(j,k)\} - \log\{F_n(j,k)\} \tag{4.38}$$

There are a total of N(N – 1) different difference or ratio pairs that may be formed from N multispectral bands. To reduce the number of combinations to be considered, the differences or ratios are often formed with respect to an average image field:

$$A(j,k) = \frac{1}{N}\sum_{n=1}^{N} F_n(j,k) \tag{4.39}$$

Unitary transforms between multispectral planes have also been employed as a means of enhancement. For N image bands, a N x 1 vector

$$x = \begin{bmatrix} F_1(j,k) \\ F_2(j,k) \\ . \\ . \\ F_N(j,k) \end{bmatrix} \tag{4.40}$$

is formed at each coordinate (j, k). Then, a transformation

$$y = A\,x \tag{4.41}$$

is formed where A is a N x N unitary matrix. A common transformation is the principal components decomposition, in which the rows of the matrix A are composed of the eigenvectors of the covariance matrix $A_X$ between the bands. The matrix A performs a diagonalization of the covariance matrix $A_X$ such that the covariance matrix of the transformed imagery bands

$$\mathbf{K_y} = \mathbf{A K_x A}^T = \Lambda \tag{4.42}$$

is a diagonal matrix whose elements are the eigen values of $K_X$ arranged in descending value. The principal components decomposition, therefore, results in a set of decorrelated data arrays whose energies are ranged in amplitude. This process, of course, requires knowledge of the covariance matrix between the multispectral bands. The covariance matrix must be either modeled, estimated or measured. If the covariance matrix is highly nonstationary, the principal components method becomes difficult to utilize. Figure 4.43 contains a set of four multispectral images, and Figure 4.44 exhibits their corresponding log ratios. Principal components bands of these multispectral images are illustrated in Figure 4.45

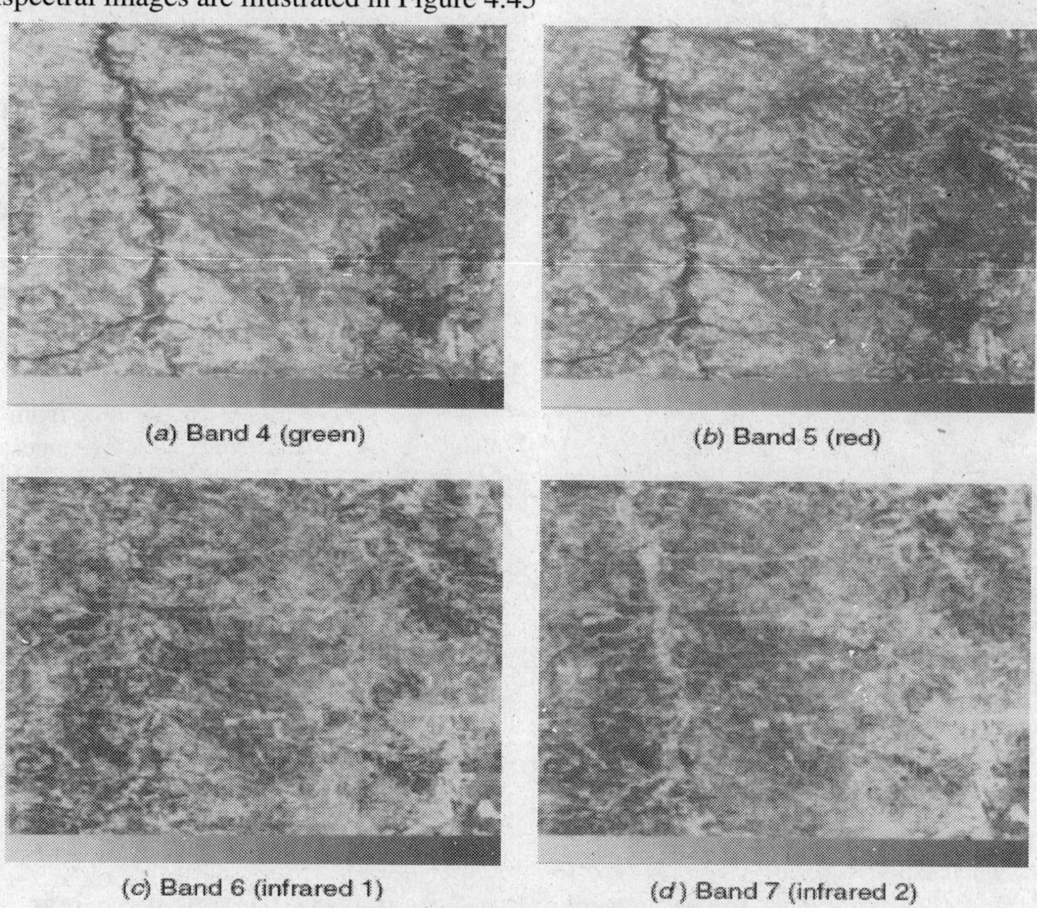

(*a*) Band 4 (green) (*b*) Band 5 (red)

(*c*) Band 6 (infrared 1) (*d*) Band 7 (infrared 2)

**Figure 4.43 Multispectral images**

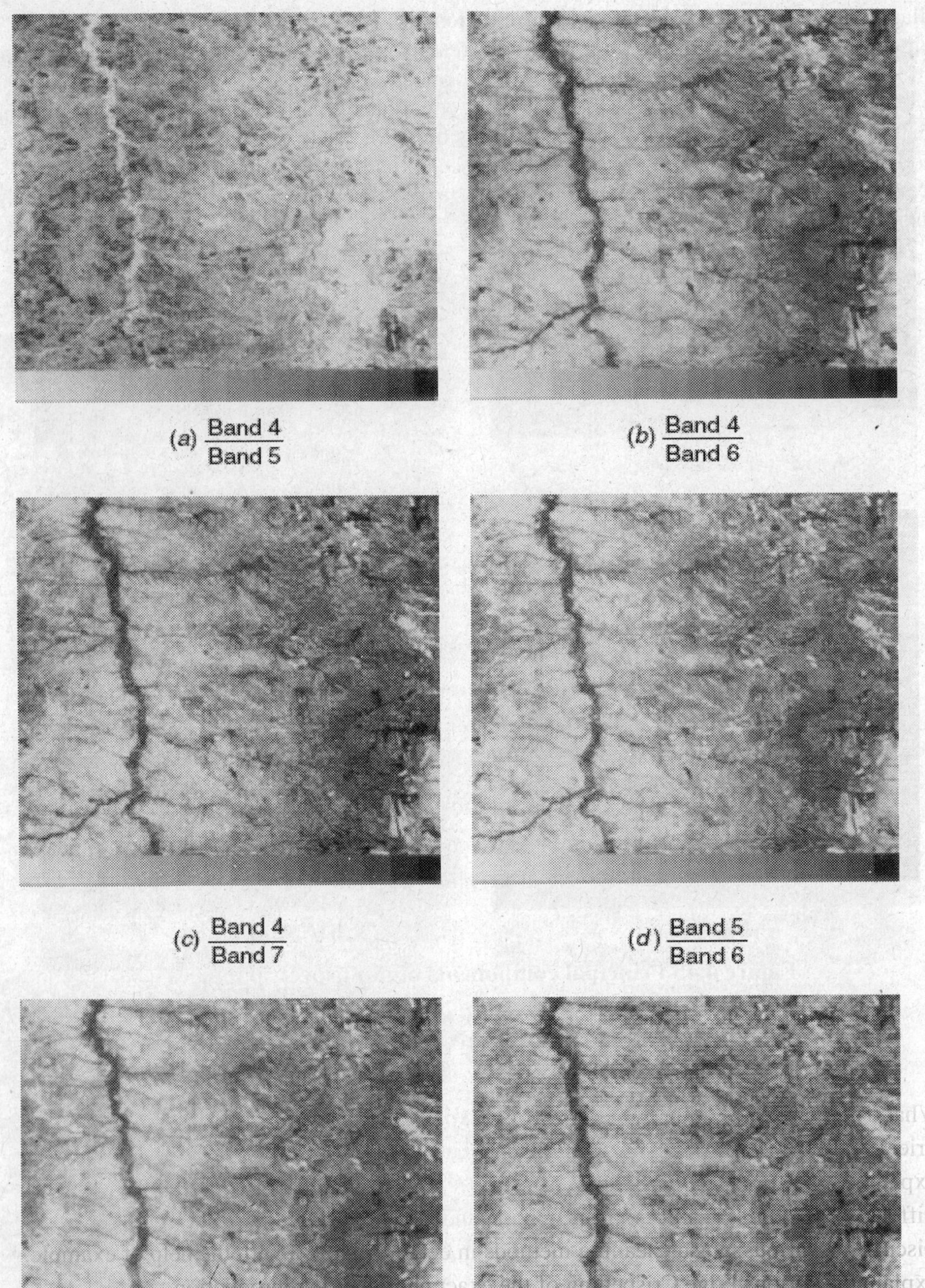

(a) $\frac{\text{Band 4}}{\text{Band 5}}$ (b) $\frac{\text{Band 4}}{\text{Band 6}}$

(c) $\frac{\text{Band 4}}{\text{Band 7}}$ (d) $\frac{\text{Band 5}}{\text{Band 6}}$

**Figure 4.44 Logarithmic ratios of multispectral images**

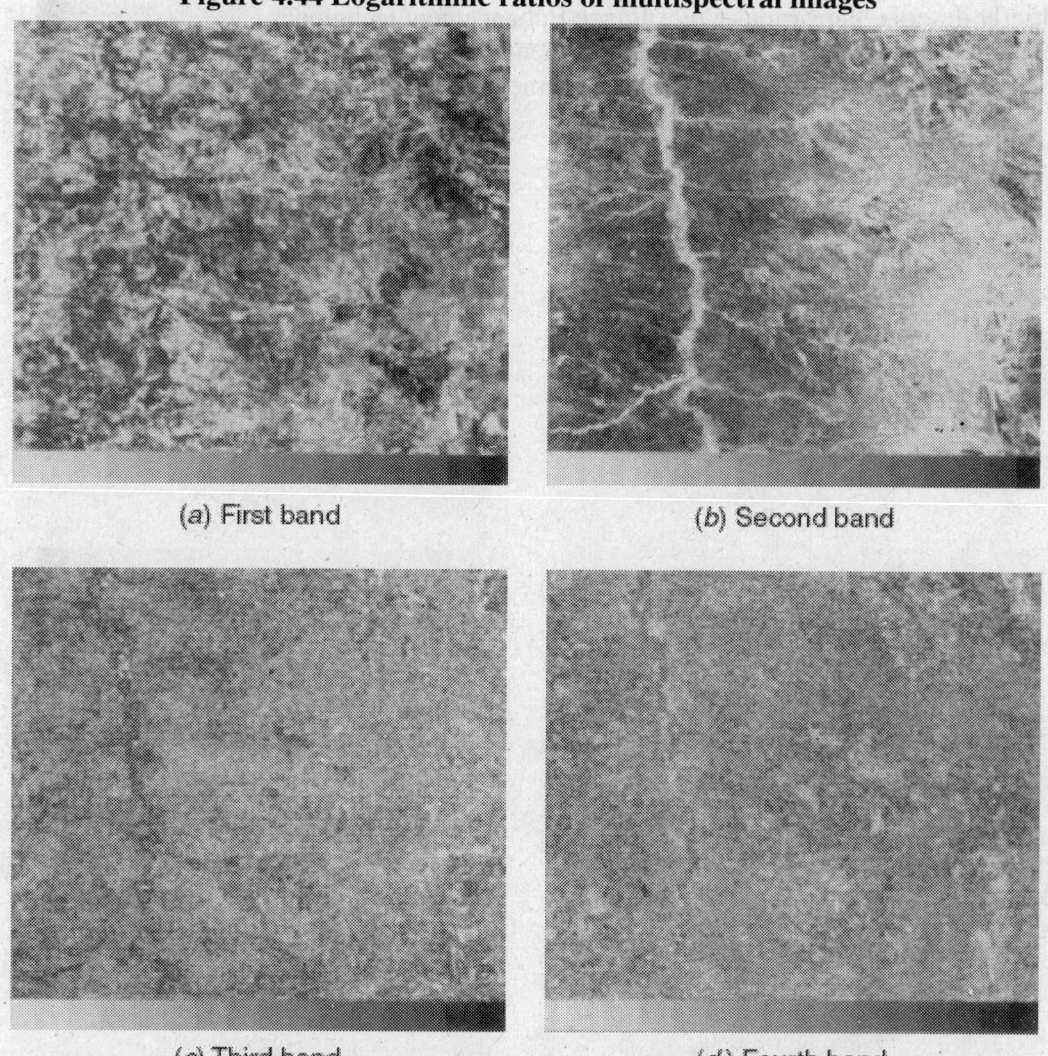

(*a*) First band (*b*) Second band

(*c*) Third band (*d*) Fourth band

**Figure 4.45 Principal components of multispectral images**

# QUESTION BANK

Q1. What do you mean by image enhancement? Explain with the help of example.
Q2. Briefly describe the various image contrast enhancements;
Q3. Explain the Histogram Modification in details?
Q4. Difference between Histogram Modification and Adaptive Histogram Modification.
Q5. Discuss the various Noise Cleaning methods in details? Explain with the help of example.
Q6. Explain the various Edge Crispening of the exact photometric reproduction.

Q7. Write a short note on the statistical differencing in details.
Q8. Briefly describe the various Color Image Enhancement techniques.
Q9. Explain the Multispectral Image Enhancement.
Q10. Difference between Color Image Enhancement and Multispectral Image Enhancement.

# CHAPTER 5

# IMAGE RESTORATION

## 5.1 INTRODUCTION

Image restoration refers to removal or minimization of known degradations in an image. This includes deblurring of images degraded by the limitations of a sensor or its environment, noise filtering and correction of geometric distortion or non-linearities due to sensors in image restoration. The image of a point source is blurred and degraded due to noise by an imaging system. If the imaging system is linear, the image of an object can be expressed as

$$g(x,y)=\int_{-\infty}^{\infty}\int_{-\infty}^{\infty}h(x,y;\alpha,\beta)f(\alpha,\beta)d\alpha d\beta+\eta(x,y)$$

Where $\eta(x,y)$ is the additive noise function , $f(\alpha,\beta)$ is the object , g(x, y) is the image and $h(x,y,\alpha,\beta)$ is called the point spreed function (PSF). A typical image restoration problem is to find an estimate of $f(\alpha,\beta)$ given the PSF, the blurred image and the statistical properties of the noise process.

A fundamental result in filtering theory used commonly for image restoration is called the wiener filter. This filter gives the best linear mean square estimate of the object from the observations. It can be implementation in frequency domain via the fast unitary transforms, in spatial domain by two dimensional recursive techniques similar to Kalman filtering, or by FIR nonrecursive filters. It can also be implemented as a semirecursive filter that employs a unitary transform in one of the dimensions and a recursive filter in the other.

Several other image restoration methods such as least squares, constrained least squares and sline interpolation methods can be shown to belong to the class of wiener filtering algorithms. other methods such as maximum likelihood , maximum entropy and maximum a posteriori are nonlinear techniques that require iterative solutions.

## 5.2 GENERAL IMAGE RESTORATION MODELS

In order effectively to design a digital image restoration system, it is necessary quantitatively to characterize the image degradation effects of the physical imaging system, the image digitizer and the image display. Basically, the procedure is to model the image degradation effects and then perform operations to undo the model to obtain a restored image. It should be emphasized that accurate image modeling is often the key to effective image restoration. There are two basic approaches to the modeling of image degradation effects: a priori modeling and a posteriori modeling. In the former case, measurements are made on the physical imaging system, digitizer and display to determine their response for an arbitrary image field. In some instances, it will be possible to model the system response deterministically, while in other situations it will only be possible to determine the system response in a stochastic sense. The a posteriori modeling approach is to develop the model for the image degradations based on measurements of a particular image to be restored.

Basically, these two approaches differ only in the manner in which information is gathered to describe the character of the image degradation. Figure 5.1 shows a general model of a digital imaging system and restoration process. In the model, a continuous image light distribution $C(x, y, t, \lambda)$ dependent on spatial coordinates (x, y), time (t) and spectral wavelength $(\lambda)$ is assumed to exist as the driving force of a physical imaging system subject to point and spatial degradation effects and corrupted by deterministic and stochastic disturbances.

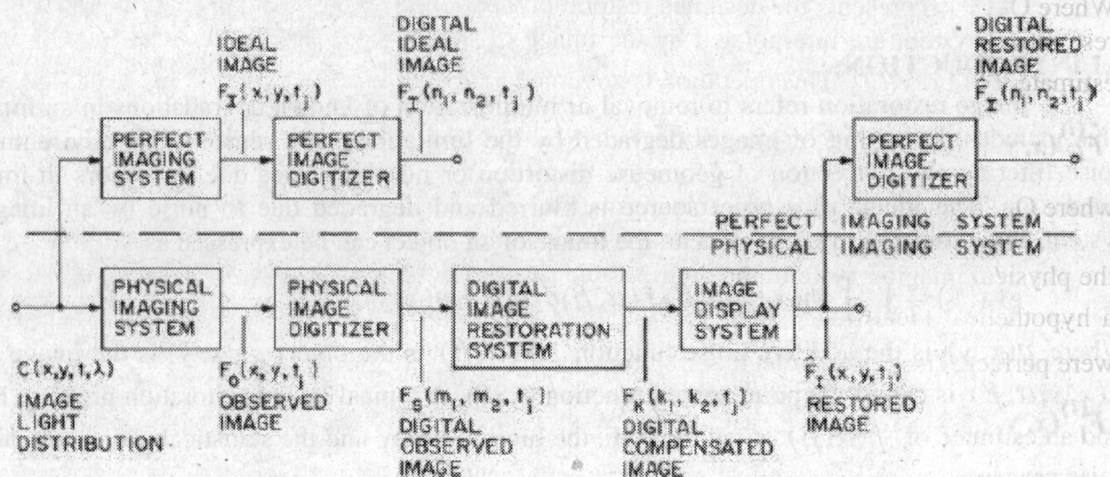


**Figure 5.1. Digital image restoration model**

Potential degradations include diffraction in the optical system, sensor nonlinearities, optical system aberrations, film nonlinearities, atmospheric turbulence effects, image motion blur and geometric distortion. Noise disturbances may be caused by electronic imaging sensors or film granularity. In this model, the physical imaging system produces a set of output image fields $F_o^{(i)}(x, y, t_j)$ at time instant $t_j$ described by the general relation

$$F_O^{(i)}(x, y, t_j) = O_P\{C(x, y, t, \lambda)\} \tag{5.1}$$

Where $O_P\{\ .\ \}$ represents a general operator that is dependent on the space coordinates (x, y), the time history (t), the wavelength $(\lambda)$ and the amplitude of the light distribution (C). For a monochrome imaging system, there will only be a single output field, while for a natural color imaging system, $F_o^{(i)}(x, y, t_j)$ may denote the red, green and blue tristimulus bands for i = 1, 2, 3, respectively. Multispectral imagery will also involve several output bands of data.

In the general model of Figure 5.1, each observed image field $F_o^{(i)}(x, y, t_j)$ is digitized, following the techniques outlined in Part 2, to produce an array of image samples $F_S^{(i)}(m_1, m_2, t_j)$ at each time instant $t_j$. The output samples of the digitizer are related to the input observed field by

$$F_S^{(i)}(m_1, m_2, t_j) = O_G\{F_O^{(i)}(x, y, t_j)\} \tag{5.2}$$

Where $O_G\{\ .\ \}$ is an operator modeling the image digitization process.

A digital image restoration system that follows produces an output array $F_K^{(i)}(K_1, K_2, t_j)$ by the transformation

$$F_K^{(i)}(k_1, k_2, t_j) = O_R\{F_S^{(i)}(m_1, m_2, t_j)\} \tag{5.3}$$

Where $O_R\{\ .\ \}$ represents the designed restoration operator. Next, the output samples of the digital restoration system are interpolated by the image display system to produce a continuous image estimate $F_l^{(i)}(x, y, t_j)$. This operation is governed by the relation

$$\hat{F}_I^{(i)}(x, y, t_j) = O_D\{F_K^{(i)}(k_1, k_2, t_j)\} \tag{5.4}$$

where $O_D\{\ .\ \}$models the display transformation.

The function of the digital image restoration system is to compensate for degradations of the physical imaging system, the digitizer and the image display system to produce an estimate of a hypothetical ideal image field $F_l^{(i)}(x, y, t_j)$ that would be displayed if all physical elements were perfect. The perfect imaging system would produce an ideal image field modeled by

$$F_I^{(i)}(x, y, t_j) = O_I\left\{\int_0^{\infty}\int_{t_j-T}^{t_j} C(x, y, t, \lambda) U_i(t, \lambda)\, dt\, d\lambda\right\} \tag{5.5}$$

where $U_i(t, \lambda)$is a desired temporal and spectral response function, T is the observation period and $O_I\{\ .\ \}$is a desired point and spatial response function. Usually, it will not be possible to restore perfectly the observed image such that the output image field is identical to the ideal image field. The design objective of the image restoration processor is to minimize some error measure between

$F_I^{(i)}(x, y, t_j)$ and $\hat{F}_I^{(i)}(x, y, t_j)$.

The discussion here is limited, for the most part, to a consideration of techniques that minimize the mean-square error between the ideal and estimated image fields as defined by

$$\mathcal{E}_i = E\left\{[F_I^{(i)}(x, y, t_j) - \hat{F}_I^{(i)}(x, y, t_j)]^2\right\} \tag{5.6}$$

where E{.}denotes the expectation operator. Often, it will be desirable to place side constraints on the error minimization, for example, to require that the image estimate be strictly positive if it is to represent light intensities that are positive. Because the restoration process is to be performed digitally, it is often more convenient to restrict the error measure to discrete points on the ideal and estimated image fields. These discrete arrays are obtained by mathematical models of perfect image digitizers that produce the arrays

$$F_I^{(i)}(n_1, n_2, t_j) = F_I^{(i)}(x, y, t_j)\delta(x - n_1\Delta, y - n_2\Delta) \tag{5.7 (a)}$$

$$\hat{F}_I^{(i)}(n_1, n_2, t_j) = \hat{F}_I^{(i)}(x, y, t_j)\delta(x - n_1\Delta, y - n_2\Delta) \tag{5.7 (b)}$$

It is assumed that continuous image fields are sampled at a spatial period $\Delta$ satisfying the Nyquist criterion. Also, quantization error is assumed negligible. It should be noted that the processes indicated by the blocks of Figure 5.1 above the dashed division line represent mathematical modeling and are not physical operations performed on physical image fields and arrays. With this discretization of the continuous ideal and estimated image fields, the corresponding mean-square restoration error becomes

$$\mathcal{E}_i = E\left\{[F_I^{(i)}(n_1, n_2, t_j) - \hat{F}_I^{(i)}(n_1, n_2, t_j)]^2\right\} \tag{5.8}$$

With the relationships of Figure 5.1 quantitatively established, the restoration problem may be formulated as follows:

Given the sampled observation $F_S^{(i)}(m_1, m_2, t_j)$ expressed in terms of the image light distribution $C(x, y, t, \lambda)$, determine the transfer function O$_k${.} that minimizes the error measure between $F_I^{(i)}(x, y, t_j)$ and $F_I^{(-i)}(x, y, t_j)$ subject to desired constraints.

There are no general solutions for the restoration problem as formulated above because of the complexity of the physical imaging system. To proceed further, it is necessary to be more specific about the type of degradation and the method of restoration. The following sections describe models for the elements of the generalized Imaging system of Figure 5.1.

## 5.3 OPTICAL SYSTEMS MODELS

One of the major advances in the field of optics during the past 50 years has been the application of system concepts to optical imaging. Imaging devices consisting of lenses, mirrors, prisms and so on, can be considered to provide a deterministic transformation of an input spatial light distribution to some output spatial light distribution. Also, the system concept can be extended to encompass the spatial propagation of light through free space or some dielectric medium.

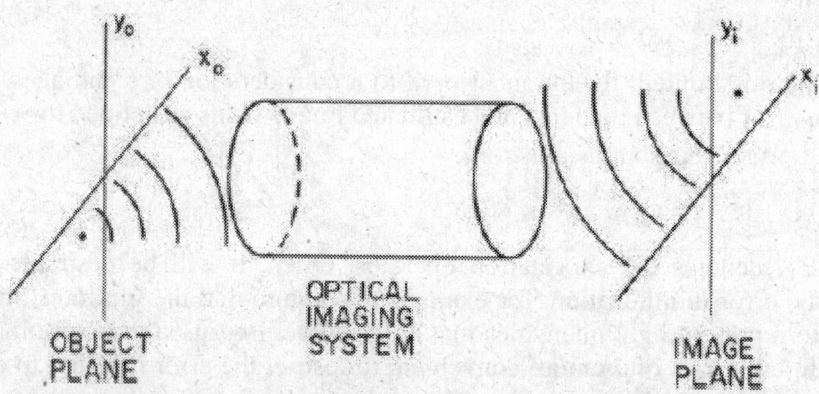


**Figure 5.2 Generalized optical imaging system.**

In the study of geometric optics, it is assumed that light rays always travel in a straight-line path in a homogeneous medium. By this assumption, a bundle of rays passing through a clear aperture onto a screen produces a geometric light projection of the aperture. However, if the light distribution at the region between the light and dark areas on the screen is examined in detail, it is found that the boundary is not sharp. This effect is more pronounced as the aperture size is decreased. For a pinhole aperture, the entire screen appears diffusely illuminated. From a simplistic viewpoint, the aperture causes a bending of rays called diffraction. Diffraction of light can be quantitatively characterized by considering light as electromagnetic radiation that satisfies Maxwell's equations. The formulation of a complete theory of optical imaging from the basic electromagnetic principles of diffraction theory is a complex and lengthy task. Figure 5.2 is a diagram of a generalized optical imaging system. A point in the object plane at coordinate $(x_\sigma, y_\sigma)$ of intensity $I_o(x_\sigma, y_\sigma)$ radiates energy toward an imaging system characterized by an entrance pupil, exit pupil and intervening system transformation. Electromagnetic waves emanating from the optical system are focused to a point $(x_i, y_i)$ on the image plane producing intensity $I_i(x_i, y_i)$. .

The imaging system is said to be diffraction limited if the light distribution at the image plane produced by a point-source object consists of a converging spherical wave whose extent is limited only by the exit pupil. If the wavefront of the electromagnetic radiation emanating from the exit pupil is not spherical, the optical system is said to possess aberrations.

In most optical image formation systems, the optical radiation emitted by an object arises from light transmitted or reflected from an incoherent light source. The image radiation can often be regarded as quasi monochromatic in the sense that the spectral bandwidth of the image radiation detected at the image plane is small with respect to the center wavelength of the radiation. Under these joint assumptions, the imaging system Figure 5.2 will respond as a linear system in terms of the intensity of its input and output fields. The relationship between the image intensity and object intensity for the optical system can then be represented by the superposition integral equation

$$I_i(x_i, y_i) = \int_{-\infty}^{\infty}\int_{-\infty}^{\infty} H(x_i, y_i;\, x_o, y_o) I_o(x_o, y_o)\, dx_o\, dy_o \tag{5.9}$$

Where $H(x_i, y_i; x_\sigma, y\sigma)$ represents the image intensity response to a point source of light. Often, the intensity impulse response is space invariant and the input–output relationship is given by the convolution equation

$$I_i(x_i, y_i) = \int_{-\infty}^{\infty}\int_{-\infty}^{\infty} H(x_i - x_o, y_i - y_o) I_o(x_o, y_o)\, dx_o\, dy_o \tag{5.10}$$

In this case, the normalized Fourier transforms

$$\mathcal{I}_o(\omega_x, \omega_y) = \frac{\int_{-\infty}^{\infty}\int_{-\infty}^{\infty} I_o(x_o, y_o) \exp\{-i(\omega_x x_o + \omega_y y_o)\}\, dx_o\, dy_o}{\int_{-\infty}^{\infty}\int_{-\infty}^{\infty} I_o(x_o, y_o)\, dx_o\, dy_o} \tag{5.11 (a)}$$

$$\mathcal{I}_i(\omega_x, \omega_y) = \frac{\int_{-\infty}^{\infty}\int_{-\infty}^{\infty} I_i(x_i, y_i) \exp\{-i(\omega_x x_i + \omega_y y_i)\}\, dx_i\, dy_i}{\int_{-\infty}^{\infty}\int_{-\infty}^{\infty} I_i(x_i, y_i)\, dx_i\, dy_i} \tag{5.11 (b)}$$

of the object and image intensity fields are related by

$$\mathcal{I}_o(\omega_x, \omega_y) = \mathcal{H}(\omega_x, \omega_y)\mathcal{I}_i(\omega_x, \omega_y) \tag{5.12}$$

where $|\mathrm{H}(\omega_x, \omega_y)|$, which is called the optical transfer function (OTF), is defined by

$$\mathcal{H}(\omega_x, \omega_y) = \frac{\int_{-\infty}^{\infty}\int_{-\infty}^{\infty} H(x, y) \exp\{-i(\omega_x x + \omega_y y)\}\, dx\, dy}{\int_{-\infty}^{\infty}\int_{-\infty}^{\infty} H(x, y)\, dx\, dy} \tag{5.13}$$

The absolute value $\left|H(\omega_x, \omega_y)\right|$ of the OTF is known as the modulation transfer function (MTF) of the optical system. The most common optical image formation system is a circular thin lens. Figure 5.3 illustrates the OTF for such a lens as a function of its degree of misfocus (1, p. 486; 4). For extreme misfocus, the OTF will actually become negative at some spatial frequencies. In this state, the lens will cause a contrast reversal: Dark objects will appear light, and vice versa. Earth's atmosphere acts as an imaging system for optical radiation transversing a path through the atmosphere. Normally, the index of refraction of the atmosphere remains relatively constant over the optical extent of an object, but in some instances atmospheric turbulence can produce a spatially variable index of

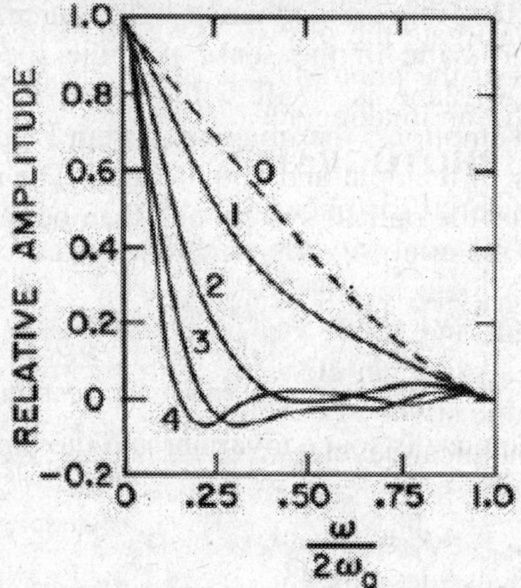


**Figure 5.3 Cross section of transfer function of a lens. Numbers indicate degree of misfocus**

Refraction that leads to an effective blurring of any imaged object. An equivalent impulse response

$$H(x, y) = K_1 \exp\left\{-(K_2 x^2 + K_3 y^2)^{5/6}\right\} \tag{5.14}$$

where the $K_n$ are constants, has been predicted and verified mathematically by experimentation for long-exposure image formation. For convenience in analysis, the function 5/6 is often replaced by unity to obtain a Gaussian-shaped impulse response model of the form

$$H(x, y) = K \exp\left\{-\left(\frac{x^2}{2b_x^2} + \frac{y^2}{2b_y^2}\right)\right\} \tag{5.15}$$

where K is an amplitude scaling constant and $b_x$ and $b_y$ are blur-spread factors. Under the assumption that the impulse response of a physical imaging system is independent of spectral wavelength and time, the observed image field can be modeled by the superposition integral equation

$$F_O^{(i)}(x, y, t_j) = O_C\left\{\int_{-\infty}^{\infty}\int_{-\infty}^{\infty} C(\alpha, \beta, t, \lambda) H(x, y; \alpha, \beta)\, d\alpha\, d\beta\right\} \tag{5.16}$$

Where $O_C\{\ .\ \}$ is an operator that models the spectral and temporal characteristics of the physical imaging system. If the impulse response is spatially invariant, the model reduces to the convolution integral equation

$$F_O^{(i)}(x, y, t_j) = O_C\left\{\int_{-\infty}^{\infty}\int_{-\infty}^{\infty} C(\alpha, \beta, t, \lambda) H(x-\alpha, y-\beta)\, d\alpha\, d\beta\right\} \tag{5.17}$$

## 5.4. PHOTOGRAPHIC PROCESS MODELS

There are many different types of materials and chemical processes that have been utilized for photographic image recording. No attempt is made here either to survey the field of photography or to deeply investigate the physics of photography. Rather, the attempt here is to develop mathematical models of the photographic process in order to characterize quantitatively the photographic components of an imaging system.

### 5.4.1. MONOCHROMATIC PHOTOGRAPHY

The most common material for photographic image recording is silver halide emulsion, depicted in Figure 5.4. In this material, silver halide grains are suspended in a transparent layer of gelatin that is deposited on a glass, acetate or paper backing. If the backing is transparent, a transparency can be produced, and if the backing is a white paper, a reflection print can be obtained. When light strikes a grain, an electrochemical conversion process occurs, and part of the grain is converted to metallic silver. A development center is then said to exist in the grain. In the development process, a chemical developing agent causes grains with partial silver content to be converted entirely to metallic silver. Next, the film is fixed by chemically removing unexposed grains.

The photographic process described above is called a nonreversal process. It produces a negative image in the sense that the silver density is inversely proportional to the exposing light. A positive reflection print of an image can be obtained in a two-stage process with nonreversal materials. First, a negative transparency is produced, and then the negative transparency is illuminated to expose negative reflection print paper. The resulting silver density on the developed paper is then proportional to the light intensity that exposed the negative transparency. A positive transparency of an image can be obtained with a reversal type of film. This film is exposed and undergoes a first development similar to that of a nonreversal film. At this stage in the photographic process, all grains that have been exposed to light are converted completely to metallic silver. In the next step, the metallic silver grains are chemically removed. The film is then uniformly exposed to light, or alternatively, a chemical process is performed to expose the remaining silver halide grains. Then the exposed grains are developed and fixed to produce a positive transparency whose density is proportional to the original light exposure.

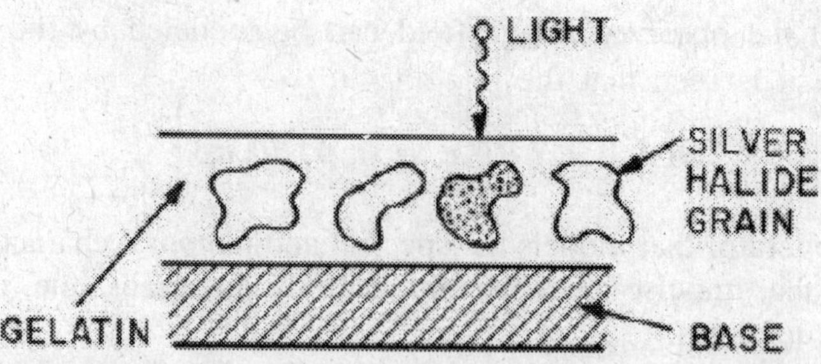


**Figure 5.4. Cross section of silver halide emulsion**

The relationships between light intensity exposing a film and the density of silver grains in a transparency or print can be described quantitatively by sensitometric measurements. Through sensitometry, a model is sought that will predict the spectral light distribution passing through an illuminated transparency or reflected from a print as a function of the spectral light distribution of the exposing light and certain physical parameters of the photographic process. The first stage of the photographic process, that of exposing the silver halide grains, can be modeled to a first-order approximation by the integral equation

$$X(C) = k_x \int C(\lambda)L(\lambda)\,d\lambda \tag{5.18}$$

where X(C) is the integrated exposure, $C(\lambda)$ represents the spectral energy distribution of the exposing light, $L(\lambda)$ denotes the spectral sensitivity of the film or paper plus any spectral losses resulting from filters or optical elements and $K_x$ is an exposure constant that is controllable by an aperture or exposure time setting. Equatión 5.18 assumes a fixed exposure time. Ideally, if the exposure time were to be increased by a certain factor, the exposure would be increased by the same factor.

Unfortunately, this relationship does not hold exactly. The departure from linearity is called a reciprocity failure of the film. Another anomaly in exposure prediction is the intermittency effect, in which the exposures for a constant intensity light and for an intermittently flashed light differ even though the incident energy is the same for both sources. Thus, if Eq. 5.18 is to be utilized as an exposure model, it is necessary to observe its limitations: The equation is strictly valid only for a fixed exposure time and constant-intensity illumination. The transmittance $\tau(\lambda)$ of a developed reversal or nonreversal transparency as a function of wavelength can be ideally related to the density of silver grains by the exponential law of absorption as given by

$$\tau(\lambda) = \exp\{-d_e D(\lambda)\} \tag{5.19}$$

where $D(\lambda)$ represents the characteristic density as a function of wavelength for a reference exposure value and $d_e$ is a variable proportional to the actual exposure. For monochrome transparencies, the characteristic density function $D(\lambda)$ is reasonably constant over the visible region. As Eq. 5.19 indicates, high silver densities result in low transmittances, and vice versa. It is common practice to change the proportionality constant of Eq. 5.19 so that measurements are made in exponent ten units. Thus, the transparency transmittance can be equivalently written as

$$\tau(\lambda) = 10^{-d_x D(\lambda)} \tag{5.20}$$

where $d_x$ is the density variable, inversely proportional to exposure, for exponent 10 units. From Eq. 5.20, it is seen that the photographic density is logarithmically related to the transmittance. Thus,

$$d_x D(\lambda) = -\log_{10} \tau(\lambda) \tag{5.21}$$

The reflectivity $r_o(\lambda)$ of a photographic print as a function of wavelength is also inversely proportional to its silver density, and follows the exponential law of absorption of Eq. 5.19. Thus, from Eqs. 5.20 and 5.21, one obtains directly

$$r_o(\lambda) = 10^{-d_x D(\lambda)} \tag{5.22}$$

$$d_x D(\lambda) = -\log_{10} r_o(\lambda) \tag{5.23}$$

where $d_x$ is an appropriately evaluated variable proportional to the exposure of the photographic paper. The relational model between photographic density and transmittance or reflectivity is straightforward and reasonably accurate.

The major problem is the next step of modeling the relationship between the exposure X(C) and the density variable $d_x$. Figure 5.5(a) shows a typical curve of the transmittance of a nonreversal transparency as a function of exposure. It is to be noted that the curve is highly nonlinear except for a relatively narrow region in the lower exposure range. In Figure 5.5(b), the curve of Figure 5.5(a) has been replotted as transmittance versus the logarithm of exposure. An approximate linear relationship is found to exist between transmittance and the logarithm of exposure, but operation in this exposure region is usually of little use in imaging systems.

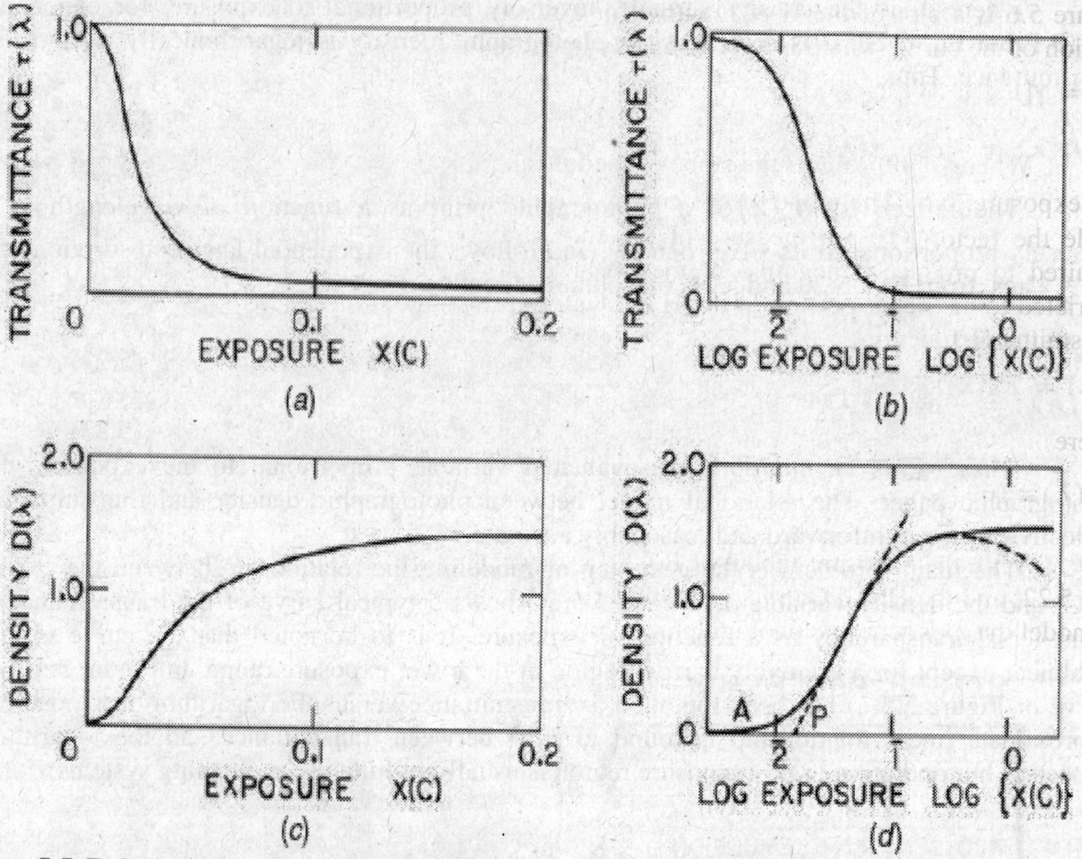

**Figure 5.5 Relationships between transmittance, density and exposure for a nonreversal film**

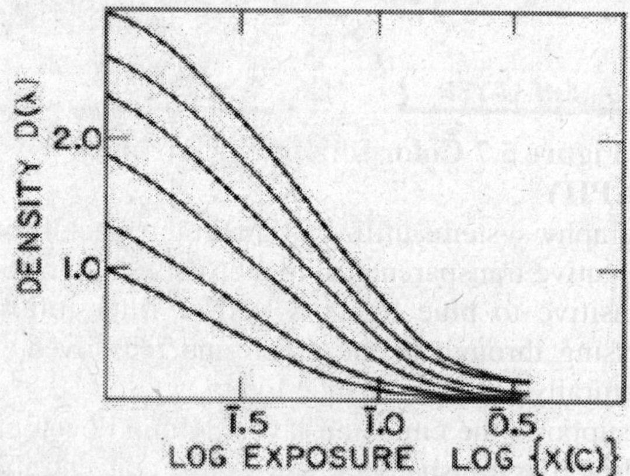


**Figure 5.6 H & D curves for a reversal film as a function of development time**

The parameter of interest in photography is the photographic density variable $d_x$, which is plotted as a function of exposure and logarithm of exposure in Figure 5.5(c) and 5.5(d). The plot of density versus logarithm of exposure is known as the H & D curve after Hurter and Driffield, who performed fundamental investigations of the relationships between density and exposure.

Figure 5.6 is a plot of the H & D curve for a reversal type of film. In figure 5.5(d), the central portion of the curve, which is approximately linear, has been approximated by the line defined by

$$d_x = \gamma[\log_{10} X(C) - K_F] \tag{5.24}$$

Where $\lambda$ represents the slope of the line and KF denotes the intercept of the line with the log exposure axis. The slope of the curve $\lambda$ (gamma) is a measure of the contrast of the film, while the factor KF is a measure of the film speed; that is, a measure of the base exposure required to produce a negative in the linear region of the H & D curve. If the exposure is restricted to the linear portion of the H & D curve, substitution of Eq. 5.24 into Eq. 5.20 yields a transmittance function

$$\tau(\lambda) = K_\tau(\lambda)[X(C)]^{-\gamma D(\lambda)} \tag{5.25}$$

where

$$K_\tau(\lambda) \equiv 10^{\gamma K_F D(\lambda)} \tag{5.26}$$

With the exposure model of Eq. 5.18, the transmittance or reflection models of Eqs. 5.20 and 5.22, and the H & D curve, or its linearized model of Eq. 5.24, it is possible mathematically to model the monochrome photographic process.

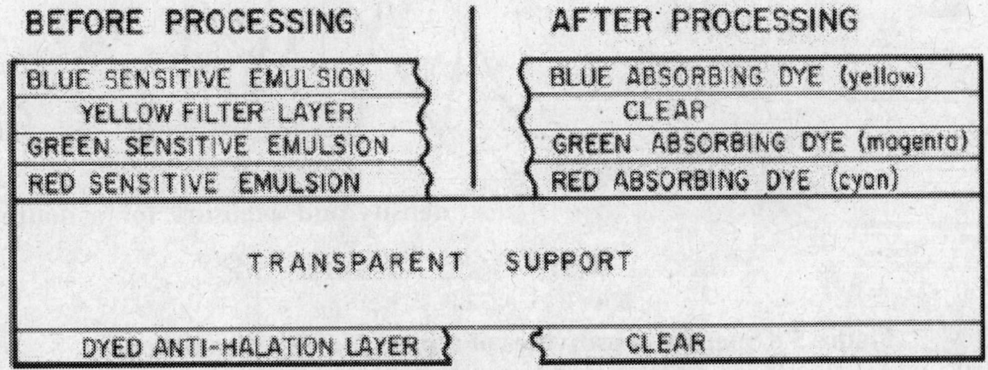


**Figure 5.7 Color film integral tripack**

### 5.4.2 COLOR PHOTOGRAPHY

Modern color photography systems utilize an integral tripack film, as illustrated in Figure 5.7, to produce positive or negative transparencies. In a cross section of this film, the first layer is a silver halide emulsion sensitive to blue light. A yellow filter following the blue emulsion prevents blue light from passing through to the green and red silver emulsions that follow in consecutive layers and are naturally sensitive to blue light.

A transparent base supports the emulsion layers. Upon development, the blue emulsion layer is converted into a yellow dye transparency whose dye concentration is proportional to the blue exposure for a negative transparency and inversely proportional for a positive transparency. Similarly, the green and red emulsion layers become magenta and cyan dye layers, respectively. Color prints can be obtained by a variety of processes. The most common technique is to produce a positive print from a color negative transparency onto nonreversal color paper. In the establishment of a mathematical model of the color photographic process, each emulsion layer can be considered to react to light as does an emulsion layer of a monochrome photographic material. To a first approximation, this assumption is correct.

However, there are often significant interactions between the emulsion and dye layers, Each emulsion layer possesses a characteristic sensitivity, as shown by the typical curves of Figure 5.8. The integrated exposures of the layers are given by

$$X_R(C) = d_R \int C(\lambda) L_R(\lambda)\, d\lambda \tag{5.27 (a)}$$

$$X_G(C) = d_G \int C(\lambda) L_G(\lambda)\, d\lambda \tag{5.27 (b)}$$

$$X_B(C) = d_B \int C(\lambda) L_B(\lambda)\, d\lambda \tag{5.27 (c)}$$

where $d_R$, $d_G$, $d_B$ are proportionality constants whose values are adjusted so that the exposures are equal for a reference white illumination and so that the film is not saturated. In the chemical development process of the film, a positive transparency is produced with three absorptive dye layers of cyan, magenta and yellow dyes.

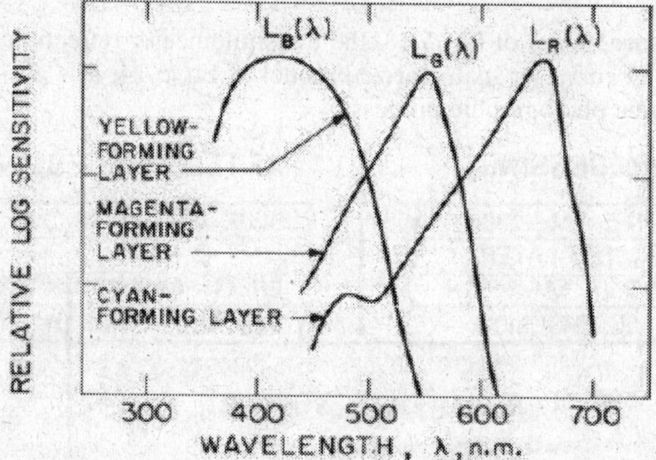


**Figure 5.8 Spectral sensitivities of typical film layer emulsions**

The transmittance $\tau_T(\lambda)$ of the developed transparency is the product of the transmittance of the cyan $\tau_{TC}(\lambda)$, the magenta $\tau_{TM}(\lambda)$ and the yellow $\tau_{TY}(\lambda)$ dyes. Hence,

$$\tau_T(\lambda) = \tau_{TC}(\lambda)\tau_{TM}(\lambda)\tau_{TY}(\lambda) \tag{5.28}$$

The transmittance of each dye is a function of its spectral absorption characteristic and its concentration. This functional dependence is conveniently expressed in terms of the relative density of each dye as

$$\tau_{TC}(\lambda) = 10^{-cD_{NC}(\lambda)} \tag{5.29 (a)}$$

$$\tau_{TM}(\lambda) = 10^{-mD_{NM}(\lambda)} \tag{5.29 (b)}$$

$$\tau_{TY}(\lambda) = 10^{-yD_{NY}(\lambda)} \tag{5.29 (c)}$$

where c, m, y represent the relative amounts of the cyan, magenta and yellow dyes, and $D_{NC}(\lambda), D_{NM}(\lambda), D_{NY}(\lambda)$ denote the spectral densities of unit amounts of the dyes. For unit amounts of the dyes, the transparency transmittance is

$$\tau_{TN}(\lambda) = 10^{-D_{TN}(\lambda)} \tag{5.30 (a)}$$

Where

$$D_{TN}(\lambda) = D_{NC}(\lambda) + D_{NM}(\lambda) + D_{NY}(\lambda) \tag{5.30 (b)}$$

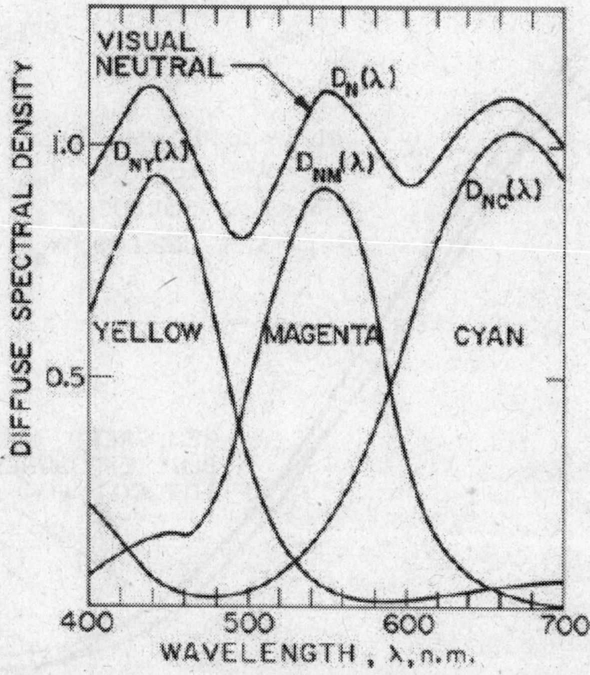


**Figure 5.9 Spectral dye densities and neutral density of a typical reversal color film**

Such a transparency appears to be a neutral gray when illuminated by a reference white light. Figure 5.9 illustrates the typical dye densities and neutral density for a reversal film. The relationship between the exposure values and dye layer densities is, in general, quite complex. For example, the amount of cyan dye produced is a nonlinear function not only of the red exposure, but is also dependent to a smaller extent on the green and blue exposures. Similar relationships hold for the amounts of magenta and yellow dyes produced by their exposures. Often, these interimage effects can be neglected, and it can be assumed that the cyan dye is produced only by the red exposure, the magenta dye by the green exposure, and the blue dye by the yellow exposure.

For this assumption, the dye density–exposure relationship can be characterized by the Hurter–Driffield plot of equivalent neutral density versus the logarithm of exposure for each dye. Figure 5.10 shows a typical H & D curve for a reversal film. In the central portion of each H & D curve, the density versus exposure characteristic can be modeled as

$$c = \gamma_C \log_{10} X_R + K_{FC} \tag{5.31 (a)}$$

$$m = \gamma_M \log_{10} X_G + K_{FM} \tag{5.31 (b)}$$

$$y = \gamma_Y \log_{10} X_B + K_{FY} \tag{5.31 (c)}$$

Where $\lambda_C, \lambda_M, \lambda_Y$ representing the slopes of the curves in the linear region, are called dye layer gammas.

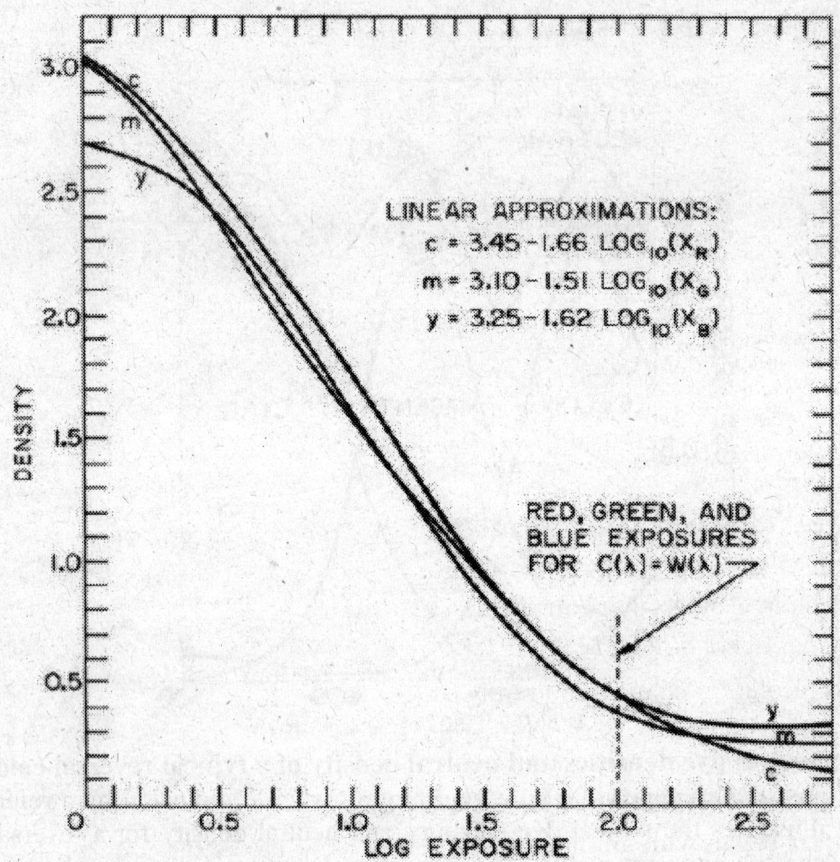


**Figure 5.10 H & D curves for a typical reversal color film**

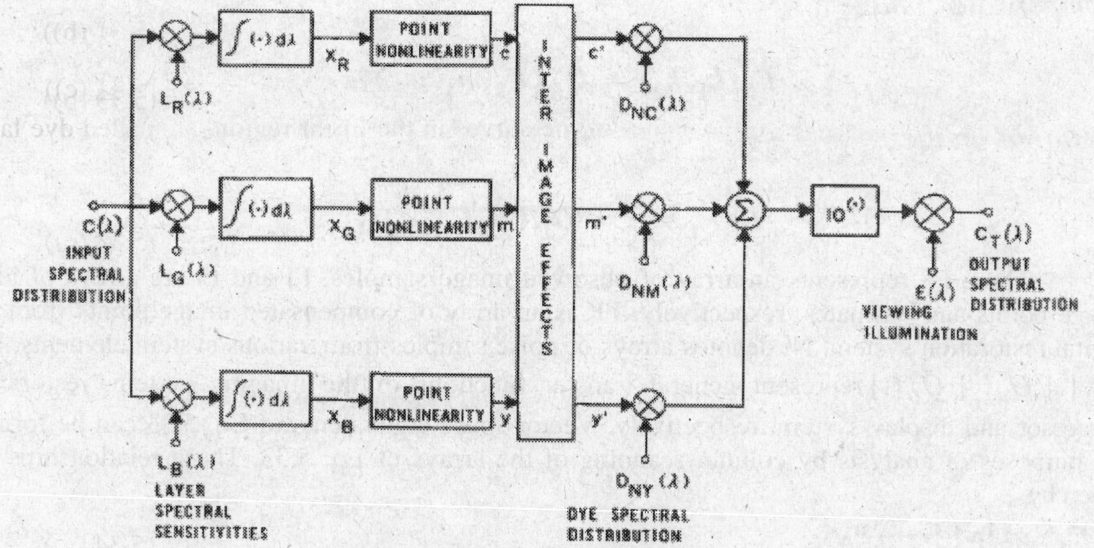


**Figure 5.11 Color Film Model**

The spectral energy distribution of light passing through a developed transparency is the product of the transparency transmittance and the incident illumination spectral energy distribution $E(\lambda)$ as given by

$$C_T(\lambda) = E(\lambda)\,10^{-[cD_{NC}(\lambda) + mD_{NM}(\lambda) + yD_{NY}(\lambda)]} \tag{5.32}$$

Figure 5.11 is a block diagram of the complete color film recording and reproduction process. The original light with distribution $C(\lambda)$ and the light passing through the transparency $C_T(\lambda)$at a given resolution element are rarely identical. That is, a spectral match is usually not achieved in the photographic process. Furthermore, the lights C and CT usually do not even provide a colorimetric match.

## 5.5 DISCRETE IMAGE RESTORATION MODELS

This chapter began with an introduction to a general model of an imaging system and a digital restoration process. Next, typical components of the imaging system were described and modeled within the context of the general model. Now, the discussion turns to the development of several discrete image restoration models. In the development of these models, it is assumed that the spectral wavelength response and temporal response characteristics of the physical imaging system can be separated from the spatial and point characteristics. The following discussion considers only spatial and point characteristics.

After each element of the digital image restoration system of Figure 5.1 is modeled, following the techniques described previously, the restoration system may be conceptually distilled to three equations:

*Observed image:*

$$F_S(m_1, m_2) = O_M\{F_I(n_1, n_2), N_1(m_1, m_2), \ldots, N_N(m_1, m_2)\} \tag{5.33 (a)}$$

***Compensated image:***

$$F_K(k_1, k_2) = O_R\{F_S(m_1, m_2)\} \tag{5.33 (b)}$$

***Restored image:***

$$\bar{F}_I(n_1, n_2) = O_D\{F_K(k_1, k_2)\} \tag{5.33 (c)}$$

where FS represents an array of observed image samples, FI and Fl are arrays of ideal image points and estimates, respectively, FK is an array of compensated image points from the digital restoration system, Ni denotes arrays of noise samples from various system elements, and $O_M\{.\}, O_R\{.\}, O_D\{.\}$ represent general transfer functions of the imaging system, restoration processor and display system, respectively. Vector-space equivalents of Eq. 5.33 can be formed for purposes of analysis by column scanning of the arrays of Eq. 5.33. These relationships are given by

$$\mathbf{f}_S = O_M\{\mathbf{f}_I, \mathbf{n}_1, \ldots, \mathbf{n}_N\} \tag{5.34 (a)}$$

$$\mathbf{f}_K = O_R\{\mathbf{f}_S\} \tag{5.34 (b)}$$

$$\bar{\mathbf{f}}_I = O_D\{\mathbf{f}_K\} \tag{5.34 (c)}$$

Unfortunately, general solutions have not been found; recourse must be made to specific solutions for less general models. The most common digital restoration model is that of Figure 5.12(a), in which a continuous image field is subjected to a linear blur, the electrical sensor responds nonlinearly to its input intensity, and the sensor amplifier introduces additive Gaussian noise independent of the image field. The physical image digitizer that follows may also introduce an effective blurring of the sampled image as the result of sampling with extended pulses. In this model, display degradation is ignored.

(a) Imaging model

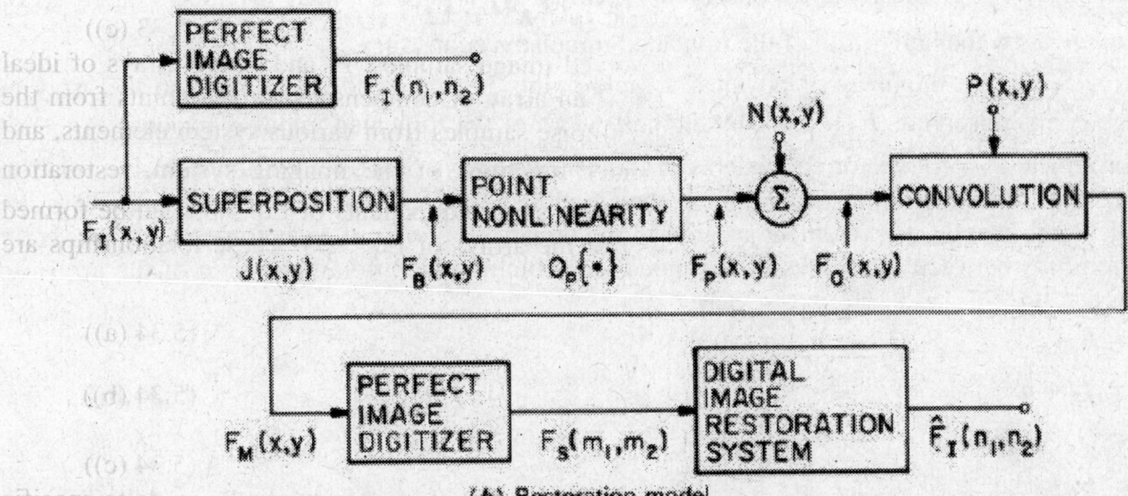


(b) Restoration model

**Figure 5.12. Imaging and restoration models for a sampled blurred image with additive noise**

Figure 5.12(b) shows a restoration model for the imaging system. It is assumed that the imaging blur can be modeled as a superposition operation with an impulse response J(x, y) that may be space variant. The sensor is assumed to respond nonlinearly to the input field FB(x, y) on a point-by-point basis, and its output is subject to an additive noise field N(x, y). The effect of sampling with extended sampling pulses, which are assumed symmetric, can be modeled as a convolution of FO(x, y) with each pulse P(x, y) followed by perfect sampling.

The objective of the restoration is to produce an array of samples $\tilde{F}1(n_1, n_2)$ that are estimates of points on the ideal input image field FI(x, y) obtained by a perfect image digitizer sampling at a spatial period $\Delta l$. To produce a digital restoration model, it is necessary quantitatively to relate the physical image samples $F_S(m_1, m_2)$ to the ideal image points $F_1(n_1, n_2)$. This is accomplished by truncating the sampling pulse equivalent impulse response P(x, y) to some spatial limits $\pm T_p$, and then extracting points from the continuous observed field FO(x, y) at a grid spacing $\Delta p$.

The discrete representation must then be carried one step further by relating points on the observed image field FO(x, y) to points on the image field FP(x, y) and the noise field N(x, y). The final step in the development of the discrete restoration model involves discretization of the superposition operation with J(x, y). There are two potential sources of error in this modeling process: truncation of the impulse responses J(x, y) and P(x,y) and quadrature integration errors.

Both sources of error can be made negligibly small by choosing the truncation limits TB and TP large, and by choosing the quadrature spacings $\Delta$I and $\Delta$P small. This, of course, increases the sizes of the arrays, and eventually, the amount of storage and processing required.

Actually, as is subsequently shown, the numerical stability of the restoration estimate may be impaired by improving the accuracy of the discretization process. The relative dimensions of the various arrays of the restoration model are important. Figure 5.13 shows the nested nature of the arrays. The image array observed, $F_O(k_1,k_2)$, is smaller than the ideal image array, $F_1(n_1,n_2)$ , by the half-width of the truncated impulse response J(x, y).

Similarly, the array of physical sample points FS(m1, m2) is smaller than the array of image points observed, $F_O(k_1,k_2)$by the half-width of the truncated impulse response P(x,y). It is convenient to form vector equivalents of the various arrays of the restoration model in order to utilize the formal structure of vector algebra in the subsequent restoration analysis. arrays are reindexed so that the first element appears in the upper-left corner of each array. Next, the vector relationships between the stages of the model are obtained by column scanning of the arrays to give

$$f_S = B_p f_O \tag{5.35(a)}$$

$$f_O = f_P + n \tag{5.35(b)}$$

$$f_P = O_P\{f_B\} \tag{5.35(c)}$$

$$f_B = B_B f_I \tag{5.35(d)}$$

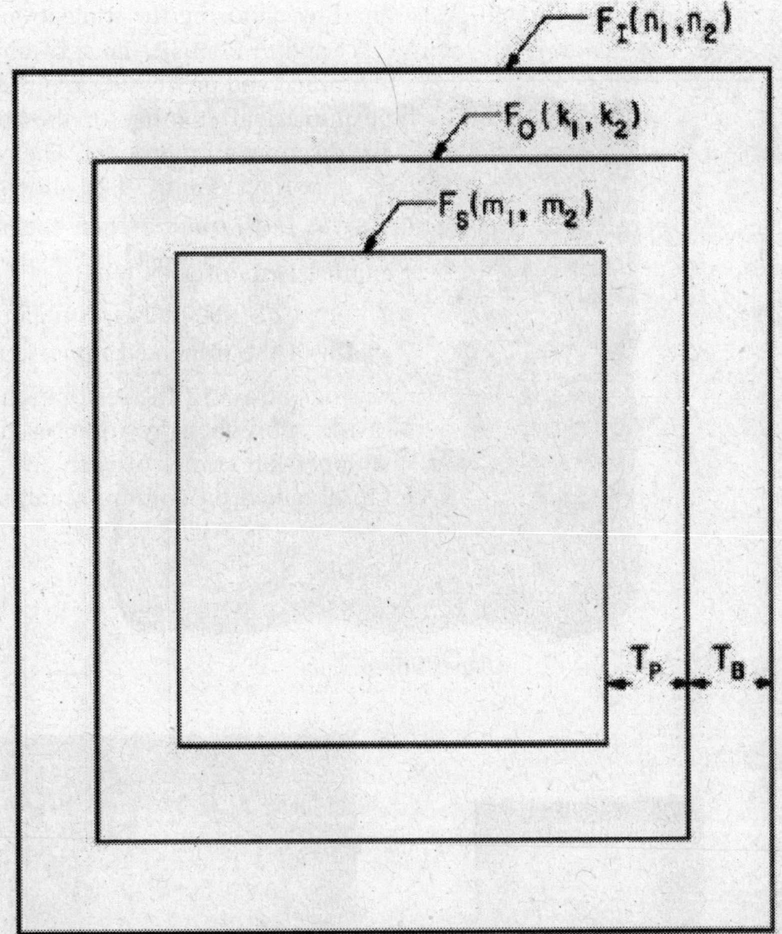


**Figure 5.13. Relationships of sampled image arrays**

where the blur matrix BP contains samples of P(x, y) and BB contains samples of J(x, y). The nonlinear operation of Eq. 5.34c is defined as a point-by-point nonlinear transformation. That is,

$$f_P(i) = O_P\{f_B(i)\} \tag{5.36}$$

Equations 5.35(a) to 5.35(d) can be combined to yield a single equation for the observed physical image samples in terms of points on the ideal image:

$$\mathbf{f}_S = \mathbf{B}_P O_P\{\mathbf{B}_B \mathbf{f}_I\} + \mathbf{B}_P \mathbf{n} \tag{5.37}$$

Several special cases of Eq. 5.37 will now be defined. First, if the point nonlinearity is absent,

$$\mathbf{f}_S = \mathbf{B}\mathbf{f}_I + \mathbf{n}_B \tag{5.38}$$

where B = BPBB and $n_B = B_p$ n. This is the classical discrete model consisting of a set of linear equations with measurement uncertainty. Another case that will be defined for later discussion occurs when the spatial blur of the physical image digitizer is negligible. In this case,

$$\mathbf{f}_S = O_P\{\mathbf{B}\mathbf{f}_I\} + \mathbf{n} \tag{5.39}$$

where
B = BB.

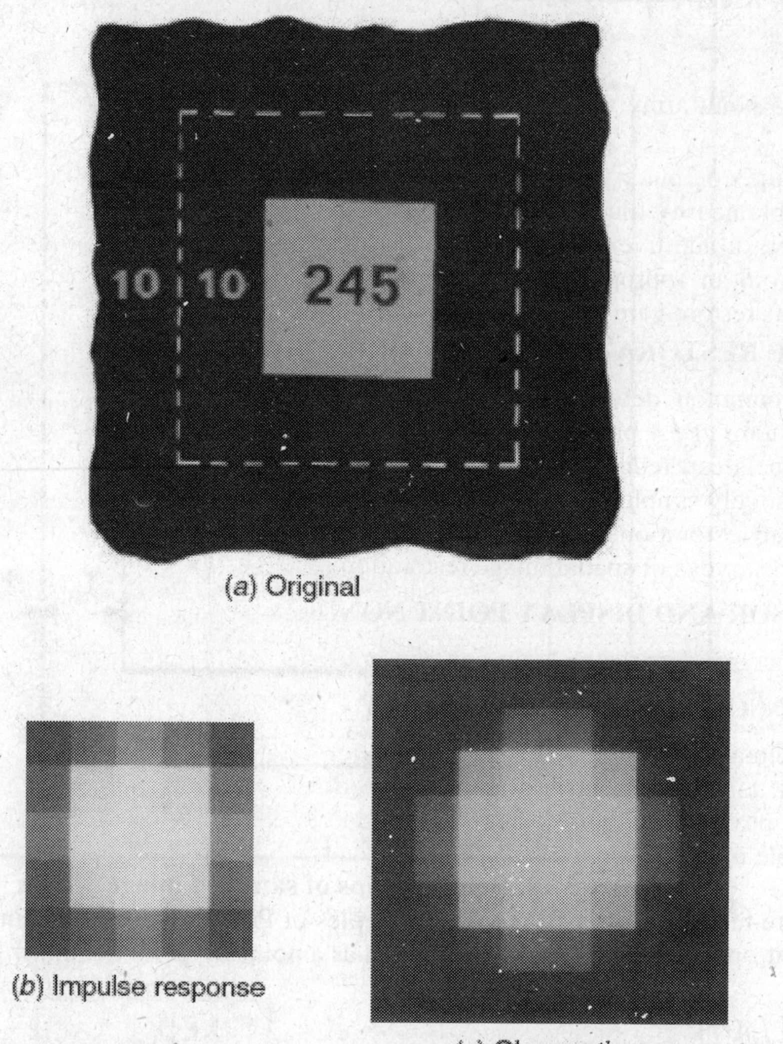


(*a*) Original

(*b*) Impulse response

(*c*) Observation

**Figure 5.14 Image arrays for underdetermined model**

Image restoration experiments based on the restoration model defined by Eq. 5.38. An artificial image has been generated for these computer simulation experiments . The original image used for the analysis of underdetermined restoration techniques, shown in Figure 5.14(a), consists of a 4 x 4 pixel square of intensity 245 placed against an extended background of intensity 10 referenced to an intensity scale of 0 to 255. All images are zoomed for display purposes.

The Gaussian-shaped impulse response function is defined as

$$H(l_1, l_2) = K \exp\left\{-\left(\frac{l_1}{2b_C^2} + \frac{l_2}{2b_R^2}\right)\right\} \tag{5.40}$$

over a 5 x 5 point array where K is an amplitude scaling constant and $b_C$ and $b_R$ are blur-spread constants.

In the computer simulation restoration experiments, the observed blurred image model has been obtained by multiplying the column-scanned original image of eq. 5.35(a) by the blur matrix B. Next, additive white Gaussian observation noise has been simulated by adding output variables from an appropriate random number generator to the blurred images. For display, all image points restored are clipped to the intensity range 0 to 255.

## 5.6 IMAGE RESTORATION TECHNIQUES

A common defect in imaging systems is unwanted nonlinearities in the sensor and display systems. Post processing correction of sensor signals and pre-processing correction of display signals can reduce such degradations substantially. Such point restoration processing is usually relatively simple to implement. One of the most common image restoration tasks is that of spatial image restoration to compensate for image blur and to diminish noise effects. References 2 to 6 contain surveys of spatial image restoration methods.

### 5.6.1 SENSOR AND DISPLAY POINT NONLINEARITY CORRECTION

This section considers methods for compensation of point nonlinearities of sensors and displays.

#### 5.6.1.1 SENSOR POINT NONLINEARITY CORRECTION

In imaging systems in which the source degradation can be separated into cascaded spatial and point effects, it is often possible directly to compensate for the point degradation. Consider a physical imaging system that produces an observed image field $F_O(x, y)$ according to the separable model

$$F_O(x, y) = O_Q\{O_D\{C(x, y, \lambda)\}\} \tag{5.41}$$

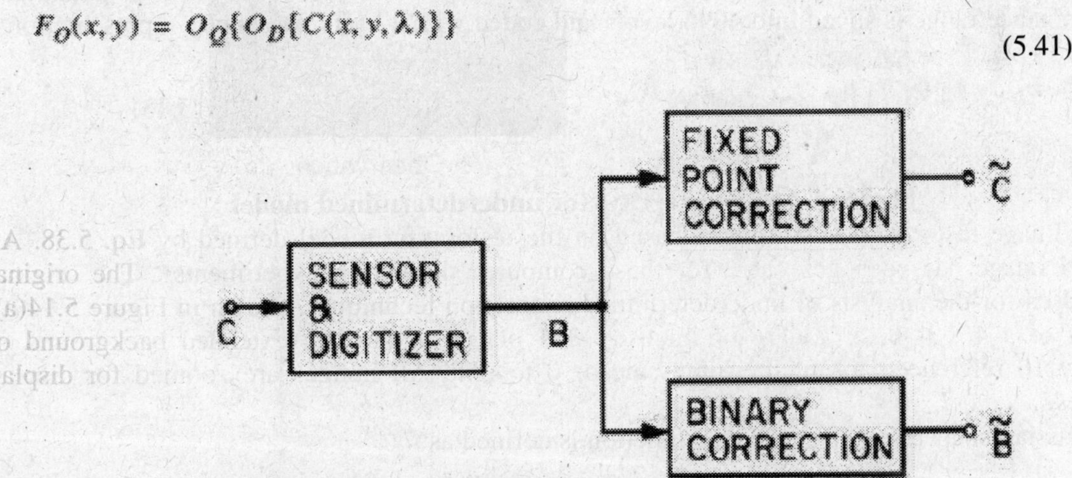


**Figure 5.15 Point luminance correction for an image sensor**

where $C(x, y, \lambda)$ is the spectral energy distribution of the input light field, $O_Q\{.\}$ represents the point amplitude response of the sensor and $O_D\{.\}$ denotes the spatial and wavelength responses. Sensor luminance correction can then be accomplished by passing the observed image through a correction system with a point restoration operator $O_R\{.\}$ ideally chosen such that

$$O_R\{O_Q\{\cdot\}\} = 1 \tag{5.42}$$

For continuous images in optical form, it may be difficult to implement a desired point restoration operator if the operator is nonlinear. Compensation for images in analog electrical form can be accomplished with a nonlinear amplifier, while digital image compensation can be performed by arithmetic operators or by a table look-up procedure.

Figure 5.15 is a block diagram that illustrates the point luminance correction methodology. The sensor input is a point light distribution function C that is converted to a binary number B for eventual entry into a computer or digital processor.

In some imaging applications, processing will be performed directly on the binary representation, while in other applications, it will be preferable to convert to a real fixed-point computer number linearly proportional to the sensor input luminance. In the former case, the binary correction unit will produce a binary number $\tilde{B}$ that is designed to be linearly proportional to C, and in the latter case, the fixed-point correction unit will produce a fixed-point number $\tilde{C}$ that is designed to be equal to C.

Typical measured response B versus sensor input luminance level C is shown in Figure 5.16(a), while Figure 5.16(b) shows the corresponding compensated response that is desired. The measured response can be obtained by scanning a gray scale test chart of known luminance values and observing the digitized binary value B at each step. Repeated measurements should be made to reduce the effects of noise and measurement errors. For calibration purposes, it is convenient to regard the binary-coded luminance as a fixed-point binary number. As an example, if the luminance range is sliced into 4096 levels and coded with 12 bits, the binary representation would be

$$B = b_8 b_7 b_6 b_5 b_4 b_3 b_2 b_1 . b_{-1} b_{-2} b_{-3} b_{-4} \tag{5.43}$$

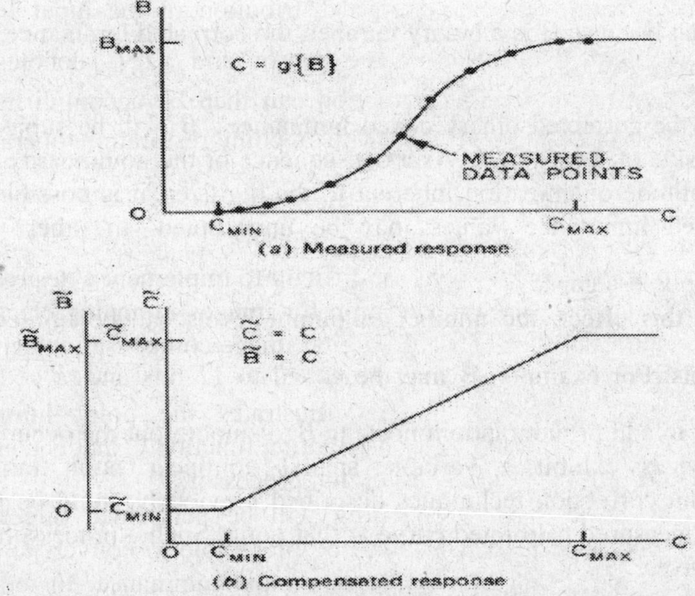


**Figure 5.16 Measured and compensated sensor luminance response**

The whole-number part in this example ranges from 0 to 255, and the fractional part divides each integer step into 16 subdivisions. In this format, the scanner can produce output levels over the range.

$$255.9375 \leq B \leq 0.0 \tag{5.44}$$

After the measured gray scale data points of Figure 5.16(a) have been obtained, a smooth analytic curve

$$C = g\{B\} \tag{5.45}$$

is fitted to the data. The desired luminance response in real number and binary number forms is

$$\tilde{C} = C \tag{5.46(a)}$$

$$\tilde{B} = B_{max} \frac{C - C_{min}}{C_{max} - C_{min}} \tag{5.46(b)}$$

Hence, the required compensation relationships are

$$\tilde{C} = g\{B\} \tag{5.47(a)}$$

$$\tilde{B} = B_{max} \frac{g\{B\} - C_{min}}{C_{max} - C_{min}} \tag{5.47(b)}$$

The limits of the luminance function are commonly normalized to the range 0.0 to 1.0.

To improve the accuracy of the calibration procedure, it is first wise to perform a rough calibration and then repeat the procedure as often as required to refine the correction curve. It should be observed that because B is a binary number, the corrected luminance value $\tilde{C}$ will be a quantized real number.

Furthermore, the corrected binary coded luminance $\tilde{B}$ will be subject to binary round off of the right-hand side of Eq. 5.47(b). As a consequence of the nonlinearity of the fitted curve C=g{B} and the amplitude quantization inherent to the digitizer, it is possible that some of the corrected binary-coded luminance values may be unoccupied. In other words, the image histogram $\tilde{B}$ of may possess gaps.

To minimize this effect, the number of output levels can be limited to less than the number of input levels. For example, B may be coded to 12 bits and $\tilde{B}$ coded to only 8 bits. Another alternative is to add pseudorandom noise to $\tilde{B}$ to smooth out the occupancy levels. Many image scanning devices exhibit a variable spatial nonlinear point luminance response. Conceptually, the point correction techniques described previously could be performed at each pixel value using the measured calibrated curve at that point. Such a process, however, would be mechanically prohibitive.

An alternative approach, called gain correction, that is often successful is to model the variable spatial response by some smooth normalized two-dimensional curve G(j, k) over the sensor surface. Then, the corrected spatial response can be obtained by the operation

$$\tilde{F}(j,k) = \frac{F(j,k)}{G(j,k)} \tag{5.48}$$

where F(j, k) and $\tilde{F}(j,k)$ represent the raw and corrected sensor responses, respectively. Figure 5.17 provides an example of adaptive gain correction of a charge coupled device (CCD) camera. Figure 5.17(a) is an image of a spatially flat light box surface obtained with the CCD camera. A line profile plot of a diagonal line through the original image is presented in Figure 5.17(b). Figure 5.17(c) is the gain-corrected original, in which G(j, k) is obtained by Fourier domain low-pass filtering of the original image. The line profile plot of Figure 5.17(d) shows the "flattened" result.

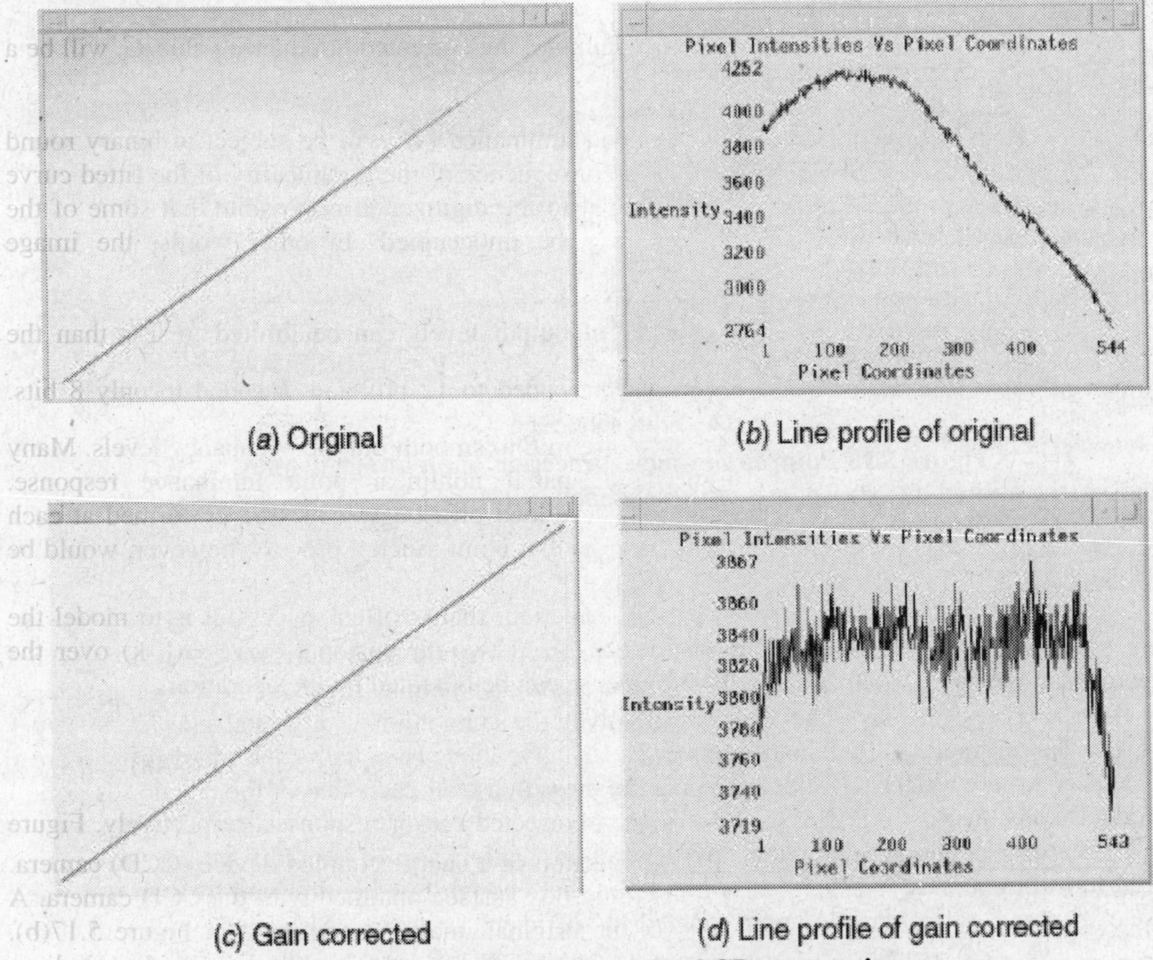


(*a*) Original (*b*) Line profile of original

(*c*) Gain corrected (*d*) Line profile of gain corrected

**Figure 5.17 Gain correction of a CCD camera image**

### 5.6.1.2. DISPLAY POINT NONLINEARITY CORRECTION

Correction of an image display for point luminance nonlinearities is identical in principle to the correction of point luminance nonlinearities of an image sensor. The procedure illustrated in Figure 5.18 involves distortion of the binary coded image luminance variable B to form a corrected binary coded luminance B function so that the displayed luminance $\tilde{C}$ will be linearly proportional to B. In this formulation, the display may include a photographic record of a displayed light field. The desired overall response is

$$\tilde{C} = B\,\frac{\tilde{C}_{max} - \tilde{C}_{min}}{B_{max}} + \tilde{C}_{min} \tag{5.49}$$

Normally, the maximum and minimum limits of the displayed luminance function $\tilde{C}$ are not absolute quantities, but rather are transmissivities or reflectivities normalized over a unit range. The measured response of the display and image reconstruction system is modeled by the nonlinear function

$$C = f\{B\} \tag{5.50}$$

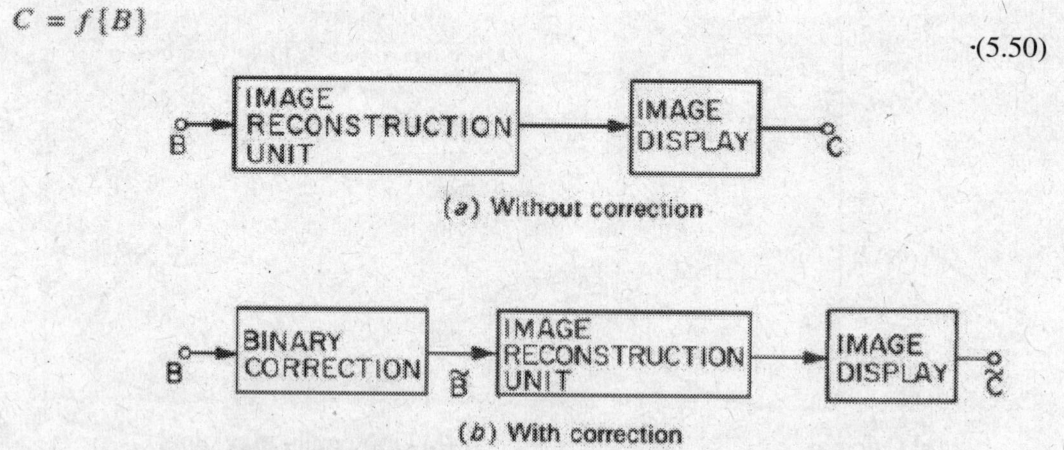


**Figure 5.18 Point luminance correction of an image display**

Therefore, the desired linear response can be obtained by setting

$$\tilde{B} = g\left\{B\frac{\tilde{C}_{max} - \tilde{C}_{min}}{B_{max}} + \tilde{C}_{min}\right\} \tag{5.51}$$

where g{ . }is the inverse function of f{ . }. The experimental procedure for determining the correction function g{ . } will be described for the common example of producing a photographic print from an image display. The first step involves the generation of a digital gray scale step chart over the full range of the binary number B. Usually, about 16 equally spaced levels of B are sufficient. Next, the reflective luminance must be measured over each step of the developed print to produce a plot such as in Figure 5.19.

The data points are then fitted by the smooth analytic curve B=g{C}, which forms the desired transformation of Eq. 5.50. It is important that enough bits be allocated to B so that the discrete mapping g{ . } can be approximated to sufficient accuracy. Also, the number of bits allocated to $\tilde{B}$ must be sufficient to prevent gray scale contouring as the result of the nonlinear spacing of display levels. A 10- bit representation of B and an 8-bit representation of $\tilde{B}$ should be adequate in most applications.

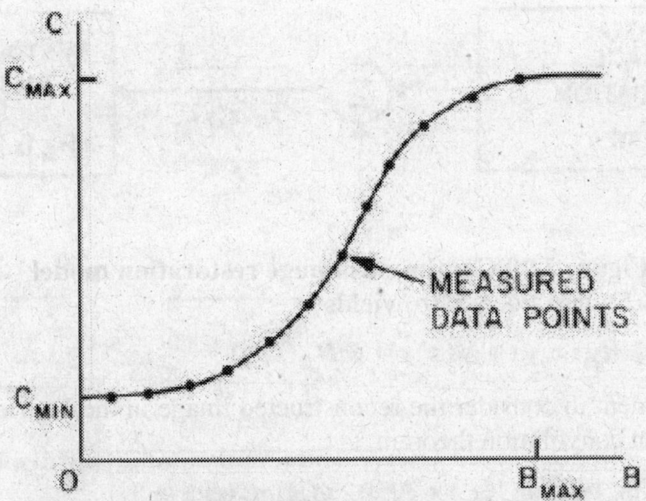


**Figure 5.19 Measured image display response**

Image display devices such as cathode ray tube displays often exhibit spatial luminance variation. Typically, a displayed image is brighter at the center of the display screen than at its periphery. Correction techniques, as described by Eq. 5.48, can be utilized for compensation of spatial luminance variations.

## 5.6.2 CONTINUOUS IMAGE SPATIAL FILTERING RESTORATION

For the class of imaging systems in which the spatial degradation can be modeled by a linear-shift-invariant impulse response and the noise is additive, restoration of continuous images can be performed by linear filtering techniques. Figure 5.20 contains a block diagram for the analysis of such techniques. An ideal image $F_I(x,y)$ passes through a linear spatial degradation system with an impulse response $H_D(x,y)$ and is combined with additive noise $N(x,y)$. The noise is assumed to be uncorrelated with the ideal image. The image field observed can be represented by the convolution operation as

$$F_O(x, y) = \int_{-\infty}^{\infty}\int_{-\infty}^{\infty} F_I(\alpha, \beta)\, H_D(x-\alpha, y-\beta)\, d\alpha\, d\beta + N(x, y) \quad (5.52)$$

or

$$F_O(x, y) = F_I(x, y) \circledast H_D(x, y) + N(x, y) \quad (5.53)$$

The restoration system consists of a linear-shift-invariant filter defined by the impulse response $H_R(x,y)$ . After restoration with this filter, the reconstructed image becomes

$$\hat{F}_I(x, y) = \int_{-\infty}^{\infty}\int_{-\infty}^{\infty} F_O(\alpha, \beta) H_R(x-\alpha, y-\beta)\, d\alpha\, d\beta \quad (5.54(a))$$

or

$$\hat{F}_I(x, y) = F_O(x, y) \circledast H_R(x, y) \quad (5.54(b))$$

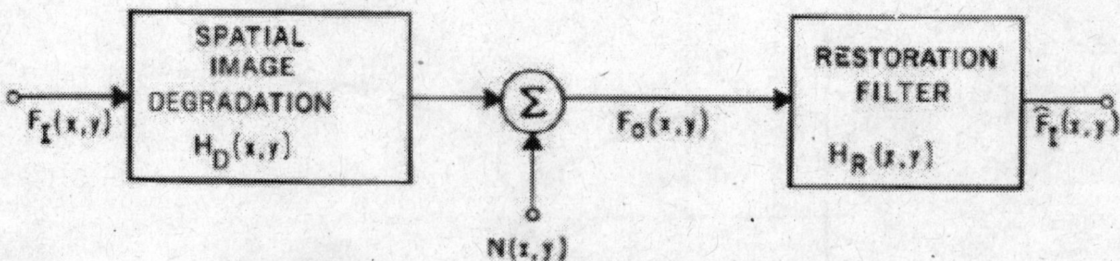


**Figure 5.20 Continuous image restoration model**

Substitution of Eq. 5.53(b) into Eq. 5.54(b) yields

$$\hat{F}_I(x, y) = [F_I(x, y) \circledast H_D(x, y) + N(x, y)] \circledast H_R(x, y) \tag{5.55}$$

It is analytically convenient to consider the reconstructed image in the Fourier transform domain. By the Fourier transform convolution theorem,

$$\hat{\mathcal{F}}_I(\omega_x, \omega_y) = [\mathcal{F}_I(\omega_x, \omega_y)\mathcal{H}_D(\omega_x, \omega_y) + \mathcal{N}(\omega_x, \omega_y)]\mathcal{H}_R(\omega_x, \omega_y) \tag{5.56}$$

where

$\mathcal{F}_I(\omega_x, \omega_y)$ , $\hat{\mathcal{F}}_I(\omega_x, \omega_y)$ , $\mathcal{N}(\omega_x, \omega_y)$ , $\mathcal{H}_D(\omega_x, \omega_y)$ , $\mathcal{H}_R(\omega_x, \omega_y)$

are the two dimensional Fourier transforms of $F_1(x, y), F_1(x, y), N(x, y), H_D(x, y), H_R(x, y)$ respectively. The following sections describe various types of continuous image restoration filters.

### 5.6.2.1 INVERSE FILTER

The earliest attempts at image restoration were based on the concept of inverse filtering, in which the transfer function of the degrading system is inverted to yield a restored image. If the restoration inverse filter transfer function is chosen so that

$$\mathcal{H}_R(\omega_x, \omega_y) = \frac{1}{\mathcal{H}_D(\omega_x, \omega_y)} \tag{5.57}$$

then the spectrum of the reconstructed image becomes

$$\hat{\mathcal{F}}_I(\omega_x, \omega_y) = \mathcal{F}_I(\omega_x, \omega_y) + \frac{\mathcal{N}(\omega_x, \omega_y)}{\mathcal{H}_D(\omega_x, \omega_y)} \tag{5.58}$$

Upon inverse Fourier transformation, the restored image field

$$\hat{F}_I(x, y) = F_I(x, y) + \frac{1}{4\pi^2} \int_{-\infty}^{\infty}\int_{-\infty}^{\infty} \frac{\mathcal{N}(\omega_x, \omega_y)}{\mathcal{H}_D(\omega_x, \omega_y)} \exp\{i(\omega_x x + \omega_y y)\}\, d\omega_x\, d\omega_y \tag{5.59}$$

is obtained. In the absence of source noise, a perfect reconstruction results, but if source noise is present, there will be an additive reconstruction error whose value can become quite large at spatial frequencies for which $H_D(\omega_x, \omega_y)$ is small. Typically, $H_D(\omega_x, \omega_y)$ and $F_l(\omega_x, \omega_y)$ and are small at high spatial frequencies, hence image quality becomes severely impaired in high-detail regions of the reconstructed image. Figure 5.21 shows typical frequency spectra involved in inverse filtering.

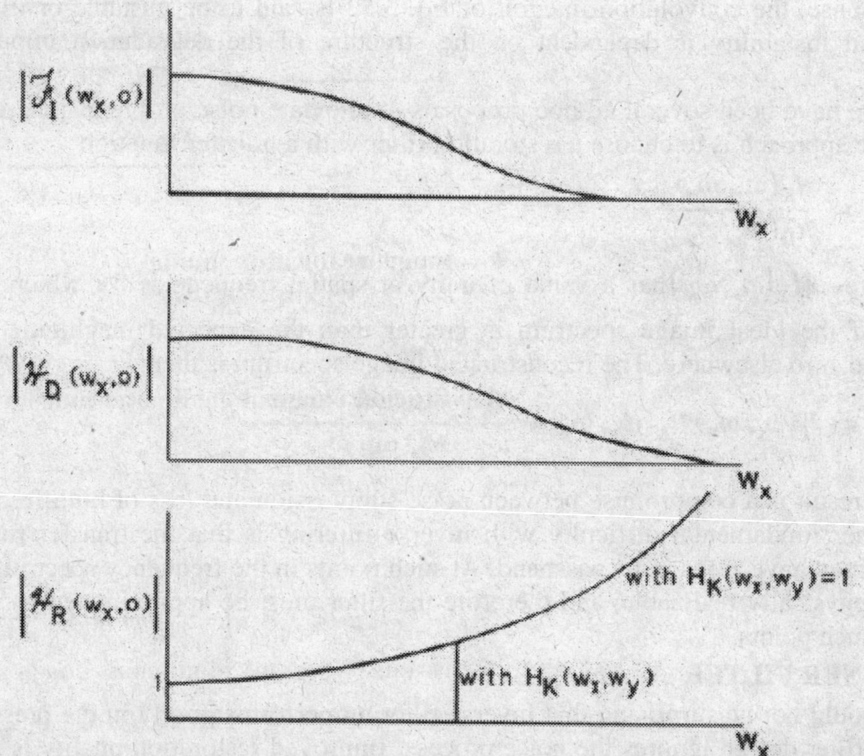


**Figure 5.21 Typical spectra of an inverse filtering image restoration system**

The presence of noise may severely affect the uniqueness of a restoration estimate. That is, small changes in N(x,y) may radically change the value of the estimate $\tilde{F}_I(x,y)$. For example, consider the dither function Z(x,y) added to an ideal image to produce a perturbed image

$$F_Z(x,y) = F_I(x,y) + Z(x,y) \tag{5.60}$$

There may be many dither functions for which

$$\left|\int_{-\infty}^{\infty}\int_{-\infty}^{\infty} Z(\alpha,\beta)H_D(x-\alpha,y-\beta)\;d\alpha\;d\beta\right| < |N(x,y)| \tag{5.61}$$

For such functions, the perturbed image field $F_Z(x,y)$ may satisfy the convolution integral of Eq. 5.53 to within the accuracy of the observed image field. Specifically, it can be shown that if the dither function is a high-frequency sinusoid of arbitrary amplitude, then in the limit

$$\lim_{n\to\infty}\left\{\int_{-\infty}^{\infty}\int_{-\infty}^{\infty} \sin\{n(\alpha+\beta)\}H_D(x-\alpha,y-\beta)\;d\alpha\;d\beta\right\} = 0 \tag{5.62}$$

For image restoration, this fact is particularly disturbing, for two reasons. High-frequency signal components may be present in an ideal image, yet their presence may be masked by observation noise. Conversely, a small amount of observation noise may lead to a reconstruction of $F_I(x,y)$that contains very large amplitude high-frequency components. If relatively small perturbations N(x,y) in the observation result in large dither functions for a particular degradation impulse response, the convolution integral of Eq. 5.53 is said to be unstable or ill conditioned. This potential instability is dependent on the structure of the degradation impulse response function.

There have been several ad hoc proposals to alleviate noise problems inherent to inverse filtering. One approach is to choose a restoration filter with a transfer function

$$\mathcal{H}_R(\omega_x, \omega_y) = \frac{\mathcal{H}_K(\omega_x, \omega_y)}{\mathcal{H}_D(\omega_x, \omega_y)} \tag{5.63}$$

where $H_k(\omega_x, \omega_y)$ has a value of unity at spatial frequencies for which the expected magnitude of the ideal image spectrum is greater than the expected magnitude of the noise spectrum, and zero elsewhere. The reconstructed image spectrum is then

$$\hat{\mathcal{F}}_I(\omega_x, \omega_y) = \mathcal{F}_I(\omega_x, \omega_y)\mathcal{H}_K(\omega_x, \omega_y) + \frac{\mathcal{N}(\omega_x, \omega_y)\mathcal{H}_K(\omega_x, \omega_y)}{\mathcal{H}_D(\omega_x, \omega_y)} \tag{5.64}$$

The result is a compromise between noise suppression and loss of high-frequency image detail. Another fundamental difficulty with inverse filtering is that the transfer function of the degradation may have zeros in its passband. At such points in the frequency spectrum, the inverse filter is not physically realizable, and therefore the filter must be approximated by a large value response at such points.

#### 5.6.2.2 WIENER FILTER

It should not be surprising that inverse filtering performs poorly in the presence of noise because the filter design ignores the noise process. Improved restoration quality is possible with Wiener filtering techniques, which incorporate a priori statistical knowledge of the noise field. In the general derivation of the Wiener filter, it is assumed that the ideal image $F_I(x,y)$ and the observed image $F_O(x,y)$ of Figure 5.20 are samples of two dimensional, continuous stochastic fields with zero-value spatial means. The impulse response of the restoration filter is chosen to minimize the mean-square restoration error

$$\mathcal{E} = E\left\{[F_I(x, y) - \hat{F}_I(x, y)]^2\right\} \tag{5.65}$$

The mean-square error is minimized when the following orthogonality condition is met:

$$E\{[F_I(x, y) - \hat{F}_I(x, y)]F_O(x', y')\} = 0 \tag{5.66}$$

for all image coordinate pairs (x,y) and (x',y'). Upon substitution of Eq. 5.54(a) for the restored image and some linear algebraic manipulation, one obtains

$$E\{F_I(x, y)F_O(x, y)\} = \int_{-\infty}^{\infty}\int_{-\infty}^{\infty} E\{F_O(\alpha, \beta)F_O(x', y')\}H_R(x - \alpha, y - \beta)\, d\alpha\, d\beta \tag{5.67}$$

Under the assumption that the ideal image and observed image are jointly stationary, the expectation terms can be expressed as covariance functions. This yields

$$K_{F_I F_O}(x - x', y - y') = \int_{-\infty}^{\infty}\int_{-\infty}^{\infty} K_{F_O F_O}(\alpha - x', \beta - y')H_R(x - \alpha, y - \beta)\, d\alpha\, d\beta \tag{5.68}$$

Then, taking the two-dimensional Fourier transform of both sides of Eq. 5.58 and solving for $H_R(\omega_x, \omega_y)$, the following general expression for the Wiener filter transfer function is obtained:

$$\mathcal{H}_R(\omega_x, \omega_y) = \frac{\mathcal{W}_{F_I F_O}(\omega_x, \omega_y)}{\mathcal{W}_{F_O F_O}(\omega_x, \omega_y)} \tag{5.69}$$

In the special case of the additive noise model of Figure 5.21:

$$\mathcal{W}_{F_I F_O}(\omega_x, \omega_y) = \mathcal{H}_D^*(\omega_x, \omega_y)\mathcal{W}_{F_I}(\omega_x, \omega_y) \tag{5.70 (a)}$$

$$\mathcal{W}_{F_O F_O}(\omega_x, \omega_y) = |\mathcal{H}_D(\omega_x, \omega_y)|^2 \mathcal{W}_{F_I}(\omega_x, \omega_y) + \mathcal{W}_N(\omega_x, \omega_y) \tag{5.70 (b)}$$

This leads to the additive noise Wiener filter

$$\mathcal{H}_R(\omega_x, \omega_y) = \frac{\mathcal{H}_D^*(\omega_x, \omega_y)\mathcal{W}_{F_I}(\omega_x, \omega_y)}{|\mathcal{H}_D(\omega_x, \omega_y)|^2 \mathcal{W}_{F_I}(\omega_x, \omega_y) + \mathcal{W}_N(\omega_x, \omega_y)} \tag{5.71 (a)}$$

or

$$\mathcal{H}_R(\omega_x, \omega_y) = \frac{\mathcal{H}_D^*(\omega_x, \omega_y)}{|\mathcal{H}_D(\omega_x, \omega_y)|^2 + \mathcal{W}_N(\omega_x, \omega_y)/\mathcal{W}_{F_I}(\omega_x, \omega_y)} \tag{5.71 (b)}$$

In the latter formulation, the transfer function of the restoration filter can be expressed in terms of the signal-to-noise power ratio

$$\text{SNR}(\omega_x, \omega_y) \equiv \frac{\mathcal{W}_{F_I}(\omega_x, \omega_y)}{\mathcal{W}_N(\omega_x, \omega_y)} \tag{5.72}$$

at each spatial frequency. Figure 5.22 shows cross-sectional sketches of a typical ideal image spectrum, noise spectrum, blur transfer function and the resulting Wiener filter transfer function. As noted from the figure, this version of the Wiener filter acts as a band pass filter. It performs as an inverse filter at low spatial frequencies, and as a smooth roll off low-pass filter at high spatial frequencies. Equation 5.71 is valid when the ideal image and observed image stochastic processes are zero mean. In this case, the reconstructed image Fourier transform is

$$\hat{\mathcal{F}}_I(\omega_x, \omega_y) = \mathcal{H}_R(\omega_x, \omega_y)\mathcal{F}_O(\omega_x, \omega_y) \tag{5.73}$$

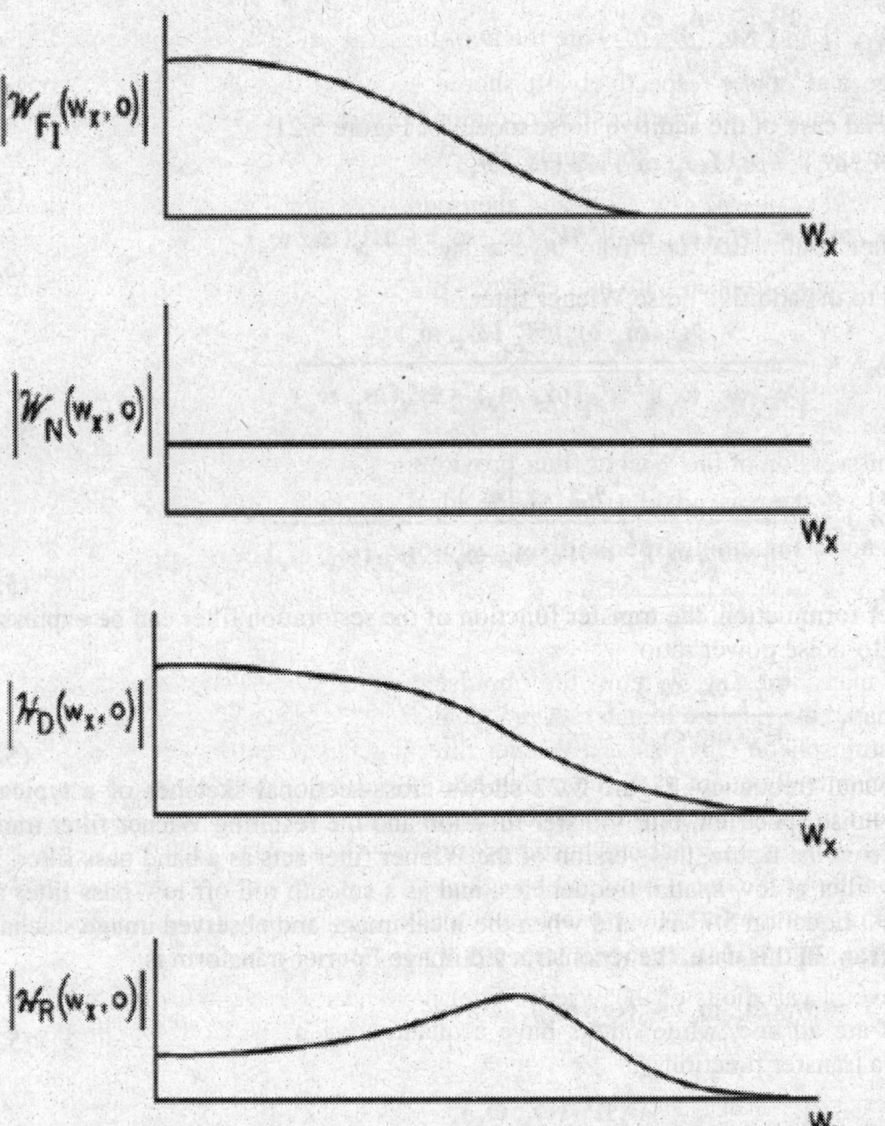


**Figure 5.22 Typical spectra of a Wiener filtering image restoration system**

If the ideal image and observed image means are nonzero, the proper form of the reconstructed image Fourier transform is

$$\mathcal{F}_{\hat{I}}(\omega_x, \omega_y) = \mathcal{H}_R(\omega_x, \omega_y)[\mathcal{F}_O(\omega_x, \omega_y) - \mathcal{M}_O(\omega_x, \omega_y)] + \mathcal{M}_I(\omega_x, \omega_y) \tag{5.74 (a)}$$

Where

$$\mathcal{M}_O(\omega_x, \omega_y) = \mathcal{H}_D(\omega_x, \omega_y)\mathcal{M}_I(\omega_x, \omega_y) + \mathcal{M}_N(\omega_x, \omega_y) \tag{5.74 (b)}$$

and $M_I(\omega_{x,y})$ and $M_N(\omega_x,\omega_y)$ are the two-dimensional Fourier transforms of the means of the ideal image and noise, respectively. It should be noted that Eq. 5.74 accommodates spatially varying mean models. In practice, it is commonto estimate the mean of the observed image by its spatial average $M_O(x,y)$ and apply the Wiener filter of Eq. 5.71 to the observed image difference $F_O(x,y)-M_O(x,y)$, and then add back the ideal image mean $M_I(x,y)$ to the Wiener filter result. It is useful to investigate special cases of Eq. 5.71. If the ideal image is assumed to be uncorrelated with unit energy, $W_{F1}(\omega_x,\omega_y)=1$ and the Wiener filter becomes

$$\mathcal{H}_R(\omega_x,\omega_y) = \frac{\mathcal{H}_D^*(\omega_x,\omega_y)}{|\mathcal{H}_D(\omega_x,\omega_y)|^2 + \mathcal{W}_N(\omega_x,\omega_y)} \tag{5.75}$$

This version of the Wiener filter provides less noise smoothing than does the general case of Eq. 5.71. If there is no blurring of the ideal image $H_D(\omega_x,\omega_y)=1$ and the Wiener filter becomes a noise smoothing filter with a transfer function

$$\mathcal{H}_R(\omega_x,\omega_y) = \frac{1}{1 + \mathcal{W}_N(\omega_x,\omega_y)} \tag{5.76}$$

In many imaging systems, the impulse response of the blur may not be fixed; rather, it changes shape in a random manner. A practical example is the blur caused by imaging through a turbulent atmosphere. Obviously, a Wiener filter applied to this problem would perform better if it could dynamically adapt to the changing blur impulse response. If this is not possible, a design improvement in the Wiener filter can be obtained by considering the impulse response to be a sample of a two-dimensional stochastic process with a known mean shape and with a random perturbation about the mean modeled by a known power spectral density. Transfer functions for this type of restoration filter have been developed by Slepian.

### 5.6.2.3 PARAMETRIC ESTIMATION FILTERS

Several variations of the Wiener filter have been developed for image restoration. Some techniques are ad hoc, while others have a quantitative basis. Cole has proposed a restoration filter with a transfer function

$$\mathcal{H}_R(\omega_x,\omega_y) = \left[\frac{\mathcal{W}_{F_I}(\omega_x,\omega_y)}{|\mathcal{H}_D(\omega_x,\omega_y)|^2\mathcal{W}_{F_I}(\omega_x,\omega_y) + \mathcal{W}_N(\omega_x,\omega_y)}\right]^{1/2} \tag{5.77}$$

The power spectrum of the filter output is

$$\mathcal{W}_{\hat{F}_I}(\omega_x,\omega_y) = |\mathcal{H}_R(\omega_x,\omega_y)|^2\mathcal{W}_{F_O}(\omega_x,\omega_y) \tag{5.78}$$

where $W_{Fo}(\omega_x,\omega_y)$ represents the power spectrum of the observation, which is related to the power spectrum of the ideal image by

$$\mathcal{W}_{F_O}(\omega_x,\omega_y) = |\mathcal{H}_D(\omega_x,\omega_y)|^2\mathcal{W}_{F_I}(\omega_x,\omega_y) + \mathcal{W}_N(\omega_x,\omega_y) \tag{5.79}$$

Thus, it is easily seen that the power spectrum of the reconstructed image is identical to the power spectrum of the ideal image field. That is,

$$\mathcal{W}_{F_I}^{*}(\omega_x, \omega_y) = \mathcal{W}_{F_I}(\omega_x, \omega_y) \tag{5.80}$$

For this reason, the restoration filter defined by Eq. 5.77 is called the image power-spectrum filter. In contrast, the power spectrum for the reconstructed image as obtained by the Wiener filter of Eq. 5.71 is

$$\mathcal{W}_{F_I}^{*}(\omega_x, \omega_y) = \frac{|\mathcal{H}_D(\omega_x, \omega_y)|^2 [\mathcal{W}_{F_I}(\omega_x, \omega_y)]^2}{|\mathcal{H}_D(\omega_x, \omega_y)|^2 \mathcal{W}_{F_I}(\omega_x, \omega_y) + \mathcal{W}_N(\omega_x, \omega_y)} \tag{5.81}$$

In this case, the power spectra of the reconstructed and ideal images become identical only for a noise-free observation. Although equivalence of the power spectra of the ideal and reconstructed images appears to be an attractive feature of the image power-spectrum filter, it should be realized that it is more important that the Fourier spectra (Fourier transforms) of the ideal and reconstructed images be identical because their Fourier transform pairs are unique, but power-spectra transform pairs are not necessarily unique. Furthermore, the Wiener filter provides a minimum mean-square error estimate, while the image power-spectrum filter may result in a large residual mean-square error. Cole has also introduced a geometrical mean filter, defined by the transfer Function

$$\mathcal{H}_R(\omega_x, \omega_y) = [\mathcal{H}_D(\omega_x, \omega_y)]^{-S} \left[\frac{\mathcal{H}_D^{*}(\omega_x, \omega_y) \mathcal{W}_{F_I}(\omega_x, \omega_y)}{|\mathcal{H}_D(\omega_x, \omega_y)|^2 \mathcal{W}_{F_I}(\omega_x, \omega_y) + \mathcal{W}_N(\omega_x, \omega_y)}\right]^{1-S} \tag{5.82}$$

Where $0 \le S \le 1$ is a design parameter. If S=1/2 and $H_D = H_D^{*}$, the geometrical mean filter reduces to the image power-spectrum filter as given in Eq. 5.77. Hunt has developed another parametric restoration filter, called the constrained least-squares filter, whose transfer function is of the form

$$\mathcal{H}_R(\omega_x, \omega_y) = \frac{\mathcal{H}_D^{*}(\omega_x, \omega_y)}{|\mathcal{H}_D(\omega_x, \omega_y)|^2 + \gamma |\mathcal{C}(\omega_x, \omega_y)|^2} \tag{5.83}$$

Where $\gamma$ is a design constant and $c(\omega_x, \omega_y)$ is a design spectral variable. If $\gamma$=1 and $|c(\omega_x, \omega_y)|^2$ is set equal to the reciprocal of the spectral signal-to-noise power ratio of Eq. 5.72, the constrained least-squares filter becomes equivalent to the Wiener filter of Eq. 5.70(b). The spectral variable can also be used to minimize higher-order derivatives of the estimate.

#### 5.6.2.4 APPLICATION TO DISCRETE IMAGES

The inverse filtering, Wiener filtering and parametric estimation filtering techniques developed for continuous image fields are often applied to the restoration of discrete images. The common procedure has been to replace each of the continuous spectral functions involved in the filtering operation by its discrete twodimensional Fourier transform counterpart. However, care must be taken in this conversion process so that the discrete filtering operation is an accurate representation of the continuous convolution process and that the discrete form of the restoration filter impulse response accurately models the appropriate continuous filter impulse response.

Figures 5.23 to 5.27 present examples of continuous image spatial filtering techniques by discrete Fourier transform filtering. The original image of Figure 5.23(A) (a) has been blurred with a Gaussian-shaped impulse response with to b=0 obtain the blurred image of Figure 5.23(A) (b). White Gaussian noise has been added to the blurred image to give the noisy blurred image of Figure 5.23(A) (c), which has a signal- to-noise ratio of 10.0. Figure 5.23(B) shows the results of inverse filter image restoration of the blurred and noisy-blurred images. In Figure 5.23(B) *(a)*, the inverse filter transfer function follows (i.e., no high-frequency cutoff). The restored image for the

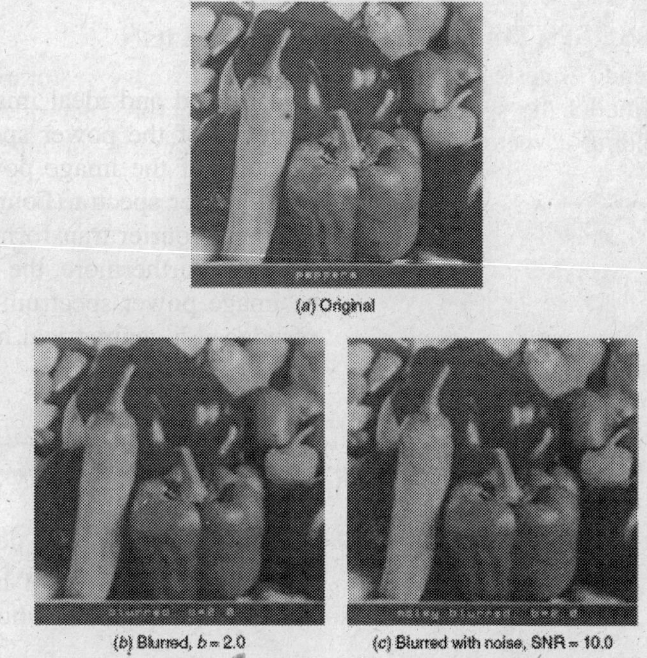

(*a*) Original

(*b*) Blurred, *b* = 2.0 (*c*) Blurred with noise, SNR = 10.0

**Figure 5.23(A) Blurred test images.**

noise-free observation is corrupted completely by the effects of computational error. The computation was performed using 32-bit floating-point arithmetic. In Figure 5.23(B) *c,* the inverse filter restoration is performed with a circular cutoff inverse filter as defined by Eq. with C=200 for the pixel 512 X 512 noise-free observation. Some faint artifacts are visible in the restoration. In Figure 12.2-5*e,* the cutoff frequency is reduced to C=50 . The restored image appears relatively sharp and free of artifacts. Figure 5.23(B) *b*, *d* and *f* show the result of inverse filtering on the noisy-blurred observed image with varying cutoff frequencies. These restorations illustrate the trade-off between the level of artifacts and the degree of deblurring. Figure 5.24 shows the results of Wiener filter image restoration. In all cases, the noise power spectral density is white and the signal power spectral density is circularly symmetric Markovian with a correlation factor $\rho$ . For the noise-free observation, the Wiener filter provides restorations that are free of artifacts but only slightly sharper than the blurred observation. For the noisy observation, the restoration artifacts are less noticeable than for an inverse filter. Figure 5.25 presents restorations using the power spectrum filter. For a noise-free observation, the power spectrum filter gives a restoration of similar quality to an inverse filter with a low cutoff frequency. For a noisy observation, the power spectrum filter restorations appear to be grainier than for the Wiener filter. The continuous image field restoration techniques derived in this section are advantageous in that they are relatively simple to understand and to implement using Fourier domain processing. However, these techniques face several important limitations. First, there is no provision for aliasing error effects caused by physical undersampling of the observed image. Second, the formulation inherently assumes that the quadrature spacing of the convolution integral is the same as the physical sampling. Third, the methods only permit restoration for linear, space-invariant degradation. Fourth, and perhaps most important, it is difficult to analyze the effects of numerical errors in the restoration process and to develop methods of combating such errors.

### 5.6.3 PSEUDOINVERSE SPATIAL IMAGE RESTORATION

The matrix pseudo inverse can be used for spatial image restoration of digital images when it is possible to model the spatial degradation as a vector-space operation on a vector of ideal image points yielding a vector of physical observed samples obtained from the degraded image.

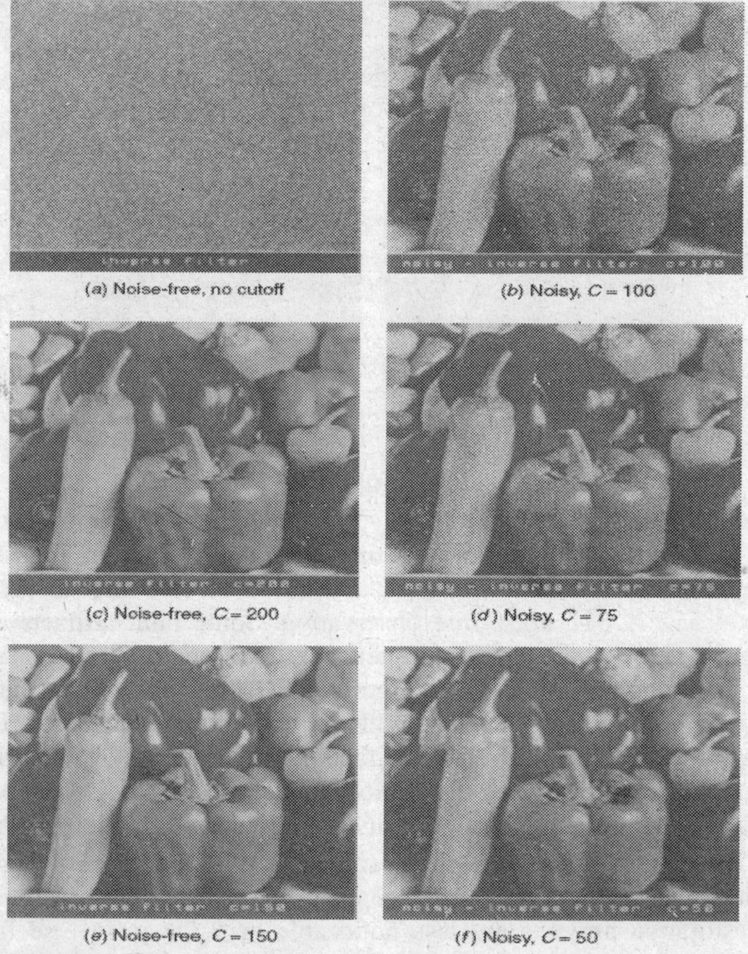

(*a*) Noise-free, no cutoff

(*b*) Noisy, $C = 100$

(*c*) Noise-free, $C = 200$

(*d*) Noisy, $C = 75$

(*e*) Noise-free, $C = 150$

(*f*) Noisy, $C = 50$

**Figure 5.23(B) Inverse filter image restoration on the blurred test images**

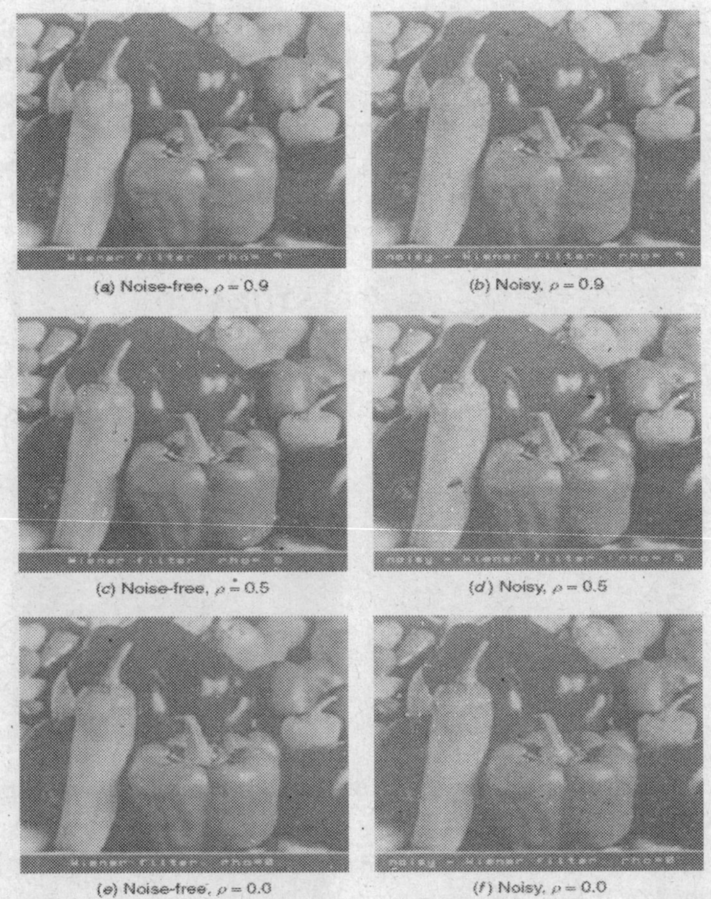

(*a*) Noise-free, $\rho = 0.9$ (*b*) Noisy, $\rho = 0.9$

(*c*) Noise-free, $\rho = 0.5$ (*d*) Noisy, $\rho = 0.5$

(*e*) Noise-free, $\rho = 0.0$ (*f*) Noisy, $\rho = 0.0$

**Figure 5.24 Wiener filter image restoration on the blurred test images; SNR = 10.0**

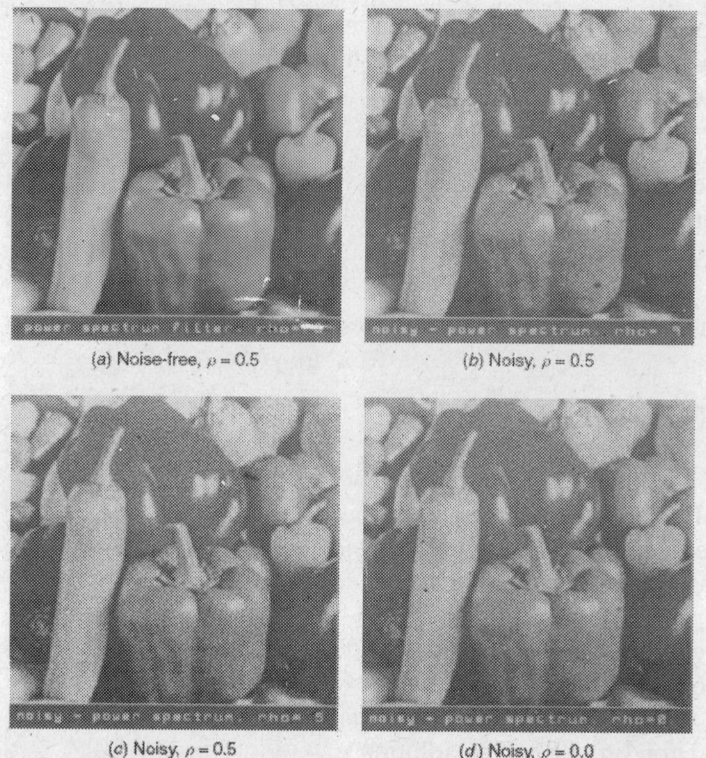

(a) Noise-free, $\rho = 0.5$ (b) Noisy, $\rho = 0.5$

(c) Noisy, $\rho = 0.5$ (d) Noisy, $\rho = 0.0$

**Figure 5.25 Power spectrum filter image restoration on the blurred test images; SNR = 10.0**

### 5.6.3.1 PSEUDOINVERSE: IMAGE BLUR

The first application of the pseudoinverse to be considered is that of the restoration of a blurred image described by the vector-space model

$$G=Bf \tag{5.84}$$

as derived in Eq. 5.84, where g is a P x 1vector ($P=M^2$) containing the M x M physical samples of the blurred image, f is a Q x 1vector ($Q=N^2$) containing N x N points of the ideal image and B is the P x Q matrix whose elements are points on the impulse function. If the physical sample period and the quadrature representation period are identical, P will be smaller than Q, and the system of equations will be underdetermined.

By oversampling the blurred image, it is possible to force P>Q or even P = Q . In either case, the system of equations is called overdetermined. An overdetermined set of equations can also be obtained if some of the elements of the ideal image vector can be specified through a priori knowledge. For example, if the ideal image is known to contain a limited size object against a black background (zero luminance), the elements of f beyond the limits may be set to zero. In discrete form, the restoration problem reduces to finding a solution f to Eq. 5.84 in the sense that

$$\mathbf{Bf} = \mathbf{g} \tag{5.85}$$

Because the vector g is determined by physical sampling and the elements of B are specified independently by system modeling, there is no guarantee that a $\tilde{f}$ even exists to satisfy Eq. 5.85.

If there is a solution, the system of equations is said to be consistent; otherwise, the system of equations is inconsistent. In Appendix 1, it is shown that inconsistency in the set of equations of Eq. 5.84 can be characterized as

$$\mathbf{g} = \mathbf{Bf} + \mathbf{e}\{\mathbf{f}\} \tag{5.86}$$

Where e{f} is a vector of remainder elements whose value depends on f. If the set of equations is inconsistent, a solution of the form

$$\hat{\mathbf{f}} = \mathbf{Wg} \tag{5.87}$$

is sought for which the linear operator W minimizes the least-squares modeling error

$$\mathcal{E}_M = [\mathbf{e}\{\hat{\mathbf{f}}\}]^T[\mathbf{e}\{\hat{\mathbf{f}}\}] = [\mathbf{g} - \mathbf{B}\hat{\mathbf{f}}]^T[\mathbf{g} - \mathbf{B}\hat{\mathbf{f}}] \tag{5.88}$$

This error is shown, to be minimized when the operator $W=B^{\$}$ is set equal to the least-squares inverse of B. The least-squares inverse is not necessarily unique. It is also proved that the generalized inverse operator $W=B^{-}$ which is a special case of the least-squares inverse, is unique, minimizes the least-squares modeling error, and simultaneously provides a minimum norm estimate.

That is, the sum of the squares of f is a minimum for all possible minimum least-square error estimates. For the restoration of image blur, the generalized inverse provides a lowest-intensity restored image. If Eq. 5.84 represents a consistent set of equations, one or more solutions may exist for Eq. 5.85. The solution commonly chosen is the estimate that minimizes the least-squares estimation error defined in the equivalent forms

$$\mathcal{E}_E = (\mathbf{f} - \hat{\mathbf{f}})^T(\mathbf{f} - \hat{\mathbf{f}}) \tag{5.89 (a)}$$

$$\mathcal{E}_E = \mathrm{tr}\left\{(\mathbf{f} - \hat{\mathbf{f}})(\mathbf{f} - \hat{\mathbf{f}})^T\right\} \tag{5.89 (b)}$$

it is proved that the estimation error is minimum for a generalized inverse ($W=B^{-}$)estimate. The resultant residual estimation error then becomes

$$\mathcal{E}_E = \mathbf{f}^T[\mathbf{I} - [\mathbf{B}^{-}\ \mathbf{B}]]\mathbf{f} \tag{5.90 (a)}$$

or

$$\mathcal{E}_E = \mathrm{tr}\{\mathbf{f}\mathbf{f}^T[\mathbf{I} - [\mathbf{B}^{-}\ \mathbf{B}]]\} \tag{5.90 (b)}$$

The estimate is perfect, of course, if $B^{-}B = 1$ Thus, it is seen that the generalized inverse is an optimal solution, in the sense defined previously, for both consistent and inconsistent sets of equations modeling image blur. From, the generalized inverse has been found to be algebraically equivalent to

$$\mathbf{B}^{-} = [\mathbf{B}^T\mathbf{B}]^{-1}\mathbf{B}^T \tag{5.91 (a)}$$

if the P x Q matrix B is of rank Q. If B is of rank P, then

$$\mathbf{B}^{-} = \mathbf{B}^{T}[\mathbf{B}^{T}\mathbf{B}]^{-1} \tag{5.91 (b)}$$

For a consistent set of equations and a rank Q generalized inverse, the estimate

$$\hat{\mathbf{f}} = \mathbf{B}^{-}\mathbf{g} = \mathbf{B}^{-}\mathbf{B}\mathbf{f} = [[\mathbf{B}^{T}\mathbf{B}]^{-1}\mathbf{B}^{T}]\mathbf{B}\mathbf{f} = \mathbf{f} \tag{5.92}$$

is obviously perfect. However, in all other cases, a residual estimation error may occur. Clearly, it would be desirable to deal with an overdetermined blur matrix of rank Q in order to achieve a perfect estimate. Unfortunately, this situation is rarely achieved in image restoration. Oversampling the blurred image can produce an overdetermined set of equations (P > Q), but the rank of the blur matrix is likely to be much less than Q because the rows of the blur matrix will become more linearly dependent with finer sampling.

A major problem in application of the generalized inverse to image restoration is dimensionality. The generalized inverse is a Q x P matrix where P is equal to the number of pixel observations and Q is equal to the number of pixels to be estimated in an image. It is usually not computationally feasible to use the generalized inverse operator, defined by Eq. 5.70, over large images because of difficulties in reliably computing the generalized inverse and the large number of vector multiplications associated with Eq. 5.65. Computational savings can be realized if the blur matrix B is separable such that

$$\mathbf{B} = \mathbf{B}_{C} \otimes \mathbf{B}_{R} \tag{5.93}$$

where BC and BR are column and row blur operators. In this case, the generalized inverse is separable in the sense that

$$\mathbf{B}^{-} = \mathbf{B}_{C}^{-} \otimes \mathbf{B}_{R}^{-} \tag{5.94}$$

Where $B_{C}^{-} and B_{R}^{-}$ and are generalized inverses of BC and BR, respectively. Thus, when the blur matrix is of separable form, it becomes possible to form the estimate of the image by sequentially applying the generalized inverse of the row blur matrix to each row of the observed image array and then using the column generalized inverse operator on each column of the array.

Pseudo inverse restoration of large images can be accomplished in an approximate fashion by a block mode restoration process, similar to the block mode filtering technique, in which the blurred image is partitioned into small blocks that are restored individually. It is wise to overlap the blocks and accept only the pixel estimates in the center of each restored block because these pixels exhibit the least uncertainty. Figure 5.26(a) shows a blurred image based on the model. Figure 5.26(b) shows a restored image using generalized inverse image restoration. An efficient computational algorithm for pseudo inverse restoration for space-invariant blur. In this example, the observation is noise free and the blur impulse response function is Gaussian shaped, with $b_R = b_C = 1.2$. Only the center 8 x 8 region of the 12 x 12 blurred picture is displayed, zoomed to an image size of 256 x 256 pixels. The restored image appears to be visually improved compared to the blurred image, but the restoration is not identical to the original unblurred image of Figure 5.14(a).

The figure also gives the percentage least-squares error (PLSE) between the blurred image and the original unblurred image, and between the restored image and the original. The restored image has less error than the blurred image.

#### 5.6.3.2 PSEUDOINVERSE: IMAGE BLUR PLUS ADDITIVE NOISE

In many imaging systems, an ideal image is subject to both blur and additive noise; the resulting vector-space model takes the form

$$G=Bf+n \tag{5.95}$$

where g and n are P x 1vectors of the observed image field and noise field, respectively, f is a Q x 1 vector of ideal image points, and B is a P x Q blur matrix. The vector n is composed of two additive components: samples of an additive external noise process and elements of the vector difference (g – Bf) arising from modeling errors in the formulation of B. As a result of the noise contribution, there may be no vector solutions $\tilde{f}$ that satisfy Eq. 5.95

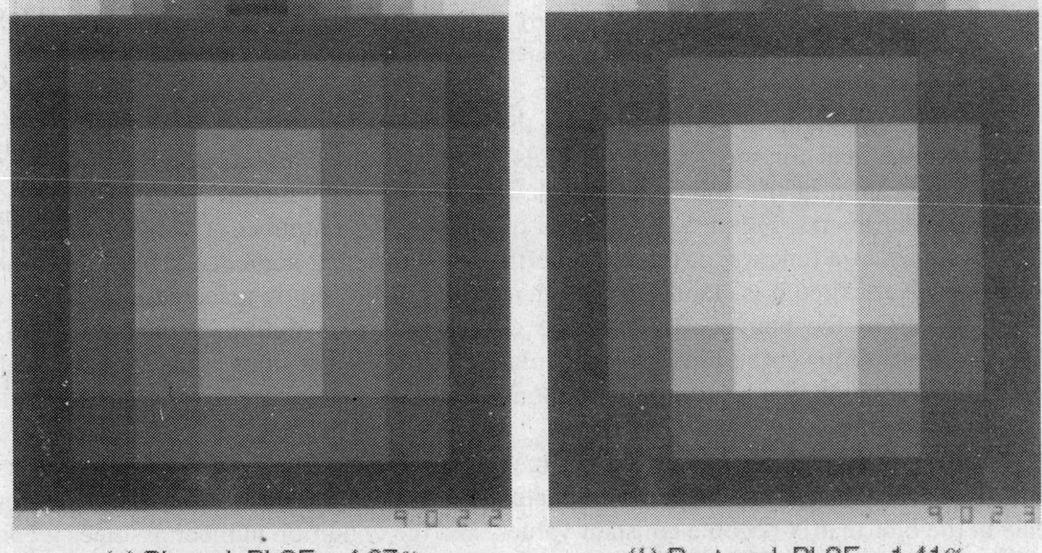


**Figure 5.26 Pseudoinverse image restoration for test image blurred with Gaussian shape impulse response. M = 8, N = 12, L = 5; $b_R = b_C = 1.2$; noise-free observation**

However, the generalized inverse $B^{-}$ can be utilized to determine a least-squares error, minimum norm estimate. In the absence of modeling error, the estimate

$$\hat{f} = B^{-} g = B^{-} Bf + B^{-} n \tag{5.96}$$

differs from the ideal image because of the additive noise contribution $B^{-}n$. . Also, for the underdetermined model, $B^{-}B$ will not be an identity matrix. If B is an over determined rank Q matrix, as defined in Eq. 5.91a, then $B^{-}B=I$, and the resulting estimate is equal to the original image vector f plus a perturbation vector $\Delta f = B^{-}n$.. The perturbation error in the estimate can be measured as the ratio of the vector norm of the perturbation to the vector norm of the estimate. It can be shown (25, p.52) that the relative error is subject to the bound

$$\frac{\|\Delta f\|}{\|f\|} < \|B^{-}\| \cdot \|B\| \frac{\|n\|}{\|g\|} \tag{5.97}$$

The product $\|B^{-}\|$. . $\|B\|$, which is called the condition number C{B} of B, determines the relative error in the estimate in terms of the ratio of the vector norm of the noise to the vector norm of the observation. The condition number can be computed directly or found in terms of the ratio

$$C\{\mathbf{B}\} = \frac{W_1}{W_N}$$

(5.98)

of the largest W1 to smallest WN singular values of B. The noise perturbation error for the underdetermined matrix B. if WN is defined to be the smallest nonzero singular value of B (25, p. 41). Obviously, the larger the condition number of the blur matrix, the greater will be the sensitivity to noise perturbations. Figure 5.27 contains image restoration examples for a Gaussian-shaped blur function for several values of the blur standard deviation and a noise variance of 10.0 on an amplitude scale of 0.0 to 255.0. As expected, observation noise degrades the restoration. Also as expected, the restoration for a moderate degree of blur is worse than the restoration for less blur.

However, this trend does not continue; the restoration for severe blur is actually better in a subjective sense than for moderate blur. This seemingly anomalous behavior, which results from spatial truncation of the point-spread function, can be explained in terms of the condition number of the blur matrix. Figure 5.28 is a plot of the condition number of the blur matrix of the previous examples as a function of the blur coefficient . For small amounts of blur, the condition number is low. A maximum is attained for moderate blur, followed by a decrease in the curve for increasing values of the blur coefficient. The curve tends to stabilize as the blur coefficient approaches infinity. This curve provides an explanation for the previous experimental results. In the restoration operation, the blur impulse response is spatially truncated over a square region of 5 x 5 quadrature points.

As the blur coefficient increases, for fixed M and N, the blur impulse response becomes increasingly wider, and its tails become truncated to a greater extent. In the limit, the nonzero elements in the blur matrix become constant values, and the condition number assumes a constant level. For small values of the blur coefficient, the truncation effect is negligible, and the condition number curve follows an ascending path toward infinity with the asymptotic value obtained for a smoothly represented blur impulse response.

As the blur factor increases, the number of nonzero elements in the blur matrix increases, and the condition number stabilizes to a constant value. In effect, a trade-off exists between numerical errors caused by ill-conditioning and modeling accuracy. Although this conclusion is formulated on the basis of a particular degradation model, the inference seems to be more general because the inverse of the integral operator that describes the blur is unbounded. Therefore, the closer the discrete model follows the continuous model, the greater the degree of ill-conditioning. A move in the opposite direction reduces singularity but imposes modeling errors. This inevitable dilemma can only be broken with the intervention of correct a priori knowledge about the original image.

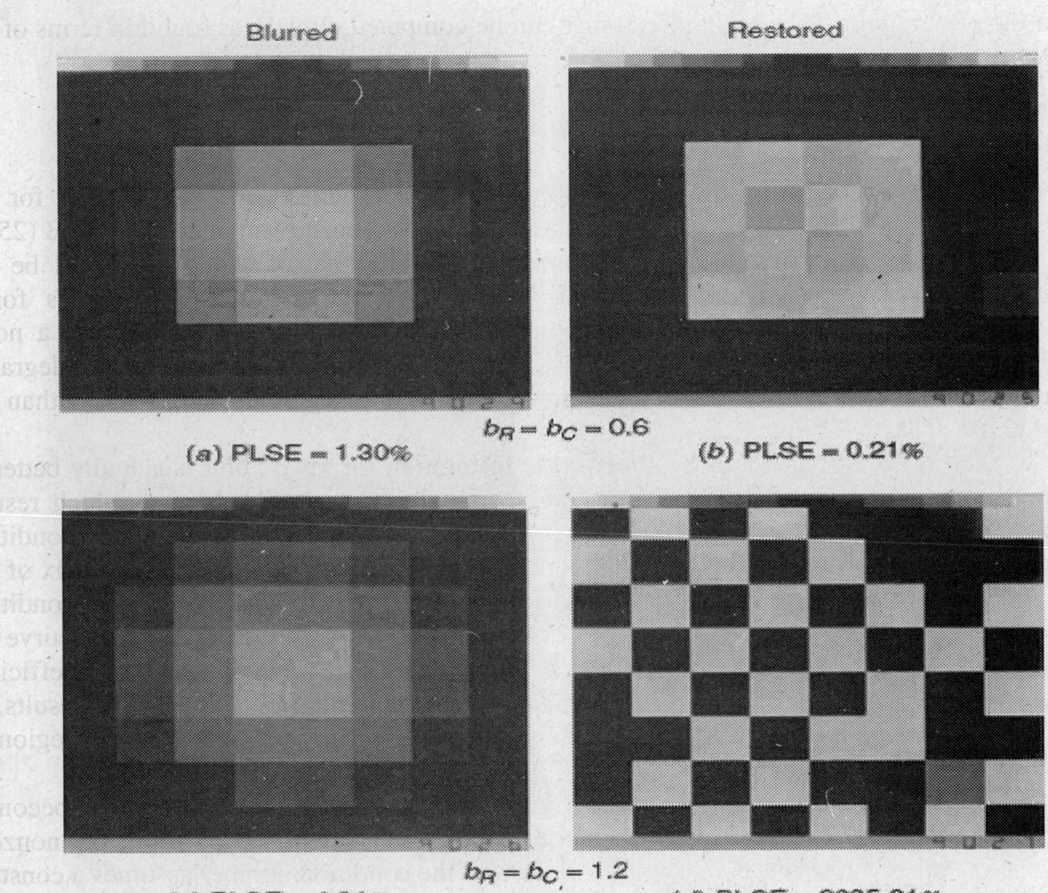


(*a*) PLSE = 1.30% (*b*) PLSE = 0.21%

(*c*) PLSE = 4.91% (*d*) PLSE = 2695.81%

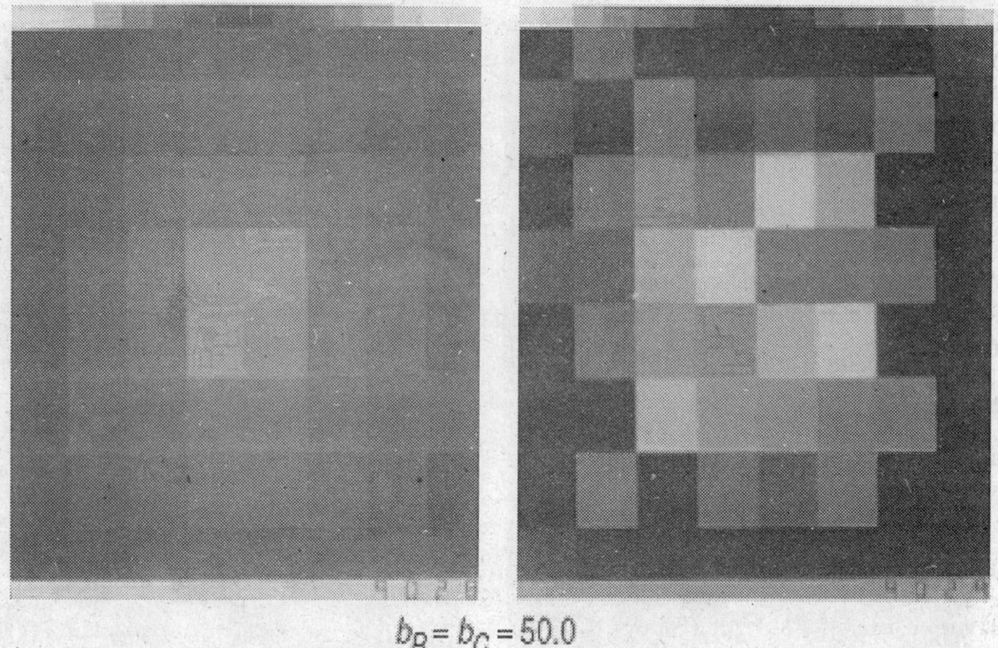


**Figure 5.27 Pseudoinverse image restoration for test image blurred with Gaussian shape impulse response. M = 8, N = 12, L = 5; noisy observation, Var = 10.0**

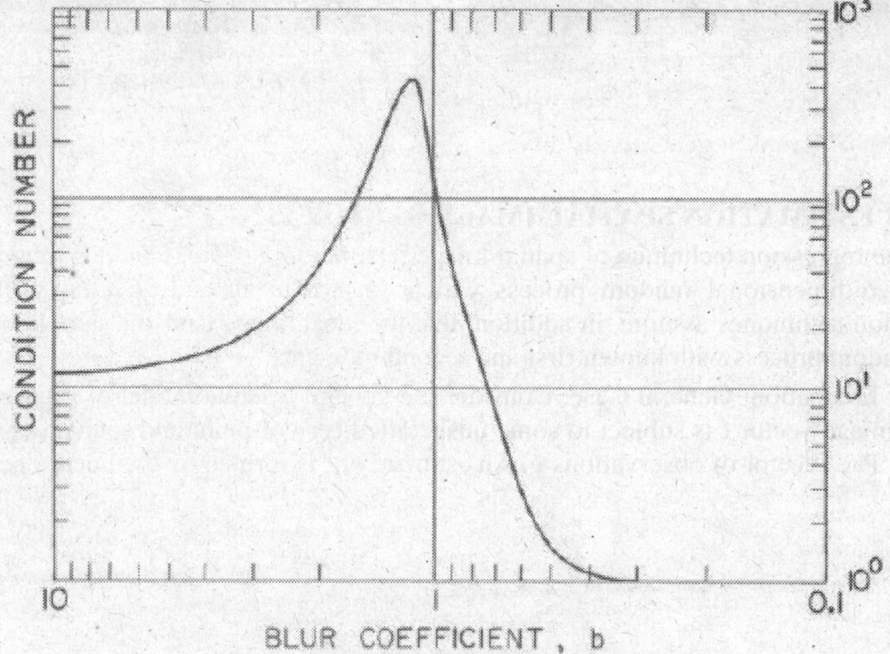


**Figure 5.28 Condition number curve**

## 5.7 STATISTICAL ESTIMATION SPATIAL IMAGE RESTORATION

A fundamental limitation of pseudo inverse restoration techniques is that observation noise may lead to severe numerical instability and render the image estimate unusable. This problem can be alleviated in some instances by statistical restoration techniques that incorporate some a priori statistical knowledge of the observation noise.

### 5.7.1 REGRESSION SPATIAL IMAGE RESTORATION

Consider the vector-space model

$$g = Bf + n \tag{5.99}$$

for a blurred image plus additive noise in which B is a P x Q blur matrix, and the noise is assumed to be zero mean with known covariance matrix Kn. The regression method seeks to form an estimate

$$\hat{\mathbf{f}} = \mathbf{W}\mathbf{g} \tag{5.100}$$

where W is a restoration matrix that minimizes the weighted error measure

$$\Theta\{\hat{\mathbf{f}}\} = [\mathbf{g} - \mathbf{B}\hat{\mathbf{f}}]^T \mathbf{K}_n^{-1} [\mathbf{g} - \mathbf{B}\hat{\mathbf{f}}] \tag{5.101}$$

Minimization of the restoration error can be accomplished by the classical method of setting the partial derivative of $\Theta\{\tilde{f}\}$ with respect to $\tilde{f}$ to zero. In the underdetermined case, for which P < Q, it can be that the minimum norm estimate regression operator is

$$\mathbf{W} = [\mathbf{K}^{-1}\mathbf{B}]^{-} \mathbf{K}^{-1} \tag{5.101}$$

where K is a matrix obtained from the spectral factorization

$$\mathbf{K}_n = \mathbf{K}\mathbf{K}^T \tag{5.102}$$

of the noise covariance matrix $K_n$. For white noise, $K = \sigma_n^2 I$, and the regression operator assumes the form of a rank P generalized inverse for an underdetermined system as given by Eq. 5.93(b).

### 5.7.2 WIENER ESTIMATION SPATIAL IMAGE RESTORATION

With the regression technique of spatial image restoration, the noise field is modeled as a sample of a two-dimensional random process with a known mean and covariance function. Wiener estimation techniques assume, in addition, that the ideal image is also a sample of a two-dimensional random process with known first and second moments.

Wiener Estimation: General Case. Consider the general discrete model of Figure 5.29 in which a Q x 1 image vector f is subject to some unspecified type of point and spatial degradation resulting in the P x 1vector of observations g. An estimate of f is formed by the linear operation

$$\hat{\mathbf{f}} = \mathbf{W}\mathbf{g} + \mathbf{b} \tag{5.103}$$

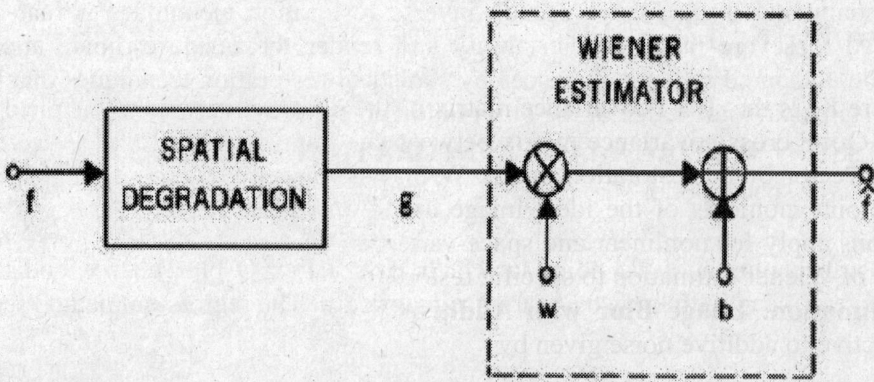


**Figure 5.29. Wiener estimation for spatial image restoration**

where W is a Q x P restoration matrix and b is a Q x 1 bias vector. The objective of Wiener estimation is to choose W and b to minimize the mean-square restoration error, which may be defined as

$$\mathcal{E} = E\left\{[\mathbf{f}-\hat{\mathbf{f}}]^T[\mathbf{f}-\hat{\mathbf{f}}]\right\} \qquad (5.104\ (a))$$

or

$$\mathcal{E} = \text{tr}\left\{E\left\{[\mathbf{f}-\hat{\mathbf{f}}][\mathbf{f}-\hat{\mathbf{f}}]^T\right\}\right\} \qquad (5.104\ (b))$$

Equation 5.104(a) expresses the error in inner-product form as the sum of the squares of the elements of the error vector [f – f], while Eq. 5.104(b) forms the covariance matrix of the error, and then sums together its variance terms (diagonal elements) by the trace operation. Minimization of Eq. 5.104 in either of its forms can be accomplished by differentiation of $\mathcal{E}$ with respect to $\tilde{f}$.

An alternative approach, which is of quite general utility, is to employ the orthogonality principle (33, p. 219) to determine the values of W and b that minimize the mean-square error. In the context of image restoration, the orthogonality principle specifies two necessary and sufficient conditions for the minimization of the mean-square restoration error:

1. The expected value of the image estimate must equal the expected value of the image

$$E\{\tilde{\mathbf{f}}\} = E\{\mathbf{f}\} \qquad (5.105)$$

2. The restoration error must be orthogonal to the observation about its mean

$$E\{[\mathbf{f}-\hat{\mathbf{f}}][\mathbf{g}-E\{\mathbf{g}\}]^T\} = \mathbf{0} \qquad (5.106)$$

From condition 1, one obtains

$$\mathbf{b} = E\{\mathbf{f}\} - \mathbf{W}E\{\mathbf{g}\} \qquad (5.107)$$

and from condition 2

$$E\{[\mathbf{W}+\mathbf{b}-\mathbf{f}][\mathbf{g}-E\{\mathbf{g}\}]^T\} = \mathbf{0} \qquad (5.108)$$

Upon substitution for the bias vector b from Eq. 5.107 and simplification, Eq. 5.108 yields

$$\mathbf{W} = \mathbf{K}_{fg}[\mathbf{K}_{gg}]^{-1} \tag{5.109}$$

where $K_{gg}$is the P x Pcovariance matrix of the observation vector (assumed nonsingular) and $_{fg}$ is the Q x P cross-covariance matrix between the image and observation vectors. Thus, the optimal bias vector b and restoration matrix W may be directly determined in terms of the first and second joint moments of the ideal image and observation vectors. It should be noted that these solutions apply for nonlinear and space-variant degradations. Subsequent sections describe applications of Wiener estimation to specific restoration models.

**Wiener Estimation: Image Blur with Additive Noise**. For the discrete model for a blurred image subjective to additive noise given by

$$g=Bf+n \tag{5.110}$$

the Wiener estimator is composed of a bias term

$$\mathbf{b} = E\{\mathbf{f}\} - \mathbf{W}E\{\mathbf{g}\} = E\{\mathbf{f}\} - \mathbf{WB}E\{\mathbf{f}\} + \mathbf{W}E\{\mathbf{n}\} \tag{5.111}$$

and a matrix operator

$$\mathbf{W} = \mathbf{K}_{fg}[\mathbf{K}_{gg}]^{-1} = \mathbf{K}_f\mathbf{B}^T[\mathbf{BK}_f\mathbf{B}^T + \mathbf{K}_n]^{-1} \tag{5.112}$$

If the ideal image field is assumed uncorrelated, $K_f = \sigma_f^2 I$ where $\sigma_f^2$ represents the image energy. Equation 5.112 then reduces to

$$\mathbf{W} = \sigma_f^2\mathbf{B}^T[\sigma_f^2\mathbf{BB}^T + \mathbf{K}_n]^{-1} \tag{5.113}$$

For a white-noise process with energy $\sigma_n^2$, the Wiener filter matrix becomes

$$\mathbf{W} = \mathbf{B}^T\left(\mathbf{BB}^T + \frac{\sigma_n^2}{\sigma_f^2}\mathbf{I}\right) \tag{5.114}$$

As the ratio of image energy to noise energy $(\sigma_f^2 / \sigma_n^2)$ approaches infinity, the Wiener estimator of Eq. 5.114 becomes equivalent to the generalized inverse estimator.

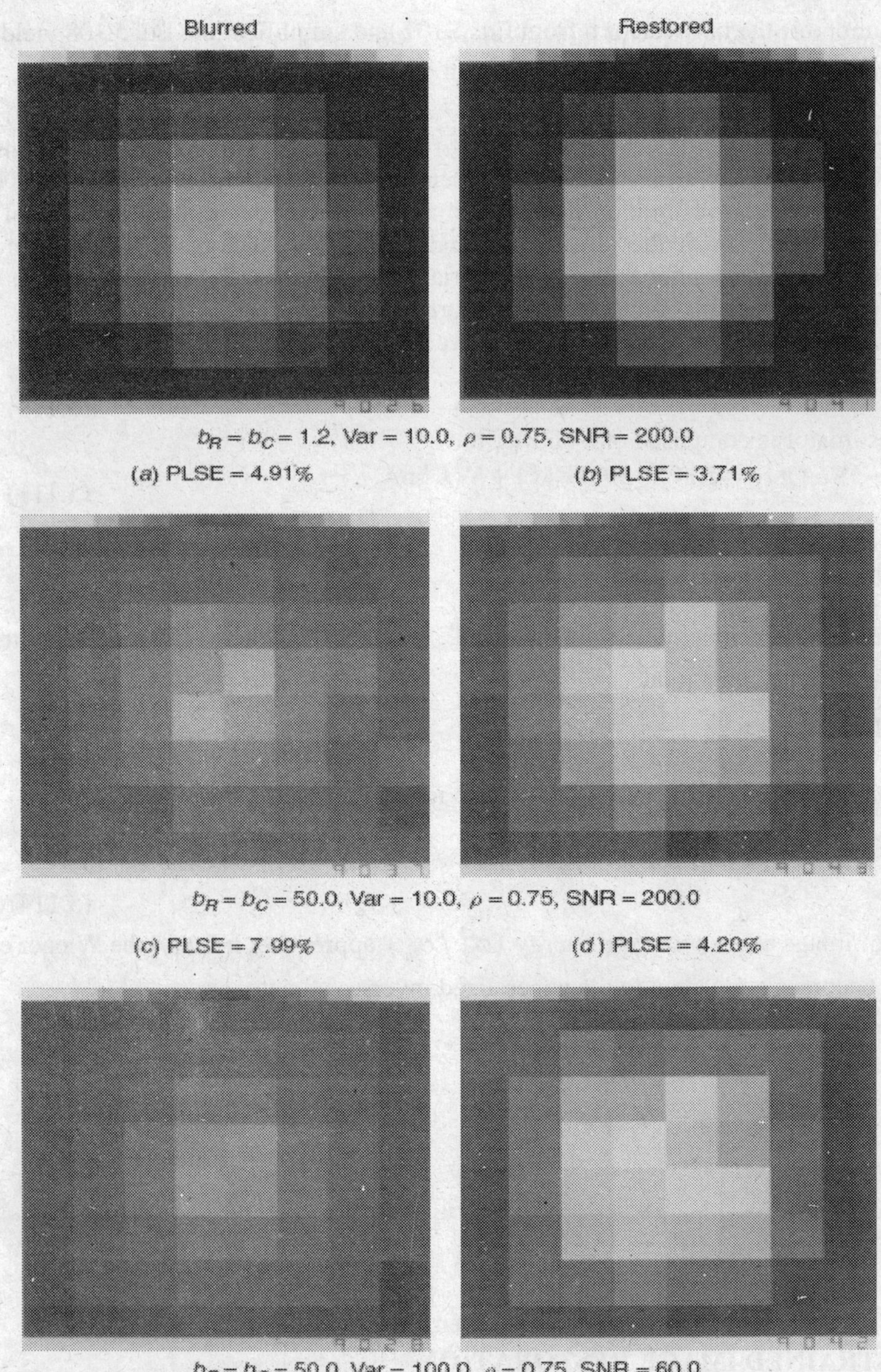


**Figure 5.30 Wiener estimation for test image blurred with Gaussian-shaped impulse response. M = 8, N = 12, L = 5**

Figure 5.30 shows restoration examples for the model for a Gaussian-shaped blur function. In the example of Figure 5.31(a) illustrating horizontal image motion blur, the impulse response is of rectangular shape of length $L = 11$. The center pixels have been restored and replaced within the context of the blurred image to show the visual restoration improvement. The noise level and blur impulse response of the electron microscope original image of Figure 5.31(c) were estimated directly from the photographic transparency using techniques. The parameters were then utilized to restore the center pixel region, which was then replaced in the context of the blurred original.

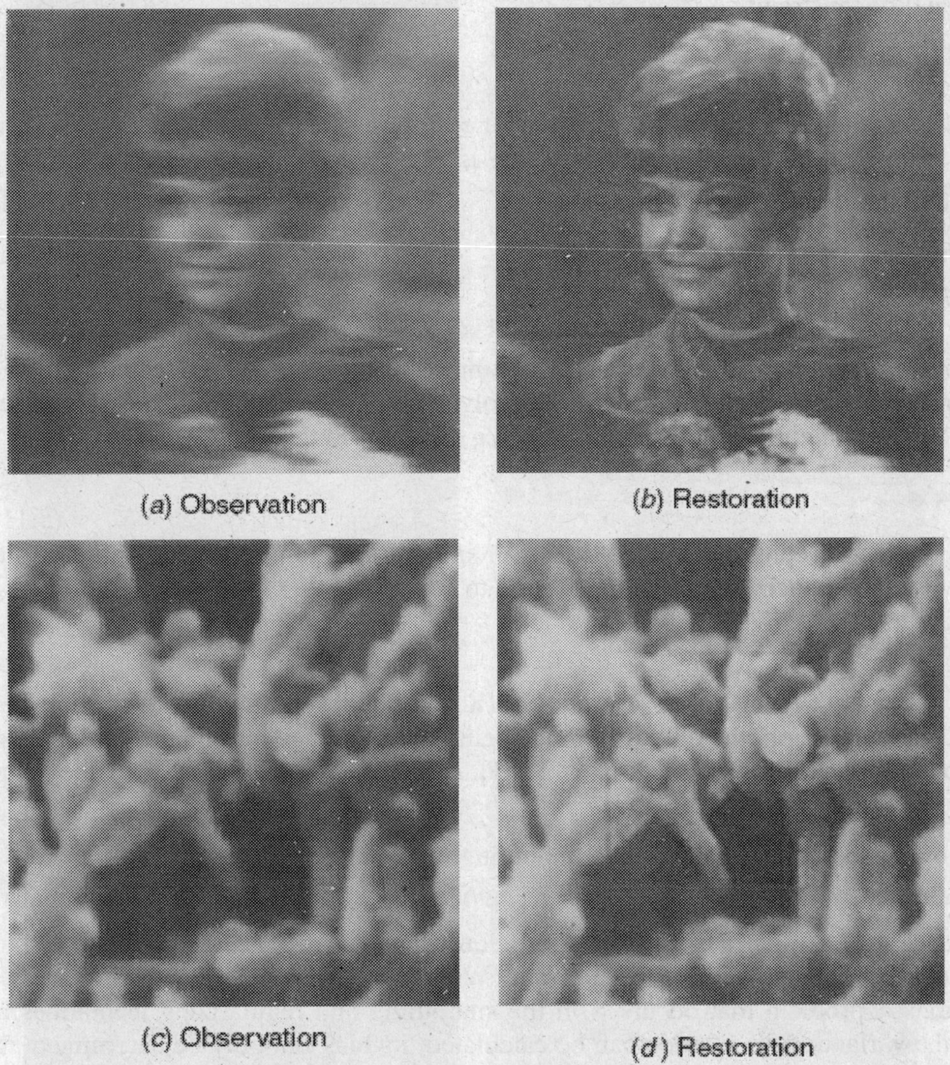

(*a*) Observation (*b*) Restoration

(*c*) Observation (*d*) Restoration

**Figure 5.31 Wiener image restoration**

## 5.8. CONSTRAINED IMAGE RESTORATION

The previously described image restoration techniques have treated images as arrays of numbers. They have not considered that a restored natural image should be subject to physical constraints. A restored natural image should be spatially smooth and strictly positive in amplitude.

### 5.8.1. SMOOTHING METHODS

Smoothing and regularization techniques have been used in an attempt to overcome the ill-conditioning problems associated with image restoration. Basically, these methods attempt to force smoothness on the solution of a least-squares error problem. Two formulations of these methods are considered. The first formulation consists of finding the minimum of $f^{-T}Sf$ subject to the equality constraint

$$[\mathbf{g}-\mathbf{B}\hat{\mathbf{f}}]^T\mathbf{M}[\mathbf{g}-\mathbf{B}\hat{\mathbf{f}}] = e \tag{5.115}$$

where S is a smoothing matrix, M is an error-weighting matrix, and e denotes a residual scalar estimation error. The error-weighting matrix is often chosen to be equal to the inverse of the observation noise covariance matrix, $M = K_n^{-1}$. The Lagrangian estimate satisfying Eq. 5.115 is

$$\hat{\mathbf{f}} = \mathbf{S}^{-1}\mathbf{B}^T\left[\mathbf{B}\mathbf{S}^{-1}\mathbf{B}^T + \frac{1}{\gamma}\mathbf{M}^{-1}\right]^{-1}\mathbf{g} \tag{5.116}$$

In Eq. 5.96, the Lagrangian factor $\gamma$ is chosen so that Eq. 5.115 is satisfied; that is, the compromise between residual error and smoothness of the estimator is deemed satisfactory. Now consider the second formulation, which involves solving an equality-constrained least-squares problem by minimizing the left-hand side of Eq. 5.115 such that

$$\hat{\mathbf{f}}^T\mathbf{S}\hat{\mathbf{f}} = d \tag{5.117}$$

where the scalar d represents a fixed degree of smoothing. In this case, the optimal solution for an underdetermined nonsingular system is found to be

$$\hat{\mathbf{f}} = \mathbf{S}^{-1}\mathbf{B}^T[\mathbf{B}\mathbf{S}^{-1}\mathbf{B}^T + \gamma\mathbf{M}^{-1}]^{-1}\mathbf{g} \tag{5.118}$$

A comparison of Eqs. 5.116 and 5.118 reveals that the two inverse problems are solved by the same expression, the only difference being the Lagrange multipliers, which are inverses of one another. The smoothing estimates of Eq. 5.118 are closely related to the regression and Wiener estimates derived previously. If $\gamma = 0, S = 1$, and $M = K_n^{-1}$ where $K_n$ is the observation noise covariance matrix, then the smoothing and regression estimates become equivalent. Substitution of $\gamma$=1, $S = K_f^{-1} andM = K_n^{-1} whereK_f$ is the image covariance matrix results in equivalence to the Wiener estimator. These equivalences account for the relative smoothness of the estimates obtained with regression and Wiener restoration as compared to pseudoinverse restoration. A problem that occurs with the smoothing and regularizing techniques is that even though the variance of a solution can be calculated, its bias can only be determined as a function of f.

### 5.8.2. CONSTRAINED RESTORATION TECHNIQUES

Equality and inequality constraints have been suggested as a means of improving restoration performance for ill-conditioned restoration models. Examples of constraints include the specification of individual pixel values, of ratios of the values of some pixels, or the sum of part or all of the pixels, or amplitude limits of pixel values. Quite often a priori information is available in the form of inequality constraints involving pixel values. The physics of the image formation process requires that pixel values be non-negative quantities.

Furthermore, an upper bound on these values is often known because images are digitized with a finite number of bits assigned to each pixel. Amplitude constraints are also inherently introduced by the need to "fit" a restored image to the dynamic range of a display. One approach is linearly to rescale the restored image to the display image. This procedure is usually undesirable because only a few out-of-range pixels will cause the contrast of all other pixels to be reduced. Also, the average luminance of a restored image is usually affected by rescaling. Another common display method involves clipping of all pixel values exceeding the display limits.

Although this procedure is subjectively preferable to rescaling, bias errors may be introduced. If a priori pixel amplitude limits are established for image restoration, it is best to incorporate these limits directly in the restoration process rather than arbitrarily invoke the limits on the restored image. Several techniques of inequality constrained restoration have been proposed. Consider the general case of constrained restoration in which the vector estimate $\tilde{f}$ is subject to the inequality constraint

$$\mathbf{l} \leq \mathbf{f} \leq \mathbf{u} \quad (5.119)$$

where u and L are vectors containing upper and lower limits of the pixel estimate, respectively. For least-squares restoration, the quadratic error must be minimized subject to the constraint of Eq. 5.119. Under this framework, restoration reduces to the solution of a quadratic programming problem. In the case of an absolute error measure, the restoration task can be formulated as a linear programming problem. The a priori knowledge involving the inequality constraints may substantially reduce pixel uncertainty in the restored image; however, as in the case of equality constraints, an unknown amount of bias may be introduced. Figure 5.32 is an example of image restoration for the Gaussian blur model of pseudoinverse restoration and with inequality constrained in which the scaled luminance of each pixel of the restored image has been limited to the range of 0 to 255. The improvement obtained by the constraint is substantial. Unfortunately, the quadratic programming solution employed in this example requires a considerable amount of computation. A brute-force extension of the procedure does not appear feasible. Several other methods have been proposed for constrained image restoration.

One simple approach, based on the concept of homomorphic filtering, is to take the logarithm of each observation. Exponentiation of the corresponding estimates automatically yields a strictly positive result. Burg , Edward and Fitelson and Frieden have developed restoration methods providing a positivity constraint, which are based on a maximum entropy principle originally employed to estimate a probability density from observation of its moments. Huang et al. have introduced a projection method of constrained image restoration in which the set of equations g=Bf are iteratively solved by numerical means. At each stage of the solution the intermediate estimates are amplitude clipped to conform to amplitude limits.

(a) Blurred observation

(b) Unconstrained restoration (c) Constrained restoration

**Figure 5.32. Comparison of unconstrained and inequality constrained image restoration for a test image blurred with Gaussian-shaped impulse response. $B_R = b_C = 1.2$, M = 12, N = 8, L = 5; noisy observation, Var = 10.0**

## 5.9. BLIND IMAGE RESTORATION

Most image restoration techniques are based on some a priori knowledge of the image degradation; the point luminance and spatial impulse response of the system degradation are assumed known. In many applications, such information is simply not available. The degradation may be difficult to measure or may be time varying in an unpredictable manner. In such cases, information about the degradation must be extracted from the observed image either explicitly or implicitly. This task is called blind image restoration . Discussion here is limited to blind image restoration methods for gamma corrected images and to blurred images subject to additive noise. There are two major approaches to blind image restoration: direct measurement and indirect estimation. With the former approach, the unknown system parameters, e.g. blur impulse response and noise level, are first measured from an image to be restored, and then these parameters are utilized in the restoration. Indirect estimation methods employ techniques to either obtain a restoration or to determine key elements of a restoration algorithm.

### 5.9.1. DIRECT MEASUREMENT METHODS

Direct measurement blind restoration of a blurred and noisy image usually requires measurement of the blur impulse response and noise power spectrum or covariance function of the observed image. The blur impulse response is usually measured by isolating the image of a suspected object within a picture. By definition, the blur impulse response is the image of a point-source object. Therefore, a point source in the observed scene yields a direct indication of the impulse response. The image of a suspected sharp edge can also be utilized to derive the blur impulse response. Averaging several parallel line scans normal to the edge will significantly reduce noise effects. The noise covariance function of an observed image can be estimated by measuring the image covariance over a region of relatively constant background luminance. Most techniques are limited to symmetric impulse response functions of simple parametric form.

## 5.9.2. INDIRECT ESTIMATION METHODS

Gamma Estimation. video images are usually gamma corrected to compensate for the nonlinearity of display devices, especially cathode ray tube displays. Gamma correction is performed by raising the unit range camera signal s to a power

$$g(s) = s^{\gamma} \tag{5.120}$$

Where $\gamma$ typically is about 0.45 for a CRT display. Most digital cameras use different amounts of gamma, whose values, generally, are not made available to the camera user. In many image processing applications, it is advantageous to perform inverse gamma correction

$$g^{-1}(s) = s^{1/\gamma} \tag{5.121}$$

before processing to eliminate the point nonlinearity. Thus, some means is needed to estimate the gamma of an unknown image. Farid has developed a clever means of gamma estimation, which is based upon the observation that gamma correction of an image introduces high-order correlations in the Fourier spectrum of an image. The amount of gamma correction can be found by a minimization of the correlations. Because gamma correction is a point process, gamma estimation can be determined by one-dimensional Fourier transforms along rows or columns of an image. The gamma estimation algorithm , which is similar to the estimation of a power spectrum using a Fast Fourier transform , follows:

1. Perform inverse gamma correction to an image for a range of suspected gamma values.
2. Extract one-dimensional signals x(n) from rows of the image.
3. Subdivide each x(n) into K possibly overlapping segments $y_k(m)$.
4. Form the discrete Fourier transform y(u) of the kth segment.
5. Form the two-dimensional bicoherence function estimate.1

$$\hat{B}(u_1, u_2) = \frac{\left|\frac{1}{K}\sum_k y_k(u_1)y_k(u_2)y_k^*(u_1+u_2)\right|}{\sqrt{\frac{1}{K}\sum_k |y_k(u_1)y_k(u_2)|^2 \frac{1}{K}\sum_k |y_k(u_1+u_2)|^2}} \tag{5.122}$$

6. Form the third-order correlation measure.

$$c = \sum_{u_1=-\pi}^{\pi} \sum_{u_2=-\pi}^{\pi} \left|\hat{B}(u_1, u_2)\right| \tag{5.123}$$

7. Determine the gamma value that minimizes Eq. 5.123 Accurate results have been reported for usage of this algorithm.

# QUESTION BANK

Q1. What is the Digital image restoration model? Explain with the help of example.

Q2. What do you mean by Optical Systems Models?

Q3. Discuss the various photographic process models in details.

Q4. Write short note on the (a) monochromatic photography and (b) color photography.

Q5. Briefly describe the Discrete Image Restoration Models. Explain with the help of Example.

Q6. Difference between sensor point nonlinearity correction and display point nonlinearity Correction.

Q7. Discuss the various continuous image spatial filtering restoration with example.

Q8. Explain the various applications to the discrete images.

Q9. Explain the various Image Restoration Techniques in details?

Q10. Describe the Pseudoinverse Spatial Image Restoration

Q11. Briefly describe the various statistical estimation spatial image restorations.

Q12. Explain the various constrained image restoration.

Q13. Briefly describe the blind image restoration.

# CHAPTER 6

# IMAGE FEATURE EXTRACTION

## 6.1 INTRODUCTION

An image feature is a distinguishing primitive characteristic or attribute of an image. Some features are natural in the sense that such features are defined by the visual appearance of an image, while other, artificial features result from specific manipulations of an image. Natural features include the luminance of a region of pixels and gray scale textural regions. Image amplitude histograms and spatial frequency spectra are examples of artificial features. Image features are of major importance in the isolation of regions of common property within an image (image segmentation) and subsequent identification or labeling of such regions (image classification).

## 6.2 IMAGE FEATURE EVALUATION

There are two quantitative approaches to the evaluation of image features: prototype performance and figure of merit. In the prototype performance approach for image classification, a prototype image with regions (segments) that have been independently categorized is classified by a classification procedure using various image features to be evaluated. The classification error is then measured for each feature set.

The best set of features is, of course, that which results in the least classification error. The prototype performance approach for image segmentation is similar in nature. A prototype image with independently identified regions is segmented by a segmentation procedure using a test set of features. Then, the detected segments are compared to the known segments, and the segmentation error is evaluated.

The problems associated with the prototype performance methods of feature evaluation are the integrity of the prototype data and the fact that the performance indication is dependent not only on the quality of the features but also on the classification or segmentation ability of the classifier or segmenter. The figure-of-merit approach to feature evaluation involves the establishment of some functional distance measurements between sets of image features such that a large distance implies a low classification error, and vice versa. Faugeras and Pratt have utilized the Bhattacharyya distance figure-of-merit for texture feature evaluation. The method should be extensible for other features as well. The Bhattacharyya distance (B-distance for simplicity) is a scalar function of the probability densities of features of a pair of classes defined as

$$B(S_1, S_2) = -\ln\left\{\int [p(\mathbf{x}|S_1)p(\mathbf{x}|S_2)]^{1/2} d\mathbf{x}\right\} \tag{6.1}$$

where x denotes a vector containing individual image feature measurements with conditional density $p(x \mid S_i)$. It can be shown that the B-distance is related monotonically to the Chernoff bound for the probability of classification error using a Bayes classifier. The bound on the error probability is

$$P \le [P(S_1)P(S_2)]^{1/2} \exp\{-B(S_1, S_2)\} \qquad (6.2)$$

where $P(S_i)$ represents the a priori class probability. For future reference, the Chernoff error bound is tabulated in Table 6.1 as a function of B-distance for equally likely feature classes. For Gaussian densities, the B-distance becomes

$$B(S_1, S_2) = \frac{1}{8}(\mathbf{u}_1 - \mathbf{u}_2)^T\left(\frac{\Sigma_1 + \Sigma_2}{2}\right)^{-1}(\mathbf{u}_1 - \mathbf{u}_2) + \frac{1}{2}\ln\left\{\frac{\frac{1}{2}|\Sigma_1 + \Sigma_2|}{|\Sigma_1|^{1/2}|\Sigma_2|^{1/2}}\right\} \qquad (6.3)$$

where $u_i$ and $\Sigma_i$ represent the feature mean vector and the feature covariance matrix of the classes, respectively. Calculation of the B-distance for other densities is generally difficult. Consequently, the B-distance figure of merit is applicable only for Gaussian-distributed feature data, which fortunately is the common case. In practice, features to be evaluated by Eq. 6.3 are measured in regions whose class has been determined independently. Sufficient feature measurements need be taken so that the feature mean vector and covariance can be estimated accurately.

| $B(S_1, S_2)$ | Error Bound |
|---|---|
| 1 | $1.84 \times 10^{-1}$ |
| 2 | $6.77 \times 10^{-2}$ |
| 4 | $9.16 \times 10^{-3}$ |
| 6 | $1.24 \times 10^{-3}$ |
| 8 | $1.68 \times 10^{-4}$ |
| 10 | $2.27 \times 10^{-5}$ |
| 12 | $2.07 \times 10^{-6}$ |

**Table 6.1 Relationship of Bhattacharyya Distance and Chernoff Error Bound**

## 6.2.1 AMPLITUDE FEATURES

The most basic of all image features is some measure of image amplitude in terms of luminance, tristimulus value, spectral value or other units. There are many degrees of freedom in establishing image amplitude features. Image variables such as luminance or tristimulus values may be utilized directly, or alternatively, some linear, nonlinear, or perhaps non-invertible transformation can be performed to generate variables in a new amplitude space.

Amplitude measurements may be made at specific image points, e.g., the amplitude F(j,k) at pixel coordinate (j , k) , or over a neighborhood centered at (j , k). For example, the average or mean image amplitude in a W x W pixel neighborhood is given by

$$M(j,k) = \frac{1}{W^2} \sum_{m=-w}^{w} \sum_{n=-w}^{w} F(j+m, k+n) \qquad (6.4)$$

where W = 2w + 1. An advantage of a neighborhood, as opposed to a point measurement, is a diminishing of noise effects because of the averaging process. A disadvantage is that object edges falling within the neighborhood can lead to erroneous measurements. The median of pixels within a W x W neighborhood can be used as an alternative amplitude feature to the mean measurement of Eq. 6.4, or as an additional feature. The median is defined to be that pixel amplitude in the window for which one-half of the pixels are equal or smaller in amplitude, and one-half are equal or greater in amplitude. Another useful image amplitude feature is the neighborhood standard deviation, which can be computed as

$$S(j,k) = \frac{1}{W}\left[\sum_{m=-w}^{w}\sum_{n=-w}^{w}[F(j+m,k+n) - M(j+m,k+n)]^2\right]^{1/2} \tag{6.5}$$

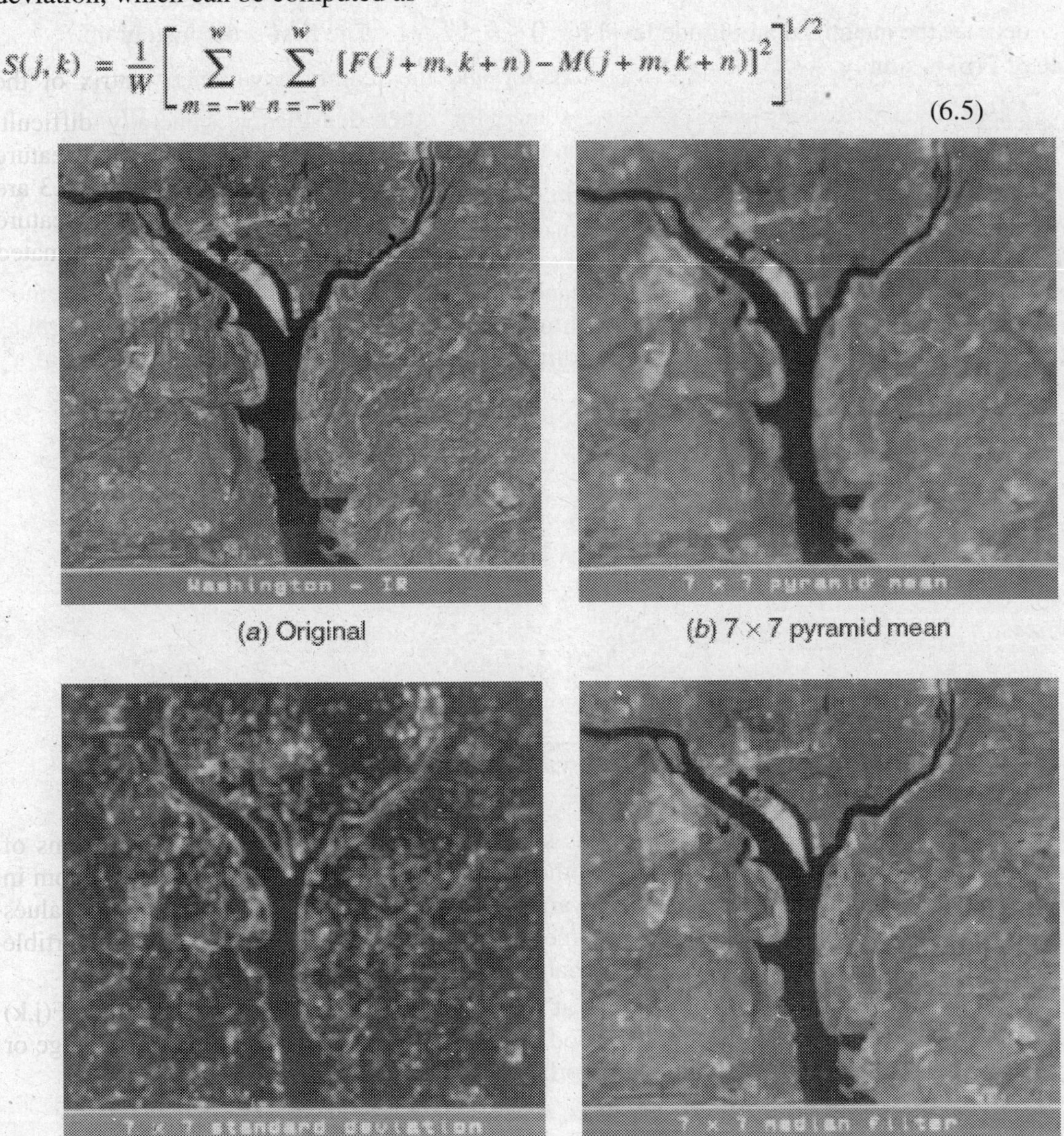


(*a*) Original (*b*) 7 × 7 pyramid mean

(*c*) 7 × 7 standard deviation (*d*) 7 × 7 plus median

**Figure 6.1 Image amplitude features of the washington_ir image**

In the literature, the standard deviation image feature is sometimes called the image dispersion. Figure 6.1 shows an original image and the mean, median and standard deviation of the image computed over a small neighborhood. The mean and standard deviation of Eqs. 6.4 and 6.5 can be computed indirectly in terms of the histogram of image pixels within a neighborhood. This leads to a class of image amplitude histogram features. The first-order probability distribution of the amplitude of a quantized image may be defined as

$$P(b) = P_R[F(j,k) = r_b] \tag{6.6}$$

where $r_b$ denotes the quantized amplitude level for $0 \le b \le L-1$ . The first-order histogram estimate of P(b) is simply

$$P(b) \approx \frac{N(b)}{M} \tag{6.7}$$

where M represents the total number of pixels in a neighborhood window centered about (j,k), and N(b) is the number of pixels of amplitude $r_b$ in the same window. The shape of an image histogram provides many clues as to the character of the image. For example, a narrowly distributed histogram indicates a low-contrast image. A bimodal histogram often suggests that the image contains an object with a narrow amplitude range against a background of differing amplitude. The following measures have been formulated as quantitative shape descriptions of a first-order histogram.

*Mean:*

$$S_M \equiv \bar{b} = \sum_{b=0}^{L-1} bP(b) \tag{6.8}$$

*Standard deviation:*

$$S_D \equiv \sigma_b = \left[ \sum_{b=0}^{L-1} (b-\bar{b})^2 P(b) \right]^{1/2} \tag{6.9}$$

*Skewness:*

$$S_S = \frac{1}{\sigma_b^3} \sum_{b=0}^{L-1} (b-\bar{b})^3 P(b) \tag{6.10}$$

*Kurtosis:*

$$S_K = \frac{1}{\sigma_b^4} \sum_{b=0}^{L-1} (b-\bar{b})^4 P(b) - 3 \tag{6.11}$$

*Energy:*

$$S_N = \sum_{b=0}^{L-1} [P(b)]^2 \tag{6.12}$$

*Entropy:*

$$S_E = -\sum_{b=0}^{L-1} P(b) \log_2\{P(b)\} \tag{6.13}$$

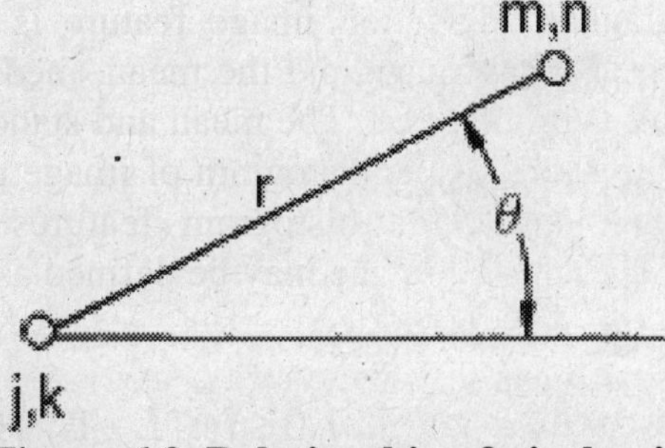


**Figure 6.2. Relationship of pixel pairs**

The factor of 3 inserted in the expression for the Kurtosis measure normalizes SK to zero for a zero-mean, Gaussian-shaped histogram. Another useful histogram shape measure is the histogram mode, which is the pixel amplitude corresponding to the histogram peak (i.e., the most commonly occurring pixel amplitude in the window). If the histogram peak is not unique, the pixel at the peak closest to the mean is usually chosen as the histogram shape descriptor. Second-order histogram features are based on the definition of the joint probability distribution of pairs of pixels. Consider two pixels F(j , k) and F(m,n) that are located at coordinates (j , k) and (m , n), respectively, and, as shown in Figure 6.2, are separated by r radial units at an angle $\theta$ with respect to the horizontal axis. The joint distribution of image amplitude values is then expressed as

$$P(a,b) = P_R\,[F(j,k) = r_a, F(m,n) = r_b] \tag{6.14}$$

where $r_a$ and $r_b$ represent quantized pixel amplitude values. As a result of the discrete rectilinear representation of an image, the separation parameters (r, $\theta$) may assume only certain discrete values. The histogram estimate of the second-order distribution is

$$P(a,b) \approx \frac{N(a,b)}{M} \tag{6.15}$$

where M is the total number of pixels in the measurement window and N(a,b) denotes the number of occurrences for which $F(j,k)=r_a$ and $F(m,n)=r_b$ If the pixel pairs within an image are highly correlated, the entries in P(a,b) will be clustered along the diagonal of the array. Various measures, listed below, have been proposed as measures that specify the energy spread about the diagonal of P(a,b).

$$\textit{Autocorrelation:} \quad S_A = \sum_{a=0}^{L-1} \sum_{b=0}^{L-1} abP(a,b) \tag{6.16}$$

$$\textit{Covariance:} \quad S_C = \sum_{a=0}^{L-1} \sum_{b=0}^{L-1} (a-\bar{a})(b-\bar{b})P(a,b) \tag{6.17(a)}$$

Where

$$\bar{a} = \sum_{a=0}^{L-1} \sum_{b=0}^{L-1} aP(a,b) \tag{6.17(b)}$$

$$\bar{b} = \sum_{a=0}^{L-1} \sum_{b=0}^{L-1} bP(a,b) \tag{6.17(c)}$$

*Inertia:* $$S_I = \sum_{a=0}^{L-1} \sum_{b=0}^{L-1} (a-b)^2 P(a,b) \tag{6.18}$$

*Absolute value:* $$S_V = \sum_{a=0}^{L-1} \sum_{b=0}^{L-1} |a-b| P(a,b) \tag{6.19}$$

*Inverse difference:* $$S_F = \sum_{a=0}^{L-1} \sum_{b=0}^{L-1} \frac{P(a,b)}{1+(a-b)^2} \tag{6.20}$$

*Energy:* $$S_G = \sum_{a=0}^{L-1} \sum_{b=0}^{L-1} [P(a,b)]^2 \tag{6.21}$$

*Entropy:* $$S_T = -\sum_{a=0}^{L-1} \sum_{b=0}^{L-1} P(a,b) \log_2\{P(a,b)\} \tag{6.22}$$

The utilization of second-order histogram measures for texture analysis.

### 6.2.2 TRANSFORM COEFFICIENT FEATURES

The coefficients of a two-dimensional transform of a luminance image specify the amplitude of the luminance patterns (two-dimensional basis functions) of a transform such that the weighted sum of the luminance patterns is identical to the image. By this characterization of a transform, the coefficients may be considered to indicate the degree of correspondence of a particular luminance pattern with an image field.

If a basis pattern is of the same spatial form as a feature to be detected within the image, image detection can be performed simply by monitoring the value of the transform coefficient. The problem, in practice, is that objects to be detected within an image are often of complex shape and luminance distribution, and hence do not correspond closely to the more primitive luminance patterns of most image transforms. Lendaris and Stanley have investigated the application of the continuous two dimensional Fourier transform of an image, obtained by a coherent optical processor, as a means of image feature extraction. The optical system produces an electric field radiation pattern proportional to

$$\mathcal{F}(\omega_x, \omega_y) = \int_{-\infty}^{\infty}\int_{-\infty}^{\infty} F(x,y) \exp\{-i(\omega_x x + \omega_y y)\}\, dx\, dy \tag{6.23}$$

where $(\omega_x, \omega_y)$ are the image spatial frequencies. An optical sensor produces an output

$$\mathcal{M}(\omega_x, \omega_y) = |\mathcal{F}(\omega_x, \omega_y)|^2 \tag{6.24}$$

proportional to the intensity of the radiation pattern. It should be observed that $F(\omega_x, \omega_y)$ and F(x,y) are unique transform pairs, but $M(\omega_x, \omega_y)$ is not uniquely related to F(x,y) . For example, $M(\omega_x, \omega_y)$ does not change if the origin of F(x,y) is shifted. In some applications, the translation invariance of $M(\omega_x, \omega_y)$ may be a benefit. Angular integration of $M(\omega_x, \omega_y)$ over the spatial frequency plane produces a spatial frequency feature that is invariant to translation and rotation. Representing $M(\omega_x, \omega_y)$ in polar form, this feature is defined as

$$\mathcal{N}(\rho) = \int_0^{2\pi} \mathcal{M}(\rho, \theta)\, d\theta \tag{6.25}$$

where $\theta = \arctan\{\omega_x / \omega_y\}$ and $P^2 = \omega_x^2 + \omega_y^2$ . Invariance to changes in scale is an attribute of the feature

$$\mathcal{P}(\theta) = \int_0^{\infty} \mathcal{M}(\rho, \theta)\, d\rho \tag{6.26}$$

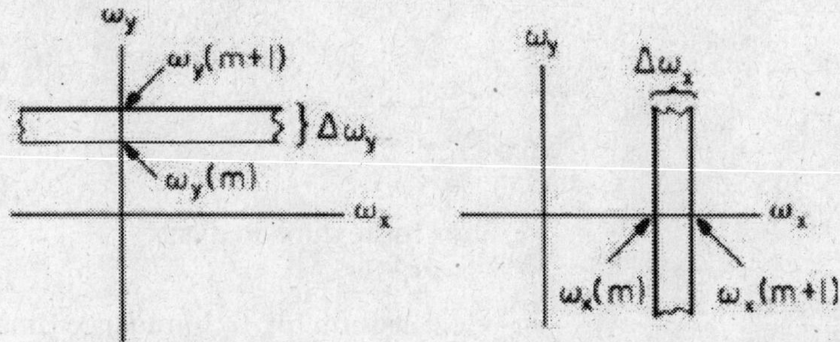


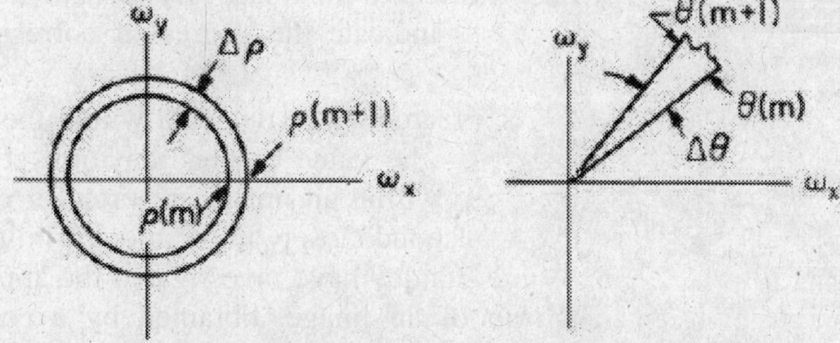


**Figure 6.3 Fourier transform feature masks**

The Fourier domain intensity pattern $M(\omega_x, \omega_y)$ is normally examined in specific regions to isolate image features. As an example, Figure 6.3 defines regions for the following Fourier features:

*Horizontal slit:*

$$S_1(m) = \int_{-\infty}^{\infty} \int_{\omega_y(m)}^{\omega_y(m+1)} \mathcal{M}(\omega_x, \omega_y)\; d\omega_x\, d\omega_y \tag{6.27}$$

*Vertical slit:*

$$S_2(m) = \int_{\omega_x(m)}^{\omega_x(m+1)} \int_{-\infty}^{\infty} \mathcal{M}(\omega_x, \omega_y)\, d\omega_x\, d\omega_y \tag{6.28}$$

*Ring:*

$$S_3(m) = \int_{\rho(m)}^{\rho(m+1)} \int_0^{2\pi} \mathcal{M}(\rho, \theta)\; d\rho\; d\theta \tag{6.29}$$

*Sector:* $$S_4(m) = \int_0^{\infty} \int_{\theta(m)}^{\theta(m+1)} \mathcal{M}(\rho, \theta)\, d\rho\, d\theta \tag{6.30}$$

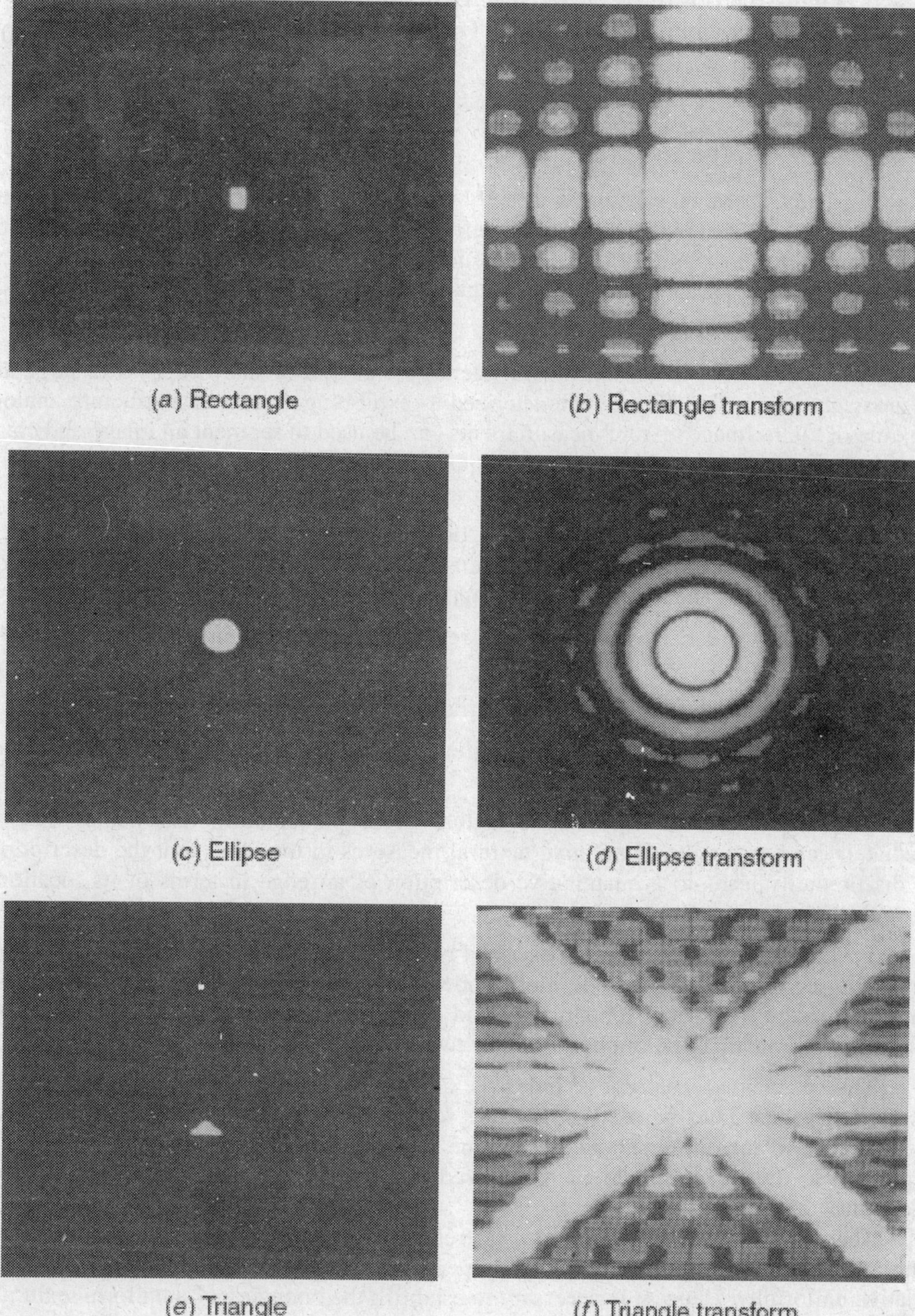

(*a*) Rectangle

(*b*) Rectangle transform

(*c*) Ellipse

(*d*) Ellipse transform

(*e*) Triangle

(*f*) Triangle transform

**Figure 6.4 Discrete Fourier spectra of objects; log magnitude displays**

For a discrete image array F(j,k) , the discrete Fourier transform

$$\mathcal{F}(u,v) = \frac{1}{N}\sum_{j=0}^{N-1}\sum_{k=0}^{N-1} F(j,k)\exp\left\{\frac{-2\pi i}{N}(ux+vy)\right\} \tag{6.31}$$

for u,v=0,……,N-1 can be examined directly for feature extraction purposes. Horizontal slit, vertical slit, ring and sector features can be defined analogous to Eqs. 6.27 to 6.30. This concept can be extended to other unitary transforms, such as the Hadamard and Haar transforms. Figure 6.4 presents discrete Fourier transform log magnitude displays of several geometric shapes.

### 6.2.3 TEXTURE DEFINITION

Many portions of images of natural scenes are devoid of sharp edges over large areas. In these areas, the scene càn often be characterized as exhibiting a consistent structure analogous to the texture of cloth. Image texture measurements can be used to segment an image and classify its segments. Several authors have attempted qualitatively to define texture. Pickett states that "texture is used to describe two dimensional arrays of variations...

The elements and rules of spacing or arrangement may be arbitrarily manipulated, provided a characteristic repetitiveness remains." Hawkins (10) has provided a more detailed description of texture: "The notion of texture appears to depend upon three ingredients:

1. some local 'order' is repeated over a region which is large in comparison to the order's size,
2. the order consists in the nonrandom arrangement of elementary parts and
3. the parts are roughly uniform entities having approximately the same dimensions everywhere within the textured region."

Although these descriptions of texture seem perceptually reasonable, they do not immediately lead to simple quantitative textural measures in the sense that the description of an edge discontinuity leads to a quantitative description of an edge in terms of its location, slope angle and height.

Texture is often qualitatively described by its coarseness in the sense that a patch of wool cloth is coarser than a patch of silk cloth under the same viewing conditions. The coarseness index is related to the spatial repetition period of the local structure. A large period implies a coarse texture; a small period implies a fine texture.

This perceptual coarseness index is clearly not sufficient as a quantitative texture measure, but can at least be used as a guide for the slope of texture measures; that is, small numerical texture measures should imply fine texture, and large numerical measures should indicate coarse texture. It should be recognized that texture is a neighborhood property of an image point.

Therefore, texture measures are inherently dependent on the size of the observation neighborhood. Because texture is a spatial property, measurements should be restricted to regions of relative uniformity. Hence it is necessary to establish the boundary of a uniform textural region by some form of image segmentation before attempting texture measurements.

Texture may be classified as being artificial or natural. Artificial textures consist of arrangements of symbols, such as line segments, dots and stars placed against a neutral background. Several examples of artificial texture are presented in Figure 6.5. As the name implies, natural textures are images of natural scenes containing semirepetitive arrangements of pixels. Examples include photographs of brick walls, terrazzo tile, sand and grass. Brodatz has published an album of photographs of naturally occurring textures. Figure 6.6 shows several natural texture examples obtained by digitizing photographs from the Brodatz album.

**Figure 6.5 Artificial texture**

**Figure 6.6 Brodatz texture fields**

### 6.2.4 VISUAL TEXTURE DISCRIMINATION

A discrete stochastic field is an array of numbers that are randomly distributed in amplitude and governed by some joint probability density. When converted to light intensities, such fields can be made to approximate natural textures surprisingly well by control of the generating probability density. This technique is useful for generating realistic appearing artificial scenes for applications such as airplane flight simulators. Stochastic texture fields are also an extremely useful tool for investigating human perception of texture as a guide to the development of texture feature extraction methods.

In the early 1960s, Julesz attempted to determine the parameters of stochastic texture fields of perceptual importance. This study was extended later by Julesz et al. Further extensions of Julesz's work have been made by Pollack ,

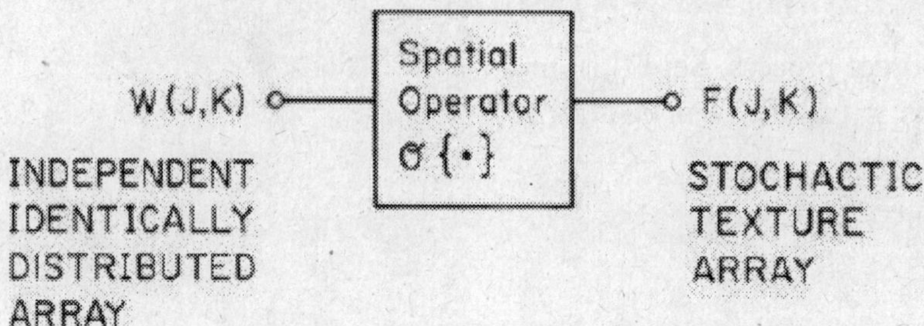


**Figure 6.7 Stochastic texture field generation model**

Purks and Richards and Pratt et al. These studies have provided valuable insight into the mechanism of human visual perception and have led to some useful quantitative texture measurement methods. Figure 6.7 is a model for stochastic texture generation. In this model, an array of independent, identically distributed random variables W(j,k) passes through a linear or nonlinear spatial operator O{.} to produce a stochastic texture array F(j,k) . By controlling the form of the generating probability density and the spatial operator, it is possible to create texture fields with specified statistical properties. Consider a continuous amplitude pixel at some coordinate (j,k) in F(j,k). Let the set $\{z_1, z_2,.......z_J\}$ denote neighboring pixels but not necessarily nearest geometric neighbors, raster scanned in a conventional top-to-bottom, left-to-right fashion. The conditional probability density of $x_o$ conditioned on the state of its neighbors is given by

$$p(x_0|z_1, \dots, z_J) = \frac{p(x_0, z_1, \dots, z_J)}{p(z_1, \dots, z_J)} \tag{6.32}$$

The first-order density $P(x_o)$ employs no conditioning, the second-order density $P(x_o \mid z_1)$ implies that J = 1, the third-order density implies that J = 2, and so on.

### 6.2.4.1. JULESZ TEXTURE FIELDS

In his pioneering texture discrimination experiments, Julesz utilized Markov process state methods to create stochastic texture arrays independently along rows of the array. The family of Julesz stochastic arrays are defined below.

1. Notation. Let $X_n$ = F (j , k - n) denote a row neighbor of pixel $x_o$ and let P(m), for m = 1, 2,..., M, denote a desired probability generating function.
2. First-order process. Set $x_o$ = m for a desired probability function P(m). The resulting pixel probability is

$$P(x_0) = P(x_0 = m) = P(m) \tag{6.33}$$

3. Second-order process. Set F(j , i) =m for P(m)=1/M, and set $x_o$ =( $x_1$ +m)MOD{M}, where the modulus function $P^{MOD}$ {q}=p-[qx(p/q)] for integers p and q. This gives a first-order probability

$$P(x_0) = \frac{1}{M} \tag{6.34(a)}$$

and a transition probability

$$p(x_0|x_1) = P[x_0 = (x_1 + m)\text{ MOD}\{M\}] = P(m) \tag{6.34(b)}$$

4. Third-order process. Set F(j,i)=m for P(m)=1/M, and set F(j,2)=n for P(n)=1/M . Choose $x_o$ to satisfy $2x_O = (x_1 + x_2 + m)MOD\{M\}$. The governing probabilities then become

$$P(x_0) = \frac{1}{M} \tag{6.35(a)}$$

$$p(x_0|x_1) = \frac{1}{M} \tag{6.35(b)}$$

$$p(x_0|x_1, x_2) = P[2x_0 = (x_1 + x_2 + m)\text{ MOD }\{M\}] = P(m) \tag{6.35(c)}$$

This process has the interesting property that pixel pairs along a row are independent, and consequently, the process is spatially uncorrelated. Figure 6.8 contains several examples of Julesz texture field discrimination tests performed by Pratt et al. In these tests, the textures were generated according to the presentation format of Figure 6.9. In these and subsequent visual texture discrimination tests, the perceptual differences are often small. Proper discrimination testing should be performed using high-quality photographic transparencies, prints or electronic displays. The following moments were used as simple indicators of differences between generating distributions and densities of the stochastic fields.

$$\eta = E\{x_0\} \tag{6.36(a)}$$

$$\sigma^2 = E\{[x_0 - \eta]^2\} \tag{6.36(b)}$$

$$\alpha = \frac{E\{[x_0 - \eta][x_1 - \eta]\}}{\sigma^2} \tag{6.36(c)}$$

$$\theta = \frac{E\{[x_0 - \eta][x_1 - \eta][x_2 - \eta]\}}{\sigma^3} \tag{6.36(d)}$$

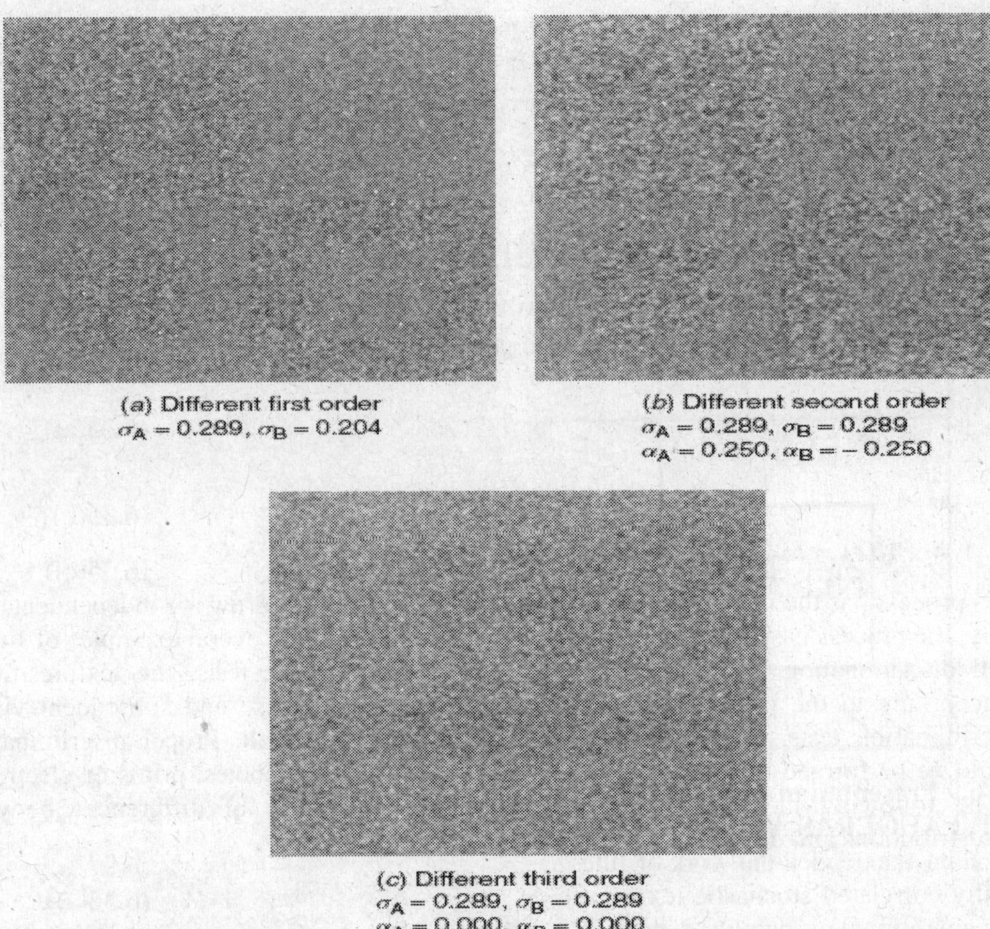


**Figure 6.8 Field comparison of Julesz stochastic fields; $\eta_A = \eta_B = 0.500$**

The examples of Figure 6.8(a) and (b) indicate that texture field pairs differing in their first- and second-order distributions can be discriminated. The example of Figure 6.8(c) supports the conjecture, attributed to Julesz, that differences in third-order, and presumably, higher-order distribution texture fields cannot be perceived provided that their first- and second-order distributions are pairwise identical.

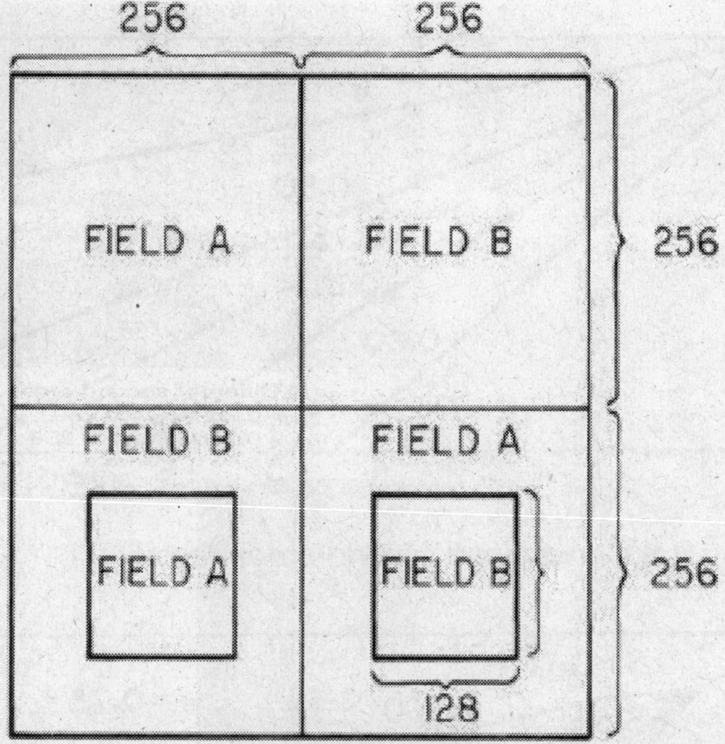


**Figure 6.9 Presentation format for visual texture discrimination experiments**

### 6.2.4.2. PRATT, FAUGERAS AND GAGALOWICZ TEXTURE FIELDS

Pratt et al.have extended the work of Julesz et al. in an attempt to study the discrimination ability of spatially correlated stochastic texture fields. A class of Gaussian fields was generated according to the conditional probability density

$$p(x_0|z_1,\ldots,z_J) = \frac{\left[(2\pi)^{J+1}|\mathbf{K}_{J+1}|\right]^{-1/2} \exp\left\{-\frac{1}{2}(\mathbf{v}_{J+1}-\eta_{J+1})^T(\mathbf{K}_{J+1})^{-1}(\mathbf{v}_{J+1}-\eta_{J+1})\right\}}{\left[(2\pi)^{J}|\mathbf{K}_{J}|\right]^{-1/2} \exp\left\{-\frac{1}{2}(\mathbf{v}_{J}-\eta_{J})^T(\mathbf{K}_{J})^{-1}(\mathbf{v}_{J}-\eta_{J})\right\}} \quad (6.37(a))$$

where

$$v_j = \begin{bmatrix} Z_1 \\ \vdots \\ \vdots \\ Z_j \end{bmatrix} \quad (6.37(b))$$

$$v_{J+1} = \begin{bmatrix} x_O \\ \hline v_J \end{bmatrix} \quad (6.37(c))$$

The covariance matrix of Eq. 6.37(a) is of the parametric form

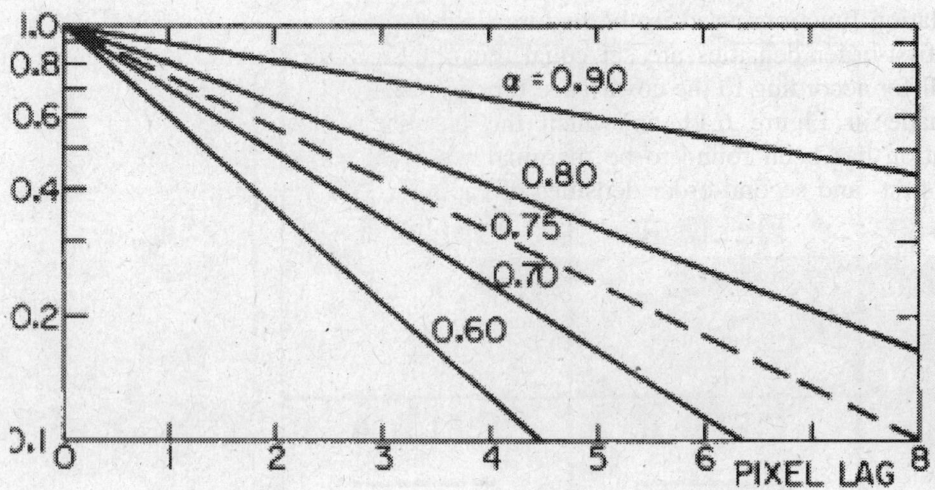


(*a*) Constrained second-order density

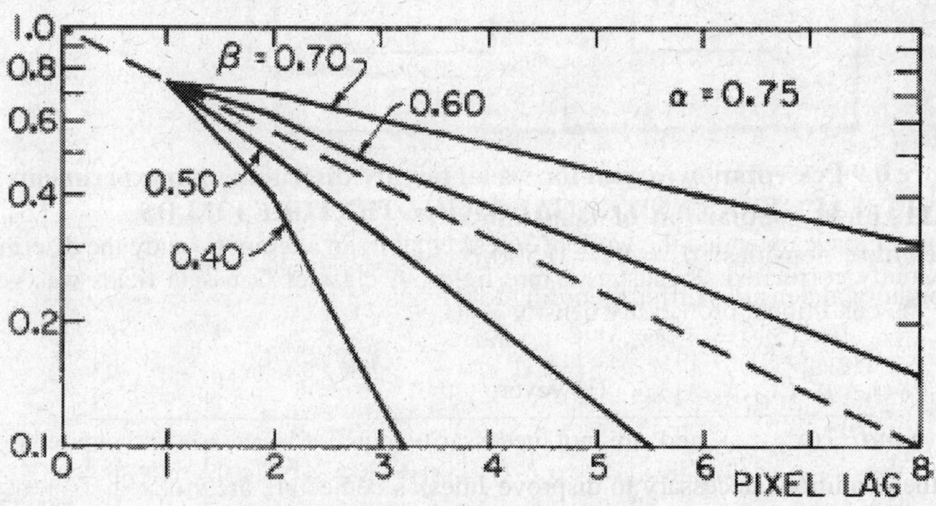


(*b*) Constrained third-order density

**Figure 6.10. Row correlation factors for stochastic field generation. Dashed line, field A; solid line, field B**

$$\mathbf{K}_{J+1} = \begin{bmatrix} 1 & \alpha & \beta & \gamma & \cdots \\ \alpha & & & & \\ \beta & & \sigma^{-2}\mathbf{K}_J & & \\ \gamma & & & & \\ \vdots & & & & \end{bmatrix} \tag{6.38}$$

where $\alpha, \beta, \lambda, ....$ denote correlation lag terms. Figure 6.10 presents an example of the row correlation functions used in the texture field comparison tests described below. In Figure 6.11, the first-order densities are set equal, but the second-order nearest neighbor conditional densities differ according to the covariance function plot of Figure 6.10(a). Visual discrimination can be made in Figure 6.11, in which the correlation parameter differs by 20%. Visual discrimination has been found to be marginal when the correlation factor differs by less than 10%. The first- and second-order densities of each field are fixed in Figure 6.12, and the third-order

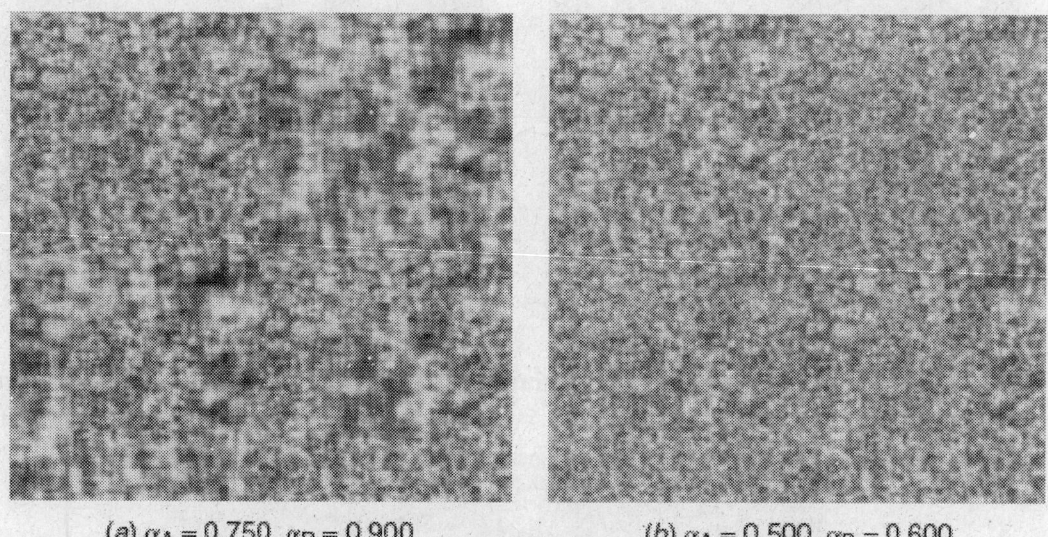

(a) $\alpha_A = 0.750, \alpha_B = 0.900$ (b) $\alpha_A = 0.500, \alpha_B = 0.600$

**Figure 6.11. Field comparison of Gaussian stochastic fields with different second-order nearest neighbor densities; $\eta_A = \eta_B = 0.500, \sigma_A = \sigma_B = 0.167$**

conditional densities differ according to the plan. Visual discrimination is possible. In this test, $[p^A(x_O) = p^B(x_O)]$ and $p^A(x_O, x_1) = p^B(x_O, x_1)$ , but $p^A(x_O, x_1, x_2) \neq p^B(x_O, x_1, x_2)$. However, the general second-order density pairs $p^A(x_O, z_j) and P^B(x_O, z_j)$ and are not necessarily equal for an arbitrary neighbor $z_j$, and therefore the conditions necessary to disprove Julesz's conjecture are violated. To test the Julesz conjecture for realistically appearing texture fields, it is necessary to generate a pair of fields with identical first-order densities, identical .

(a) $\beta_A = 0.563$, $\beta_B = 0.600$ (b) $\beta_A = 0.563$, $\beta_B = 0.400$

**Figure 6.12 Field comparison of Gaussian stochastic fields with different third-order nearest neighbor densities;** $\eta_A = \eta_B = 0.500, \sigma_A = \sigma_B = 0.167$ $\alpha_A = \alpha_B = 0.750$

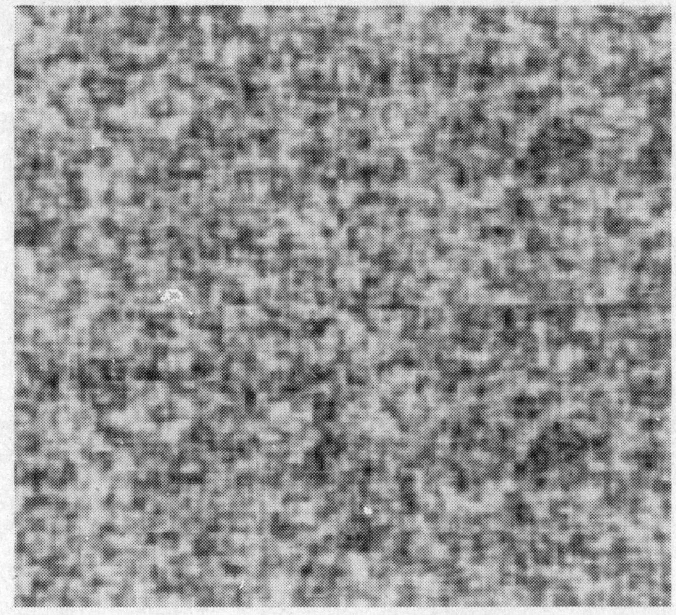

$\eta_A = 0.500$, $\eta_B = 0.500$
$\sigma_A = 0.167$, $\sigma_B = 0.167$
$\alpha_A = 0.850$, $\alpha_B = 0.850$
$\theta_A = 0.040$, $\theta_B = -0.027$

**Figure 6.13 Field comparison of correlated Julesz stochastic fields with identical first and second-order densities, but different third-order densities**

Markovian type second-order densities, and differing third-order densities for every pair of similar observation points in both fields. An example of such a pair of fields is presented in Figure 6.13 for a non-Gaussian generating process . In this example, the texture appears identical in both fields, thus supporting the Julesz conjecture. Gagalowicz has succeeded in generating a pair of texture fields that disprove the Julesz conjecture. However, the counterexample, shown in Figure 6.14, is not very realistic in appearance. Thus, it seems likely that if a statistically based

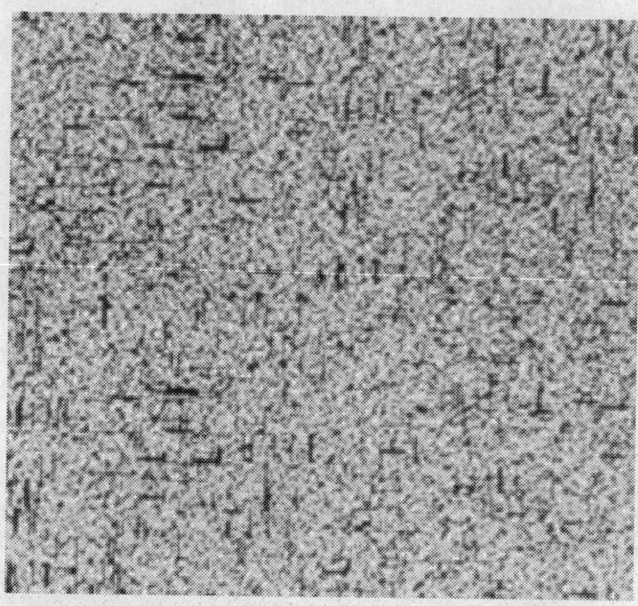

**Figure 6.14 Gagalowicz counter example**

$\eta_A = 0.413, \eta_B = 0.412$
$\sigma_A = 0.078, \sigma_B = 0.078$
$\alpha_A = 0.915, \alpha_B = 0.917$
$\theta_A = 1.512, \theta_B = 0.006$

**Figure 6.15 Field comparison of correlated stochastic fields with identical means, variances and autocorrelation functions, but different nth-order probability densities generated by different processing of the same input field. Input array consists of uniform random variables raised to the 256th power. Moments are computed**

texture measure can be developed, it need not utilize statistics greater than second-order. Because a human viewer is sensitive to differences in the mean, variance and autocorrelation function of the texture pairs, it is reasonable to investigate the sufficiency of these parameters in terms of texture representation. Figure 6.15 presents examples of the comparison of texture fields with identical means, variances and autocorrelation functions, but different nth-order probability densities. Visual discrimination is readily accomplished between the fields. This leads to the conclusion that these low-order moment measurements, by themselves, are not always sufficient to distinguish texture fields.

### 6.2.5 TEXTURE FEATURES

There is no commonly accepted quantitative definition of visual texture. As a consequence, researchers seeking a quantitative texture measure have been forced to search intuitively for texture features, and then attempt to evaluate their performance by techniques. The following subsections describe several texture features of historical and practical importance. Randen and Husoy have performed a comprehensive study of many texture feature extraction methods.

#### 6.2.5.1. FOURIER SPECTRA METHODS

Several studies have considered textural analysis based on the Fourier spectrum of an image region. Because the degree of texture coarseness is proportional to its spatial period, a region of coarse texture should have its Fourier spectral energy concentrated at low spatial frequencies. Conversely, regions of fine texture should exhibit a concentration of spectral energy at high spatial frequencies. Although this correspondence exists to some degree, difficulties often arise because of spatial changes in the period and phase of texture pattern repetitions. Experiments have shown that there is considerable spectral overlap of regions of distinctly different natural texture, such as urban, rural and woodland regions extracted from aerial photographs. On the other hand, Fourier spectral analysis has proved successful in the detection and classification of coal miner's black lung disease, which appears as diffuse textural deviations from the norm.

### 6.2.5.2. EDGE DETECTION METHODS

Rosenfeld and Troy have proposed a measure of the number of edges in a neighborhood as a textural measure. As a first step in their process, an edge map array E(j,k) is produced by some edge detector such that E(j,k)=1 for a detected edge and E(j,k)=0 otherwise. Usually, the detection threshold is set lower than the normal setting for the isolation of boundary points. This texture measure is defined as

$$T(j,k) = \frac{1}{W^2} \sum_{m=-w}^{w} \sum_{n=-w}^{w} E(j+m, k+n) \tag{6.39}$$

where W=2w+1 is the dimension of the observation window. A variation of this approach is to substitute the edge gradient G(j,k) for the edge map array in Eq. 6.39.

### 6.2.5.3. AUTOCORRELATION METHODS

The autocorrelation function has been suggested as the basis of a texture measure. Although it has been demonstrated in the preceding section that it is possible to generate visually different stochastic fields with the same autocorrelation function, this does not necessarily rule out the utility of an autocorrelation feature set for natural images. The autocorrelation function is defined as

$$A_F(m,n) = \sum_j \sum_k F(j,k)F(j-m, k-n) \tag{6.40}$$

for computation over a W x W window with $-T \le m,n \le T$ pixel lags. Presumably, a region of coarse texture will exhibit a higher correlation for a fixed shift (m,n) than will a region of fine texture. Thus, texture coarseness should be proportional to the spread of the autocorrelation function. Faugeras and Pratt have proposed the following set of autocorrelation spread measures:

$$S(u,v) = \sum_{m=0}^{T} \sum_{n=-T}^{T} (m-\eta_m)^u (n-\eta_n)^v A_F(m,n) \tag{6.41(a)}$$

where

$$\eta_m = \sum_{m=0}^{T} \sum_{n=-T}^{T} m A_F(m, n) \tag{6.41(b)}$$

$$\eta_n = \sum_{m=0}^{T} \sum_{n=-T}^{T} n A_F(m, n) \tag{6.41(c)}$$

In Eq. 6.41, computation is only over one-half of the autocorrelation function because of its symmetry. Features of potential interest include the profile spreads S(2, 0) and S(0, 2), the cross-relation S(1, 1) and the second-degree spread S(2, 2). Figure 6.16 shows perspective views of the autocorrelation functions of the four Brodatz texture examples. Bhattacharyya distance measurements of these texture fields, performed by Faugeras and Pratt. are presented in Table 6.2. These B-distance measurements indicate that the autocorrelation shape features are marginally adequate for the set of four shape features, but unacceptable for fewer features. Tests by Faugeras and Pratt verify that the B-distances are low for

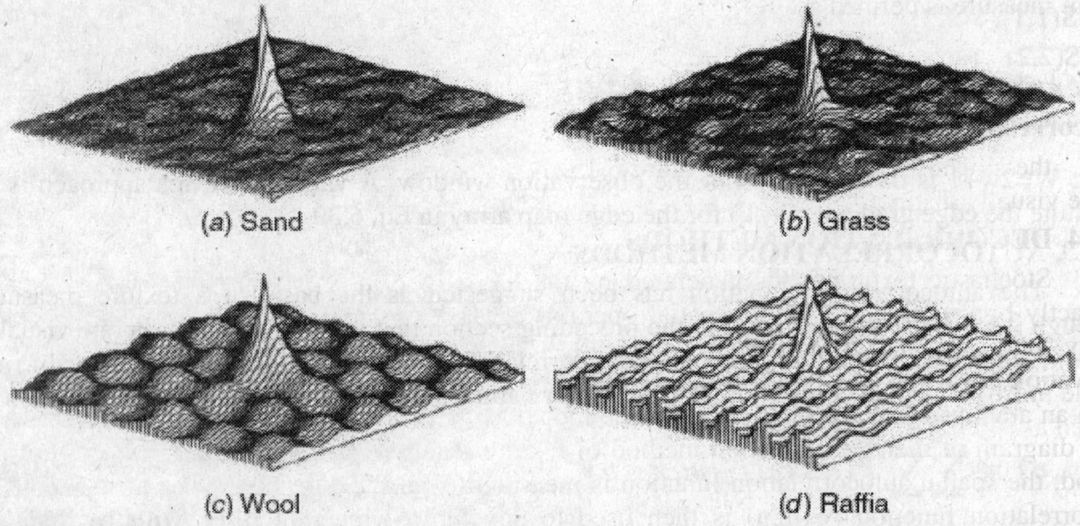


**Figure 6.16 Perspective views of autocorrelation functions of Brodatz texture fields**

| Field Pair | Set 1[a] | Set 2[b] | Set 3[c] |
|---|---|---|---|
| Grass – sand | 5.05 | 4.29 | 2.92 |
| Grass – raffia | 7.07 | 5.32 | 3.57 |
| Grass – wool | 2.37 | 0.21 | 0.04 |
| Sand – raffia | 1.49 | 0.58 | 0.35 |
| Sand – wool | 6.55 | 4.93 | 3.14 |
| Raffia – wool | 8.70 | 5.96 | 3.78 |
| Average | 5.21 | 3.55 | 2.30 |

[a]1: S(2, 0), S(0, 2), S(1, 1), S(2,2).
[b]2: S(1,1), S(2,2).
[c]3: S(2,2).

**Table 6.2 Bhattacharyya Distance of Texture Feature sets for prototype Texture Fields: Autocorrelation Features**

the stochastic field pairs of Figure 6.15 , which have the same autocorrelation functions but are visually distinct.

### 6.2.5.4. DECORRELATION METHODS

Stochastic texture fields generated by the model of Figure 6.7 can be described quite compactly by specification of the spatial operator O{.}and the stationary first-order probability density p(W) of the independent, identically distributed generating process W(j,k). This observation has led to a texture feature extraction procedure, developed by Faugeras and Pratt , in which an attempt has been made to invert the model and estimate its parameters. Figure 6.17 is a block diagram of their decorrelation method of texture feature extraction. In the first step of the method, the spatial autocorrelation function is measured over a texture field to be analyzed. The autocorrelation function $A_F(m,n)$ is then used to develop a whitening filter, with an impulse response $H_W(j,k)$, using techniques. The whitening filter is a special type of decorrelation operator. It is used to generate the whitened field

$$\hat{W}(j, k) = F(j, k) \circledast H_W(j, k) \tag{6.42}$$

This whitened field, which is spatially uncorrelated, can be utilized as an estimate of the independent generating process W(j,k) by forming its first-order histogram.

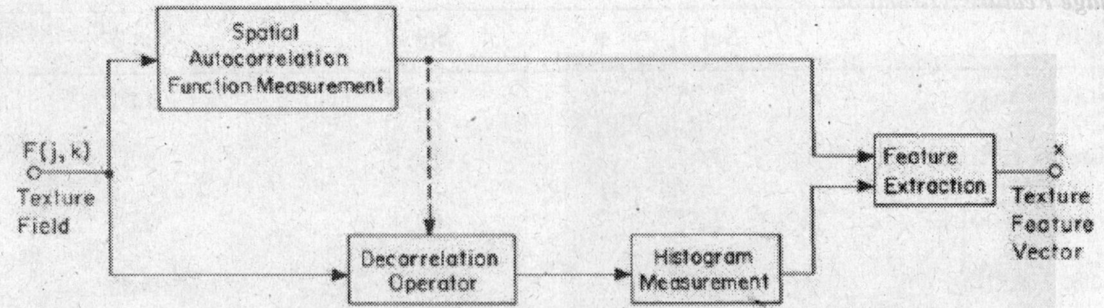


**Figure 6.17 Decorrelation method of texture feature extraction**

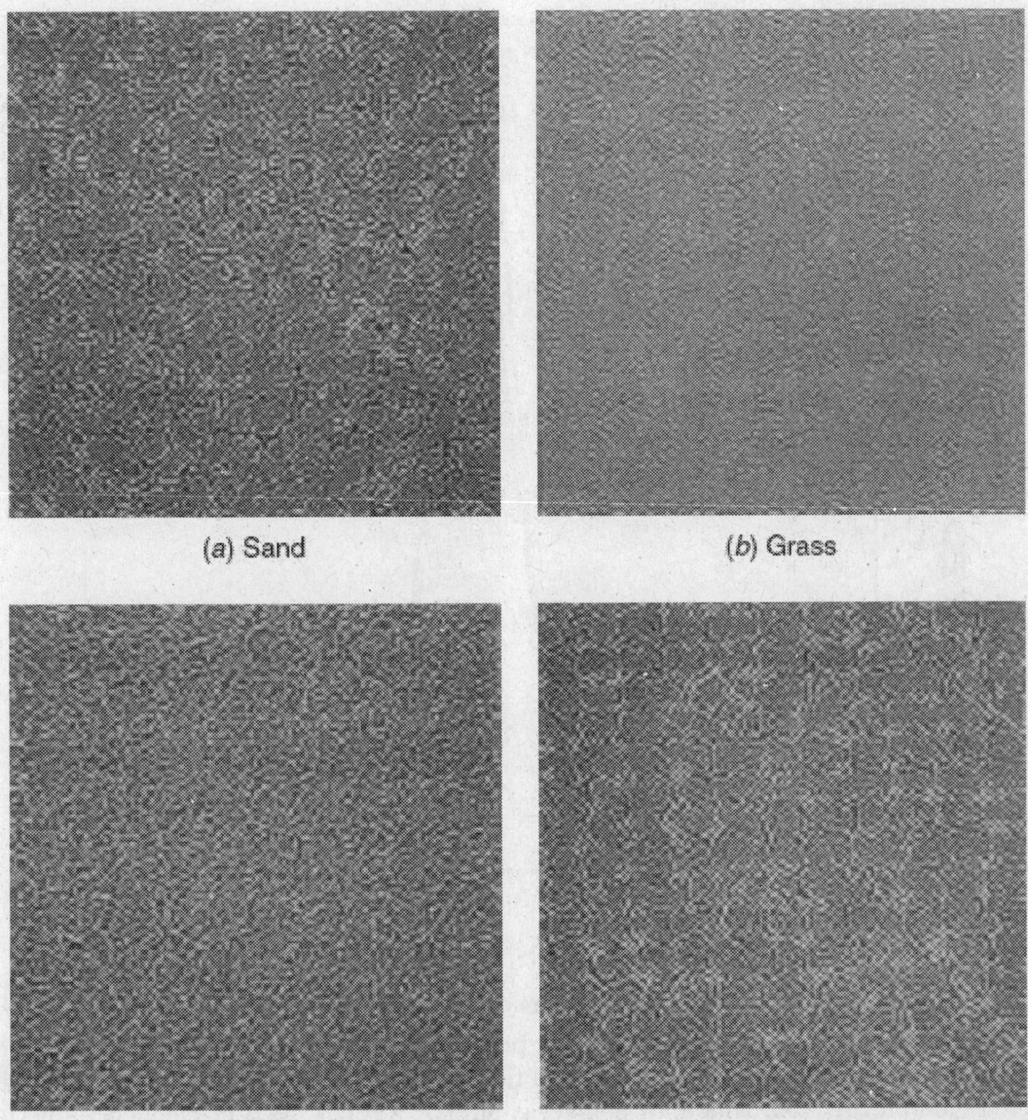

(*a*) Sand (*b*) Grass

(*c*) Wool (*d*) Raffia

**Figure 6.18 Whitened Brodatz texture fields**

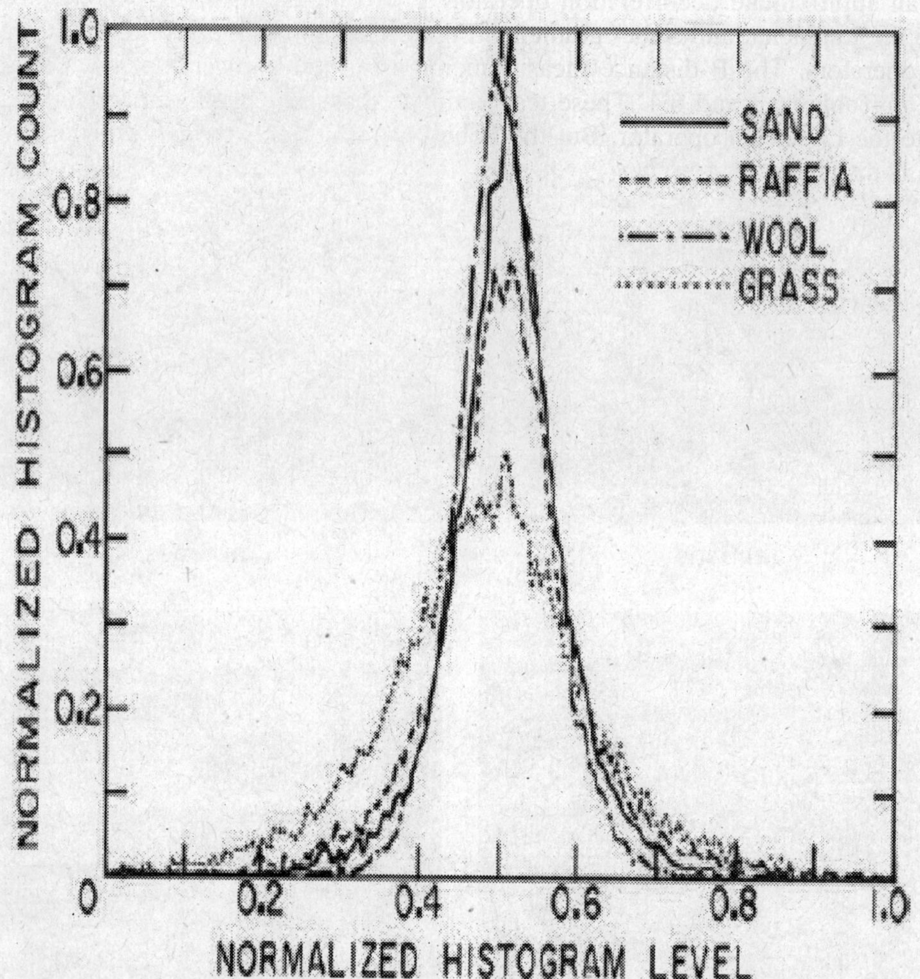


**Figure 6.19 First-order histograms of whitened Brodatz texture fields**

If W(j,k) were known exactly, then, in principle, it could be used to identify O{.} from the texture observation F(j,k). But, the whitened field estimate W(j,k) can only be used to identify the autocorrelation function, which, of course, is already known. As a consequence, the texture generation model cannot be inverted.

However, the shape of the histogram of W(j,k) augmented by the shape of the autocorrelation function have proved to be useful texture features. Figure 6.18 shows the whitened texture fields of the Brodatz test images. Figure 6.19 provides plots of their histograms. The whitened fields are observed to be visually distinctive; their histograms are also different from one another. Tables 6.3 and 6.4 list, respectively, the B-distance measurements for histogram shape features alone, and histogram and autocorrelation shape features. The B-distance is relatively low for some of the test textures for histogram-only features. A combination of the autocorrelation shape and histogram shape features provides good results, as noted in Table 6.4. An obvious disadvantage of the decorrelation method of texture measurement, as just described, is the large amount of computation involved in generating the whitening operator. An alternative is to use an approximate decorrelation operator. Two candidates, investigated by Faugeras and Pratt , are the Laplacian and Sobel gradients. Figure 6.20 shows the resultant decorrelated fields for these operators. The B-distance measurements using the Laplacian and Sobel gradients are presented in Tables 6.3 and 6.4. These tests indicate that the whitening operator is superior, on average, to the Laplacian operator. But the Sobel operator yields the largest average and largest minimum B-distances.

| | Texture Feature | | | | | | | | | | | |
|---|---|---|---|---|---|---|---|---|---|---|---|---|
| | Whitening | | | | Laplacian | | | | Sobel | | | |
| Field Pair | Set 1[a] | Set 2[b] | Set 3[c] | Set 4[d] | Set 1 | Set 2 | Set 3 | Set 4 | Set 1 | Set 2 | Set 3 | Set 4 |
| Grass – sand | 4.61 | 4.52 | 4.04 | 0.77 | 1.29 | 1.28 | 0.19 | 0.66 | 9.90 | 7.15 | 4.41 | 2.31 |
| Grass – raffia | 1.15 | 1.04 | 0.51 | 0.52 | 3.48 | 3.38 | 0.55 | 1.87 | 2.20 | 1.00 | 0.27 | 0.02 |
| Grass – wool | 1.68 | 1.59 | 1.07 | 0.14 | 2.23 | 2.19 | 1.76 | 0.13 | 2.98 | 1.67 | 1.01 | 1.46 |
| Sand – raffia | 12.76 | 12.60 | 10.93 | 0.24 | 2.23 | 2.14 | 1.57 | 0.28 | 5.09 | 4.79 | 3.51 | 2.30 |
| Sand – wool | 12.61 | 12.55 | 8.24 | 2.19 | 7.73 | 7.65 | 7.42 | 1.40 | 9.98 | 5.01 | 1.67 | 0.56 |
| Raffia – wool | 4.20 | 3.87 | 0.39 | 1.47 | 4.59 | 4.43 | 1.53 | 3.13 | 7.73 | 2.31 | 0.41 | 1.41 |
| Average | 6.14 | 6.03 | 4.20 | 0.88 | 3.59 | 3.51 | 2.17 | 1.24 | 6.31 | 3.66 | 1.88 | 1.35 |

[a]Set 1: $S_M, S_D, S_S, S_K$
[b]Set 2: $S_S, S_K$
[c]Set 3: $S_S$.
[d]Set 4: $S_K$.

**Table 6.3 Bhattacharyya Distance of Texture Feature sets for prototype Texture Fields: Histogram Features.**

| | Texture Feature | | | | | | | | | | | |
|---|---|---|---|---|---|---|---|---|---|---|---|---|
| | Whitening | | | | Laplacian | | | | Sobel | | | |
| Field Pair | Set 1[a] | Set 2[b] | Set 3[c] | Set 4 | Set 1 | Set 2 | Set 3 | Set 4 | Set 1 | Set 2 | Set 3 | Set 4 |
| Grass – sand | 9.80 | 9.72 | 8.94 | 7.48 | 6.39 | 6.37 | 5.61 | 4.21 | 15.34 | 12.34 | 11.48 | 10.12 |
| Grass – raffia | 8.47 | 8.34 | 6.56 | 4.66 | 10.61 | 10.49 | 8.74 | 6.95 | 9.46 | 8.15 | 6.33 | 4.59 |
| Grass – wool | 4.17 | 4.03 | 1.87 | 1.70 | 4.64 | 4.59 | 2.48 | 2.31 | 5.62 | 4.05 | 1.87 | 1.72 |
| Sand – raffia | 15.26 | 15.08 | 13.22 | 12.98 | 3.85 | 3.76 | 2.74 | 2.49 | 6.75 | 6.40 | 5.39 | 5.13 |
| Sand – wool | 19.14 | 19.08 | 17.43 | 15.72 | 14.43 | 14.38 | 12.72 | 10.86 | 18.75 | 12.3 | 10.52 | 8.29 |
| Raffia – wool | 13.29 | 13.14 | 10.32 | 7.96 | 13.93 | 13.75 | 10.90 | 8.47 | 17.28 | 11.19 | 8.24 | 6.08 |
| Average | 11.69 | 11.57 | 9.72 | 8.42 | 8.98 | 8.89 | 7.20 | 5.88 | 12.20 | 9.08 | 7.31 | 5.99 |

[a]Set 1: $S_M$, $S_D$, $S_S$, $S_K$, $S(2,0)$, $S(0,2)$, $S(1,1)$, $S(2,2)$.

[b]Set 2: $S_S$, $S_K$, $S(2,0)$, $S(0,2)$, $S(1,1)$, $S(2,2)$.

[c]Set 3: $S_S$, $S_K$, $S(1,1)$, $S(2,2)$.

[d]Set 4: $S_S$, $S_K$, $S(2,2)$.

**Table 6.4 Bhattacharyya Distance of Texture Features sets for prototype Texture Fields: Autocorrelation and histogram Features**

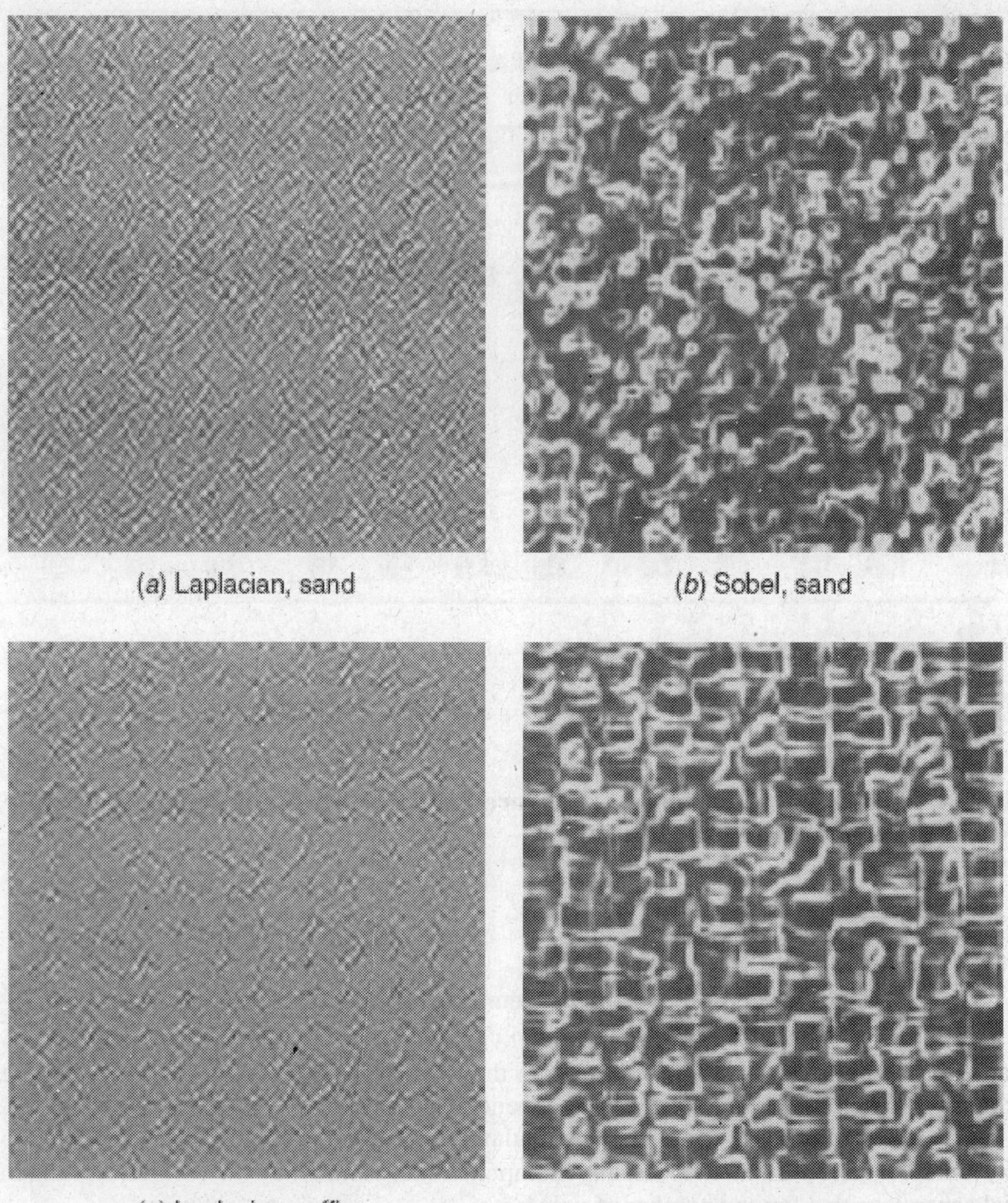


**Figure 6.20 Laplacian and Sobel gradients of Brodatz texture fields**

### 6.2.5.5. DEPENDENCY MATRIX METHODS

Haralick et al. have proposed a number of textural features based on the joint amplitude histogram of pairs of pixels. If an image region contains fine texture, the two-dimensional histogram of pixel pairs will tend to be uniform, and for coarse texture, the histogram values will be skewed toward the diagonal of the histogram. Consider the pair of pixels F(j,k) and F(m,n) that are separated by r radial units at an angle $\theta$ with respect to the horizontal axis. Let $p(a,b;j,k,r,\theta)$ represent the two-dimensional histogram measurement of an image over some window where each pixel is quantized over a range $0 \le a,b \le L-1$. The two-dimensional histogram can be considered as an estimate of the joint probability distribution

$$P(a, b; j, k, r, \theta) \approx P_R[F(j, k) = a, F(m, n) = b] \quad (6.43)$$

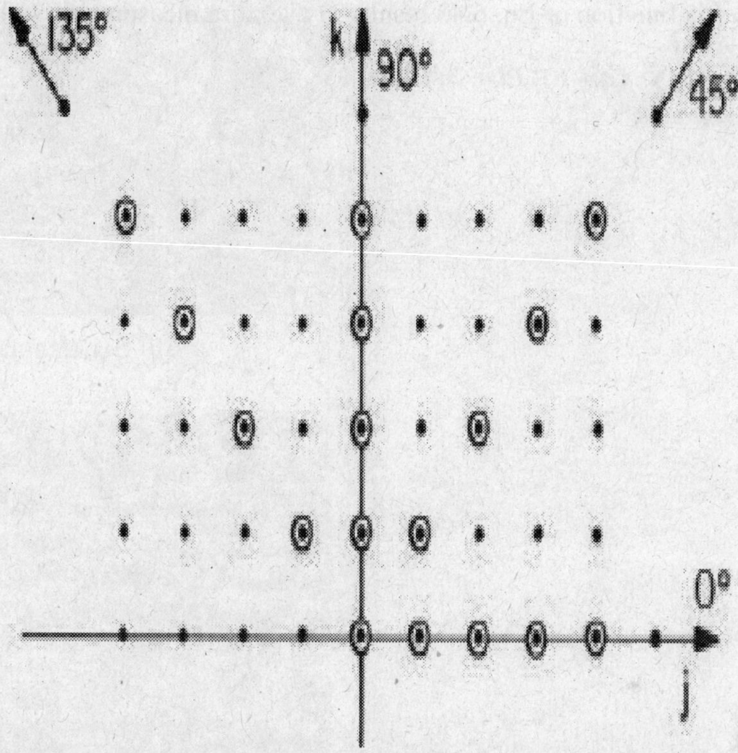


**Figure 6.21 Geometry for measurement of gray scale dependency matrix.**

For each member of the parameter set (j,k,r, $\theta$) , the two-dimensional histogram may be regarded as a L x L array of numbers relating the measured statistical dependency of pixel pairs. Such arrays have been called a gray scale dependency matrix or a co-occurrence matrix. Because a L x L histogram array must be accumulated for each image point (j,k) and separation set (r, $\theta$) under consideration, it is usually computationally necessary to restrict the angular and radial separation to a limited number of values.

Figure 6.21 illustrates geometrical relationships of histogram measurements made for four radial separation points and angles of $\theta = 0, \pi/4, \pi/2, 3\pi/4$ radians under the assumption of angular symmetry. To obtain statistical confidence in estimation of the joint probability distribution, the histogram must contain a reasonably large average occupancy level. This can be achieved either by restricting the number of amplitude quantization levels or by utilizing a relatively large measurement window. The former approach results in a loss of accuracy in the measurement of low-amplitude texture, while the latter approach causes errors if the texture changes over the large window. A typical compromise is to use 16 gray levels and a window of about 30 to 50 pixels on each side. Perspective views of joint amplitude histograms of two texture fields are presented in Figure 6.22.

For a given separation set (r, $\theta$), the histogram obtained for fine texture tends to be more uniformly dispersed than the histogram for coarse texture. Texture coarseness can be measured in terms of the relative spread of histogram occupancy cells about the main diagonal of the histogram. Haralick et al. have proposed a number of spread indicators for texture measurement. an example, the inertia function of Eq. 6.43 results in a texture measure of the form

$$T(j, k, r, \theta) = \sum_{a=0}^{L-1} \sum_{b=0}^{L-1} (a-b)^2 P(a, b; j, k, r, \theta) \tag{6.44}$$

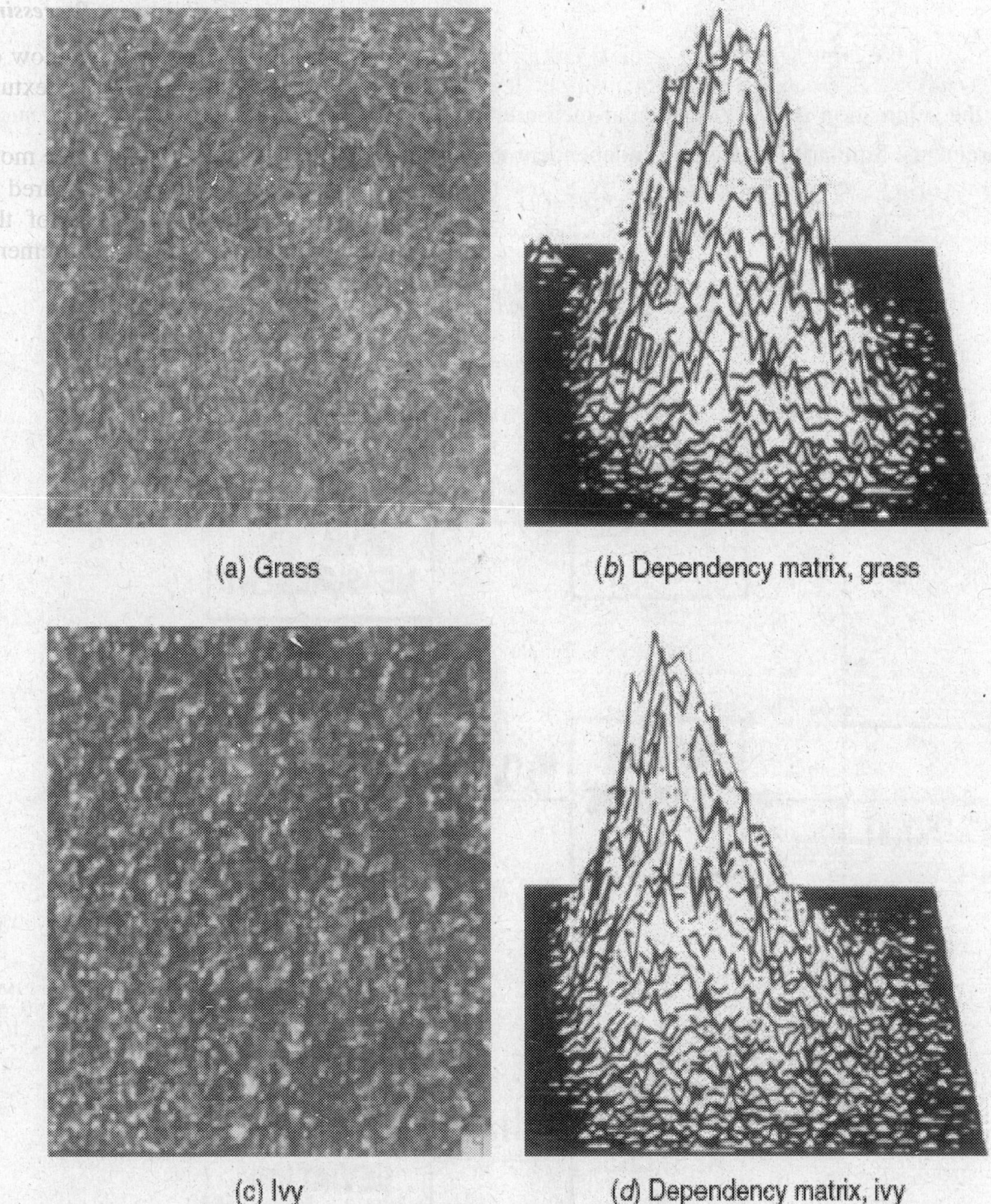

(a) Grass (b) Dependency matrix, grass

(c) Ivy (d) Dependency matrix, ivy

**Figure 6.22 Perspective views of gray scale dependency matrices for** $r = 4, \theta = 0$

If the textural region of interest is suspected to be angularly invariant, it is reasonable to average over the measurement angles of a particular measure to produce the mean textural measure

$$M_T(j,k,r) = \frac{1}{N_\theta} \sum_\theta T(j,k,r,\theta) \tag{6.45}$$

where the summation is over the angular measurements, and $N_\theta$ represents the number of such measurements. Similarly, an angular-independent texture variance may be defined as

$$V_T(j,k,r) = \frac{1}{N_\theta} \sum_\theta [T(j,k,r,\theta) - M_T(j,k,r)]^2 \tag{6.46}$$

$$M_i(j,k) = F(j,k) \circledast H_i(j,k)$$

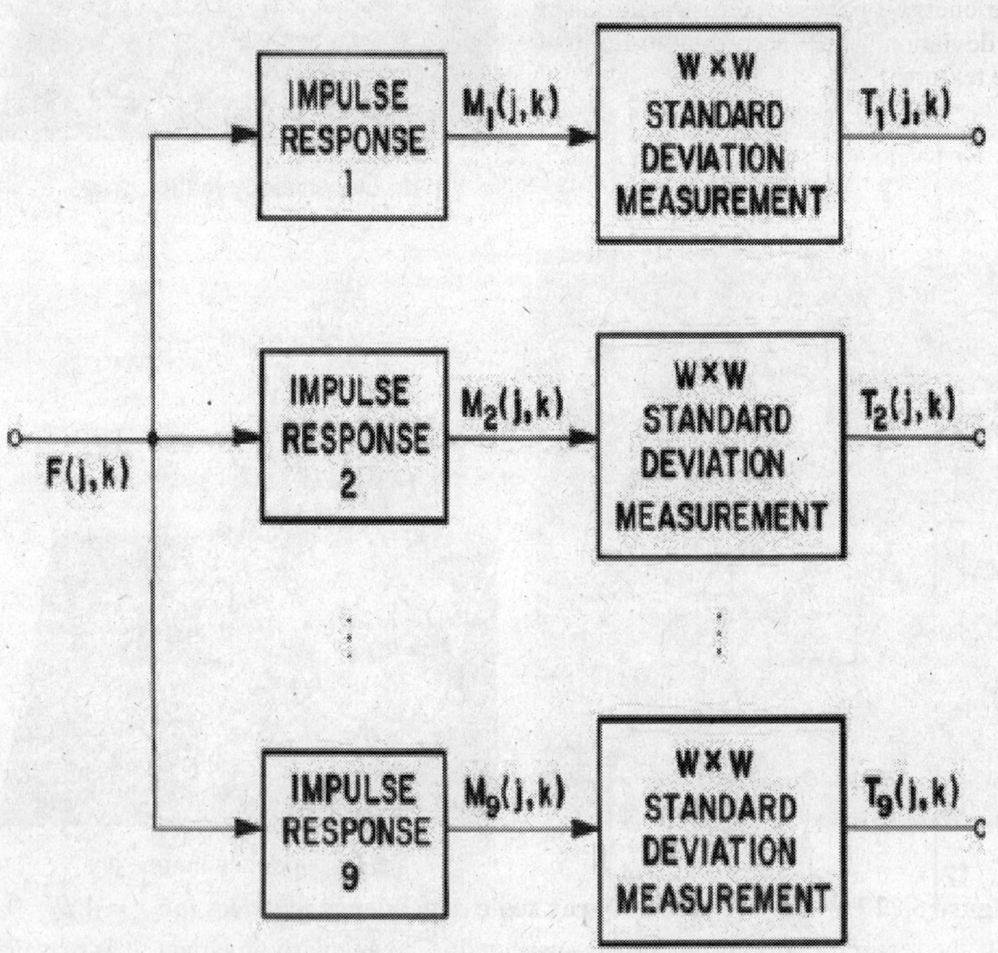


**Figure 6.23 Laws microstructure texture feature extraction method**

Another useful measurement is the angular independent spread defined by

$$S(j,k,r) = \underset{\theta}{\mathrm{MAX}}\{T(j,k,r,\theta)\} - \underset{\theta}{\mathrm{MIN}}\{T(j,k,r,\theta)\} \quad (6.47)$$

**6.2.5.6. MICROSTRUCTURE METHODS**

Examination of the whitened, Laplacian and Sobel gradient texture fields of Figures 5.20 to 5.18 reveals that they appear to accentuate the microstructure of the texture. This observation was the basis of a texture feature extraction scheme developed by Laws , and described in Figure 6.23 Laws proposed that the set of nine 3 x 3 pixel impulse response arrays $H_i(j,k)$ shown in Figure 6.24, be convolved with a texture field to accentuate its microstructure. The ith microstructure array is defined as

$$M_i(j,k) = F(j,k) \circledast H_i(j,k) \quad (6.48)$$

Then, the energy of these microstructure arrays is measured by forming their moving window standard deviation $T_i(j,k)$ according to Eq. 6.40, over a window that contains a few cycles of the repetitive texture.

$$\frac{1}{36}\begin{bmatrix} 1 & 2 & 1 \\ 2 & 4 & 2 \\ 1 & 2 & 1 \end{bmatrix} \quad \frac{1}{12}\begin{bmatrix} 1 & 0 & -1 \\ 2 & 0 & -2 \\ 1 & 0 & -1 \end{bmatrix} \quad \frac{1}{12}\begin{bmatrix} -1 & 2 & -1 \\ -2 & 4 & -2 \\ -1 & 2 & -1 \end{bmatrix}$$

Laws 1 Laws 2 Laws 3

$$\frac{1}{12}\begin{bmatrix} -1 & -2 & -1 \\ 0 & 0 & 0 \\ 1 & 2 & 1 \end{bmatrix} \quad \frac{1}{4}\begin{bmatrix} 1 & 0 & -1 \\ 0 & 0 & 0 \\ -1 & 0 & 1 \end{bmatrix} \quad \frac{1}{4}\begin{bmatrix} -1 & 2 & -1 \\ 0 & 0 & 0 \\ 1 & -2 & 1 \end{bmatrix}$$

Laws 4 Laws 5 Laws 6

$$\frac{1}{12}\begin{bmatrix} -1 & -2 & -1 \\ 2 & 4 & 2 \\ -1 & -2 & -1 \end{bmatrix} \quad \frac{1}{4}\begin{bmatrix} -1 & 0 & 1 \\ 2 & 0 & -2 \\ -1 & 0 & 1 \end{bmatrix} \quad \frac{1}{4}\begin{bmatrix} 1 & -2 & 1 \\ -2 & 4 & -2 \\ 1 & -2 & 1 \end{bmatrix}$$

Laws 7 Laws 8 Laws 9

**Figure 6.24. Laws microstructure impulse response arrays**

Figure 6.25 shows a mosaic of several Brodatz texture fields that have been used to test the Laws feature extraction method. Note that some of the texture fields appear twice in the mosaic. Figure 6.26 illustrates the texture arrays $T_i(j,k)$. In classification tests of the Brodatz textures performed by Laws, the correct texture was identified in nearly 90% of the trials. The pyramid average, the Sobel horizontal and vertical gradients, the weighted line horizontal and vertical gradients and the cross second derivative. The nine Laws operators form a basis set that can be generated from all outer product combinations of the three vectors

$$v_1 = \frac{1}{6}\begin{bmatrix} 1 \\ 2 \\ 1 \end{bmatrix} \qquad (6.49(a))$$

$$\mathbf{v}_2 = \frac{1}{2}\begin{bmatrix} 1 \\ 0 \\ -1 \end{bmatrix} \qquad (6.49(b))$$

$$\mathbf{v}_3 = \frac{1}{2}\begin{bmatrix} 1 \\ -2 \\ 1 \end{bmatrix} \qquad (6.49(c))$$

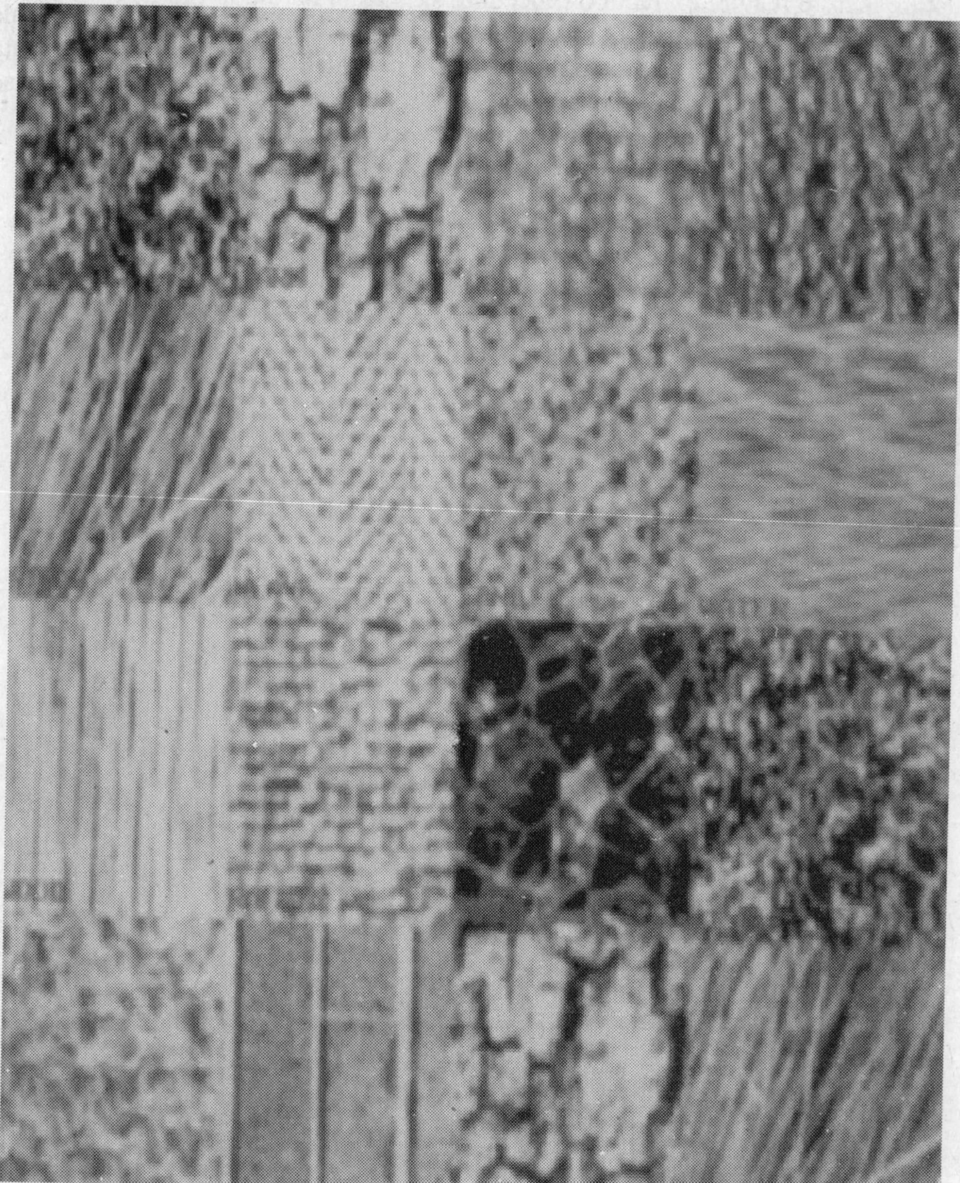

**Figure 6.25 Mosaic of Brodatz texture fields.**

Alternatively, the 3 x 3 Chebyshev basis set proposed by Haralick for edge detection, can be used for texture measurement. The first Chebyshev basis vector is

$$\mathbf{v}_1 = \frac{1}{3}\begin{bmatrix} 1 \\ 1 \\ 1 \end{bmatrix} \tag{6.50}$$

The other two are identical to Eqs. 6.49(b) and 6.49(c). The Laws procedure can be extended by using larger size Chebyshev arrays or other types of basis arrays . Ade has suggested a microstructure texture feature extraction procedure similar in nature to the Laws method, which is based on a principal components transformation of a texture sample. In the development of this transformation, pixels within a 3 x 3 neighborhood are regarded as being column stacked into a 9 x 1vector, as shown in Figure 6.27. Then a 9 x 9 covariance matrix K that specifies all pairwise covariance relationships of pixels within the stacked vector is estimated from a set of prototype texture fields.

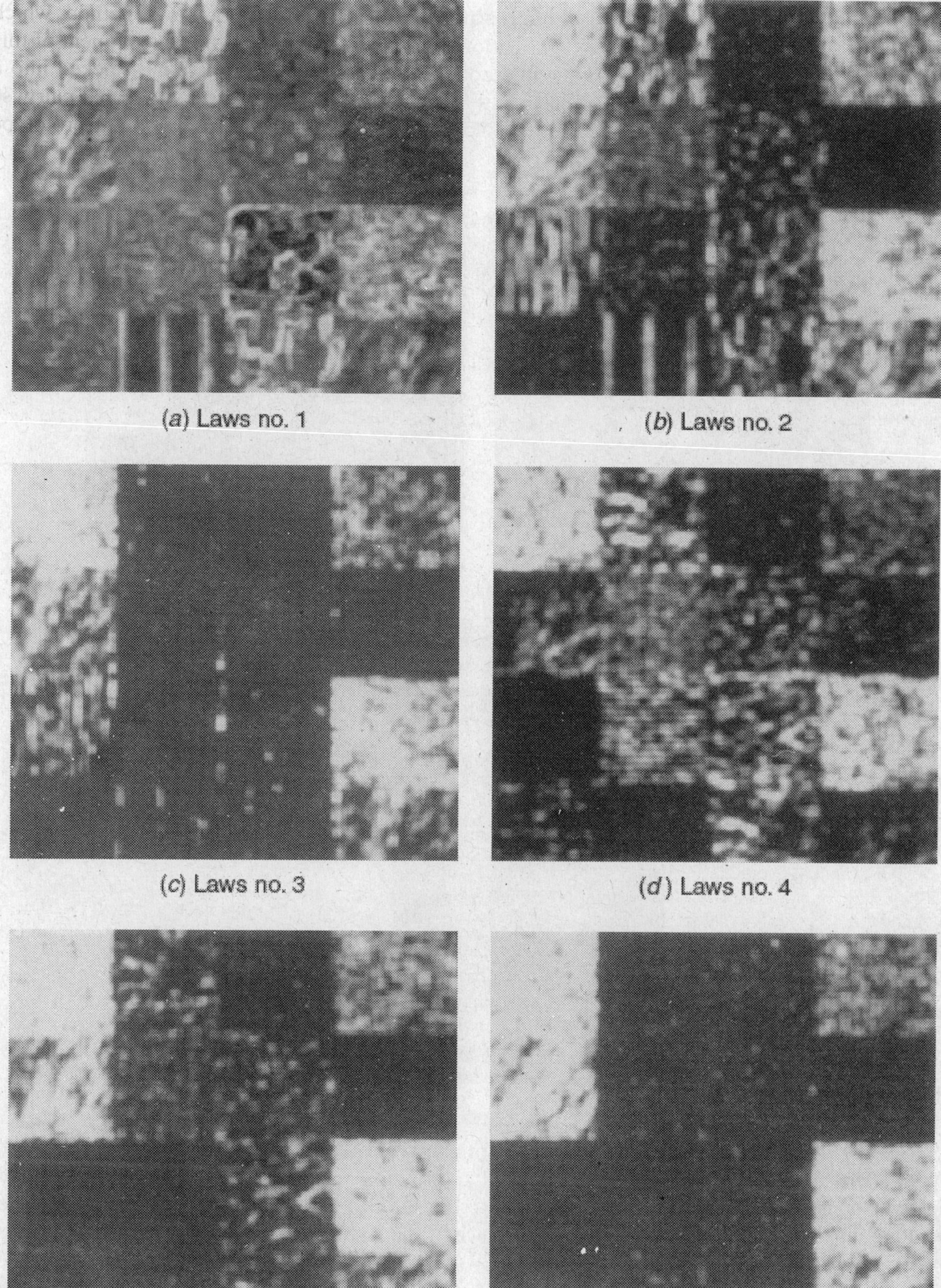

(a) Laws no. 1

(b) Laws no. 2

(c) Laws no. 3

(d) Laws no. 4

**Figure 6.26 Laws microstructure texture features**

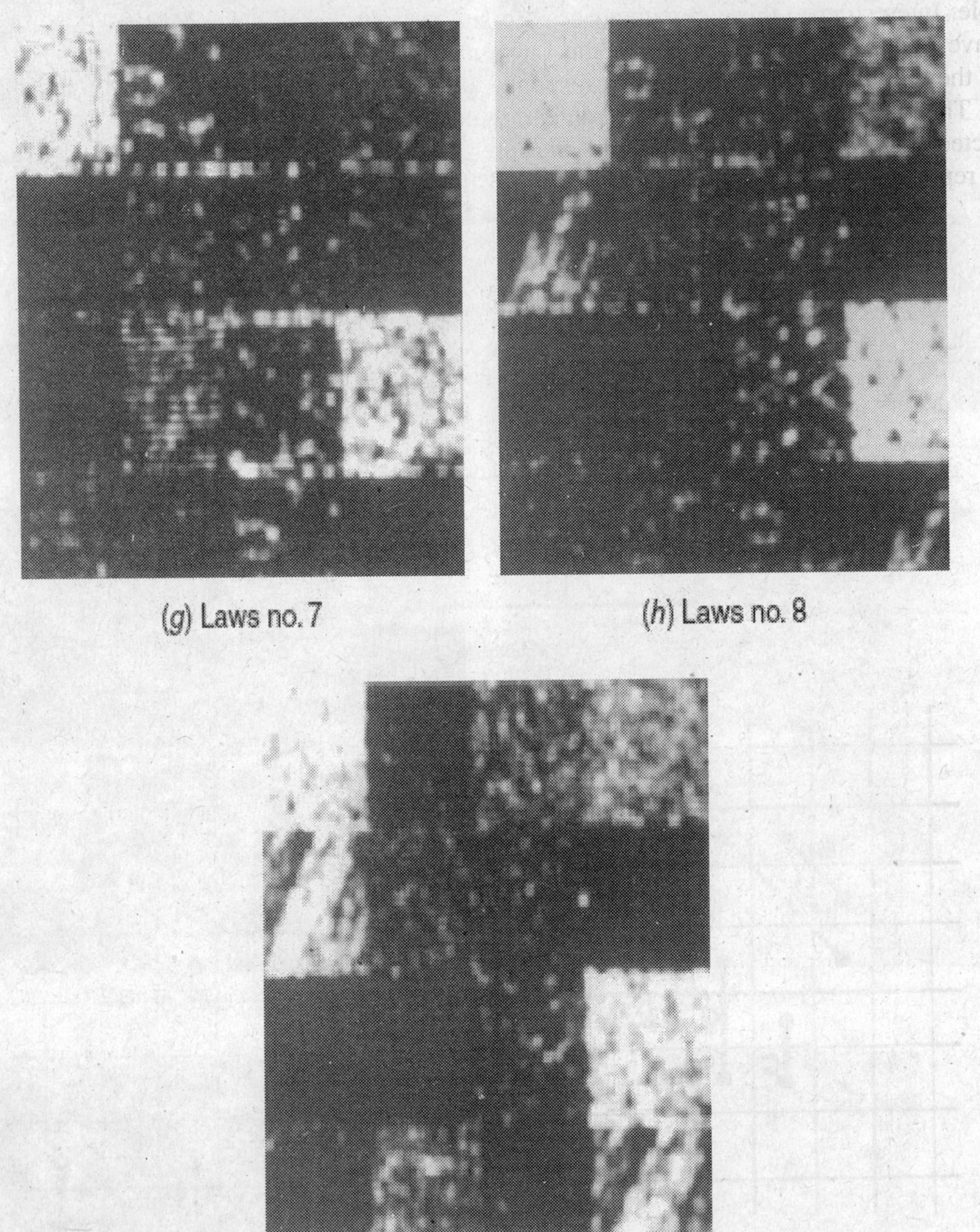

(*g*) Laws no. 7 (*h*) Laws no. 8

(*i*) Laws no. 9

**Figure 6.27. (continued) Laws microstructure texture features.**

The rows of T are eigenvectors of the principal components transformation. Each eigenvector is then cast into a 3 x 3 impulse response array by the destacking operation. The resulting nine eigen matrices are then used in place of the Laws fixed impulse response arrays, as shown in Figure 6.24. Ade has computed eigenmatrices for a Brodatz texture field and a cloth sample. Interestingly, these eigenmatrices are similar in structure to the Laws arrays. Manian et al. have also developed a variant of the Laws microstructure method. With reference to Figure 6.24, they use the six 2 x 2 impulse response arrays, called logical operators, shown in Figure 6.29. The standard deviation measurement is over a 5 x 5 pixel window. Next, features are extracted from the standard deviation measurements using the four zonal filter feature masks. They report good classification results for the Brodatz texture set (36).

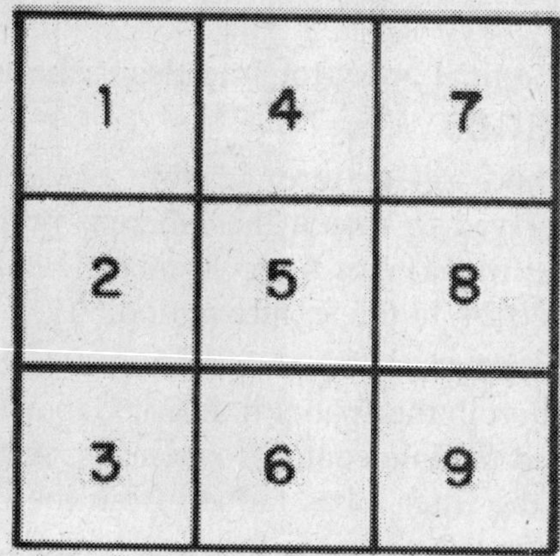


(*a*) 3 × 3 neighborhood

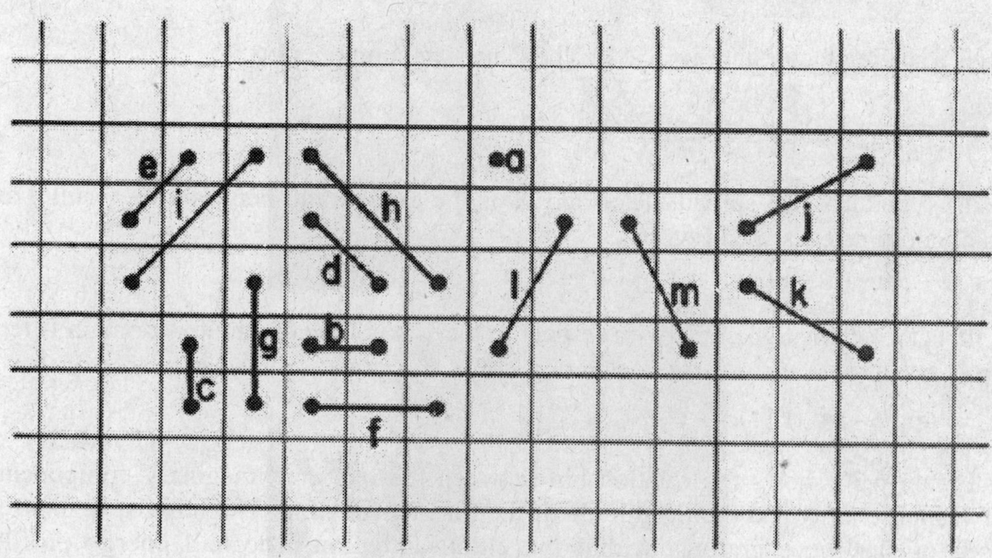


(*b*) Pixel relationships

**Figure 6.28 Neighborhood covariance relationships**

$$\begin{bmatrix} 1 & 1 \\ 1 & -1 \end{bmatrix} \quad \begin{bmatrix} 1 & 0 \\ 1 & 1 \end{bmatrix} \quad \begin{bmatrix} 1 & 0 \\ -1 & 1 \end{bmatrix}$$

$$\begin{bmatrix} 1 & 0 \\ 0 & 1 \end{bmatrix} \quad \begin{bmatrix} 0 & 0 \\ 0 & 1 \end{bmatrix} \quad \begin{bmatrix} 0 & 1 \\ 1 & 1 \end{bmatrix}$$

**Figure 6.29 Logical operator impulse response arrays**

### 6.2.5.7. GABOR FILTER METHODS

The microstructure method of texture feature extraction is not easily scalable. Microstructure arrays must be derived to match the inherent periodicity of each texture to be characterized. Bovik et al. have utilized Gabor filters as an efficient means of scaling the impulse response function arrays of Figure 6.24 to the texture periodicity.

A two-dimensional Gabor filter is a complex field sinusoidal grating that is modulated by a two-dimensional Gaussian function in the spatial domain. Gabor filters have tunable orientation and radial frequency passbands and tunable center frequencies. A special case of the Gabor filter is the daisy petal filter, in which the filter lobes radiate from the origin of the spatial frequency domain. The continuous domain impulse response function of the daisy petal Gabor filter is given by

$$H(x, y) = G(x', y') \exp\{2\pi i F x'\} \tag{6.51}$$

where F is a scaling factor and $i = \sqrt{-1}$. The Gaussian component is

$$G(x, y) = \frac{1}{2\pi\lambda\sigma^2} \exp\left\{-\frac{(x/\lambda)^2 + y^2}{2\sigma^2}\right\} \tag{6.52}$$

Where $\sigma$ is the Gaussian spread factor and $\lambda$ is the aspect ratio between the x and y axes. The rotation of coordinates is specified by

$$(x', y') = (x\cos\phi + y\sin\phi, -x\sin\phi + y\cos\phi) \tag{6.53}$$

Where $\Phi$ is the orientation angle with respect to the x axis. The continuous domain filter transfer function is given by

$$\mathcal{H}(u, v) = \exp\{-2\pi^2\sigma^2[(u' - F)^2 + (v')^2]\} \tag{6.54}$$

Figure 6.30 shows the relationship between the real and imaginary components of the impulse response array and the magnitude of the transfer function. The impulse response array is composed of sine-wave gratings within the elliptical region. The half energy profile of the transfer function is shown in gray. Grigorescu et al. have performed a comprehensive comparison of Gabor filter texture features. In the comparative study of texture classification methods by Randen and Husoy, the Gabor filter method, like many other methods, gave mixed results. It performed well on some texture samples, but poorly on others.

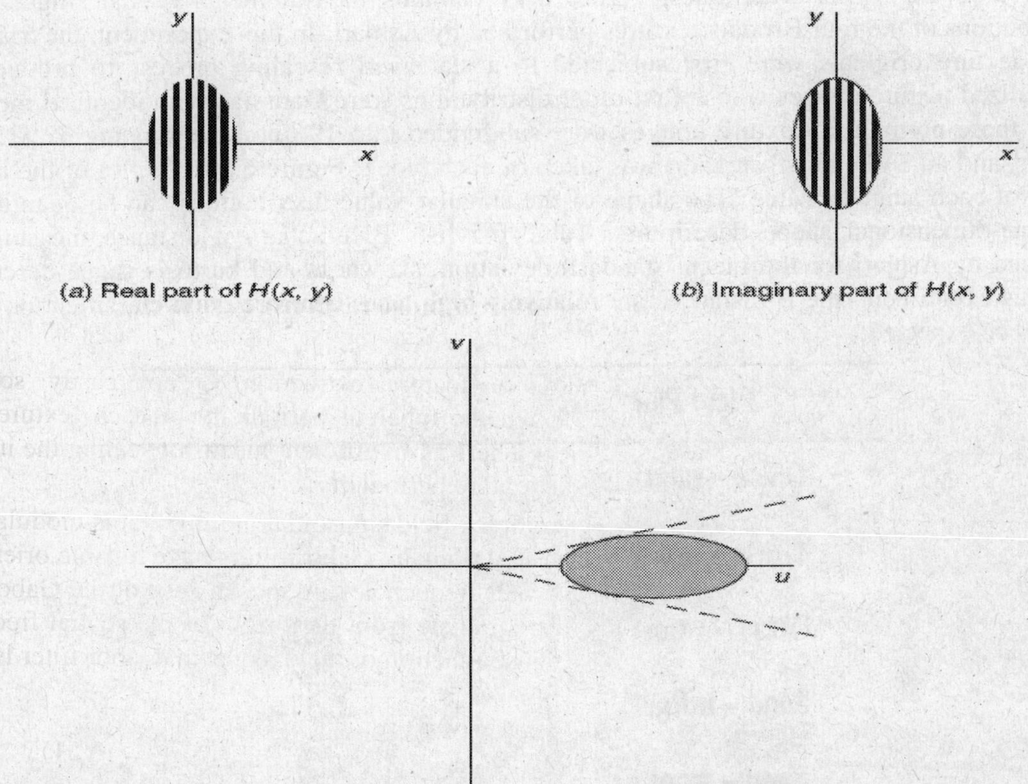


**Figure 6.30 Relationship between impulse response array and transfer function of a Gabor filter**

## 6.2.5.8. TRANSFORM AND WAVELET METHODS

The Fourier spectra method of texture feature extraction can be generalized to other unitary transforms. The concept is straightforward. A N x N texture sample is subdivided into M x M pixel arrays, and a unitary transform is performed for each array yielding a $M^2$ x 1 feature vector. The window size needs to large enough to contain several cycles of the texture periodicity. Mallat has used the discrete wavelet transform, based on Haar wavelets as a means of generating texture feature vectors. Improved results have been obtained by Unser , who has used a complete Haar-based wavelet transform for an 8 x 8 window. In their comparative study of texture classification, Randen and Husoy used several types of Daubechies transforms up to size 10. The transform and wavelet methods provide reasonably good classification for many texture samples. However, the computational requirement is high for large windows.

## 6.2.5.9. SINGULAR-VALUE DECOMPOSITION METHODS

Ashjari has proposed a texture measurement method based on the singular value decomposition of a texture sample. In this method, a N x N texture sample is treated as a N x N matrix X, and the amplitude-ordered set of singular values s(n) for n = 1, 2,. .., N is computed. If the elements of X are spatially unrelated to one another, the singular values tend to be uniformly distributed in amplitude. On the other hand, if the elements of X are highly structured, the singular-value distribution tends to be skewed such that the lower-order singular values are much larger than the higher-order ones. Figure 6.31 contains measurements of the singular-value distributions of the four Brodatz textures performed by Ashjari. In this experiment, the 512 x 512 pixel texture originals were first subjected to a statistical rescaling process to produce four normalized texture images whose first-order distributions were Gaussian with identical moments. Next, these normalized texture images were subdivided into 196 non-overlapping 32 x 32pixel blocks, and an SVD transformation was taken of each block. Figure 6.30 is a plot of the average value of each singular value. The shape of the singular-value distributions can be quantified by the one-dimensional shape descriptors. Table 6.5 lists Bhattacharyya distance measurements obtained by Ashjari for the mean, standard deviation, skewness and kurtosis shape descriptors. For this experiment, the B-distances are relatively high, and therefore good classification results should be expected.

| Field Pair | |
|---|---|
| Grass – sand | 1.25 |
| Grass – raffia | 2.42 |
| Grass – wool | 3.31 |
| Sand – raffia | 6.33 |
| Sand – wool | 2.56 |
| Raffia – wool | 9.24 |
| Average | 4.19 |

**Table 6.5 Bhattacharyya Distance of SVD Texture Features sets for prototype Texture Fields: SVD Features**

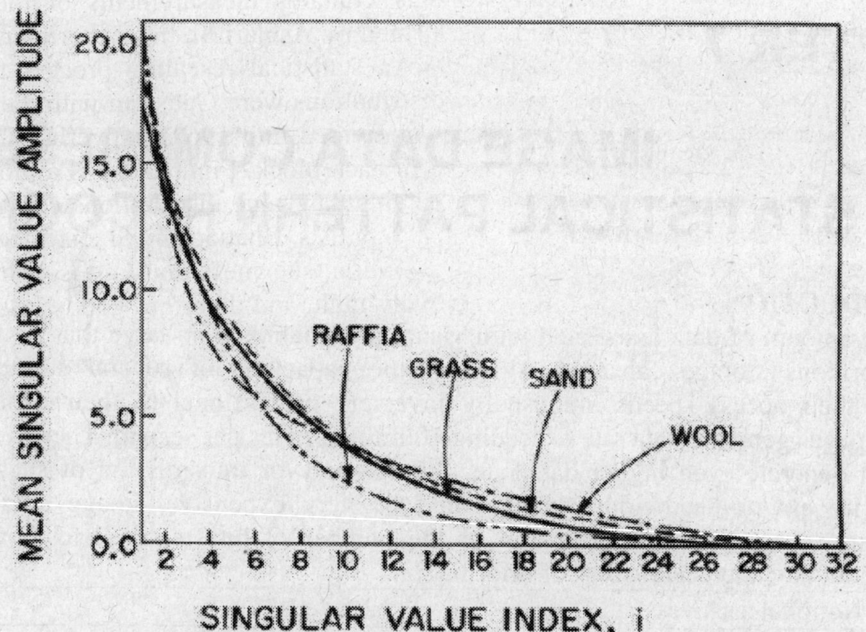


**Figure 6.31 Singular-value distributions of Brodatz texture fields**

# QUESTION BANK

Q1. Briefly explain the various image feature extraction?

Q2. Difference between the amplitude features and transform coefficient features.

Q3. Write short note on the texture definition?

Q4. Explain the various visual texture discrimination?

Q5. Briefly describe the various texture features? Explain with the help of example.

# CHAPTER 7

# IMAGE DATA COMPRESSION & STATISTICAL PATTERN RECOGNITION

## 7.1 INTRODUCTION

The amount of data associated with visual information is so large that its storage would require enormous storage capacity. Although the capacities of several storage media are substantial, their access speeds are usually inversely proportional to their capacity. Typical television images generate data rate exceeding 10 million bytes per second. There are other image sources that generate even higher data rate. Storage and /or transmission of such data require large capacity and/or bandwidth, which could be very expensive. Image data compression techniques are concerned with reduction of the number of bits required to store or transmit images without any appreciable loss of information.

| | |
|---|---|
| National archives | $12.5 \times 10^9$ |
| I h of color television | $28 \times 10^3$ |
| Encyclopedia Britannica | $12.5 \times 10^3$ |
| Book (200 pages of text characters) | 1 3 |
| One page viewed as an image | 13 |

**Table 7.1 Data volumes of image sources (in millions of bytes)**

| | |
|---|---|
| Human brain | 125,000,000 |
| Magnetic Cartridge | 250,000 |
| Optical Disc Memory | 12,500 |
| Magnetic Disc | 760 |
| 2400-ft Magnetic tape | 200 |
| Floppy Disc | 1.25 |
| Solid –State Memory Modules | 0.25 |

**Table 7.2 Storage Capacities (in Millions of bytes)**

Uncompressed multimedia (graphics, audio and video) data requires considerable storage capacity and transmission bandwidth. Despite rapid progress in mass-storage density, processor speeds, and digital communication system performance, demand for data storage capacity and data-transmission bandwidth continues to outstrip the capabilities of available technologies. The recent growth of data intensive multimedia-based web applications have not only sustained the need for more efficient ways to encode signals and images but have made compression of such signals central to storage and communication technology.

For still image compression, the `Joint Photographic Experts Group' or JPEG standard has been established by ISO (International Standards Organization) and IEC (International Electro-Technical Commission). The performance of these coders generally degrades at low bit-rates mainly because of the underlying block-based Discrete Cosine Transform (DCT) scheme. More recently, the wavelet transform has emerged as a cutting edge technology, within the field of image compression. Wavelet-based coding provides substantial improvements in picture quality at higher compression ratios.

Over the past few years, a variety of powerful and sophisticated wavelet-based schemes for image compression, have been developed and implemented. Because of the many advantages, the top contenders in the upcoming JPEG-2000 standard are all wavelet-based compression algorithms.

The goal of this article is two-fold. First, for readers new to compression, we briefly review some basic concepts on image compression and present a short overview of the DCT-based JPEG standard and the more popular wavelet-based image coding schemes. Second, for more advanced readers, we mention a few sophisticated, modern, and popular wavelet-based techniques including one we are currently pursuing. The goal of the upcoming JPEG-2000 image compression standard, which is going to be wavelet-based, is briefly presented. For those who are curious, a number of useful references are given. There is also abundance of information about image compression on the Internet.

## 7.2 WHAT ARE THE PRINCIPLES BEHIND COMPRESSION?

A common characteristic of most images is that the neighboring pixels are correlated and therefore contain redundant information. The foremost task then is to find less correlated representation of the image. Two fundamental components of compression are redundancy and irrelevancy reduction. Redundancy reduction aims at removing duplication from the signal source (image/video). Irrelevancy reduction omits parts of the signal that will not be noticed by the signal receiver, namely the Human Visual System (HVS). In general, three types of redundancy can be identified:

- Spatial Redundancy or correlation between neighboring pixel values.
- Spectral Redundancy or correlation between different color planes or spectral bands.
- Temporal Redundancy or correlation between adjacent frames in a sequence of images (in video applications).

Image compression research aims at reducing the number of bits needed to represent an image by removing the spatial and spectral redundancies as much as possible. Since we will focus only on still image compression, we will not worry about temporal redundancy.

### 7.2.1 WHAT ARE THE DIFFERENT CLASSES OF COMPRESSION TECHNIQUES?

Two ways of classifying compression techniques are mentioned here.

**(a) Lossless vs. Lossy compression**: In lossless compression schemes, the reconstructed image, after compression, is numerically identical to the original image. However lossless compression can only a achieve a modest amount of compression. An image reconstructed following lossy compression contains degradation relative to the original. Often this is because the compression scheme completely discards redundant information. However, lossy schemes are capable of achieving much higher compression. Under normal viewing conditions, no visible loss is perceived (visually lossless).

**(b) Predictive vs. Transform coding:** In predictive coding, information already sent or available is used to predict future values, and the difference is coded. Since this is done in the image or spatial domain, it is relatively simple to implement and is readily adapted to local image characteristics. Differential Pulse Code Modulation (DPCM) is one particular example of predictive coding. Transform coding, on the other hand, first transforms the image from its spatial domain representation to a different type of representation using some well-known transform and then codes the transformed values (coefficients). This method provides greater data compression compared to predictive methods, although at the expense of greater computation.

### 7.2.2 WHAT DOES A TYPICAL IMAGE CODER LOOK LIKE?

A typical lossy image compression system is shown in Fig. 7.1. It consists of three closely connected components namely (a) Source Encoder (b) Quantizer, and (c) Entropy Encoder. Compression is accomplished by applying a linear transform to decorrelate the image data, quantizing the resulting transform coefficients, and entropy coding the quantized values.

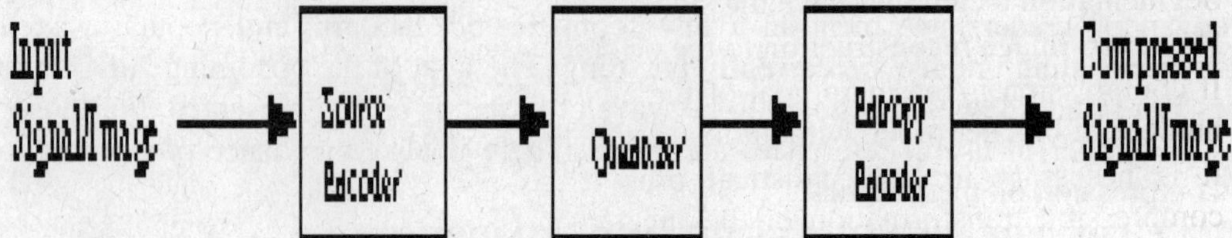


**Figure 7.1 A Typical Lossy Signal/Image Encoder**

#### 7.2.2.1. SOURCE ENCODER (OR LINEAR TRANSFORMER)

Over the years, a variety of linear transforms have been developed which include Discrete Fourier Transform (DFT), Discrete Cosine Transform (DCT) , Discrete Wavelet Transform (DWT) and many more, each with its own advantages and disadvantages.

#### 7.2.2.2. QUANTIZER

A quantizer simply reduces the number of bits needed to store the transformed coefficients by reducing the precision of those values. Since this is a many-to-one mapping, it is a lossy process and is the main source of compression in an encoder. Quantization can be performed on each individual coefficient, which is known as Scalar Quantization (SQ). Quantization can also be performed on a group of coefficients together, and this is known as Vector Quantization (VQ). Both uniform and non-uniform quantizers can be used depending on the problem at hand. For an analysis on different quantization schemes.

#### 7.2.2.3. ENTROPY ENCODER

An entropy encoder further compresses the quantized values losslessly to give better overall compression. It uses a model to accurately determine the probabilities for each quantized value and produces an appropriate code based on these probabilities so that the resultant output code stream will be smaller than the input stream. The most commonly used entropy encoders are the Huffman encoder and the arithmetic encoder, although for applications requiring fast execution, simple run-length encoding (RLE) has proven very effective.

It is important to note that a properly designed quantizer and entropy encoder are absolutely necessary along with optimum signal transformation to get the best possible compression.

#### 7.2.2.4. COMPRESSION

- Large amounts of data are used to represent an image.
- Technology permits ever-increasing image resolution (spatially and in gray levels), increasing numbers of spectral bands, and there is a consequent need to limit the resulting data volume.

- Example from the remote sensing domain - Landsat D satellite broadcasts 85 x 10^6 bits of data every second and a typical image from one pass consists of 6100 x 6100 pixels in 7 spectral bands - 260 megabytes of image data.
- Japanese Advanced Earth Observing Satellite (ADEOS) has spatial resolution of 8 meters for the polychromatic band and 16 meters for the multispectral bands has the transmitted data rate of 120 Mbps.
- The amount of storage media needed is enormous.
- One possible approach to decreasing the necessary amount of storage is to work with compressed image data.
- Segmentation techniques have the side effect of image compression.
- However, image reconstruction to the original, uncompressed image is not possible.
- If compression is the main goal of the algorithm, an image is represented using a lower number of bits per pixel, without losing the ability to reconstruct the image.
- It is necessary to find statistical properties of the image to design an appropriate compression transformation of the image; the more correlated the image data are, the more data items can be removed.

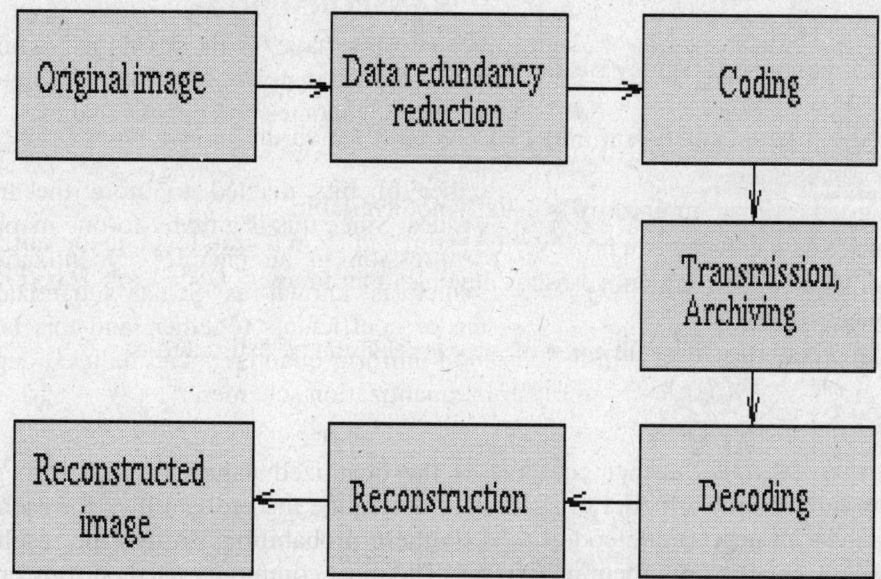


**Figure 7.2 Data Compression and Image reconstruction**

- Data compression methods can be divided into two principal groups:
- Information preserving compression permit error-free data reconstruction (lossless compression).
- Compression methods with loss of information do not preserve the information completely (lossy compression).
- In image processing, a faithful reconstruction is often not necessary in practice and then the requirements are weaker, but the image data compression must not cause significant changes in an image.

- Data compression success is usually measured in the reconstructed image by the mean squared error (MSE), signal to noise ratio etc. although these global error measures do not always reflect subjective image quality.
- Image data compression design - 2 parts.

  1) Image data properties determination

     gray level histogram

     image entropy

     various correlation functions etc.

  2) Appropriate compression technique design.
- Data compression methods with loss of information are typical in image processing.

**7.2.2.5. IMAGE DATA PROPERTIES**

- Entropy - measure of image information content
- If an image has G gray levels, and the probability of gray level k is P(k), then entropy $H_e$, not considering correlation of gray levels, is defined as

$$H_e = -\sum_{k=0}^{G-1} P(k)\log_2(P(k)) \qquad (7.1)$$

- Information redundancy r is defined as

  $R = b - H_e$ (7.2)
- where b is the smallest number of bits with which the image quantization levels can be represented.
- A good estimate of entropy is usually not available.
- Image data entropy can however be estimated from a gray level histogram.
- Let h(k) be the frequency of gray level k in an image f, 0 <= k <= 2^b -1, and let the image size be M x N.
- The probability of occurrence of gray level k can be estimated as

$$\tilde{P}(k) = \frac{h(k)}{MN} \qquad (7.3)$$

and the entropy can be estimated as

$$\tilde{H}_e = -\sum_{k=0}^{2^b-1} \tilde{P}(k)\log_2(\tilde{P}(k)) \qquad (7.4)$$

The information redundancy estimate is $r = b - H_e$. The definition of the compression ratio K is then

$$K = \frac{b}{\tilde{H}_e} \qquad (7.5)$$

These formulae give theoretical limits of possible image compression.

**EXAMPLE**

The entropy of satellite remote sensing data may be between 4 and 5, considering 8 bits per pixel the information redundancy is between 3 and 4 bits these data can be represented by an average data volume of 4 to 5 bits per pixel with no loss of information, and the compression ratio would be between 1.6 and 2.

### 7.2.2.6. JPEG: DCT-BASED IMAGE CODING STANDARD

The idea of compressing an image is not new. The discovery of DCT in 1974 is an important achievement for the research community working on image compression. The DCT can be regarded as a discrete-time version of the Fourier-Cosine series. It is a close relative of DFT, a technique for converting a signal into elementary frequency components. Thus DCT can be computed with a Fast Fourier Transform (FFT) like algorithm in O(n log n) operations. Unlike DFT, DCT is real-valued and provides a better approximation of a signal with fewer coefficients. The DCT of a discrete signal x(n), n=0, 1, .. , N-1 is defined as:

$$X(u) = \sqrt{\frac{2}{N}}\, C(u) \sum_{n=0}^{N-1} x(n) \cos\left(\frac{(2n+1)u\pi}{2N}\right)$$

where, C(u) = 0.707 for u = 0 and
= 1 otherwise.

An excellent analysis of DCT and related transforms and their applications can be found in. In 1992, JPEG established the first international standard for still image compression where the encoders and decoders are DCT-based. The JPEG standard specifies three modes namely sequential, progressive, and hierarchical for lossy encoding, and one mode of lossless encoding. The `baseline JPEG coder' which is the sequential encoding in its simplest form, will be briefly discussed here. Fig. 7.3(a) and 7.3(b) show the key processing steps in such an encoder and decoder for grayscale images. Color image compression can be approximately regarded as compression of multiple grayscale images, which are either compressed entirely one at a time, or are compressed by alternately interleaving 8x8 sample blocks from each in turn. In this article, we focus on grayscale images only.

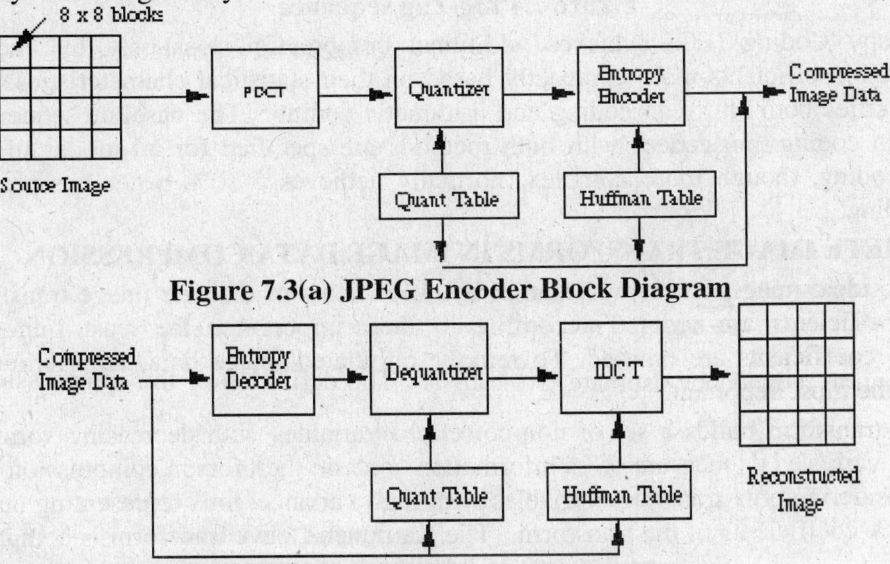


**Figure 7.3(a) JPEG Encoder Block Diagram**

**Figure 7.3(b) JPEG Decoder Block Diagram**

The DCT-based encoder can be thought of as essentially compression of a stream of 8x8 blocks of image samples. Each 8x8 block makes its way through each processing step, and yields output in compressed form into the data stream. Because adjacent image pixels are highly correlated, the `forward' DCT (FDCT) processing step lays the foundation for achieving data compression by concentrating most of the signal in the lower spatial frequencies. For a typical 8x8 sample block from a typical source image, most of the spatial frequencies have zero or near-zero amplitude and need not be encoded. In principle, the DCT introduces no loss to the source image samples; it merely transforms them to a domain in which they can be more efficiently encoded.

After output from the FDCT, each of the 64 DCT coefficients is uniformly quantized in conjunction with a carefully designed 64-element Quantization Table (QT). At the decoder, the quantized values are multiplied by the corresponding QT elements to recover the original unquantized values. After quantization, all of the quantized coefficients are ordered into the "zig-zag" sequence as shown in Fig. 7.4. This ordering helps to facilitate entropy encoding by placing low-frequency non-zero coefficients before high-frequency coefficients. The DC coefficient, which contains a significant fraction of the total image energy, is differentially encoded.

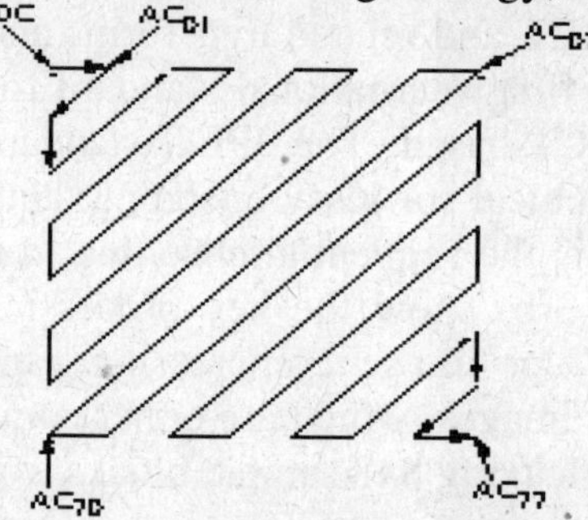


**Figure 7.4 Zig-Zag sequence**

Entropy Coding (EC) achieves additional compression losslessly by encoding the quantized DCT coefficients more compactly based on their statistical characteristics. The JPEG proposal specifies both Huffman coding and arithmetic coding. The baseline sequential codec uses Huffman coding, but codecs with both methods are specified for all modes of operation. Arithmetic coding, though more complex, normally achieves 5-10% better compression than Huffman coding.

### 7.2.3 DISCRETE IMAGE TRANSFORMS IN IMAGE DATA COMPRESSION

Basic idea: image data representation by coefficients of discrete image transforms. The transform coefficients are ordered according to their importance the least important (low contribution) coefficients are omitted. To remove correlated image data, the Karhunen-Loeve transform is the most important.

This transform builds a set of non-correlated variables with decreasing variance. The variance of a variable is a measure of its information content; therefore, a compression strategy is based on considering only transform variables with high variance, thus representing an image by only the first k coefficients of the transform. The Karhunen-Loeve transform is computationally expensive.

Other discrete image transforms discussed in the previous chapter are computationally less demanding.

Cosine, Fourier, Hadamard, Walsh, or binary transforms are all suitable for image data compression. If an image is compressed using discrete transforms, it is usually divided into subimages of 8 x 8 or 16 x 16 pixels to speed up calculations, and then each subimage is transformed and processed separately.

The same is true for image reconstruction, with each subimage being reconstructed and placed into the appropriate image position

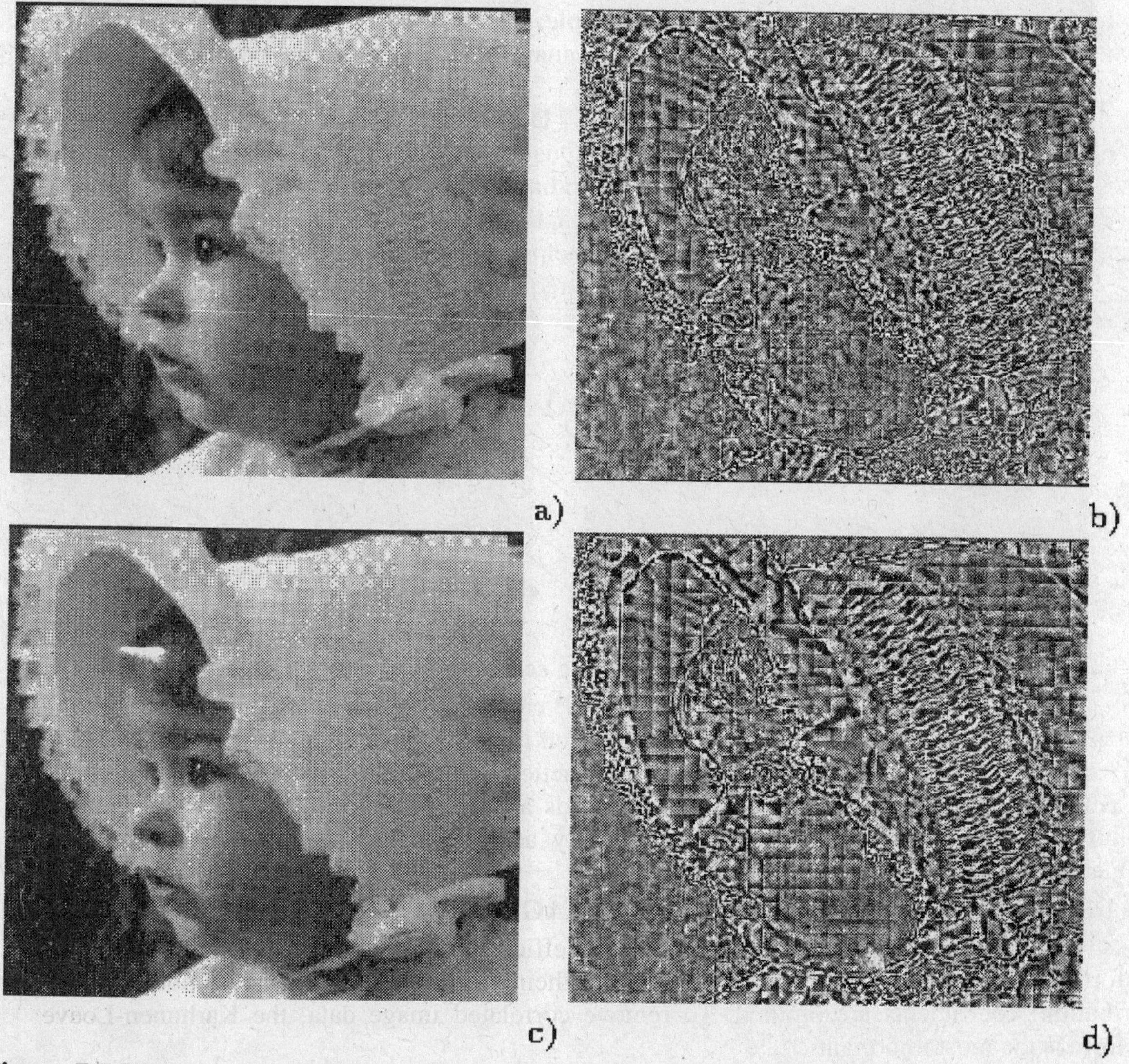


**Figure 7.5 Discrete cosine image compression : (a) Reconstructed image, compression ratio K=4.2 , (b) difference image – differences between pixel values in the original and the constructed image (K=4.2); the maximum difference is 78 grey level, mean squared reconstruction error MSE = XXX; (image is histogram equalized for visualization purposes), (c) reconstructed image, compression ration K=5.6 , (d) difference image – differences between pixel values in the original and the reconstructed image (K=5.6); the maximum difference is 125 grey level , MSE = XXX**

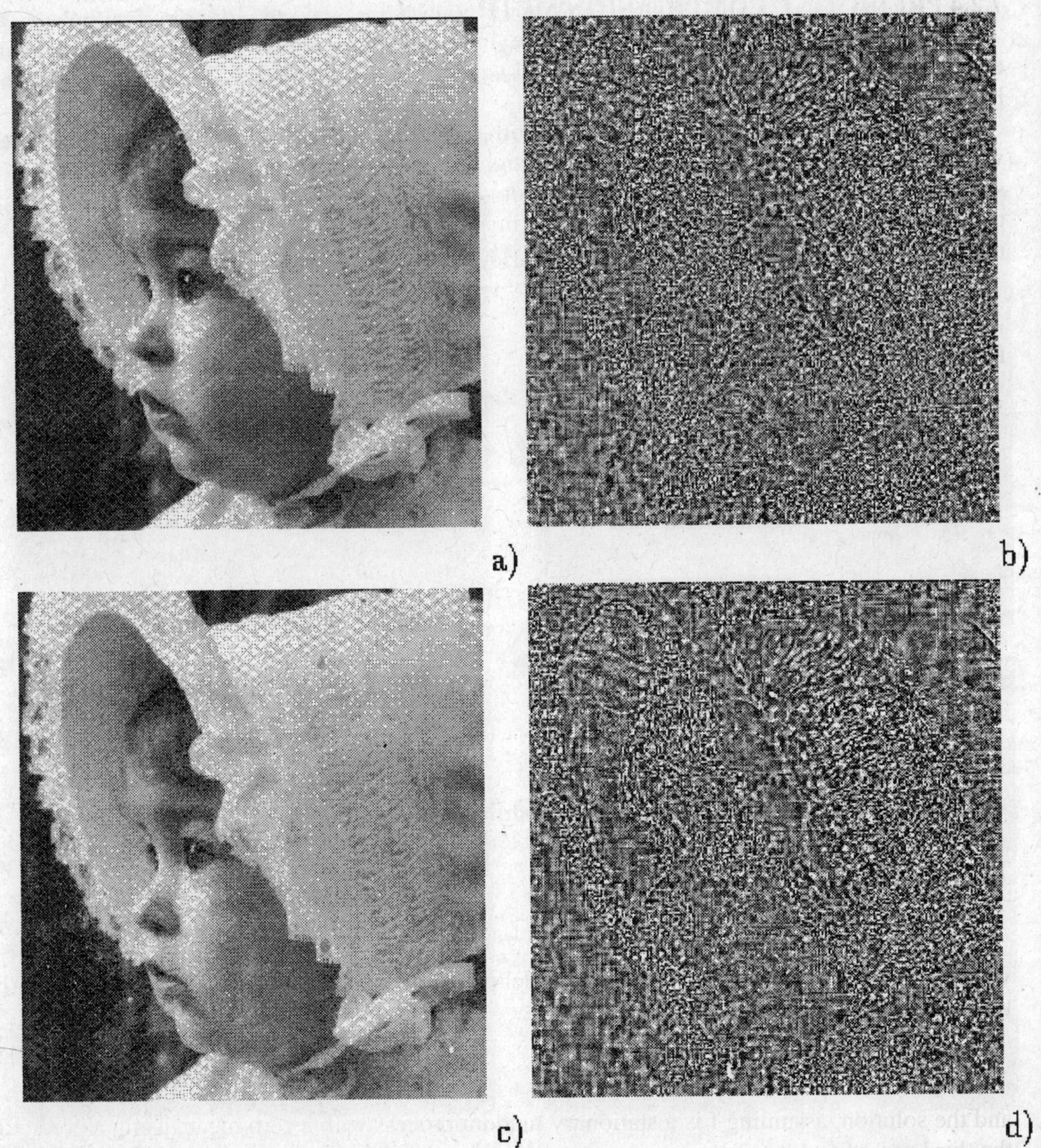


**Figure 7.6 Wavelet image compression: (a) Reconstructed image compression ration K=4.2 ,(b) difference image – differences between pixel values in the original and the reconstructed image (K=4.2) ; the maximum difference is 21 grey level, mean squared reconstruction error MSE=13.9 grey level; (c) reconstructed image compression ration k=5.6 , (d) difference image – differences between pixel values in the original and the reconstructed image (k=5.6); the maximum difference is grey level, MSE=24.7 grey level (image is histogram equalized for visualization purpose)**

### 7.2.4 PREDICTIVE COMPRESSION METHODS

Predictive compressions use image information redundancy (correlation of data) to construct an estimate ~f(i,j) of the gray level value of an image element (i,j) from values of gray levels in the neighborhood of (i,j).

In image parts where data are not correlated, the estimate ~f will not match the original value. The differences between estimates and reality, which may be expected to be relatively small in absolute terms, are coded and transmitted together with prediction model parameters -- the whole set now represents compressed image data. The gray value at the location (i,j) is reconstructed from a computed estimate ~f(i,j) and the stored difference d(i,j)

$$d(i,j) = \tilde{f}(i,j) - f(i,j) \tag{7.6}$$

Differential Pulse Code Modulation (DPCM)

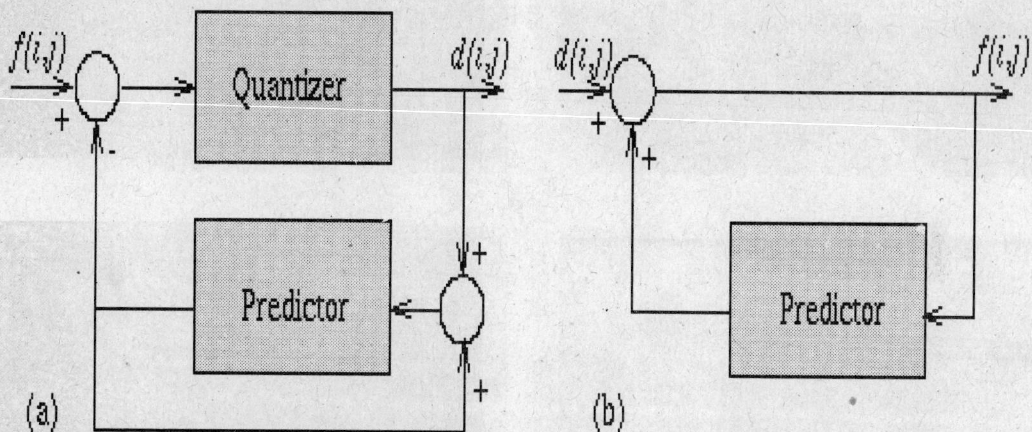


**Figure 7.7 Differential pulse code modulation: (a) Compression (b) reconstruction**

Linear predictor of the third order is sufficient for estimation in a wide variety of images. The estimate ~f can be computed as

$$\tilde{f}(i,j) = a_1 f(i,j-1) + a_2 f(i-1,j-1) + a_3 f(i-1,j) \tag{7.7}$$

where a_1,a_2,a_3 are image prediction model parameters. These parameters are set to minimize the mean quadratic estimation error e,

$$e = \mathcal{E}([\tilde{f}(i,j) - f(i,j)]^2) \tag{7.8}$$

and the solution, assuming f is a stationary random process with a zero mean, using a predictor of the third order, is

$$\begin{aligned} a_1 R(0,0) + a_2 R(1,0) + a_3 R(1,1) &= R(0,1) \\ a_1 R(1,0) + a_2 R(0,0) + a_3 R(0,1) &= R(1,1) \\ a_1 R(1,1) + a_2 R(0,1) + a_3 R(0,0) &= R(1,0) \end{aligned} \tag{7.9}$$

where R(m,n) is the autocorrelation function of the random process f.

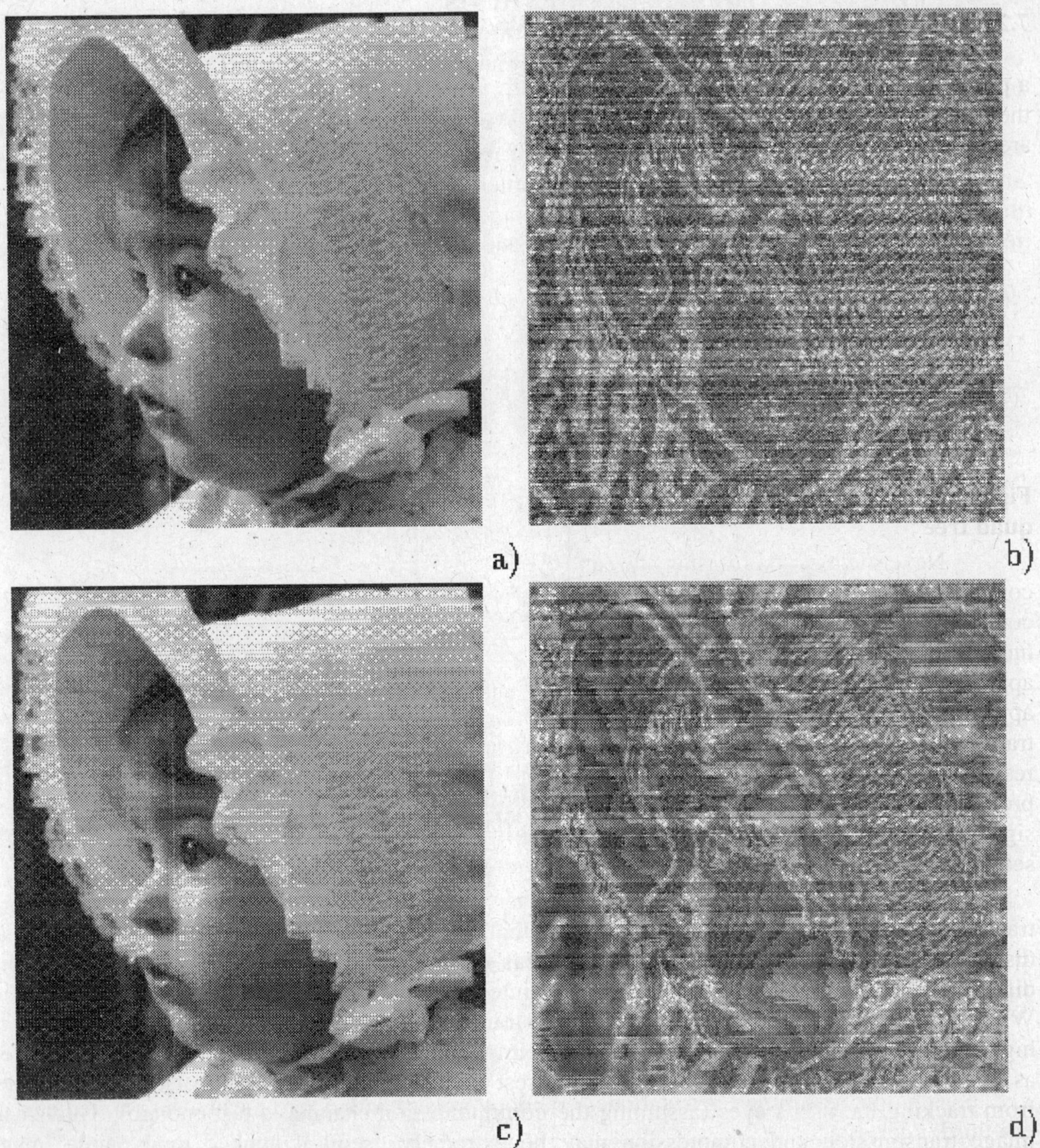


**Figure 7.8 Predictive compression: (a) Reconstructed image , compression ration k=3.8, (b) difference image – differences between pixel values in the original and the reconstructed image (k=3.8); the maximum difference is 6 grey level, mean squared reconstruction MSE=XXX; (c) reconstructed image , compression ration k=6.2, (d) difference image – differences between pixel values in the original and the reconstructed image (k=6.2); the maximum difference is 140 grey level, MSE=XXX; (image is histogram equalized for visualization purpose)**

### 7.2.5 HIERARCHICAL AND PROGRESSIVE COMPRESSION TECHNIQUES

A substantial reduction in bit volume can be obtained by merely representing a source as a pyramid. Approaches exist for which the entire pyramid requires data volume equal to that of the full resolution image.. Even more significant reduction can be achieved for images with large areas of the same gray level if a quad tree coding scheme is applied.

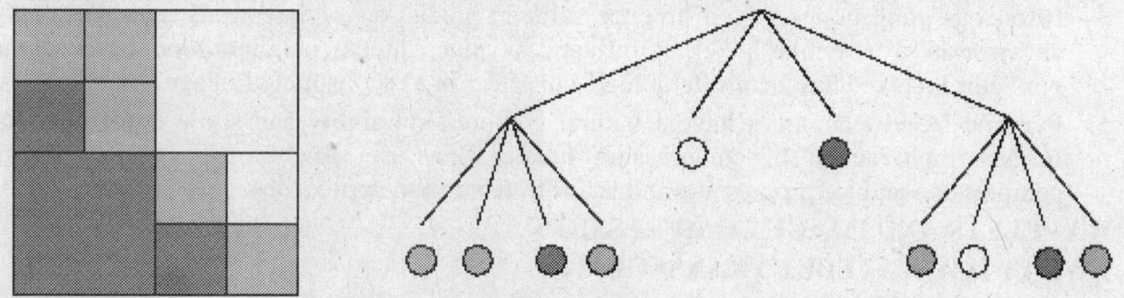

**Figure 7.9 Principle of quad tree image compression; original image and the corresponding quad tree**

Nevertheless, there may be an even more important aspect connected with this compression approach - the feasibility of progressive image transmission and the idea of smart compression. Progressive image transmission - transmitting all image data may not be necessary under some circumstances - e.g., searching an image database looking for a particular image. This approach is also commonly used to decrease the waiting time needed for the image to start appearing after transmission and is used by World Wide Web image transmissions. In progressive transmission, the images are represented in a pyramid structure, the higher pyramid levels (lower resolution) being transmitted first. The concept of smart compression is based on the sensing properties of human visual sensors. The spatial resolution of the human eye decreases significantly with increasing distance from the optical axis. Therefore, the human eye can only see in high resolution in a very small area close to the point where the eye is focused.

Similarly as with image displays, where it does not make sense to display or even transmit an image in higher resolution than that of the display device, it is not necessary to display an image in full resolution in image areas where the user's eyes are not focused. The main difficulty remains in determining the areas of interest in the image on which the user will focus. When considering a smart progressive image transmission, the image should be transmitted in higher resolution in areas of interest first - this improves a subjective rating of transmission speed as sensed by a human user. The areas of interest may be obtained in a feedback control manner from tracking the user's eyes (assuming the communication channel is fast enough). This smart image transmission and compression may be extremely useful if applied to dynamic image generators in driving or flight simulators, or to high definition television.

### 7.2.6 COMPARISON OF COMPRESSION METHODS

1) Transform-based methods better preserve subjective image quality, and are less sensitive to statistical image property changes both inside a single image and between images.
2) Prediction methods, on the other hand, can achieve larger compression ratios in a much less expensive way, tend to be much faster than transform-based or vector quantization compression schemes, and can easily be realized in hardware.

3) If compressed images are transmitted, an important property is insensitivity to transmission channel noise. Transform-based techniques are significantly less sensitive to the channel noise - if a transform coefficient is corrupted during transmission, the resulting image distortion is homogeneously spread through the image or image part and is not too disturbing.
4) Erroneous transmission of a difference value in prediction compressions causes not only an error in a particular pixel, it influences values in the neighborhood because the predictor involved has a considerable visual effect in a reconstructed image.
5) Pyramid based techniques have a natural compression ability and show a potential for further improvement of compression ratios. They are suitable for dynamic image compression and for progressive and smart transmission approaches.

## 7.3 WAVELETS AND IMAGE COMPRESSION

### 7.3.1 WHAT IS A WAVELET TRANSFORM?

Wavelets are functions defined over a finite interval and having an average value of zero. The basic idea of the wavelet transform is to represent any arbitrary function (t) as a superposition of a set of such wavelets or basis functions. These basis functions or baby wavelets are obtained from a single prototype wavelet called the mother wavelet, by dilations or contractions (scaling) and translations (shifts). The Discrete Wavelet Transform of a finite length signal x(n) having N components, for example, is expressed by an N x N matrix.. For a thorough analysis and applications of wavelets and filterbanks.

### 7.3.2 WHY WAVELET-BASED COMPRESSION?

Despite all the advantages of JPEG compression schemes based on DCT namely simplicity, satisfactory performance, and availability of special purpose hardware for implementation, these are not without their shortcomings. Since the input image needs to be ``blocked," correlation across the block boundaries is not eliminated. This results in noticeable and annoying ``blocking artifacts" particularly at low bit rates as shown in Fig. 7.10. Lapped Orthogonal Transforms (LOT) attempt to solve this problem by using smoothly overlapping blocks. Although blocking effects are reduced in LOT compressed images, increased computational complexity of such algorithms do not justify wide replacement of DCT by LOT.

7.10 (a)

**7.10 (b)**

**Figure 7.10(a) Original Lena Image, and (b) Reconstructed Lena with DC component only, to show blocking artifacts**

Over the past several years, the wavelet transform has gained widespread acceptance in signal processing in general, and in image compression research in particular. In many applications wavelet-based schemes (also referred as subband coding) outperform other coding schemes like the one based on DCT. Since there is no need to block the input image and its basis functions have variable length, wavelet coding schemes at higher compression avoid blocking artifacts. Wavelet-based coding is more robust under transmission and decoding errors, and also facilitates progressive transmission of images. In addition, they are better matched to the HVS characteristics. Because of their inherent multiresolution nature, wavelet coding schemes are especially suitable for applications where scalability and tolerable degradation are important.

### 7.3.3 SUBBAND CODING

The fundamental concept behind Subband Coding (SBC) is to split up the frequency band of a signal (image in our case) and then to code each subband using a coder and bit rate accurately matched to the statistics of the band. SBC has been used extensively first in speech coding and later in image coding because of its inherent advantages namely variable bit assignment among the subbands as well as coding error confinement within the subbands.

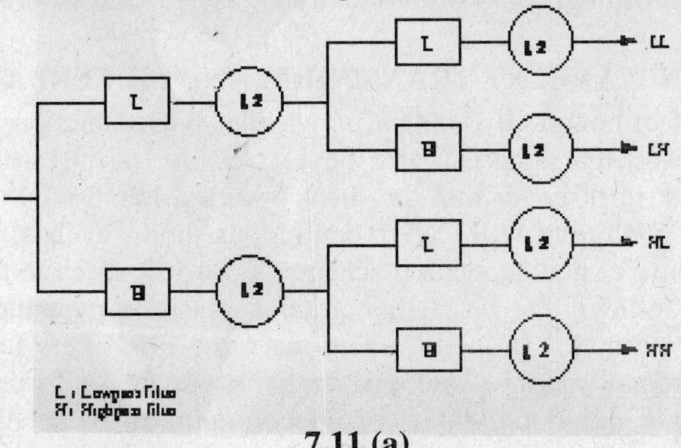


**7.11 (a)**

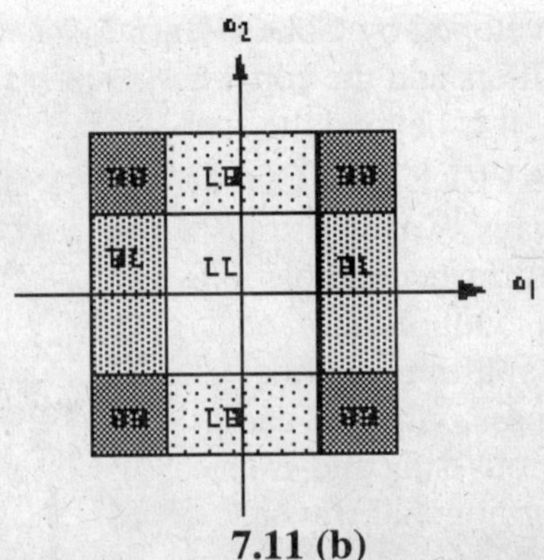


7.11 (b)

**Figure 7.11(a) Separable 4-subband Filterbank and (b) Partition of the Frequency Domain**

Woods and O'Neil used a separable combination of one-dimensional Quadrature Mirror Filterbanks (QMF) to perform a 4-band decomposition by the row-column approach as shown in Figure 7.11(a). Corresponding division of the frequency spectrum is shown in Figure 7.11(b). The process can be iterated to obtain higher band decomposition filter trees. At the decoder, the subband signals are decoded, upsampled and passed through a bank of synthesis filters and properly summed up to yield the reconstructed image. Interested readers may look into a number of books and papers dealing with single and multi-dimensional QMF design and applications.

### 7.3.4 FROM SUBBAND TO WAVELET CODING

Over the years, there have been many efforts leading to improved and efficient design of filterbanks and subband coding techniques. Since 1990, methods very similar and closely related to subband coding have been proposed by various researchers under the name of Wavelet Coding (WC) using filters specifically designed for this purpose. Such filters must meet additional and often conflicting requirements. These include short impulse response of the analysis filters to preserve the localization of image features as well as to have fast computation, short impulse response of the synthesis filters to prevent spreading of artifacts (ringing around edges) resulting from quantization errors, and linear phase of both types of filters since nonlinear phase introduce unpleasant waveform distortions around edges. Orthogonality is another useful requirement since orthogonal filters, in addition to preservation of energy, implement a unitary transform between the input and the subbands. But, as in the case of 1-D, in two-band Finite Impulse Response (FIR) systems linear phase and orthogonality are mutually exclusive, and so orthogonality is sacrificed to achieve linear phase.

### 7.3.5 LINK BETWEEN WAVELET TRANSFORM AND FILTERBANK

Construction of orthonormal families of wavelet basis functions can be carried out in continuous time. However, the same can also be derived by starting from discrete-time filters. Daubechies was the first to discover that the discrete-time filters or QMFs can be iterated and under certain regularity conditions will lead to continuous-time wavelets. This is a very practical and extremely useful wavelet decomposition scheme, since FIR discrete-time filters can be used to implement them. It follows that the orthonormal bases in correspond to a subband coding scheme with exact reconstruction property, using the same FIR filters for reconstruction as for decomposition. So, subband coding developed earlier is in fact a form of wavelet coding in disguise. Wavelets did not gain popularity in image coding until Daubechies established this link in late 1980s. Later a systematic way of constructing a family of compactly supported biorthogonal wavelets was developed by Cohen, Daubechies, and Feauveau (CDF). Although the design and choice of various filters and the construction of different wavelets from the iteration of such filters are very important, it is beyond the scope of this article.

### 7.3.6 AN EXAMPLE OF WAVELET DECOMPOSITION

There are several ways wavelet transforms can decompose a signal into various subbands. These include uniform decomposition, octave-band decomposition, and adaptive or wavelet-packet decomposition. Out of these, octave-band decomposition is the most widely used. This is a non-uniform band splitting method that decomposes the lower frequency part into narrower bands and the high-pass output at each level is left without any further decomposition. Figure 7.12(a) shows the various subband images of a 3-level octave-band decomposed Lena using the popular CDF-9/7 biorthogonal wavelet.

**7.12 (a)**

LLL, LLL | LLL, LLH | LLH, LLL | LLH, LLH | LL, LH | L, H | LH, LL | LH, LH | H, L | H, H

**7.12 (b)**

**Figure 7.12 (a) Three level octave-band decomposition of Lena image, (b) Spectral decomposition and ordering.**

Most of the subband and wavelet coding schemes can also be described in terms of the general framework depicted as in Fig7.1. The main difference from the JPEG standard is the use of DWT rather than DCT. Also, the image need not be split into 8 x 8 disjoint blocks. Of course, many enhancements have been made to the standard quantization and encoding techniques to take advantage of how the wavelet transforms works on an image and the properties and statistics of transformed coefficients so generated.

## 7.4 ADVANCED WAVELET CODING SCHEMES

### 7.4.1 RECENT DEVELOPMENTS IN SUBBAND AND WAVELET CODING

The interplay between the three components of any image coder cannot be over-emphasized since a properly designed quantizer and entropy encoder are absolutely necessary along with optimum signal transformation to get the best possible compression. Many enhancements have been made to the standard quantizers and encoders to take advantage of how the wavelet transform works on an image, the properties of the HVS, and the statistics of transformed coefficients. A number of more sophisticated variations of the standard entropy encoders have also been developed. These include Q, QM, ELS, Z, and ZP coders. These have lead to improved results in terms of lower bit rates for a required image quality and better image quality for a given bit rate.

Over the past few years, a variety of novel and sophisticated wavelet-based image coding schemes have been developed. These include EZW, SPIHT, SFQ, CREW, EPWIC, EBCOT, SR, Second Generation Image Coding, Image Coding using Wavelet Packets, Wavelet Image Coding using VQ, and Lossless Image Compression using Integer Lifting. This list is by no means exhaustive and many more such innovative techniques are being developed as this article is written. We will briefly discuss a few of these interesting algorithms here.

#### 7.4.1.1 EMBEDDED ZEROTREE WAVELET (EZW) COMPRESSION

In octave-band wavelet decomposition, shown in Fig. 7.13 each coefficient in the high-pass bands of the wavelet transform has four coefficients corresponding to its spatial position in the octave band above in frequency. Because of this very structure of the decomposition, it probably needed a smarter way of encoding its coefficients to achieve better compression results. Lewis and Knowles in 1992 were the first to introduce a tree-like data structure to represent the coefficients of the octave decomposition.

Later, in 1993 Shapiro called this structure zerotree of wavelet coefficients, and presented his elegant algorithm for entropy encoding called Embedded Zerotree Wavelet (EZW) algorithm. The zerotree is based on the hypothesis that if a wavelet coefficient at a coarse scale is insignificant with respect to a given threshold T, then all wavelet coefficients of the same orientation in the same spatial location at a finer scales are likely to be insignificant with respect to T. The idea is to define a tree of zero symbols which starts at a root which is also zero and labeled as end-of-block. Fig. 7.13 and 7.13 shows a similar zerotree structure.

Many insignificant coefficients at higher frequency subbands (finer resolutions) can be discarded, because the tree grows as powers of four. The EZW algorithm encodes the tree structure so obtained. This results in bits that are generated in order of importance, yielding a fully embedded code. The main advantage of this encoding is that the encoder can terminate the encoding at any point, thereby allowing a target bit rate to be met exactly. Similarly, the decoder can also stop decoding at any point resulting in the image that would have been produced at the rate of the truncated bit stream. The algorithm produces excellent results without any pre-stored tables or codebooks, training, or prior knowledge of the image source.

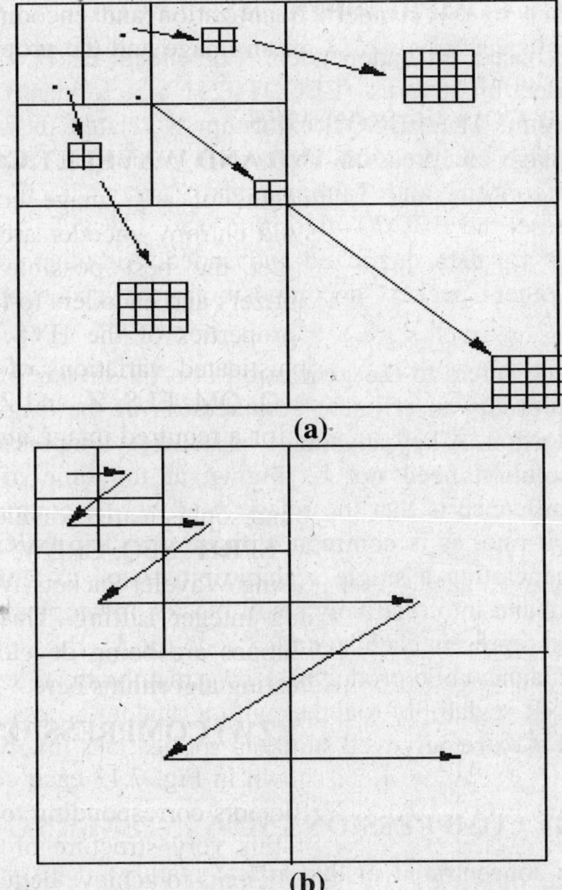


**Figure 7.13(a) Structure of zerotrees, and 7(b) Scanning order of subbands for encoding**

Since its inception in 1993, many enhancements have been made to make the EZW algorithm more robust and efficient. One very popular and improved variation of the EZW is the SPIHT algorithm.

### 7.4.1.2. SET PARTITIONING IN HIERARCHICAL TREES (SPIHT) ALGORITHM

Said and Pearlman, offered an alternative explanation of the principles of operation of the EZW algorithm to better understand the reasons for its excellent performance. According to them, partial ordering by magnitude of the transformed coefficients with a set partitioning sorting algorithm, ordered bitplane transmission of refinement bits, and exploitation of self-similarity of the image wavelet transform across different scales of an image are the three key concepts in EZW. In addition, they offer a new and more effective implementation of the modified EZW algorithm based on set partitioning in hierarchical trees, and call it the SPIHT algorithm. They also present a scheme for progressive transmission of the coefficient values that incorporates the concepts of ordering the coefficients by magnitude and transmitting the most significant bits first. They use a uniform scalar quantizer and claim that the ordering information made this simple quantization method more efficient than expected. An efficient way to code the ordering information is also proposed. According to them, results from the SPIHT coding algorithm in most cases surpass those obtained from EZQ algorithm.

#### 7.4.1.3 SCALABLE IMAGE COMPRESSION WITH EBCOT

This algorithm is based on independent Embedded Block Coding with Optimized Truncation of the embedded bit-streams (EBCOT)[25] which identifies some of the major contributions of the algorithm. The EBCOT algorithm is related in various degrees to much earlier work on scalable image compression. Noteworthy among its early predecessors are: the EZW algorithm, SPIHT algorithm, and Taubman and Zakhor's LZC (Layered Zero Coding) algorithm. Like each of these, the EBCOT algorithm uses a wavelet transform to generate the subband coefficients which are then quantized and coded. Although the usual dyadic wavelet decomposition is typical, other "packet" decompositions are also supported and occasionally preferable.

Scalable compression refers to the generation of a bit-stream which contains embedded subsets, each of which represents an efficient compression of the original image at a reduced resolution or increased distortion. A key advantage of scalable compression is that the target bit-rate or reconstruction resolution need not be known at the time of compression. Another advantage of practical significance is that the image need not be compressed multiple times in order to achieve a target bit-rate, as is common with the existing JPEG compression standard. Rather than focusing on generating a single scalable bit-stream to represent the entire image, EBCOT partitions each subband into relatively small blocks of samples and generates a separate highly scalable bit-stream to represent each so-called code-block. The algorithm exhibits state-of-the-art compression performance while producing a bit-stream with an unprecedented feature set, including resolution and SNR scalability together with a random access property. The algorithm has modest complexity and is extremely well suited to applications involving remote browsing of large compressed images.

#### 7.4.1.4 LOSSLESS IMAGE COMPRESSION USING INTEGER TO INTEGER WT

Although we have concentrated in this article mainly on lossy image coding, lossless coding is important for high-fidelity images like medical images, seismic data, satellite images, and images generated from studio-quality video. The JPEG standard specifies a lossless coding scheme which simply codes the difference between each pixel and the predicted value for the pixel. The sequence of differences is encoded using Huffman or arithmetic encoding. Unfortunately, the huge size of the images for which lossless compression is required makes it necessary to have encoding methods that can support storage and progressive transmission of images at a spectrum of resolutions and encoding fidelities from lossy to lossless.

The multiresolution nature of the wavelet transform makes it an ideal candidate for progressive transmission. However, when wavelet filtering is applied to an input image (set of integer pixel values), since the filter coefficients are not necessarily integers, the resultant filtered output is no longer integers but floating point values. For lossless encoding, to make the decoding process exactly reversible, it is required that the filtered coefficients should be represented with integer values. In approaches to build invertible wavelet transforms that map integers to integers are described. These invertible integer-to-integer wavelet transforms are useful for lossless image coding. The approach is based upon the idea of factoring wavelet transforms into lifting steps thereby, allowing the construction of an integer version of every wavelet transform. The construction is based on writing a wavelet transform in terms of lifting, which is a flexible technique that has been applied to the construction of wavelets through an iterative process of updating subbands and from an appropriate linear combination of the other subbands. A number of invertible integer wavelet transforms are implemented and applied to lossless compression of images. Although the results are mixed in terms of performance of these newly developed filters, it is concluded that using such wavelet transforms permits lossless representation of images thereby easily allowing progressive transmission where a lower resolution version of the image is transmitted first followed by transmission of successive details.

### 7.4.1.5 IMAGE CODING USING ADAPTIVE WAVELETS

Now a few words about image coding using adaptive wavelets. The main idea behind the research work that we are currently pursuing is that all images are not equal, and so in wavelet-based image coding, the wavelet filter should be chosen adaptively depending on the statistical nature of image being coded. We have experimented with a variety of wavelets to compress a variety of images of different types at various compression ratios. Our results show that the performance in lossy coders is image dependent; while some wavelet filters perform better than others depending on the image, no specific wavelet filter performs uniformly better than others on all images. Similar results have also been observed in the context of lossless compression using various integer-to-integer wavelet transforms. This adaptive filter selection is important because, when the performance of the wavelet filter is poor in the first place, use of even sophisticated quantization and context modeling of the transform coefficients may not always provide significant enough gain. Hence, the importance of searching and using good wavelet filters in most coding schemes cannot be over emphasized. We are currently working on algorithms to dynamically determine the right wavelet filter based on the type and statistical nature of the input image to be coded.

### 7.4.2 PERFORMANCE COMPARISON: DCT VS. DWT

A final word on the performance of wavelet-based and JPEG coders. The peak signal to noise ratios (PSNR) of several different wavelet compression techniques applied to the 512 x 512, 8-bpp Lena image as well as the performance of a baseline JPEG image compressor are compared and are reproduced in Figure 7.14. It is seen that, at compression ratios less than 25:1 or so, the JPEG performs better numerically than the simple wavelet coders. At compression ratios above 30:1, JPEG performance rapidly deteriorates, while wavelet coders degrade gracefully well beyond ratios of 100:1. The graphs also show that both the encoding technique and the particular wavelet used can make a significant difference in the performance of a compression system: the zerotree coder performs the best; biorthogonal perform better than W6; and variable length coders(VLC) perform better than fixed length coders(FLC).

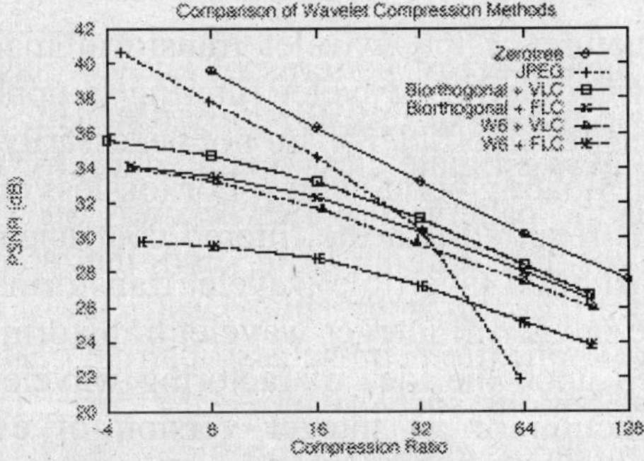


**Figure 7.14 Comparison of Wavelet Compression methods**

## 7.5 STATISTICAL PATTERN RECOGNITION

Pattern recognition as a field of study developed significantly in the 1960s. It was very much an interdisciplinary subject, covering developments in the areas of statistics, engineering, artificial intelligence, computer science, psychology and physiology, among others. Some people entered the field with a real problem to solve. The large numbers of applications, ranging from the classical ones such as automatic character recognition and medical diagnosis to the more recent ones in data mining (such as credit scoring, consumer sales analysis and credit card transaction analysis), have attracted considerable research effort, with many methods developed and advances made. Other researchers were motivated by the development of machines with 'brain-like' performance that in some way could emulate human performance. There were many over-optimistic and unrealistic claims made, and to some extent there exist strong parallels with the growth of research on knowledge-based systems in the 1970s and neural networks in the 1980s.

Nevertheless, within these areas significant progress has been made, particularly where the domain overlaps with probability and statistics, and within recent years there have been many exciting new developments, both in methodology and applications. These build on the solid foundations of earlier research and take advantage of increased computational resources readily available nowadays. These developments include, for example, kernel-based methods and Bayesian computational methods. The emphasis in machine learning is perhaps more on computationally intensive methods and less on a statistical approach, but there is strong overlap between the research areas of statistical pattern recognition and machine learning.

Since many of the techniques we shall describe have been developed over a range of diverse disciplines, there is naturally a variety of sometimes contradictory terminology. We shall use the term 'pattern' to denote the p-dimensional data vector $x = (x1, \ldots, x_p)^T$ of measurements ($^T$ denotes vector transpose), whose components xi are measurements of the features of an object. Thus the features are the variables specified by the investigator and thought to be important for classification. In discrimination, we assume that there exist C groups or classes, denoted $\omega 1, \ldots, \omega C$, and associated with each pattern x is a categorical variable z that denotes the class or group membership; that is, if z = i, then the pattern belongs to $\omega i$, $i \in \{1, \ldots, C\}$.

Examples of patterns are measurements of an acoustic waveform in a speech recognition problem; measurements on a patient made in order to identify a disease (diagnosis); measurements on patients in order to predict the likely outcome (prognosis); measurements on weather variables (for forecasting or prediction); and a digitised image for character recognition. Therefore, we see that the term 'pattern', in its technical meaning, does not necessarily refer to structure within images.

We assume that we have a set of patterns of known class $\{(xi, zi), i = 1, \ldots, n\}$ (the training or design set) that we use to design the classifier (to set up its internal parameters). Once this has been done, we may estimate class membership for an unknown pattern x.

The form derived for the pattern classifier depends on a number of different factors. It depends on the distribution of the training data, and the assumptions made concerning its distribution. Another important factor is the misclassification cost – the cost of making an incorrect decision. In many applications misclassification costs are hard to quantify, being combinations of several contributions such as monetary costs, time and other more subjective costs. For example, in a medical diagnosis problem, each treatment has different costs associated with it. These relate to the expense of different types of drugs, the suffering the patient is subjected to by each course of action and the risk of further complications.

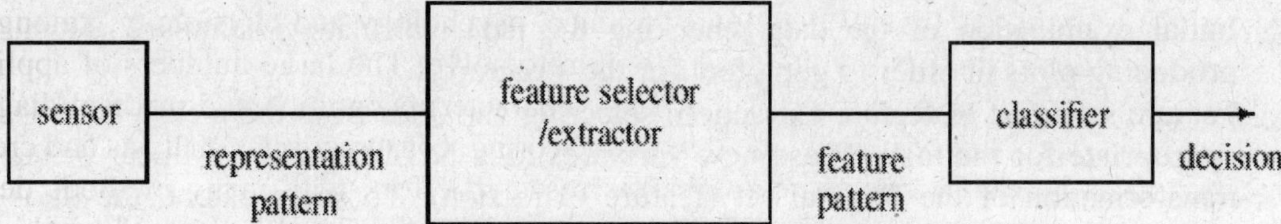


**Figure 7.15 Pattern classifier**

Figure 7.15 grossly oversimplifies the pattern classification procedure. Data may undergo several separate transformation stages before a final outcome is reached. These transformations (sometimes termed preprocessing, feature selection or feature extraction) operate on the data in a way that usually reduces its dimension (reduces the number of features), removing redundant or irrelevant information, and transforms it to a form more appropriate for subsequent classification. The term intrinsic dimensionality refers to the minimum number of variables required to capture the structure within the data. In the speech recognition example mentioned above, a preprocessing stage may be to transform the waveform to a frequency representation. This may be processed further to find formants (peaks in the spectrum). This is a feature extraction process (taking a possible nonlinear combination of the original variables to form new variables). Feature selection is the process of selecting a subset of a given set of variables.

Terminology varies between authors. Sometimes the term 'representation pattern' is used for the vector of measurements made on a sensor (for example, optical imager, radar) with the term 'feature pattern' being reserved for the small set of variables obtained by transformation (by a feature selection or feature extraction process) of the original vector of measurements. In some problems, measurements may be made directly on the feature vector itself. In these situations there is no automatic feature selection stage, with the feature selection being performed by the investigator who 'knows' (through experience, knowledge of previous studies and the problem domain) those variables that are important for classification. In many cases, however, it will be necessary to perform one or more transformations of the measured data.

In some pattern classifiers, each of the above stages may be present and identifiable as separate operations, while in others they may not be. Also, in some classifiers, the preliminary stages will tend to be problem-specific, as in the speech example. In this book, we consider feature selection and extraction transformations that are not application- specific. That is not to say all will be suitable for any given application, however, but application-specific preprocessing must be left to the investigator.

### 7.5.1 STAGES IN THE PATTERN RECOGNITION PROBLEM

A pattern recognition investigation may consist of several stages, enumerated below. Further details are given in Appendix D. Not all stages may be present; some may be merged together so that the distinction between two operations may not be clear, even if both are carried out; also, there may be some application-specific data processing that may not be regarded as one of the stages listed. However, the points below are fairly typical.

1. Formulation of the problem: gaining a clear understanding of the aims of the investigation

and planning the remaining stages.

2. Data collection: making measurements on appropriate variables and recording details of the data collection procedure (ground truth).
3. Initial examination of the data: checking the data, calculating summary statistics and producing plots in order to get a feel for the structure.
4. Feature selection or feature extraction: selecting variables from the measured set that are appropriate for the task. These new variables may be obtained by a linear or nonlinear transformation of the original set (feature extraction). To some extent, the division of feature extraction and classification is artificial.
5. Unsupervised pattern classification or clustering. This may be viewed as exploratory data analysis and it may provide a successful conclusion to a study. On the other hand, it may be a means of preprocessing the data for a supervised classification procedure.
6. Apply discrimination or regression procedures as appropriate. The classifier is designed using a training set of exemplar patterns.
7. Assessment of results. This may involve applying the trained classifier to an independent test set of labelled patterns.
8. Interpretation.

The above is necessarily an iterative process: the analysis of the results may pose further hypotheses that require further data collection. Also, the cycle may be terminated at different stages: the questions posed may be answered by an initial examination of the data or it may be discovered that the data cannot answer the initial question and the problem must be reformulated. The emphasis of this book is on techniques for performing steps 4, 5 and 6.

### 7.5.2 ISSUES

There are a number of very important points to make about the sentence above, straightforward as it seems. The first is that we are given a finite design set. If the classifier is too complex (there are too many free parameters) it may model noise in the design set. This is an example of over-fitting. If the classifier is not complex enough, then it may fail to capture structure in the data. An example of this is the fitting of a set of data points by a polynomial curve. If the degree of the polynomial is too high, then, although the curve may pass through or close to the data points, thus achieving a low fitting error, the fitting curve is very variable and models every fluctuation in the data (due to noise). If the degree of the polynomial is too low, the fitting error is large and the underlying variability of the curve is not modelled.

Thus, achieving optimal performance on the design set (in terms of minimising some error criterion perhaps) is not required: it may be possible, in a classification problem, to achieve 100% classification accuracy on the design set but the generalisation performance – the expected performance on data representative of the true operating conditions (equivalently, the performance on an infinite test set of which the design set is a sample) – is poorer than could be achieved by careful design. Choosing the 'right' model is an exercise in model selection.

In practice we usually do not know what is structure and what is noise in the data. Also, training a classifier (the procedure of determining its parameters) should not be considered as a separate issue from model selection, but it often is.

A second point about the design of optimal classifiers concerns the word 'optimal'. There are several ways of measuring classifier performance, the most common being error rate, although this has severe limitations. Other measures, based on the closeness of the estimates of the probabilities of class membership to the true probabilities, may be more appropriate in many cases. However, many classifier design methods usually optimise alternative criteria since the desired ones are difficult to optimise directly. For example, a classifier may be trained by optimising a squared error measure and assessed using error rate.

Finally, we assume that the training data are representative of the test conditions. If this is not so, perhaps because the test conditions may be subject to noise not present in the training data, or there are changes in the population from which the data are drawn (population drift), then these differences must be taken into account in classifier design.

### 7.5.3 SUPERVISED VERSUS UNSUPERVISED

There are two main divisions of classification: supervised classification (or discrimination) and unsupervised classification (sometimes in the statistics literature simply referred to as classification or clustering).

In supervised classification we have a set of data samples (each consisting of measurements on a set of variables) with associated labels, the class types. These are used as exemplars in the classifier design.

Why do we wish to design an automatic means of classifying future data? Cannot the same method that was used to label the design set be used on the test data? In some cases this may be possible. However, even if it were possible, in practice we may wish to develop an automatic method to reduce labour-intensive procedures. In other cases, it may not be possible for a human to be part of the classification process. An example of the former is in industrial inspection. A classifier can be trained using images of components on a production line, each image labelled carefully by an operator. However, in the practical application we would wish to save a human operator from the tedious job, and hopefully make it more reliable. An example of the latter reason for performing a classification automatically is in radar target recognition of objects. For vehicle recognition, the data may be gathered by positioning vehicles on a turntable and making measurements from all aspect angles. In the practical application, a human may not be able to recognise an object reliably from its radar image, or the process may be carried out remotely.

In unsupervised classification, the data are not labelled and we seek to find groups in the data and the features that distinguish one group from another. Clustering techniques, can also be used as part of a supervised classification scheme by defining prototypes. A clustering scheme may be applied to the data for each class separately and representative samples for each group within the class (the group means, for example) used as the prototypes for that class.

### 7.5.4 APPROACHES TO STATISTICAL PATTERN RECOGNITION

Given a set of measurements obtained through observation and represented as a pattern vector x, we wish to assign the pattern to one of C possible classes $\omega$, i =1, . .., C. A decision rule partitions the measurement space into C regions $\Omega i$, i =1, . . . , C. If an observation vector is in $\Omega i$ then it is assumed to belong to class $\omega i$. Each region may be multiply connected – that is, it may be made up of several disjoint regions. The boundaries between the regions $\Omega i$ are the decision boundaries or decision surfaces. Generally, it is in regions close to these boundaries that the highest proportion of misclassifications occurs. In such situations, we may reject the pattern or withhold a decision until further information is available so that a classification may be made later. This option is known as the reject option and therefore we have C +1 outcomes of a decision rule (the reject option being denoted by $\omega 0$) in a C-class problem.

The first assumes a knowledge of the underlying class-conditional probability density functions (the probability density function of the feature vectors for a given class). Of course, in many applications these will usually be unknown and must be estimated from a set of correctly classified samples termed the design or training set.

The second approach introduced in this section develops decision rules that use the data to estimate the decision boundaries directly, without explicit calculation of the probability density functions.

### 7.5.5 ELEMENTARY DECISION THEORY

#### 7.5.5.1 BAYES DECISION RULE FOR MINIMUM ERROR

Consider C classes, $\omega 1, \ldots, \omega C$, with a priori probabilities (the probabilities of each class occurring) $p(\omega 1), \ldots, p(\omega C)$, assumed known. If we wish to minimise the probability of making an error and we have no information regarding an object other than the class probability distribution then we would assign an object to class $\omega j$ if

$p(\omega j) > p(\omega k)$ $k = 1, \ldots, C$; $k \neq j$

This classifies all objects as belonging to one class. For classes with equal probabilities, patterns are assigned arbitrarily between those classes.

However, we do have an observation vector or measurement vector x and we wish to assign x to one of the C classes. A decision rule based on probabilities is to assign x to class $\omega j$ if the probability of class $\omega j$ given the observation x, $p(\omega j|)$, is greatest over all classes $\omega 1, \ldots, \omega$. That is, assign x to class $\omega$ if

$$p(\omega j|) > p(\omega k|) \quad k = 1, \ldots, C;\ k \neq j \qquad (7.10)$$

This decision rule partitions the measurement space into C regions $\Omega 1, \ldots, \Omega C$ such that if $x \in \Omega j$ then x belongs to class $\omega j$. The a posteriori probabilities $p(\omega j|)$ may be expressed in terms of the a priori probabilities and the class-conditional density functions $p(x|\omega i)$ using Bayes' theorem as

$$p(\omega_i \mid x) = \frac{p(x \mid \omega_i)p(\omega_i)}{p(x)}$$

and so the decision rule (7.10) may be written: assign x to $\omega j$ if

$$p(x|\omega j)p(\omega j) > p(x|\omega k)p(\omega k) \quad k = 1, \ldots, C;\ k \neq j \qquad (7.11)$$

This is known as Bayes' rule for minimum error. For two classes, the decision rule (7.11) may be written

$$l_r(x) = \frac{p(x \mid \omega 1)}{p(x \mid \omega 2)} > \frac{p(\omega 2)}{p(\omega 1)} \text{ implies } x \in class\,\omega 1$$

The function $l_r(x)$ is the likelihood ratio. Figures 7.16 and 7.17 give a simple illustration for a two-class discrimination problem. Class co1 is normally distributed with zero mean and unit variance, $p(x|\omega 1) = N(x|0, 1)$ (see Appendix E). Class co2 is a normal mixture (a weighted sum of normal densities) $p(x|\omega 2) = 0.6N(x|1, 1) + 0.4N(x|-1, 2)$.

Figure 7.16 plots $p(x|\omega i)p(\omega i)$, i = 1, 2, where the priors are taken to be $p(\omega 1) = 0.5$, $p(\omega 2) = 0.5$. Figure 7.17 plots the likelihood ratio $l_r(x)$ and the threshold $p(\omega 2)/p(\omega 1)$. We see from this figure that the decision rule (7.11) leads to a disjoint region for class $\omega 2$.

The fact that the decision rule (7.11) minimises the error may be seen as follows. The probability of making an error, p(error), may be expressed as

$$p(error) = \sum_{i=1}^{c} p(error \mid \omega i)\, p(\omega i) \tag{7.12}$$

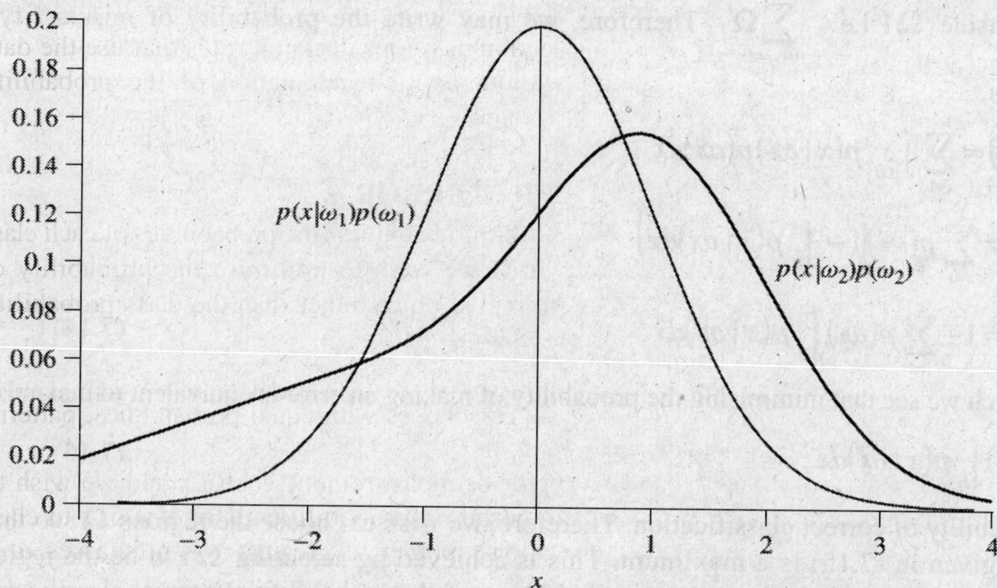


**Figure 7.16 p(x|ω i)p(ω i), for classes ω 1 and ω 2**

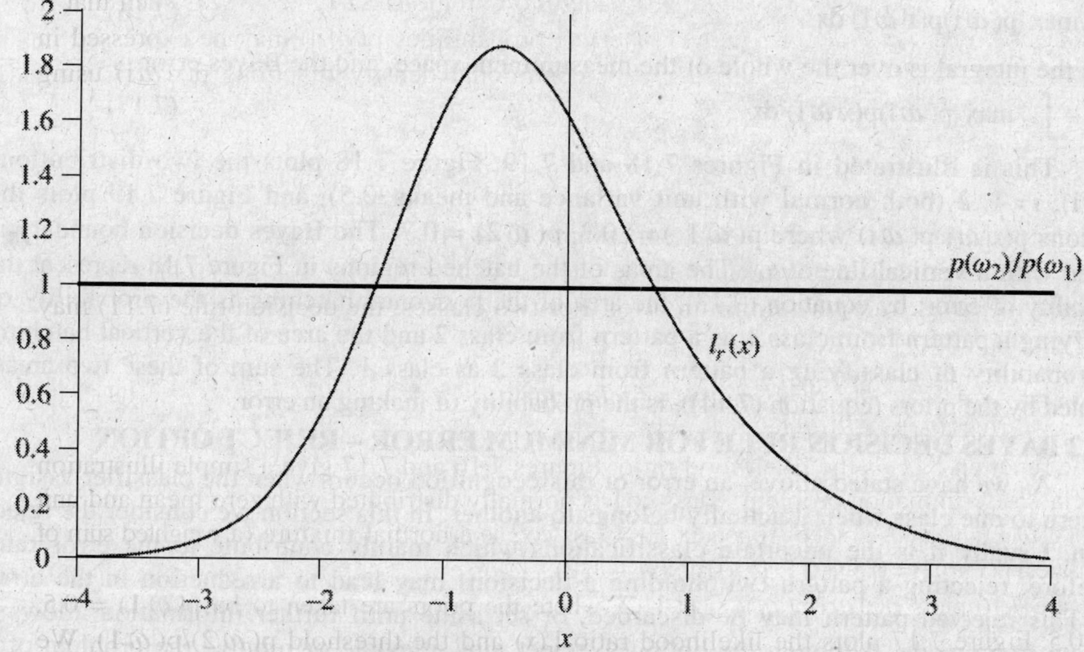


**Figure 7.17 Likelihood function**

where p(error| $\omega$ i) is the probability of misclassifying patterns from class $\omega$ i. This is given by

$$p(error \mid \omega_i) = \int_{c(\Omega_i)} p(x \mid \omega_i) dx \tag{7.13}$$

the integral of the class-conditional density function over C[$\Omega$ i], the region of measurement space outside $\Omega$ I i.e $\sum_{j=1, j\neq i}^{c} \Omega_j$ Therefore, we may write the probability of misclassifying a pattern as

$$p(error) = \sum_{i=1}^{c} \int_{c[\Omega i]} p(x \mid \omega i) p(\omega i) dx$$

$$= \sum_{i=1}^{c} p(\omega i)\left(1 - \int_{\Omega i} p(x \mid \omega i) dx\right)$$

$$= 1 - \sum_{i=1}^{c} p(\omega i) \int_{\Omega i} p(x \mid \omega i) dx \tag{7.14}$$

from which we see that minimising the probability of making an error is equivalent to maximizing

$$\sum_{i=1}^{c} p(\omega i) \int_{\Omega i} p(x \mid \omega i) dx \tag{7.15}$$

the probability of correct classification. Therefore, we wish to choose the regions $\Omega$ i so that the integral given in (7.15) is a maximum. This is achieved by selecting $\Omega$ i to be the region for which p( $\omega$ i)p(x| $\omega$ i) is the largest over all classes and the probability of correct classification, c, is

$$c = \int \max_i p(\omega i) p(x \mid \omega i)\, dx \tag{7.16}$$

where the integral is over the whole of the measurement space, and the Bayes error is

$$eB = 1 - \int \max_i p(\omega i) p(x \mid \omega i)\, dx \tag{7.17}$$

This is illustrated in Figures 7.18 and 7.19. Figure 7.18 plots the two distributions p(x| $\omega$ i), i = 1, 2 (both normal with unit variance and means ±0.5), and Figure 7.19 plots the functions p(x| $\omega$ i)p( $\omega$ i) where p( $\omega$ 1 ) = 0.3, p( $\omega$ 2) = 0.7. The Bayes decision boundary is marked with a vertical line at $x_B$. The areas of the hatched regions in Figure 7.18 represent the probability of error: by equation (7.13), the area of the horizontal hatching is the probability of classifying a pattern from class 1 as a pattern from class 2 and the area of the vertical hatching the probability of classifying a pattern from class 2 as class 1. The sum of these two areas, weighted by the priors (equation (7.14)), is the probability of making an error.

### 7.5.5.2 BAYES DECISION RULE FOR MINIMUM ERROR – REJECT OPTION

As we have stated above, an error or misrecognition occurs when the classifier assigns a pattern to one class when it actually belongs to another. In this section we consider the reject option. Usually it is the uncertain classifications which mainly contribute to the error rate. Therefore, rejecting a pattern (withholding a decision) may lead to a reduction in the error rate. This rejected pattern may be discarded, or set aside until further information allows a decision to be made. Although the option to reject may alleviate or remove the problem of a high misrecognition rate, some otherwise correct

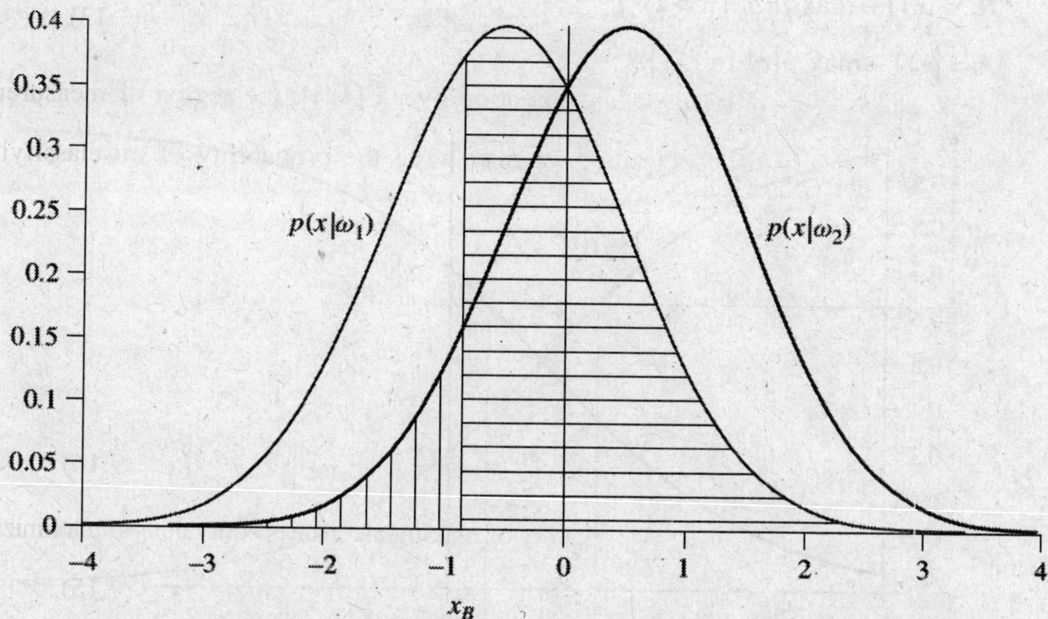


**Figure 7.18 Class-conditional densities for two normal distributions**

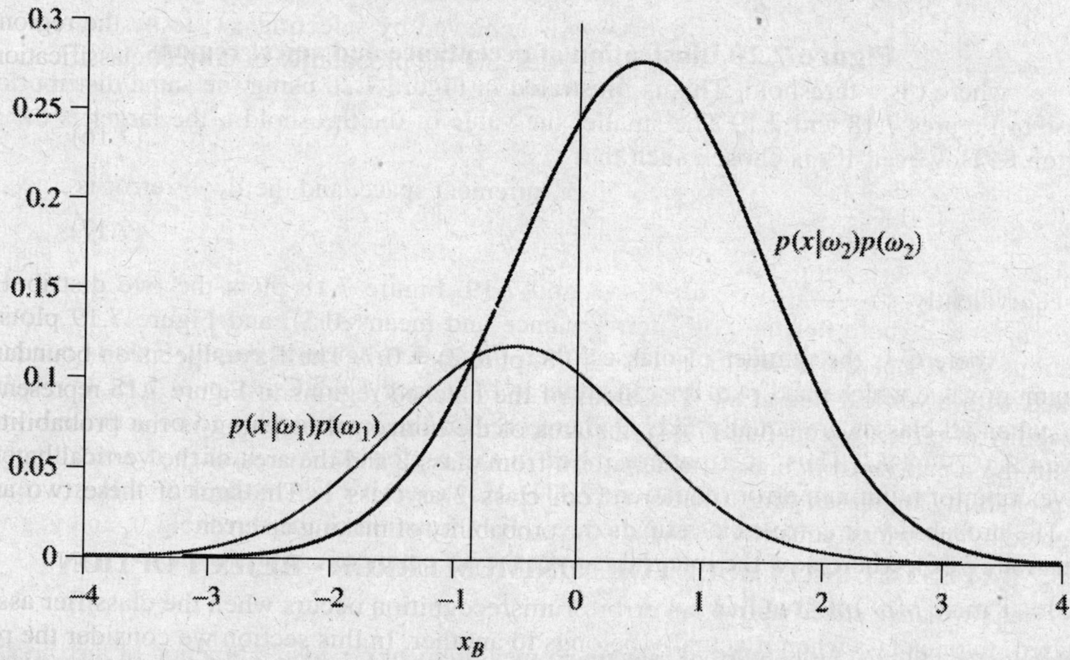


**Figure 7.19 Bayes decision boundary for two normally distributed classes with unequal priors**

classifications are also converted into rejects. Here we consider the trade-offs between error rate and reject rate. Firstly, we partition the sample space into two complementary regions: R, a reject region, and A, an acceptance or classification region. These are defined by

$$R_1 = \{x \mid 1 - \max_i p(\omega_i \mid x > t)\ \}$$

$$A = \{x \mid 1 - \max_i p(\omega_i \mid x) \leq t\}$$

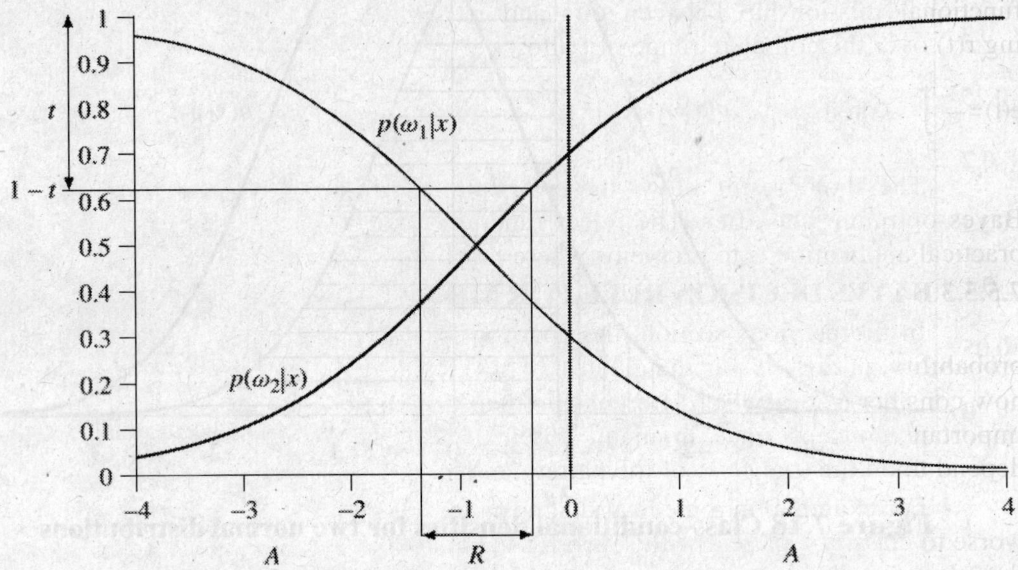


**Figure 7.20 Illustration of acceptance and reject regions**

where t is a threshold. This is illustrated in Figure 7.20 using the same distributions as those in Figures 7.18 and 7.19 The smaller the value of the threshold t, the larger is the reject region R. However, if t is chosen such that

$$1\text{-}t < \frac{1}{c}$$

Or equivalently $t > \dfrac{c-1}{c}$

where C is the number of classes, then the reject region is empty. This is because the minimum value which maxi p( ω i|x) can attain is 1/C (since 1 = Σ C i=1 p( ω i|x) ≤ C maxi p( ω |x)), when all classes are equally likely. Therefore, for the reject option to be activated, we must have t ≤ (C — 1)/C. Thus, if a pattern x lies in the region A, we classify it according to the Bayes rule for minimum error (equation (7.11)). However, if x lies in the region R, we reject x.

The probability of correct classification, c(t), is a function of the threshold, t, and is given by equation (7.16), where now the integral is over the acceptance region, A, only

$$c(t) = \int_A \max\left[p(\omega_i)p(x \mid \omega_i)\right]dx$$

and the unconditional probability of rejecting a measurement x, r, also a function of the threshold t is

$$r(t) = \int_R p(x)dx \qquad (7.18)$$

Therefore, the error rate, e (the probability of accepting a point for classification and incorrectly classifying it), is

$e(t) = \int (1 - \max p(\omega i|x))p(x)\, dx$

$A = 1\text{-}C(t)\text{-}R(t)$

Thus, the error rate and reject rate are inversely related. Chow (1970) derives a simple functional relationship between e(t) and r(t) which we quote here without proof. Knowing r(t) over the complete range of t allows e(t) to be calculated using the relationship

$$e(t) = -\int_0^1 s\, dr(s) \qquad (7.19)$$

The above result allows the error rate to be evaluated from the reject function for the Bayes optimum classifier. The reject function can be calculated using unlabelled data and a practical application is to problems where labelling of gathered data is costly.

### 7.5.5.3 BAYES DECISION RULE FOR MINIMUM RISK

In the previous section, the decision rule selected the class for which the a posteriori probability, $p(\omega j\,|x)$, was the greatest. This minimised the probability of making an error. We now consider a somewhat different rule that minimises an expected loss or risk. This is a very important concept since in many applications the costs associated with misclassification depend upon the true class of the pattern and the class to which it is assigned.

For example, in a medical diagnosis problem in which a patient has back pain, it is far worse to classify a patient with severe spinal abnormality as healthy (or having mild back ache) than the other way round.

We make this concept more formal by introducing a loss that is a measure of the cost of making the decision that a pattern belongs to class $\omega i$ when the true class is $\omega j$. We define a loss matrix $\Lambda$ with components

$\lambda ji$ = cost of assigning a pattern x to $\omega i$ when $x \in \omega j$

In practice, it may be very difficult to assign costs. In some situations, A may be measured in monetary units that are quantifiable. However, in many situations, costs are a combination of several different factors measured in different units – money, time, quality of life. As a consequence, they may be the subjective opinion of an expert. The conditional risk of assigning a pattern x to class $\omega i$ is defined as

$$l^i(x) = \sum_{j=1}^{C} \lambda jip(\omega_j \mid x)$$

The average risk over region $\Omega i$ is

$$ri = \int_{\Omega i} l^i(x)p(x)\, dx$$

$$= \int_{\Omega i} \sum_{j=1}^{C} \lambda jip(\omega_j \mid x)p(x)dx$$

and the overall expected cost or risk is

$$r = \sum_{r=1}^{c} r^i = \sum_{i=1}^{c} \int_{\Omega i} \sum_{j=1}^{c} \lambda jip(\omega_j \mid x)p(x)dx \qquad (7.20)$$

The above expression for the risk will be minimised if the regions $\Omega i$ are chosen such that if

$$\sum_{j=1}^{c} \lambda jip(\omega_i \mid x)p(x) \leq \sum_{j=1}^{c} \lambda jkp(\omega_j \mid x)p(x)...k = 1,......, C \qquad (7.21)$$

then x∈ Ω Qi. This is the Bayes decision rule for minimum risk, with Bayes risk, $r^*$, given by

$$r^* = \int_x \min i = 11,......, c\sum_{i=1}^{c} \lambda jip(\omega_j \mid x)p(x)dx$$

One special case of the loss matrix A is the equal cost loss matrix for which

$$\lambda ji = \int \frac{1...i \neq j}{0....i = j}$$

Substituting into (1.12) gives the decision rule: assign x to class $\omega$i if

$$\sum_{i=1}^{c} p(\omega_j \mid x)p(x) - p(\omega_i \mid x)p(x) \leq \sum_{j=1}^{c} p(\omega_j \mid x)p(x) - p(\omega_k \mid x)p(x)....k = 1,.........., c$$

That is,

$$p(x \mid \omega_i)p(\omega_i) \geq p(x \mid \omega_k)p(\omega_k)....k = 1,........., C$$

implies that x∈ class $\omega$ i; this is the Bayes rule for minimum error.

### 7.5.5.4 BAYES DECISION RULE FOR MINIMUM RISK – REJECT OPTION

As with the Bayes rule for minimum error, we may also introduce a reject option, by which the reject region, R, is defined by

$$R = \{x \mid \min l^i(x) > t\}$$

where t is a threshold. The decision is to accept a pattern x and assign it to class $\omega$i if

li (x) = min $l^j$(x)≤ t

and to reject x if

$l^i$(x) = min lj(x)>t

This decision is equivalent to defining a reject region Ω 0 with a constant conditional risk

$$l^o(x) = t$$

so that the Bayes decision rule is: assign x to class $\omega$i if

$$l^i(x) \leq l^j(x)....j = 0,1,......., c$$

with Bayes risk

$$r^* = \int_R tp(x)dx + \int_A \min ..i = 1,....,c\sum_{j=1}^{c} \lambda jip(\omega j \mid x)p(x)dx \qquad (7.22)$$

### 7.5.5.5 NEYMAN–PEARSON DECISION RULE

An alternative to the Bayes decision rules for a two-class problem is the Neyman–Pearson test. In a two-class problem there are two possible types of error that may be made in the decision process. We may classify a pattern of class $\omega$1 as belonging to class $\omega$2 or a pattern from class !2 as belonging to class $\omega$1. Let the probability of these two errors be ∈ 1 and ∈ 2 respectively, so that

$$\in_1 = \int_{\Omega 2} p(x \mid \omega_i)dx = \text{error probability of Type I}$$

and

$\in_2 = \int_{\Omega 1} p(x \mid \omega_2)dx$ = error probability of Type II

The Neyman–Pearson decision rule is to minimise the error ∈ 1 subject to ∈ 2 being equal to a constant, ∈ 0, say. If class $\omega$ 1 is termed the positive class and class $\omega$ 2 the negative class, then ž1 is referred to as the false negative rate, the proportion of positive samples incorrectly assigned to the negative class; ∈ 2 is the false positive rate, the proportion of negative samples classed as positive.

An example of the use of the Neyman–Pearson decision rule is in radar detection where the problem is to detect a signal in the presence of noise. There are two types of error that may occur; one is to mistake noise for a signal present. This is called a false alarm. The second type of error occurs when a signal is actually present but the decision is made that only noise is present. This is a missed detection. If $\omega$ 1 denotes the signal class and $\omega$ 2 denotes the noise then ∈ 2 is the probability of false alarm and ∈ 1 is the probability of missed detection. In many radar applications, a threshold is set to give a fixed probability of false alarm and therefore the Neyman–Pearson decision rule is the one usually used. We seek the minimum of

$$r = \int_{\Omega_2} p(x \mid \omega_1)dx + \mu\left\{\int_{\Omega_1} p(x \mid \omega_2)dx - \in 0\right\}$$

where $\mu$ is a Lagrange multiplier[1] and ∈ 0 is the specified false alarm rate. The equation may be written

$$r = (1 - \mu \in 0) + \int_{\Omega 1} \{\mu\, p(x|(\omega 2)\, dx - p(x|(\omega 1)\, dx\}$$

This will be minimised if we choose Ω 1 such that the integrand is negative, i.e

if ' $\mu$ p(x+( $\omega$ 2) — p(x|( $\omega$ 1) < 0, then x∈ Ω 1

or, in terms of the likelihood ratio,

$$\text{if}\ \frac{p(x \mid \omega 1)}{p(x \mid \omega 2)} > \mu, then..x \in \Omega 1 \qquad (7.23)$$

Thus the decision rule depends only on the within-class distributions and ignores the a priori probabilities. The threshold $\mu$ is chosen so that

$$\int_{\Omega 1} p(x \mid \omega 2)dx = \in 0$$

the specified false alarm rate. However, in general 'L cannot be determined analytically and requires numerical calculation. often, the performance of the decision rule is summarised in a receiver operating characteristic (ROC) curve, which plots the true positive against the false positive (that is, the probability of detection (1-∈ 1 = $\int_{\Omega 1}$ p(x|( $\omega$ 1) dx) against the probability of false alarm (∈ 2 = $\int_{\Omega 1}$ p(x|( $\omega$ 2) dx)) as the threshold $\mu$ is varied.

This is illustrated in Figure 7.21 for the univariate case of two normally distributed classes of unit variance and means separated by a distance, d. All the ROC curves pass through the (0, 0) and (1, 1) points and as the separation increases the curve moves into the top left corner. Ideally, we would like 100% detection for a 0% false alarm rate; the closer a curve is to this the better.

For the two-class case, the minimum risk decision equation (7.20) defines the decision rules on the basis of the likelihood ratio ( $\lambda$ ii = 0):

$$\text{If } \frac{p(x \mid \omega 1)}{p(x \mid \omega 2)} > \frac{\lambda_{21} p(\omega 2)}{\lambda_{12} p(\omega 1)}, then, x \in \Omega 1$$

The threshold defined by the right-hand side will correspond to a particular point on the ROC curve that depends on the misclassification costs and the prior probabilities.

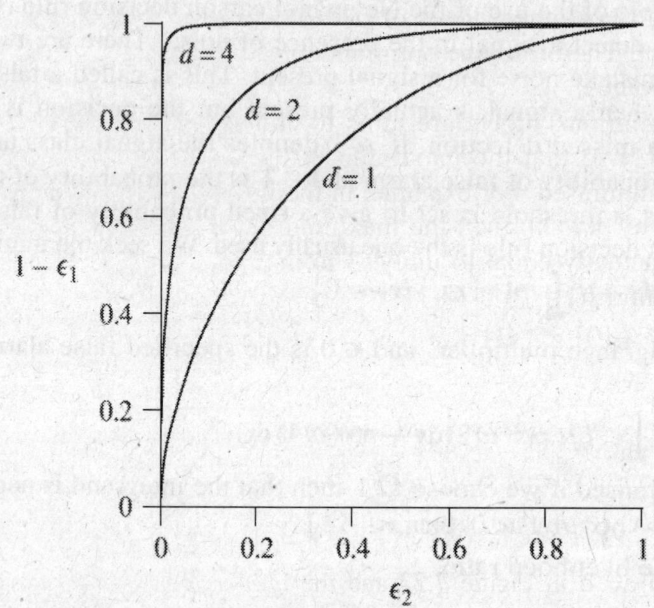


**Figure 7.21 Receiver operating characteristic for two univariate normal distributions of unit variance and separation d; 1-$\in$ 1 = $\int_{\Omega 1}$ p(x | $\omega$ 1) dx is the true positive (the probability of detection) and $\in$ 2= $\int_{\Omega 1}$ p(x | $\omega$ 2) dx is the false positive (the probability of false alarm)**

### 7.5.5.6 MINIMAX CRITERION

The Bayes decision rules rely on a knowledge of both the within-class distributions and the prior class probabilities. However, situations may arise where the relative frequencies of new objects to be classified are unknown. In this situation a minimax procedure may be employed. The name minimax is used to refer to procedures for which either the maximum expected loss or the maximum of the error probability is a minimum. We shall limit our discussion below to the two-class problem and the minimum error probability procedure.

Consider the Bayes rule for minimum error. The decision regions $\Omega$ 1 and $\Omega$ 2 are defined by

$$p(x \mid \omega 1)p(\omega 1) > p(x \mid \omega 2)p(\omega 2) \text{ implies } x \in \Omega 1 \qquad (7.24)$$

and the Bayes minimum error, $e_B$, is

$$e_B = p(\omega 2) \int_{\Omega 1} p(x \mid \omega 2)\, dx + p(\omega 1) \int_{\Omega 2} p(x \mid \omega 1)\, dx \qquad (7.25)$$

where $p(\omega 2) = 1 - p(\omega 1)$.

For fixed decision regions $\Omega 1$ and $\Omega 2$, $e_B$ is a linear function of $p(\omega 1)$ (we denote this function $\Omega$ $e_B$) attaining its maximum on the region [0, 1] either at $p(\omega 1) = 0$ or $p(\omega 1) = 1$. However, since the regions $\Omega 1$ and $\Omega 2$ are also dependent on $p(\omega 1)$ through the Bayes decision criterion (7.23), the dependency of $e_B$ on $p(\omega 1)$ is more complex, and not necessarily monotonic.

If $\Omega 1$ and $\Omega 2$ are fixed (determined according to (7.24) for some specified $p(\omega i)$), the error given by (7.25) will only be the Bayes minimum error for a particular value of p(co1), say $p^{Ł}{}_1$. For other values of $p(\omega 1)$, the error given by (7.25) must be greater than the minimum error. Therefore, the optimum curve touches the line at a tangent at $p^*{}_1$ and is concave down at that point.

The minimax procedure aims to choose the partition $\Omega 1$, $\Omega 2$, or equivalently the value of $p(\omega 1)$ so that the maximum error (on a test set in which the values of $p(\omega i)$ are unknown) is minimised. For example, in the figure, if the partition were chosen to correspond to the value $p^*{}_1$ of $p(\omega 1)$, then the maximum error which could occur would be a value of b if $p(\omega 1)$ were actually equal to unity. The minimax procedure aims to minimise this maximum value, i.e. minimise

$$\max\left\{\tilde{e}_B(0), \tilde{e}_B(1)\right\}$$

or minimize

$$\max\left\{\int_{\Omega 2} p(x \mid \omega 1)dx, \int_{\Omega 1} p(x \mid \omega 2)dx\right\}$$

This is a minimum when

$$\left\{\int_{\Omega 2} p(x \mid \omega 1)dx, \int_{\Omega 1} p(x \mid \omega 2)dx\right\} \qquad (7.26)$$

which is when a= b in Figure 7.22 and the line $\tilde{e}B(p(\omega 1))$ is horizontal and touches the Bayes minimum error curve at its peak value.

Therefore, we choose the regions $\Omega 1$ and $\Omega 2$ so that the probabilities of the two types of error are the same. The minimax solution may be criticised as being over-pessimistic since it is a Bayes solution with respect to the least favorable prior distribution.

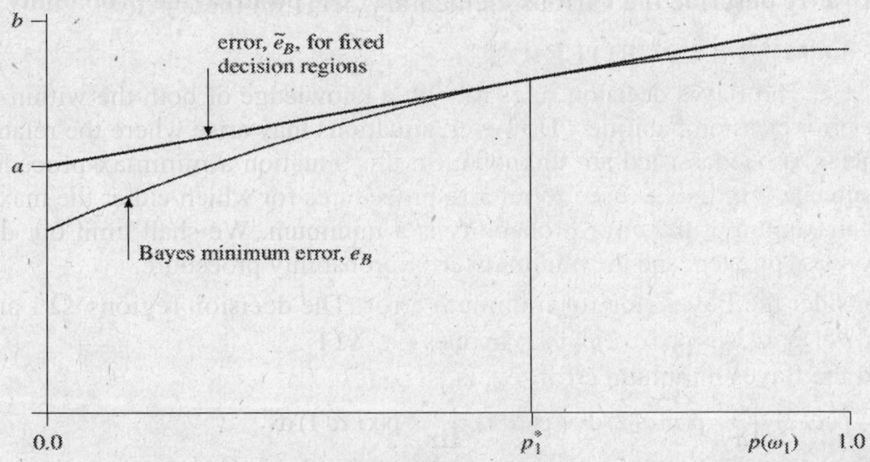


**Figure 7.22 Minimax illustration**

strategy may also be applied to minimising the maximum risk. In this case, the risk is

$$\int_{\Omega 21}[\lambda_{11}p(\omega 1\,|\,x)\lambda_{12}p(\omega 2\,|\,x)]p(x)dx+\int_{\Omega 22}[\lambda_{12}p(\omega 1\,|\,x)\lambda_{22}p(\omega 2\,|\,x)]p(x)dx$$

$$=p(\omega 1)\left[\lambda_{11}+(\lambda_{12}-\lambda_{11})\int_{\Omega 22}p(x\,|\,\omega 1)dx\right]+p(\omega 2)\left[\lambda_{22}+(\lambda_{22}-\lambda_{21})\int_{\Omega 21}p(x\,|\,\omega 2)dx\right]$$

and the boundary must therefore satisfy,

$$\lambda_{11}-\lambda_{22}+(\lambda_{12}-\lambda_{11})\int_{\Omega 22}p(x\,|\,\omega 1)dx-(\lambda_{21}-\lambda_{22})\int_{\Omega 21}p(x\,|\,\omega 2)dx=0$$

For $\lambda_{11}=\lambda_{22}$ and $\lambda_{21}=\lambda_{12}$, this reduces to condition (7.26).

# QUESTION BANK

Q1. What is the Digital image data compression? Explain with the help of example.
Q2. What are the different classes of compression techniques?
Q3. Describe the various typical image coders? Explain with the help of example.
Q4. Explain the discrete image transforms in image data compression?
Q5. Discuss the various predictive compression methods?
Q6. Explain the hierarchical and progressive compression techniques?
Q7. Write short note on the comparison of compression methods
Q8. Briefly describe the various wavelets and image compression? Explain with the help of example.
Q9. Explain the various advanced wavelet coding schemes? Explain with the help of example.
Q10. Briefly describe the various statistical pattern recognition? Explain with the help of example.
Q11. Explain the various stages in the pattern recognition problem.
Q12. Difference between supervised versus unsupervised?
Q13. Explain the approaches to statistical pattern recognition?
Q14. Briefly describe the various elementary decision theory?

# CHAPTER 8

# HARDWARE ARCHITECTURE FOR IMAGE PROCESSING

## 8.1 INTRODUCTION

Hardware architecture refers to the identification of a system's physical components and their interrelationships. This description, often called a hardware design model, allows hardware designers to understand how their components fit into system architecture and provides software component designers important information needed for software development and integration. Clear definition of a hardware architecture allows the various traditional engineering disciplines (e.g., electrical and mechanical engineering) to work more effectively together to develop and manufacture new machines, devices and components.

Hardware is also an expression used within the computer engineering industry to explicitly distinguish the (electronic computer) hardware from the software which runs in it. But hardware, within the automation and software engineering disciplines, need not simply be a computer of some sort. A modern automobile runs vastly more software than the Apollo spacecraft. Also, modern aircraft cannot function without running tens of millions of computer instructions embedded and distributed throughout the aircraft and resident in both standard computer hardware and in specialized hardward components such as IC wired logic gates, analog and hybrid devices, and other digital components. The need to effectively model how separate physical components combine to form complex systems is important over a wide range of applications, including computers, personal digital assistants (PDAs), cell phones, surgical instrumentation, satellites, and submarines.

Hardware architecture is therefore the representation of an engineered (or to be engineered) electronic or electromechanical hardware system, and the process and discipline for effectively implementing the design(s) for such a system. It is generally part of a larger integrated system encompassing information, software, and device prototyping.

It is a representation because it is used to convey information about the related elements comprising a hardware system, the relationships among those elements, and the rules governing those relationships.

It is a process because a sequence of steps is prescribed to produce or change the architecture, and/or a design from that architecture, of a hardware system within a set of constraints.

It is a discipline because a body of knowledge is used to inform practitioners as to the most effective way to design the system within a set of constraints.

A hardware architecture is primarily concerned with the internal electrical (and, more rarely, the mechanical) interfaces among the system's components or subsystems, and the interface between the system and its external environment, especially the devices operated by or the electronic displays viewed by a user. (This latter, special interface is known as the computer human interface, AKA human computer interface, or HCI; formerly called the man-machine interface.) Integrated circuit (IC) designers are driving current technologies into innovative approaches for new products. Hence, multiple layers of active devices are being proposed as single chip, opening up opportunities for disruptive microelectronic, optoelectronic, and new microelectromechanical.

A programmable hardware artifact, or machine, that lacks its software program is impotent; even as a software artifact, or program, is equally impotent unless it can be used to alter the sequential states of a suitable (hardware) machine. However, a hardware machine and its software program can be designed to perform an almost illimitable number of abstract and physical tasks. Within the computer and software engineering disciplines (and, often, other engineering disciplines, such as communications), then, the terms hardware, software, and system came to be used to distinguish among the hardware which could run a software program, the software program itself, and the hardware device complete with its program, respectively.

The hardware engineer or architect deals (more or less) exclusively with the hardware device; the software engineer or architect deals (more or less) exclusively with the software program; and the systems engineer or systems architect is responsible for seeing that the software program is capable of properly running within the hardware device, and that the system composed of the two entities is capable of properly interacting with its external environment, especially the user, and performing its intended function.

Hardware architecture, then, is an abstract representation of an electronic and/or an electromechanical device which is capable of running a fixed or changeable program.

Hardware architecture generally includes some form of analog, digital, or hybrid electronic computer, along with electronic and mechanical sensors and actuators. Hardware architecting may be viewed as a 'partitioning scheme,' or algorithm, which considers all of the system's present and foreseeable requirements and arranges the necessary hardware components into a workable set of cleanly bounded subsystems with no more parts than are required. That is, it is a partitioning scheme which is exclusive, inclusive, and exhaustive. A major purpose of the partitioning is to arrange the elements in the hardware subsystems so that there is a minimum of electrical connections and electronic communications needed among them. In both software and hardware, a good subsystem tends to be seen as a meaningful "object." Moreover, a clear allocation of user requirements to the architecture (hardware and software) provides an effective basis for validation tests of the user's requirements in the as-built system.

## 8.2 DISTRIBUTED PROCESSING OF IMAGE DATA

Distribution of applications and business logic across multiple processing platforms. Distributed processing implies that processing will occur on more than one processor in order for a transaction to be completed. In other words, processing is distributed across two or more machines and the processes are most likely not running at the same time, i.e. each process performs part of an application in a sequence. Often the data used in a distributed processing environment is also distributed across Platforms. Digital images, several prior art systems for image processing and storage have burgeoned. The prior art image processing and storage systems have become very popular because they allow photographers to make their images available for viewing to a large number of potential customers that may be located in random locations around the globe. The prior art systems include host sites that offer digital images for viewing by potential customers who may wish to purchase the digital images.

Hundreds of digital images are typically captured at events, such as weddings, by photographers, and the potential customers may have attended the event. The host sites are in communication with image laboratories and customer computers via a communication system, such as the Internet; and, photographer computers are in communication with the image laboratories. In this manner, photographers may send film, if the images were captured on traditional film, or a CD, which includes the digital images, to the image laboratory. If the photographer sent film to the image laboratory, the laboratory would convert the pictures taken on film to digital images. The image laboratory then sends the images to the host site for uploading. In other prior art a system, the photographer computers are in communication with the host site, and the photographers send the digital images to the host site by using the File Transfer Protocol (FTP). The photographers must manually send digital images to the host site, which is a lengthy and cumbersome process that can take as much as thirty hours to complete. The prior art systems impose an undue burden on photographers to upload images because the prior art systems either require photographers to physically ship the captured images to a laboratory for uploading or require photographers to spend a great deal of time to manually FTP digital images to the host site.

After the photographer ships the hundreds of images to the image laboratory, the image laboratory stores the hundreds of digital images, in high resolution format, and uploads the hundreds of digital images, in high resolution format, to the host site. The photographer may then access the host site and select a small subset of the uploaded images that the photographer believes potential customers may select for purchasing. At the host site, the selected images are converted from a high resolution format to a low resolution and/or a thumbnail format and are converted into a JPEG format.

The photographer may also crop or rotate the selected images as desired. The small subsets of selected and converted images are then made available to customers for viewing. Of the small subset of images, customers choose an even smaller subset for purchasing. The chosen smaller subsets of images are then retransmitted, in high resolution format, from the host site back to the image laboratory for printing.

By requiring the image laboratory to store the hundreds of images in a high resolution format, the image laboratory is required to have large storage resources; and, by requiring the image laboratory to send the hundreds of images to the host site, the image laboratory is required to have large bandwidth resources. Further, the host site must also have large storage and bandwidth resources to receive and store the hundreds of high resolution images that are transmitted to the host site from the image laboratory. Moreover, by requiring the images to be converted into low resolution and/or thumbnail formats and into JPEG format at the host site, the host site must have tremendous processing resources to accommodate the conversion of thousands of images that are being transmitted to the host site from several image laboratories. While the image laboratory and the host site must invest in a large amount of storage, bandwidth and processing resources to accommodate uploading and processing of the hundreds of high resolution images, the storage, bandwidth and processing resources of the user computer are being unutilized.

When the processed images are stored at the host site, the images are stored at a remote image file and image related data that describe the images are stored at a host database. Pointers, which indicate where the images are stored, must also be stored at the host database. When a customer wishes to view an image, it sends an image request to the host site. The host site retrieves image related data, which pertains to the requested images, from the host database; and, in a second step, retrieves the requested images from the remote image file. The host site uses the pointers stored in the host database to determine the location of the requested images in the remote image file. To ensure that the pointers indicate the location of the correct image, the integrity of the pointers must constantly be maintained by the host site.

The steps of retrieving pointers from the host database and of retrieving the images from the remote file location are burdensome and, oftentimes, result in incorrect pointers—preventing a database user from viewing the image. Because the prior art systems require such steps, processing power of the host site is wasted and the period of time required for viewers, such as customers and users, to view the images is prolonged.

In sum, although the prior art image processing and storage systems facilitate image viewing, the prior art image processing and storage systems have several inefficiencies. The inefficiencies of prior art systems result in an extra burden for photographers while uploading or sending their images to the host site, a wastage of storage resources at both the image laboratory and the host site, a wastage of processing resources at the host site, an extended delay in the time that images are uploaded onto the host site, and an extended delay in the amount of time it takes viewers to view the images.

As a result, a need remains for an image processing and storage method and system that does not create an extra burden for photographers, a wastage of storage resources, a wastage of processing resources, an extended delay for image uploading, and an extended delay in the amount of time it takes viewers to view images.

### 8.2.1 DISTRIBUTED PROCESSING OF VIDEO DATA

Video processing and analysis systems pose high demands on the computation platform in terms of processing speed, memory bandwidth, and storage capacity. Requirements grow even further if real-time processing speed is needed for analysis and visualization applications. On current commodity hardware, this processing power is not available. For example, simultaneous capturing of two 640 × 480@25fps videos from IEEE-1394 cameras already fills the full bus bandwidth. The straightforward solution for this problem is to use computation clusters instead of expensive specialized hardware. However, the design of distributed systems is a troublesome task, prone to design flaws.

Most previous approaches to parallel computation have concentrated on fine- granular data-parallelism. In this approach, the algorithms themselves are parallelized, which requires a reimplementation of the algorithms. This is difficult, especially because computer-vision engineers are rarely experts in distributed processing. Since complex systems are composed of many processing steps, parallelization can also be carried out by keeping the (sequential) algorithms as atomic processing steps.

This has two advantages:

1. Algorithms are easier to implement
2. Algorithm development stays independent of the parallelization.

It is still possible to use the distributed-processing framework to also parallelize the algorithms itself by splitting the task into smaller sub-tasks that can be computed independently. A generic framework for distributed real-time processing, into which existing software components (algorithms) can be integrated effortlessly. Algorithm parallelization is achieved by splitting the processing into a set of processing tiles (PT). Each processing tile performs a specific operation on a set of inputs and generates one or several outputs. The inputs and outputs of the PTs can be connected to build arbitrary processing graphs, describing the order and dependencies of processing. The framework software takes care about the appropriate distribution of the algorithms over the processing resources and the control of execution.

#### 8.2.1.1 THE PROPOSED FRAMEWORK PROVIDES THE FOLLOWING FEATURES.

The processing graph is not limited to a certain topology (like processing pipelines). In particular, PT outputs can be efficiently connected to the inputs of several PTs.

**(i) Automatic parallelization:-** While the processing within one PT is considered an atomic operation, parallelism is obtained by running PTs in parallel. The framework also allows to process data from different time instances in parallel, such that not only horizontal parallelism (concurrency of independent tasks), but also vertical parallelism (pipelining) is exploited. The framework is network transparent. The processing graph can be distributed over a cluster of computers and still be accessed in a uniform way. If data has to be sent across the network, this is done transparently by the framework. The framework supports operations on arbitrary data-types. Hence, not only image data can be processed, but also structured data-types like mesh-based geometry. An important alternative view onto this is that data can be processed in different representations. For example, low-level processing tasks (lens-distortion correction, image-rectification, depth estimation) can be implemented more efficiently on the graphics processor (GPU). In this case, the image data is loaded into the texture memory of the graphics card. Since the overhead of transferring the image data between main memory and the graphics card would annihilate the performance gain of processing on the GPU, it should be avoided whenever possible. This is achieved by passing only handles to the texture data between PTs and doing the conversion to image data in main memory only when necessary.

### 8.2.2 DESIGN OF THE DISTRIBUTED PROCESSING

#### 8.2.2.1 DESIGN CONSIDERATIONS

The design of our Distributed Processing(DP) was driven by the following requirements.

**(i) Fine-grained vs. coarse-grained parallelization**:- Previous work on parallel algorithms has mostly considered parallelization using a fine-granular data- parallelism within a single algorithm. The difficulty with this approach is that it complicates the implementation of the algorithm, because it requires knowledge of the image-processing algorithms as well as knowledge about parallel and distributed programming. On the other hand, large applications consist of a multitude of processing steps. This allows to apply parallel processing on a coarser level, at which every algorithm is (conceptually) implemented in a sequential program.

Since we are targeting complex video-processing systems comprising several algorithms, we have chosen the coarse-grained parallelization because it simplifies the implementation of each algorithm. Furthermore, the coarse-grained parallelization has a lower communication overhead, which is usually one of the most restricting bottlenecks.

**(ii) SMP and cluster parallelization:-** Currently, multi-core processors begin to replace single-core processors because they allow to increase the computation speed more economically than by increasing the processor frequency. While current processors have two or four cores, the number of cores is expected to increase further in the future. But even with multi-core processors, the processing speed is limited because of the limited memory-bandwidth, limited I/O bandwidth, or simply because the computation speed of these processors is still not sufficient for the application. To overcome these limitations, processing in a cluster of computers is a viable approach .

For these reasons, the DP should enable parallel processing in both ways, by exploiting multiple processing cores within one shared-memory system (SMP), and by distributing the work over a cluster of computers.

**(iii) Automatic parallelization vs. manual splitting of tasks:-** In designing a system using our DP, it must be decided which processing tiles should be processed on which computer. The optimal design of the processing network can be determined automatically, but we still prefer to specify the assignment of the processing tiles to the computers by hand for the following reasons. First, the number of processing tiles is rather limited for most systems, and the placement of some of these tiles is dictated by the hardware (the camera capturing must take place at the computer to which the cameras are connected). Second, for an automatic optimal distribution of the tasks, exact knowledge about the processing times, the required bandwidths, or the available computation resources is required. These are often difficult to specify formally, particularly in a heterogeneous architecture with special-purpose processors.

**(iv) Flexibility:-** Our intention in designing the DP was to provide a general framework for a wide area of applications. Hence, the design should not impose a specific processing architecture, like a fixed processing pipeline, which might be unsuitable for many applications. Furthermore, the framework should strengthen the reuse of processing tiles for different applications. This is supported by allowing processing tiles to have a flexible number of inputs and outputs, which do not have to be connected all. Unconnected outputs can indicate to the processing tile to disable part of its processing, and optional inputs can be used for optional hints that may help the algorithm.

**(v) Special-purpose processor utilization:-** Many low-level image-processing tasks are well suited for parallel processing, but this parallelism cannot be achieved with standard general-purpose processors. Even though these processors nowadays have support for SIMD instructions, especially designed for multimedia applications, (like MMX on x86, or Altivec on PowerPC architectures), the degree of parallelism is limited and restricted to simple processing. Additional to the CPU, specific media-processors do exist which offer higher parallelization factors than regular CPUs. When utilizing special-purpose processors with independent memory (like the GPU on graphics cards), it should be considered that the image data to be processed has to be stored in its local memory. The time to transfer the image between different memories is not negligible, and can even exceed the actual computation time. For this reason, it is important to avoid unnecessary memory transfers wherever possible. This has to be considered in the design of the DPF by providing several options how the image data is transferred between successive processing tiles.

#### 8.2.2.2 CORE OF DISTRIBUTED PROCESSING

The core of our distributed processing (DP) is a set of user-definable processing tiles (PT). A processing tile conducts an operation on its input data and generates new output. The number of inputs and outputs is flexible. In order to define the data-flow through the PTs, they can be connected to form a processing graph of an arbitrary topology (without cycles).

A Processing Graph Control (PGC) distributes the tasks to carry out in the graph of PTs over a set of worker threads, hereby exploiting multi-processor parallelism in an SMP system.

The scheduling is determined by splitting the processing into a set of "(PT, sequence-number)" pairs. Each of these pairs represents a processing task that can be issued to a thread. The scheduler maintains the set of tasks in three queues: the tasks that are currently processed, tasks that are ready to run (all input dependencies are met), and tasks that cannot be started yet because of unmet dependencies. These queues are updated whenever a PT has finished its computation.

For specifying processing graphs that are distributed over several computers in a cluster, the PGC can be wrapped into a Distributed Processing Graph (DPG). The DPG provides a uniform access to all PTs even though they might be distributed over different computers. Whenever data is to be transferred between computers, a network connection is established transparently to the user. From a user point-of-view, a DPG looks like a local processing graph, because most of the network distribution is hidden from the user. It should be emphasized here that the DPF is organized in three separate layers that represent subsets of the features made available by the DPF. The idea is to provide simpler APIs to the programmer when the full-featured framework is not required. The typical usage of these three layers is briefly explained below.

A system building upon the first layer includes only the PT objects, which are connected to a graph. There is no central scheduler organizing the data processing. Data can be processed directly by pushing new data into some PT input. This will trigger the processing of this tile and also the successive tiles, where additional input is requested as required. On the other hand, the graph of PTs can also be used in a pull mode, where new output data is requested at some PT, which again triggers the processing of the tile. If there is missing input, the PT first acquires the required inputs from the preceding tiles.

The second layer adds a scheduler (PGC) to the graph of connected tiles. This scheduler manages multiple worker threads to carry out the computations in parallel.

The third layer adds a network-transparent distribution of the processing graph (DPG) over a cluster of computers. To this end, a server application is run on every computer in the network, and the servers are registered at a central control computer. PTs can be instantiated at any arbitrary computer through a uniform API at the control computer. Connecting two PTs across the network is possible and handled transparently to the user.

### 8.2.3 IMPLEMENTATION DETAILS

#### 8.2.3.1 PROCESSING TILES

All algorithms are wrapped into Processing Tile (PT) objects. Each PT can accept a number of inputs and can also create several outputs. For the DP, a PT appears like an atomic operation (however, the algorithm in the PT may itself be implemented as a parallel algorithm, independent to the parallelization performed in the DP). Each PT provides the memory for storing the computed results, but it does not include buffers for holding its own input data. The input data is accessed directly from the output buffers of the connected tiles. This prevents that data is unnecessarily copied between PTs, which could constitute a considerable part of the computation time.

On the other hand, this blocks the PT that provides the input from already starting the work on the next Data- Unit. If this is a problem, an additional buffering PT can be inserted in-between the two PTs to decouple the data-dependency between these two PTs. Every output can be connected to several inputs, without any extra cost.

Moreover, inputs and outputs can also be left unconnected. While the algorithm within the PT might simply proceed as usual even when there are unconnected outputs, it can be more efficient by disabling generating the data for this output. This feature can be used, for example, to create outputs that provide a visualization of the algorithm. When the visualization is not required, the output can be left unconnected. Connecting only some of the inputs can be used, for example, for operations that work with a varying number of inputs (like composition of images, depth estimation from multiple cameras), or to support additional hints for the algorithm (segmentation masks that can help to increase the quality of the result, but which are not required). Each PT also saves a sequence-number, indicating which frame was processed in the last step, now being available at the outputs. Using this sequence-number, a PT can check if all its inputs are available such that it can start processing.

#### 8.2.3.2 DATA-UNITS

Data that should be passed between PTs is encapsulated in Data-Unit objects. Each Data-Unit provides a uniform interface for communicating with the DPF, but it can nevertheless hold arbitrary types of data. The Data-Unit must provide a function to serialize the data and to reconstruct the Data-Unit again from the serialized data. This is used by the DPF in order to send data across the network, transparently for the user.

#### 8.2.3.3 USING A GRAPH OF PTS WITHOUT PROCESSING GRAPH CONTROL

It is possible to use a graph of connected PTs without any further central control. For simple pipelined processing, this comes close to the Decorator design-pattern used in software engineering. However, processing in our graph of PTs is more flexible than a straight processing pipeline. We do not only allow arbitrary (acyclic) graphs of PTs, but also allow a push-data semantic as well as a pull-data semantic. Using a graph of PTs without a central Processing Graph Control (see next section) is simple to use, but note that parallel processing is not available. Processing of a new unit of data is triggered at an arbitrary PT in the graph. If new input is fed into the graph, then triggering happens at the moment when the new data is passed into one PT. Whenever a PT is triggered, it checks if the data at its inputs are already available. This is visible from the sequence- numbers in the predecessor PTs. If some input is missing, this predecessor PT is triggered. When all input is available, the tile performs its operation and triggers all output PTs if they are not yet at the same sequence-number (this can happen if triggering one output PT has propagated to another output).

#### 8.2.3.4 PROCESSING GRAPH CONTROL

The Processing Graph Contol (PGC) comprises a scheduler that distributes the processing tasks in a graph of PTs over several processors running in parallel. To this end, a pool-of-tasks scheme is applied. The PGC maintains a set of PTs that are ready to process the next Data-Unit. A PT is ready if all the input data is available at the connected inputs, if the PT is not internally blocked, and if the outputs of the PT are not required by any other PT anymore. The PGC maintains three sets of "(PT, sequence-number)" pairs to schedule the tasks to the threads. The to-be-processed set is initially filled with all tasks for the first sequence-number. Whenever the first task with the latest sequence-number has started, all tasks for the next sequence-number are added to this set.

After a PT has finished its processing, the successor and predecessor PTs are examined if they are now ready to be processed. If they are, the corresponding task is moved from the to-be-processed set into the ready-to-run set. Whenever a working thread has finished a task, it gets a new task from the ready-to-run set, moves this task into the in-progress set and starts processing. In order to efficiently test if a task can be processed, an active-edges set is maintained. An active edge is an edge in the PT graph, connecting an already- processed output of a tile PTo with a not-yet processed tile PTi. This active edge represents a data-dependency which prevents that PTo can process another unit before PTi has finished using this output data.

An example of this scheduling algorithm is presented in Figure 8.1. In this figure, PTs that are ready-to-run are indicated with a black bar at the left (input) side. PTs that are currently being processed are depicted in grey color. When they have their output data available, this is indicated with a black bar at the right (output) side. Active edges between PTs are shown with bold lines. The number in the PT denotes the current sequence-number of the outputs. In this example, we have assumed that processing takes equal time-periods for every tile.

### 8.2.3.5 NETWORK TRANSFER

In order to connect two processing graphs on two different computers, the data processed on one computer must be sent to the input at the second computer. This is realized with a network-sender PT and a network-receiver PT. The network-sender PT uses the Serialize method of the Data-Unit interface to generate a bit-stream representation of the data. This bit-stream is then stored in a FIFO buffer from which it is sent over the network. The sending is carried out in a separate thread which is managed by the PT itself instead of a global scheduler. This has the two fold advantages that (1) streaming can run with maximum throughput because the thread is always active, and (2) the network- connection PTs can also be used without any PGC. Since the sending thread is almost always blocked in the system-function for network transmission, its computation time is negligible.

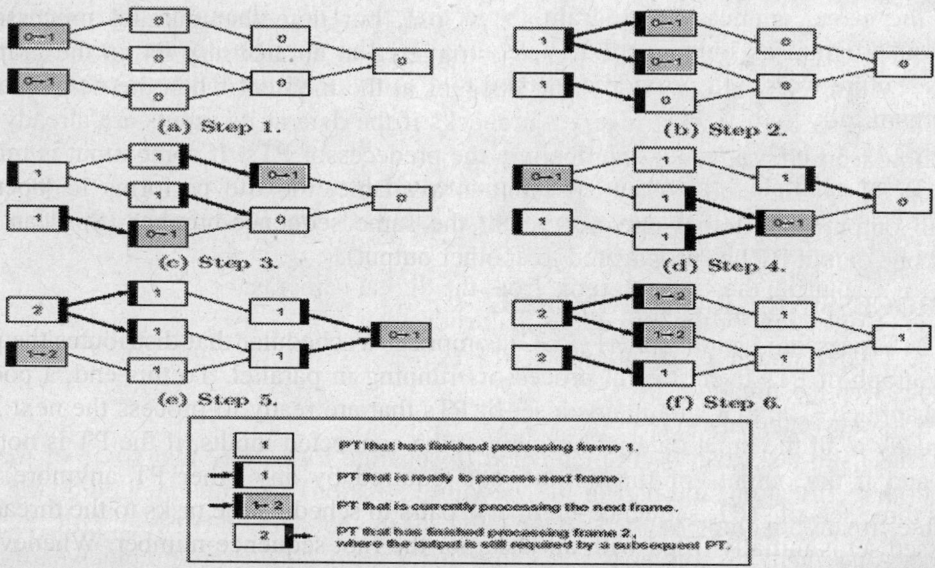


**Figure 8.1. Example processing graph running on two cpus. It is assumed here that processing of each tile takes the same time**

The network-receiver PT at the other side works similarly to the network- sender. A separate thread is responsible for receiving new data bit-streams from the network. Whenever the PT is triggered, one data packet is removed from the FIFO and used to reconstruct a Data-Unit.

#### 8.2.3.6 DISTRIBUTED PROCESSING GRAPH

A Distributed Processing Graph (DPG) wraps a PGC into a network interface. When DPGs are created on different computers, they can be joined together with a control connection. From that moment onwards, both graphs in the DPGs appear as a joint graph and can also be controlled in a unified way, even though the PTs might be on different computers. New tiles can be created on any computer via the DPG interface by specifying the name of the PT and the system on which it should be instantiated. Universally Unique Identifiers (UUIDs) are used to access the PTs in the network.

In the general case, many computers with DPG daemons running on them can be connected into a control tree. Each DPG stores which PTs can be reached via each of its neighboring computers. Control commands for a non-local PT are forwarded to the closest neighbor DPG, which then further handles the request.

The DPG interface can also be used to connect pairs of PTs. If both PTs are on the same computer, a simple direct connection is established like before. If the PTs are on different computers, special PTs are added that serialize the data into a network stream on one computer, and then reconstruct the Data- Unit on the receiving computer. These network- transmission PTs are connected to the pair of PTs that originally should be connected. This process is transparent to the user of the DPF. Note that the data-transfer connections are independent from the control connections between DPGs. Hence, while the control connections always have a tree topology, data is transferred directly between the involved pair of computers.

In order to run our distributed processing framework on a cluster of computers, a DPG is started as a daemon process on each computer. One computer acts as the control computer, running the actual application program. Note that the DPG daemons are independent of the application program as long as all PTs required by the application are compiled in the DPG daemons. Future work will provide a method to also transmit the PT code over the network and link it dynamically to the DPG.

### 8.2.4 APPLICATION

As an example application, we implemented a multi-camera view-interpolation system which allows to synthesize images along a set of cameras. For the view-interpolation system, the following tasks have to be carried out.

1. Capturing the video streams from the digital cameras.
2. Correction for the radial lens distortion.
3. Stereo image rectification.
4. Depth estimation.
5. View interpolation.

These sub-tasks can be implemented in separate PTs. Note that some of the tasks (lens undistortion, rectification, and part of the view interpolation) are implemented on the GPU, while the depth estimation is implemented on the CPU. At the connection between GPU processing and CPU processing, there are conversion PTs to transfer the data between graphics-card memory and main memory. Because the depth-estimation process is computationally expensive, it is attractive to parallelize this algorithm itself. Even though parallelization within one PT is not supported directly by our framework, it can be easily achieved by splitting the PT into separate PTs which compute a partial solution each. The results are then combined into a final solution in a multiplexer PT.

## 8.3 ROLE OF ARRAY PROCESSING

Array is a temporary grouping of SAS variables that are arranged in a particular order and identified by an array-name. The array exists only for the duration of the current DATA step. The array-name distinguishes it from any other arrays in the same DATA step; it is not a variable. Note: Arrays in SAS are different from those in many other programming languages. In SAS, an array is not a data structure but is just a convenient way of temporarily identifying a group of variables.

Array processing is a method that enables you to perform the same tasks for a series of related variables. Array reference is a method to reference the elements of an array. One-dimensional array is a simple grouping of variables that, when processed, results in output that can be represented in simple row format. Multidimensional array is a more complex grouping of variables that, when processed, results in output that could have two or more dimensions, such as columns and rows.

## BASIC ARRAY PROCESSING INVOLVES THE FOLLOWING STEPS:

1. Grouping variables into arrays
2. Selecting a current variable for an action
3. Repeating an action

### 8.3.1 ONE-DIMENSIONAL ARRAY

The following figure is a conceptual representation of two one-dimensional arrays, MISC and MDAY.

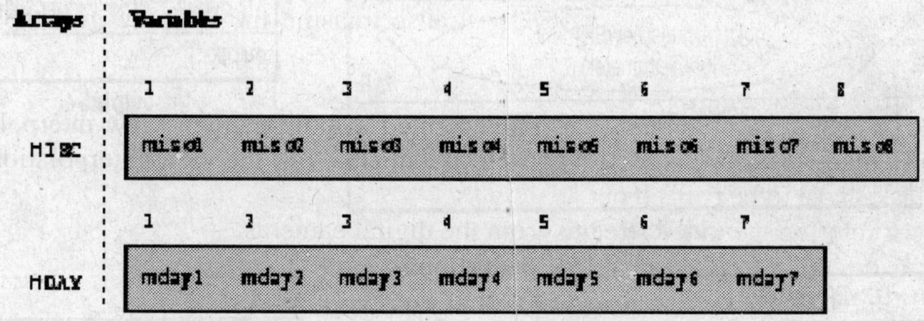

**Figure 8.2 One-Dimensional Array**

MISC contains eight elements, the variables MISC1 through MISC8. To reference the data in these variables, use the form MISC{n}, where n is the element number in the array. For example, MISC is the sixth element in the array. MDAY contains seven elements, the variables MDAY1 through MDAY7. MDAY is the third element in the array.

### 8.3.2 TWO-DIMENSIONAL ARRAY

The following figure is a conceptual representation of the two-dimensional array EXPENSES.

| First Dimension | | Second Dimension | | | | | | | |
|---|---|---|---|---|---|---|---|---|---|
| Expense Categories | | Days of the Week | | | | | | | Total |
| | | 1 | 2 | 3 | 4 | 5 | 6 | 7 | 8 |
| Hotel | 1 | hotel1 | hotel2 | hotel3 | hotel4 | hotel5 | hotel6 | hotel7 | hotel8 |
| Phone | 2 | phone1 | phone2 | phone3 | phone4 | phone5 | phone6 | phone7 | phone8 |
| Pers. Auto | 3 | peraut1 | peraut2 | peraut3 | peraut4 | peraut5 | peraut6 | peraut7 | peraut8 |
| Rental Car | 4 | carrnt1 | carrnt2 | carrnt3 | carrnt4 | carrnt5 | carrnt6 | carrnt7 | carrnt8 |
| Airfare | 5 | airlin1 | airlin2 | airlin3 | airlin4 | airlin5 | airlin6 | airlin7 | airlin8 |
| Dues | 6 | dues1 | dues2 | dues3 | dues4 | dues5 | dues6 | dues7 | dues8 |
| Registration Fees | 7 | regfee1 | regfee2 | regfee3 | regfee4 | regfee5 | regfee6 | regfee7 | regfee8 |
| Other | 8 | other1 | other2 | other3 | other4 | other5 | other6 | other7 | other8 |
| Tips (non-meal) | 9 | tips1 | tips2 | tips3 | tips4 | tips5 | tips6 | tips7 | tips8 |
| Meals | 10 | meals1 | meals2 | meals3 | meals4 | meals5 | meals6 | meals7 | meals8 |

**Figure 8.3 Example of a Two-Dimensional Array**

The EXPENSES array contains ten groups of eight variables each. The ten groups (expense categories) comprise the first dimension of the array, and the eight variables (days of the week) comprise the second dimension. To reference the data in the array variables, use the form EXPENSES{m,n}, where m is the element number in the first dimension of the array, and n is the element number in the second dimension of the array. EXPENSES{6,4} references the value of dues for the fourth day (the variable is DUES4).

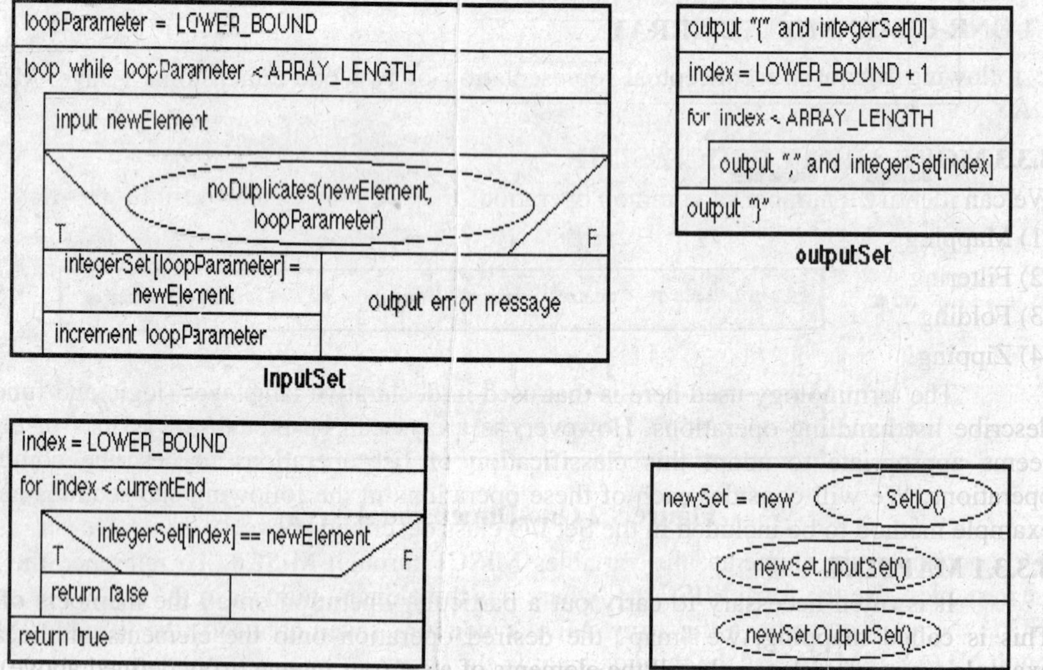


**Figure 8.4 Input Sets and Output Sets**

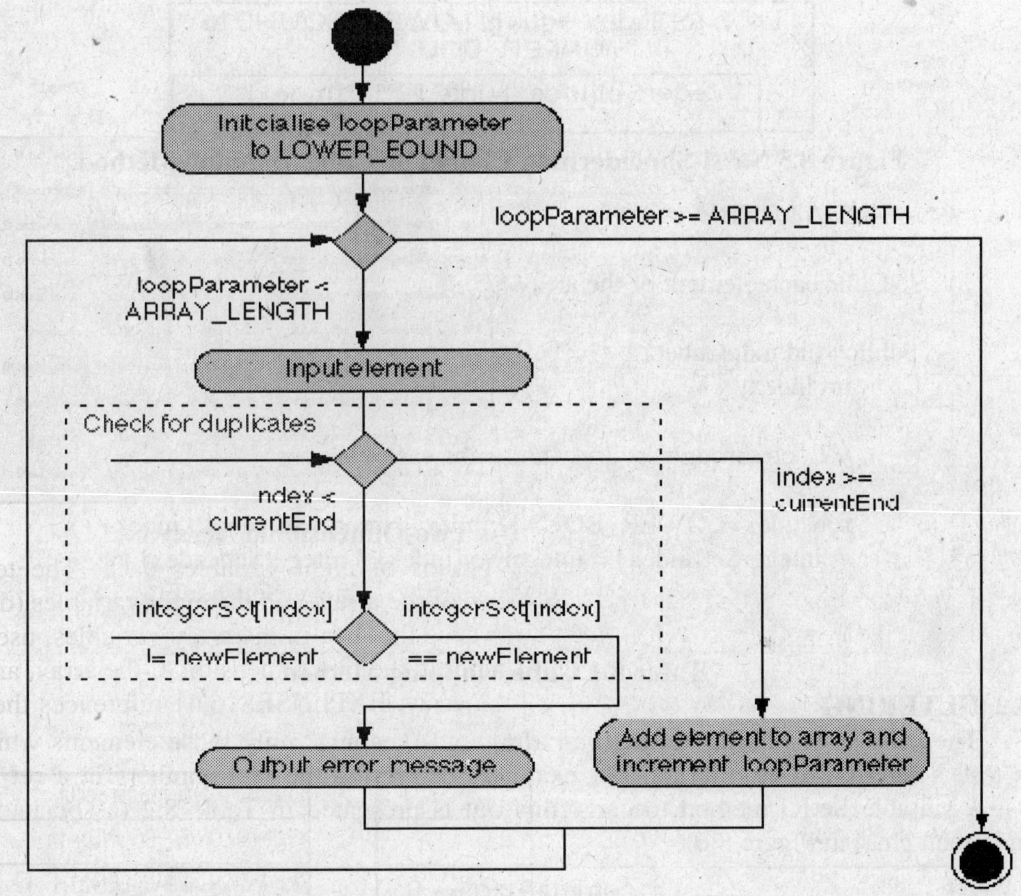


## 8.3.3 MORE ARRAY PROCESSING

We can identify a number of common operations that we may wish to perform on arrays:

(1) Mapping

(2) Filtering

(3) Folding

(4) Zipping

The terminology used here is that used in declarative languages (logic and functional) to describe list handling operations. However, as arrays can be thought of as lists of elements, it seems appropriate to adopt this classification of list operations to describe common array operations. We will consider each of these operations in the following sub-sections and give an example method to be included in the Set I/O class described above.

### 8.3.3.1 MAPPING

It is often necessary to carry out a particular operation on all the members of an array. This is called mapping, we "map" the desired operation onto the elements of the array. For example we may wish to cube all the elements of a set (our integer array defined above) as shown in the Nassi-Shneiderman chart given in Figure 8.5 and the method in Table 8.1.

Loop for index equals LOWER_BOUND to UPPER_BOUND

integerSet[index]=integerSet[index]^3

**Figure 8.5 Nassi-Shneiderman Chart For Cube Mapping Method**

```
/* ------ MAP CUBE ------ */

   /* Cube each element of the array */

   public void mapCube() {
         int index;

         // Loop through set array and cube each element

         for(index=LOWER_BOUND;index < integerSet.length;index++)
            integerSet[index] = integerSet[index] * integerSet[index] *
                                                    integerSet[index];
         }
```

**Table 8.1 Cube Mapping Method**

### 8.3.3.2 FILTERING

The process of running through an array and "keeping" only those elements which pass some test is referred to as filtering. For example identifying the odd numbers in a set (integer array). A suitable SetIO method to carry this out is presented in Table 8.2 (associated Nassi-Shneiderman chart in Figure 8.6).

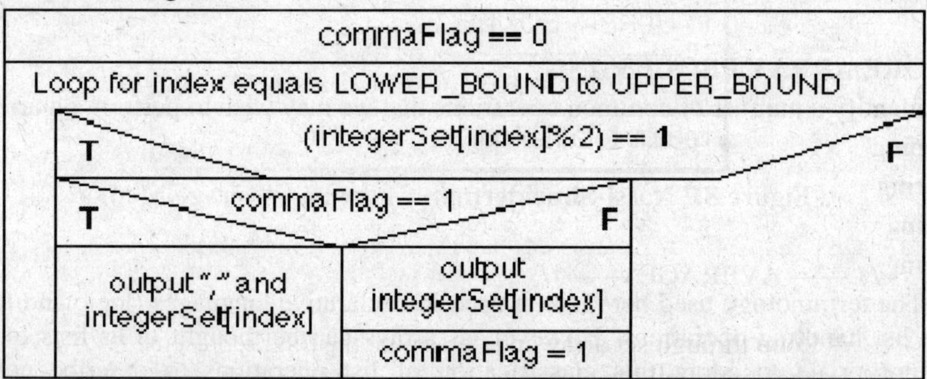


**Figure 8.6 Nassi-Shneiderman Chart For Odd Number Filter Method**

```
/* ------ ODD NUMBER FILTER ------ */
/* Loop through set array and output only those elements that represent
   an odd number */
     public void oddNumberFilter() {
         int index, commaFlag=0;
         // Loop through set array and cube each element
```

```
        System.out.print("Odd numbers = {");
        for(index=LOWER_BOUND;index                                    <
integerSet.length;index++) {
            if (integerSet[index]%2 == 1) {
                if (commaFlag == 1) System.out.print("," +
                                                integerSet[index]);
                else {
                    System.out.print(integerSet[index]);
                    commaFlag=1;
                    }
                }
            }
        // End
        System.out.println("}");
        }
```

**Table 8.2 Odd Number Filter Method**

### 8.3.3.3 FOLDING

The process of putting an operator between each pair of elements in an array to produce a single data item is called folding. For example adding up all the elements of a numeric array (set) for the purpose of finding (say) an average value or a total value. An example average method and associated Nassi-Shneiderman chart are presented in Table 8.3 and Figure 8.7,

| total = 0 |
|---|
| loop for index equals LOWER BOUND to UPPER_BOUND |
|     total = total + integerSet[index] |
| return total/length |

**Figure 8.7 Nassi-Shneiderman Chart For Average Method**

```
/* ------ AVERAGE ------ */

   /* Loop through set array and determine the total represented
   by the sum of all the elements. */

   public double average() {
        int index, total=0;

        // Loop through set array and add value of each element to total

        for(index=LOWER_BOUND;index < integerSet.length;index++)
```

```
        total = total + integerSet[index];

    // Return

    return((double) total/(double) integerSet.length);
    }
```

**Table 8.3 Average Method**

### 8.3.3.4 ZIPPING

The process of combining two arrays to form a third is called zipping. For example we may wish to add the elements of two arrays to each other to form a third array ( Table 8.4 and Figure 8.8 ).

```
loop for index equals LOWER BOUND
to UPPER_BOUND
    integerSet[index] = set1.integerSet[index] +
              set2.integerSet[index]
```

**Figure 8.8 Nassi-Shneiderman Chart For Zip Method**

```
/* ------ ZIP ------ */

  /* Loop through two given set arrays to form a new array. */

  public void zip(SetIO set1, SetIO set2) {
        int index;

        // Loop through set arrays and combine each pair of
elements
        // to form a new element

        for(index=LOWER_BOUND;index < set1.length;index++)
           integerSet[index] = set1.integerSet[index] +
                                        set2.integerSet[index];
        }
```

**Table 8.4 Zip Method**

### 8.3.4 IMAGE REPRESENTATION

This loads the package.

In[1]:=<< Image Processing

A digital image is a two-dimensional (2-D) discrete signal. Mathematically, such signals can be represented as functions of two independent variables, for example, a brightness function of two spatial variables. A monochrome digital image $f(x, y)$ is a 2-D array of luminance values,

$$f(x, y) = \begin{pmatrix} f(0, 0) & f(0, 1) & . & f(0, N-1) \\ f(1, 0) & f(1, 1) & . & f(1, N-1) \\ . & . & . & . \\ f(M-1, 0) & f(M-1, 1) & . & f(M-1, N-1) \end{pmatrix}$$

with $0 \leq \int(x, y) \leq 0 \leq £$ and typically £=255. Each element of the array is called a pel (picture element), or more commonly pixel. Typical image dimensions are M*N =256 x 256 and 512 x 512.

Consider a small portion of the "head" image, one of the monochrome example images. We read the image and extract the raw pixel data. The example images included in the ImageProcessing package are located in the Data directory of the root ImageProcessing directory. The location on any system, is given by the system variable $ImageDataDirectory. In a typical , Windows installation the path may be as follows.

```
In[2] := $ImageDataDirectory
Out[2] = {C:\Program~1\WOLFRA~1\MATHEM~1\4.0\Add0ns\
        Application\Imageprocessing\Data\}
```

The directory paths listed in this system variable are automatically searched for named files in an ImageRead operation.

```
In[3]:= H= ImageRead["head.tif"];
In[4]:- Take[RawImageData[H], {64,71}, {64,71}] //
        MatrixForm
Out[4] // MatrixForm =
```

$$\begin{pmatrix} 87 & 60 & 51 & 100 & 151 & 155 & 149 & 142 \\ 84 & 56 & 61 & 81 & 149 & 145 & 150 & 152 \\ 70 & 61 & 49 & 49 & 152 & 150 & 150 & 162 \\ 43 & 38 & 44 & 60 & 145 & 164 & 160 & 150 \\ 34 & 48 & 47 & 57 & 112 & 70 & 94 & 138 \\ 53 & 58 & 58 & 132 & 131 & 71 & 121 & 135 \\ 59 & 60 & 51 & 52 & 46 & 75 & 99 & 108 \\ 132 & 82 & 76 & 60 & 107 & 133 & 115 & 134 \end{pmatrix}$$

Small values represent dark areas of an image, while large values represent bright pixels.

A color digital image is typically represented by a triplet of values, one for each of the color channels, as in the frequently used RGB color scheme. The individual color values are almost universally 8-bit values, resulting in a total of 3 bytes (or 24-bits) per pixel. This yields a three-fold increase in the storage requirements for color versus monochrome images. Naturally, there are a number of alternative methods of storing the image data. Most widely used are the so-called pixel-interleaved (or meshed) and color interleaved (or planar) formats. Less frequent, but possible are row-wise or column-wise interleaving methods. In a pixel-interleaved format every image pixel is represented by a list of three values:

$$, f(x, y) = \begin{bmatrix} r_{0.0}, g_{0.0}, b_{0.0} & r_{0.1}, g_{0.1}, b_{0.1} & r_{0.N-1}, g_{0.M-1} \\ r_{1.0}, g_{1.0}, b_{1.0} & r_{1.1}, g_{1.1}, b_{1.1} & r_{1.N-1}, g_{1.M-1} \\ . & . & . \\ r_{M-1.0}, g_{M-1.0}, b_{M-1.0} & r_{M-1.1}, g_{M-1.1}, b_{M-1.1} & r_{M-1,N-1}, g_{m-1} \end{bmatrix}$$

whereas in the color-interleaved format, the color information is separated into three matrices, one for each of the three color channels:

$$f(x, y) = \left\{\begin{pmatrix} r_{0,0} & r_{0,1} & \cdot & r_{0,N-1} \\ r_{0,1} & r_{1,1} & \cdot & r_{1,N-1} \\ \cdot & \cdot & \cdot & \cdot \\ r_{M-1,0} & r_{M-1,1} & \cdot & r_{M-1,N-1} \end{pmatrix}, \begin{pmatrix} g_{0,0} & g_{0,1} & \cdot & g_{0,N-1} \\ g_{0,1} & g_{1,1} & \cdot & g_{1,N-1} \\ \cdot & \cdot & \cdot & \cdot \\ g_{M-1,0} & g_{M-1,1} & \cdot & g_{M-1,N-1} \end{pmatrix}, \begin{pmatrix} b_{0,0} & b_{0,1} & \cdot & b_{0,N-1} \\ b_{0,1} & b_{1,1} & \cdot & b_{1,N-1} \\ \cdot & \cdot & \cdot & \cdot \\ b_{M-1,0} & b_{M-1,1} & \cdot & b_{M-1,N-1} \end{pmatrix}\right\}$$

Here we read the color example image - "beans".

In[5]:= B=ImageRead[“beans.tif”];

Here we extract a 4x4 region and display it in a meshed format.

In[6]:= RawImageData[ImageTake[B , {25 , 28} ,{ 25 , 28 }]] //MatrixForm

Out[6]//MatrixForm=

$$\begin{pmatrix} \begin{pmatrix}137\\107\\62\end{pmatrix} & \begin{pmatrix}137\\62\\50\end{pmatrix} & \begin{pmatrix}167\\49\\48\end{pmatrix} & \begin{pmatrix}192\\52\\48\end{pmatrix} \\ \begin{pmatrix}157\\135\\75\end{pmatrix} & \begin{pmatrix}140\\74\\53\end{pmatrix} & \begin{pmatrix}161\\49\\46\end{pmatrix} & \begin{pmatrix}188\\50\\47\end{pmatrix} \\ \begin{pmatrix}158\\150\\83\end{pmatrix} & \begin{pmatrix}134\\84\\56\end{pmatrix} & \begin{pmatrix}150\\49\\45\end{pmatrix} & \begin{pmatrix}181\\47\\44\end{pmatrix} \\ \begin{pmatrix}129\\122\\69\end{pmatrix} & \begin{pmatrix}115\\71\\54\end{pmatrix} & \begin{pmatrix}134\\46\\47\end{pmatrix} & \begin{pmatrix}170\\45\\44\end{pmatrix} \end{pmatrix}$$

Here, the same region of the color image is displayed in a planar format.

In[7]:=MatrixForm /@ RawImageData[PlanarImageData[ImageTake[B, {25,28} , {25,28}]]]

Out[7]=

$$\left\{\begin{pmatrix} 137 & 137 & 167 & 192 \\ 157 & 140 & 161 & 188 \\ 158 & 134 & 150 & 181 \\ 129 & 115 & 134 & 170 \end{pmatrix}, \begin{pmatrix} 107 & 62 & 49 & 52 \\ 135 & 74 & 49 & 50 \\ 150 & 84 & 49 & 47 \\ 122 & 71 & 46 & 45 \end{pmatrix}, \begin{pmatrix} 62 & 50 & 48 & 48 \\ 75 & 53 & 46 & 47 \\ 83 & 56 & 45 & 44 \\ 69 & 54 & 47 & 44 \end{pmatrix}\right\}$$

The RGB color scheme is just one of many color representation methods used in practice. The letters R, G, B stand for red, green and blue, the three primary colors used to synthesize any one of 224 or approximately 16 million colors. Equal quantities of the three color values result in shades of gray in the range {0, 255}. Other supported color models, include monochrome, HSV which stands for hue, saturation, value and CMYK which stands for cyan, magenta, yellow. The latter has found application primarily in the printing and graphics markets. HSV is useful in color image processing, since it separates the color information from brigthness.

#### 8.3.4.1 STRUCTURE OF IMAGEDATA

The color image data structure is encapsulated in an ImageData Mathematica expression. ImageData is a graphics primitive that facilitates the easy manipulation and handling of single and multi-channel images. This reads in a small example image in RGB color format.

In[8]:= R=ImageRead["rgb.tif"];

ImageData like other graphics primitives may be displayed using Show command.

In[9]:= Show[Graphics[R]];

**Figure 8.9 Graphics Primitives**

Here is the input form of ImageData.

In[10]:=R//InputForm

```
ImageData[{{{255, 0, 0}, {0, 255, 0}, {0, 0, 255}, {255, 255, 255}, {0, 0, 0}},
    {{255, 0, 0}, {0, 255, 0}, {0, 0, 255}, {255, 255, 255}, {0, 0, 0}},
    {{196, 225, 242}, {96, 204, 248}, {106, 122, 211}, {219, 112, 131},
    {144, 42, 55}}, {{202, 172, 172}, {111, 229, 152}, {227, 140, 232},
    {175, 149, 115}, {249, 229, 3}}, {{2, 168, 101}, {176, 116, 98}, {206, 37, 113},
    {185, 107, 237}, {76, 76, 45}}}, PixelInterleave -> True,
 ColorFunction -> RGBColor]
```

The default ... This converts the image to a planar format.

In[11]:= PlanarImageData[R] //InputForm

```
ImageData[{{{255, 0, 0, 255, 0}, {255, 0, 0, 255, 0}, {196, 96, 106, 219, 144},
    {202, 111, 227, 175, 249}, {2, 176, 206, 185, 76}},
    {{0, 255, 0, 255, 0}, {0, 255, 0, 255, 0}, {225, 204, 122, 112, 42},
    {172, 229, 140, 149, 229}, {168, 116, 37, 107, 76}},
    {{0, 0, 255, 255, 0}, {0, 0, 255, 255, 0}, {242, 248, 211, 131, 55},
    {172, 152, 232, 115, 3}, {101, 98, 113, 237, 45}}}, PixelInterleave -> False,
 ColorFunction -> {RGBColor[#1, 0, 0] & , RGBColor[0, #1, 0] & ,
  RGBColor[0, 0, #1] & }]
```

This returns a monochrome (i.e. single channel) image.

In[12]:= ToGrayLevel[R] //InputForm

```
ImageData[{{85., 85., 85., 255., 0}, {85., 85., 85., 255., 0},
    {221., 182.66666666666666, 146.33333333333331, 154., 80.33333333333333},
    {182., 164., 199.66666666666666, 146.33333333333331, 160.33333333333331},
    {90.33333333333333, 130., 118.66666666666666, 176.33333333333331,
       65.66666666666666}}, PixelInterleave -> None, ColorFunction -> GrayLevel]
```

This converts from the default RGB format to HSV.

In[13]:= ToHSVColor[R] //InputForm

```
ImageData[{{{0., 1., 1.}, {0.33333333333333337, 1., 1.},
  {0.6666666666666666, 1., 1.}, {0, 0, 1.}, {0, 0, 0}},
 {{0., 1., 1.}, {0.33333333333333337, 1., 1.}, {0.6666666666666666, 1., 1.},
  {0, 0, 1.}, {0, 0, 0}}, {{0.5595413379513471, 0.1900826446280991,
```

0.9490196078431372}, {0.5453797791150686, 0.6129032258064515, 0.9725490196078431}, {0.6440842331116621, 0.4976303317535545З, 0.8274509803921568}, {0.973391114828529, 0.4885844748858448, 0.8588235294117647}, {0.9813236988642904, 0.7083333333333334, 0.5647058823529412}}, {{2.371593461809983*^-9, 0.1485148514851484 2, 0.792156862745098}, {0.3889176340426471, 0.5152838427947598, 0.8980392156862745}, {0.8256392086959877, 0.3965517241379З094, 0.9098039215686274}, {0.09556097125631627, 0.3428571428571428б, 0.6862745098039216}, {0.1550068744474194, 0.9879518072289156, 0.9764705882352941}}, {{0.4343074457102995, 0.9880952380952381, 0.6588235294117647}, {0.03536257718999525 5, 0.4431818181818182 3, 0.6901960784313725}, {0.9258994821488294, 0.8203883495145632, 0.807843137254902}, {0.7682965987600818, 0.5485232067510548, 0.9294117647058824}, {0.1666666666666666б, 0.4078947368421053, 0.2980392156862745}}}, PixelInterleave -> True, ColorFunction -> Hue]

### 8.3.4.2 IMAGE DISPLAY

All image data imported into Mathematica using the ImageRead command may be displayed using Show, since ImageRead returns an ImageData object that is Show compatible.

In[14]:=Show[GraphicsArray[Graphics /@ {B , G = ToGrayLevel[B]}]];

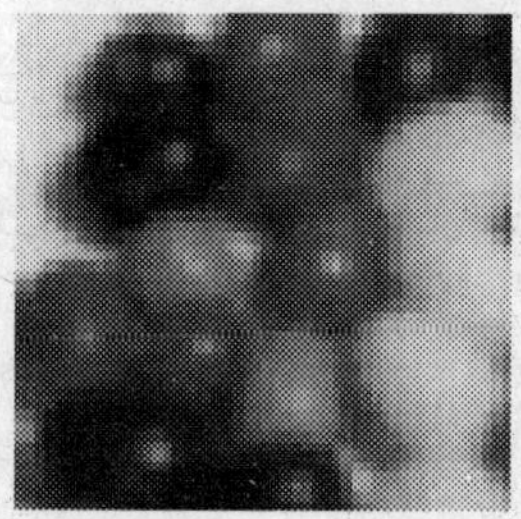
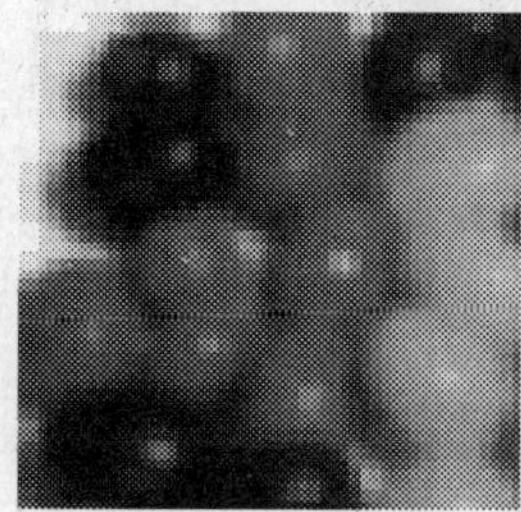

**Figure 8.10**

Raw monochrome image data may be visualized in any number of ways, such as surface plots, contour plots and intensity plots. The latter is the most natural (see ListDensityPlot, Raster). Here is a 32-by-32 fragment of the example image.

In[15]:=

```
tmp = RawImageData[
   ImageTake[G, {12, 43}, {12, 43}]];
Show[GraphicsArray[
   {{ListDensityPlot[tmp, Mesh -> False,
      DisplayFunction -> Identity],
    Graphics[Raster[tmp, {{0, 0}, {32, 32}},
      {0, 255}], AspectRatio → Automatic]},
   {ListPlot3D[tmp, DisplayFunction ->
      Identity],
    ListContourPlot[tmp, Contours → 6,
      DisplayFunction -> Identity]}}]];
```

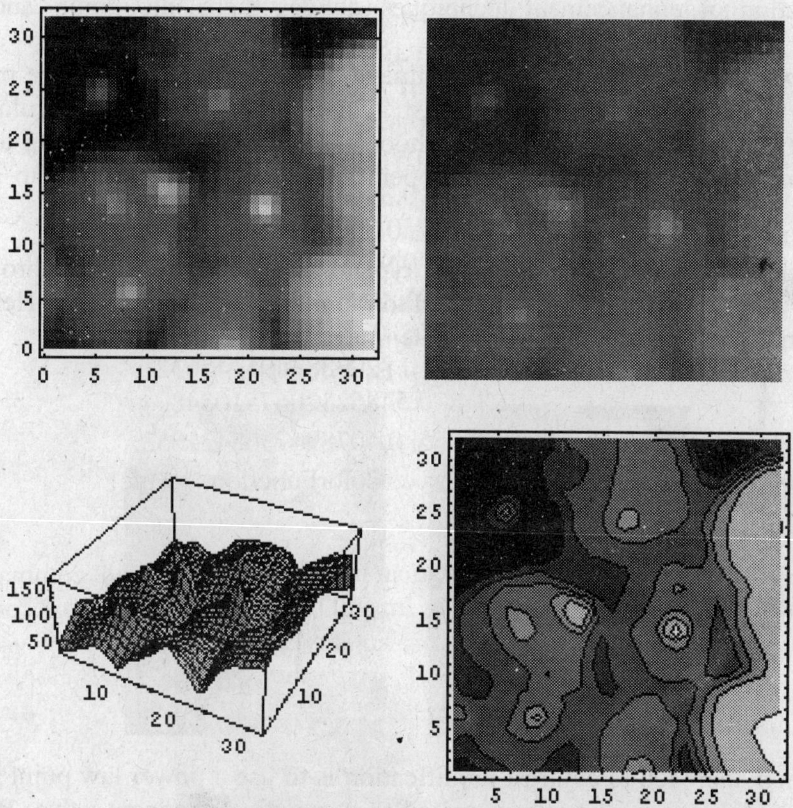


**Figure 8.11 32-By-32 Fragment of the Example Image**

According to (3), color image data in a planar format may be treated as three separate single color images, one for each of the color channels. Here, the three channels are displayed as a GraphicsArray.

In[17]:=Show[GraphicsArray[Graphics /@ToChannels[B]]];

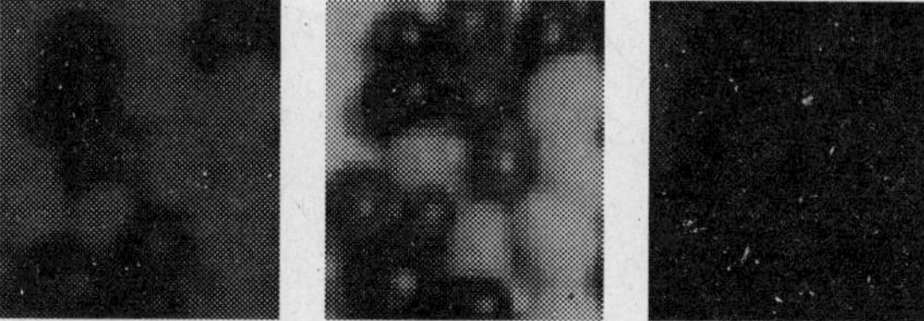

Alternatively, the three individual color channels may be viewed as separate monochrome images. This is a convenient conceptualization of color images allowing the simple and immediate extension of many monochrome image processing techniques to the color image domain.

Image processing with point operations

Image enhancement refers to any technique that improves or modifies the image data, either for purposes of subsequent visual evaluation or further numerical processing. Image enhancement techniques include gray level and contrast manipulation, noise reduction, edge sharpening, linear and non-linear filtering, magnification, pseudocoloring, and so on. One useful, broad categorization of enhancement techniques divides them into point- and region-based operations.

Point operations modify pixels of an image based on the value of the pixel. These are also called zero memory operations. In contrast, region-based operations calculate a new pixel value based on the values in a local neighborhood (typically small). Negating an image is the simplest image modification operation. This operation changes large values to small and vice versa, according to $\tilde{x} = 2^{\pi} - 1 - x$

Where X is a pixel value and n=8 for the typical 8-bits-per-pixel monochrome image. For color images the same transformation is applied to the individual color values. Here we show the effect of negation on both the color and grayscale images.

In[18]:=Show[GraphicsArray[Graphics/@{255 – B, 255-G}]];

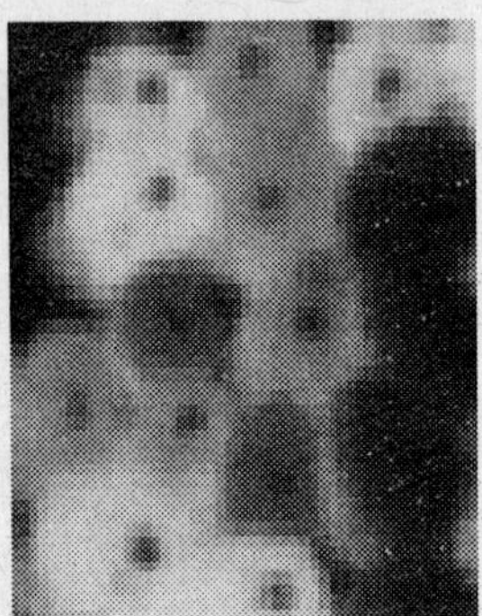
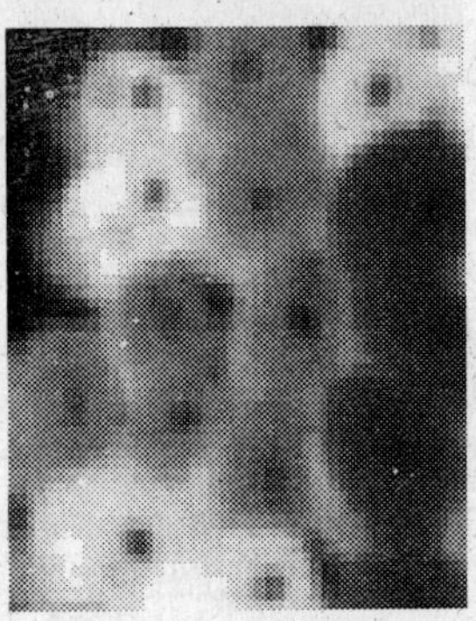

A common approach to contrast modification is to use a power law point transformation, where each pixel of the original image is raised to a specified exponent value. By selecting the exponent values appropriately, either high or low luminance values can be boosted. A simple, yet useful contrast manipulation technique, is to define a piecewise linear transformation to selectively stretch and/or compress a range of luminance values. The slope of the transformation is chosen greater than 1 in the region of stretch and less than 1 in the region of compression. Examples of the effect of selected point operations on the color "beans" image are displayed below.

In[19]:= X=Range[0,255];

In[20]:=

```
{{ListPlot[ScaleLinear[x^3, {0, 255}],
   PlotJoined -> True,
   DisplayFunction → Identity],
  ListPlot[ScaleLinear[Log[1 + x], {0, 255}],
   PlotJoined -> True,
   DisplayFunction → Identity]},
 {Graphics[ScaleLinear[B^3, {0, 255}]],
  Graphics[
   ScaleLinear[Log[1 + B], {0, 255}]]}};
```

In[21]:=Show[GraphicsArray[%]];

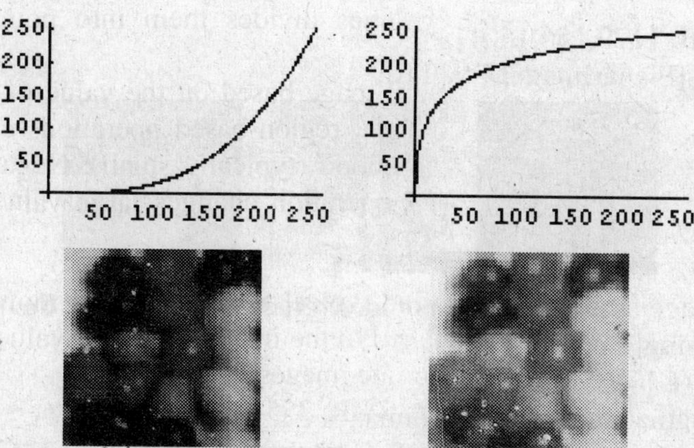


The image histogram is an estimate of the probability density of the image pixels. As such, it measures the frequency of occurance of the pixel luminance values. Many higher-level image processing tasks require the calculation of a histogram. Here we present the histograms of each of the three color channels in the "beans" image.

In[22]:= ImageHistogram[B];
In[23]:= Show[GraphicsArray[
    ListPlot[#, PlotJoined -> {0,0.04}, AspectRation -> 1/3 ,
    DisplayFunction -> Identify] &/@%]];

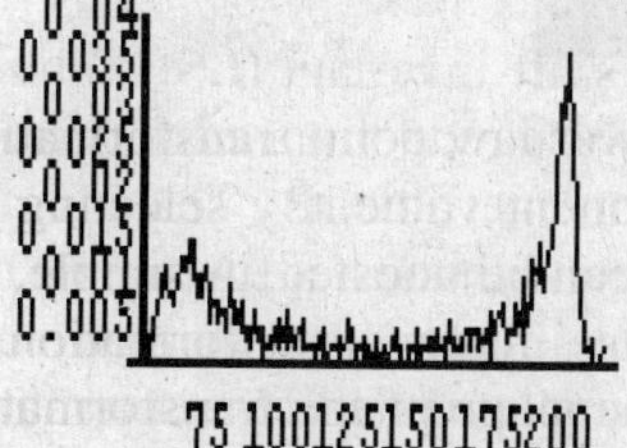


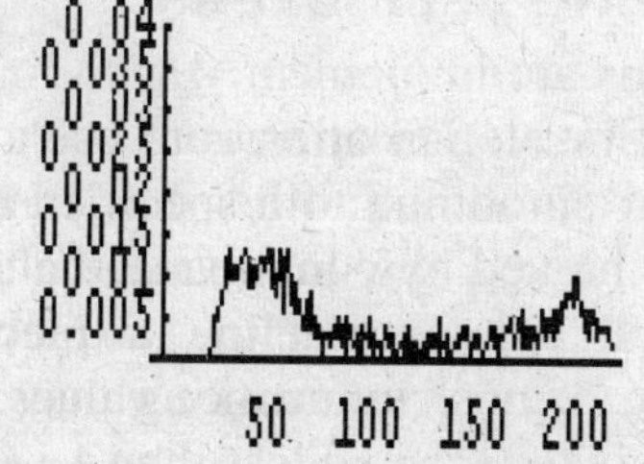


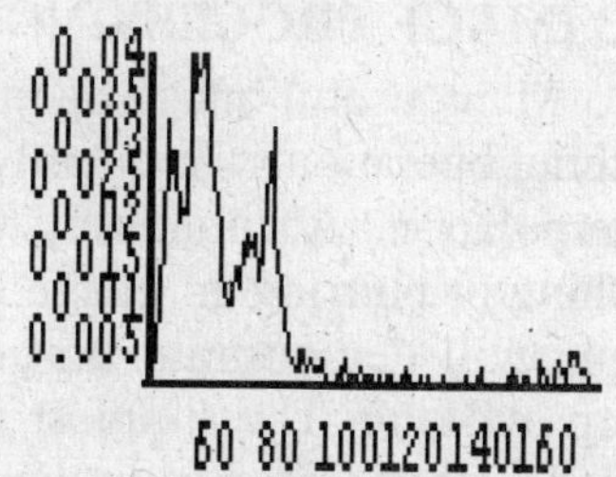


Image equalization, or linearization, is a common image enhancement technique. Here is a linearized version of the beans image.

In[24]:=Show[GraphicsArray[Graphics /@{B,HistogramEqualize[B]}]];

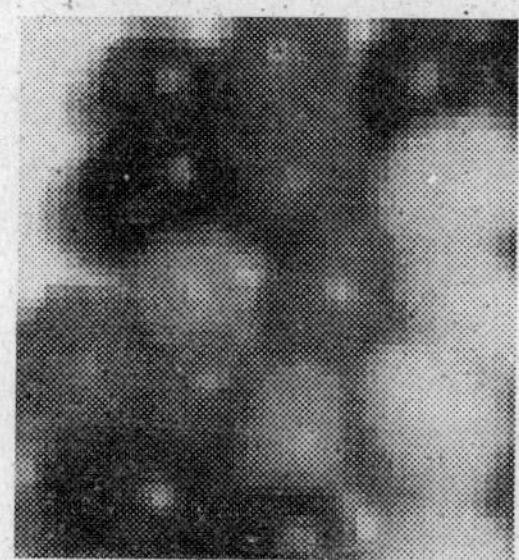

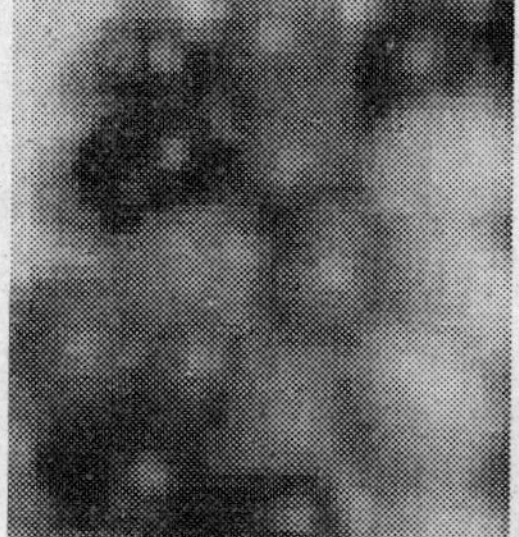

Amplitude thresholding is one of many segmentation techniques. Two-level or binary thresholding changes a value to 0 or 1 depending on the setting of a threshold value. Here is an image segmentation example where we extract the green beans by thresholding the individual color channels. The respective thresholds were selected from an examination of the channel histograms.

In[25]:= T=Threshold[B, {170,150,150}];
In[26]:=Show[Graphics[PlanarImageData[T]]];

 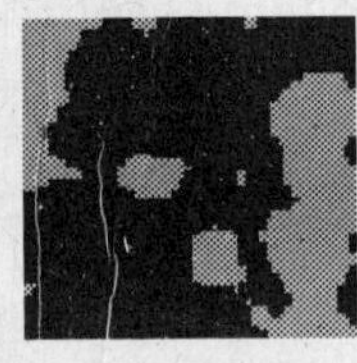 

We now find all the image regions that do not have green pixels and set them to black.
In[27]:= RegionProcessing[0 &, B,
 Where[T, _ ? (# != {0,1,0} &}]];
Here we display the original and segmented images.
In[28]:= Show[GraphicsArray[Graphics /@{B,%}]];

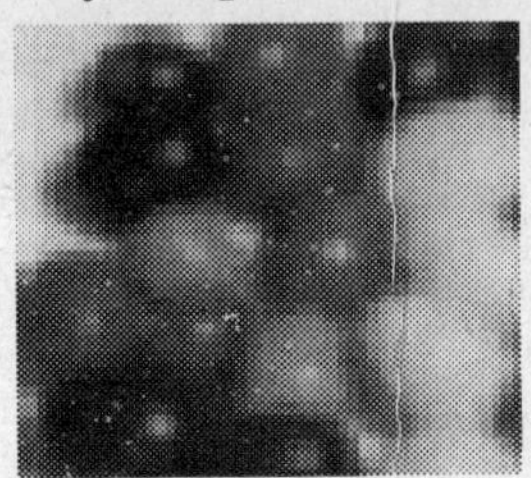 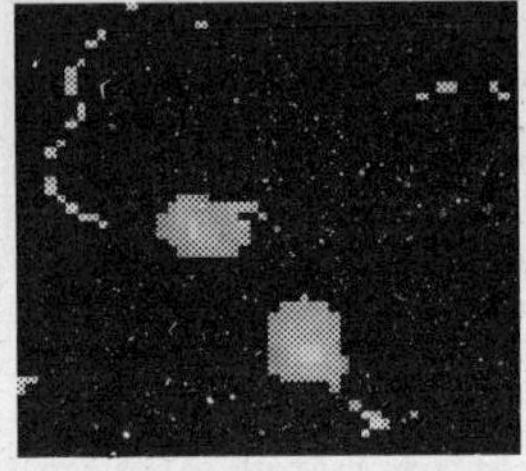

### 8.3.4.3 IMAGE PROCESSING USING LSI FILTERS

Many useful image operations are implemented with linear shift-invariant (LSI) filters. A smoothing operation is frequently a first step in operations such as noise reduction, edge detection or interpolation. A commonly used smoothing filter has constant coefficients. The effect of smoothing or blurring an image is achieved by convolving the image with such a filter. The third example will demonstrate the use of convolution to "sharpen" an image by a method called unsharp masking. The simplest form of unsharp masking may be implemented by subtracting a scaled smoothed image from the original.

Here we smooth and sharpen image the "head" example image.
In[29]:=

$H_S$ = **DiscreteConvolve**[H, $\frac{1}{9.}$
 {{1., 1., 1.}, {1., 1., 1.}, {1., 1., 1.}}];

$H_U$ = **ImagePlus**[ $\frac{5}{4}$ H, - $\frac{1}{4}$ $H_S$];

Here we display the three results.
In[31]:=Show[GraphicsArray[Graphics /@ {Hs , Hv}]];

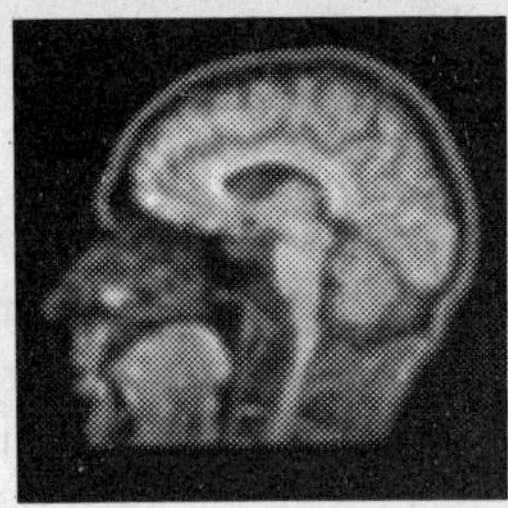 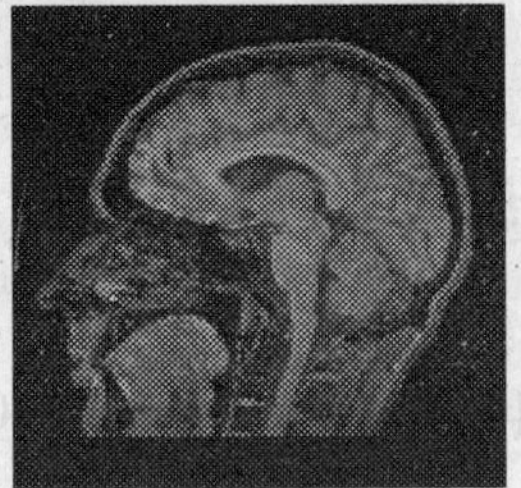

Edge detection is an important step in many shape-based recognition tasks. Edge detection is typically implemented as a convolution operation with appropriately chosen differentiating filters. Two examples of edge detection using two common edge filters, the Sobel gradient edge detector and the Laplacian-of-Gaussian edge detector, conclude this section.

In[32]:=

```
Show[GraphicsArray[
  Graphics /@ {Threshold[EdgeMagnitude[H,
     N[SobelFilter]], 50], ZeroCrossing[
    EdgeMagnitude[H, LoGFilter[21, 21]]]}]];
```

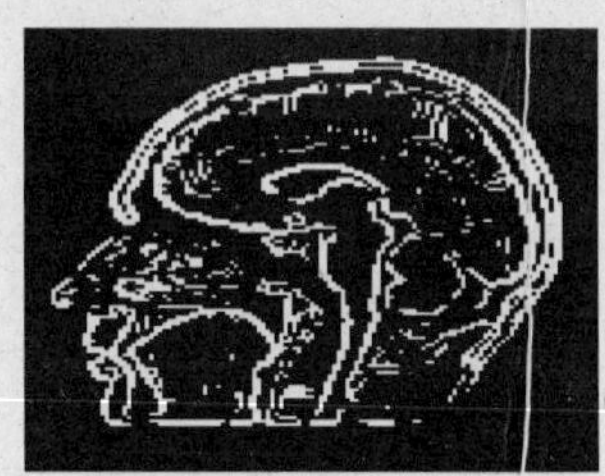
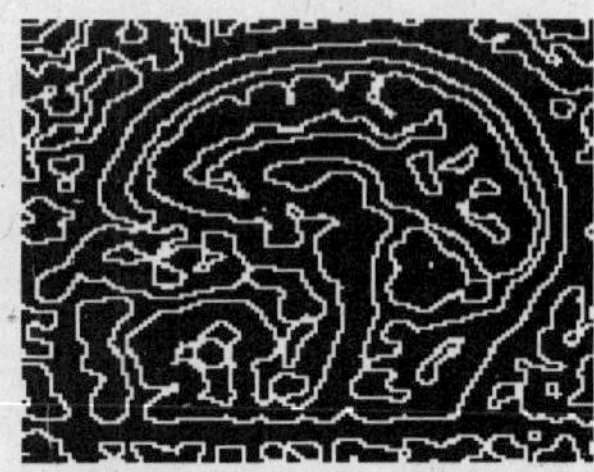

### 8.3.4.4 IMAGE TRANSFORMS: DCT

It is well known that LTI operators may be implemented in the Fourier transform domain, leading to computational efficiencies. The energy compaction property of transforms such as the discrete Fourier transform (DFT), discrete cosine transform (DCT) or discrete wavelet transform (DWT) plays an important role in many image/video compression techniques. Here we demonstrate image compression using the DCT transform. Here we take the block cosine transform of the head image. The blocks are non-overlapping, of dimensions 8x8.

In[36]:= H=BloxkProcessing[DCT[# - 128] &, RawImageData[H],
{8 , 8} , {8 , 8} , MatrixJoin];

Here we show a fragment of the head image and the DCT coefficients.

In[37]:= Show[GraphicsArray[ListDensityPlot[Take [#, {64 , 95} , {64 , 95}],
Mesh → False, DisplayFunction → Identify] & /@
{RawImageData[H] , Abs[H]}]];

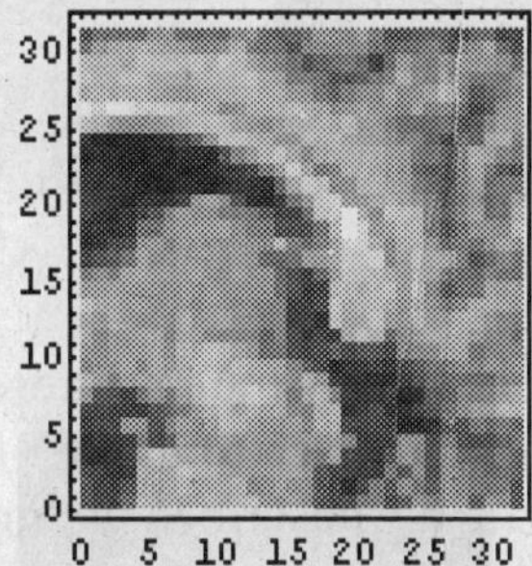

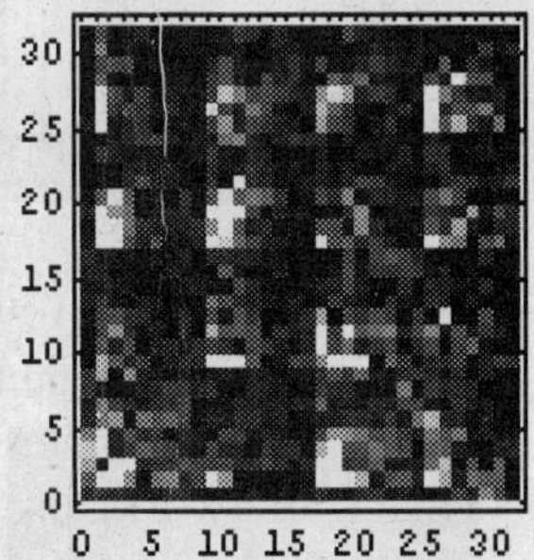


We now retain cosine coefficients located in a low-frequency zone of each block. We then use the inverse DCT to calculate an approximation to the original image. Here is a typical zonal mask.

In[38]:=(M=ZeroPad [{{1 , 1 , 1 , 1 , 1} , {1 , 1 , 1 , 1 , 0 } , {1 , 1 , 1 , 0 , 0} ,
{1 , 1 , 0 , 0 , 0} , {1, 0 , 0 , 0 , 0}} , {0 , 3} , {0 , 3}] ) // MatrixForm

Out[38] //MatrixForm=

$$\begin{pmatrix} 1 & 1 & 1 & 1 & 1 & 0 & 0 & 0 \\ 1 & 1 & 1 & 1 & 0 & 0 & 0 & 0 \\ 1 & 1 & 1 & 0 & 0 & 0 & 0 & 0 \\ 1 & 1 & 0 & 0 & 0 & 0 & 0 & 0 \\ 1 & 0 & 0 & 0 & 0 & 0 & 0 & 0 \\ 0 & 0 & 0 & 0 & 0 & 0 & 0 & 0 \\ 0 & 0 & 0 & 0 & 0 & 0 & 0 & 0 \\ 0 & 0 & 0 & 0 & 0 & 0 & 0 & 0 \end{pmatrix}$$

In[39]:=

```
H̃ = BlockProcessing[Round[IDCT[M * #]] &,
   ℋ, {8, 8}, {8, 8}, MatrixJoin] + 128;
```

In[40]:=

```
Show[GraphicsArray[
      ListDensityPlot[#, Mesh → False,
   Frame → False, PlotRange → {0, 255},
   DisplayFunction -> Identity] & /@
 {RawImageData[H], H̃,
  RawImageData[H] - H̃ + 128}]];
```

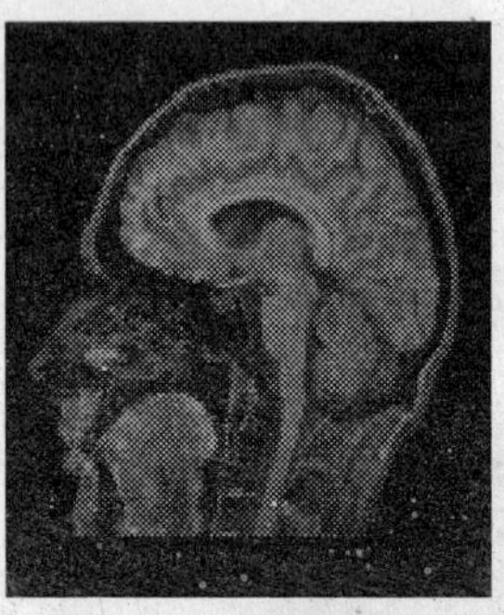
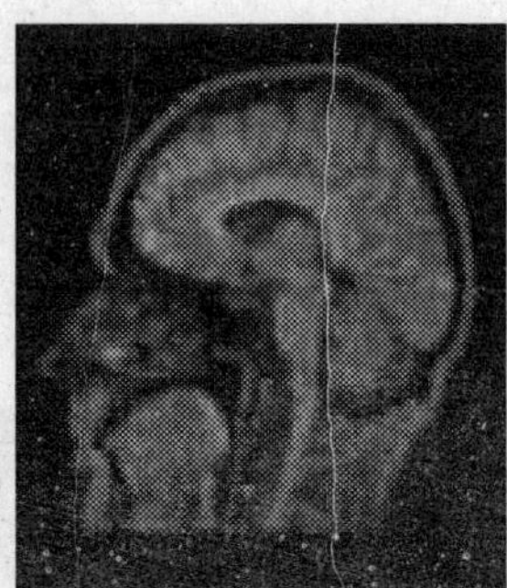
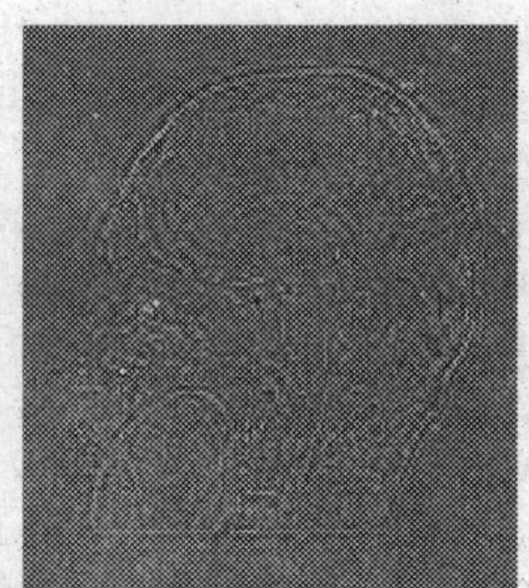

### 8.3.5 ARRAY SIGNAL PROCESSING

Sensor array signal processing emerged as an active area of research and was centered on the ability to fits data collected at several sensors in order to carry out a given estimation task (space-time processing). This framework, as will be described in more detail below, uses to advantage prior information on the data acquisition system (i.e., array geometry, sensor characteristics, etc.). The methods have proven useful for solving several real-world problems; perhaps most notably source localization in radar and sonar.

The first approach to carrying out space-time processing of data sampled at an array of sensors was spatial filtering or beam forming. The conventional (Bartlett) beam former dates back to the second world-war, and is a mere application of Fourier-based spectral analysis to spatiotemporally sampled data. Later, adaptive beam formers and classical time delay estimation techniques were applied to enhance one's ability to resolve closely spaced signal sources. The spatial filtering approach, however, suffers from fundamental limitations: its performance, in particular, is directly dependent upon the physical size of the array (the aperture), regardless of the available data collection time and signal-to-noise ratio (SNR). From a statistical point of view, the classical techniques can be seen as spatial extensions of spectral Wiener filtering (or matched filtering).

The extension of the time-delay estimation methods to more than one signal (these techniques originally used only two sensors), and the limited resolution of beam forming together with an increasing number of novel applications, renewed interest of researchers in statistical signal processing. We might add at this stage, that the word resolution is used in a rather informal way. It generally refers to the ability to distinguish closely spaced signal sources. One typically refers to some spectral-like measure, which would exhibit peaks at the locations of the sources. Whenever there are two peaks near two actual emitters, the latter are said to be resolved.

However, for parametric techniques, the intuitive notion of resolution is non-trivial to define in precise terms. This in turn, resulted in the emergence of the parameter estimation approach as an active research area. Important inspirations for the subsequent effort include the Maximum Entropy (ME) spectral estimation method in geophysics by and early applications of the maximum likelihood principle. The introduction of subspace-based estimation techniques marked the beginning of a new era in the sensor array signal processing literature. The subspace-based approach relies on certain geometrical properties of the assumed data model, resulting in a resolution capability which (in theory) is not limited by the array aperture, provided the data collection time and/or SNR are sufficiently large and assuming the data model accurately reflects the experimental scenario.

The quintessential goal of sensor array signal processing is the estimation of parameters by fusing temporal and spatial information, captured via sampling a wavefield with a set of judiciously placed antenna sensors. The wave field is assumed to be generated by a finite number of emitters, and contains information about signal parameters characterizing the emitters. Given the great number of existing applications for which the above problem formulation is relevant, and the number of newly emerging ones, we feel that a review of the area, with the hindsight and perspective provided by time, is in order. The focus is on parameter estimation methods, and many relevant problems are only briefly mentioned. The manuscript is clearly not meant to be exhaustive, but rather as a broad review of the area, and more importantly as a guide for a first time exposure to an interested reader.

#### 8.3.5.1. BACKGROUND AND FORMULATION

We motivate the data model assumed throughout this paper, via its derivation from first principles in physics. Statistical assumptions about data collection are stated and basic geometrical properties of the model are reviewed.

#### 8.3.5.2. WAVE PROPAGATION

Many physical phenomena are either a result of waves propagating through a medium (displacement of molecules) or exhibit a wave-like physical manifestation. A wave propagation which may take various forms (with variations depending on the phenomenon and on the medium, e.g. an electro-magnetic (EM) wave in free space or an acoustic wave in a pipe), generally follows from the homogeneous solution of the wave equation.

The models of interest in this paper may equally apply to an EM wave as well as to an acoustic wave (e.g., SONAR). Given that the propagation model is fundamentally the same, we will for analytical expediency, show that it can follow from the solution of Maxwell's equations, which, clearly are only valid for EM waves. In empty space (no current or charge) the following holds

V -E = 0

V • B = 0

V x E - as
at

V x B = Eolito
dr

Where and x, respectively, denote the "divergence" and "curl." Further, B is the magnetic induction, E is the electric field, whereas 40 and co are the magnetic and dielectric constants. Invoking Eq. 1 the following curl property results,

$$\nabla\times(\nabla\times\mathbf{E})=\nabla(\nabla\cdot\mathbf{E})-\nabla^2\mathbf{E}=-\nabla^2\mathbf{E}. \tag{8.3}$$

Using Equation 8.1 and 8.2 leads to

$$\nabla\times(\nabla\times\mathbf{E})=-\frac{\partial}{\partial t}(\nabla\times\mathbf{B})=-\varepsilon_0\mu_0\frac{\partial^2\mathbf{E}}{\partial t^2}, \tag{8.4}$$

which, when combined with Eq. 8.3, yields the fundamental wave equation

$$\nabla^2\mathbf{E}-\frac{1}{c^2}\frac{\partial^2}{\partial t^2}\mathbf{E}=\mathbf{0}. \tag{8.5}$$

The constant c is generally referred to as the speed of propagation, and for EM-waves in free space it follows from the above derivation $C=1/\sqrt{\varepsilon_\theta\mu_\theta}\cong 3*10m/s$. The homogeneous (no forcing function) wave equation (Eq. 8.5) constitutes the physical motivation for our assumed data model. This is regardless of the type of wave or medium (EM or acoustic). In some applications, the underlying physics are irrelevant, it is merely the mathematical structure of the data model that counts.

Though Eq. 8.5 is a vector equation, we only consider one of its components, say E(r,t) where r is the radius vector. It will later be assumed that the measured sensor outputs are proportional to E(r,t). Interestingly enough, any field of the form E(r,t) =1(t—rTOC) satisfies Eq. 8.5, provided l c = 1/c, with "T" denoting transposition. Through its dependence on t—ria only,. the solution can be interpreted as a wave traveling in the direction a, with the speed of propagation 1, al = c. For the latter reason, a is referred to as the slowness vector. The chief interest herein is in narrowband (This is not really a restriction, since any signal can be expressed as a linear combination of narrowband components.) forcing functions. The details of generating such a forcing function (i.e. radiation of an antenna) can be found in the classic book by Jordan . In complex notation and taking the origin as a reference, a narrowband transmitted waveform can be expressed as (uppercase and lowercase Greek letters are to be understood as vectors or matrices within their context)

$$E(0,t) = s(t)e^{j}\omega^{t},$$

Where s(t) is slowly time-varying compared to the carrier $e^{j}\omega^{t}$. For |r| <<c/B, where B is the bandwidth of s(t), we can write

$$E(\mathbf{r},t) = s(t-\mathbf{r}^{T}\alpha)e^{j\omega(t-\mathbf{r}^{T}\alpha)} \cong s(t)e^{j(\omega t-\mathbf{r}^{T}\mathbf{k})} \quad (8.6)$$

In the last equality the so-called wave-vector k = ao) was introduced, and its magnitude 1k I = k = colc is the wave- number. One can also write k = 27c1X, where X is the wavelength. Note that k also points in the direction of propagation. For example, in the xy-plane we have k = k(cose Ø sin Ø) r ,where Ø is the direction of propagation, defined counterclockwise relative the x-axis.

It should be noted that Eq. 8.6 implicitly assumed far-field conditions, since an isotropic (Isotropic refers to uniform propagation/transmission in all directions.) point source gives rise to a spherical traveling wave whose amplitude is inversely proportional to the distance to the source. All points lying on the surface of a sphere of radius R will then share a common phase and are referred to as a wavefront. This indicates that the distance between the emitters and the receiving antenna array determines whether the sphericity of the wave should be taken into account. The reader is referred to e.g., for treatments of near field reception. Far- field receiving conditions imply that the radius of propagation is so large (compared to the physical size of the array) that a flat plane of constant phase can be considered, thus resulting in a plane wave as indicated in Eq. 8.6. Though not necessary, the latter will be our assumed working model for convenience of exposition.

A linear medium implies the validity of the superposition principle, and thus allows for more than one traveling wave. Equation 8.6 carries both spatial and temporal information and represents an adequate model for distinguishing signals with distinct spatio-temporal parameters. These may come in various forms, such as DOA (in general azimuth and elevation), signal polarization (if more than one component of the wave is taken into account), transmitted waveforms, temporal frequency etc. Each emitter is generally associated with a set of such characteristics. The interest in unfolding the signal parameters forms the essence of sensor array signal processing as presented herein, and continues to be an important and active topic of research.

### 8.3.5.3 PARAMETRIC DATA MODEL

Most modern approaches to signal processing are model- based, in the sense that they rely on certain assumptions made on the observed data. In this section we describe the prevailing model used in the remainder of this article. A sensor is represented as a point receiver at given spatial coordinates. In the 2D-case and as shown in Fig. 8.12, we have ri = (xi yi)T Using Eqs, 8.6, the field measured at sensor land due to a source at azimuthally DOA 0 is given by

$$\mathrm{E}(r_{l},t) = s(t)\ell^{[j\omega t - k(x_{j}Cos\theta + ylSin\theta)]} \quad (8.7)$$

If a flat frequency response, say gi(0), is assumed for the sensor / over the signal bandwidth, its measured output will be proportional to the field at rt. Dropping the carrier term el cot for convenience (in practice, the signal is usually down- converted to baseband before sampling), the output is modeled by

$$x_l(t) = g_l(\theta)\ell^{-jk(x_l Cos\theta + y_l Sin\theta)} s(t) = a_l \theta s(t) \qquad (8.8)$$

Referring to Eq. 8.6, we see that Eq. 8.8 requires that the array aperture (i.e. the physical size measured in wavelengths) be much less than the inverse relative bandwidth f/B.

In the array processing literature, this is referred to as the narrowband assumption. For an L-element antenna array of arbitrary geometry, the array output vector is obtained as x(t) = a(Ø)s(t).

A single signal at the DOA 0, thus results in a scalar multiple of the steering vector (Other popular names for a(0) include action vector, array propagation vector and signal replica vector.) $a(\theta) = [a_1(\theta),....,a_L(\theta)]^T$ as the array output.

Common array geometries are depicted in Figure. 8.13 and 8.14. For the uniform linear array (ULA) we have ri = ((/ — 1)d 0)T, and assuming that all elements have the same directivity gi(0) = = We) = g(0), the ULA steering vector takes the form (cf. (11))

$$a_{ULA}(\theta) = g(\theta)\left[1\ell^{-jkdCos\theta}...\ell^{-j(L-1)kdCos\theta}\right]^T \qquad (8.9)$$

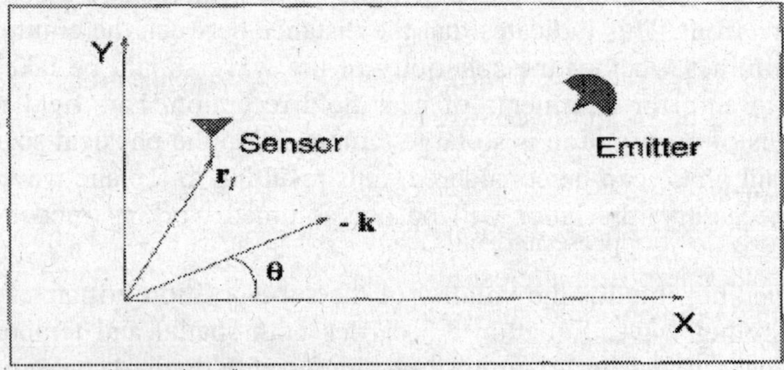


*1. Two-dimensional array geometry*

**Figure 8.12 Two-dimensional array geometry**

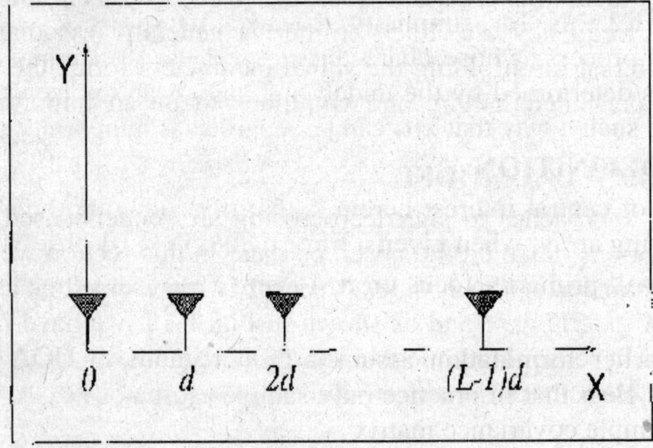


*2. Uniform Linear Array geometry*

**Figure 8.13 Uniform Linear Array Geometry**

where d denotes the inter-element distance. The radius vectors of the uniform circular array (UCA) have the form ri = R(cos(2t(l — 1)/L) sin(2td/ — 1)/L))T , from which thė form of the UCA steering vector can easily be derived. As previously alluded to, a signal source can be associated with a number of characteristic parameters.

For the sake of clarity and ease of presentation by referring to Figure 8.13 and 8.14, we assume that 0 is a real-valued scalar referred to as the DOA. For most of the discussed methods the extension to the multiple parameter per source case is straightforward.

As noted earlier, the superposition principle is applicable assuming a linear receiving system. If M signals impinge on an L-dimensional array from distinct DOAs 01 0/1/r, the output vector takes the form x(t) - t a(0),(t)

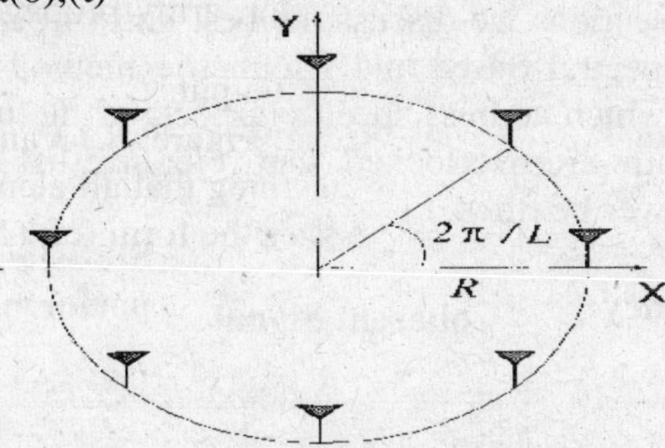


**Figure 8.14. Uniform Circular Array Geometry**

In the presence of an additive noise n(t) we now get the model commonly used in array processing

$$x(t) = A(\theta)S(t) + n(t) \tag{8.10}$$

The methods to be presented all require that M < L, which is therefore assumed throughout the development. It is interesting to note that in the noiseless case, the array output is then confined to an M-dimensional subspace of the complex L-space, which is spanned by the steering vectors. This is the signal subspace, and this observation forms the basis of subspace-based methods.

The sensor outputs are appropriately pre-processed and sampled at arbitrary time instances, labeled t 1,2,...,N for simplicity. Clearly, the process x(t) can be viewed as a multichannel random process, whose characteristics can be well understood from its first and second order statistics determined by the underlying signals and noise. The preprocessing of the signal is often done in such a way that x(t) can be regarded as temporally white.

### 8.3.5.4 PROBLEM DEFINITION

The problem of central interest herein is that of estimating the DOAs of emitter signals impinging on a receiving array, when given a finite data set { x(01 observed over t = 1,2,

As noted earlier, we will primarily focus on reviewing a number of techniques based on second-order statistics of data.

All of the earlier formulation assumed the existence of exact quantities, i.e. infinite observation time. It is clear that in practice only sample estimates i.e., A, are available. A natural estimate of R is the sample covariance matrix

$$\hat{\mathbf{R}} = \frac{1}{N}\sum_{t=1}^{N}\mathbf{x}(t)\mathbf{x}^{H}(t), \tag{8.11}$$

for which a spectral representation similar to that of R is defined as

$$\hat{\mathbf{R}} = \hat{\mathbf{U}}_s \hat{\Lambda}_s \hat{\mathbf{U}}_s^H + \hat{\mathbf{U}}_n \hat{\Lambda}_n \hat{\mathbf{U}}_n^H \quad (8.12)$$

This representation will be extensively used in the description and implementation of the subspace-based estimation algorithms. Indeed, if x(t) is a stationary white Gaussian process with unknown structure (i.e., the data model is not used), then R and its eigen-elements are maximum likelihood estimates of the corresponding exact quantities .

Throughout the paper, the number of underlying signals, M, in the observed process is considered known. There are, however, good and consistent techniques for estimating the M signals present in the event that such information is not available (see also the "Additional Topics"). In the following two sections we discuss the best known parameter estimation techniques, respectively classified as Spectral-Based and Parametric methods. Due to space limitations, a number of good variations which address specific aspects of the underlying problem and which have appeared in the literature are overlooked. Our reference list attempts to cover a portion of the gap which clearly can never be filled.

| **Method** | **Consistency** | **Coherent Signal** | **Statistical performance** | **Computations** |
|---|---|---|---|---|
| Bartlett | M= 1 | | | 1-D Search |
| Capon | No | No | Poor | 1-D Search |
| MUSIC | Yes | No | Good | EVD, 1-D Search |
| Min-Norm | Yes | No | Good | EVD, 1-D Search |
| DML | Yes | Yes | Good | M-D Search |
| SML | Yes | Yes | Efficient | M-D Search |
| WSF | Yes | Yes | Efficient | EVD, M-D Search |

**Table 8.5: Estimation Applicable of Arbitrary Array Geometrics**

| **Method** | **Consistency** | **Coherent Signals** | **Statistical Performance** | **Computations** |
|---|---|---|---|---|
| Root-Music | Yes | Yes | Good | EVD, polynomial |
| ESPRIT | Yes | Yes | Good | EVD Iterative |
| IQML | Yes | Yes | Good | |
| Root-WSF | Yes | Yes | Efficient | EVD, LS |

**Table8.6: Estimation Applicable of Uniform Linear Array**

### 8.3.5.5 NUMBER OF SIGNALS ESTIMATION

In applications of model-based methods, an important problem is the determination of M, the number of signals. In the case of non-coherent signals, the number of signals is equal to the number of "large" eigen values of the array covariance matrix. This fact is used to obtain relatively simple non-parametric algorithms for determining M. The most frequently used approach emanates from the factor analysis literature. The idea is to determine the multiplicity of the smallest eigen value, which theoretically equals L — M.

In the presence of coherent signals, the methods as just stated will fail, since the dimension of the signal subspace is in this case smaller than M. A more systematic approach to estimating the number of signals is possible if the maximum likelihood estimator is employed. A classical generalized likelihood ratio test (GLRT). For determining the number of signals the model-based methods require signal parameter estimates for an increasing hypothesized number of signals, until some pre-specified criterion is met. The approach is thus inherently more computationally intensive than the non-parametric tests. Its performance in difficult signal scenarios is, however, improved and is in addition less sensitive to small perturbations of the assumed noise covariance matrix.

### 8.3.5.6 REDUCED DIMENSION BEAMSPACE PROCESSING

At the exception of the beamforming-based methods, the estimation techniques discussed herein require that the outputs of all elements of the sensor array be available in digital form. In many applications, the required n umber of high-precision receiver front-ends and AID converters may be prohibitive. Arrays of 104 elements are not uncommon, for example in radar applications. Techniques for reducing the dimensionality of the observation vector with minimal effect on performance, are therefore of great interest. As already discussed previously, a useful idea is to employ a linear transformation

z(t) — T*x(t),

where T is L R, with (usually) R << L. The transformation is typically implemented in analog hardware, thus significantly reducing the number of required AJD converters. The reduced-dimension observation vector z(t) is usually referred to as the beamspace data, and T is a beamspace transformation.

Naturally, processing the beamspace data significantly reduces the computational load of the digital processor. How ever, reducing the dimension of the data also implies a loss of information. The beamspace transformation can be thought of as a multichannel beamformer. By designing the beamformers (the columns of T) so that they focus on a relatively narrow DOA sector, the essential information in x(t) regarding sources in that sector can be retained in z(t). With further a priori information on the locations of sources, the beamspace transformation can in fact be performed with no loss of information. As previously alluded to, beamspace processing can even improve the resolution (the bias) of spectral-based methods.

The beamspace transformation effectively changes the array propagation vectors from a(0) into T*a(0). It is possible to utilize this freedom to give the beamspacc array manifold a simpler form, such as that of a ULA. Hence, the computationally efficient ULA techniques are applicable in beamspace. In, a transformation that maps a uniform circular array into a ULA is proposed and analyzed, enabling computationally efficient estimation of both azimuth and elevation.

### 8.3.5.7 ESTIMATION UNDER MODEL UNCERTAINTY

As implied by the terminology, model-based signal processing relies on the availability of a precise mathematical description of the measured data. When the model fails to reflect the physical phenomena with a sufficient accuracy, the performance of the methods will clearly degrade. In particular, deviations from the assumed model will introduce bias in the estimates, which for spectral-based methods is manifested by a loss of resolving power and a presence of spurious peaks. In principle, the various sources of modeling errors can be classified into noise covariance and array response perturbations.

In many applications of interest, such as communication, sonar and radar, the background noise is dominated by manmade noise. While the noise generated in the receiving equipment is likely to fulfill the spatially white assumption, the man-made noise tends to be quite directional. One could in principle envision extending the model-based estimation techniques to also include estimation of the noise covariance matrix. However, for low SNR's, this solution is less than adequate.

The simultaneous estimation of a completely unknown noise covariance matrix and of the signal parameters poses a problem unless some additional information which enables us to separate signal from noise, is available. It is; for example, always possible to infer that the received data is nothing but noise, and that the (unknown) noise covariance matrix is precisely the observed array sample covariance matrix. At high SNR, the modeling errors are usually dominated by errors in the assumed signal model.

The signals have a non-zero bandwidth, the sensor positions may be uncertain, the receiving equipment may not be perfectly calibrated, etc. In some cases it is possible to physically quantify the error sources. In, robust techniques for unstructured sensor modeling errors are considered, Wideband Data Processing

The methods presented herein are essentially limited to processing narrowband data. In many applications (e.g. radar and communication), this is indeed a realistic assumption. However, in other cases (e.g. sonar), the received signal may be broadband. A natural extension of all these methods is to employ narrowband filtering, for example using the Fast Fourier Transform (FFT). A simpler suboptimal approach is to process the different FFT channels separately using a standard narrowband method, whereafter the DOA estimates at different bins must be combined in some appropriate way.

Another approach is to explicitly model the array output as a multidimensional time series, using an autoregressive moving average (ARMA) model. The poles of the system are estimated, e.g. using the ovcrdctermincd Yule-Walker equations. A narrowband technique can subsequently be employed using the estimated spectral density matrix, evaluated at the system poles.

A wideband DOA estimation approach inspired hy beam- space processing is the so-called coherently averaged signal subspace method. The idea is to first estimate the signal subspace at a number of FFT channels. The information from different frequency bins is subsequently merged by employing linear transformations. The objective is to make the transformed steering matrices A at different frequencies as identical as possible, for example by focusing at the center frequency of the signals.

### 8.3.5.8 FAST SUBSPACE CALCULATION AND TRACKING

The implementation of subspace-based methods in applications with real-time operation usually experiences a bottleneck in the calculation of the signal subspace. The idea is to exploit the "low-rank plus 62I" structure of the ideal array covariance matrix. An alternative gradient-based technique for subspace tracking. Therein, it is observed that the solution W, of the constrained optimization problem, max Tr {WilW} subject to W'W = I spans the signal subspace.

For some methods, estimates of the individual principal eigenvectors are required, in addition to the subspace they span. A number of different methods for eigenvalue/vector (The referenced paper considers tracking of the principal left singular values of the data matrix. The so-called fast subspace decomposition (FSD) technique is based on a Lanczos method for calculating the eigendccomposition. It is observed that the Lanczos iterations can be prematurely terminated without any significant performance loss.

### 8.3.5.9 SIGNAL STRUCTURE METHODS

Most "standard" approaches to array signal processing make no use of any available information about the signal structure. However, many man-made signals have a rich structure that can be used to improve the estimator performance. In digital communication applications, the transmitted signals are often cyclostationary, which implies that their autocorrelation functions are periodic. This additional information is exploited and algorithms for DOA estimation of cyclostationary signals are derived and analyzed. In this approach, the wideband signals are easily incorporated into the framework, and the number of signals may exceed the number of sensors with the provision that they do not all share the same cyclic frequency (which refers to the frequency at which the spatial correlation function repeats itself).

A different approach utilizing signal structure is based on high-order statistics. As is well-known, all information about a Gaussian signal is conveyed in the first and second order moments. However, for non-Gaussian signals, there is potentially more to be gained by using higher moments. This is particularly so if the noise can be regarded as Gaussian. Then, the high-order cumulants will be theoretically noise-free, as they vanish for Gaussian signals.

A common criticism of both approaches (those based on cyclostationarity and those based on high-order statistics) is that they require a considerable amount of data to yield reliable results. This is due to the slower convergence of the estimated cyclic and high-order moments to their theoretical values as the number of data is increased compared to that of second order moments.

### 8.3.5.10 POLARIZATION SENSITIVITY

Most antenna arrays used in electro-magnetic applications are sensitive to polarization differences among the received signals. Provided that each polarization component can be calibrated separately, the signal polarization can be utilized for improving the DOA estimation performance, even if the array only measures the sum of the polarization components. In , it is shown that polarization diversity can also significantly improve the signal waveform estimates, a fact which has long been known in microwave communications and which could be of considerable interest in array processing applications, e.g. communication applications. Therein, it is assumed that the receiving sensors measure all six field components of the electric and magnetic fields. This allows source localization using only one so-called vector sensor.

### 8.3.5.11 TIME SERIES ANALYSIS

The DOA estimation problem employing a ULA shares some common aspects with time series analysis. Indeed, an important pre-cursor of the MUSIC algorithm is Pisarenko's method for estimation of the frequencies of damped/undamped sinusoids in noise, whose covariance function measurements are given. Similarly, Kung's algorithm for stale-space realization of a measured impulse response is an early version of the. ESPRIT algorithm. An important difference between the time series case and the (standard) DOA estimation problem is that the time series data is usually estimated using a sliding window. A "sensor array-like data vector" x(t) is formed from the scalar time series v(t) by using

x(t)=[y(t),y(t +1),. ..y(t + L

The windowing transformation induces a temporal correlation in the L-dimensional time series x(t), even if the scalar process y(t) is temporally white. This fact complicates the analysis, as in the case of spatial smoothing in DOA estimation. A further complication arises in time series analysis problems when there is a known input signal present. This problem has fortunately, also been successfully tackled using ideas from sensor array signal processing.

### 8.3.6 APPLICATIONS

The research progress of parameter estimation and detection in array processing has resulted in a great diversity of applications, and continues to provide fertile ground for new ones. In this section we discuss three important application areas.

### 8.3.6.1 PERSONAL COMMUNICATIONS

Receiving arrays and related estimation/detection techniques have long been used in High Frequency communications. These applications have recently reemerged and received a significant attention by researchers, as a potentially useful "panacea" for numerous problems in personal communications. They are expected to play a key role in accommodating a multiuser communication environment, subject to severe multipath.

One of the most important problems in a multiuser asynchronous environment is the inter-user interference, which can degrade the performance quite severely. This is also the case in a practical Code-Division Multiple Access (CDMA) system, because the varying delays of different users induce non-orthogonal codes. The base stations in mobile communication systems have long been using spatial diversity for combating fading due to the severe multipath. However, using an antenna array of several elements introduces additional degrees of freedom, which can be used to obtain higher selectivity. An adaptive receiving array can be steered in the direction of one user at a time, while simultaneously nulling interference from other users, much in the the same way as the beamforming techniques described previously.

The multipath which may be caused by buildings reflections or hills, etc. introduces difficulties for conventional adaptive array processing. Undesired cancelation may occur 11491, and spatial smoothing may be required to achieve a proper selectivity. It is proposed to identify all signal paths emanating from each user, whereafter an optimal signal combination is performed. A configuration equivalent to the beamspace array processing with a simple energy differencing scheme serves in localizing incoming users waveforms.

Communication signals have a rich structure that can be exploited for signal separation using antenna arrays. Indeed, the DOAs need not be estimated. Instead, signal structure methods such as the constant-modulus beamformer have been proposed for directly estimating the steering vectors of the signals, thereby allowing for blind (i.e., not requiring a training sequence) signal separation. It is important to note that the various optimal and/or suboptimal proposed methods are of current research interest, and that i n practice, many challenging and interesting problems remain to be addressed.

### 8.3.6.2 RADAR AND SONAR

The classical application of array signal processing is in radar and sonar, and modern model-based techniques. The antenna array is, for example, used for source localization, interference cancellation and ground clutter suppression.

In radar applications, the mode of operation is referred to as active. This is on account of the role of the antenna array based system which radiates pulses of electro-magnetic energy and listens for the return. The parameter space of interest may vary according to the geometry and sophistication of the antenna array. The radar returns enable estimation of parameters such as velocity (Doppler frequency), range and DOAs of targets of interest. Using passive far-field listening arrays, only the DOAs can be estimated.

In sonar applications, on the other hand, the signal energy is usually acoustic, and measured using arrays of hydro- phones. The sonar can operate in an active as well as passive mode. In a passive mode, the receiving array has the capability of detecting and locating distant sources. Deformable array models are often used in sonar, as the receiving antenna is typically towed under water. Techniques with piecewise linear subarrays are used in the construction of the overall solution

In an active mode, a sonar system emits acoustic (electromagnetic arrays are also used underwater) energy and monitors and retrieves any existing echo. This again can be used for parameter estimation, such as bearings and velocity etc., using the delay of the echo. Despite its limitations due to the bending speed-of-propagation profiles and the high propagation losses, sonar together with related estimation techniques, remains a reliable tool for range, bearing estimation and other imaging tasks in underwater applications.

### 8.3.6.3 INDUSTRIAL APPLICATIONS

Sensor array signal processing techniques have drawn much interest from industrial applications, such as manufacturing and medical applications. In medical imaging and hyperthermia treatment , circular arrays are commonly used as a means to focus energy in both an injection mode as well as reception mode. It has also been used in treatment of tumors [36]. In electrocardiograms, planar arrays are used to track the evolution of wavefronts which in turn provide information about the condition of a patient's heart.

Array processing methods have also been adopted to localize brain activity using biomagnetic sensor arrays, so-called super-conducting quantum interference device (SQUID) magnetometers . It is expected that the medical applications will proliferate as more resolution is sought, e.g. signals emanating from a womb may be of more interest than those of a mother.

Other applications in industry are almost exclusively in automatic monitoring and fault detection/localization. In engines, sensors are placed in a judicious and convenient way to detect and potentially localize faults such as knocks or broken gears. Another emerging and important application of array signal processing is in using notions from optics to carry out tasks in product quality assurance in a manufacturing environment and in object shape characterization in tomography . An example is provided in "Radar Example."

## 8.4 STANDARD IMAGE PROCESSOR CHIPS

Image quality is clearly one of the most important features of any camera, if not the most important. This is particularly so in surveillance and monitoring applications, where lives and property may be at stake.

By developing image processing chips and sophisticated algorithms tailored for network camera applications, image quality has been improved to a degree never before seen at lower cost levels. As digital technology becomes commonplace and replaces analog solutions, there will be further advances in areas such as high resolution and advanced video compression, but success will ultimately depend on how well the initial information is captured and handled.

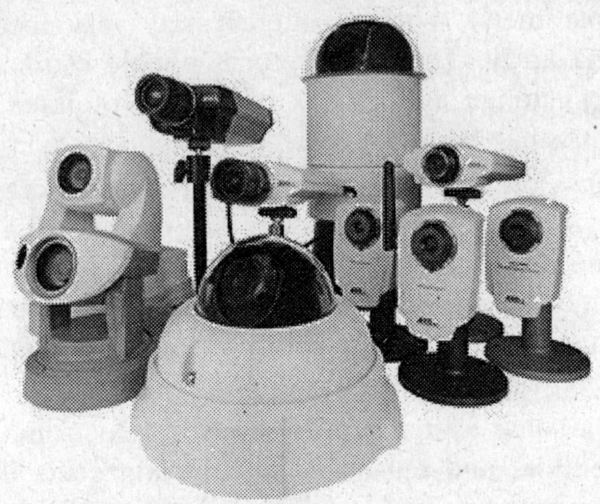

**Figure 8.15 Camera**

In the fast-growing segment of network cameras, which are used for surveillance and remote monitoring, there are many factors that influence image quality. Axis, which set the standards for network cameras in 1996, identified right from the start the need for advanced image handling, and has continued to invest in research in its Axis Superior Image Quality initiative.

Superior image quality enables the user to:

1. More closely follow details and changes in images, making for better and faster decisions concerning the safety of people and property.
2. With greater accuracy use automated analysis and alarm tools, such as face recognition, with fewer false positives.

Digital network cameras are equipped with the processing power not only to capture and present images, but also to digitally manage and compress them for network transport. Image quality can vary considerably and is dependent on the choice of optics and image sensor, the available processing power and the level of sophistication of the algorithms in the processing chip.

There are two types of image sensors:

1. CCD (Charged Coupled Device)
2. CMOS (Complementory Metal Oxide Semiconductor)

CCD sensors are produced using a technology developed specifically for the camera industry, while CMOS sensors are produced by the same technology used for the chips used in computers.

**Figure 8.16.1 1/3 inch CCD Sensor**

**Figure 8.16.2 1/4 –inch CMOS sensor**

**1. Low light capabilities**

A camera might deliver reasonable image quality in bright light conditions, but it may be unsuitable for typical indoor situations.

**2. Lens replacement**

A high quality lens can deliver better images. Most professional level cameras use a so-called C or CS mount, and some lenses feature auto-iris control for improving the dynamic range.

**3. Image resolution**

Higher resolution means more detail, and as cameras now deploy mega pixel sensors that make it possible to capture even more detail, analog CCTV cameras--which are bound to resolutions used in TV standards are being surpassed.

**4. Backlight compensation**

While a camera's automatic exposure control tries to get the lightness of an image to appear as the human eye would see a scene, it can be easily fooled. Think of the case where a person walks into a fairly dark room with a flashlight in her hand and directs this flashlight to the camera. Although the light source is quite small, it makes the camera believe the scene has become brighter and the camera's exposure control automatically adjusts to it, resulting in a darker image. To avoid this, a mechanism called backlight compensation is introduced. It strives to ignore small areas of high illumination, just as if they were not present at all. With backlight compensation, the image from the example above would have the same exposure regardless of whether the flashlight was present or not. The resulting image enables the person to be visually seen and identified. Without backlight compensation, the image would be too dark, and identification would be impossible.

**5. Ability to correctly capture moving objects**

In addition to good light sensitivity, another key feature to look for is progressive scan. That the camera has progressive scan means that images do not suffer from the "saw" effect that hampers interlaced video technologies The interlace mode is used in TVs and traditional analog CCTV cameras in order to enhance the image frequency in moving images. The "saw" effect becomes apparent when the picture is frozen.

**6. Additional image enhancements**

The functions that drive these reside in the chip that handles the image processing, and affects color, sharpness, exposure and the white balance.

**7. File size and bandwidth requirements**

Digital cameras use image compression. There is a trade off here between high quality images and compressed images that require much less bandwidth. The JPEG standard is used to achieve the highest possible quality, and MPEG is optimized for lower bandwidth requirements.

High-speed analog VLSI image acquisition and low-level image processing system are presented. The architecture of the chip is based on a dynamically reconfigurable SIMD processor array. The chip features a massively parallel architecture enabling the computation of programmable mask-based image processing in each pixel. Extraction of spatial gradients and convolutions such as Sobel operators are implemented on the circuit. Each pixel includes a photodiode, an amplifier, two storage capacitors, and an analog arithmetic unit based on a four-quadrant multiplier architecture. A 64×64 pixel proof-of-concept chip was fabricated in a 0.35μm standard CMOS process, with a pixel size of 35μm × 35μm. A dedicated embedded platform including FPGA and ADCs has also been designed to evaluate the vision chip. The chip can capture raw images up to 10000 frames per second and runs low-level image processing at a framerate of 2000 to 5000 frames per second.

Today, digital cameras are rapidly becoming ubiquitous, due to reduced costs and increasing demands of multimedia applications. Improvements in the growing digital imaging world continue to be made with two main image sensor technologies: charge-coupled devices (CCDs) and CMOS sensors. Historically, CCDs have been the dominant image-sensor technology. However, the continuous advances in CMOS technology for processors and DRAMs have made CMOS sensor arrays a viable alternative to the popular CCD sensors. This led to the adoption of CMOS image sensors in several high-volume products, such as webcams, mobile phones, PDAs, for example. Furthermore, new recent technologies provide the ability to integrate complete CMOS imaging systems at focal plane, with analog-to-digital conversion, memory and processing . By exploiting these advantages, innovative CMOS sensors have been developed and have demonstrated fabrication cost reduction, low power consumption, and size reduction of the camera.

The main advantage of CMOS image sensors is the flexibility to integrate processing down to the pixel level. As CMOS image sensors technologies scale to 0.18¼m processes and under, processing units can be realized at chip level (system-on-chip approach), at column level by dedicating processing elements to one or more columns, or ar pixel-level by integrating a specific unit in each pixel or local of neighboring pixels. Most of the researches deal with chip and column level. Indeed, pixel-level processing is generally dismissed because pixel sizes are often too large to be of practical use. However, as CMOS scales, integrating a processing element at each pixel or group of neighboring pixels becomes more feasible since the area occupied by the pixel transistors decreases, leading to an acceptable small pixel size. A fundamental tradeoff must be made between three dependent and correlated variables: pixel size, processing element area, and fill-factor.

This implies various points of view:

1. For a fixed fill-factor and a given processing element area, the pixel size is reduced with technology improvements, as a consequence, reducing pixel size increases spatial resolution for a fixed sensor die size;
2. For a fixed pixel size and a given processing element area, the photodiode area and the fill-factor increase as technology scales since the area occupied by the pixel transistors in each processing element decreases. It results in better sensibility, higher dynamic range and signal-to-noise ratio;
3. For a fixed pixel size and a given fill-factor, the processing element can integrate more functionality since the transistors require less area as technology scales. Consequently, the image processing capabilities of the sensor increase. Each new technology process

offers (1) to integrate more processing functions in a given silicon area, or (2) to integrate the same functionalities in a smaller silicon area. This can benefit the quality of imaging in terms of resolution, noise, for example, by integrating specific processing functions such as correlated double sampling, antiblooming, high dynamic range, and even all basic camera functions (color processing functions, color correction, white balance adjustment, gamma correction) onto the same camera-on-chip. Furthermore, employing a processing element per pixel offers the ability to exploit the high speed imaging capabilities of the CMOS technology by achieving massively parallel computations.

Hardware implementation issues of a high-speed CMOS imaging system embedding low-level image processing. For this purpose, we designed, fabricated, and tested a proof-of-concept $64 \times 64$ pixel CMOS analog sensor with per-pixel programmable processing element in a standard 0.35¼m double-poly quadruple-metal CMOS technology.

### 8.4.1 HIGH SPEED FOCAL PLANE IMAGE-PROCESSING CAPABILITIES

In an increasingly digital world, the most part of imaging systems has become almost entirely digital, using only an analog-to-digital (ADC) between the sensor and the processing operators. However, low-level image processing usually involves basic operations using local masks. These local operations are spatially dependent on other pixels around the processed pixel, since the same type of operations is applied to a very large dataset, these low-level tasks are computationally intensive and require a high bandwidth between the image memory and the digital processor. In this case, an analog or a mixed-approach can offer superior performance leading to a smaller, faster, and lower power solution than a digital processor. Low-level image processing tasks are inherently pixel-parallel in nature. Integrating a processing element within each pixel based on a single instruction multiple data (SIMD) architecture is a natural candidate to cope with the processing constraints.

This approach is quite interesting for several aspects. First, SIMD image-processing capabilities at focal plane have not been fully exploited because the silicon area available for the processing elements is very limited. Nevertheless, this enables massively parallel computations allowing high framerates up to thousands of images per second. The parallel evaluation of the pixels by the SIMD operators leads to processing times, independent of the resolution of the sensor. In a classical system, in which low-level image processing is externally implemented after digitization, processing times are proportional to the resolution leading to lower framerates as resolution increases. Several papers have demonstrated the potentially outstanding performance of CMOS image sensors. Krymski et al. describe a high speed (500 frames/s) large format $1024 \times 1024$ active pixel sensor (APS) with 1024 ADCs. Stevanovic et al. describe a $256 \times 256$ APS which achieves more than 1000 frames/s with variable integration times. Kleinfelder et al. describe a $352 \times 288$ digital pixel sensor (DPS) with per pixel bit parallel ADC achieving 10000 frames/s or 1Giga-pixels/s.

Secondly, the high speed imaging capability of CMOS image sensors can benefit the implementation of new complex applications at standard rates and improve the performance of existing video applications such as motion vector estimation, multiple capture with dynamic range, motion capture, and pattern recognition. Indeed, standard digital systems are unable to operate at high framerates, because of the high output data rate requirements for the sensor, the memory, and the processing elements. Integrating the memory and processing with the sensor on the same chip removes the classical input output bottleneck between the sensor and the external processors in charge of processing the pixel values. Indeed, the bandwidth of the communication between the sensor and the external processors is known as a crucial aspect, especially with high resolution sensors. In such cases, the sensor output data flow can be very high, and needs a lot of hardware resources to convert, process and transmit a lot of information. So, integrating image processing at the sensor level can alleviate the high data rate problem because the pixel values are pre-processed on-chip by the SIMD operators before sending them to the external world via the communication channel. This will result in data reduction, which allows sending the data at lower data-rates, and reduces the effect of the computational-load bottleneck.

Thirdly, one of the main drawbacks to design specific circuits integrating sensing and processing on the same chip is that these vision chips are often built as special-purpose devices, performing specific and dedicated tasks, and not reusable in another context. So, it can be widely beneficial to integrate a versatile device, whose functionality can be easily modified. Moreover, except the basic operations such as convolutions with small masks, the majority of computer vision algorithms require the sequential execution of different successive low-level image processing on the same data. So, each processing element must be built around a programmable execution unit, communication channels, and local memories dedicated to intermediate results. Because of the very limited silicon area, the processing units are necessarily very simple, providing the best compromise between various factors such as versatility, complexity, parallelism, processing speeds and resolution.

The flexibility to integrate processing down to the pixel level allows us to rearchitect the entire imaging system to achieve much higher performances.

The key idea is :-

(1) to capture images at a very high framerate,
(2) to process the data on each pixel with an SIMD programmable architecture exploiting the high on-chip bandwidth between the sensor, the memory and the elementary processors,
(3) to provide results at the best framerate depending on the complexity of the image processing. In this paper, we present our approach to the design of a massively parallel, SIMD vision chip based implementing low level image processing based on local masks. Our analog processing operators are fully programmable devices by dynamic reconfiguration, and can be viewed as a software-programmable image processor dedicated to low-level image processing.
(4) The main objectives of our design are
    a. To evaluate the potential for high-speed snapshot imaging and, in particular, to reach a 10000 frames/s rate.
    b. To demonstrate a versatile and reconfigurable processing unit at pixel level
    c. To provide an original platform for experimenting with low-level image processing algorithms that exploit high-speed imaging.

## 8.4.2 DESCRIPTION OF THE ARCHITECTURE

The proof-of-concept chip presented in this paper is depicted in Figure 8.17. The core includes a two-dimensional array of $64 \times 64$ identical processing element (PE). It follows the single instruction multiple data (SIMD) computing paradigm. Each of the PE is able to convolve the pixel value issued from the photodiode by applying a set of mask coefficients to the image pixel values located in a small neighborhood. The key idea is that a global control unit can dynamically reconfigure the convolution kernel masks and then implements the most part of low-level image processing algorithms. This confers the functionality of programmable processing devices to the PEs embedded in the circuit.

**Figure 8.17 : Image sensor with a processor-per-pixel array**

Each individual PE includes the following elements.

(1) A photodiode dedicated to the optical acquisition of the visual information and the light-to-voltage transduction.

(2) Two analog memory, amplifier and multiplexer structures called [AM]2, which serve as intelligent pixel memories and are able to dissociate the acquisition of the current frame in the first memory and the processing of the previous frames in the second memory.

(3) An analog arithmetic unit named A2U based on four analog multipliers, which performs the linear combination of the four adjacent pixels using a $2 \times 2$ convolution kernel.

Each PE includes 38 transistors integrating all the analog circuitry dedicated to the image processing algorithms. The global size of the PE is 35¼m × 35¼m (1225¼m2). The active area of the photodiode is 300¼m2, giving a fill-factor of 25%. The chip has been realized in a standard 0.35¼m double-poly quadruple-metal CMOS technology and contains about 160000 transistors on a 3.67mm × 3.77mm die (13.83mm2). The chip also contains test structures on the bottom left of the chip. These structures are used for detailed characterization of the photodiodes and processing units.

### 8.4.2.1 CIRCUIT DESIGN

#### 1. PIXEL STRUCTURE

Each pixel in the CMOS image sensor array consists of a photodiode and a processing unit dedicated to low-level image processing based on neighborhoods. In our chip, the type of photodiodes is one of the simplest photo element in CMOS image sensor technology. It consists of N-type photodiodes based on an n+-type diffusion in a p-type silicon substrate. The depletion region is formed in the neighborhood of the photodiode cathode. Optically generated photocarriers diffuse to neighboring junctions. In order to achieve good performances, the photodiodes should be designed and optimized carefully, in order to minimize critical parameters such as the dark current and the spectral response. The shape of photodiode layout, the structure of the photodiode, and the layout have significant influences on the performance of the whole The active area of the photodiode absorbs the illumination energy and turns that energy into charge carriers. This active area must be large as possible in order to absorb a maximum of photons. In the mean time, the control circuitry required for the readout of the collected charges and the interelement isolation area must be as small as possible in order to obtain the best fill factor.

The second part of the pixel is the analog processing unit. Existing works on analog pixel-level image processing can be classified into two main categories. The first one is intra pixel, in which processing is performed on the individual pixels in order to improve image quality, such as the classical active pixel sensor or APS . The second category is intra pixel, where the processing is dedicated to groups of pixels in order to perform some early vision processing and not merely to capture images. Our work clearly takes place in this category because our main objective is the implementation of various in situ image processing using local neighborhoods. Based on this design concept, this forces a rethinking of the spatial distribution of the processing resources, so that each computational unit can easily use a programmable neighborhood of pixels. For this purpose, the pixels are mirrored about the horizontal and the vertical axes in order to share the different analog arithmetic units (A2Us). As example, a block of $2\times2$ pixels is depicted in Figure 1. The main feature of its innovative distribution is to optimize the compactness of the metal interconnections with pixels, to contribute to a better fill factor, and to provide generality of high-speed processing based on neighborhood of pixels.

## 2. ANALOG MEMORY, AMPLIFIER AND MULTIPLEXER: [AM]2

In order to increase the algorithmic possibilities of the architecture, the key point is the separation of the acquisition of the light inside the photodiode and the readout of the stored value at pixel-level. Thus, the storage element should keep the output voltage of the previous frames whereas the sensor integrates photocurrent for a new frame. So, we have designed and implemented dedicated pixels including a light sensitive structure and two specific circuits called analog memory, amplifier, and multiplexer ([AM]2), as shown in Figure 8.18.

**Figure 8.18: The [AM]2 structure.**

The system has five successive operation modes: reset, integration, storage, amplification, and readout. All these phases are externally controlled by global signals common to the full array of pixels. They all occur in parallel over the sensor (snapshot mode) in order to avoid any distortion due to a row-by-row reset. In each pixel, the photosensor is an N-type photodiode associated with a PMOS transistor reset. This switch resets the integrating node to the fixed voltage $V_{dd}$.

The pixel array is held in the reset mode until the init signal raises, turning the PMOS transistor off. Then, the photodiode discharges for a fixed period, according to the incidental luminous flow. The first NMOS transistor acts as a transconductance, producing the voltage $V_{Ph}$, directly proportional to the incident light intensity.

The integrated voltage is polarized around $V_{dd}/2$ by the second NMOS transistor. The calibration of the structure is ensured by the positive reference bias voltage ($V_{bias} = 1.35V$ ).

Following the acquisition stage, two identical subcircuits $[Am]_i^2$ (with $i = 1, 2$) take place to realize the storage phase of $V_{Ph}$ Each [AM]2 includes three pairs of NMOS and PMOS transistors and a capacitor which acts as an analog memory. The subcircuit $[Am]_i^2$ is selected when the $st_i$ signal is turned on. Then, the associated analog switch is open allowing the integration of the photogenerated current in the corresponding $C_i$ capacitor. Consequently, the capacitors are able to store the pixel value during the frame capture from one of the two switches. The capacitors are implemented with double-polysilicium. The size of the capacitors is as large as possible in order to respect the fill-factor and the pixel-size requirements.

The capacitors values are about 40F. They are able to store the pixel value for 20 milliseconds with an error lower than 4%. Behind the storage subcircuit, a basic CMOS inverter is integrated. This inverter serves as a linear high-gain amplifier since the pixel signal is polarized around $V_{dd}$ /2 Finally, the last phase consists in the readout of the stored values in the capacitors $C_i$. The integrated voltage across the capacitor $C_i$ can be readout on the output $out_i$ through one of the two switches, controlled by the $r_i$ signals.

Figure 8.19 describes the experimental results of successive acquisitions in an individual pixel. The acquisitions occur when one of the two signals $St_1$ or $St_2$ goes high. The two combinations of acquisitions are presented in this example. After the first reset, $St_2$ is followed by $St_1$ whereas the inverted sequence of acquisitions is realized after the second reset. The signal $V_{Ph}$ gives the voltage corresponding to the incidental illumination on the pixel and the the two outputs (out1 and out2 give the voltage stored in each of the capacitors when the associated readout signal raises.

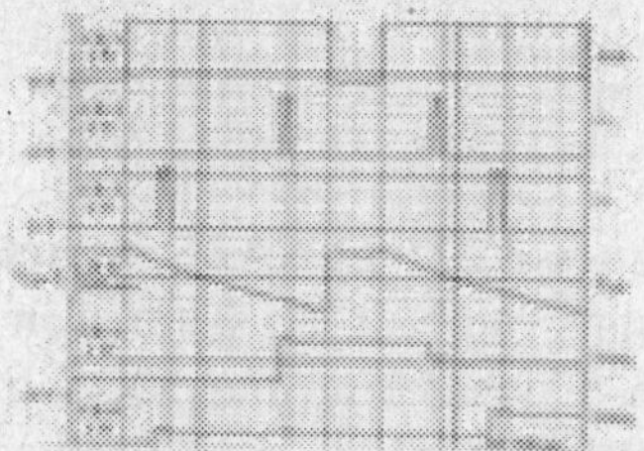

**Figure 8.19: High-speed sequence capture with basic image processing**

One of the main advantages of the two [AM]2 structures is that the capture sequence can be made in the first memory in parallel with a readout sequence and/or processing sequence of the previous image stored in the second memory, as shown in Figure 8.20.

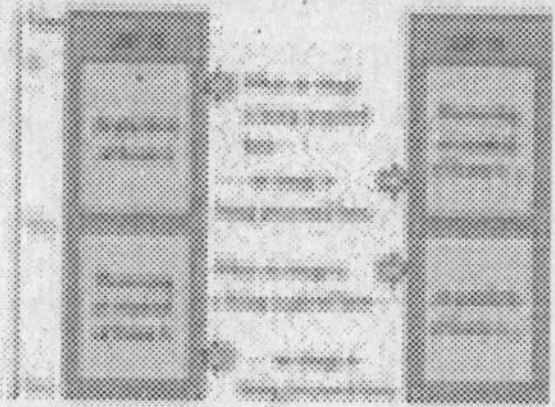

**Figure 8.20: Parallelism between capture sequence and readout sequence**

Such a strategy has several advantages.

(1) The framerate can be increased (up to 2 ×) without reducing the exposure time.

(2) The image acquisition is time-decorrelated from image processing, implying that the architecture performance is always the highest, and the processing framerate is maximum.

(3) A new image is always available without spending any integration time.

### 3. ANALOG ARITHMETIC UNIT: A2U

When designing a pixel-level processing unit, you should consider adopting efficient strategies to minimize the silicon area occupied by the processor. To that end, we designed an analog arithmetic unit (A2U) which is able to perform convolution of the pixels with a 22 dynamic kernel. This unit is based on four-quadrant analog multipliers named M1, M2, M3, and M4, as illustrated in Figure 8.21. Each multiplier requires 5 transistors. So, the transistor count of the complete unit is only 22 transistors. The last two transistors not depicted on the Figure 5 serve as an output switch, driven by the column signal.

It features relative small area, simplicity, and high speed. These characteristics make it an interesting choice in low-level image processing embedded at focal plane. Each multiplier $M_i$ (with $i = 1, \ldots, 4$) takes two analog signals $V_{i1}$ and $V_{i2}$ and produces an output $V_{iS}$ which is their product. The outputs of multipliers are all interconnected with a diode-connected transistor employed as load. Consequently, the global operation result at the VS point is a linear combination of the four products $V_{iS}$. Image processing operations such as spatial convolution can be easily performed by connecting the inputs $V_{i1}$ to the kernel coefficients and the inputs $V_{i2}$to the corresponding pixel values.

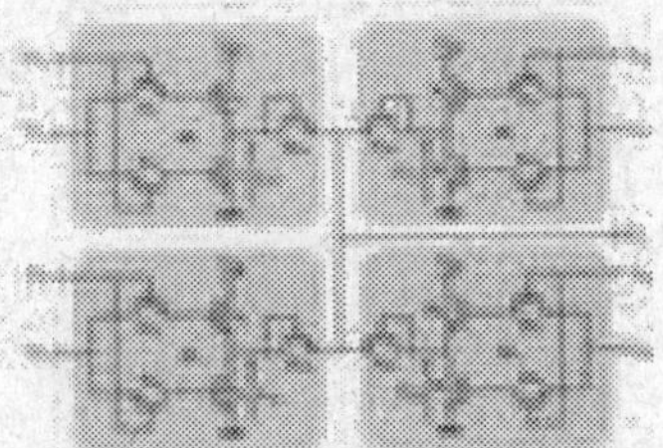

**Figure 8.21: The A2U structure**

In order to keep the analysis simple, it is assumed in this section that the contribution of parasitic capacitances is negligible. Considering the MOS transistors operating in subthreshold region, the output node $V_{iS}$ of a multiplier can be expressed as a function of the two inputs $V_{i1}$and $V_{i2}$as follows: $K_r(V_{ThN} - V_{i1})(V_{i1} - V_{i2} - V_{ThN}) = (V_{i1} - V_{iS} - V_{ThN})(V_{i2} - V_{iS} - V_{ThN} - V_{ThP})$

(8.131)

with $k_r$represents the transconductance factor, $V_{Thn}$ and $V_{Thp}$ are the threshold voltages for the NMOS and PMOS transistors. Around the operating point ($V_{dd}/2$), the variations of the output node mainly depend on the product $V_{i1}\, V_{i2}$.

So, the equation 8.13 can be simplified and finally, the output node $V_{iS}$ can be expressed as a simple first-order of the two input voltages $V_{i1}$ and $V_{i2}$.

$$V_{iS} = MV_{i1}V_{i2} with.M = \frac{k_r - 1}{2V_{ThN} + V_{ThP}} \approx 8.07/V \tag{8.14}$$

The important value of the coefficient M gives to the structure a good robustness by limiting the impact of the second-order intermodulation products. The first consequence is a better linearity of our multiplier design integrating only 5 transistors.

The theoretical analysis has been validated by an experimental study realized on the test structures embedded on the chip. Figure 8.22 shows the experimental measures obtained with two cosine signals as inputs of the multiplier structure.

$$V_{i1} = A\cos(2nf_1) with f_1 = 2.5KHz, \quad V_{i2} = B\cos(2nf_2) with f_2 = 20KHz, \tag{8.15}$$

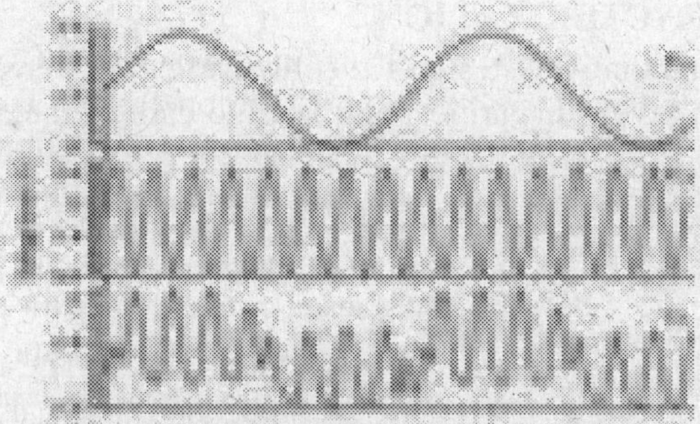

**Figure 8.22: Experimental results of the multiplication of two cosine signals by the four-quadrant multiplier**

In an ideal case, the voltage $V_S$ at the output of the multiplier can be expressed as

$$V_S = \frac{AB}{2}[\cos(2n(f_2 - f_1)) + \cos(2n(f_2 + f_1))] \tag{8.16}$$

The frequency spectrum, represented in Figure 8.22 contains two main frequencies (17.5Hz and 22.5Hz) around the carrier frequency. The residues which appear in the spectrum are known as intermodulation products. Intermodulation is caused by nonlinear behavior of the structure (around 10kHz and 30kHz) and the insulation defects of input pads (at 40kHz). Nevertheless, the amplitude of these intermodulation products is significantly lower than the two main frequencies. Therefore, the contribution of the insulation defect is eight times smaller than the main signals.

Furthermore, the experimental measures highlighted that the linearity of the multiplier is maximum for input signals with amplitude range between 0.6V and 2.6V. This corresponds to the typical range of values coming from the pixel since the [AM]2 structures provide values around $V_{dd}/2 = 1.65V$.

## 4. CHIP CHARACTERIZATION

An experimental $64 \times 64$ pixel image sensor has been developed in a 0.35¼m, 3.3V, standard CMOS process with poly-poly capacitors. Its functional testing and its characterization were performed using a specific hardware platform. The hardware part of the imaging system contains a one million Gates Spartan-3 FPGA board with 32MB SDRAM embedded. This FPGA board is the XSA-3S1000 from XESS Corporation. An interface acquisition circuit includes three ADCs from analog device (AD9048), high-speed LM6171 amplifiers and others elements such as the motor lens. Figure 8.23 shows the schematic and some pictures of the experimental platform.

**Figure 8.23: Block diagram and pictures of the hardware platform including FPGA board and CMOS sensor**

## 5. ELECTRICAL CHARACTERIZATION

The sensor was quantitatively tested for conversion gain, sensitivity, fixed pattern noise, thermal reset noise, output levels disparities, and voltage gain of the amplifier stage, linear flux, and dynamic range.

To determine these values, the sensor included specific test pixels in which some internal node voltages can be directly read. The test equipment hardware is based on a light generator with wavelength of 400nm to 1100nm. The sensor conversion gain was evaluated to 54¼V/e⁻ RMS with a sensitivity of 0.15V/lux.s, thanks to the octagonal shape of the photodiode and the fill-factor of 25%. At 10000 frames/s, measured nonlinearity is 0.12% over a 2V range. According to the experimental results, the voltage gain of the amplifier stage of the two [AM]2 is $Av = 12$and the disparities on the output levels are about 4.3%.

## 6. FIXED PATTERN NOISE

Image sensors always suffer from technology related nonidealities that can limit the performances of the vision system. Among them, fixed pattern noise (FPN) is the variation in output pixel values, under uniform illumination, due to device and interconnect mismatches across the image sensor. Two main types of FPN occur in CMOS sensors. First, offset FPN which takes place into the pixel is due to fluctuations in the threshold voltage of the transistors. Second, the most important source of FPN is introduced by the column amplifiers used in standard APS systems. In our approach, the layout is symmetrically built in order to reduce the offset FPN among each block of four pixels and to ensure uniform spatial sampling.

Furthermore, our chip does not include any column amplifier since the amplification of the pixel values takes place into the pixel by means of an inverter. So, the gain FPN is very limited and only depends on the mismatch of the two transistors. FPN can be reduced by correlated double sampling (CDS). To implement CDS, each pixel output needs to be read twice, once after reset and a second time at the end of integration. The correct pixel signal is obtained by substracting the two values. A CDS can be easily implemented in our chip.

**Figure 8.24: Images of fixed pattern noise (a) without CDS and (b) with CDS for an integration time of 1 millisecond**

For this purpose, the first analog memory stores the pixel value just after the reset signal and the second memory stores the value at the end of integration. Then, at the end of the image acquisition, the two values can be transferred to the FPGA, responsible for producing the difference. In Figure 8.24 the two images show fixed pattern noise with and without CDS using a 1 millisecond integration time. On the left image, the FPN is mainly due to the random variations in the offset voltages of the pixel-level analog structures. The experimental benchmarks of our chip reveal an FPN value of 225¼V RMS. The right picture shows the same image after analog CDS, performed as described above. The final FPN has been reduced by a factor of 34 to 6.6¼V.

In the rest of the results, CDS has not been implemented since FPN has low values. Only, an entire dark image is substracted from the output images on the FPGA. Focus has been made on the development of low-level image processing using the two analog memories and the associated processing unit.

### 8.4.3 HIGH-SPEED IMAGE PROCESSING APPLICATIONS

In this section, we provide experimental results of image processing implemented on our high-speed vision chip. First, we demonstrate the possibility of acquisition of raw images at different framerates, up to 10000 frames/s. Secondly, we present an implementation of edge detection, based on the well-known Sobel operator.

#### 8.4.3.1 SAMPLE IMAGES

The prototype chip was used for acquisition of raw images. First, sample raw images of stationary scenes were captured at different framerates, as shown in Figure 8.25. In the three views, no image processing is performed on the video stream, except for amplification of the photodiodes signal. From left to right, we can see a human face obtained at 1000 frames/s, a static electric fan at 5000 frames/s, and an electronic chip at 10000 frames/s.

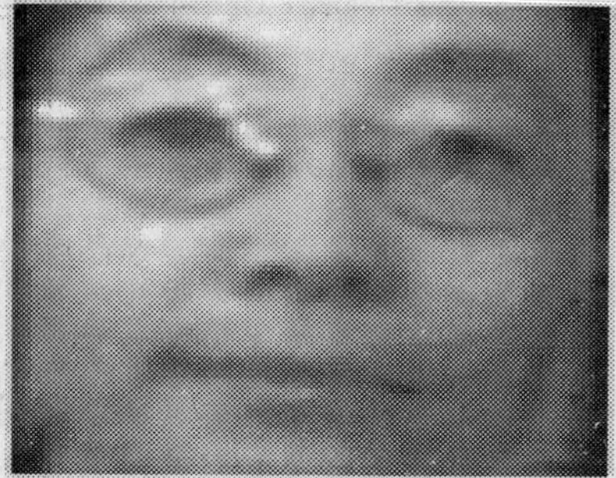

**Figure 8.25: Various raw images acquisition at 1000, 5000 and 10000 frames/s**

Figure 8.26 represents different frames of a moving object, namely, a milk drop splashing sequence. In order to capture the details of such a rapidly moving scene, the sensor operates at 2500 frames/s. and stores a sequence of 50 images. The frames 1, 5, 10, 15, 20, 25, 30, and 40 are shown in the figure.

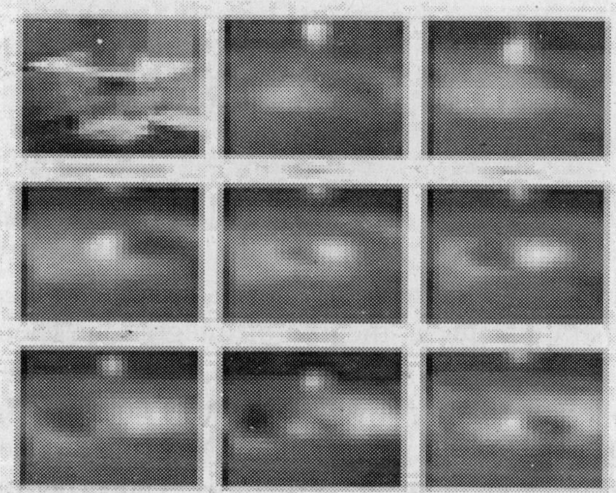

**Figure 8.26: A 2500 frames/s video sequence of a milk drop splashing**

### 8.4.3.2 SOBEL OPERATOR

The characteristics of our sensor, especially the analog processing unit, make it extremely useful for low-level image processing based on convolution masks. In this paragraph, we report an edge detector, the Sobel detector. The Sobel operator estimates the gradient of a 2D image. This algorithm is used for edge detection in the preprocessing stage of computer vision systems. The classical algorithm uses a pair of convolution kernels (8.17), one to detect changes along the vertical axis ($h_1$) and another one to detect horizontal contrast ($h_2$). For this purpose, the algorithm performs a convolution between the image and the sliding convolution mask over the image. It manipulates 9 pixels for each value to produce. The value corresponds to an approximation of the gradient centered on the processed image area:

$$h_1 = \begin{pmatrix} -1 & 0 & 1 \\ -2 & 0 & 2 \\ -1 & 0 & 1 \end{pmatrix}, \quad h_2 = \begin{pmatrix} -1 & -2 & -1 \\ 0 & 0 & 0 \\ 1 & 2 & 1 \end{pmatrix}. \tag{8.17}$$

The structure of our architecture is well adapted to the evaluation of the Sobel algorithm. It leads to the result directly centered on the photosensor and directed along the natural axes of the image. The gradient is computed in each pixel of the image by performing successive linear combinations of the 4 adjacent pixels. For this purpose, each kernel mask is decomposed into two 22 masks that successively operate on the whole image.

For the kernel $h_1$ the corresponding 22 masks are:

$$m_1 = \begin{pmatrix} -1 & 0 \\ -1 & 0 \end{pmatrix}, \quad m_2 = \begin{pmatrix} 0 & 1 \\ 0 & 1 \end{pmatrix} \tag{8.18}$$

Figure 8.27 represents the 33 mask centered on the pixel $ph_5$ Each octagonal photodiode $ph_i(i=1,\ldots\ldots,9)$ is associated with a processing element $PE_i$ represented with a circle on the figure. Each $PE_i$ is positioned on the bottom right of its photodiode, as in the real layout of the circuit.

The first mask $m_1$ contributes to evaluate the following series of operations for the four $PE_i$ is:

$$\begin{aligned} V_{11} &= -(V_{ph_1} + V_{ph_4}), \\ V_{12} &= -(V_{ph_2} + V_{ph_5}), \\ V_{14} &= -(V_{ph_4} + V_{ph_7}), \\ V_{15} &= -(V_{ph_5} + V_{ph_8}), \end{aligned} \tag{8.19}$$

and the second mask $m_2$ computes:

$$\begin{aligned} V_{21} &= +(V_{ph_2} + V_{ph_5}), \\ V_{22} &= +(V_{ph_3} + V_{ph_6}), \\ V_{24} &= +(V_{ph_5} + V_{ph_8}), \\ V_{25} &= +(V_{ph_6} + V_{ph_9}) \end{aligned} \tag{8.20}$$

with $V_{ij}$ corresponding to the result provided by the processing element $PE_j$ $(j=1,2,\ldots\ldots,9)$ with the mask $m_i(i=1,2)$, and $V_{phk}(k=1,2,\ldots\ldots,9)$, the voltages representing the incidental illumination on each photodiode $ph_K$. Then, the evaluation of the gradient at the center of the mask can be computed by summing the different values on the external FPGA.

Note that $V_{12} = -V_{21}$ and $V_{15} = -V_{24}$. So, the final sum can be simplified and written as $V_{h1} = V_{11} + V_{22} + V_{25} + V_{14}$. If we define a retina cycle as the time spent for the configuration of the coefficients kernel and the preprocessing of the image, the evaluation of the gradient on the vertical direction only spends a frame acquisition and two retina cycles. By generalization, the estimation of the complete gradient along the two axes spend 4 cycles because it involves 4 dynamic configurations.

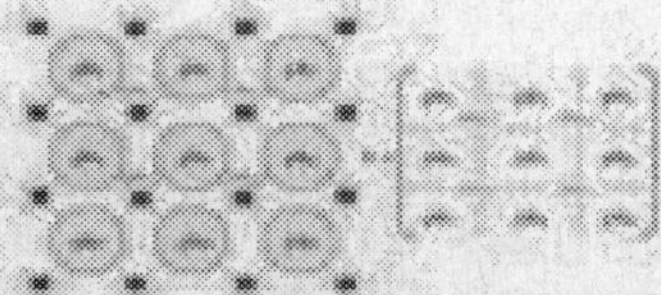

**Figure 8.27: kernel used by the 4 processing elements**

In short, the dynamic assignment of coefficient values from the external processor gives the system some interesting dynamic properties. The system can be easily reconfigured by changing the internal coefficients for the masks between two successive computations. First, this allows the possibility to dynamically change the image processing algorithms embedded in the sensor. Secondly, this enables the evaluation of some complex pixel-level algorithms, implying different successive convolutions. The images can be captured at higher framerates than the standard framerate, processed by exploiting the the analog memories and the reconfigurable processing elements and output at a lower framerate depending of the number of the dynamic reconfigurations.

Moreover, the analog arithmetic units implementing these pixel-level convolutions drastically decrease the number of single operations such as additions and multiplications executed by an external processor (an FPGA in our case) as shown in Figure 8.23. Indeed, in the case of our experimental $64 \times 64$ pixel sensor, the peak performance is equivalent to 4 parallel signed multiplications by pixel at 10000 frames/s, that is, more than 160 million multiplications per second. With a VGA resolution ($640 \times 480$), the performance level would increase to a factor of 75, leading to about 12 billion multiplications per second. Processing this data flow by external processors will imply important hardware resources in order to cope with the temporal constraints.

As an illustration of the Sobel algorithm, Figure 8.28 is an example sequence of 16 images of a moving object, namely., an electric fan. Two white specific markers are placed on the fan, that is a small circle near the rotor and a painted blade. The speed rotation of the fan is 3750rpm. In order to capture such a rapidly moving object, a short integration time (100 microseconds) was used for the frames acquisition. The Sobel algorithm allows to distinguish clearly the two white markers even with a high framerate.

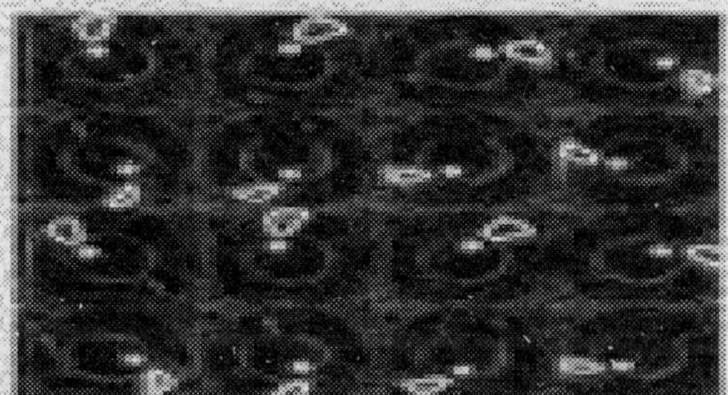

**Figure 8.28: Sequence of 16 images with Sobel operator**

### 8.4.4. AN IMAGE PROCESSOR DEVELOPED BY PANASONIC

They are being used in almost all the digital cameras featuring in the Lumix series. Generally image processors work in four stages. Firstly they receive data from the CCD sensors, then they create Y-Colour differences i.e. image processing is done, then JPEG compression is done and lastly the image data is saved. With the introduction of Venus Image Processing Engine series; the latest being Venus Engine HD, Panasonic is claiming faster shutter speeds along with lower energy consumption.

**Figure 8.29 Venus Image Processing Chip**

Venus II, is the successor of Venus engine and is known for its enhanced resolution and super fast shutter response, this image processor has been incorporated in its Lumix DMC-FZ7 camera. Now with all the basic properties of Venus II, Panasonic developed the Venus III image processing engine that also provides better noise reduction at high ISO speeds and offers lower power consumption. But it was later discovered that along with noise reduction, some fine image details were eliminated, thus to overcome this defect of the Venus III; the Venus IV Engine was developed.

**Figure 8.30 Panasonic MN895 10RF EA (Chip)**

The Venus Engine IV claims higher quality images as well as includes accurate tracking and correction of of stabilisation and ISO control. It also provides better noise reduction, preserves the finer image details, a faster shutter response along with great power efficiency. It provides superior quality images by using advanced signal processing that provides blur-free images that are rich in colour and depth. Advanced signal processing is done by adding two more circuits that help in reducing both low frequency as well as chromatic noise. Thus y6ou are sure to get superior quality images even in dimly lit situations. Panasonic has incorporated this advanced image processor in its Lumix DMC LS85 and Lumix DMC TZ6 Digital Cameras.

Panasonic's Image Processors is the Venus Engine V; which uses advanced signal processing to generate beautiful images under high sensitivities. Multi-task signal processing is applied to all images for empowering higher performance and faster shooting. This image processor also increases the accuracy of many features such as MEGA Optical Image Stabilisation technique and the Intelligent ISO Control. A lot of energy efficiency improvements have been incorporated in this one, thus it provides better power efficiency. The cameras which come with this feature include the Lumix DMC FX40 and the Lumix DMC FX550 Digital Cameras.

A large scale image processing engine is the Venus Engine HD. It ensures high quality pictures and supports high definition television screen. It can handle dimly-lit subjects as well as fast moving high definition movies very well. It allows you to shoot in 720p AVCHD Lite and performs advanced signal processing for the best quality images and videos. Cameras using this image processor include the Lumix DMC G1 and Lumix DMC TZ7 Digital Cameras. With the Venus image processor you are sure to get the best quality of images and movies along with the almost nil amount of noise and distortion. It also ensures maximum power consumption.

#### 8.4.4.1 BIONZ IMAGE PROCESSING ENGINE – THE BRAIN BEHIND SONY CAMERAS

An image processor is a chip that is in-built into a digital camera. Image processing is a form of signal processing that transforms the image signal into a clear and precise image file. These days digital cameras include a dedicated image processing chips that convert the RAW data obtained from image sensors into a standard image format with the respective colour combinations. Due to these image processors the digital cameras always have an upper hand over conventional film cameras. This is because the image processing is done by special software that can manipulate the image in a number of ways. You can come across a variety of image processors have been introduced by different manufacturers. Like Canon who founded DIGIC III processor and Nikon which uses EXPEED processor, Sony has established the BIONZ Image Processing Engine. This BIONZ Imaging Processor has been incorporated into all Sony's latest compact and professional cameras as well as camcorders

**Figure 8.31 BIONZ Image Processor**

An image sensor is the heart of any digital camera. Usually CCD sensors were used for small and digital cameras, however these days they are being gradually replaced by CMOS sensors for higher quality and battery life. Sony has instituted the concept of High Definition video with the ClearVid CMOS Sensor. This CMOS sensor features Exmor technology that enables it to provide higher resolution and better sensitivity with a large dynamic range.

Image processor converts the raw data into a complete image. However the image processing engine is a major deciding factor that determines the clarity and precision with which the conversion is done. To support enhanced details reproduction, Sony's BIONZ Image Processing Engine inculcates a sense of realism in each and every shot. It renders colours and adds rich texture and depth to convert it as the human eye would be able to view it. It works in conjunction with Exmor CMOS sensor that eliminates noise during the raw data conversion and image processing periods. The image thus reproduced is a realistic one that is rich in colour and detail. In cases where the background is very bright, this image processor suppresses the colour and luminance and noise to deliver a true-to-life photo.

Sony's BIONZ processor has revolutionised the digital camera industry and it unquestionably portrays the quality level of Sony Electronics.

### 8.4.4.2 TECHNOLOGY BEHIND CANON'S 'DIGIC-III PROCESSOR'

**Figure 8.32 DIGIC Image Processor Chip**

DIGIC Processing technology was introduced by Canon, which it uses in all its models. This Image processor uses signal processing to augment the picture quality, as well as the image processing speed.

**(i) Evolution of DIGIC Processors:-**

Canon had set its R&D team to develop a technology that could change the way the images were produced. It was on the lookout for a technique, using which the processing speed, the automatic focus and the image quality could be improved. The outcome was the development of the Digital Imaging Core (DIGIC) technology by Canon.

There is an image sensor in the digital camera, which converts the light that enters the camera through its lens into electrical signals. Now a Digital Image Processor is a technicality that removes the noise from these signals and generates images with natural colours and realistic effects. The DIGIC is an image processor that reduces the false colours and moiré patterns in the pictures and cancels the noise that is generated during long exposures.

The original DIGIC was used on the Canon S1 IS and other cameras. This technology was used to improve the image quality and reduce the processing speed. However, it consisted of three separate chips: a video processing integrated circuit, an image processing integrated circuit, and a camera control integrated circuit.

The DIGIC II; unlike the initial DIGIC, was all about a single chip, thus the design becoming more compact. This new version was enhanced by the addition of a large buffer and faster processing speed. It uses a Double Data Rate Synchronous Dynamic Static RAM (DDR-SDRAM), which improves the start-up time, as well as the Auto-Focus speed. DIGIC II also improves the colour, white balance and sharpness. This technology is used in Canon EOS 400D Digital Camera, Canon EOS 5D Digital Camera, etc.

The DIGIC III processor is the advanced version of the DIGIC II processor. It has all the above mentioned qualities. Additionally, it can extend the battery life, deliver better quality images, and improve the operating speed as well. It also provides for a faster interface to the SD card memory. It also provides Face Detection Technicality, using which it can track about 9 faces in the frame and adjust the exposure, focus and flash, and provide proper lighting effects to produce explicitly realistic images. It also helps in improving the LCD screen resolution.

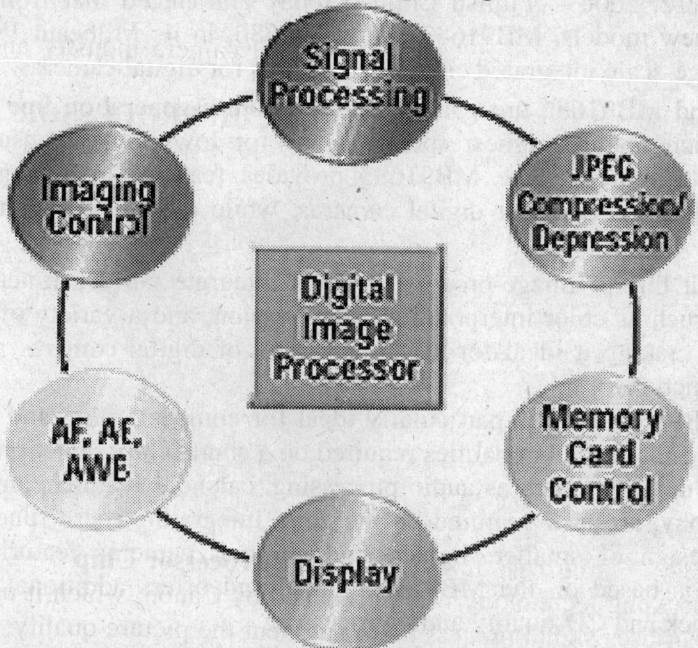


**Figure 8.33 1 DIGIC III Image Processor**

**(ii) DIGIC III Processor:-**

The circuit board of DIGIC contains a x86 compatible processor, a Datalight ROM-DOS operating system and the image processor. The DIGIC III processor consists of an embedded 32-bit ARM architecture processor.

DIGIC III Image Processor enhances the performance of the digital cameras in the following areas:-

- JPEG Compression or Expansion
- Memory Card Control
- LCD Control
- Video Processing

DIGIC III uses Advanced Noise Reduction Technology, due to which high light sensitivity can be produced. The cameras with higher light sensitivities are capable of capturing images in low light conditions with no loss to image quality and clarity. A higher light sensitivity also ensures faster shutter speed, thus reducing blurs in the images, or in fast moving pictures that refer to sports events or wildlife in action.

DIGIC III Processor has a superior processing speed, accurate auto-focus functionality, a fast camera response and continuous shooting capability. Its rate of operation and accuracy of colour reproduction, enables it to be used in Professional EOS Cameras; the Canon EOS 1000D Digital Camera, Canon S5 IS, etc.

Canon's DIGIC technology is considered as a revolution in the digital camera industry and it emphatically displays Canon's leadership in this industry.

### 8.4.4 3 FUJITSU LAUNCHES NEW IMAGE-PROCESSING CHIPS FOR COMPACT DIGITAL CAMERAS WITH VIDEO

Tokyo, July 12, 2006 — Fujitsu Limited today announced that from August 1 it will begin sales of two new models, MB91683 and MB91686, in its Milbeaut ™ line of advanced image processing large-scale integrated circuit (LSI) chips for digital cameras.

MB91683 and MB91686 are part of the new fourth-generation line (M-4) of Fujitsu's Milbeaut chips, which feature highest specifications for low power consumption and high-resolution imaging technology. The MB91683 provides features in a single chip numerous functions that are ideal for compact digital cameras, while the MB91686 in addition features video functionality.

The Milbeaut line of image-processing chips integrate various functions necessary for image processing - such as color interpolation, compression, and a variety of interfaces - into a single chip, thereby making it ideal for use in a variety of digital cameras and mobile phones featuring imaging functions.

The new MB91683 chip is particularly ideal for compact, slim, and lightweight digital cameras, as it provides basic functionalities required on a single chip. Functions which in the past required peripherals devices - such as audio processing, calendar features, anti-shake with high-sensitivity photography, are now featured on the chip. Integrating these functions into a single chip enables the design of smaller, lighter, and slimmer cameras featuring high-resolution imaging. MB91686 is based on the MB91683 model and offers additional features for video recording and playback and CD-quality audio processing.

Both chip models are manufactured at Fujitsu's leading-edge advance semiconductor fab in Mie, Japan using 300-mm wafers and 90 nanometer (nm) process technology, resulting in industry-leading levels of power saving. The new chips were developed in collaboration with Fujitsu VLSI Limited, Fujitsu Micro Solutions Limited, and Fujitsu Laboratories Limited.

**Key Features**

1. Peripherals functions now embedded in single chip; enables smaller camera size and lowers overall cost (for both MB91683 and MB91686) Built-in calendar function, voice recording and playback amplifier and codec Programs stored on NAND flash memory can boot system, eliminating the need for external memory to program.
2. World's first: Built-in high-sensitivity photography and anti-shake image processing functions (for both MB91683 and MB91686) Increased image sensitivity for a faster shutter and less distortion from shaking is made possible through digital processing New

noise-reduction function for high-sensitivity photography. These new chips are the first in the industry to integrate these functions into a single chip. Fujitsu's new Milbeaut chips enable high-sensitivity photography and high-precision anti-shake functions that are desired for high-resolution compact digital cameras.

3. Built-in MPEG4 video for digital cameras (MB91686 only) MPEG4 codec is embedded, offering both high-quality imagery and high compression rates. It also enables high-quality video recording and playback at 30 frames per second with video graphics array (VGA) (640 x 480) resolution 16-bit digital signal processor (DSP) built in for audio processing Includes an HDMI interface and REC656 input interface to easily enable connections to a variety of audio/video equipment.

# QUESTION BANK

Q1. What do you mean by hardware architecture for image processing?

Q2. Briefly describe the various distributed processing of image data? Explain with the help of example.

Q3. Explain the various design of the distributed processing?

Q4. Write short note on the core of distributed processing.

Q5. Explain the various implementation details of the distributed processing of image data. Also explain its Applications.

Q6. Describe the various role of array processing in details?

Q7. Write short note on the Mapping, Filtering, Folding and Zipping?

Q8. Briefly describe the various image representations? Explain with the help of example.

Q9. Explain the various array signals processing in details?

Q10. Write short note on the wave propagation?

Q11. Briefly explain the parametric data model?

Q12. Explain the applications of array signal processing.

Q13. What are the standard image processor chips? Explain with the help of example.

Q14. Briefly explain the Architecture of the image processor chips?

Q15. Explain the various high-speed image processing applications.

Q16. Explain the DIGIC- III Image Processor Chip? Explain with the help of example.

# CHAPTER 9

# TECHNIQUES OF COLOR IMAGE PROCESSING

## 9.1 INTRODUCTION

In our daily life, our vision and actions are influenced by an abundance of geometry and color information. When crossing a street, we identify a technical apparatus by its geometry as a traffic light. However, only by analyzing color information do we subsequently decide whether we are to continue, if the light is green, or stop, if the light is red. A camera-assisted driving information system should be able to evaluate similar information and either pass the information on to the driver of a vehicle or directly influence the behavior of the vehicle. The latter is of importance, for example, for the guidance of an autonomous vehicle on a public road. Something similar to this applies to traffic signs, which can be classified as prohibitive, regulatory, or informative signs based on color and geometry.

The assessment of color information also plays an important role in our individual object identification. We usually do not search in a bookcase for a book known to us solely by its title. We try to remember the color of the cover (e.g., blue) and then search among all of the books with a blue cover for the one with the correct title. The same applies to recognizing an automobile in a parking lot. In general, we do not search for model X of company Y, but rather we look for a red car, for example. Only when we see a red vehicle do we decide, according to its geometry, whether that vehicle is the one for which we are looking. The search strategy is driven by a hierarchical combination of color and form. Such hierarchical strategies are also implemented in automatic object recognition systems.

While in the past color image processing was limited essentially to satellite imagery, it has gained importance in recent years on account of new possibilities. This is due, among other things, to the high information level that color images contain in relation to gray-level images. This information allows color image processing to succeed in areas where "classical gray-level image processing" currently dominates. The decision confidence level for various techniques can be greatly improved by the additional classification markers color can provide. The applied procedures are thereby made simpler, more robust, or even applicable in the first place.

The fundamental difference between color images and gray-level images is that in a color space, a color vector (which generally consists of three components) is assigned to a pixel of a color image, while a scalar gray value is assigned to a pixel of a gray-level image. Thus, in color image processing, vector-valued image functions are treated instead of the scalar image functions used in gray-level image processing. Color image processing techniques can be subdivided 011 the basis of their principal procedures into two classes:

1. Monochromatic-based techniques first treat information from the individual color channels or color vector components separately and then combine the individual results.
2. Vector-valued techniques treat the color information as color vectors in a vector space provided with a vector norm.

The techniques from the first class can also be designated as rental schemes, since they frequently borrow methods from gray-level image processing and implement them separately on each color component. Thereby the dependencies between the individual color components (or vector components) are usually ignored. The monochromatic-based techniques make it clear that the transition from scalar to vector-valued functions, which can be mastered with color image analysis, is not yet generally known.

Color attributes such as hue or saturation are also used in monochromatic based techniques. However, the analysis or processing of color information occurs separately for each component, for example, only the hue component or only the saturation component is treated (as in a gray-level image). In contrast, vector valued techniques treat the color information in its entirety and not separately for each vector component. While monochromatic-based techniques were predominantly regarded in the early days of color image processing, in recent times vector-valued techniques are being more frequently discussed.

The difference between the two techniques serves as a systematization of the procedure in order to point out the respective conditions of developments from monochromatic-based techniques to vector valued techniques. Better or more robust results are often attained with monochromatic-based techniques for color image processing than with techniques for gray-level processing. The monochromatic-based techniques, however, do not define a new way of image processing but rather demonstrate only transference of known techniques to color images. In contrast, the analysis and processing of vector-valued image information establishes a new step in image processing that simultaneously presents a challenge and a new possibility for analyzing image information. One difficulty with vector-valued techniques has been that the signal theoretical basics for vector-valued color signals have not yet been presented.

In the past, the application of techniques for color image processing was restricted by additional factors. One factor was limited data memory and the "slow" processors: a three-channel color image of 1024 x 1024 pixels occupies, for example, 3 MB. For a geometric stereo analysis technique at least two images (6 MB) are needed, and for a photometric stereo analysis technique generally three images (9 MB) are necessary. These must be treated at a processing speed appropriate for the requirements of the application. Using more modern computers, the limitations on memory space and processing speed are not totally eliminated; however, the importance of this problem continues to decrease. Thus, the processor requirements for implementing digital color image processing today are satisfied.

Another factor that limited the applicability of color image processing in the past was color camera technology. In recent years, the availability of robust and low-cost color CCD cameras has made the acquisition of high-quality color images feasible under many varying acquisition conditions. However, in spite of enormous advances in camera technology there is a lack, as already mentioned, of extensive signal-theory investigations of vector-valued color signals. Here an urgent need for basic research exists. In areas such as photo grammetry and remote sensing, images with more than three "color" channels are frequently analyzed. Newer areas of application analyze color images that represent three-channel spectral transmissions of visible light. Knowledge of the processing occurring in the human eye and brain of the signals that come from the three sensitive (with regard to different wavelengths) receptors in the retina can be used for the development and evaluation of techniques for color image processing.

The three different receptor types in the human retina are also the reason that commercial CCD-color cameras likewise implement measurements in three different wavelength areas of visible light. These cameras deliver a three-channel signal and the three channels are represented separately on a monitor or screen for the observer. Furthermore, the color attributes hue and saturation are defined only within the spectral area of visible light. As an example, correspondence analysis in stereo images shows that red pixels do not correspond with blue pixels, even when their intensity values are similar. The segmentation of color images based on classification of color values is generally substantially more differentiated than segmentation based exclusively on intensity values.

The evaluation of color information in the image creates additional new possibilities for solving problems in computer vision. Many image processing techniques still assume that only matte (Lambertian) surfaces in the scene are analyzed. This assumption does not hold for real scenes with several reflecting (non-Lambertian) surfaces.

However, this limitation can be overcome under certain conditions by highlight elimination in color images. Furthermore, physically determined phenomena, such as shadows or interreflections, can be analyzed more easily in color images than in gray-level images. For this, predominantly vector-valued image processing techniques are used that employ reflection models derived from physical optics for modeling image functions. These techniques are denoted as physics-based vision techniques. The invariant extraction of color information in relation to varying lighting conditions and description of image characteristics represents another problem in computer vision. Here promising vector-valued techniques for so-called color constancy can make an important contribution.

## 9.2 COLOR IMAGE SIGNAL REPRESENTATION

The Image Processing Toolbox handles color image either as indexed images or RGB (red, green, blue) images. In this section we discuss these two image types in some detail.

### 9.2.1 RGB IMAGES

An RGB color image is an MX N X 3 array of color pixels, where each cold pixel is a triplet corresponding to the red, green, and blue components of RGB image at a specific spatial location (see Figure 9.1). An RGB image may h viewed as a "stack" of three gray-scale images that, when fed into the re. green, and blue inputs of a color monitor, produce a color image on the screen By convention, the three images forming an RGB color image are referred" as the red, green, and blue component images. The data class of the component images determines their range of values. If an RGB image is of class double the range of values is [0, 1]. Similarly, the range of values is [0,255] or [0, 65535 for RGB images of class uint8 or uint16, respectively. The number of bit used to represent the pixel values of the component images determines the b depth of an RGB image.

For example, if each component image is an 8-bi image, the corresponding RGB image is said to be 24 bits deep. Generally, number of bits in all component images is the same. In this case, the number of possible colors in an RGB image is (2"), where b is the number of bits in each component image. For the 8-bit case, the number is 16,777,216 colors.

Let fR, fG, and fB represent three RGB component images. An RGB image is formed from these images by using the cat (concatenate) operator to stack the images:

```
rgb_image = cat(3, fR, fG, fB)
```

The order in which the images are placed in the operand matters. In general, cat (dim, Al , A2, . . . ) concatenates the arrays along the dimension specified by dim. For example, if dim = 1, the arrays are arranged vertically, if dim = - 2, they are arranged horizontally, and, if dim = 3, they are stacked in the third dimension, as in Figure 9.1.

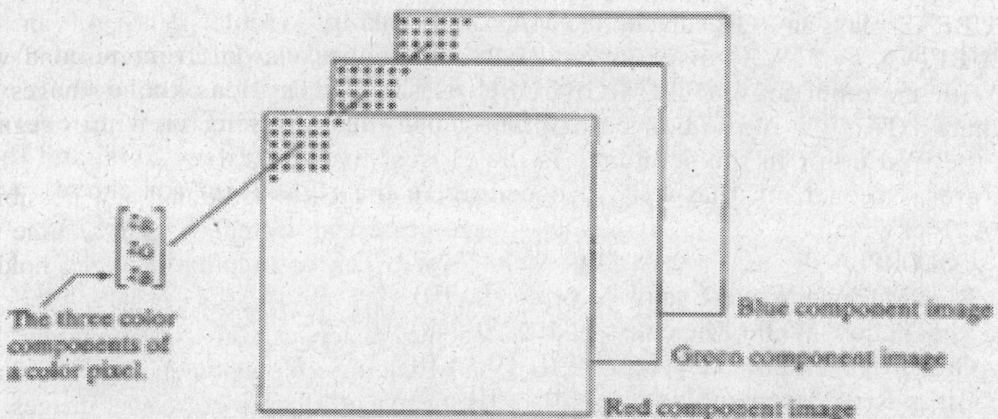


**Figure 9.1 Schematic showing how pixels of an RGB color image are formed from the corresponding pixels of the three component images**

If all component images are identical, the result is a gray-scale image. Let rgb_image denote an RGB image. The following commands extract the three component images:

```
>> fR = rgb_image(:    1 );
>> fG = rgb_image(:    2) ;
>> fB  = rgb_image(:   3);
```

The RGB color space usually is shown graphically as an RGB color cube, as depicted in Figure 9.2. The vertices of the cube are the primary (red, green, and blue) and secondary (cyan, magenta, and yellow) colors of light.

Often, it is useful to be able to view the color cube from any perspective. Function rgbcube is used for this purpose. The syntax is

```
rgbcube(vx, vy, vz)
```

Typing rgbcube (vx , vy, vz) at the prompt produces an RGB cube on the MATLAB desktop, viewed from point ( vx , vy, vz ). The resulting image can be saved to disk using function print. The code for this function follows. It is self-explanatory.

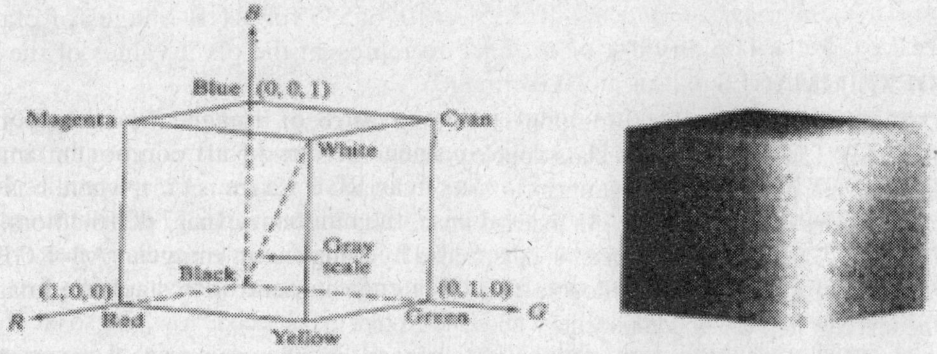


**Figure 9.2 (a)Schematic of the RGB color cube showing the primary and secondary colors of light at the vertices. Points along the main diagonal have gray values from black at the origin to white at point (1, 1, 1) .(b)The RGB color cube**

function rgbcube(vx, vy, vz)
RGBCUBE Displays an RGB cube on the MATLAB desktop.
RGBCUBE(VX, VY, VZ) displays an RGB color cube, viewed from point (VX, VY, VZ). With no input arguments, RGBCUBE uses (10, 10, 4) as the default viewing coordinates. To view individual color planes, use the following viewing coordinates, where the first color in the sequence is the closest to the viewing axis, and the other colors are as seen from that axis, proceeding to the right right (or above), and then moving clockwise.

| COLORPLANE | ( vx, vy, vz) |
|---|---|
| Blue-Magenta-White-Cyan | ( 0, 0, 10) |
| Red-Yellow-White-Magenta | ( 10, 0, 0) |
| Green-Cyan-White-Yellow | ( 0, 10, 0) |
| Black-Red-Magenta-Blue | ( 0, —10, 0) |
| Black-Blue-Cyan-Green | (-10, 0, 0) |
| Black-Red-Yellow-Green | ( 0, 0, —10) |

Set up parameters for function patch.
vertices_matrix = [0 0 0;0 0 1;0 1 0;0 1 1;1 0 0;1 0 1;1 1 0;1 1 1];
faces_matrix = [1 5 6 2;1 3 7 5;1 2 4 3;2 4 8 6;3 7 8 4;5 6 8 7];
colors = vertices_matrix;
The order of the cube vertices was selected to be the same as the order of the (R,G,B) colors (e.g., (0,0,0) corresponds to % black, (1,1,1) corresponds to white, and so on.)
Generate RGB cube using function patch.
patch( 'Vertices' , vertices_matrix, 'Faces', faces_matrix, 'FaceVertexCData' ,colors, 'FaceColor ' , 'interp' , 'EdgeAlpha' , 0)
Set up viewing point.

```
if nargin == 0
vx = 10; vy = 10; vz = 4;
elseif nargin —= 3
  error('Wrong number of inputs.')
end
axis off
view([vx, vy, vz]) axis square
```

### 9.2.2 INDEXED IMAGES

An indexed image has two components: a data matrix of integers, X, and a color map matrix, map. Matrix map is an m X 3 array of class double containing floating-point values in the range [0, 1]. The length, m, of the map is equal to the number of colors it defines. Each row of map specifies the red, green, and blue components of a single color. An indexed image uses "direct mapping" of pixel intensity values to color map values. The color of each pixel is determined by using the corresponding value of integer matrix X as a pointer into map. If X is of class double, then all of its components with values less than or equal to 1 point to the first row in map, all components with value 2 point to the second row, and so on. If X is of class uint 8 or uint 16, then all components with value 0 point to the first row in map, all components with value 1 point to the second row, and so on. These concepts are illustrated in Figure 9.3.

To display an indexed image we write

```
>> imshow(X, map)
```

or, alternatively,

>> image ( X )

>> color map (map )

A color map is stored with an indexed image and is automatically loaded with the image when function imread is used to load the image.

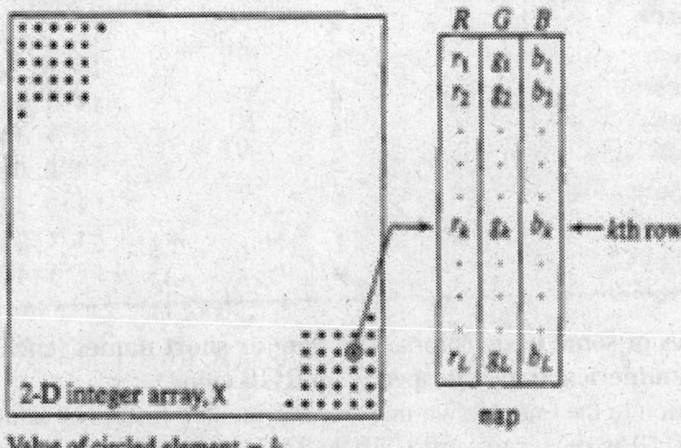


**Figure 9.3 Elements of an indexed image. Note that the value of an element of integer array X determines the row number in the colormap. Each row contains an RGB triplet, and L is the total number of rows**

Sometimes it is necessary to approximate an indexed image by one with fewer colors. For this we use function imapprox, whose syntax is

[Y, newmap] = imapprox(X, map, n)

This function returns an array Y with colormap newmap, which has at most n colors.

The input array X can be of class uint8, u in t 16, or do u ble. The output Y is of class uint8 if n is less than or equal to 256. If n is greater than 256, Y is of class double.

When the number of rows in map is less than the number of distinct integer values in X, multiple values in X are displayed using the same color in map. For example, suppose that X consists of four vertical bands of equal width, with values 1, 64, 128, and 256. If we specify the colormap map = [ 0 0 0; 1 1 1], then all the elements in X with value 1 would point to the first row (black) of the map and all the other elements would point to the second row (white). Thus, the command imshow(X, map) would display an image with a black band followed by three white bands. In fact, this would be true until the length of the map became 65, at which time the display would be a black band, followed by a gray band, followed by two white bands. Nonsensical image displays can result if the length of the map exceeds the allowed range of values of the elements of X.

There are several ways to specify a color map. One approach is to use the statement

» map(k, :) = [r(k) g(k) b(k)]

where [r(k) g(k) b(k) ] are RGB values that specify one row of a color map. The map is filled out by varying k.

Table 9.1 lists the RGB values for some basic colors. Any of the three formats shown in the table can be used to specify colors. For example, the background color of a figure can be changed to green by using any of the following three statements:

```
>> whitebg('g')
>> whitebg('green')
>> whitebg([0 1 0])
```

| Long name | Short name | RGB values |
|---|---|---|
| Black | k | [0 0 0] |
| Blue | b | [0 0 1] |
| Green | g | [0 1 0] |
| Cyan | c | [0 1 1] |
| Red | r | [1 0 0] |
| Magenta | m | [1 0 1] |
| Yellow | y | [1 1 0] |
| White | w | [1 1 1] |

**Table 9.1 RGB values of some basic colors. The long or short names (enclosed by quotes) can be used instead of the numerical triplet to specify an RGB color**

Other colors in addition to the ones shown in Table 9.1 involve fractional values. For instance, [ .5 .5 .5] is gray, [ .5 0 0] is dark red, and [ .49 1 .83] is aquamarine.

MATLAB provides several predefined color maps, accessed using the command..

```
>> colormap(map_name)
```

which sets the colormap to the matrix map_name; an example is

```
>> colormap (copper)
```

where copper is one of the prespecified MATLAB colormaps. The colors in this map vary smoothly from black to bright copper. If the last image displayed was an indexed image, this command changes its colormap to copper. Alternatively, the image can be displayed directly with the desired colormap:

```
>> imshow(X, copper)
```

Table 9.2 lists some of the colormaps available in MATLAB. The length (number of colors) of these colormaps can be specified by enclosing the number in parentheses. For example, gray (16) generates a colormap with 16 shades of gray.

### 9.2.3 IPT FUNCTIONS FOR MANIPULATING RGB AND INDEXED IMAGES

Table 9.3 lists the IPT functions suitable for converting between RGB, indexed, and gray-scale images. For clarity of notation in this section, we use rgb_image to denote RGB images, gray_image to denote gray-scale images, bw to denote black and white images, and X, to denote the data matrix component of indexed images. Recall that an indexed image is composed of an integer data matrix and a colormap matrix.

Function dither is applicable both to gray-scale and color images. Dithering is a process used mostly in the printing and publishing industry to give the visual impression of shade variations on a printed page that consists of dots. In the case of gray-scale images, dithering attempts to capture shades of gray by producing a binary image of black dots on a white background (or vice versa). The sizes of the dots vary, from small dots in light areas to increasingly larger dots for dark areas. The key issue in implementing a dithering algorithm is a tradeoff between "accuracy" of visual perception and computational complexity. The dithering approach used in IPT is based on the Floyd-Steinberg algorithm . The syntax used by function dither for gray-scale images is

```
bw = dither(gray_image)
```

Where, as noted earlier, gray_image is a gray-scale image and bw is the dithered result (a binary image).

| Name | Description |
|---|---|
| autumn | Varies smoothly from red, through orange, to yellow. |
| bone | A gray-scale colormap with a higher value for the blue component. This colormap is useful for adding an "electronic" look to gray-scale images. |
| colorcube | Contains as many regularly spaced colors in RGB color space as possible, while attempting to provide more steps of gray, pure red, pure green, and pure blue. |
| cool | Consists of colors that are shades of cyan and magenta. It varies smoothly from cyan to magenta. |
| copper | Varies smoothly from black to bright copper. |
| flag | Consists of the colors red, white, blue, and black. This colormap completely changes color with each index increment. |
| gray | Returns a linear gray-scale colormap. |
| hot | Varies smoothly from black, through shades of red, orange, and yellow, to white. |
| hsv | Varies the hue component of the hue-saturation-value color model. The colors begin with red, pass through yellow, green, cyan, blue, magenta, and return to red. The colormap is particularly appropriate for displaying periodic functions. |
| jet | Ranges from blue to red, and passes through the colors cyan, yellow, and orange. |
| lines | Produces a colormap of colors specified by the ColorOrder property and a shade of gray. Consult online help regarding function ColorOrder. |
| pink | Contains pastel shades of pink. The pink colormap provides sepia tone colorization of grayscale photographs. |
| prism | Repeats the six colors red, orange, yellow, green, blue, and violet. |
| spring | Consists of colors that are shades of magenta and yellow. |
| summer | Consists of colors that are shades of green and yellow. |
| white | This is an all white monochrome colormap. |
| winter | Consists of colors that are shades of blue and green. |

**Table 9.2 Some of the MATLAB predefined colormaps**

| Function | Purpose |
|---|---|
| dither | Creates an indexed image from an RGB image by dithering. |
| grayslice | Creates an indexed image from a gray-scale intensity image by multilevel thresholding. |
| gray2ind | Creates an indexed image from a gray-scale intensity image. |
| ind2gray | Creates a gray-scale intensity image from an indexed image. |
| rgb2ind | Creates an indexed image from an RGB image. |
| ind2rgb | Creates an RGB image from an indexed image. |
| rgb2gray | Creates a gray-scale image from an RGB image. |

**Table 9.3 IPT functions for converting between RGB, indexed, and gray- scale intensity images.**

When working with color images, dithering is used principally in conjunction with function rgb2ind to reduce the number of colors in an image. This function is discussed later in this section. Function grayslice has the syntax

X = grayslice (gray_image, n)

this function produces an indexed image by thresholding gray_image with threshold values

$$\frac{1}{n},\frac{2}{n},\ldots\ldots\ldots,\frac{n-1}{n}$$

As noted earlier, the resulting indexed image can be viewed with the cornniand ims how ( X , map ) using a map of appropriate length [e.g., j et (16)]. An alternate syntax is

X = grayslice(gray_image, v)

where v is a vector whose values are used to threshold gray_image. When used in conjunction with a colormap, grayslice is a basic tool for pseudo color image processing, where specified gray intensity bands are assigned different colors. The input image can be of class unit 8, unit 16, or double. The threshold values in v must between 0 and 1, even if the input image is of class uint8 or uint16. The function performs the necessary scaling.

Function gray2ind, with syntax

[X, map] = gray2ind(gray_image, n)

scales, then rounds image gray_image to produce an indexed image X with colormap gray ( n ) . If n is omitted, it defaults to 64. The input image can be of class uint8, uintl 6, or double. The class of the output image X is unit 8 if n is less than or equal to 256, or of class unit 16 if n is greater than 256.

Function ind2gray, with the syntax

gray_image = ind2gray(X, map)

converts an indexed image, composed of X and map, to a gray-scale image. Array X can be of class uint8, uint16, or double. The output image is of class double.

The syntax of interest in this chapter for function rgb2ind has the form

[X, map] = rgb2ind(rgb_image, n, dither_option)

where n determines the length (number of colors) of map, and dither_option can have one of two values: ' dither' (the default) dithers, if necessary, to achieve better color resolution at the expense of spatial resolution; conversely ' nodither ' maps each color in the original image to the closest color in the new map (depending on the value of n). No dithering is performed. The input image can be of class uint 8, uint 16, or double. The output array, X, is of class uint8 if n is less than or equal to 256; otherwise it is of class uint16. Example 9.1 shows the effect that dithering has on color reduction.

Function ind2rgb, with syntax

ind2rgb rgb_image = ind2rgb(X, map)

converts the matrix X and corresponding colormap map to RGB format; X can be of class uint8, uintl6, or double. The output RGB image is an M x N x 3 array of class double.

Finally, function rg b2g ray, with syntax

rgb2gray gray_image = rgb2gray(rgb_image)

converts an RGB image to a gray-scale image. The input RGB image can be of class uint8, uint 1 6, or double; the output image is of the same class as the input.

**EXAMPLE 9.1: ILLUSTRATION OF SOME OF THE FUNCTIONS IN TABLE 9.3.**

Function rgb2ind is quite useful for reducing the number of colors in an RGB image. As an illustration of this function, and of the advantages of using the dithering option, consider Figure 9.4(a), which is a 24-bit RGB image, f Figures 9.4(b) and (c) show the results of using the commands

```
>> [X1, map1] = rgb2ind(f, 8, 'nodither'); >> imshow(X1, map1)
```

and

```
>> [X2, map2] = rgb2ind(f, 8, 'dither'); >> figure, imshow(X2, map2)
```

Both images have only 8 colors, which is a significant reduction in the number of possible colors in f, which, for a 24-bit RGB image exceeds 16 million, as mentioned earlier. Figure 9.4(b) has noticeable false contouring, especially in the center of the large flower. The dithered image shows better tonality, and considerably less false contouring, a result of the "randomness" introduced by dithering. The image is a little blurred, but it certainly is visually superior to Figure 9.4(b).

The effects of dithering are usually better illustrated with gray-scale images. Figures 9.4(d) and (e) were obtained using the commands

```
>> g rgb2gray(f);
>> gi = dither(g);
>> figure, imshow(g); figure, imshow(g1)
```

**Figure 9.4**

**(a) RGB image.**

**(b) Number of colors reduced to 8 without dithering.**

**(c) Number of colors reduced to 8 with dithering.**

**(d) Gray-scale version of (a) obtained using function rgb2gray.**

**(e) Dithered gray- scale image**

The image in Figure 9.4(e) is a binary image, which again represents a significant degree of data reduction. By looking at Figure 9.4(c) and (e), it is clear why dithering is such a staple in the printing and publishing industry, especially $i_n$ situations (such as in newspapers) where paper quality and printing resolution are low.

## 9.2.4 THE BASICS OF COLOR IMAGE PROCESSING

In this section we begin the study of processing techniques applicable to color images. Although they are far from being exhaustive, the techniques developed in the sections that follow are illustrative of how color images are handled for a variety of image-processing tasks.

For the purposes of the following discussion we subdivide color image processing into three principal areas:

(1) Color transformations (also called color mappings)

(2) Spatial processing of individual color planes

(3) Color vector processing.

The first category deals with processing the pixels of each color plane based strictly on their values and not on their spatial coordinates. The second category deals with spatial (neighborhood) filtering of individual color planes and is analognus and spatial filtering.

The third category deals with techniques based on processing all components of a color image simultaneously. Because full-color images have at least three components, color pixels really are vectors. For example, in the RGB system, each color point can be interpreted as a vector extending from the origin to that point in the RGB coordinate system.

Let c represent an arbitrary vector in RGB color space.

$$c = \begin{bmatrix} C_R \\ C_G \\ C_B \end{bmatrix} = \begin{bmatrix} R \\ G \\ B \end{bmatrix}$$

This equation indicates that the components of c are simply the RGB components of a color image at a point. We take into account the fact that the color components are a function of coordinates (x, y) by using the notation.

$$C(x, y) = \begin{bmatrix} C_R(x, y) \\ C_G(x, y) \\ C_B(x, y) \end{bmatrix} = \begin{bmatrix} R(x, y) \\ G(x, y) \\ B(x, y) \end{bmatrix}$$

For an image of size M x N, there are MN such vectors, c(x, y), for x = 0, 1, 2, ... , M — 1 and y = 0, 1, 2, ... , N — 1.

In some cases, equivalent results are obtained whether color images are processed one plane at a time or as vector quantities.

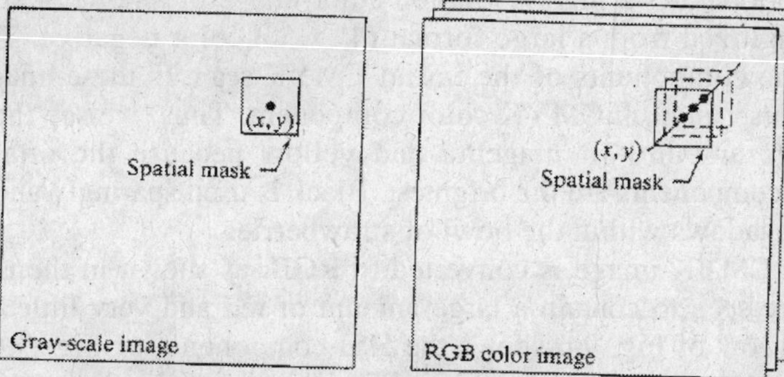


**Figure 9.5 Spatial masks for gray-scale and RGB color images**

In order for independent color component and vector-based processing to be equivalent, two conditions have to be satisfied: First, the process has to be applicable to both vectors and scalars. Second, the operation on each component of a vector must be independent of the other components. As an illustration, Fig. 9.5 shows spatial neighborhood processing of gray-scale and full-color images. Suppose that the process is neighborhood averaging. In Fig. 9.5(a), averaging would be accomplished by summing the gray levels of all the pixels in the neighborhood and dividing by the total number of pixels in the neighborhood. In Fig. 9.5(b) averaging would be done by summing all the vectors in the neighborhood and dividing each component by the total number of vectors in the neighborhood. But each component of the average vector is the sum of the pixels in the image corresponding to that component, which is the same as the result that would be obtained if the averaging were done on the neighborhood of each component image individually, and then the color vector were formed.

## 9.4 COLOR TRANSFORMATIONS

The techniques described in this section, collectively called *color transformations,* deal with processing the components of a color image within the context of a *single* color model, as opposed to the conversion of those components between models.

### 9.4.1 FORMULATION

As with the gray-level transformation techniques, we model color transformations using the expression

$$g(x, y) = T[f(x, y)] \qquad (1)$$

where $f(x, y)$ is a color input image, $g(x, y)$ is the transformed or processed color output image, and $T$ is an operator on $f$ over a spatial neighborhood of $(x, y)$. *The* principal difference between this equation and is in its interpretation. The pixel values here are triplets or quartets (i.e., groups of three or four values)from the color space chosen to represent the images.

Analogous to the approach we used to introduce the basic gray-level transformations, we will restrict attention in this section to color transformations of the form

$$s_i = T_i(r_1, r_2, \ldots, r_n), \qquad i = 1, 2, \ldots, n \tag{2}$$

where, for notational simplicity, $r_i$ and $s_i$ are variables denoting the color components of $f(x, y)$ and $g(x, y)$ at any point $(x, y)$, $n$ is the number of color components, and $\{ T_1, T_2, \ldots T_n \}$ *is a.* set of *transformation* or *color mapping functions* that operate on $r_i$ to produce $s_i$. Note that $n$ transformations, $T_i$ combine to implement the single transformation function, $T$, in Eq. (1). The color space chosen to describe the pixels of $f$ and $g$ determines the value of n. If the RGB color space is selected, for example, $n=3$ and $r_1$. $r_2$, and $r_3$ denote the red, green, and blue components of the input image, respectively. If the CMYK or HSI color spaces are chosen, n = 4 or $n = 3$.

Figure 9.6(a) shows a high-resolution color image of a bowl of strawberries and cup of coffee that was digitized from a large format (4" x 5") color negative. The second row of the figure contains the components of the initial CMYK scan. In these images, black represents 0 and white represents 1 in each CMYK color component. Thus, we see that the strawberries are composed of large amounts of magenta and yellow because the images corresponding to these two CMYK components are the brightest. Black is used sparingly and is generally confined to the coffee and shadows within the bowl of strawberries.

When the CMYK image is converted to RGB, as shown in the third row of the figure. the strawberries are seen to contain a large amount of red and very little (although some) green and blue. The last row of Fig. 9.6 shows the HSI components of Fig. 9.6(a). As expected, the intensity component is a monochrome rendition of the full-color original. In addition, the strawberries are relatively pure in color; they possess the highest saturation or least dilution by white Eight of any of the hues in the image. Finally, we note some difficulty in interpreting the hue component. The problem is compounded by the fact that (1) there is a discontinuity in the HSI model where 0° and 360° meet, and (2) hue is undefined for a saturation of 0 (i.e., for white, black, and pure grays). The discontinuity of the model is most apparent around the strawberries, which are depicted in gray level values near both black (0) and white (1). The result is an unexpected mixture of highly contrasting gray levels to represent a single color—red.

Any of the color space components in Fig. 9.6 can he used in conjunction with Eq. (2). In theory, any transformation can be performed in any color model. In practice. however, some operations are better suited to specific models. For a given transformation, the cost of converting between representations must be factored into the decision regarding the color space in which to implement it. Suppose, for example, that we wish to modify the intensity of the image in Fig. 9.6(a) using

$$g(x. y) = kf(x, y) \tag{3}$$

where $0 < k < 1$. *In* the HSI color space, this can be done with the simple transformation

$$s_3 = kr_3 \tag{4}$$

where $s_i = r_1$ and $s_2 = r_2$. Only HSI intensity component $r_3$ is modified. In the RGB color space. three components must be transformed:

$$s_i = kr_i, \quad i = 1, 2, 3. \tag{5}$$

The CMY space requires a similar set of linear transformations:

$$s_i = kr_i + (1 - k) \qquad 1 = 1, 2, 3. \qquad (6)$$

Although the HSI transformation involves the fewest number of operations, the computations required to convert an RGB or CMY(K) image to the HSI space more than offsets (in this case) the advantages of the simpler transformation-

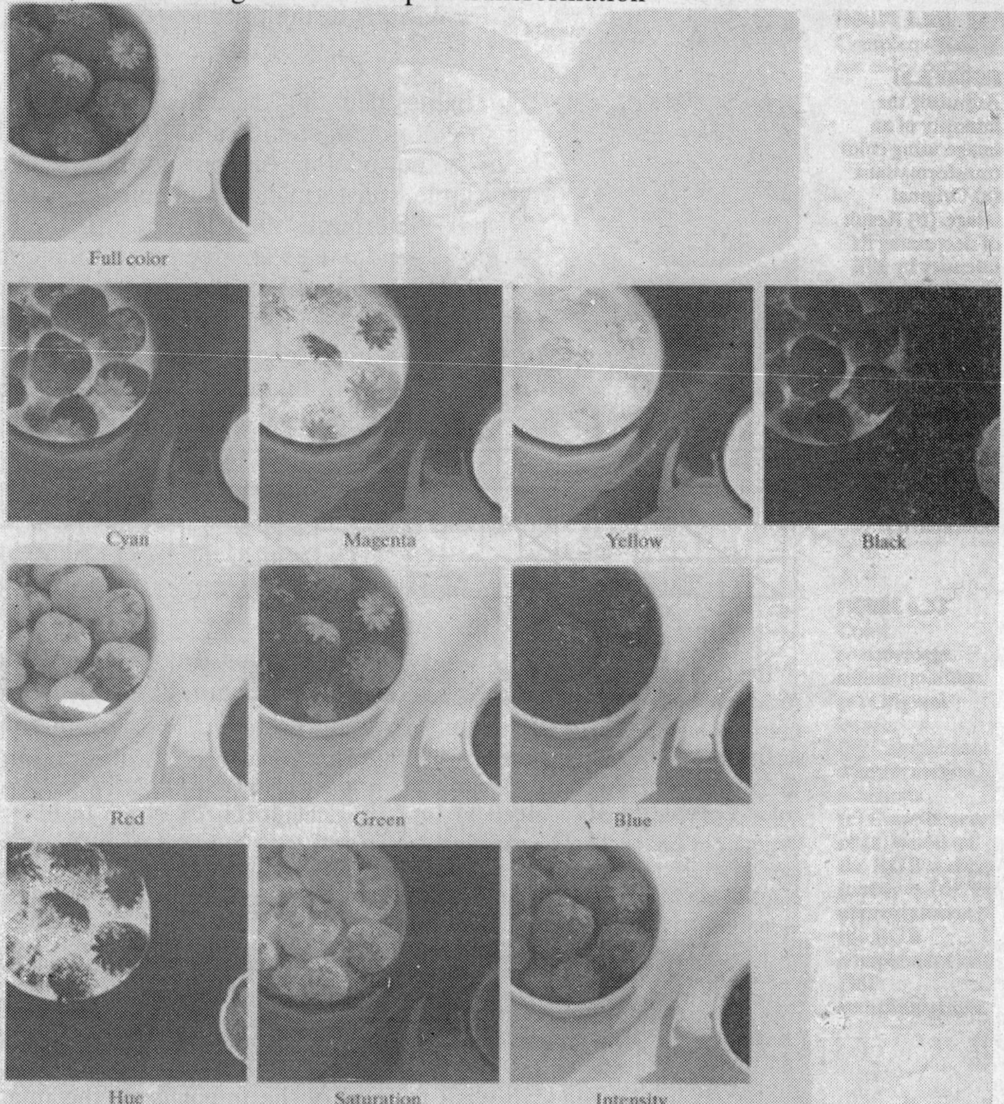


**Figure 9.6 A full-color image and its various color-space components. (Original image courtesy of MedData interactive.)**

the conversion calculations are more computationally intense than the intensity transformation itself. Regardless of the color space selected, however, the output is the same. Figure 9.7(h) shows the result of applying any of the transformations in Eqs. (4) through (6) to the image of Fig. 9.6(a) using $k$=0.7.The mapping functions themselves are depicted graphically in Figs. 9.7(c) through (e).

**Figure 9.7 Adjusting the intensity of an image using color transformations. (a) Original image. (b) Result of decreasing its intensity by 30% (i.e.. letting $k$ = 0.7).(c)—(e) The required_RGB CMY, and H,S transformation _ functions. (Original image courtesy of MedData Interactive.)**

It is important to note that each transformation defined in Eqs. (4) through (6) depends only on one component within its color space. For example, the red output component, $s_1$, in Eq. (5) is independent of the green ($r_2$) and blue $r_3$ inputs; it depends only on the red ($r_1$) input Transformations of this type are among the simplest and most used color processing tools and can he carried out on a percolor-component basis, as mentioned at the beginning of our discussion. In the remainder of this section we examine several such transformations and discuss a case in which the component transformation functions are dependent on all the color components of the input image and, therefore, cannot be done on an individual color component basis.

### 9.4.2 COLOR COMPLEMENTS

The hues directly opposite one another on the *color circle' of* Fig. 9.8 are called *complements, Our* interest in complements stems from the fact that they are analogous to the gray-scale negatives.. As in the gray-scale case, color complements are useful for enhancing detail that is embedded in dark regions of a color image—particularly when the regions are dominant in size.

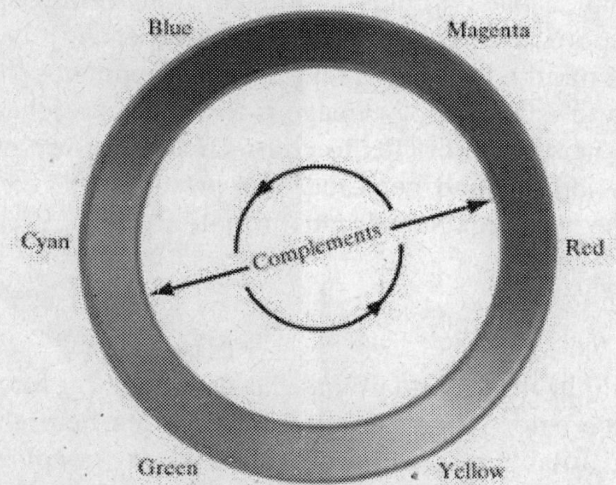


**Figure 9.8 Complements On The Color Circle**

**Figure 9.9 Color Complement Transformation (A) Original Image (B) Complement Transformation Functions (C) Complement Of (A) Base On The Rgb Mapping Function (D) Approximation Of The Rgb Complements Using His Transformation.**

### 9.4.3 COLOR SLICING

Highlighting a specific range of colors in an image is useful for separating objects from their surrounding& Tile basic idea is either to (1) display the colors of interest so that they stand outer the background or (2) use the region defined by the colors as a mask for fuller processing. The most straightforward approach is to expand the gray¯-level slicing technique . Because a color pixel is an n-dimensional quantity. however, the resulting color transformation functions are more complicated than their gray-scale counterparts.In fact. the required transformations are more complex than the color component transforms considered thus far. This is because all practical color slicing approaches require each pixel's transformed color components to he a function of all *n* original pixel's color components.

One of the simplest ways to "slice" a color image is to map the colors outside some range of interest to a nonprominent neutral color. If the color Of interest are enclosed by a cube (or *hypercube* for $n > 3$) of width W and centered at a prototypical (e.g., average) color with components $(a_1, a_2, \ldots, a_n)$, the necessary set of transformations is

$$s_i = \begin{cases} 0.5 & \text{if } \left[ |r_j - a_j| > \frac{W}{2} \right]_{\text{any } 1 \le j \le n} \\ r_i & \text{otherwise} \end{cases} \quad (7)$$

These transformations highlight the colors around the prototype by forcing ail other colors to the midpoint of the reference color space (an arbitrarily chosen neutral point). For the RGB color space, for example, a suitable neutral point is middle gray or color (0.5, 0.5, 0.5).

If a sphere is used to specify the colors of interest, Eq. (7) becomes

$$s_i = \begin{cases} 0.5 & \text{if } \sum_{j=1}^{n} (r_j - a_j)^2 > R_0^2 \\ r_i & \text{otherwise} \end{cases} \qquad i = 1, 2, \ldots, n. \quad (8)$$

Here, $R_0$ is the radius of the enclosing sphere (or hypersphere for $n > 3$) and $(a_1, a_2, \ldots a_n)$ arc the components of its center (i.e., the prototypical color). Other useful variations of Eqs. (7) and (8) include implementing multiple color prototypes and reducing the intensity of the colors outside the region of interest—rather than setting them to a neutral constant.

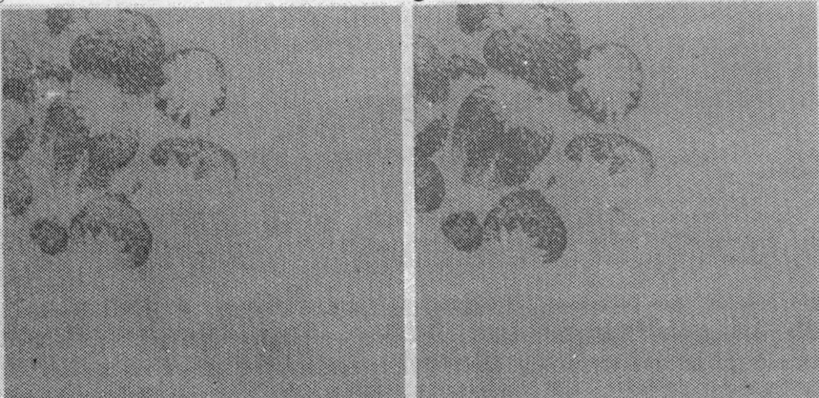

**FIGURE 9.10 Color slicing transformations that detect (a) reds within an RGB cube of width W = 0.2549 centered at (0.6863, 0.1608, 0.1922), and (b) reds within an RGB sphere of radius 0.1765 centered at the same point. Pixels outside the cube and sphere were replaced by color (0.5. 0.5, 0.5).**

### 9.4.4 TONE AND COLOR CORRECTIONS

Color transformations can be performed on most desktop computers. In conjunction with digital cameras, flatbed scanners, and inkjet printers, they turn a personal computer into a digital darkroom—allowing tonal adjustments and color corrections, the mainstays of high-end color reproduction systems, to be performed without the need for traditionally outfitted wet processing (i.e., darkroom) facilities. Although tone and color corrections are useful in other areas of imaging,the focus of the current discussion is on the most common uses. photo enhancement and color reproduction.

The effectiveness of the transformations examined in this section is judged ultimately in print. Since these transformations are developed, refined, and evaluated on monitors, it **is** necessary to maintain a high degree of color consistency between the monitors used and the eventual output devices. In fact, the colors of the monitor should represent accurately any digitally scanned source images, as well as the final printed output. This is best accomplished with a *device- independent color model* that relates the color gamuts of the monitors and output devices, as well as any other devices being used, to one another. The success of this approach is a function of the quality of the *color profiles* used to map each device to the model and the model itself. The model of choice for many *color management systems* (CMS) is the CIE $L^*a^*b^*$ model, also called CIELAB . The $L^*a^*h^*$ color components are given by the following equations:

$$L^* = 116 \cdot h\left(\frac{Y}{Y_W}\right) - 16 \tag{9}$$

$$a^* = 500\left[h\left(\frac{X}{X_W}\right) - h\left(\frac{Y}{Y_W}\right)\right] \tag{10}$$

$$b^* = 200\left[h\left(\frac{Y}{Y_W}\right) - h\left(\frac{Z}{Z_W}\right)\right] \tag{11}$$

Where

$$h(q) = \begin{cases} \sqrt[3]{q} & q > 0.008856 \\ 7.787q + 16/116 & q \le 0.008856 \end{cases} \tag{12}$$

and $X_W$, $Y_W$, and $Z_W$ are reference white tristimulus values—typically the white of **a perfectly** reflecting diffuser under CIE standard D65 illumination (defined by $x = 0.3127$ and $y = 0.3290$ in the CIE chromaticity ). The $L^*a^*b^*$ color space is *colorimetric* (i.e., colors perceived as matching are encoded identically), *perceptually uniform* (i.e , color differences among various hues are perceived uniformly, and *device independent.* While not a directly displayable format (conversion to another color space is required), its gamut encompasses the entire visible spectrum and can represent accurately the colors of any display, print, or input device. Like the HSI system, the $L^*a^*b^*$ system is an excellent decoupler of intensity (represented by lightness $L^*$) and color (represented by $a^*$ for red minus green and $b^*$ for green minus blue). making it useful in both image manipulation (tone and contrast editing) and image compression applications.

The principal benefit of calibrated imaging systems is that they allow tonal and color imbalances to be corrected interactively and independently—that is, in two sequential operations. Before color irregularities, like over- and under- saturated colors, are resolved, problems involving the image's tonal range are corrected. The *tonal range* of an image, also called its *key type,* refers to its general distribution of color intensities. Most of the information in *high-key* images is concentrated at high (or light) intensities; the colors of *low-key* images are located predominantly at low intensities; *middle-key* images lic in between. As in the monochrome case, it is often desirable to distribute the intensities of a color image equally between the highlights and the shadows. The following examples demonstrate a variety of color transformations for the correction of tonal and color imbalances.

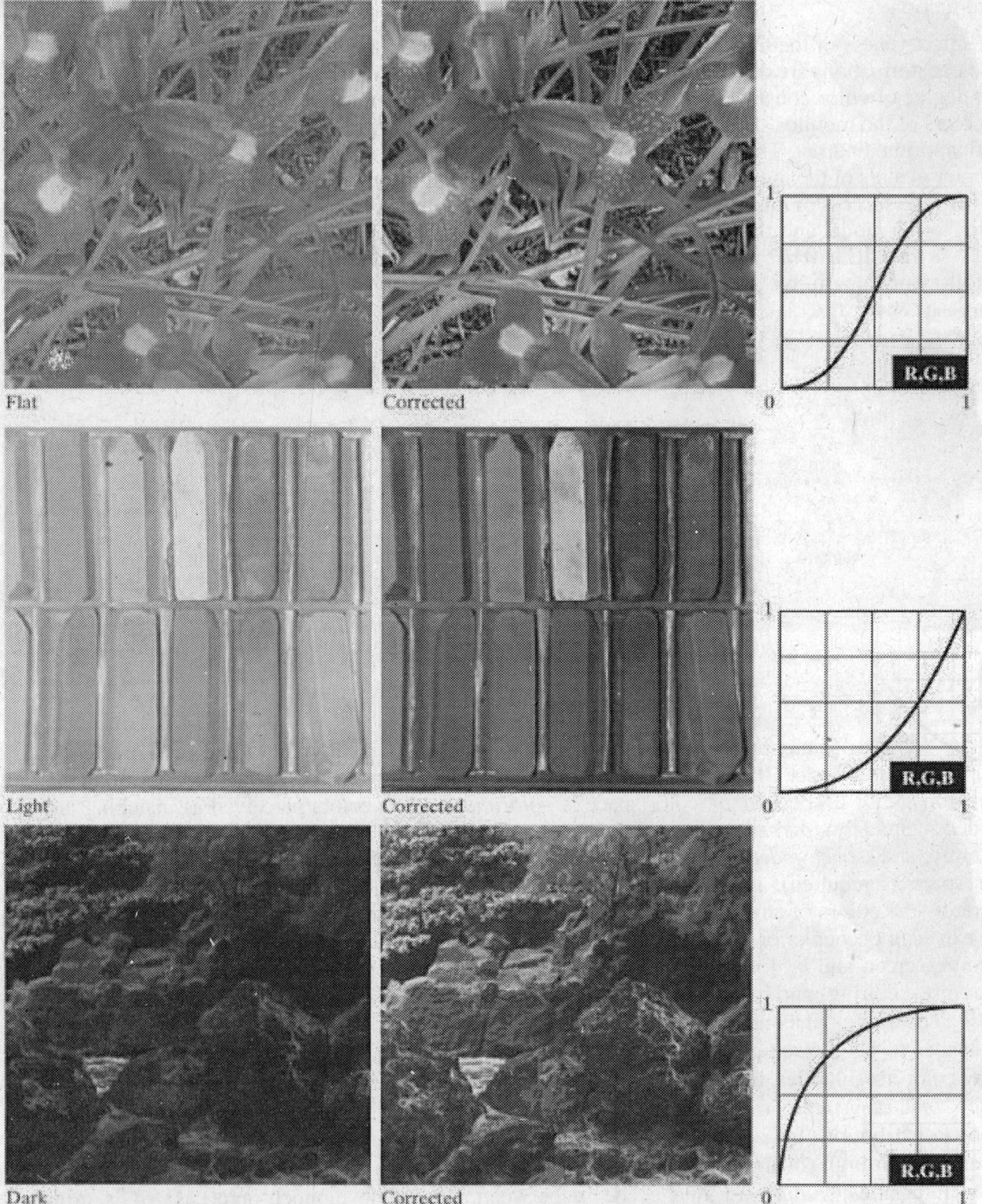


**Figure 9.11 Tonal corrections for flat, light and dark color images. Adjusting red, green and blue components equally does not always alter the image hues significantly.**

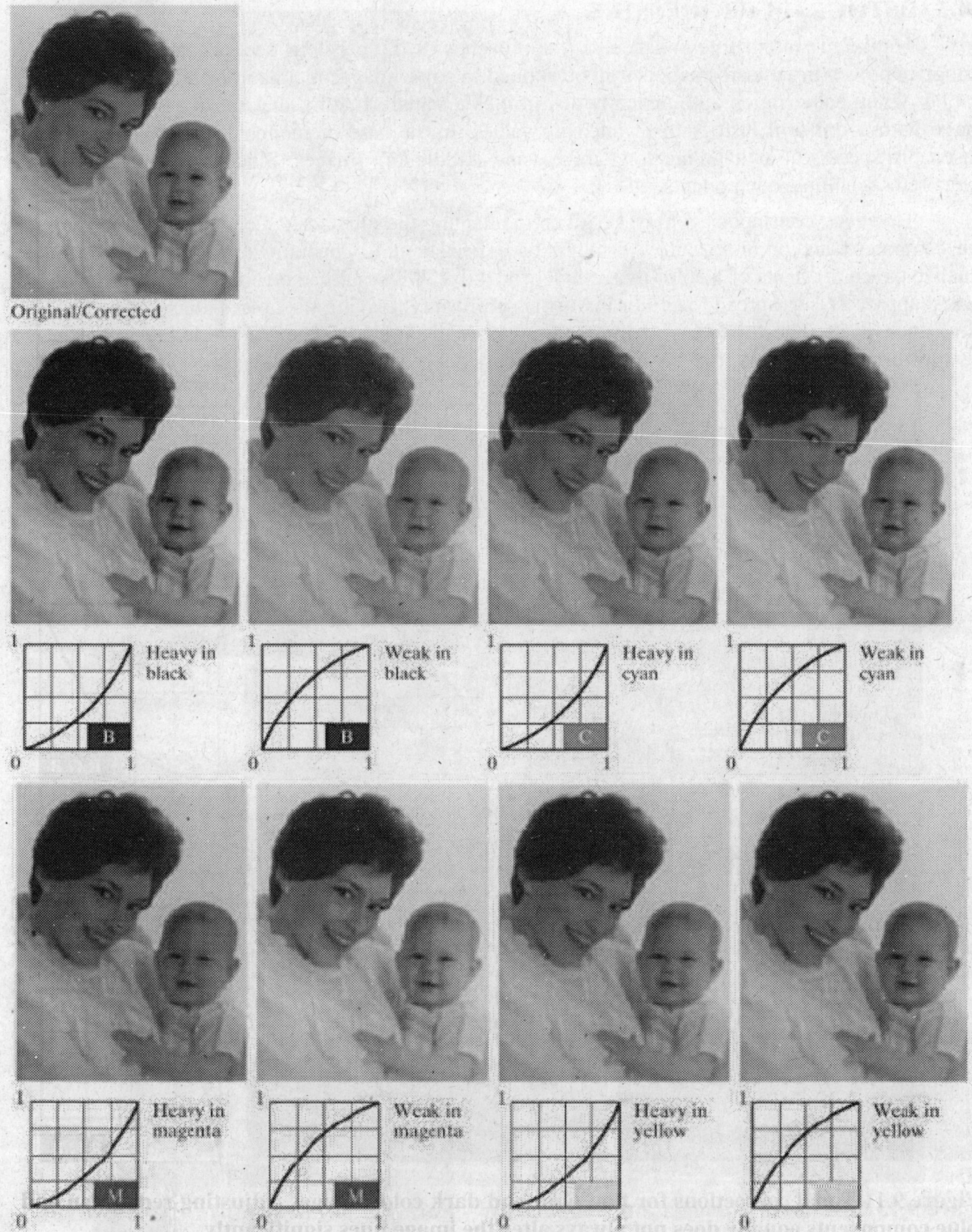


**Figure 9.12 Color balancing corrections for CMYK color images.**

### 9.4.5 HISTOGRAM PROCESSING

Unlike the interactive enhancement approaches of the previous section. the gray- level histogram processing transformations can be applied to color images in an automated way. Recall that histogram equalization automatically determines a transformation that seeks to produce an image with a uniform histogram of intensity values. In the case of monochrome images to be reasonably successful at handling low-, high-, and middle-key images. Since color images are composed of multiple components.

However, consideration must be given to adapting the gray-scale technique to more than one component and/or histogram. As might be expected, it is generally unwise to histogram equalize the components of a color image independently. This results in erroneous color. A more logical approach is to spread the color intensities uniformly, leaving the colors themselves (e.g.. hues) unchanged. The following example shows that the HSI color space is ideally suited to this type of approach.

**Figure 9.13 Histogram equalization (followed by saturation adjustment) in the HIS color space.**

## 9.4 EXTENSION OF PROCESSING TECHNIQUES TO COLOR DOMAIN

Image processing is becoming a common tool to analyze multidimensional scientific data in all areas of natural science. For more and more scientists, processing of monochrome and especially multichannel images is the key to study complex scientific problems, they could not have dreamed to tackle only a few years ago.

Multichannel signal processing is of paramount importance in application areas such as biomedicine, computer and machine vision, robotics, entertainment and multimedia applications, industrial inspection, remote sensing and many others. In all these areas the users and system developers work with multidimensional data sets. It is well known that humans and computer vision systems use color information to sense the environment and that the correct perception of color can help in different tasks of image understanding and pattern recognition. Unfortunately, noise and other impairments associated with the measurement or the transmission apparatus can significantly degrade the value of the color information carried by the digital images. This usually declines their perceptual fidelity and also decreases the performance of the task for which the image was created. It comes therefore as no surprise that the most common signal processing task is the noise filtering. Noise filtering is an essential part of any image processing based system, whether the final information is used for human perception or for an automatic inspection and analysis.

The amount of research published in the last ten years indicates a growing interest in the area of color image processing and analysis. Furthermore, the surge of emerging applications such as web-based processing of color images and videos, image retrieval systems indexing large multimedia databases, enhancement of medical and biological images, digital archiving, cultural heritage preservation projects and the proliferation of smart devices such as video- enabled wireless phones, wearable computers and personal digital assistant tools, suggests that the demand for new, more powerful and cost effective multichannel filtering solutions will continue. The correction of the signal distortions is a digital process, by which disturbances introduced by the sensor system are rectified, with the goal being to obtain the image or generally the signal, which corresponds as closely as possible to the output of an ideal imaging system. Thus, correcting signal artifacts, in practice means adjusting the characteristics of the imaging system to meet specific demands of the human observer or the computer vision system.

Digital image processing is based on the conversion of a continuous image field into an equivalent digital form. The synthesis of images from the signals arising from various sensor systems is accomplished by a digital process directed to transforming the signal into a form allowing visual or machine perception. The requirements for an ideal conversion system are usually expressed in terms of certain technical properties such as the resolution of the imaging systems, photometric accuracy, quantization levels, intensity of intrinsic noise and many others. Improvement of the quality of images has always been one of the central tasks of digital image processing. In modern terms, improvements in sensitivity, resolution and noise reduction have equated higher quality with greater informational throughput. Image noise is an unwanted feature, which is either contained in the relevant light signal or is added by the imaging process and it compromises a precise evaluation of the light signal distribution, which should be measured. The analysis of the image noise in digital image acquisition systems often focuses on random noise sources, such as those associated with quantum signal detection (shot noise) and signal independent fluctuations (dark current, readout noise). Other important source of image noise is the in homogeneity of the responsiveness of the sensor elements and signal disturbances that introduce repeatable patterns into image data.

During image formation, acquisition, storage and transmission many additional types of distortions limit the quality of digital images. Transmission errors, periodic or random motion of the camera system during exposure, electronic instability of the image signal, electromagnetic interferences from natural or man-made sources, sensor malfunctions, optic imperfections, electronics interference or aging of the storage material all disturb the image quality.

In the last years, the area of vector valued (multichannel, multispectral, multicomponent) signal processing has dramatically increased. The leading edge of development and interest is in the domain of remote sensing, but the classical color imaging still remains the preferred research domain.

Typically, a color image is represented in each pixel by a three component vector. The vector components quantify in general the amounts of pure red, green and blue that compose the local color. These vector valued signals cannot be reduced to a stack of separately processed scalar components, due to the inherent correlation between the channels. In the literature, several noise reduction techniques have been proposed. They can be divided into linear and nonlinear techniques.

Linear processing techniques have been widely used in digital signal processing applications, since their mathematical simplicity and the availability of a unifying linear system theory make them relatively easy to analyze and implement. Unfortunately, most of the linear techniques tend to blur structural elements such as lines, edges and fine image details and therefore many multichannel image processing tasks cannot be efficiently accomplished by linear techniques.

Image signals are nonlinear in nature, due to the presence of structural information and are perceived through the human visual system, which has strong nonlinear characteristics. Nonlinear methods are able to preserve important multichannel structural elements and eliminate degradations occurring during signal formation or transmission through nonlinear channels and they proved to be efficient in the suppression of impulsive, Gaussian and mixed type of noise.The most popular nonlinear filters are based on order statistics. However their common drawback is that they ignore the temporal or spatial information of the signal samples. Therefore many different techniques alleviating this problem have been proposed to date. The algorithms developed by the author of this tutorial are oriented towards the improvement of the efficiency of the standard filtering approaches and are especially focused on the impulsive noise removal. The special emphasis will be placed on the suppression of impulsive and mixed noise, as the nonlinear techniques are especially well suited to this particular task. The purpose of this tutorial is to present the state of the art in nonlinear color image noise removal techniques and also to present author's original contributions to the dynamic development of this field.

### 9.4.1 THE CONTENT OF STRUCTURED INTO 7 PARTS

The first part is devoted to the overview of the problems of noise reduction in color images. Its purpose is to give some insight into the fundamentals of color image processing and basic color image filtering designs. This part also covers the various color image noise sources, their models and measures of the quality of image restoration.

The second part is devoted to the adaptive schemes of noise reduction in gray scale images, as many techniques primarily developed for monochrome images can be reformulated to work in the multichannel domain. In this part special emphasis is put on the weighted median filters and their optimization, as this filter family, extended to the vectorial case is considered at the and of the tutorial.

The next topic is the overview of the noise reduction filters used in color imaging. This part provides the state of the art in color image filtering and serves as a basis for the remainder of the tutorial. The following part covers the anisotropic diffusion technique in the scalar and multichannel case. The evaluation of the efficiency of this nonlinear technique shows that the approach, in which the central pixel of the filtering window is excluded from the processing, yields much better results and increases the robustness of the anisotropic diffusion method and its various modifications.

Part 5 is devoted to the digital paths approach to color image filtering, originally developed by the author for the gray scale imaging using the concept of random and self-avoiding walks. This novel technique, based on the exploration of the local neighborhood through digital paths and on the utilization of the fuzzy concepts, can be seen as a powerful generalization of the anisotropic diffusion approach. The performed simulations indicate that the new filter class excels significantly over the currently used nonlinear multichannel techniques especially in the case of mixed noise.

In the next part the problem of nonparametric impulsive noise reduction in multichannel images is addressed. A new family of filters for noise attenuation elaborated by the author, based on nonparametric probability density estimation of sample data, is introduced and its relationship to commonly used filtering techniques is investigated. Extensive simulation experiments indicate that the presented family of filters outperform the standard techniques used to eliminate impulsive noise in color images.

The last part deals with the adaptive optimization of the weighted vector median filters and also introduces the new technique based on the so called sigma-filtering, which can be seen as an extension of the rank conditioned vector median. This novel adaptive filtering technique is based on robust order statistic concepts and simplified statistical measures of vectors' dispersion. Simulation studies indicate that the presented filters are computationally attractive, yield good performance and are able to preserve fine details, while efficiently suppressing impulsive noise.

Multichannel images refer to the type of data obtained from multiple frequency bands, multiple time frames, or multiple sensors. Such images have numerous applications in practice, such as, medical diagnosis, forensic sciences, industrial automation, space and satellite imagery. For the sake of terminology, we are going to use the term multichannel throughout this paper to refer to an image obtained by an imaging system that uses more than one sensor for the same scene.

Processing multichannel images, such as smoothing, restoration, and enhancement is an important step before any further use or analysis. The degradation sources for the single channel case, such as noise and blur, apply to the multichannel case, too. However, an additional and important type of degradation that is natural to the multichannel imaging is the cross-channel or cross-spectral degradation. For example, the overlapping in the cutoff frequency characteristics of the detectors results in cross-spectral mixing of adjacent spectral bands. As in the single channel case, the multichannel identification techniques have not received much attention as the restoration techniques have. As a matter of fact, even the restoration techniques for multichannel imaging have not received much attention. Although it seems a straightforward extension of the single channel methods, the lack of multichannel image processing theories, the complexity of the computation involved, and the consideration of the cross-spectral effects between frames make the problem more difficult.

In general, restoring each channel independently does not necessarily produce useful results because of neglecting the information between the channels. Following this approach, Bescos et al. applied conventional restoration techniques to individual color components without using the cross-channel information. Also, Angwin and Kaufman presented adaptive filtering for color images without taking into account the correlation between the color components. This resulted in a suboptimal solution. Thus, solutions which are optimal for the single channel case may be suboptimal for the multichannel image when restored independently. One of the successful approaches to overcome this problem is to model the correlation between the channels and incorporate it explicitly into the filtering procedure. Pavlovic' and Tekalp employed this approach using the Kalman filtering and least squares parameter identification of the image parameters. Ozkan et al. applied this approach to Wiener restoration filters. In an extensive study, Galatsanos presented and applied this approach using an efficient and feasible computation algorithms including Wiener, Kalman, and least squares techniques, however, blur parameters were assumed to be known. In , a multi channel Wiener filter was proposed in both the spatial and frequency domains that showed a reduction in computation. Almost all of these researches deals with restoration techniques of multichannel images rather than the identification process. Up-to-date, techniques that study the multichannel identification problem are very limited. Among the rare papers in this subject is the work of Pavlovic et al. Thus, this area needs to be extensively studied.

Considering the two familiar types of blur that can be represented in a closed form parametric description in the continuous domain, namely, the 1-D uniform motion blur and the 2-D out of focus blur, we will show how to identify the blur extent from noisy color images. Then, by implementing some restoration methods available for multichannel imaging, the identified parameters will be used to restore the original image. Employing the cross-channel information will be an important factor in the modeling. It is shown that incorporation of these components produces more accurate results.

### 9.4.2 MODELING AND FORMULATION

Following the AR image and observation models formulations given in we consider here the multichannel modeling where the image and observation models for the p$^{th}$ channel are represented as

$$s_p(m,n) = \sum_{q=1}^{N} \sum_{R_{pq}} c^{pq}(k,l)\, s_q(m-k,n-l) + w_p(m,n) \tag{9.1}$$

$$r_p(m,n) = \sum_{q=1}^{N} \sum_{(k,l)\in \mathbf{S}_h} h^{pq}(k,l)\, s_q(m-k,n-l) + v_p(m,n) \tag{9.2}$$

respectively, where $N$ is the number of spectral channels, $c^{pq}(k,l)$ represent the model coefficients coupling the $p^{th}$ and $q^{th}$ channels, $R_{pq}$ denotes the support of the coefficients $c^{pq}(k,l)$, $s_q(m,n)$ is the undistorted image for the $q^{th}$ channel and $w_p(m,n)$ is the zero mean white Gaussian noise for the $p^{th}$ channel. Equations (9.1) and (9.2) can be written in a matrix form as

$$\mathbf{s}_p = \mathbf{C}^{pq}\mathbf{s}_p + \mathbf{w}_p \tag{9.3}$$

$$\mathbf{r}_p = \mathbf{H}^{pq}\mathbf{s}_p + \mathbf{v}_p \tag{9.4}$$

where, $\mathbf{s}_p$, $\mathbf{r}_p$, $\mathbf{w}_p$ , and $\mathbf{v}_p$ are the lexicographic order of the corresponding terms in equations (9.1) and (9.2), $\mathbf{C}^{pq}$ and $\mathbf{H}^{pq}$ represent the appropriate ordering of the model and blur coefficients, respectively. Further, we may write the set of equations (9.3) and (9.4) in lexicographic orders to get

$$\boldsymbol{s} = \boldsymbol{Cs} + \boldsymbol{w} \tag{9.5}$$

$$\boldsymbol{r} = \boldsymbol{Hs} + \boldsymbol{v} \tag{9.6}$$

where now, the $NM^2 \times 1$ vectors $\boldsymbol{r}, \boldsymbol{s}, \boldsymbol{v}$, and $\boldsymbol{w}$ are the lexicographic order of $\mathbf{s}_p$, $\mathbf{r}_p$, $\mathbf{w}_p$, and $\mathbf{v}_p$, for, $p = 1,2,\ldots,N$ and $q = 1,2,\ldots,N$ , respectively, and where $\boldsymbol{C}$ is the image model matrix and $\boldsymbol{H}$ is the degradation or blur matrix, and both are block matrices of size $(NM^2 \times NM^2)$. Following the procedure used to derive the PDF of the observed image for the single channel case [9,12], we may now express the PDF of $\boldsymbol{r}$ ,which is also Gaussian, as

$$p(\boldsymbol{r};\Theta) = \frac{1}{\sqrt{(2\pi)^{N^2}|\boldsymbol{P}_{rr}|}} \exp\left(\frac{1}{2}\boldsymbol{r}^t \boldsymbol{P}_{rr}{}^{-1}\boldsymbol{r}\right) \tag{9.7}$$

where now, the vector $\Theta$ represents the unknown parameters, $h_{i,j}(k,l), c_{ij}(m,n), \sigma^2_{v_{ij}}, \sigma^2_{w_i}$. $\boldsymbol{P}_{rr}$ is the covariance matrix of block structure where elements of each block of $\boldsymbol{P}_{rr}$ are computed as

$$\mathbf{P}^{ij}_{rr}(k,l) = E[r_i(m,n)r_j(m+k,n+l)] \tag{9.8}$$

for $i, j = 1,2,\ldots,N$ where $N$ is the number of channels. Notice that the matrix of $\boldsymbol{P}_{rr}$ is not Toeplitz because of the structure of C , where cross-spectral components are not the same in each channel. However, each block element of $\boldsymbol{P}_{rr}$ is a Toeplitz matrix and $\mathbf{P}^{ij}_{rr} = [\mathbf{P}^{ij}_{rr}]^t$. We may now express $\boldsymbol{P}_{rr}$ in terms of C and H as

$$\begin{aligned} \boldsymbol{P}_{rr} &= E[\boldsymbol{rr}^t] \\ &= E[\{\boldsymbol{H}(\boldsymbol{I}-\boldsymbol{C})^{-1}\boldsymbol{w} + \boldsymbol{v}\}\{\boldsymbol{H}(\boldsymbol{I}-\boldsymbol{C})^{-1}\boldsymbol{w} + \boldsymbol{v}\}^t] \end{aligned} \tag{9.9}$$

which can be simplified as

$$\boldsymbol{P}_{rr} = \boldsymbol{H}(\boldsymbol{I}-\boldsymbol{C})^{-1}\boldsymbol{P}_{ww}(\boldsymbol{I}-\boldsymbol{C})^{-t}\boldsymbol{H}^t + \boldsymbol{P}_{vv} \tag{9.10}$$

#### 9.4.2.1 MAXIMUM LIKELIHOOD ESTIMATOR

The maximum likelihood estimate is obtained by maximizing the LF . Using (9.7) and (9.10), dropping all terms independent of $\Theta$ and simplifying, the ML identification problem can be expressed as

$$\begin{aligned} L(\Theta) &= -\log\{p(\boldsymbol{r};\Theta)\} \\ &= -\{\log(|\boldsymbol{P}_{rr}|) + \boldsymbol{r}^t\boldsymbol{P}^{-1}_{rr}\boldsymbol{r}\} \end{aligned} \tag{9.11}$$

The parameters that maximize the LF can be obtained by equating all the partial derivatives of the LF to zero. However, this optimization problem is so extensive because of the number of unknowns involved. Therefore some simplifications are necessary. We will make the assumption that the model coefficients, $c_{ij}(m,n)$ and $\sigma^2_{w_i}$ , are estimated using the least square procedure.

Also, the observation noise, $\sigma^2_{v_{ij}}$ , will be estimated as the variance of a uniform region in the different channels. Further, we make the following practical assumption. We assume that the cross channel blur is not significant. This means that although the channels exhibit cross-correlation, the contribution of the blur to this correlation is minimal or negligible. The major contributor to the cross-correlation is the image signal. Our experimental results demonstrate this. To be able to compute the conditional likelihood function, we make use of the structure of $\boldsymbol{P}_{rr}$ and apply the Toeplitz-to-circular approximation through the DFT for each block element of $\boldsymbol{P}_{rr}$. Thus, the CLF can be written in the frequency domain as

$$L(\Theta) = -\sum_k \sum_l \left\{ \log(\left|\mathbf{S}_{r_p r_p}(k,l)\right|) + \frac{1}{M^2} \frac{\left|R_p(k,l)\right|^2}{\mathbf{S}_{r_p r_p}(k,l)} \right\} \tag{9.12}$$

Following the formulation used in [9.9,9.10], we first express the blur PSF as a function of parameters $\Theta = [\theta_1, \theta_2, \ldots, \theta_n]$ in the continuous domain for channel $p$, as

$$h_p(x,y) = h_p(x,y;\Theta) \quad \text{for } (x,y) \in \Re_p(\Theta) \tag{9.13}$$

where $\Re_p(\Theta)$ denotes the PSF support for channel $p$. The observed image in continuous domain can be written as

$$r_p(m,n) = \int_{\Re(\Theta)} h_p(\xi,\eta;\Theta)\, s(m\Delta x - \xi, n\Delta y - \eta)\, d\xi\, d\eta + v(m,n) \tag{9.14}$$

by sampling at the points $(x,y) = (m\Delta x, n\Delta y)$, where the two intervals $\Delta x$ and $\Delta y$ denote the horizontal and vertical sampling distances, respectively, $(m,n)$ denotes discrete spatial domain coordinates, and $r_p(m,n)$ are the observed samples of $r_p(x,y)$. This accuracy in this form of modeling overcomes the bandliminting assumption of the discrete model. Also, it will enable us to differentiate with respect to the variable appearing in the integration limits for estimating the blur extent. We may now write the cross-correlation components, $P_{r_p r_q}(i,j)$, as

$$\begin{aligned} P_{r_p r_q}(i,j) &= E[r_p(m,n) r_q(m+i, n+j)] \\ &= \int_{\Re_p(\Theta)} \int_{\Re_q(\Theta)} h_p(\xi,\eta) h_q(\psi,\zeta) P_{s_p s_q}(i - \xi + \psi, j - \eta + \zeta)\, d\xi\, d\eta\, d\psi\, d\zeta \\ &\quad + \delta(i,j)\sigma_{v_p}\sigma_{v_q} \end{aligned} \tag{9.15}$$

where $P_{s_p s_q}(x,y) = E\{s_p(\xi,\eta) s_q(\xi + x, \eta + y)\}$ is the cross-correlation function of the ideal continuous domain image $s(m,n)$. Then, taking the DFT of (9.15), we have

$$S_{r_p r_q}(k,l) = S_{s_p s_q}(k,l) H_p(k,l) H_q^*(k,l) + \sigma_{v_p}\sigma_{v_q} \tag{9.16}$$

where $S_{r_p r_q}(k,l)$ represents the DFT of $P_{r_p r_q}(i,j)$ which denotes the samples of $P_{r_p r_q}(x,y)$, and $H_p(k,l)$ denotes the samples of the continuous Fourier transform of $h_p(x,y;\Theta)$ for the *pth* channel given by

$$H_p(k,l) = \int_{\Re_p(\Theta)} h_p(x,y;\Theta)\exp\left(-j\frac{2\pi}{N}kx\right)\exp\left(-j\frac{2\pi}{N}ly\right)dxdy \tag{9.17}$$

Thus, the power spectrum for each channel reduces to

$$S_{r_p r_p}(k,l) = S_{s_p s_p}(k,l)\left|H_p(k,l)\right|^2 + \sigma^2_{v_p} \tag{9.18}$$

The key point here is to incorporate the cross-spectral components and to include them in the computation of the power spectrum of the ideal image, $S_{s_p s_q}(k,l)$, which can be obtained from the AR model of (9.1 ) as

$$S_{s_p s_p}(k,l) = \frac{\sigma^2_{w_p} + \sum_{q,q\neq p}\sum_{(m,n)} C^{pq}(m,n)S_{s_p s_q}(k,l)}{\left|1 - \sum_{(m,n)} C^{pp}(m,n)\right|^2} \tag{9.19}$$

where $C^{pq}(k,l)$ are the DFT of the correlation coefficients computed using a least squares procedure. For example, for the RGB color image, the power spectrum for the red channel is fully computed using the power spectrum of the red spectral component including the power spectra of the green and blue components. Now, we need to compute the derivative of the CLF for each channel as

$$\frac{\partial}{\partial\theta_i}\mathrm{L}(\Theta|c_{i,j}(m,n),\sigma^2_{v\,i},\sigma^2_{w_i}) =$$

$$-\sum_k\sum_l\left\{\left(\frac{1}{Sr_p r_p(k,l)} - \frac{1}{N^2}\frac{\left|R_p(k,l)\right|^2}{S^2_{r_p r_p}(k,l)}\right)\frac{\partial}{\partial\theta_i}Sr_p r_p(k,l)\right\} \tag{9.20}$$

Here, the derivative of the power spectrum component, $\frac{\partial}{\partial\theta_i}Sr_p r_p(k,l)$, can be computed depending on the particular parametric form of the unknown PSF. For example, for a uniform motion blur, [9.9,9.10]

$$\frac{\partial}{\partial\theta_i}Sr_p r_p(k,l) =$$

$$\frac{1}{a}\left\{-2\left|H_p(k,l)\right|^2 + \exp\left(j\frac{2\pi}{N}ka\right)H_p(k,l) + \exp\left(-j\frac{2\pi}{N}ka\right)H_p^{*}(k,l)\right\}S_{s_p s_p}(k,l) \tag{9.21}$$

where $H_p(k,l)$ for this form is given by

$$H_p(k,l) = \left(-j\frac{2\pi}{N}k\frac{a-1}{2}\right)\frac{\sin\frac{2\pi}{N}k\frac{a}{2}}{\frac{2\pi}{N}k\frac{a}{2}} \tag{9.22}$$

Also, for the out-of-focus blur, $\frac{\partial}{\partial \theta_i} S_{r,r}(K,l)$ is given by

$$\frac{d}{d\theta} S_{r_p r_p}(k,l) =$$

$$\left\{ \frac{-4}{R} |H_p(k,l)|^2 + \frac{2}{R} J_0\left(\frac{2\pi}{N} R\sqrt{k^2+l^2}\right)(H_p(k,l) + H_p^*(k,l)) \right\} S_{s_p s_p}(k,l) \tag{9.23}$$

where in this case $H_p(k,l)$

$$H(k,l) = NR \frac{J_1\left(\frac{2\pi}{N} R\sqrt{k^2+l^2}\right)}{\sqrt{k^2+l^2}} \tag{9.24}$$

### 9.4.2.2 IMPLEMENTATION OF THE ML ESTIMATOR

The multichannel estimation procedure can be described by the following algorithm:

1) Estimate $\{c^{pq}(m,n)\}$ and $\sigma_{w_i}^2$ for the different channels using least squares procedure

2) Estimate $\sigma_v^2$ from a uniform region in the different channels

3) Compute $S_{s_p s_p}(k,l)$ using (19) and employing the cross spectral components.

4) Use the parametric form of the specific PSF, namely uniform blur or out-of focus blur, and set the parameter, $\Theta$, to some initial values.

DO UNTIL convergence criterion is satisfied

5) Compute $|H_p(k,l)|^2$ using (9.22) or (9.24) depending on the parametric form chosen.

6) Given $\sigma_v^2$, compute $S_{r_p r_p}(k,l)$ using (9.18).

7) Compute the value of CLF using (9.12).

8) Compute the derivative of the CLF with respect to the unknown parameter using (20) and either (9.21) or (9.23). Again depending on the parametric form chosen.

9) Update $\Theta$ using a gradient based numerical optimization technique.

END UNTIL

### 9.4.2.3. EXPERIMENTAL RESULTS

Using the above described procedure for blur identification, several experiments were successfully conducted on color images that were blurred by uniform linear motion or out-of-focus blur. Here, we present the results uniform motion blur experiments that were conducted using the original color image of "TANK" as in Figure 9.14. We blurred this image by uniform motion blur of size $a$ =10 and additive noise equivalent to $SNR$=40 dB as shown in Figure 9.15.

The identified parameter was computed without cross spectral correlation (i.e. independent channels) and the blur extent estimated was about $a$=7.5 for each channel. The blur extent estimated by the above multichannel procedure, i.e. including the cross spectral components, was estimated as $a$=9. The restoration results using the estimated parameters of the two cases are shown in Figure. 9.16 and 9.17, respectively. We note here that we are dealing with PSF that is expressed as a function of one parameter. The identified parameter $a$ was computed for each channel while including the cross-spectral components of the other channels. Clearly, since the channels were blurred with the same PSF, we should expect the estimated extent $a$ to be the same in all channels.

To test the performance of this method with noise, we blurred the "TANK" image with a uniform motion blur of extent $a=10$ and separately added Gaussian noise that corresponds to *SNR* of 10, 20, 30, 40, and 50 dB. The blur extent we estimated using both the independent identification method and the multichannel approach described here. The results are shown in Table 9.7. We observe that the multichannel approach gives better results than the independent identification. Obviously, this improvement is due to the inclusion of the cross-spectral components. Although at low *SNR* levels the improvement is moderate, the fact that cross-spectral component incorporation produce better results is still valid.

**9.4.2.4. CONCLUSION**

We may say that the novel approach outlined in this paper is very useful in identifying blur extents of uniform motion or out-of-focus degradations and can be used satisfactory for *SNR* levels more than 20dB. This contribution is very important in the field of image restoration since multichannel identification techniques are few and limited in performance.

**Figure 9.14** The original color "TANK" image

**Figure 9.15.** The blurred "TANK" image with uniform motion blur of extent $a=10$

**Figure 9.16**. The restored "TANK" image using the identified parameter of $a$ =7.5 without including the cross-spectral correlation

**Figure 9.17** The restored " TANK" image using the identified parameter of $a$ =9 including the cross-spectral correlation.

| SNR (dB) | Independent blur identification | | | Multichannel blur identification | | |
|---|---|---|---|---|---|---|
| | Channel R | Channel G | Channel B | Channel R | Channel G | Channel B |
| 10 | 7.1 | 7 | 7.1 | 7.5 | 7.5 | 7.6 |
| 20 | 7.2 | 7.3 | 7.2 | 8.2 | 8.1 | 8.1 |
| 30 | 7.3 | 7.3 | 7.3 | 8.5 | 8.5 | 8.5 |
| 40 | 7.5 | 7.4 | 7.5 | 9 | 8.9 | 9 |
| 50 | 7.8 | 7.8 | 7.9 | 9.3 | 9.3 | 9.4 |

**Table 9.7 The identified blur extents for the TANK image that was degraded by unifie motion blur of size l=10 at different noise levels. The independent blur identification and th multichannel blur identification refer to estimating the blur from each channel without an with cross-spectral components, respectively**

### 9.4.3 COMPRESSED DOMAIN TECHNIQUES TO SUPPORT INFORMATIO RETRIEVAL APPLICATIONS FOR BROADCAST NEWS VIDEOS

Large video repositories are getting into the mainstream with the advent c information technology. High speed Internet and commoditization of storage hardwa catalyzes this trend. The increasing number of news channels results in an abundance of data which makes it difficult for the users to visualize and comprehend the available information. In India, a typical cable or satellite TV distribution network daily delivers approximately 200 hours of news in English, Hindi and regional languages. Users can never afford to view this entire news broadcast. They are interested to (a) Avoid watching irrelevant videos like advertisements and other repetitive content like channel logos, program lead-in and lead- outs. (b) Search for videos similar to a particular news story. (c) Watch the most important news stories over a duration, say a day or week. (d) Keep track of the developments in a particular news story.

We focus on presenting techniques which can effectively support applications like above. A spotting technique has been proposed to address (a) which enables real time recognition of query clips in online video feeds. An LSH based indexing scheme is presented which supports near neighbor queries at interactive speeds. This forms a core component for applications like (b). (c) and (d) can be solved by exploiting the occurrence of common video clips in different news broadcasts across channels and time. Relationships can be established between news stories by clustering such visually similar clips which leads to importance ranking of news stories based on cluster size. Developments to news stories can be tracked by analyzing the growth of clusters and addition of new videos to them. Significant gains in computation of the clusters can be achieved by using the LSH index.

Video content is often represented using key frames which reduces the problem of video retrieval to CBIR. Early systems based on this approach include QBIC and VisualSeek. The general solution for content based image and video retrieval has traditionally been to build feature descriptions of the content and then defining distance measures between these features for matching. Features can typically be grouped into two categories - low level and high level. Low level features are compact, mathematical representations of the physical properties of video data like color atmosphere, texture, shape, edge information and motion. Popular high level representations attempt at representing video content in terms of objects, faces, activities, etc. There exist specialized techniques developed for addressing specific categories like sports videos. However, they are not necessarily effective for general and diverse content like broadcast news. A lot of work has been done on hierarchical representation of structure for easy browsing of video content. The main objective of these methods is to accelerate the process of manual browsing of videos and thus are suitable only for access of limited video content (say a movie or a specific news broadcast).

Several algorithms represent video as a sequence of feature vectors. Each feature vector represents a frame or a group of frames. The matching is performed by determining the alignment score between the two sequences by using sequential correlation dynamic programming based techniques like Least Common Subsequence (LCS) and Approximate Subsequence Matching (ASM) with certain constraints. Such techniques lose on the computational efficiency as computing the correlation of features per frame gets expensive. These methods focus on very fine frame level matching and the efficiency of searching through large collections is neglected to some extent for the accuracy of matching. Moreover, these algorithms check for inherent temporal order of frames in the sequence representation. This further increases the order of matching. However video clips differing in only the temporal order of frames are not expected to be found in general broadcast videos. This motivates us to work with video clips as the fundamental unit and our features represent the entire clip.

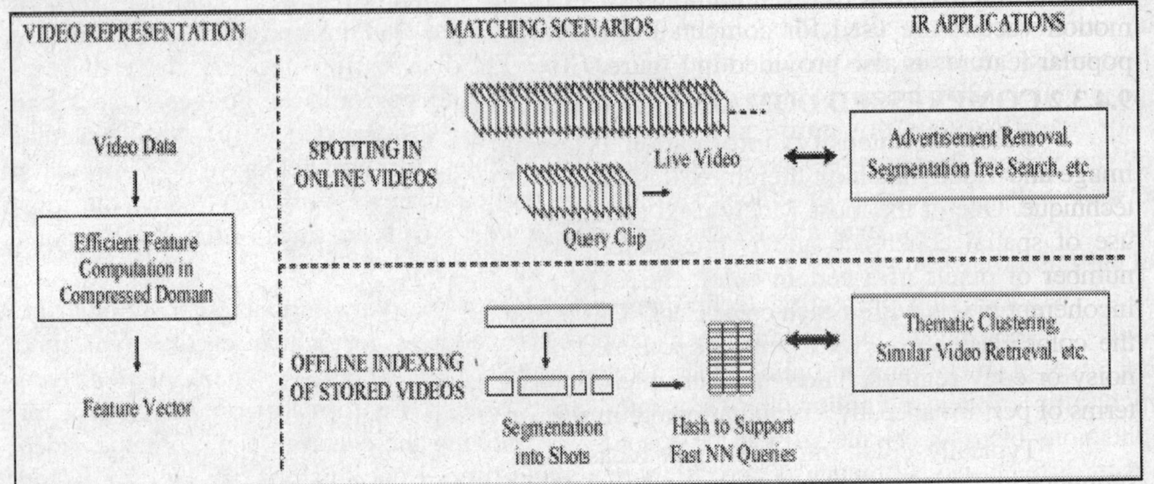


**Figure 9.18 An Overview of Techniques presented in Information Retrieval form Domain**

In the context of applications for present times, the amount of video data does not remain constant anymore. The data keeps growing every day and that too at tremendous rates. Till recently, video matching papers had been concentrating on issues pertaining to better representation of video properties and higher matching accuracy. Emergence of large scale video repositories introduced a new range of issues concerning faster offline processing and efficient search. Accuracy can be compromised to certain extent for gains in speed. For applications that require very fine level accuracy, slower sophisticated algorithms can be applied on much smaller datasets obtained after first level of coarse pruning. We propose a significantly fast approximation of a popular color feature in the compressed domain. Our implementation is capable of indexing 140 hours of video data in a day. The LSH based indexing scheme can easily search through more than 100 hours of data in few seconds.

### 9.4.3.1 EFFICIENT INDEXING IN COMPRESSED DOMAIN

The first step in our processing is to segment the broadcast news videos into shots. A shot is defined as a visually continuous sequence of successive video frames taken from one camera. The segmentation of videos is performed by automatically detecting the shot boundaries. The algorithm uses block based feature difference with an adaptive threshold, dynamically calculated over successive frames. Each shot is then processed and features are extracted for a compact representation of the shot. The feature extraction process needs to be computationally fast for handling large amounts of data. Moreover in situations when online videos need to be processed in real time, fast feature extraction mechanisms are desired.

We work in the compressed domain for extracting features. Video data is almost always found in compressed formats for efficiency of storage and transmission. Feature extraction is much more efficient in the compressed domain than that in the uncompressed domain as the overhead of decoding is removed. Memory requirements are much less while processing. Some low level features can be determined from the information directly available in the compressed domain itself which removes the overhead to compute it again in the pixel domain. JPEG and MPEG have been the most explored formats for compressed domain processing. Figure 9.19 illustrates the nature of DCT blocks in a compressed image or video frame. DCT coefficients and block motion vectors are used for computation of various low level features. An overview of the popular features is also provided in Figure 9.19.

### 9.4.3.2 COMPRESSED DOMAIN COLOR ATMOSPHERE

Color (or intensity) information is among the maximum used in the content based image and video matching literature. It is usually measured by some sort of refined color histogram technique. One of the most widely used technique is the color coherence vector (CCV). It makes use of spatial coherence and is thus much more discriminative. Instead of counting only the number of pixels of a certain color, the CCV additionally distinguishes between coherent and incoherent pixels within each color class. This essentially aims at differentiating pixels belonging to the color classes associated with smooth and homogeneous regions from those associated with noisy or edgy regions. Though it provides significant advantage over basic color histogram in terms of performance, the computational complexity is a deterrent.

Typically color information is measured in the compressed domain using DC image sequence and represented with features like DC color histograms. We propose an approximation of CCV by using information from MPEG compressed domain. This representation retains the benefits of CCV over a basic color histogram and is still a lot faster as it is directly computed from information available in the compressed domain. AC coefficients in the 8 × 8 3B DCT blocks are classified into frequency bands that roughly correspond to smooth areas, horizontal and vertical edges, and noisy areas. DCT blocks corresponding to smooth regions have low frequency and have only very few initial AC coefficients as non-zero, ideally only the DC coefficient. Whereas, blocks corresponding to noisy regions have later AC coefficients as non-zero. This information is used to classify the DC value of

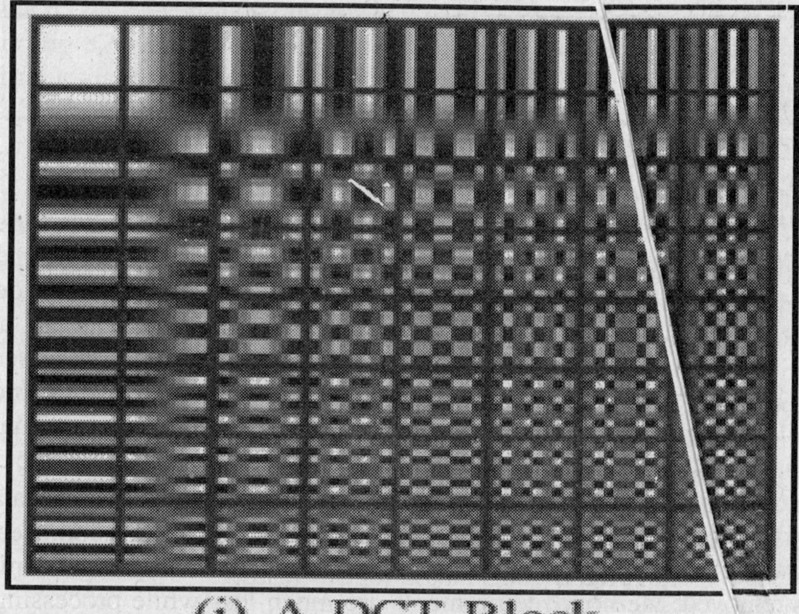

(i) A DCT Block

**Figure 9.19 (i) (8 x 8) DCT Block. Each Cell indicates the nature of the region that is represented by the particular DCT coefficient**

| Video Property | Features | Information Used |
|---|---|---|
| Color Atmosphere | DC color histogram, DC YCbCr vector | DC coefficients from all 3 color channels |
| Texture & Edge | AC coefficient energy, DCT Block edge map | AC coefficients and relationships among them |
| Motion statistics | Motion Activity, Motion Histograms | Block Motion Vectors |

(ii) Popular Compressed Domain Features [7]

**Figure 9.19 (ii) provides a review of common compressed Domain feature.**

| Method | FPS | Amount of data that can be indexed each day |
|---|---|---|
| Pixel Domain CCV | 4 | 6 hours |
| SIFT based frame representation [9], [10] | 2 | 3 hours |
| Our Compressed Domain approximation of CCV | 150 | 140 hours |

**Table 9.8 Comparison of our compressed Domain Feature Extraction with other Techniques. All the above numbers are reported on video of resolution 320 x 240**

the corresponding block as coherent or incoherent. Two values are associated with each color bin j:

- $\alpha j$ - The number of DC values corresponding to smooth DCT blocks of color class j
- $\beta_j$ - The number of DC values corresponding to noisy or edgy DCT blocks of color class j

The feature vector V is thus defined as the vector

$$V = \sim(\alpha 1, \beta 1), ...,(\alpha_n, \beta n)) \tag{9.25}$$

normalized by the number of DCT blocks. n is the number of color classes. The popular distance measure to compare CCVs can directly be adapted for our feature:

$$Dist(\mathcal{V}^1, \mathcal{V}^2) = \sum_{j=1}^{n} \left( \frac{|\alpha_j^1 - \alpha_j^2|}{\alpha_j^1 + \alpha_j^2 + 1} + \frac{|\beta_j^1 - \beta_j^2|}{\beta_j^1 + \beta_j^2 + 1} \right) \tag{9.26}$$

The Similarity measure between the two vectors is simply the inverse of the above equation

$$Sim(v^1, v^2) = \frac{1}{Dist(v^1, v^2)} \qquad (9.27)$$

Table 9.8 compares efficiency of our feature computation method with other well known standard color representations. We also compare with features used in latest video indexing schemes. It can be clearly seen from the numbers that our method of computing the approximate CCV is much superior to the standard pixel domain technique. In fact, it even turns out to be marginally faster than the computation of a basic color histogram in the pixel domain while still retaining the advantages of CCV to a large extent. Our version of the CCV is an approximation of the actual CCV and thus cannot be directly compared. We however conducted experiments which show that our approximation of the CCV is qualitatively good.

Processing video data is problematic due to the high data rates involved. Television quality video requires approximately 100 GBytes for each hour, or about 27 MBytes for each second. Such data sizes and rates severely stress storage systems and networks and make even the most trivial real-time processing impossible without special purpose hardware. Consequently, most video data is stored in a compressed format.

While compression reduces the storage and network costs, it increases the cost of processing since the data must be decompressed before it can be processed. The overhead of decompression is enormous: today's sophisticated compression algorithms, such as JPEG or MPEG, require between 150 and 300 instructions per pixel for decompression. This corresponds to a rate of 2.7 billion instructions for each second of NTSC quality video processed. Furthermore, the data must often be compressed after processing, which adds one to fifty times more overhead.

One way to circumvent these problems is to process the video data in compressed form. This technique reduces the amount of data that must be processed and avoids complex compression and decompression. Decreasing data volume has the side effect of increasing data locality and thus more efficiently uses processor cache, which further improves performance.

**1. JPEG**

JPEG is a standard for still image compression that can achieve compression ratios as high as 50 to 1. When JPEG is applied to each frame in a video sequence, the result is called "motion JPEG" video compression. The baseline JPEG algorithm is outlined in figure 9.20. Briefly, JPEG converts an RGB image into the YUV color space, subsampling the chrominance (U and V) components. Each component is divided into 8x8 pixel blocks, which are transformed using a discrete cosine transform (DCT).

The post-DCT 8x8 block is encoded as a one dimensional, 64 element vector using zig-zag scanning, a heuristic that places the low frequency coefficients, which are located in the upper left corner of the block, early in the vector. The vector is scaled by dividing each coefficient by a constant. The constant varies from element to element, and is proportional to the human eye's sensitivity to an error in each coefficient.

The scaled vector has the following property: an error of up to one half can be introduced in each element without a noticeable difference in the reconstructed image. Consequently, the elements of the scaled vector are rounded to the nearest integer, a process called quantization. Experiments reveal that typically 55 to 60 of the 64 quantized elements are zero, so they are encoded using run-length encoding (RLE), and the result is entropy coded using either Huffman or arithmetic coding.

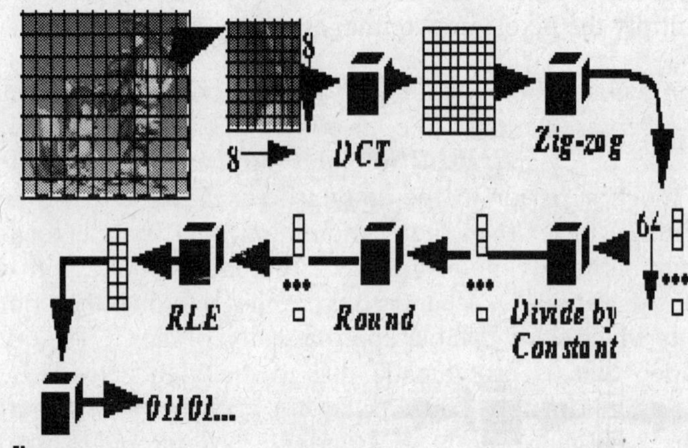

Figure 9.20: JPEG Image Compression

**JPEG IS A SEVEN STEP PROCESS**:

1. The color space of the image is converted (RGB to YUV)
2. The discrete cosine transform (DCT) is applied to each 8x8 block of pixels
3. The result is transform into a 64 element vector using zig-zag coding
4. The vector is scaled.
5. The scaled vector is quantized (rounded to the nearest integer).
6. The quantized vector is run-length encoded (RLE)
7. The RLE vector is entropy coded.

Decompression is the reverse of compression. Two important facts about JPEG compression will be needed for the discussion in the next section. First, steps 1-4 are linear operators. Second, the RLE vector is a sparse-matrix representation of the scaled, quantized DCT vector.

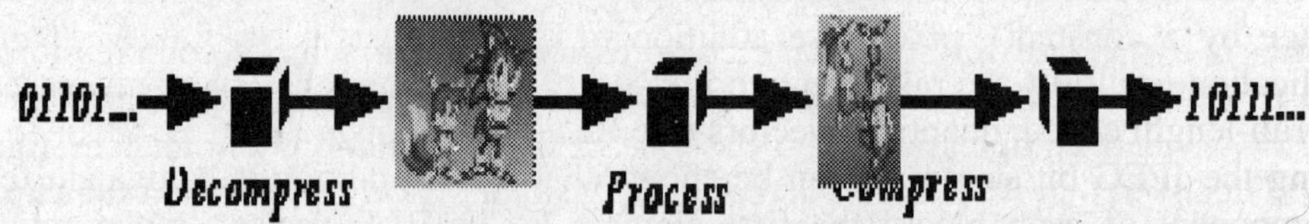

Figure 9.21: Spatial Domain Processing

We now turn to the problem of processing JPEG data. A naive approach would decompress the data, process it, and compress the result, as shown in figure 9.21. This strategy is called spatial domain processing. The basic idea of compressed domain processing is to convert the spatial domain process into its frequency domain equivalent. This conversion is accomplished by representing the spatial domain process and the transforms used in compression linear operators, and form the composite operator. Compressed data is then processed by entropy decoding the bitstream to recover the sparse vector data, applying the compressed domain operator, and quantizing and compressing the result. Figure 9.22 shows this strategy.

Perhaps the simplest type of video processing that has been mapped into the compressed domain (for JPEG) is pixel arithmetic. This type of processing consists of four operations: scalar addition (add a constant to each pixel in an image), scalar multiplication (multiply each pixel in an image by a constant), pixel-wise addition (add the pixels in two images), and pixel-wise multiplication (multiply the pixels in two images).

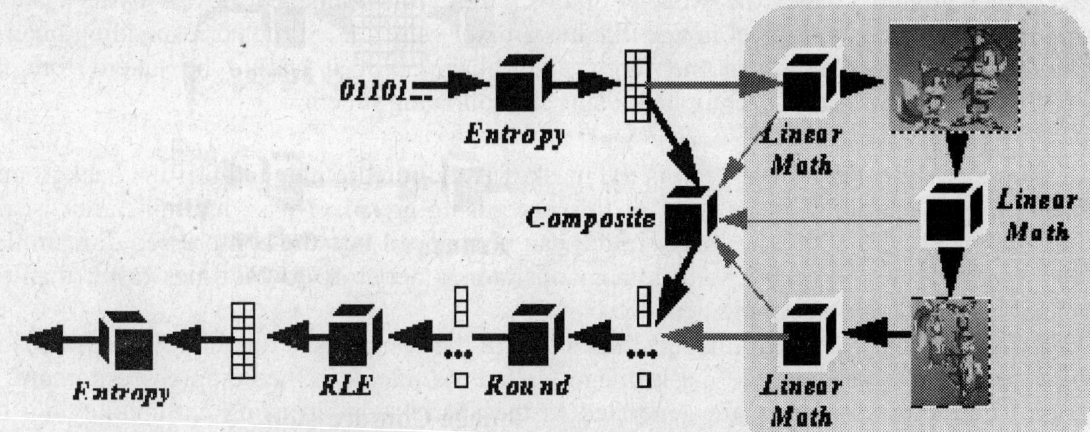


**Figure 9.22: Compressed Domain Processing**

These operations can be implemented directly on the run-length coded, quantized vectors (the RLE vectors), which can be obtained by Huffman decoding the JPEG bit stream. It can be shown that scalar addition is equivalent to altering the DC component of each block (the first element in the RLE vector), scalar multiplication is equivalent to multiplying each element of the RLE vector by a constant, and pixel-wise addition is equivalent to adding two RLE vectors. Pixel-wise multiplication is more complex: it involves the multiplication all possible pairs in the two RLE vectors. Since the vectors are relatively sparse, this operation is not too expensive in the average case.

Perhaps the simplest type of video processing that has been mapped into the compressed domain (for JPEG) is pixel arithmetic. This type of processing consists of four operations: scalar addition (add a constant to each pixel in an image), scalar multiplication (multiply each pixel in an image by a constant), pixel-wise addition (add the pixels in two images), and pixel-wise multiplication (multiply the pixels in two images). These operations can be implemented directly on the run-length coded, quantized vectors (the RLE vectors), which can be obtained by Huffman decoding the JPEG bit stream. It can be shown that scalar addition is equivalent to altering the DC component of each block (the first element in the RLE vector), scalar multiplication is equivalent to multiplying each element of the RLE vector by a constant, and pixel-wise addition is equivalent to adding two RLE vectors. Pixel-wise multiplication is more complex: it involves the multiplication all possible pairs in the two RLE vectors. Since the vectors are relatively sparse, this operation is not too expensive in the average case.

Pixel arithmetic can be used to implement a number of operations. For example, a cross-fade between two video sequences is described by the function

$$g(x, y) = \alpha f_2(x, y) + (1 - \alpha) f_1(x, y) \tag{9.28}$$

where g is an image in the output sequence, f1 and f2 are images in the source sequences, and α is a parameter that varies from 0 (beginning of the cross-fade) to 1 (end of the cross-fade). The implementation of this operation on compressed domain data is straightforward, since it involves only scalar multiplication and pixel-wise addition, and the compressed domain operator is about 100 times faster than its spatial domain equivalent.

Another application of pixel arithmetic is image composition. A familiar example of this operation is overlaying a forecaster on a weather map. The overlay is accomplished using three images: a background image (the weather map), a foreground image (the forecaster), and a masking image, which is a bi-level image that has a pixel value of 1 if the corresponding pixel in the output should be taken from the foreground image, 0 if it should be taken from the background. The output image is computed using the following function:

$$g(x, y) = m(x, y)f(x, y) + (1 - m(x, y))\, b(x, y) \tag{9.29}$$

where g is the output image, m is the mask, f is the foreground, and b is the background. Since the only operations that are used in this processing are pixel-wise multiplication, scalar addition, and pixel-wise addition, the operation can be mapped into the compressed domain. For typically applications, the compressed domain operator is about 10 to 50 times faster than the corresponding spatial domain implementation.

Two problems arise with image composition in the compressed domain. First, there is no known simple way to generate the mask image (called the matte) in the compressed domain. In television studios, these images are generated in the spatial domain using chroma-keying: the forecaster is placed in front of a bright green or blue screen, and that color is used to generate the mask image. No one has determined how to generate a matte directly on compressed data.

A second problem is that the edges of the foreground object and the edges in the matte are often highly correlated, since they both lie on the foreground object's boundary. The presence of edges increases the size of the RLE vectors, which makes the masking operation can be relatively expensive for the foreground image, since the cost of implementing a pixel-wise multiply on two RLE vectors is proportional to the product of the size of the two vectors. Often, the compressed domain operation is slower for these blocks than the spatial domain equivalent. But since there are relatively few edge blocks in typical mattes (maybe 10%), operating in the compressed domain is many times faster than in the spatial domain.

The four operations described above, pixel and scalar addition and multiplication, are local operations: the value of a pixel in the output is uniquely determined by the value of the corresponding pixel(s) in the source image(s). A more complicated type of processing uses global operations, where the value of a pixel in the output image is a function of many pixels in the source image. Linear global operations, where each output pixel is a linear combination of input pixels, can be implemented in the JPEG domain.

The basic idea of compressed domain global processing is to factor JPEG into steps that can be written mathematically as linear operators (scaling, DCT, zigzag scanning) and steps that can not (quantization, run-length and Huffman coding). Once JPEG compression, JPEG decompression, and the spatial domain operation (i.e., the processing) are written as linear operators, they can be combined. Two complications muddy this otherwise simple idea. First, the resulting operators can be more expensive to implement than the spatial domain equivalent, both in memory and operation count. This defect can be corrected using a scheme called condensation to approximate the compressed domain operator by a sparse operator. The image that results from using the sparse operator is nearly indistinguishable from the correct result, but its computation is much faster: about twice the time required for Huffman compression and decompression.

The second complication is that mapping global operations into the compressed domain is complicated because the spatial domain operators may cross block boundaries. For example, a common way to implement the operation of smoothing an image is to replace each pixel by an average of its immediate neighbors. Since an 8x8 pixel block in the output image is a function of a 10x10 block of pixels in the source image, the coefficients of the corresponding output RLE vector will be a complex linear combination of coefficients from nine RLE vectors in the input. Computing the appropriate linear combination is tractable if the spatial domain operators, and the operators corresponding to the compression and decompression, are written as high dimensional matrices. This technique gives rise to fairly complicated index gymnastics, but the calculation is straightforward.

Global operations in the compressed domain are several times faster than their spatial domain equivalents, but this efficiency comes at the cost of increased complexity of implementation. Moreover, this method of mapping global operations into the compressed domain results in impractically large data structures (tens of megabytes) unless the operation exhibits special symmetry.

These limitations have prompted other researchers to examine special cases that can be implemented efficiently. Two examples are the inner block operations discussed by Shen and Sethi, and the scaling operations derived by Natarajan and Bhaskaran.

Natarajan and Bhaskaran showed that the operation of shrinking an image by a factor of two could be implemented in the compressed domain using only shifts and adds. His work maps the scaling operator directly into the compressed domain and then factors the result into a sequence of operations with many common sub-expressions that consist of multiplies and divides by powers of two. The speed of the resulting operations is approximately 5:1, and the image quality is very high.

Sethi and Shen examined the special case of inner block transforms (IBTs), which are a form of factoring global operations. In IBTs, the coefficients in an output block is a function a single block in the source, but the combination of pixels in a block is a global operation. When IBTs are combined with pixel addition, IBTs can be used to implement a wide variety of operations, including image rotation.

Manipulating pixel values in the compressed domain provides the basis for implementing special effects, but does little to address image and video content. For example, it would be advantageous to search an image/video database using only compressed domain operations. Several researchers have pursued this idea. Two notable contributions are Seales work on object recognition and Arman's work on cut detection.

Seales examined searching a database of "mug shots" in the compressed domain using an eigenspace method. The basic idea of this work is to represent a large-dimensional object (an image) in a lower-dimensional subspace. The basis vectors for the subspace are images, called "eigen-faces", capture the most important features of the images in the database. Once the eigen-faces are computed, a linear combination of the eigen-faces is computed for each image in the database that closely approximates the image. The coefficients of this linear combination are used as an index in the database. To locate an image in the database, the eigen-face coefficients of the target image (the one you are searching for) are computed and compared against the database index. The matches are sorted and returned to the user.

Seales's method computes the eigen-faces directly on the RLE vectors, rather than pixel values. This allows the target image's index to be computed without decompressing the image, a significant savings. Seales showed that image searching using eigen-faces in the compressed domain was just as effective as in the image domain for moderate quality images, proving the validity of the technique and showing that the information lost during compression was insignificant.

## 2. MPEG VIDEO

Although JPEG is very effective at compressing still images, further compression can be achieved using the MPEG video standard. MPEG augments JPEG with motion compensation, a form of differential encoding, and achieves compression ratios as high as 200 to 1. In MPEG, each frame in a video sequence is encoded as either an I-frame, a P-frame, or a B-frames. A typical frame sequence is shown in figure 9.23, along with the inter-frame dependencies. I-frames are independent of other frames, and their encoding is almost identical to JPEG.

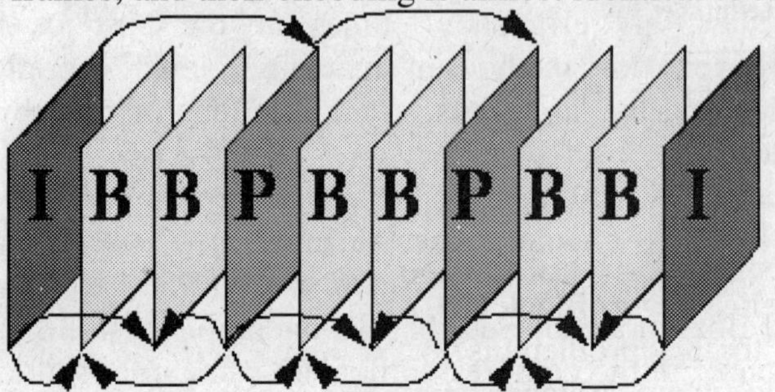


**Figure 9.23: MPEG Dependencies**

B-frames and P-frames are encoded as a difference from nearby I- or P-frames (called reference frames). P-frame encoding is shown in figure 9.24. MPEG partitions a P-frame into 16x16 pixel macroblocks. Each macroblock in the P-frame, called the target macroblock, is encoded by searching for a macroblock in the reference frame (the most recent I- or P-frame), typically using the mean squared error or mean absolute error as a metric. The difference in coordinates between the target macroblock and its best match is called the motion vector, and their pixel-wise difference is called the error term. The error term is compressed using JPEG and stored along with the motion vector in the MPEG bitstream. B-frame compression is nearly identical to P-frame compression, except that two reference frames (one from the earlier in the sequence and one from later) can be used. This extra degree of freedom can result in very high compression ratios, as high as 500 to 1.

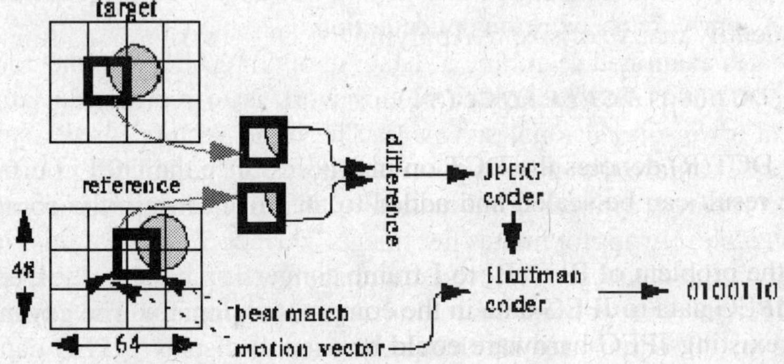


**Figure 9.24: P-frame encoding**

To decode an MPEG frame, all relevant reference frames must first be decoded. Then each error term is decompression, and the result is added pixel-wise to the 16x16 pixel block in the reference frame specified by the motion vector.

The processing in the previous section used JPEG compressed image and video data. A natural question is "can these techniques be extended to MPEG video data?" Since MPEG uses a more complex compression strategy than JPEG, the extension is non-trivial. Recall that MPEG defines three types of frames, I-, P-, and B-frames. I-frames are very similar to JPEG frames, while P- and B-frames use motion compensation. This motion compensation poses the most difficult problem for operating on MPEG data, since the motion vector may refer to a block of pixels that is not aligned on a macroblock boundary.

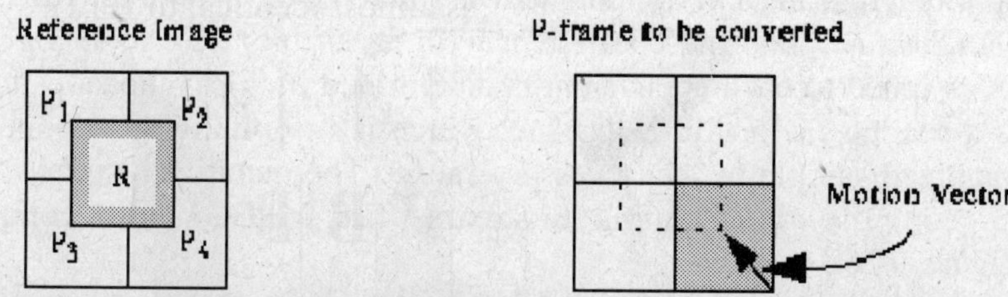


**Figure 9.25: Reference Macroblock (R), motion vector, and original macroblocks**

Chang's solution to this problem is to convert P- and B- frames into I-frames, then process the resulting frames using strategies similar to those of JPEG frames. Converting a P-or B-frame into an I-frame requires computing DCT coefficients of a motion compensated macroblock from the motion vector and the coefficients in the reference frame. Chang showed how to compute these coefficients by pre-multiplying and post-multiplying the reference macroblocks with appropriate matrices. Suppose in figure 9.25, R is the macroblock in the reference frame that we wish to derive from the four original macroblocks P1... P4. In the spatial domain, this conversion is expressed by the following equation:

$$R = \sum_{1}^{4} S_{i1} P_i S_{i2} \tag{9.30}$$

where $S_{ij}$ are matrices like

$$\begin{bmatrix} 0 & 0 \\ I_n & 0 \end{bmatrix} \quad or \quad \begin{bmatrix} 0 & I_n \\ 0 & 0 \end{bmatrix}$$

Each In is an identity matrix of size n. Applying the DCT to each side of this equation, we have

$$DCT(R) = \sum_{1}^{4} DCT(S_{i1})\, DCT(P_i)\, DCT(S_{i2})$$

where DCT(R) denotes the DCT on matrix R. Once the DCT coefficients of R have been calculated, the result can be scaled and added to the error term in the compressed domain using pixel addition.

Once the problem of P- or B- to I-frame conversion has been solved, it becomes possible to transcode MPEG data to JPEG data in the compressed domain. The advantage of this technique would be that existing JPEG hardware could be used to display MPEG data. Smith and Arachya have studied this problem recently, with promising results: MPEG to JPEG conversion can be performed at rates four to five times faster in the compressed domain than in the spatial domain. Their method caches converted motion-compensated macroblocks for additional performance.

## 3. MPEG AUDIO

The MPEG audio encoder achieves compression ratios between 6 and 12 to 1. MPEG audio converts a group samples into 32 equal width frequency bands using the subband analysis.

For example, CD quality audio digitized at 44.1 kHz would be divided into 32 bands, each 689 Hz wide. The result of the analysis is 32 amplitude coefficients, one for each band, that indicates the strength of that band. Each coefficient is then quantized using masking.

Masking is a psychoacoustic effect where larger amplitude signals obscures lower amplitude signals. Studies have shown that masking decreases with distance in the frequency domain. This fact means that, in MPEG audio, an amplitude coefficient with a large value will tend to render a neighboring coefficient with a small value inaudible. MPEG uses this fact to represent the smaller, neighboring coefficient with fewer bits than its large neighbor. The exact number of bits assigned to each coefficient is determined by a psychoacoustic model. The model also computes a scaling factor for each band, which is essentially an exponent which is used to expand the quantized sample to the necessary range. The quantized sample, bit allocations, and scaling factors comprise the resulting bitstream. The MPEG audio compression process is illustrated in figure 9.26.

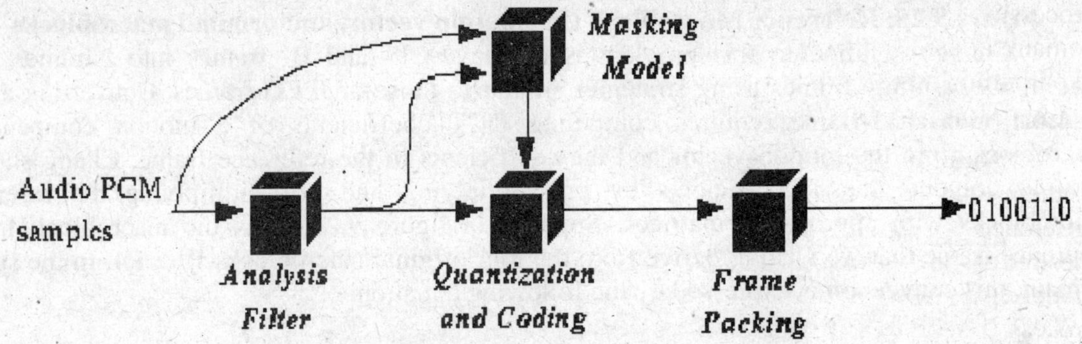


**Figure 9.26: MPEG Audio Encoding**

Few researchers have explored the possibility of directly manipulating MPEG compressed audio data. The area has attracted little attention because many researchers believe that less significant gains are possible because audio data rates are lower; CD-quality audio corresponds to a data rate of 192 KBytes/sec. But the sophisticated compression and decompression techniques used in MPEG audio compression make real-time processing of compressed audio data impossible on current generation machines.

### 9.4.4 COLOR IMAGE FILTERING AND ENHANCEMENT REFER TO THE PROCESS OF NOISE REDUCTION IN THE COLOR IMAGE AND ENHANCEMENT OF THE VISUAL QUALITY OF THE IMAGE INPUT

Noise encountered into the image data reduces the perceptual quality of an image and thus limits the performance of the imaging system. The generation of high quality color images which are visually pleasing is of great importance in a variety of application areas. That pre supposes image filtering, since images captured with sensing devices and transmitted through communication networks are often corrupted by noise. Therefore, both filtering and enhancement constitute an important part of any image processing pipeline where the final image is utilized for visual inspection or for automatic analysis.

The filtering operators applied to color images are required to preserve color information and structural content (edges and fine details), and to remove noise. The choice of these criteria follows the well-known fact that the human visual system is sensitive to changes in color appearance and fine details. Further to that, a good filtering/enhancement method should maintain the edge information while it removes image noise. Edges are important features since they indicate the presence, and the shape, of various objects in the image. From this viewpoint it is evident that the noise removal task in digital color imaging may be viewed as compromise between the noise suppression and color/structural content preservation.

Following the tristimulus theory of color representation, each pixel in a color Red-Green-Blue image can be viewed as a three-component vector $x_i = [x_{i1}, x_{i2}, x_{i3}]$ in the color RGB space (Figure 3). Thus, the color image is a vector array or a two-dimensional matrix of three-component samples $x_i$ with $x_{ik}$ denoting the R ( $k = 1$), G ( $k = 2$) or B ( $k = 3$) component (Figure 2). The chromaticity properties of color vector $x_i$ relate to its magnitude and direction (orientation in the vector space) which respectively relate to the luminance and chromaticity characteristics of the color pixel. Since both these measures are essential for human perception, color image processing techniques should preserve the color vectors' characteristics during processing. The processing operations can be performed in the magnitude domain, directional domain, or ideally both magnitude and directional information should be taken into consideration in outputting the color image with enhanced visual quality

#### 9.4.4.1 NOISE MODELING

Noise in digital images can be introduced by numerous sources, with the most common of them listed in Figure 4, and is present in almost any image processing system. Based on the difference between the observation (noisy) color vector $x_i = [x_{i1}, x_{i2}, x_{i3}]$ and the original (desired) sample $o_i = [o_{i1}, o_{i2}, o_{i3}]$, the noise corruption is modeled via the additive noise model $x_i = o_i + v_i$ with $v_i = [v_{i1}, v_{i2}, v_{i3}]$ denoting the vector which describes the noise process. The noise contribution $v_i$ can describe either signal-dependent or independent noise.

Given the definition above, color noise is the amount of color fluctuation given a certain color signal. As such the color noise signal should be considered as a three-channel perturbation vector in the RGB color space, affecting the spread of the actual color vectors in the space

#### 9.4.4.2 IMAGE FILTERING BASICS

Noise reduction techniques are most often divided into two classes linear techniques, and nonlinear techniques. Linear processing techniques have been widely used in digital signal processing applications, since their mathematical simplicity and the availability of a unifying linear system theory make these techniques relatively easy to analyze and implement. However, most of the linear techniques tend to blur structural elements such as lines, edges and other fine image details. Since image signals are nonlinear in nature due to the presence of structural information and are perceived via the human visual system which has strong nonlinear characteristics, nonlinear filters can potentially preserve important multichannel structural elements, such as color edges and eliminate degradations occurring during signal formation or transmission through nonlinear channel.

Since natural images should be considered non-stationary signals due to presence of edges, varying color information and noise, filtering schemes operate on the premise that an image can be subdivided into small regions, each of which can be treated as stationary. Most color filtering techniques operate on some type of sliding window placing the pixel $x_{(N+1)/2}$ under consideration at the center of the processing window (Figure 9.24). This pixel's value is changed as a result of a filtering operation on the vectors $x_1, x_2, x_N$ included in a local neighborhood. This window operator slides over the entire image successively placing each image pixel at its center (Figure 9.24).

The performance of a filtering scheme is generally influenced by the size of the local area inside the processing window. Some applications may require larger support to read local image features and complete the task appropriately. On the other hand, a filter operating on a smaller spatial neighborhood can better match image details. The most commonly used window is a 3×3 square shape (Figure 9.24) due to its versatility and performance, however, a particular window, such as those presented in can be designed to preserve specifically oriented image edges.

### 9.4.4.3 COMPONENT-WISE VS. VECTOR COLOR IMAGE FILTERING

Since each individual channel of a color image can be considered a monochrome (gray-scale) image (Figure 9.21), traditional image filtering techniques such as well-known (scalar) median filters often involved the application of scalar filters on each channel separately (Figure 9.25a). However, this disrupts the correlation that exists between the color components of natural images represented in a correlated color space, such as RGB or its standardized variants. Given the fact that each processing step is usually accompanied by a certain inaccuracy, the formation of the output color vector from the separately processed color components usually produces color artifacts.

It is believed that vector filtering techniques that treat the color image as a vector field (Figure 9.25b) are more appropriate for color image processing. With such an approach, the filter output is a function of the vectorial inputs x 1 , x 2 ,x N , located within the supporting window (Figure 9.24). The two basic classes of vector filters are constituted by vector median related filters vector directional filters.

The vector median filter (VMF) is a vector processing operator which has been introduced as an extension of the scalar median filter. The VMF output is the sample (lowest ranked vector or lowest order statistics) x (1) { x 1 , x 2 , x N } that minimizes the distance to the other samples inside the processing window as follows:

where L is the Minkowski metric used to quantify the distance between two color pixels x i and x j in the magnitude domain. Since the above concept can be used to determine the positions of the different input vectors without any a priori information regarding the signal distributions, VMF-related filters are robust estimators.

Vector directional filters operate on the directions of image vectors, aiming at eliminating vectors with atypical directions in the color space. The output of the basic vector directional filter (BVDF) is the sample (lowest ranked vector or lowest order statistics) x (1) ? { x 1 , x 2 , x N } which minimizes the angular ordering criteria to other samples inside the sliding filtering window:

where A(·,·) denotes the angle (angular distance) between two color vectors. Thus, the VDF filters do not take into account the brightness of color vectors. To utilize both features in color image filtering, the generalized vector directional filters (GVDF) and double window GVDF first eliminate the color vectors with atypical directions in the vector space and subsequently process the vectors with the most similar orientation according to their magnitude. In this way, the GVDF splits the color image processing into directional processing and magnitude processing.

The traditional VMF and VDF filters do not take into account neither the importance of the specific samples in the filter window or structural contents of the image. Better performance can be obtained when distances are appropriately modified by weighting coefficients representing the degree to which each input vector contributes to the output of the filte or of which the specific distances between multichannel inputs contribute to the aggregated measure serving as an ordering criterion . Such an idea is behind the weighted vector filters such as weighted VMFs, weighted VDFs and fuzzy-weighted VDFs. The selection weighted vector filters in allow for the simultaneous utilization of both the magnitude and directional characteristics of the color vectors, and generalize a number of previous filtering techniques including VMF, BVDF and their weighted modifications.

To adapt the filter weights (or parameters in general) to varying signal and noise statistics, different multichannel adaptation algorithms can be utilized The achieved weights should be sufficiently robust and their utilization should lead to the essential trade-off between noise smoothing and signal-detail preservation.

**9.4.4.4 SWITCHING VECTOR FILTERS**

Traditional filtering schemes such as VMF and BVDF which operate on a fixed supporting window introduce excessive smoothing, blur edges and eliminate fine image details. This effect should be attributed to the low-pass filtering characteristics of these color image filters. To prevent excessive smoothing and preserve fine image details, one of the most popular and computationally efficient solutions switch between a robust nonlinear smoothing mode and an identity processing mode which leaves input samples unchanged during the filtering operation Such an approach allows for the fast adaptation of the filter behavior to the statistics of the input image and it usually leads to an excellent performance in the environments with impulsive-type noise.

**9.4.4.5 EMERGING APPLICATIONS**

Robust performance characteristics and a trade-off between noise suppression and color/structural information preservation are often required in real-life imaging applications where inputs are often corrupted by noise or other visual impairments. Emerging applications include, but not limited to, virtual restoration of artworks and enhancement of the digitized images in digital artwork libraries, reconstruction of television images and old movies, microarray image processing and many others. The appearance of the noise as well as useful color/structural image information differs between the applications and thus, the designer should take into consideration the specifics of each application.

For example, strong color/structural preserving characteristics are required in the virtual restoration of artwork. In this application, noise is introduced by scanning the granulated, dirty, or damaged surface of the original artworks. To produce visually pleasing enhanced image with removed outliers and sharply looking fine details, adaptive vector filters should be used. On the other hand, cDNA microarray image processing may require the utilization of robust processing techniques such as the vector order-statistics filters or the vector fuzzy filters, which are capable to preserve the spot information and eliminate substantial noise floor in the two-channel cDNA image data.

# QUESTION BANK

Q1. What are the techniques of the color image processing?

Q2. Explain the various color image signal representation? Explain with the help of example.

Q3. What are the various basics of color image processing? Explain with the help of example.

Q4. Explain the extension of processing techniques to color domain in details?

Q5. Write short note on modeling and formulation and maximum likelihood estimator?

Q6. Explain the various compressed domain techniques to support information retrieval applications for broadcast news videos?

Q7. Write short note on the JPEG Image Compression , Spatial Domain Processing and Compressed Domain Processing.

Q8. Explain the color image filtering and enhancement refers to the process of noise reduction in the color image and enhancement of the visual quality of the image input?

Q9. Difference between the component-wise vs. vector color image filtering?

# CHAPTER 10

# APPLICATIONS OF IMAGE PROCESSING

## 10.1 INTRODUCTION

In this chapter, examples for scientific and technical applications of digital image processing are discussed. The examples demonstrate that image processing enables complex phenomena to be investigated, which could not be adequately accessed with conventional measuring techniques.

Real world applications like Picture data archival, machine vision, medical image processing. In picture data archivel we have pixel resolution Pixel resolution, Thermal sensitivity, Non-uniformity correction.

In machine vision Machine vision is a sub discipline of artificial intelligence that uses video cameras or scanners to obtain information about a given environment, and to extract data from digital images about objects in the image.

Machine vision takes an image in and outputs some level of description about the objects in it (i.e., size, position, correlation, etc.). Although applications for machine vision vary, there are generally only a few main categories:

Quality assurance, Sorting, Material handling Robot guidance, Calibration represents probably the largest number of machine vision applications in use today. As a field of scientific investigation, medical imaging constitutes a sub-discipline of biomedical engineering, medical physics or medicine depending on the context: Research and development in the area of instrumentation, image acquisition (e.g. radiography), modelling and quantification are usually the preserve of biomedical engineering, medical physics and computer science.

Medical imaging refers to the techniques and processes used to create images of the human body for clinical purposes or medical science. As a discipline and in its widest sense, it is part of biological imaging and incorporates radiology (in the wider sense), radiological sciences, endoscopy, (medical) thermography, medical hotography and microscopy (e.g. for human pathological investigations), magnetic resonance imaging (MRI).

## 10.2 PICTURE DATA ARCHIVAL

An image converter (radiant thermal energy to visible image) you need to understand only a few attributes that determine thermal image quality; resolution, thermal sensitivity and fixed pattern noise.

### 10.2.1 TOPICS:

- Pixel resolution
- Thermal sensitivity
- Non-uniformity correction

### 10.2.1.1 PIXEL RESOLUTION

The first consideration is the number of pixels. Today there are three resolution standards (some manufacturers' cameras deviate slightly):

- Low Resolution =160x120 (19,600 pixels)
- Medium Resolution = 320x240 (76,800 pixels)
- High Resolution = 640x480 (307,200 pixels)

How much resolution you need (verses want) is primarily determined by your application and by the value you give to image quality. When evaluating a digital camera with 5 verses 10 mega pixels most users will never benefit by purchasing a camera with 10 million pixels because they will never print the images on large enough paper where the resolution would provide better print quality. Whereas you will always print and display the full resolution of an infrared camera since the highest resolution available is relatively modest by today's digital camera standards. Even at 640x480 pixel resolution a high definition thermal image will only take up a fraction of today's computer displays and the resulting thermal image print quality will always be fully realized. Therefore when evaluating a thermal camera the number of pixel is relevant and increased resolution is the most significant consideration in improving image quality.

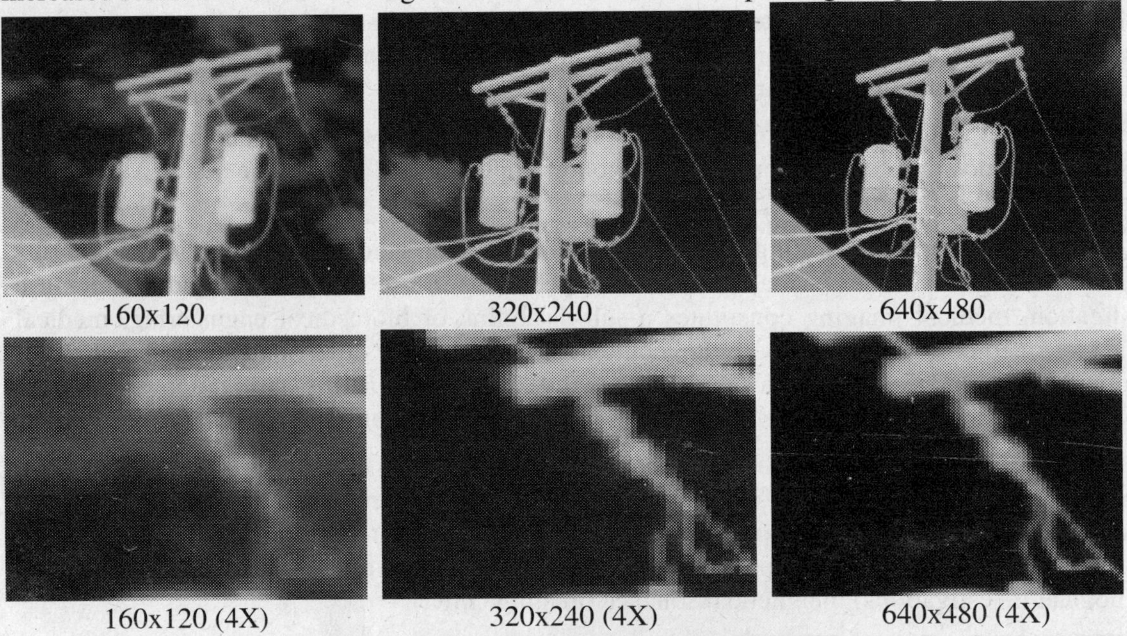


**Figure 10.1 Pixel Resolution of Thermal Camera**

Another benefit to high resolution is the ability to zoom into a scene and maintain good image quality. The majority of thermal cameras feature a standard optic with a horizontal field of view of approximately 25°. Regardless of pixel resolution the performance of a 640x480 camera set to 2X digital zoom is going to equal the performance of a 320x240 resolution camera with an optional (and often costly) 12° (2X) lens. If you anticipate the need for imaging objects at distances further than 20 feet you should consider the increased costs of a 2X lens for a 320x240 thermal camera when comparing the total costs between 320x240 and 640x480 systems.

The second major issue that impacts image quality is thermal sensitivity. While there are a number of tests used to quantify this specification, thermal sensitivity basically defines how well the camera will image as you increase image contrast. Thermal sensitivity varies with object temperature, as object temperature increases the slope of the signal output of the detector increases with increased temperature. This means that the signal (increasing) to noise (fixed) ratio improves as you view hotter objects. However this is not usually a benefit because the applications where better thermal sensitivity can be exploited are low temperature (room temperature) applications where the thermal contrast (temperature delta within an image) is very low. Typical low thermal contrast applications include building diagnosis where the camera is imaging interior walls with very little temperature variations or emissive differences and issues like moisture or insulation quality can only be visualized by increasing the contrast to the point where the cameras thermal sensitivity limits the useful temperature span settings. As you review published camera specifications you will see thermal sensitivity specifications range between 0.25°C (250mK) and 0.05°C (50mK). While you might consider a quarter of degree to be adequate thermal sensitivity as soon as you look at a low contrast scene you'll discover the image quality adversely effects the image quality as noise begins to dominate the image.

Thermal imagers usually display images in palettes comprised of 256 discreet color or gray levels. Imagine your target has a temperature difference between 0°C and 256°C each gray or color level would represent 1 degree of temperature difference. Now apply this same color mapping into a scene with temperatures between 25°C and 35°C or 10 degrees. Each color now represents 0.03°C (10°C ÷256), a value lower than the most sensitive uncoiled cameras. The result is some display of noise. There are many applications in which it is very important to set the span as narrow as possible in order to see the smallest temperature variations possible. If you are using a camera with 0.25°C sensitivity and wanted to maintain the same level of noise you would have to set a temperature range of 65°C (150°F) which would likely result in a very low contrast image. You should recognize that the difference between a camera with 50mK sensitivity verses a camera with 100mK sensitivity is 100% better and not as 0.05°C better.

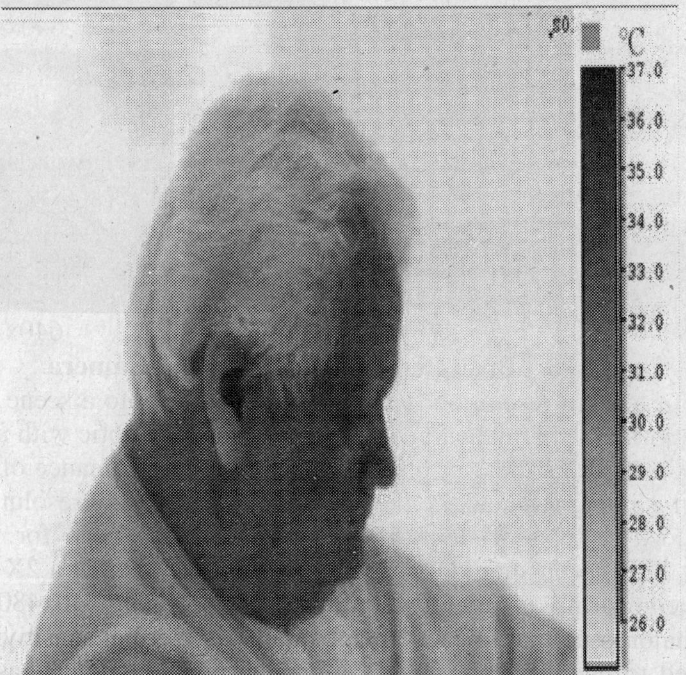

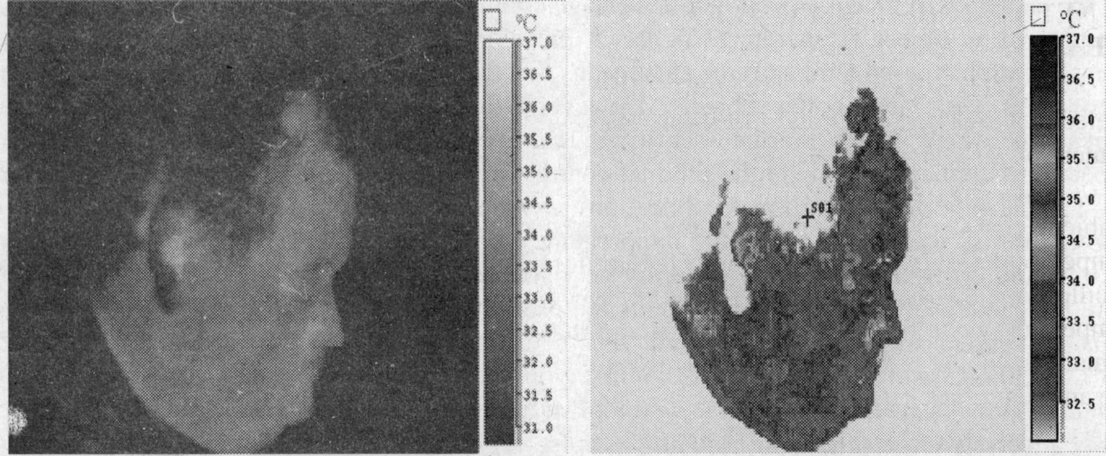


**Figure 10.2a 160x120 100mK Sensitivity is adequate for most applications where the image temperature span is >10°C, but the image degrades if you narrow the span more than 10°C**

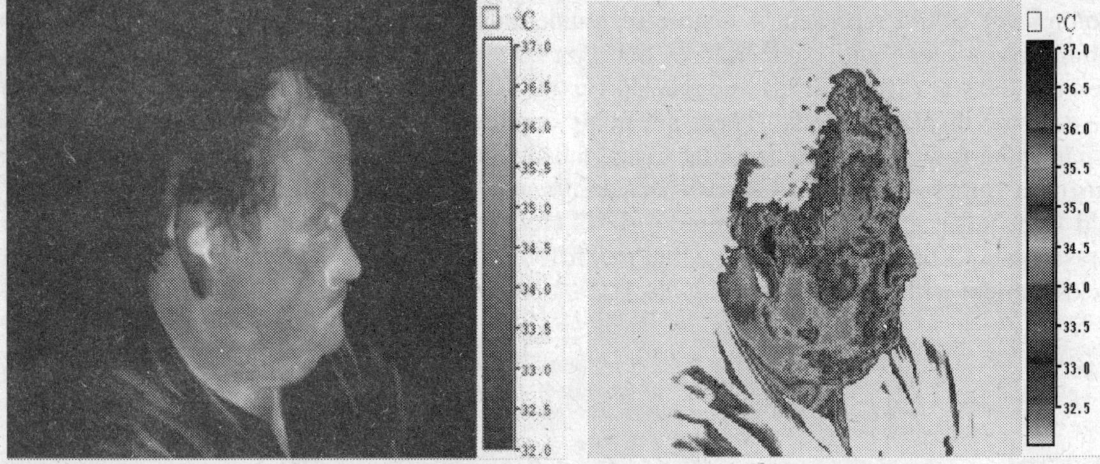


**Figure 10.2b 320x240 70mK Sensitivity lets you set a narrower span to 5°C while maintaining good image quality**

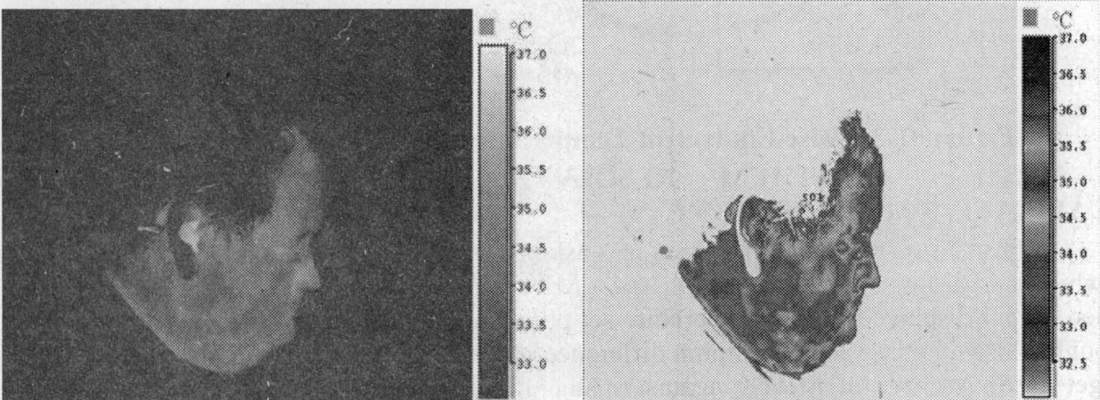


**Figure 10.2c 640x480 50mK Sensitivity creates the most smooth noise free images. This level of sensitivity rivals the thermal sensitivity of some cooled (costly) cameras.**

## 1. NETD – NOISE EQUIVALENT TEMPERATURE DIFFERENCE QUANTITATIVE MEASUREMENT

NETD is the scene temperature difference equal to either the internal noise of the detector (detector NETD) or the total electronic noise of a measurement system (system NETD). As a camera buyer you need to evaluate system NETD.

The test setup consists of temperature control blackbody reference and some type of ambient (passive) object that creates a simple slit target for the camera to visualize. The temperature of the black body is adjusted until it nearly equals the ambient target temperature. An oscilloscope measures the analog video output of one horizontal line and at the point where the temperature delta between the reference and the ambient targets no longer creates a measureable signal the NETD is determine by the measured temperature difference between the reference and the ambient reference targets. (figure 10.3 – NETD Test Setup)

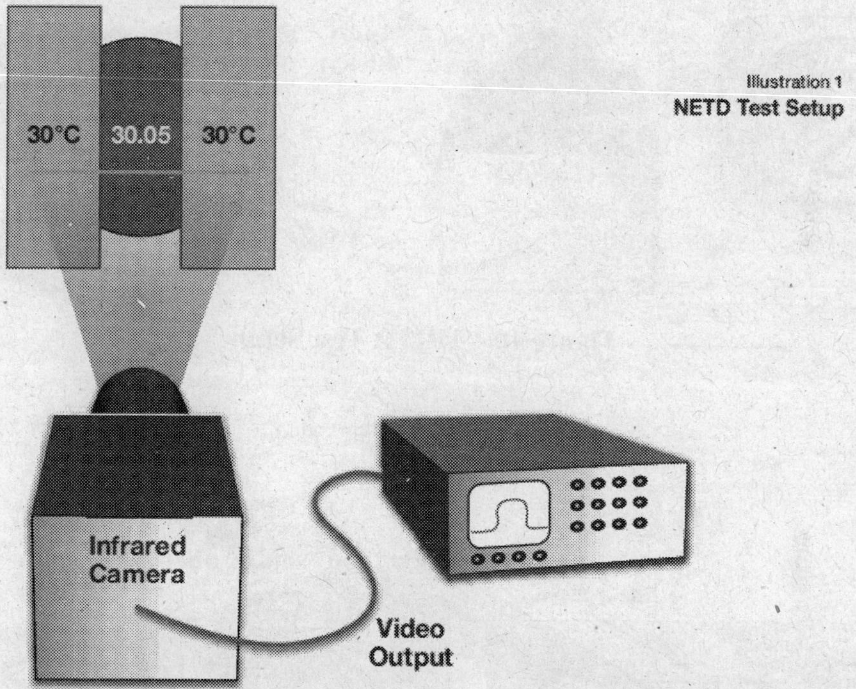


**Figure 10.3 Noise Equivalent Temperature Difference (NETD)Test Setup**

## 2. MRTD – MINIMUM RESOLVABLE TEMPERATURE DIFFERENCE QUALITATIVE MEASUREMENT

This is a system test. An observer is asked to assess the minimum temperature difference at which a 4 bar target (see Illustration 10.4 – MRTD Test Setup) can be resolved by watching the video output displayed as the temperature set points of the reference and the ambient targets are brought close together. This minimum difference will change with the spatial frequency of the bar target used. A curve of MRTD against spatial frequency is obtained which characterizes the performance of the imaging system. Modern infrared imaging systems can have low spatial frequency MRTDs of tens of milli-kelvins.

The benefits of large format cameras is significant we you combine the need for high sensitivity while viewing high spatial frequencies. To simplify explaining the fundamentals of thermal sensitivity let's focus on a single pixel of the infrared sensor in an uncooled infrared camera. Each pixel in an uncooled focal plane array image sensor is essentially a resistor fabricated using MEMS (micro electro mechanical systems).

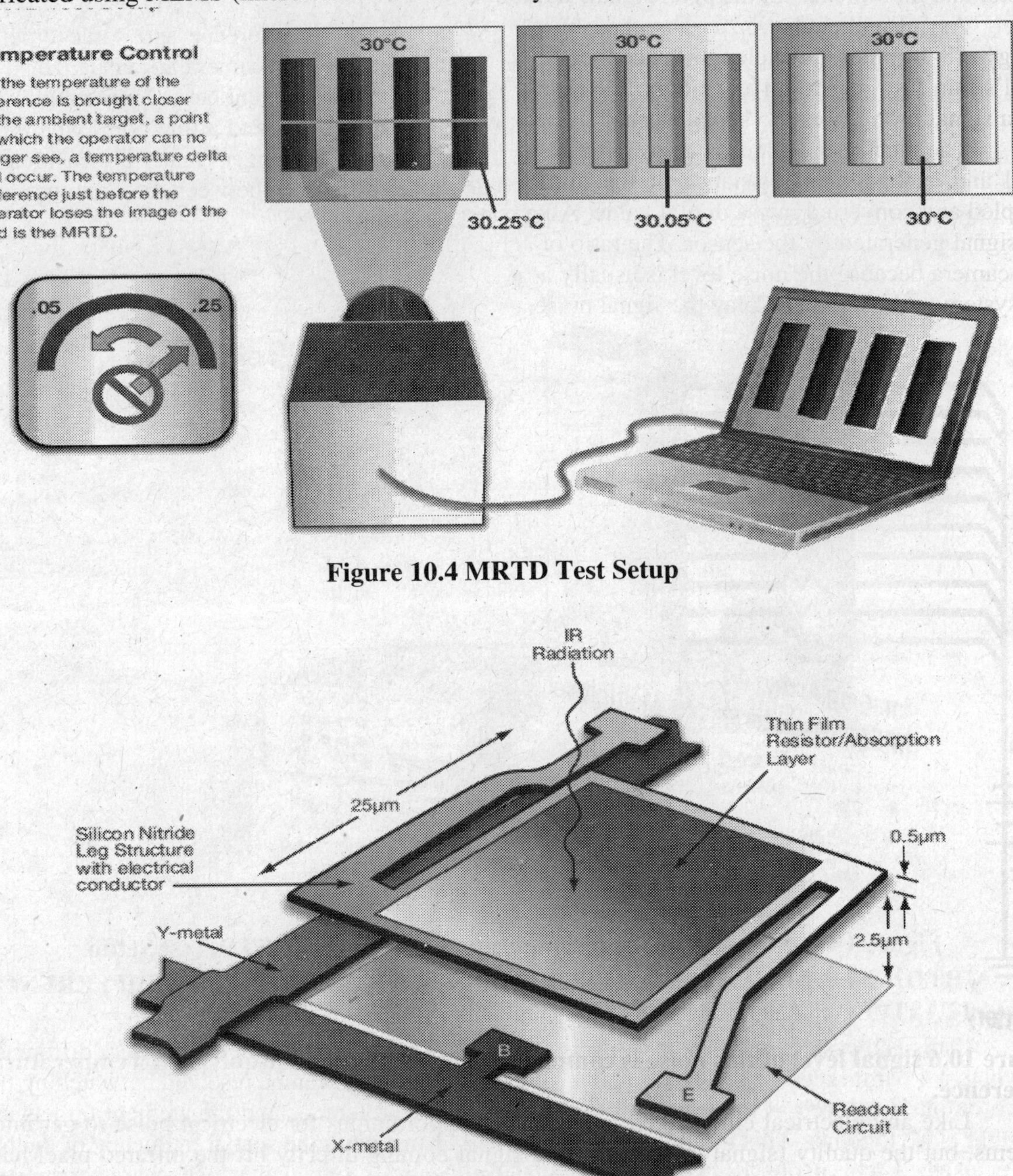


Figure 10.4 MRTD Test Setup

Figure 10.5 Structure of Thermal Uncoiled Camera

The basis structure of a thermal uncooled camera pixel is a microscopic bridge structure on which a thin resistor material and an absorbing layer have been deposited. Legs suspend the deck of bridge above an integrated circuit and provide electrical connection between the resistive bridge and the silicon readout circuit. The readout IC controls the voltage that biases the thin film resistor and multiplexes all the pixel signals out to the cameras imaging electronics.

As infrared radiation is absorbed by each pixel its temperature changes as the photon energy (8-14 micron wavelength) is converted to heat which in turn changes the resistance of the pixel's thin film resistor. The readout IC sends a voltage across each "micro bolometer" element and a signal proportional to heat absorbed by each detector is the basis of a real time video image.

The electrical circuit of an infrared sensor is very simple, a voltage is turned on to each pixel and a change in resistance of the thin film resistor based on the pixels temperature is sampled and converted into a digital value. All analog signal carry some level of noise along with the signal generated by the sensor. The ratio of signal to noise strongly impacts the image quality of a camera because the noise level is usually a fixed amount and as the detector gain is increased the system will begin to display the signal noise and you'll begin to see "snow" in the image.

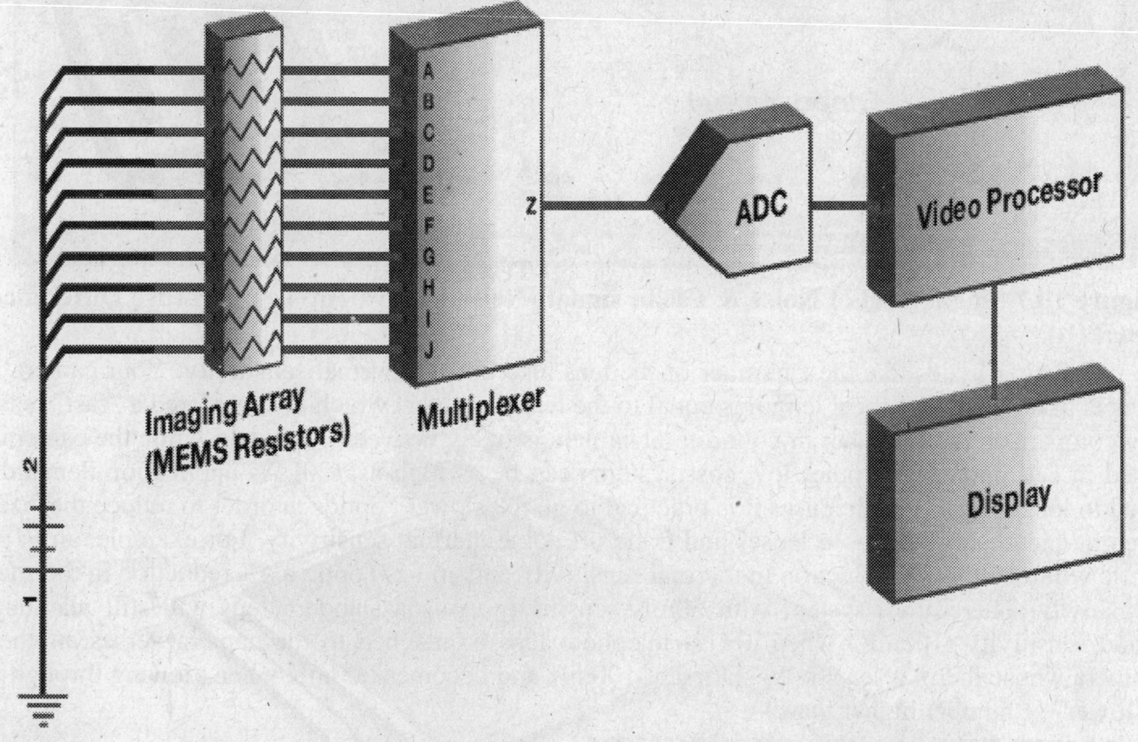


**Figure 10.6 signal level of this noise is commonly specified as Noise Equivalent Temperature Difference.**

Like any electrical circuit there are a lots of opportunities for electrical noise to get into systems, but the quality (signal to noise) of the signal coming directly off the infrared pixel has the most impact on thermal sensitivity, since nearly all camera developers have access to the same electronic components with which to create a camera. Therefore the thermal sensitivity in large part is based on the quality of the infrared imager array.

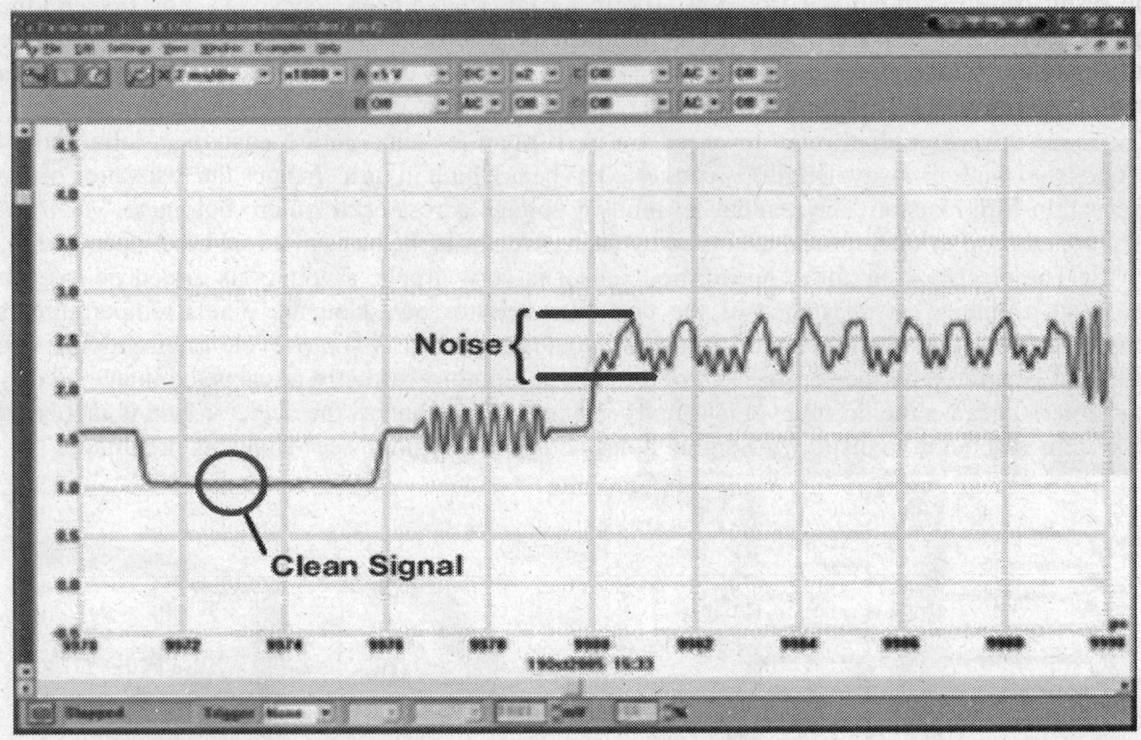


**Figure 10.7 Signal level of Noise & Clean signal (Noise Equivalent Temperature Difference (NETD))**

Other issues like the f number of the lens also impact thermal sensitivity. Your camera's lens is likely $f1.0$ (the focal length is equal to the lens diameter) which is considered a "fast" lens. By comparison the f number in your digital camera is likely between $f3$ and $f5$ while the cameras used in cell phones and other low cost systems can be as high as $f20$! As application demands lead to longer focal length lenses it is practical to go to "slower" optics in order to reduce the size, weight and cost of telephoto lenses and trade off some thermal sensitivity. For example, an F1.4 optic will result in 2X reduction in thermal sensitivity and an F2.0 optic a 4X reduction in thermal sensitivity. Therefore a system with 50mK sensitivity using a standard lens will still maintain good sensitivity (100mK) when a $f1.4$ telephoto lens is attached to the camera verses another camera whose thermal sensitivity started at 100mK and becomes 200mK when viewing through a "slower" ($f$ number higher than 1).

## 10.2.2 NON-UNIFORMITY CORRECTION

As the number of pixels increases and their sensitivity improves the quality of image is increasingly dependent on a process called Non Uniformity Correction or NUC. As we described earlier a microbolometer imaging array is essentially an array of tiny resistors and because of the micro scale of these devices there are variations in how each pixel responds to the infrared energy from an object.

During manufacturing the infrared camera's sensor must be normalized, meaning that the differences in response and DC output for each detector must be zeroed out. Here are two images from a camera. The first is what a typical image looks like without any corrections and the other the result of the calibration correction. Thermal cameras typically feature an internal flagoriris that periodically is positioned in front of the detector as a constant temperature reference to zero out differences amongst the pixels. This is a fine tuning of the factory NUC process and is sometimes referred to as a "touch up".

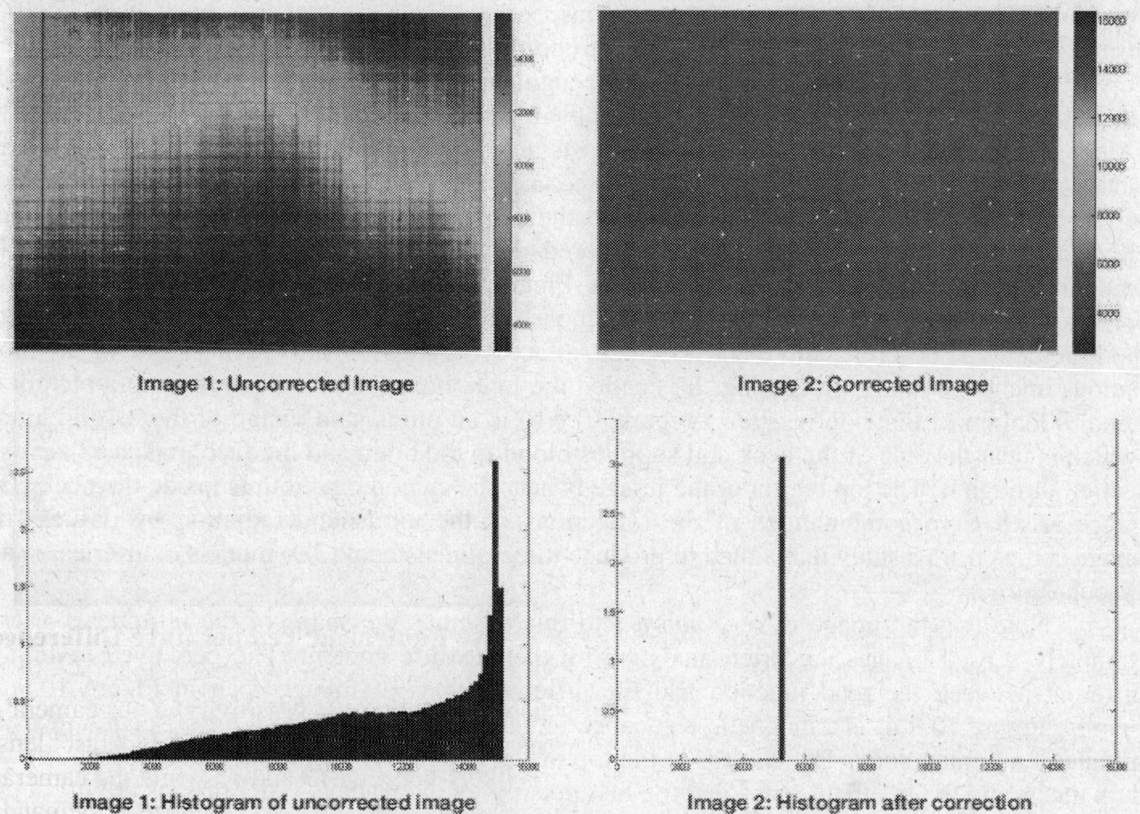


**Figure 10.8 Non Uniformity Correction (NUC)**

Because the touch up source is inside the lens, additional image quality improvements are possible when performing a touch up calibration through the lens either using a lens cap or exposing the camera to a large uniform surface. As camera performance improves the non uniformities created by the lens will begin to be seen and for the ultimate image quality a simple through the lens calibration step will ensure the highest image quality the camera is capable of generating.

**BENEFITS OF HIGH INCREASED IMAGE QUALITY**:

1. Much greater flexibility to inspect targets are varying Distances.
2. Ability to visualize low thermal contrast targets
3. More intuitive diagnosis of heat related problems
4. Improved infrared visible fused image quality due to better matching of infrared and visible camera resolution..
5. Flexibility to incorporate lower cost and lighter weight optional lenses
6. More intuitive diagnosis of temperature anomalies.

## 10.3 COMPUTER VISION OR MACHINE VISION

A computer vision system processes images acquired from an electronic camera, which is like the human vision system where the brain processes images derived from the eyes. Computer vision is a rich and rewarding topic for study and research for electronic engineers, computer scientists and many others. Increasingly, it has a commercial future. There are now many vision systems in routine industrial use: cameras inspect mechanical parts to check size, food is inspected for quality, and images used in astronomy benefit from computer vision techniques. Forensic studies and biometrics (ways to recognize people) using computer vision include automatic face recognition and recognizing people by the 'texture' of their irises.

These studies are paralleled by biologists and psychologists who continue to study how our human vision system works, and how we see and recognize objects (and people). A selection of (computer) images is given in Figure 10.9; these images comprise a set of points or picture elements (usually concatenated to pixels) stored as an array of numbers in a computer. To recognize faces, based on an image such as Figure 10.9(a), we need to be able to analyze constituent shapes, such as the shape of the nose, the eyes and the eyebrows, to make some measurements to describe, and then recognize, a face. (Figure 10.9(a) is perhaps one of the most famous images in image processing. It is called the Lena image, and is derived from a picture of Lena Sjööblom in Playboy in 1972.) Figure 10.9(b) is an ultrasound image of the carotid artery (which is near the side of the neck and supplies blood to the brain and the face), taken as a cross-section through it. The top region of the image is near the skin; the bottom is inside the neck. The image arises from combinations of the reflections of the ultrasound radiation by tissue. This image comes from a study that aimed to produce three-dimensional (3D) models of arteries, to aid vascular surgery.

Note that the image is very noisy, and this obscures the shape of the (elliptical) artery. Remotely sensed images are often analyzed by their texture content. The perceived texture is different between the road junction and the different types of foliage seen in Figure 10.9(c). Finally, Figure 10.9(d) is a magnetic resonance imaging (MRI) image of a cross-section near the middle of a human body. The chest is at the top of the image, the lungs and blood vessels are the dark areas, and the internal organs and the fat appear grey. Nowadays, MRI images are in routine medical use, owing to their ability to provide high-quality images.

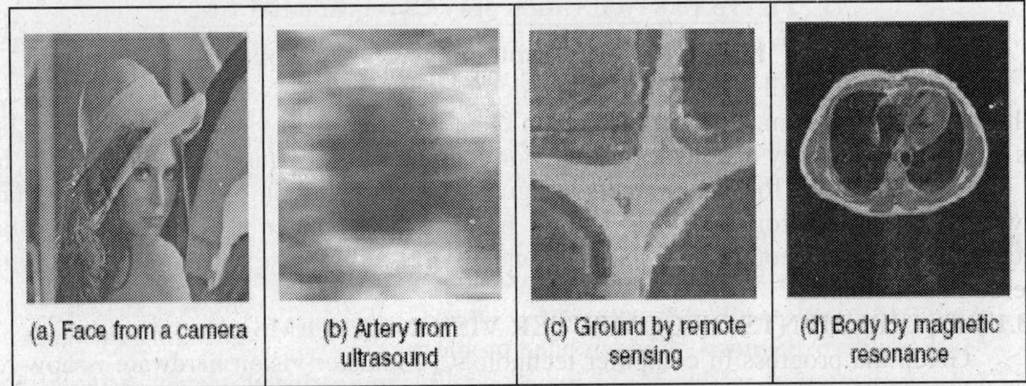


**Figure 10.9 Real images from different sources**

There are many different image sources. In medical studies, MRI is good for imaging soft tissue, but does not reveal the bone structure (the spine cannot be seen in Figure 10.9d); this can be achieved by using computed tomography (CT), which is better at imaging bone, as opposed to soft tissue. Remotely sensed images can be derived from infrared (thermal) sensors or synthetic-aperture radar, rather than by cameras, as in Figure 10.9(c). Spatial information can be provided by two-dimensional arrays of sensors, including sonar arrays.

There are perhaps more varieties of sources of spatial data in medical studies than in any other area. But computer vision techniques are used to analyse any form of data, not just the images from cameras. Synthesized images are good for evaluating techniques and finding out how they work, and some of the bounds on performance. Two synthetic images are shown in Figure 10.10. Figure 10.10(a) is an image of circles that were specified mathematically. The image is an ideal case: the circles are perfectly defined and the brightness levels have been specified to be constant. This type of synthetic image is good for evaluating techniques which find the borders of the shape (its edges) and the shape itself, and even for making a description of the shape. Figure 10.10(b) is a synthetic image made up of sections of real image data. The borders between the regions of image data are exact, again specified by a program. The image data comes from a well-known texture database, the Brodatz album of textures. This was scanned and stored as a computer image. This image can be used to analyse how well computer vision algorithms can identify regions of differing texture.

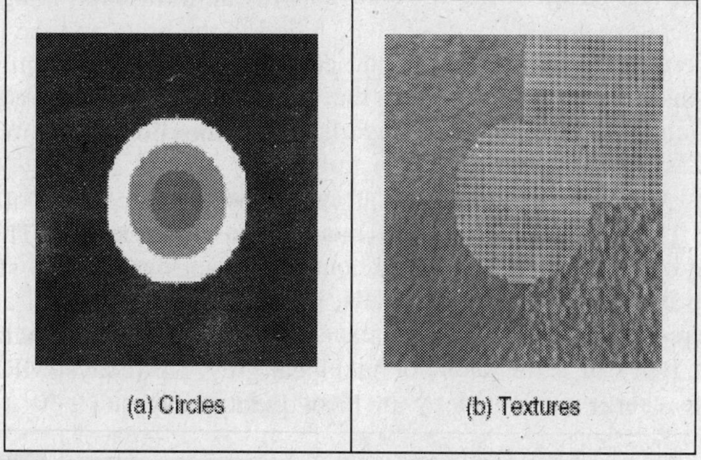

(a) Circles (b) Textures

**Figure 10.10 Examples of synthesized images**

This chapter will show you how basic computer vision systems work, in the context of the human vision system. It covers the main elements of human vision, showing you how your eyes work (and how they can be deceived). For computer vision, this chapter covers the hardware and the software used for image analysis, giving an introduction to Mathcad and Matlab, the software tools used throughout this text to implement computer vision algorithms. Finally, a selection of pointers to other material is provided, especially those for more detail on the topics covered in this chapter.

### 10.3.1 REQUIREMENTS OF COMPUTER VISION SYSTEMS

Given the progress in computer technology, computer vision hardware is now relatively inexpensive; a basic computer vision system requires, a camera, a camera interface and a computer. These days, some personal computers offer the capability for a basic vision system, by including a camera and its interface within the system. There are specialized systems for vision, offering high performance in more than one aspect.

#### 10.3.1.1 CAMERAS

A camera is the basic sensing element. In simple terms, most cameras rely on the property of light to cause hole/electron pairs (the charge carriers in electronics) in a conducting material. When a potential is applied (to attract the charge carriers), this charge can be sensed as current. By Ohm's law, the voltage across a resistance is proportional to the current through it, so the current can be turned in to a voltage by passing it through a resistor. The number of hole/electron pairs is proportional to the amount of incident light. Accordingly, greater charge (and hence greater voltage and current) is caused by an increase in brightness. In this manner cameras can provide as output, a voltage that is proportional to the brightness of the points imaged by the camera.

Cameras are usually arranged to supply video according to a specified standard. Most will aim to satisfy the CCIR standard that exists for closed circuit television (CCTV) systems. There are three main types of camera: videos, charge coupled devices (CCDs) and, more recently, CMOS cameras (complementary metal oxide silicon, now the dominant technology for logic circuit implementation). Videos are the older (analogue) technology which, although cheap (mainly by virtue of longevity in production), are being replaced by the newer CCD and CMOS digital technologies. The digital technologies now dominate much of the camera market because they are lightweight and cheap (with other advantages) and are therefore used in the domestic video market.

Videos operate in a manner akin to a television in reverse. The image is formed on a screen, and then sensed by an electron beam that is scanned across the screen. This produces an output which is continuous; the output voltage is proportional to the brightness of points in the scanned line, and is a continuous signal, a voltage which varies continuously with time. In contrast, CCDs and CMOS cameras use an array of sensors; these are regions where charge is collected which is proportional to the light incident on that region. This is then available in discrete, or sampled, form as opposed to the continuous sensing of a vidicon. This is similar to human vision with its array of cones and rods, but digital cameras use a rectangular regularly spaced lattice, whereas human vision uses a hexagonal lattice with irregular spacing.

Two main types of semiconductor pixel sensor are illustrated in Figure 10.11. In the passive sensor, the charge generated by incident light is presented to a bus through a pass transistor.

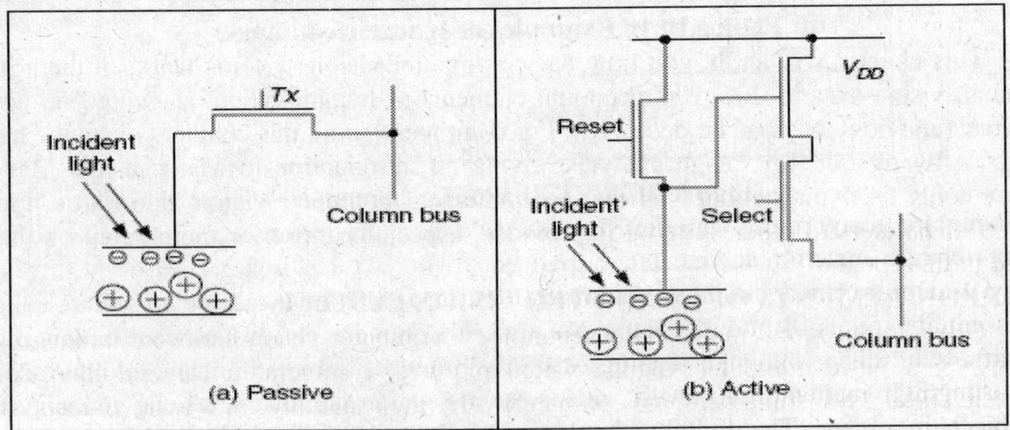


**Figure 10.11 Pixel sensors**

When the signal Tx is activated, the pass transistor is enabled and the sensor provides a capacitance to the bus, one that is proportional to the incident light. An active pixel includes an amplifier circuit that can compensate for limited fill factor of the photodiode. The select signal again controls presentation of the sensor's information to the bus. A further reset signal allows the charge site to be cleared when the image is rescanned.

The basis of a CCD sensor is illustrated in Figure 10.12. The number of charge sites gives the resolution of the CCD sensor; the contents of the charge sites (or buckets) need to be converted to an output (voltage) signal. In simple terms, the contents of the buckets are emptied into vertical transport registers which are shift registers moving information towards the horizontal transport registers. This is the column bus supplied by the pixel sensors.

The horizontal transport registers empty the information row by row (point by point) into a signal conditioning unit, which transforms the sensed charge into a voltage which is proportional to the charge in a bucket, and hence proportional to the brightness of the corresponding point in the scene imaged by the camera. The CMOS cameras are like a form of memory: the charge incident on a particular site in a two-dimensional lattice is proportional to the brightness at a point. The charge is then read like computer memory. (In fact, a computer RAM chip can act as a rudimentary form of camera when the circuit, the one buried in the chip, is exposed to light.) Horizontal transport register

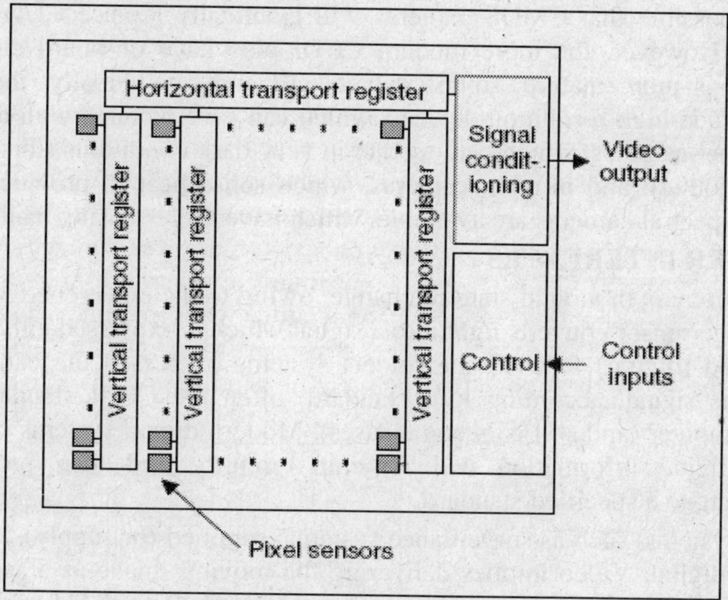


**Figure 10.12 CCD sensing element**

There are many more varieties of videos (Chalnicon, etc.) than there are of CCD technology (charge injection device, etc.), perhaps owing to the greater age of basic videos technology. Videos are cheap but have a number of intrinsic performance problems. The scanning process essentially relies on moving parts. As such, the camera performance will change with time, as parts wear; this is known as ageing. Also, it is possible to burn an image into the scanned screen by using high incident light levels; videos can also suffer lag, that is, a delay in response to moving objects in a scene. The digital technologies are dependent on the physical arrangement of charge sites and as such do not suffer from ageing, but can suffer from irregularity in the charge sites' (silicon) material. The underlying technology also makes CCD and CMOS cameras less sensitive to lag and burn, but the signals associated with the CCD transport registers can give rise to readout effects. Charge coupled devices only came to dominate camera technology when technological difficulty associated with quantum efficiency (the magnitude of response to incident light) for the shorter, blue, wavelengths was solved.

One of the major problems in CCD cameras is blooming, where bright (incident) light causes a bright spot to grow and disperse in the image (this used to happen in the analogue technologies too). This happens much less in CMOS cameras because the charge sites can be much better defined and reading their data is equivalent to reading memory sites as opposed to shuffling charge between sites. Also, CMOS cameras have now overcome the problem of fixed pattern noise that plagued earlier MOS cameras. The CMOS cameras are actually much more recent than CCDs. This begs a question as to which is better: CMOS or CCD? Given that they will be both be subject to much continued development, CMOS is a cheaper technology and it lends itself directly to intelligent cameras with on-board processing. This is mainly because the feature size of points (pixels) in a CCD sensor is limited to be about 4m so that enough light is collected. In contrast, the feature size in CMOS technology is considerably smaller, currently at around 01m.

Accordingly, it is now possible to integrate signal processing within the camera chip and thus it is perhaps possible that CMOS cameras will eventually replace CCD technologies for many applications. However, the more modern CCDs also have on-board circuitry, and their process technology is more mature, so the debate will continue. Finally, there are specialist cameras, which include high-resolution devices, which can give pictures with a great number of points, low-light level cameras, which can operate in very dark conditions (this is where vidicon technology is still found), and infrared cameras, which sense heat to provide thermal images. Increasingly, hyperspectral cameras are available, which have more sensing bands.

#### 10.3.1.2 COMPUTER INTERFACES

This technology is in a rapid state of change, owing to the emergence of digital cameras. Essentially, the image sensor converts light into a signal which is expressed either as a continuous signal or in sampled (digital) form. Some (older) systems expressed the camera signal as an analogue continuous signal, according to a standard, often the CCIR standard, and this was converted at the computer (and still is in some cases). Modern digital systems convert the sensor information into digital information with on-chip circuitry and then provide the digital information according to a specified standard.

The older systems, such as surveillance systems, supplied (or supply) video, whereas the newer systems are digital. Video implies delivering the moving image as a sequence of frames and these can be in analogue (continuous) or discrete (sampled) form, of which one format is digital video (DV). An interface that converts an analogue signal into a set of digital numbers is called a framegrabber, since it grabs frames of data from a video sequence, and is illustrated in Figure 10.13. Note that cameras that provide digital information do not need this particular interface (it is inside the camera). However, an analogue camera signal is continuous and is transformed into digital (discrete) format using an analogue-to-digital (A/D) converter.

Flash converters are usually used owing to the high speed required for conversion, say 11 MHz, which cannot be met by any other conversion technology. Usually, 8 bit A/D converters are used; at 6 dB/bit, this gives 48 dB, which just satisfies the CCIR stated bandwidth of approximately 45 dB. The output of the A/D converter is often fed to look-up tables (LUTs), which implement designated conversion of the input data, but in hardware rather than in software, and this is very fast.

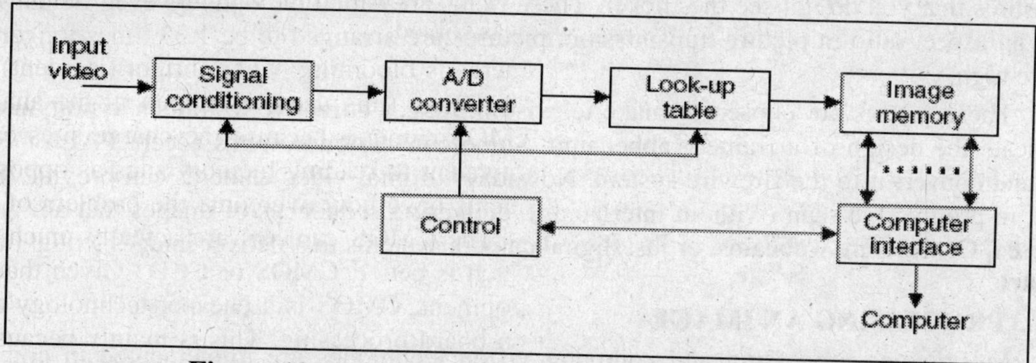


**Figure 10.13 A computer interface: a frame grabber**

The outputs of the A/D converter are then stored. Note that there are aspects of the sampling process that are of considerable interest in computer vision. In digital camera systems this processing is usually performed on the camera chip, and the camera eventually supplies digital information, often in coded form. IEEE 1394 (or firewire) is a way of connecting devices external to a computer and is often used for digital video cameras as it supports high-speed digital communication and can provide power; this is similar to universal serial bus (USB), which can be used for still cameras. Firewire needs a connection system and software to operate it, and these can be easily acquired. One important aspect of Firewire is its support of isochronous transfer operation which guarantees timely delivery of data, which is of importance in video-based systems.

There are many different ways to design framegrabber units, especially for specialist systems. Note that the control circuitry has to determine exactly when image data is to be sampled. This is controlled by synchronization pulses that are supplied within the video signal: the sync signals, which control the way video information is constructed. Television pictures are constructed from a set of lines, those lines scanned by a camera. To reduce requirements on transmission (and for viewing), the 625 lines in the PAL system (NTSC is of lower resolution) are transmitted in two fields, each of 312.5 lines, as illustrated in Figure 10.14. (Currently, in high-definition television,

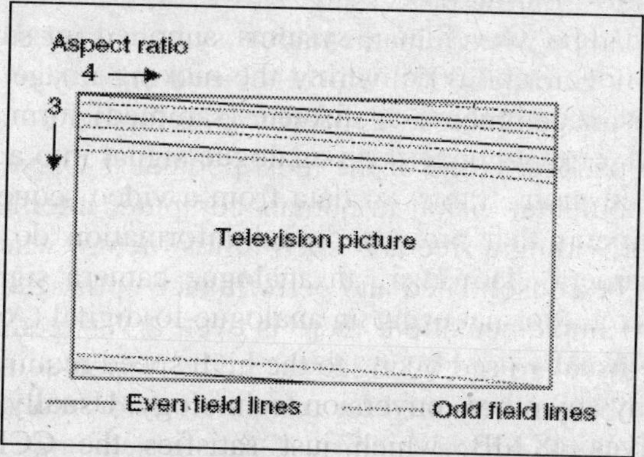


**Figure 10.14 Interlacing in television pictures**

there is some debate between the corporations who do not want interlacing, and those who do, e.g. the television broadcasters.) If you look at a television, but not directly, the flicker due to interlacing can be perceived. When you look at the television directly, persistence in the human eye ensures that you do not see the flicker. These fields are called the odd and even fields. There is also an aspect ratio in picture transmission: pictures are arranged to be 1.33 times longer than they are high.

These factors are chosen to make television images attractive to human vision, and can complicate the design of a frame grabber unit. Some conversion systems accept PAL or NTSC video and convert it to the firewire system. Nowadays, digital video cameras can provide digital output, in progressive scan (without interlacing), delivering sequences of images that are readily processed. Or there are webcams, or just digital camera systems that deliver images straight to the computer.

#### 10.3.1.3 PROCESSING AN IMAGE

Most image processing and computer vision techniques are implemented in computer software. Often, only the simplest techniques migrate to hardware, although coding techniques to maximize efficiency in image transmission are of sufficient commercial interest that they have warranted extensive, and very sophisticated, hardware development. The systems include the Joint Photographic Expert Group (JPEG) and the Moving Picture Expert Group (MPEG) image coding formats. C, C++ and Java TM are by now the most popular languages for vision system implementation, because of strengths in integrating high- and low-level functions, and the availability of good compilers. As systems become more complex, C++ and Java become more attractive when encapsulation and polymorphism may be exploited. Many people use Java as a development language partly because of platform independence, but also because of ease in implementation (although some claim that speed and efficiency are not as good as in C/C++). There is considerable implementation advantage associated with use of the Java Advanced Imaging API (application programming interface). This is based around Java, so that the site can be used over the web (as long as Java is installed and up to date). Some textbooks offer image processing systems implemented in these languages.

Many commercial packages are available, although these are often limited to basic techniques, and do not include the more sophisticated shape extraction techniques. The Visiquest (was Khoros) image processing system has attracted much interest; this is a schematic (data-flow) image processing system where a user links together chosen modules. This allows for better visualization of information flow during processing. However, the underlying mathematics is not made clear to the user, as it can be when a mathematical system is used. There is a textbook, and a very readable one at that, by Efford (2000), which is based entirely on Java and includes, via a CD, the classes necessary for image processing software development.

In terms of software packages, one of the most popular is OpenCV, whose philosophy is to 'aid commercial uses of computer vision in human–computer interface, robotics, monitoring, biometrics and security by providing a free and open infrastructure where the distributed efforts of the vision community can be consolidated and performance optimized'. This contains a wealth of technique and (optimized) implementation; there is even a Wikipedia entry and a discussion website supporting it. Then there are the VXL libraries (the Vision-something-Libraries, groan). This is 'a collection of C++ libraries designed for computer vision research and implementation'. Finally, there is Adobe's Generic Image Library (GIL), which aims to ease difficulties with writing imaging-related code that is both generic and efficient. Note that these are open source, but there are licences and conditions on use and exploitation.

A set of web links is shown in Table 10.1 for established freeware and commercial software image processing systems. Perhaps the best selection can be found at the general site, from the computer vision homepage software site at Carnegie Mellon.

| Packages (freeware or student version indicated by *) | | |
|---|---|---|
| General Site | Carnegie Mellon | http://www.cs.cmu.edu/afs/cs/project/cil/ftp/html/v-source.html (large popular index including links to research code, image processing toolkits, and display tools) |
| Visiquest (Khoros) | Accusoft | http://www.accusoft.com/ |
| | Hannover University | http://www.tnt.uni-hannover.de/soft/imgproc/khoros/ |
| AdOculos* (+ Textbook) | The Imaging Source | http://www.theimagingsource.com/ |
| CVIPtools* | Southern Illinois University | http://www.ee.siue.edu/CVIPtools/ |
| LaboImage* | Geneva University | http://cuiwww.unige.ch/~vision/LaboImage/labo.html |
| TN-Image* | Thomas J. Nelson | http://brneurosci.org/tnimage.html (scientific image analysis) |
| OpenCV | Intel | http://www.intel.com/technology/computing/opencv/index.htm and http://sourceforge.net/projects/opencvlibrary/ |
| VXL | Many international contributors | http://vxl.sourceforge.net/ |
| GIL | Adobe | http://opensource.adobe.com/gil/ |

**Table 10.1 Software websites**

### 10.3.2 USE Of COMPUTER VISION IN THE SCIENCE AND TECHNOLOGY

Computer vision is the science and technology of machines that see. As a scientific discipline, computer vision is concerned with the theory for building artificial systems that obtain information from images. The image data can take many forms, such as a video sequence, views from multiple cameras, or multi-dimensional data from a medical scanner. As a technological discipline, computer vision seeks to apply the theories and models of computer vision to the construction of computer vision systems.

Examples of applications of computer vision systems include systems for:

1. Controlling processes (e.g. an industrial robot or an autonomous vehicle).
2. Detecting events (e.g. for visual surveillance or people counting).
3. Organizing information (e.g. for indexing databases of images and image sequences).
4. Modeling objects or environments (e.g. industrial inspection, medical image analysis or topographical modeling).
5. Interaction (e.g. as the input to a device for computer-human interaction).

Computer vision can also be described as a complement (but not necessarily the opposite) of biological vision. In biological vision, the visual perception of humans and various animals are studied, resulting in models of how these systems operate in terms of physiological processes. Computer vision, on the other hand, studies and describes artificial vision systems that are implemented in software and/or hardware. Interdisciplinary exchange between biological and computer vision has proven increasingly fruitful for both fields.

Sub-domains of computer vision include scene reconstruction, event detection, tracking, object recognition, learning, indexing, motion estimation, and image restoration.

### 10.3.2.1 STATE OF THE ART

The field of computer vision can be characterized as immature and diverse. Even though earlier work exists, it was not until the late 1970s that a more focused study of the field started when computers could manage the processing of large data sets such as images. However, these studies usually originated from various other fields, and consequently there is no standard formulation of "the computer vision problem." Also, and to an even larger extent, there is no standard formulation of how computer vision problems should be solved. Instead, there exists an abundance of methods for solving various well-defined computer vision tasks, where the methods often are very task specific and seldom can be generalized over a wide range of applications. Many of the methods and applications are still in the state of basic research, but more and more methods have found their way into commercial products, where they often constitute a part of a larger system which can solve complex tasks (e.g., in the area of medical images, or quality control and measurements in industrial processes). In most practical computer vision applications, the computers are pre-programmed to solve a particular task, but methods based on learning are now becoming increasingly common.

### 10.3.2.2 RELATED FIELDS

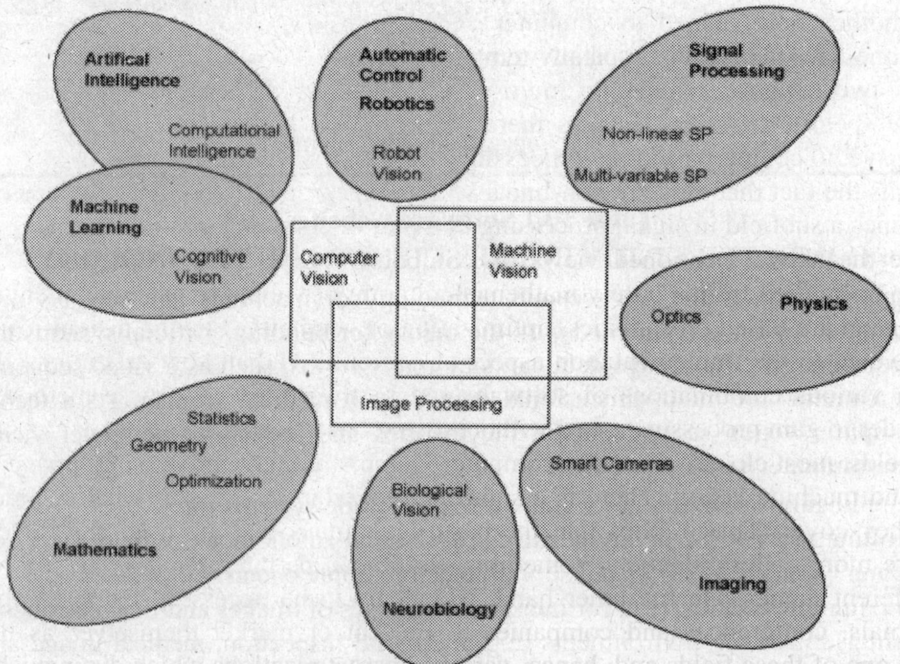


**Figure 10.15 Relation between computer vision and various other fields**

A significant part of artificial intelligence deals with autonomous planning or deliberation for systems which can perform mechanical actions such as moving a robot through some environment. This type of processing typically needs input data provided by a computer vision system, acting as a vision sensor and providing high-level information about the environment and the robot. Other parts which sometimes are described as belonging to artificial intelligence and which are used in relation to computer vision is pattern recognition and learning techniques. As a consequence, computer vision is sometimes seen as a part of the artificial intelligence field or the computer science field in general.

Physics is another field that is strongly related to computer vision. A significant part of computer vision deals with methods which require a thorough understanding of the process in which electromagnetic radiation, typically in the visible or the infra-red range, is reflected by the surfaces of objects and finally is measured by the image sensor to produce the image data. This process is based on optics and solid-state physics. More sophisticated image sensors even require quantum mechanics to provide a complete comprehension of the image formation process. Also, various measurement problems in physics can be addressed using computer vision, for example motion in fluids. Consequently, computer vision can also be seen as an extension of physics.

A third field which plays an important role is neurobiology, specifically the study of the biological vision system. Over the last century, there has been an extensive study of eyes, neurons, and the brain structures devoted to processing of visual stimuli in both humans and various animals. This has led to a course, yet complicated, description of how "real" vision systems operate in order to solve certain vision related tasks. These results have led to a subfield within computer vision where artificial systems are designed to mimic the processing and behaviour of biological systems, at different levels of complexity. Also, some of the learning-based methods developed within computer vision have their background in biology.

Yet another field related to computer vision is signal processing. Many methods for processing of one-variable signals, typically temporal signals, can be extended in a natural way to processing of two-variable signals or multi-variable signals in computer vision. However, because of the specific nature of images there are many methods developed within computer vision which have no counterpart in the processing of one-variable signals. A distinct character of these methods is the fact that they are non-linear which, together with the multi-dimensionality of the signal, defines a subfield in signal processing as a part of computer vision.

Beside the above mentioned views on computer vision, many of the related research topics can also be studied from a purely mathematical point of view. For example, many methods in computer vision are based on statistics, optimization or geometry. Finally, a significant part of the field is devoted to the implementation aspect of computer vision; how existing methods can be realized in various combinations of software and hardware, or how these methods can be modified in order to gain processing speed without losing too much performance.

The fields, most closely related to computer vision, are image processing, image analysis, robot vision and machine vision. There is a significant overlap in terms of what techniques and applications they cover. This implies that the basic techniques that are used and developed in these fields are more or less identical, something which can be interpreted as there is only one field with different names. On the other hand, it appears to be necessary for research groups, scientific journals, conferences and companies to present or market themselves as belonging specifically to one of these fields and, hence, various characterizations which distinguish each of the fields from the others have been presented.

#### 10.3.2.3 THE FOLLOWING CHARACTERIZATIONS APPEAR RELEVANT BUT SHOULD NOT BE TAKEN AS UNIVERSALLY ACCEPTED

Image processing and image analysis tend to focus on 2D images, how to transform one image to another, e.g., by pixel-wise operations such as contrast enhancement, local operations such as edge extraction or noise removal, or geometrical transformations such as rotating the image. This characterization implies that image processing/analysis neither require assumptions nor produce interpretations about the image content.

Computer vision tends to focus on the 3D scene projected onto one or several images, e.g., how to reconstruct structure or other information about the 3D scene from one or several images. Computer vision often relies on more or less complex assumptions about the scene depicted in an image.

Machine vision tends to focus on applications, mainly in industry, e.g., vision based autonomous robots and systems for vision based inspection or measurement. This implies that image sensor technologies and control theory often are integrated with the processing of image data to control a robot and that real-time processing is emphasized by means of efficient implementations in hardware and software. It also implies that the external conditions such as lighting can be and are often more controlled in machine vision than they are in general computer vision, which can enable the use of different algorithms.

There is also a field called imaging which primarily focus on the process of producing images, but sometimes also deals with processing and analysis of images. For example, medical imaging contains lots of work on the analysis of image data in medical applications.

Finally, pattern recognition is a field which uses various methods to extract information from signals in general, mainly based on statistical approaches. A significant part of this field is devoted to applying these methods to image data.

A consequence of this state of affairs is that you can be working in a lab related to one of these fields, apply methods from a second field to solve a problem in a third field and present the result at a conference related to a fourth field.

#### 10.3.2.4 APPLICATIONS FOR COMPUTER VISION

One of the most prominent application fields is medical computer vision or medical image processing. This area is characterized by the extraction of information from image data for the purpose of making a medical diagnosis of a patient. Generally, image data is in the form of microscopy images, X-ray images, angiography images, ultrasonic images, and tomography images. An example of information which can be extracted from such image data is detection of tumors, arteriosclerosis or other malign changes. It can also be measurements of organ dimensions, blood flow, etc. This application area also supports medical research by providing new information, e.g., about the structure of the brain, or about the quality of medical treatments.

A second application area in computer vision is in industry. Here, information is extracted for the purpose of supporting a manufacturing process. One example is quality control where details or final products are being automatically inspected in order to find defects. Another example is measurement of position and orientation of details to be picked up by a robot arm.

Military applications are probably one of the largest areas for computer vision. The obvious examples are detection of enemy soldiers or vehicles and missile guidance. More advanced systems for missile guidance send the missile to an area rather than a specific target, and target selection is made when the missile reaches the area based on locally acquired image data. Modern military concepts, such as "battlefield awareness", imply that various sensors, including image sensors, provide a rich set of information about a combat scene which can be used to support strategic decisions. In this case, automatic processing of the data is used to reduce complexity and to fuse information from multiple sensors to increase reliability.

**Figure 10.16 Unmanned land-based vehicles. (Notice the stereo cameras mounted on top of the Rover. (Credit: Maas Digital LLC))**

One of the newer application areas is autonomous vehicles, which include submersibles, land-based vehicles (small robots with wheels, cars or trucks), aerial vehicles, and unmanned aerial vehicles (UAV). The level of autonomy ranges from fully autonomous (unmanned) vehicles to vehicles where computer vision based systems support a driver or a pilot in various situations. Fully autonomous vehicles typically use computer vision for navigation, i.e. for knowing where it is, or for producing a map of its environment (SLAM) and for detecting obstacles. It can also be used for detecting certain task specific events, e. g., a UAV looking for forest fires. Examples of supporting systems are obstacle warning systems in cars, and systems for autonomous landing of aircraft. Several car manufacturers have demonstrated systems for autonomous driving of cars, but this technology has still not reached a level where it can be put on the market. There are ample examples of military autonomous vehicles ranging from advanced missiles, to UAVs for recon missions or missile guidance. Space exploration is already being made with autonomous vehicles using computer vision, e. g., NASA's Mars Exploration Rover.

**OTHER APPLICATION AREAS INCLUDE:**

1. Support of visual effects creation for cinema and broadcast, e.g., camera tracking (matchmoving).
2. Surveillance.

## 10.3.2.5. TYPICAL TASKS OF COMPUTER VISION

Each of the application areas described above employ a range of computer vision tasks; more or less well-defined measurement problems or processing problems, which can be solved using a variety of methods. Some examples of typical computer vision tasks are presented below.

### (i) RECOGNITION

The classical problem in computer vision, image processing and machine vision is that of determining whether or not the image data contains some specific object, feature, or activity. This task can normally be solved robustly and without effort by a human, but is still not satisfactorily solved in computer vision for the general case: arbitrary objects in arbitrary situations.

The existing methods for dealing with this problem can at best solve it only for specific objects, such as simple geometric objects (e.g., polyhedrons), human faces, printed or hand-written characters, or vehicles, and in specific situations, typically described in terms of well-defined illumination, background, and pose of the object relative to the camera.

**(ii) DIFFERENT VARIETIES OF THE RECOGNITION PROBLEM ARE DESCRIBED IN THE LITERATURE:**

1. Recognition: one or several pre-specified or learned objects or object classes can be recognized, usually together with their 2D positions in the image or 3D poses in the scene.
2. Identification: An individual instance of an object is recognized. Examples: identification of a specific person's face or fingerprint, or identification of a specific vehicle.
3. Detection: the image data is scanned for a specific condition. Examples: detection of possible abnormal cells or tissues in medical images or detection of a vehicle in an automatic road toll system. Detection based on relatively simple and fast computations is sometimes used for finding smaller regions of interesting image data which can be further analyzed by more computationally demanding techniques to produce a correct interpretation.

**(iii) SEVERAL SPECIALIZED TASKS BASED ON RECOGNITION EXIST, SUCH AS:**

1. Content-based image retrieval: finding all images in a larger set of images which have a specific content. The content can be specified in different ways, for example in terms of similarity relative a target image (give me all images similar to image X), or in terms of high-level search criteria given as text input (give me all images which contains many houses, are taken during winter, and have no cars in them).
2. Pose estimation: estimating the position or orientation of a specific object relative to the camera. An example application for this technique would be assisting a robot arm in retrieving objects from a conveyor belt in an assembly line situation.
3. Optical character recognition (or OCR): identifying characters in images of printed or handwritten text, usually with a view to encoding the text in a format more amenable to editing or indexing (e.g. ASCII).

**(iv) MOTION**

Several tasks relate to motion estimation, in which an image sequence is processed to produce an estimate of the velocity either at each points in the image or in the 3D scene. Examples of such tasks are:

1. Egomotion: determining the 3D rigid motion of the camera.
2. Tracking: following the movements of objects (e.g. vehicles or humans).

**(v) CENE RECONSTRUCTION**

Given one or (typically) more images of a scene, or a video, scene reconstruction aims at computing a 3D model of the scene. In the simplest case the model can be a set of 3D points. More sophisticated methods produce a complete 3D surface model.

**(vi) IMAGE RESTORATION**

The aim of image restoration is the removal of noise (sensor noise, motion blur, etc.) from images. The simplest possible approach for noise removal is various types of filters such as low-pass filters or median filters. More sophisticated methods assume a model of how the local image structures look like, a model which distinguishes them from the noise. By first analyzing the image data in terms of the local image structures, such as lines or edges, and then controlling the filtering based on local information from the analysis step, a better level of noise removal is usually obtained compared to the simpler approaches.

### (vii) COMPUTER VISION SYSTEMS

The organization of a computer vision system is highly application dependent. Some systems are stand-alone applications which solve a specific measurement or detection problem, while other constitute a sub-system of a larger design which, for example, also contains sub-systems for control of mechanical actuators, planning, information databases, man-machine interfaces, etc. The specific implementation of a computer vision system also depends on if its functionality is pre-specified or if some part of it can be learned or modified during operation. There are, however, typical functions which are found in many computer vision systems.

1. Image acquisition: A digital image is produced by one or several image sensor which, besides various types of light-sensitive cameras, includes range sensors, tomography devices, radar, ultra-sonic cameras, etc. Depending on the type of sensor, the resulting image data is an ordinary 2D image, a 3D volume, or an image sequence. The pixel values typically correspond to light intensity in one or several spectral bands (gray images or colour images), but can also be related to various physical measures, such as depth, absorption or reflectance of sonic or electromagnetic waves, or nuclear magnetic resonance.
2. Pre-processing: Before a computer vision method can be applied to image data in order to extract some specific piece of information, it is usually necessary to process the data in order to assure that it satisfies certain assumptions implied by the method. Examples are
    - Re-sampling in order to assure that the image coordinate system is correct.
    - Noise reduction in order to assure that sensor noise does not introduce false information.
    - Contrast enhancement to assure that relevant information can be detected.
    - Scale-space representation to enhance image structures at locally appropriate scales.
3. Feature extraction: Image features at various levels of complexity are extracted from the image data. Typical examples of such features are
    - Lines, edges and ridges.
    - Localized interest points such as corners, blobs or points.
    - More complex features may be related to texture, shape or motion.
4. Detection/Segmentation: At some point in the processing a decision is made about which image points or regions of the image are relevant for further processing. Examples are
    - Selection of a specific set of interest points.
    - Segmentation of one or multiple image regions which contain a specific object of interest.
5. High-level processing: At this step the input is typically a small set of data, for example a set of points or an image region which is assumed to contain a specific object. The remaining processing deals with, for example:

- Verification that the data satisfy model-based and application specific assumptions.
- Estimation of application specific parameters, such as object pose or object size.
- Classifying a detected object into different categories.

### 10.3.3 FACE DETECTION

Face detection is a computer technology that determines the locations and sizes of human faces in arbitrary (digital) images. It detects facial features and ignores anything else, such as buildings, trees and bodies.

Definition and relation to other tasks:-

- Face detection can be regarded as a specific case of object-class detection; In object-class detection, the task is to find the locations and sizes of all objects in an image that belong to a given class. Examples include upper torsos, pedestrians, and cars.
- Face detection can be regarded as a more general case of face localization; In face localization, the task is to find the locations and sizes of a known number of faces (usually one). In face detection, one does not have this additional information.
- Early face-detection algorithms focused on the detection of frontal human faces, whereas newer algorithms attempt to solve the more general and difficult problem of multi-view face detection. That is, the detection of faces that are either rotated along the axis from the face to the observer (in-plane rotation), or rotated along the vertical or left-right axis (out-of-plane rotation), or both.

#### 10.3.3.1 FACE DETECTION AS A PATTERN-CLASSIFICATION TASK

Implement the face-detection task as a binary pattern-classification task. That is, the content of a given part of an image is transformed into features, after which a classifier trained on example faces decides whether that particular region of the image is a face, or not.

Often, a window-sliding technique is employed. That is, the above mentioned classifier is used to classify the (usually square or rectangular) portions of an image, at all locations and scales, as either faces or non-faces (background pattern)

#### 10.3.3.2 CHALLENGES IN PATTERN CLASSIFICATION FOR FACE DETECTION

A given natural image often contains many more background patterns than face patterns. Indeed, the number of background patterns may be 1,000 to 100,000 times larger than the number of face patterns. This means that if one desires a high face-detection rate, combined with a low number of false detections in an image, one needs a very specific classifier. Publications in the field (including the two in this article's external links section) often use the rough guideline that a classifier should yield a 90% detection rate, combined with a false-positive (or type I error) rate in the order of $10^{-6}$.

The method devised by Viola and Jones, for example, uses Haar-like features. Even for a small image, the number of Haar-like features is very large (for a 24x24 pixel window one can generate more than 180000 features). They used AdaBoost to train a classifier, which allows for a feature selection. The final classifier only uses a few hundred Haar-like features. Yet, it achieves a very good hit rate with a relatively low false detection rate.

### 10.3.4 FEATURE DETECTION

Feature detection refers to methods that aim at computing abstractions of image information and making local decisions at every image point whether there is an image feature of a given type at that point or not. The resulting features will be subsets of the image domain, often in the form of isolated points, continuous curves or connected regions.

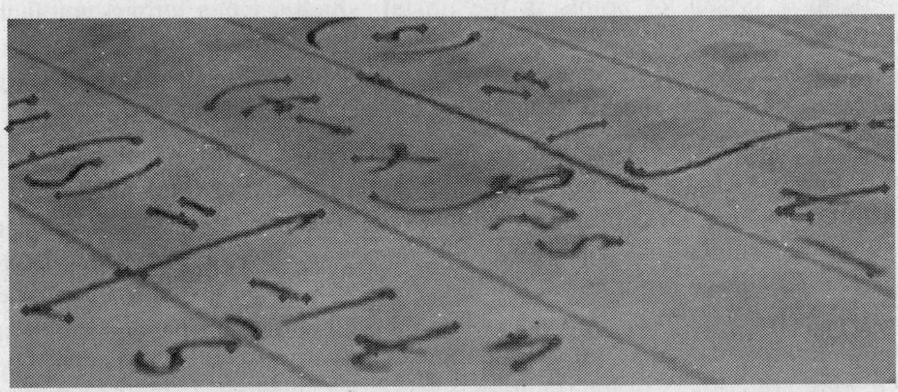

**Figure 10.17 Image domains, in the form of isolated points, continuous curves or connected regions**

### 10.3.4.1 DEFINITION OF A FEATURE

- There is no universal or exact definition of what constitutes a feature, and the exact definition often depends on the problem or the type of application. Given that, a feature is defined as an "interesting" part of an image, and features are used as a starting point for many computer vision algorithms. Since features are used as the starting point and main primitives for subsequent algorithms, the overall algorithm will often only be as good as its feature detector. Consequently, the desirable property for a feature detector is repeatability: whether or not the same feature will be detected in two or more different images of the same scene.

- Feature detection is a low-level image processing operation. That is, it is usually performed as the first operation on an image, and examines every pixel to see if there is a feature present at that pixel. If this is part of a larger algorithm, then the algorithm will typically only examine the image in the region of the features. As a built-in pre-requisite to feature detection, the input image is usually smoothed by a Gaussian kernel in a scale-space representation and one or several feature images are computed, often expressed in terms of local derivative operations.

Occasionally, when feature detection is computationally expensive and there are time constraints, a higher level algorithm may be used to guide the feature detection stage, so that only certain parts of the image are searched for features.

Where many computer vision algorithms use feature detection as the initial step, so as a result, a very large number of feature detectors have been developed. These vary widely in the kinds of feature detected, the computational complexity and the repeatability.

#### 10.3.4.2 FEATURE DETECTORS CAN (WITH SOME OVERLAP) BE DIVIDED INTO THE FOLLOWING GROUPS:

**1. EDGES**

Edges are points where there is a boundary (or an edge) between two image regions. In general, an edge can be of almost arbitrary shape, and may include junctions. In practice, edges are usually defined as sets of points in the image which have a strong gradient magnitude. Furthermore, some common algorithms will then chain high gradient points together to form a more complete description of an edge. These algorithms usually place some constraints on the properties of an edge, such as shape, smoothness, and gradient value.

**2. CORNERS / INTEREST POINTS**

The terms corners and interest points are used somewhat interchangeably and refer to point-like features in an image, which have a local two dimensional structure. The name "Corner" arose since early algorithms first performed edge detection, and then analysed the edges to find rapid changes in direction (corners). These algorithms were then developed so that explicit edge detection was no longer required, for instance by looking for high levels of curvature in the image gradient. It was then noticed that the so-called corners were also being detected on parts of the image which were not corners in the traditional sense (for instance a small bright spot on a dark background may be detected). These points are frequently known as interest points, but the term "corner" is used by tradition.

**3. BLOBS / REGIONS OF INTEREST OR INTEREST POINTS**

Blobs provide a complementary description of image structures in terms of regions, as opposed to corners that are more point-like. Nevertheless, blob descriptors often contain a preferred point (a local maximum of an operator response or a center of gravity) which means that many blob detectors may also be regarded as interest point operators. Blob detectors can detect areas in an image which are too smooth to be detected by a corner detector.

Consider shrinking an image and then performing corner detection. The detector will respond to points which are sharp in the shrunk image, but may be smooth in the original image. It is at this point that the difference between a corner detector and a blob detector becomes somewhat vague. To a large extent, this distinction can be remedied by including an appropriate notion of scale. Nevertheless, due to their response properties to different types of image structures at different scales, the LoG and DoH blob detectors are also mentioned in the article on corner detection.

**4. RIDGES**

For elongated objects, the notion of ridges is a natural tool. A ridge descriptor computed from a grey-level image can be seen as a generalization of a medial axis. From a practical viewpoint, a ridge can be thought of as a one-dimensional curve that represents an axis of symmetry, and in addition has an attribute of local ridge width associated with each ridge point. Unfortunately, however, it is algorithmically harder to extract ridge features from general classes of grey-level images than edge-, corner- or blob features. Nevertheless, ridge descriptors are frequently used for road extraction in aerial images and for extracting blood vessels in medical images.

## 10.3.5 LANE DEPARTURE

Lane departure warning system is a mechanism designed to warn a driver when the vehicle begins to move out of its lane (unless a turn signal is on in that direction) on freeways and arterial roads.

The first production lane departure warning system in Europe was the system developed by America's Iteris for Mercedes Actros commercial trucks. The system debuted in 2000 and is now available on most trucks sold in Europe. In 2002, the Iteris system became available on Freightliner Trucks' trucks in North America. In all of these systems, the driver is warned of unintentional lane departures by an audible rumble strip sound generated on the side of the vehicle drifting out of the lane. If a turn signal is used, no warnings are generated.

More effective lane departure warning systems are now combining prevention with risk reports in the transportation industry. Viewnyx applies video based technologies to assist fleets in lowering their driving liability costs. Firstly, by addressing the main causes of collisions: driving error, distraction and drowsiness. Secondly, by providing Safety Managers with driver and fleet risk assessment reports and tools to facilitate proactive coaching & training to eliminate high risk behaviors. The Lookout solution is currently being used by North American fleets.

There are two main types of systems:

1. Systems which warn the driver if the vehicle is leaving its lane.
2. Systems which warn the driver and if no action is taken automatically take steps to ensure the vehicle stays in its lane.

2001: Nissan Motors began offering a Lane Keeping Support system on the Cima sold in Japan. In 2004, the first passenger vehicle system available in North America was jointly developed by Iteris and Valeo for Nissan on the Infiniti FX and in 2005 the M vehicles. In this system, a camera mounted in the overhead console above the mirror monitors the lane markings on a roadway. A warning tone is triggered when the vehicle begins to drift over the marking to alert the driver. In 2007 Infiniti offered a newer version of this feature, which it calls the Lane Departure Prevention (LDP) system. This feature utilizes the vehicle stability control system to help assist the driver maintain lane position by applying gentle brake pressure to either the wheels.

2002: Toyota introduced its Lane Monitoring System on vehicles such as the Cardinaand Alphard sold in Japan, this system warns the driver if it appears the vehicle is beginning to drift out of its lane. In 2004, Toyota added a Lane Keeping Assist feature to the Crown Majesta which can apply a small-counter steering force to aid in keeping the vehicle in its lane. In 2006, Lexus introduced a multi-mode Lane Keeping Assist system on the LS 460 which utilizes stereo cameras along with more sophisticated object and pattern recognition processors, this system can issue an audiovisual warning and also using the Electric Power Steering (EPS) system apply counter-steering torque to help ensure the driver does not over-correct or "saw" the steering wheel while attempting to return the vehicle to its proper lane., if the radar cruise control system is engaged the Lane Keep function works to help reduce the driver's steering input burden by providing steering torque, however the driver must remain active.

2005: Citroën became first in Europe to offer LDWS on their 2005 C4 and C5 models, and now also on their C6. This system uses infrared sensors under the front bumper to monitor lane markings on the road surface. A vibration mechanism in the seat alerts the driver of deviations.

Audi began offered its Audi Lane Assist feature on the A4. This system unlike the Japanese "assist" systems will not intervene in the actual driving rather vibrate the steering wheel if the vehicle appears to be exiting its lane. Honda launched their Lane Keep Assist System (LKAS) on the Legend. It provides up to 80% of steering torque to keep the car in its lane on the highway. A camera is mounted at the top of the windshield, just above the rear-view mirror scans the road ahead in a 40-degree radius, picking up the dotted white lines used to divide lane boundaries on the highway. The computer recognizes that you're locked into a particular lane, monitors how sharp the curve is and uses factors such as yaw and vehicle speed to calculate what steering input is required.

2007: General Motors introduced Lane Departure Warning on its 2008 model year Cadillac STS, DTS and Buick Lucerne models. The General Motors system warns the driver, with an audible tone and a warning indicator in the dashboard. BMW also introduced Lane Departure Warning on the 5 series and 6 series using a vibrating steering wheel to warn the driver of unintended departures. Volvo introduced the Lane Departure Warning system along with the Driver Alert Control on its 2008 model year S80 and on the new V70 and XC70 executive cars. Volvo's lane departure warning system uses a camera to track road markings and sound an alarm when drivers depart their lane without signaling. The systems used by BMW, Volvo, and General Motors are based on technology from Mobileye. An aftermarket (retrofit) version of the technology that combines Precrash system, Lane Departure Warning (LDW) and Headway Monitoring (HWM) became available in 2006. Also in 2007, the Mitsubishi Fuso implemented the system.

2009: Mercedes-Benz began offering a Lane Keeping Assist function on the new E-class. This system warns the driver with a vibrating steering wheel if it appears the vehicle is beginning to leave its lane. And a new feature will automatically deactivate and reactivate if it ascertains the driver is intentionally leaving his lane, for instance if the driver is aggressively cornering. However this system will not automatically correct the vehicle to ensure it stays in its lane like the Japanese "assist" systems.

### 10.3.6 NON-PHOTOREALISTIC RENDERING (NPR)

Non-photorealistic rendering (NPR) is an area of computer graphics that focuses on enabling a wide variety of expressive styles for digital art. In contrast to traditional computer graphics, which has focused on photorealism, NPR is inspired by artistic styles such as painting, drawing, technical illustration, and animated cartoons. NPR has appeared in movies and video games in the form of "toon shaders," as well as in architectural illustration and experimental animation. An example of a modern use of this method is that of Cel-shaded animation.

### 10.3.6.1 THREE-DIMENSIONAL NPR TECHNIQUES

Three-dimensional NPR is the style that is most commonly seen in video games and movies. The output from this technique is almost always a 3D model that has been modified from the original input model to portray a new artistic style. In many cases, the geometry of the model is identical to the original geometry, and only the material applied to the surface is modified. The majority of NPR techniques applied to 3D geometry are intended to make the scene appear two-dimensional.

### 10.3.6.2 WO-DIMENSIONAL NPR TECHNIQUES

The input to a two-dimensional NPR system is most commonly an image; however, there are systems that take 3D geometry information as input and produce a 2D image or video as output. Again, many of the systems are intended to mimic a desired artistic style, such as watercolor, impressionism, or pen and ink drawing.

### 10.3.6.3 NPR FOR ENHANCING LEGIBILITY

The most useful illustrations in technical illustrations are not necessarily photorealistic. Non-photorealistic renderings, such as exploded view diagrams, greatly assist in showing placement of parts in a complex system.

### 10.3.6.4 INTERACTIVE TECHNIQUES

Users who are interested in having much more control in the NPR process may be more interested in interactive techniques. Many of these NPR systems provide the user with a canvas that they can "paint" on using the cursor - as the user paints, a stylized version of the image is revealed on the canvas. This is especially useful for people who want to simulate different sizes of brush strokes according to different areas of the image.

### 10.3.6.5 SIMULATING THE ARTISTIC MEDIA

Methods include simulating the diffusion of ink through different kinds of paper, and also of pigments through water for simulation of watercolor.

## 10.4 MEDICAL IMAGING

Medical imaging refers to the techniques and processes used to create images of the human body (or parts thereof) for clinical purposes (medical procedures seeking to reveal, diagnose or examine disease) or medical science (including the study of normal anatomy and physiology). As a discipline and in its widest sense, it is part of biological imaging and incorporates radiology (in the wider sense), radiological sciences, endoscopy, (medical) thermography, medical hotography and microscopy (e.g. for human pathological investigations). Measurement and recording techniques which are not primarily designed to produce images, such as electroencephalography (EEG) and magnetoencephalography (MEG) and others, but which produce data susceptible to be represented as maps (i.e. containing positional information), can be seen as forms of medical imaging.

### 10.4.1 OVERVIEW

In the clinical context, medical imaging is generally equated to radiology or "clinical imaging" and the medical practitioner responsible for interpreting (and sometimes acquiring) the images is a radiologist. Diagnostic radiography designates the technical aspects of medical imaging and in particular the acquisition of medical images. The radiographer or radiologic technologist is usually responsible for acquiring medical images of diagnostic quality, although some radiological interventions are performed by radiologists.

As a field of scientific investigation, medical imaging constitutes a sub-discipline of biomedical engineering, medical physics or medicine depending on the context: Research and development in the area of instrumentation, image acquisition (e.g. radiography), modelling and quantification are usually the preserve of biomedical engineering, medical physics and computer science; Research into the application and interpretation of medical images is usually the preserve of radiology and the medical sub-discipline relevant to medical condition or area of medical science (neuroscience, cardiology, psychiatry, psychology, etc) under investigation.

Many of the techniques developed for medical imaging also have scientific and industrial applications. Medical imaging is often perceived to designate the set of techniques that noninvasively produce images of the internal aspect of the body. In this restricted sense, medical imaging can be seen as the solution of mathematical inverse problems. This means that cause (the properties of living tissue) is inferred from effect (the observed signal). In the case of ultrasonography the probe consists of ultrasonic pressure waves and echoes inside the tissue show the internal structure. In the case of projection radiography, the probe is X-ray radiation which is absorbed at different rates in different tissue types such as bone, muscle and fat.

### 10.4.2 IMAGING TECHNOLOGY

#### 10.4.2.1 ELECTRON MICROSCOPY

The electron microscope is a microscope that can magnify very small details with high resolving power due to the use of electrons as the source of illumination, magnifying at levels up to 2,000,000 times. Electron microscopy is employed in anatomic pathology to identify organelles within the cells. Its usefulness has been greatly reduced by immunhistochemistry but it is still irreplaceable for the diagnosis of kidney disease, identification of immotile cilia syndrome and many other tasks

#### 10.4.2.2 RADIOGRAPHIC

Two forms of radiographic images are in use in medical imaging; projection radiography and fluoroscopy, with latter useful for intraoperative and catheter guidance. These 2D techniques are still in wide use despite the advance of 3D tomography due to the low cost, high resolution, and depending on application, lower radiation dosages. This imaging modality utilizes a wide beam of x rays for image acquisition and is the first imaging technique available in modern medicine.

- Fluoroscopy produces real-time images of internal structures of the body in a similar fashion to radiography, but employs a constant input of x-rays, at a lower dose rate. Contrast media, such as barium, iodine, and air are used to visualize internal organs as they work. Fluoroscopy is also used in image-guided procedures when constant feedback during a procedure is required. An image receptor is required to convert the radiation into an image after it has passed through the area of interest. Early on this was a fluorescing screen, which gave way to an Image Amplifier (IA) which was a large vacuum tube that had the receiving end coated with cesium iodide, and a mirror at the opposite end. Eventually the mirror was replaced with a TV camera.
- Projectional radiographs, more commonly known as x-rays, are often used to determine the type and extent of a fracture as well as for detecting pathological changes in the

lungs. With the use of radio-opaque contrast media, such as barium, they can also be used to visualize the structure of the stomach and intestines - this can help diagnose ulcers or certain types of colon cancer.

### 10.4.2.3 MAGNETIC RESONANCE IMAGING (MRI)

#### (i) A BRAIN MRI REPRESENTATION

A magnetic resonance imaging instrument (MRI scanner), or "nuclear magnetic resonance (NMR) imaging" scanner as it was originally known, uses powerful magnets to polarise and excite hydrogen nuclei (single proton) in water molecules in human tissue, producing a detectable signal which is spatially encoded, resulting in images of the body. MRI uses three electromagnetic fields: a very strong (on the order of units of teslas) static magnetic field to polarize the hydrogen nuclei, called the static field; a weaker time-varying (on the order of 1 kHz) field(s) for spatial encoding, called the gradient field(s); and a weak radio-frequency (RF) field for manipulation of the hydrogen nuclei to produce measurable signals, collected through an RF antenna. Like CT, MRI traditionally creates a two dimensional image of a thin "slice" of the body and is therefore considered a tomographic imaging technique.

Modern MRI instruments are capable of producing images in the form of 3D blocks, which may be considered a generalisation of the single-slice, tomographic, concept. Unlike CT, MRI does not involve the use of ionizing radiation and is therefore not associated with the same health hazards. For example, because MRI has only been in use since the early 1980s, there are no known long-term effects of exposure to strong static fields (this is the subject of some debate; see 'Safety' in MRI) and therefore there is no limit to the number of scans to which an individual can be subjected, in contrast with X-ray and CT. However, there are well-identified health risks associated with tissue heating from exposure to the RF field and the presence of implanted devices in the body, such as pace makers.

These risks are strictly controlled as part of the design of the instrument and the scanning protocols used. Because CT and MRI are sensitive to different tissue properties, the appearance of the images obtained with the two techniques differ markedly. In CT, X-rays must be blocked by some form of dense tissue to create an image, so the image quality when looking at soft tissues will be poor. In MRI, while any nucleus with a net nuclear spin can be used, the proton of the hydrogen atom remains the most widely used, especially in the clinical setting, because it is so ubiquitous and returns a large signal. This nucleus, present in water molecules, allows the excellent soft-tissue contrast achievable with MRI.

### 10.4.2.4 NUCLEAR MEDICINE

Nuclear medicine on a whole encompasses both the diagnosis and treatment of disease using nuclear properties. In imaging the energetic photons emitted from radioactive nuclei are used for enhancing and viewing various pathologies.

- Gamma cameras are used in nuclear medicine to detect regions of biological activity that are often associated with diseases. A short lived isotope, such as $^{123}$I is administered to the patient. These isotopes are more readily absorbed by biologically active regions of the body, such as tumors or fracture points in bones.
- Positron emission tomography (PET) is primarily used to detect diseases of the brain and heart. Similarly to nuclear medicine, a short-lived isotope, such as $^{18}$F, is incorporated

into a substance used by the body such as glucose which is absorbed by the tumor of interest. PET scans are often viewed alongside computed tomography scans, which can be performed on the same equipment without moving the patient. This allows the tumors detected by the PET scan to be viewed next to the rest of the patient's anatomy detected by the CT scan. Another 3D tomographic technique is SPECT but uses gamma camera like method for reconstruction.

### 10.4.2.5 PHOTOACOUSTIC IMAGING

Photoacoustic imaging is a recently developed hybrid biomedical imaging modality based on the photoacoustic effect. It combines the advantages of optical absorption contrast with ultrasonic spatial resolution for deep imaging in (optical) diffusive or quasi-diffusive regime. Recent studies have shown that photoacoustic imaging can be used in vivo for tumor angiogenesis monitoring, blood oxygenation mapping, functional brain imaging, and skin melanoma detection, etc.

### 10.4.2.6 BREAST THERMOGRAPHY

Needs main article Digital Infrared Imaging Thermography is based on the principle that metabolic activity and vascular circulation in both pre-cancerous tissue and the area surrounding a developing breast cancer is almost always higher than in normal breast tissue. Cancerous tumors require an ever-increasing supply of nutrients and therefore increase circulation to their cells by holding open existing blood vessels, opening dormant vessels, and creating new ones (neoangiogenesis). This process frequently results in an increase in regional surface temperatures of the breast. Digital Infrared Imaging uses extremely sensitive medical infrared cameras and sophisticated computers to detect, analyze, and produce high-resolution diagnostic images of these temperature variations. Because of DII's sensitivity, these temperature variations may be among the earliest signs of breast cancer and/or a pre-cancerous state of the breast.

### 10.4.2.7 TOMOGRAPHY

Tomography is the method of imaging a single plane, or slice, of an object resulting in a tomogram. There are several forms of tomography:

- Linear tomography: This is the most basic form of tomography. The X-ray tube moved from point "A" to point "B" above the patient, while the cassette holder (or "bucky") moves simultaneously under the patient from point "B" to point "A." The fulcrum, or pivot point, is set to the area of interest. In this manner, the points above and below the focal plane are blurred out, just as the background is blurred when panning a camera during exposure. No longer carried out and replaced by computed tomography.
- Poly tomography: This was a complex form of tomography. With this technique, a number of geometrical movements were programmed, such as hypocycloidic, circular, figure 8, and elliptical. Philips Medical Systems produced one such device called the 'Polytome.' This unit was still in use into the 1990s, as its resulting images for small or difficult physiology, such as the inner ear, was still difficult to image with CTs at that time. As the resolution of CTs got better, this procedure was taken over by the CT.
- Zonography: This is a variant of linear tomography, where a limited arc of movement is used. It is still used in some centres for visualising the kidney during an intravenous urogram (IVU).
- Orthopantomography (OPT or OPG): The only common tomographic examination in use. This makes use of a complex movement to allow the radiographic examination of the

mandible, as if it were a flat bone. It is often referred to as a "Panorex", but this is incorrect, as it is a trademark of a specific company's equipment

- Computed Tomography (CT), or Computed Axial Tomography (CAT): A CT scan, also known as a CAT scan, is a helical tomography (latest generation), which traditionally produces a 2D image of the structures in a thin section of the body. It uses X-rays. It has a greater ionizing radiation dose burden than projection radiography; repeated scans must be limited to avoid health effects.

#### 10.4.2.8 ULTRASOUND

Medical ultrasonography uses high frequency broadband sound waves in the megahertz range that are reflected by tissue to varying degrees to produce (up to 3D) images. This is commonly associated with imaging the fetus in pregnant women. Uses of ultrasound are much broader, however. Other important uses include imaging the abdominal organs, heart, breast, muscles, tendons, arteries and veins. While it may provide less anatomical detail than techniques such as CT or MRI, it has several advantages which make it ideal in numerous situations, in particular that it studies the function of moving structures in real-time, emits no ionizing radiation, and contains speckle that can be used in elastography.

It is very safe to use and does not appear to cause any adverse effects, although information on this is not well documented. It is also relatively inexpensive and quick to perform. Ultrasound scanners can be taken to critically ill patients in intensive care units, avoiding the danger caused while moving the patient to the radiology department. The real time moving image obtained can be used to guide drainage and biopsy procedures. Doppler capabilities on modern scanners allow the blood flow in arteries and veins to be assessed.

### 10.4.3 MEDICAL IMAGING TOPICS

#### 10.4.3.1 CREATION OF THREE-DIMENSIONAL IMAGES

Recently, techniques have been developed to enable CT, MRI and ultrasound scanning software to produce 3D images for the physician. Traditionally CT and MRI scans produced 2D static output on film. To produce 3D images, many scans are made, then combined by computers to produce a 3D model, which can then be manipulated by the physician. 3D ultrasounds are produced using a somewhat similar technique. With the ability to visualize important structures in great detail, 3D visualization methods are a valuable resource for the diagnosis and surgical treatment of many pathologies. It was a key resource for the famous, but ultimately unsuccessful attempt by Singaporean surgeons to separate Iranian twins Ladan and Laleh Bijani in 2003. The 3D equipment was used previously for similar operations with great success.

**OTHER PROPOSED OR DEVELOPED TECHNIQUES INCLUDE:**

- Diffuse optical tomography
- Elastography
- Electrical impedance tomography
- Optoacoustic imaging
- Ophthalmology
    - A-scan
    - B-scan
    - Corneal topography
    - Optical coherence tomography
    - Scanning laser ophthalmoscopy

Some of these techniques are still at a research stage and not yet used in clinical routines.

#### 10.4.3.2 NON-DIAGNOSTIC IMAGING

Neuroimaging has also been used in experimental circumstances to allow people (especially disabled persons) to control outside devices, acting as a brain computer interface.

### 10.4.4 MEDICAL APPLICATIONS FOR PATTERN CLASSIFIERS AND IMAGE PROCESSING

This section considers the role in medicine for pattern classifiers and vision inspection systems. To illustrate the points raised, three potential applications - monitoring neonatal jaundice, breast cancer screening and cervical smears - are discussed as examples.

#### 10.4.4.1. MEDICAL PATTERN CLASSIFICATION

Medicine revolves around classification and recognition. Disease diagnosis requires the interpretation of multiple parameters. The same is true for recognising asymptomatic patients who are at risk. Having made a diagnosis, the clinician is then faced with a choice of treatments, some of which will better suit certain patients. Optimally assigning treatment ensures a better prognosis and fewer side effects, leading in turn to a more economical use of resources. These are areas in which the classification and recognition of data patterns is vital.

**THE SCOPE FOR PATTERN CLASSIFIERS IN MEDICINE IS VAST.**

An early pattern classifier was built in 1973 in the London Hospital to predict the outcome of cerebral anoxia caused by cardiac arrest. This cerebral anoxia classifier, built by D E Maynard, is now on display in the London Science Museum. Other cited clinical applications are:

- Pattern Classification
  - choosing therapy for peptic ulcers
  - diagnosing breast cancer
  - interpreting tissue sections and blood chemistry
  - diagnosing dementia
  - diagnosing myocardial infarction
  - interpreting electrocardiograms
  - predicting prognosis and survival rates
- Image Analysis
  - interpreting radiograms
  - recognising macromolecules
  - monitoring diabetic retinopathies
  - assisting in breast cancer diagnosis
  - detecting cancer cells in cervical smears
  - determining lesion size
  - identifying abnormalities in assays
  - diagnosing skin cancer
  - classifying nuclei by texture

My own work in medical research has convinced me of the benefits to be gained from a practical pattern classifier. I could cite many studies to make my point, but one typical example should suffice.

In 1993 I was involved in a study that used demographic details, medical history and questionnaires to try to determine general practice patients at risk through not receiving immediate chiropody. The study was reasonably successful in that some key determinants were identified. But a practical classifier, had one been available, may well have enabled at-risk patients to be easily identified from the collected data.

### 10.4.5. MEDICAL IMAGE ANALYSIS

Medicine, like industry, needs intelligent, flexible vision systems. Medical image analysis is seen as enjoying reasonable success where quantitative issues are involved but only limited success where interpretive or diagnostic issues are involved. Systems may, for example, be able to determine the number, size and distribution of retinal microaneurysms at an acceptable accuracy, but intelligently mapping this information to a specific disease is much more challenging. This desire for intelligent vision systems is seen also in industry. Here, machine vision systems are shifting from defect detection to defect prevention.

There is a requirement in industry for systems that do not require costly reprogramming between production runs. This requirement, too, is desirable for medical vision systems. For example local or short-term screening programs require cheap, flexible image analysis systems if they are to be cost effective. Costs are reduced, and utility increased, when systems can be developed and fine-tuned by domain experts rather than systems engineers. This is true regardless of whether the application is for industry or medicine.

Indeed, it is probably misleading to distinguish between industrial and medical systems since their imaging processing techniques (such as histogram equalisation; smoothing; median filtering; edge detection and thresholding are common. Clearly, therefore, it is important for the medical community to consider the generic industrial vision systems, such as Cardiff University's Java-based Cyber Image Processing tool-set , which are currently being developed.

Colour has not been widely used by classifiers, but it could be used to classify cells and tissue.Studies into the use of colour as a classification parameter have so far been limited, possibly for reasons similar to those cited by Batchelor for the limited use of colour image processing in industry. These reasons are shown by Batchelor to be largely no longer valid. They centre on the perceived greater complexity, cost and imprecision of colour image processing systems compared with monochromatic systems.

One study which has shown the potential of colour processing is from Pavlova et al. They found that characteristic hue histograms exist for different types of blood cell. The maxima in the histograms were shown to be invariant for each cell type and were robust to changes in the staining solution. The authors acknowledge that their study has yet to create a concrete quantitative criterion for identification, but point out that similar logic could be applied to other colour microscopic images, such as bone marrow smears, tissue cultures and others. The following examples show the benefits for diagnosis and non-invasive monitoring.

The importance of computerised imaging analysis cannot be overstated; benefits are to be gained not only in better diagnoses but also in the development of less invasive monitoring techniques. The following three examples illustrate these points. Each example details a current medical problem and suggests how pattern classifiers and image processing could provide solutions.

### 10.4.6 MONITORING NEONATAL JAUNDICE

Neonatal jaundice is a major worry monitored by blood test. Jaundice is caused by an excess of the yellow bile pigment bilirubin. Neonatal jaundice occurs in 20-50% of the newborn population and is probably the most common neonatal symptom that causes professional and parental worry. High levels of bilirubin can lead to kernicterus: the staining and subsequent damaging of the brain. Bilirubin levels are monitored by blood sample. In premature babies each sample involves pricking the baby's heel to extract the blood. In the case of severe jaundice, samples must be taken frequently, often twice a day. Repeated blood sampling introduces risks of infection, anaemia and bruising, and causes pain and distress. Additionally there are the expenses of phlebotomy and biochemistry.

Skin colour is used as a guide to jaundice severity, and it might indicate potential brain damage.The severity of jaundice can also be assessed by the yellow skin colour if the skin is pressed. This is recommended only as a rough guide. Even so, there is evidence that the yellow colour of the skin should provide a better indicator of potential brain damage than does the blood bilirubin concentration.

Medical staff are advised to carry out skin colour assessment under natural or fluorescent lighting, and warned that the test can be misleading if light reflects off yellow or orange curtains or bedspreads. In dark-skinned babies the colour of the sclerea, palms and soles can be useful; although mixed ethnic standardisation curves have been suggested. An icterometer can be used. This is a piece of clear plastic that is pressed against the baby. The colour of the blanched skin is compared against five coloured strips on the plastic, which give a guide to the level of jaundice. The icterometer has been shown to be useful in reducing the need for blood samples, and may also be useful to peripheral staff in developing countries when deciding on referral to specialist centres.

Vision systems might allow continuous jaundice monitoring. Now, suppose we were able to record the colour of the blanched skin to monitor change; or compare pressed blanched skin with non-pressed skin, perhaps allowing us to account for variation in natural skin colour. A pen-sized device with shielded light-source, colour photoreceptors and learning mechanism is feasible. Could such a device provide a better guide to the level of jaundice? Moreover, could the same device be used for other conditions, such as monitoring anaemia from tissue pallor? Clearly there are confounding factors such as changes in epidermal blood flow. However, some instrumental methods for measuring skin pigmentation and skin colour change have been shown to be both sensitive and reliable. Non-invasive techniques could allow for more frequent or continuous monitoring. With over 133,000,000 babies born each year worldwide usage and sales potential could be huge.

### 10.4.7 BREAST CANCER SCREENING

Mammography is relatively reliable, but costly mistakes happen. Mammography is reported as the most reliable method for detecting lesions in the breast. Even so, interpretation of mammograms has been shown to be affected by factors such as view box luminance and masking and by ambient lighting. Contrast and definition can be degraded by under processing the mammographic film. This can be caused by physical factors (low developer temperature, inadequate development time, insufficient developer agitation) or chemical factors (developer not optimised for film type; over diluted, under replenished or contaminated developer).

The accuracy of mammography screening was recently studied in the USA, and this study is probably indicative of other countries. Of 2,400 women screened over ten years, 24% had at least one false positive mammogram (a false positive is here defined as a suspicious or abnormal finding which after one year of follow-up failed to reveal a tumour). The estimated cumulative rate for a risk of a false positive result after 10 mammographic screens was 49%. A false positive error might at first sight seem trivial - better safe than sorry. However, this study showed that for every $100 spent on screening, an additional $33 was spent to evaluate false positive results. The false positives brought unnecessary outpatient visits, biopsies, ultrasound examinations, and anxiety. A recent Swedish study concluded that examinations and investigation carried out after false positive mammography were a neglected but substantial problem.

Image processing could reduce errors, and perhaps predict tumour type.False negatives are also possible. According to Goergan et al , reportedly 11%-25% of cancers are overlooked on the initial mammogram. They found that at particular risk of being missed are cancers with a density not substantially greater than the surrounding breast tissue. Given this, image-processing options, such as segmentation or contrast expansion, seem imperative.

Computed radiography has been shown to result in high-quality images of diagnostic value equivalent to conventional film mammograms, provided image processing parameters are carefully selected. It is worth noting also that texture analysis on digital images of surrounding tissue taken during biopsy, has been shown to be useful in predicting malignant versus benign outcomes.

### 10.4.8 CERVICAL SCREENING

Failures have occurred in cervical screening programmes. Serious failures in cervical screening seem all too common. Two failures made the headlines during July 1998. At the Prince Charles Hospital, Merthyr Tydfil, inaccuracies in smear tests carried out between 1990 and 1994 were blamed for the deaths of two women and serious delays in the treatment of 12 more. While at St George's Hospital in south London, over 1,000 women had to be recalled after probable errors in colposcopy screening. There one woman died and 11 were diagnosed with cancer.

The most serious case of cervical smear test misreporting occurred at Kent and Canterbury Hospital from 1990 to 1995. More than 91,000 smears had to be re-examined in 1996. Five thousand five hundred and sixty-six women needed to be followed up, of whom 333 had moderate or severe abnormalities, including 30 who needed hysterectomies. Eight women died.

The National Audit Office has reported that only about half of the 181 laboratories in England meet recommended cervical screening quality standards. The NAO conclude that this means that many laboratories might be missing some abnormalities (false negatives) and many might be reporting abnormalities where none exist.

Errors are encouraged by the low prevalence of abnormalities. The pathologists and cytologists who screen cervical smears are dealing with a low-prevalence population. In England during 1996/97 3.8 million women were screened, involving the processing of 4.4 million smears. Only 3,500 new cases of invasive cervical cancer were expected.

The screener is searching for subtle variations in the shape, size and structure of cervical cells, but the vast majority of slides will be negative. A screener might view 50 slides a day in Britain, or up to 100 a day in the US. Each slide has 1,000 fields of view, so a screener in the US might manipulate the microscope 100,000 times a day. False negatives might be encouraged by the assimilation of each judgement to its predecessor. This is likely in screeners faced with a long sequence of similar stimuli.

The abnormal cells in false negative slides are likely to be:

- less well represented throughout the slide,
- present only as single cells rather than as groups,
- smaller in size.

Given that their characteristics are often different to genuinely positive cells, rapid re-screening of slides that are considered negative might be of limited effect. Smear testing is invaluable, but advancements are needed. Despite the scare stories it should not be forgotten that smear testing has been invaluable in reducing the incidence of cervical cancer over the past 50 years and no test ever invented has been as successful in preventing cancer.

# QUESTION BANK

Q1. Discuss the concept of picture data archival in detail.
Q2. Explain the concept of computer vision.
Q3. What are the various requirements of computer vision systems?
Q4. Write down uses of computer vision in the science and technology.
Q5. What are the various applications for computer vision?
Q6. What is medical imaging? Explain the concept of medical imaging in image processing.